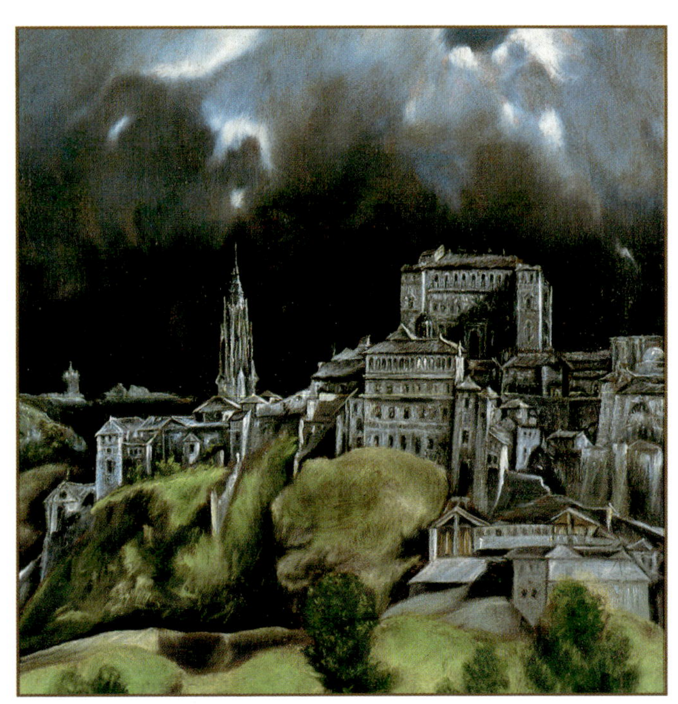

THE GOLDEN AGE *of* SPAIN

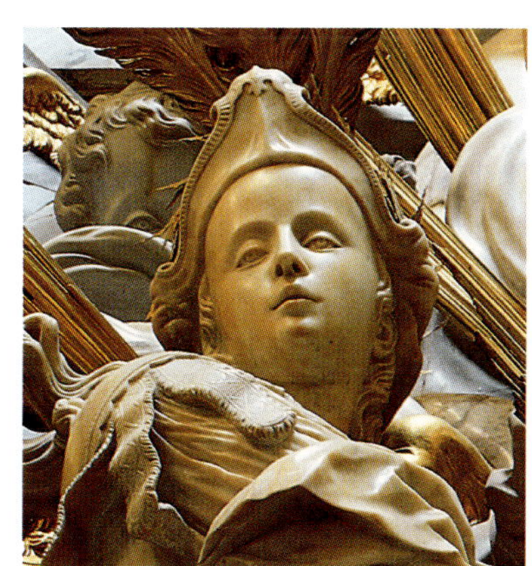

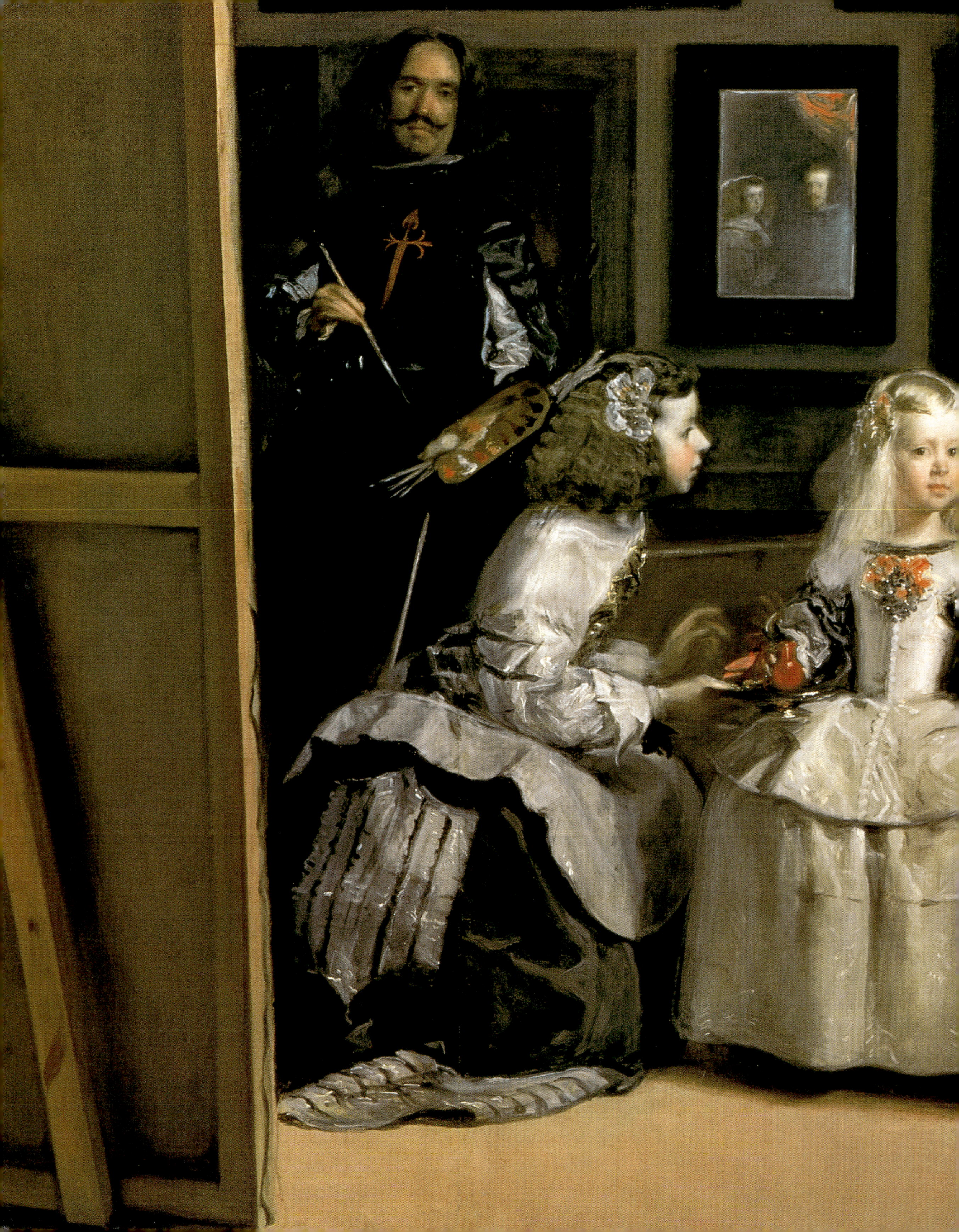

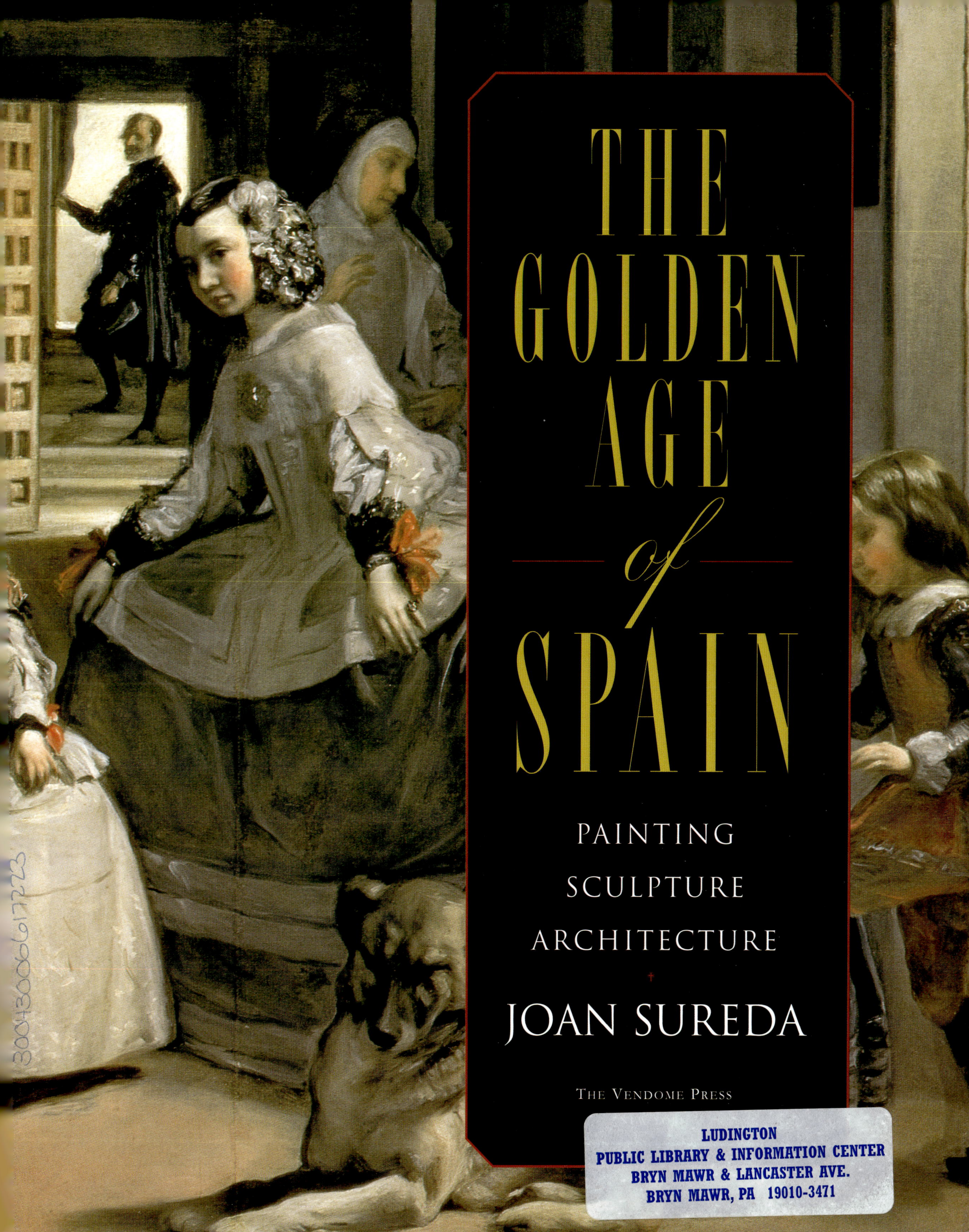

THE GOLDEN AGE *of* SPAIN

PAINTING
SCULPTURE
ARCHITECTURE

JOAN SUREDA

THE VENDOME PRESS

PAGE 1: Domenikos Theotokopoulos, called El Greco. Detail of *View of Toledo,* c. 1600 (see ill. 164).

PAGE 3: Narciso Tomé. Detail of the Glory on the *Transparente* altarpiece, 1721–32, Toledo Cathedral (see ill. 100).

PAGES 4–5: Diego Velázquez. Detail of *Las Meninas (The Family of Philip IV),* c. 1656–57 (see ill. 197).

PAGES 6–7: Diego Velázquez. Detail of *The Triumph of Bacchus,* or *The Drunkards,* 1628–29 (see ill. 56).

First published in the United States of America in 2008 by
The Vendome Press
1334 York Avenue
New York, N.Y. 10021
www.vendomepress.com

First published in Spanish by Lunwerg Editores in 2007 under the title *La gloria de los Siglos de Oro.*

ISBN 978-086565-198-2

Library of Congress Cataloging-in-Publication Data

Sureda, Joan, 1949-
[Gloria de los Siglos de Oro. English]
Golden age of Spain : painting, sculpture, architecture / by Joan Sureda.
p. cm.
ISBN 978-0-86565-198-2 (hardcover : alk. paper)
1. Art, Spanish—16th century. I. Title.
N7105.S8713 2008
709.46'09031—dc22
2008006393

Printed in Spain

First printing

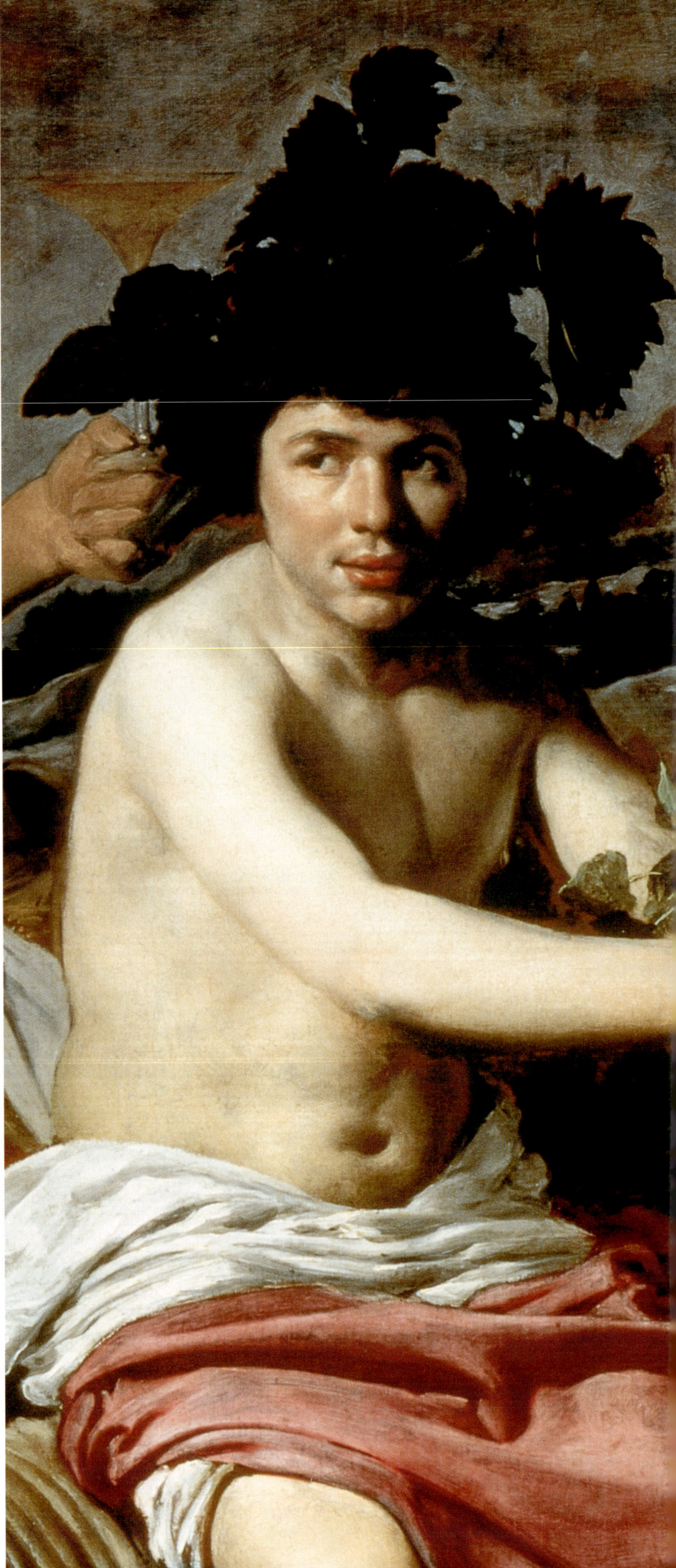

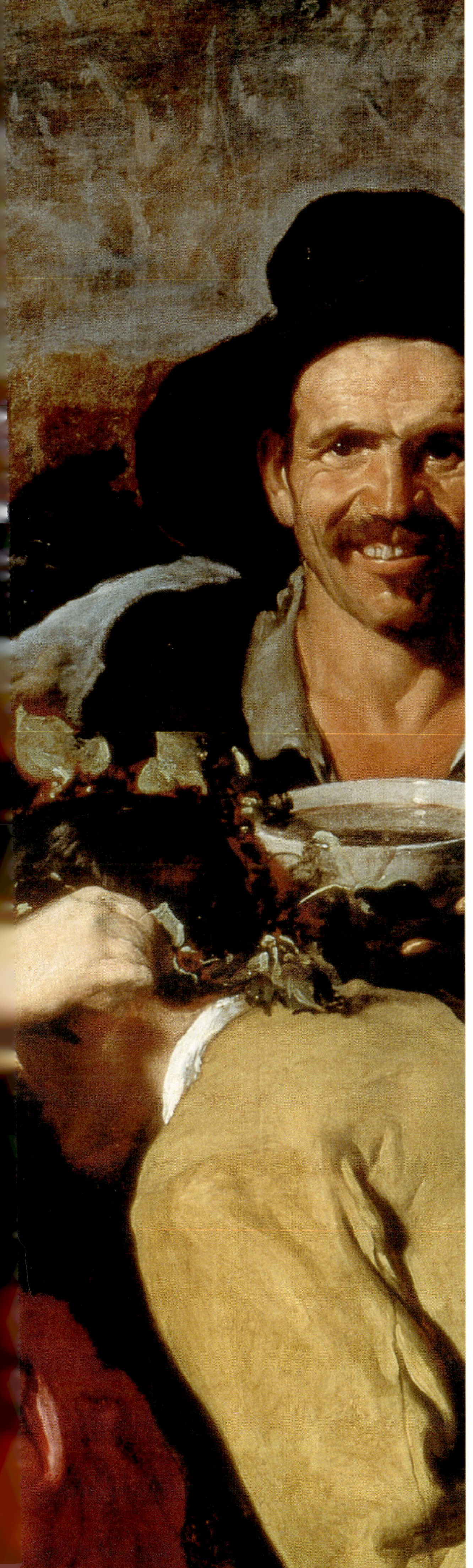

CONTENTS

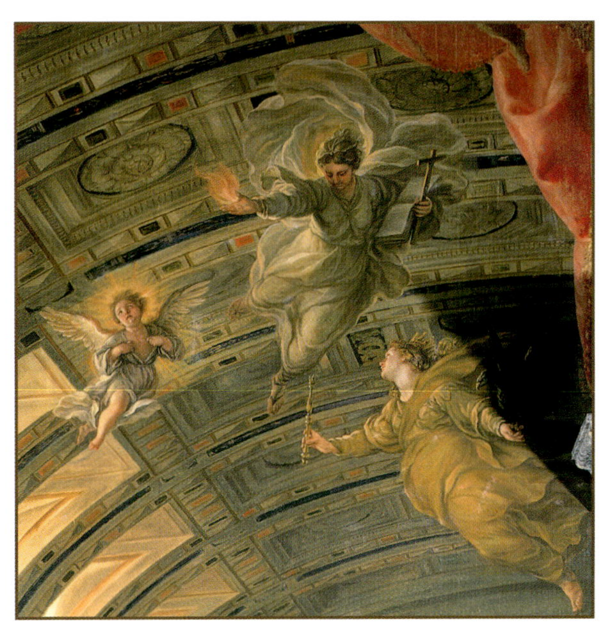

The Golden Age, or Century

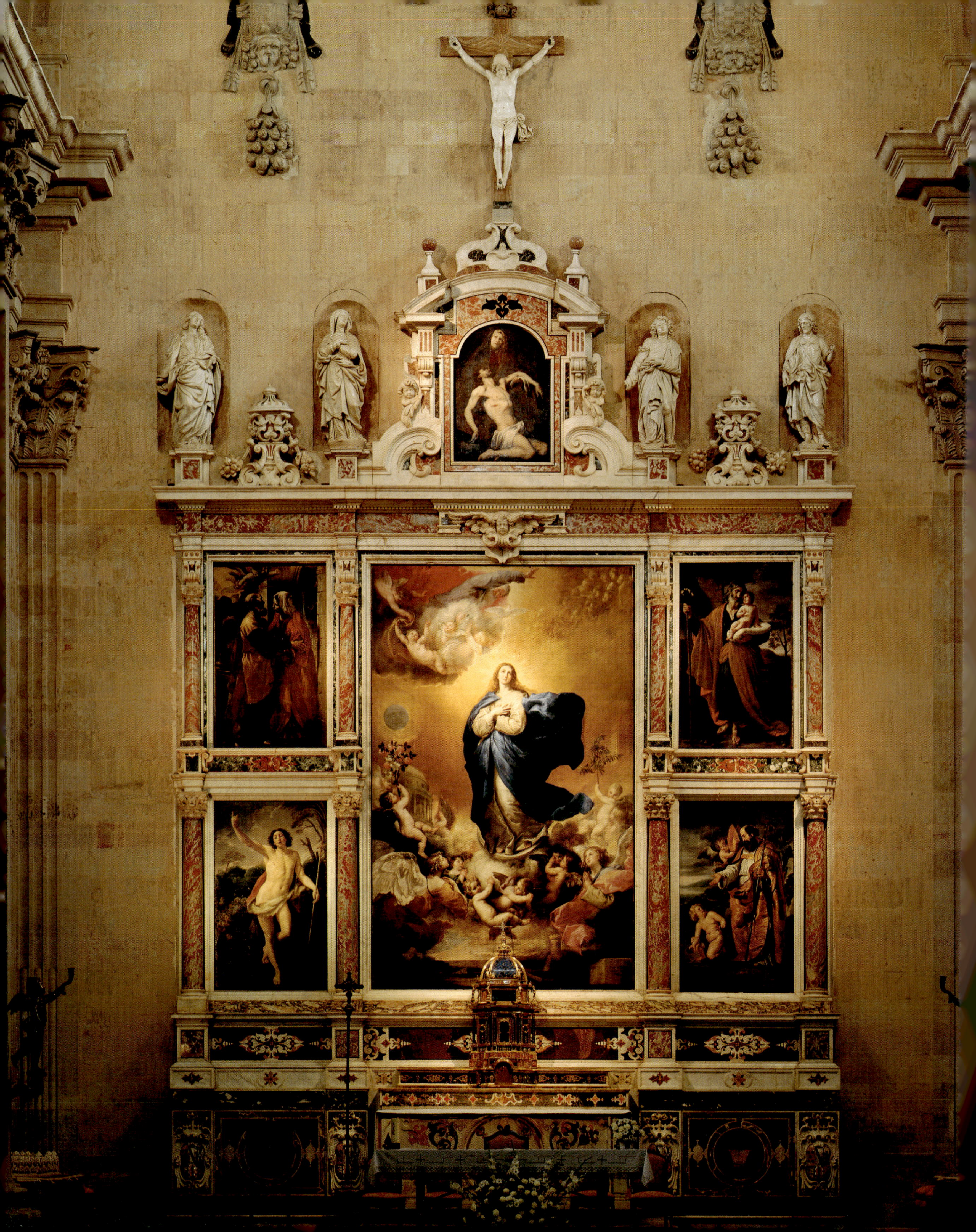

Introduction

THE GOLDEN AGE, OR CENTURY

PRECEDING PAGE:
1. Claudio Coello
1685–1686
Detail of *The Adoration of the Sacred Form.*
Sacristy, Real Monasterio de San Lorenzo, El Escorial.

LEFT:
2. High altar at the church of the Convento de las Agustinas Recoletas de Monterrey, Salamanca, with architecture and marble sculptures by Cosimo Fanzago (1633–1635) and paintings by José de Ribera (*Lamentation*, 1634; *Virgin of the Immaculate Conception*, 1635), Guido Reni, Giovanni Lanfranco, Giovanni Baglioni, and Carlo Dolci.

The Spain that witnessed the transition from the sixteenth to the seventeenth century (the age of Cervantes, broadly speaking) became aware of the advent of a new age, a golden age, like that of Petrarch's Italy, that would leave darker iron far behind. Yet at the time, few recognized its import, and it occurred to no one to use the expression *Siglo de Oro*—literally, Golden Century. The concept of a "Golden Age" began to appear in the work of certain men of letters only when the period was coming to an end and its parameters were becoming clear. For example, the Spanish writer Bartolomé de Góngora wrote in *The Wise Magistrate* (1656): "Leaving aside now those men of letters of King Philip II's time, suffice it to say that the sixteenth century was when the king himself prospered, and I close this account of the most outstanding talents of an age I regard as the Golden Century with the end of his reign [1598]."

But it was the Enlightenment, that defender of historical progress and the tireless debate between "the old" and "the modern," that conferred full recognition on the *Siglo de Oro* as a peak of Spanish cultural accomplishment, particularly in the field of literature, a period associated not only with the seventeenth-century Baroque, which immediately preceded the Enlightenment, but also with the Renaissance, which was cultivated and enhanced by Isabel and Ferdinand, the "Catholic Monarchs"; Charles V (Holy Roman Emperor who was King Charles I of Spain); and his son Philip II, who saw themselves in the mirror of Italy. In 1737 the Valencian scholar Gregorio Mayans y Siscar referred to the *Siglo de Oro* as an "age" in his dedication to Juan Barón de Carteret, which is included in the first biography of Cervantes he wrote for the London edition of *Don Quixote:* "A person [Cervantes] most worthy of a better century; for although they say that the age in which he lived was of gold, I know that for him and a number of other personages it was of iron." And the *Siglo de Oro* was defined in 1754 as a "century" by Luis José Velázquez de Velasco in his *Origins of Castilian Poetry*. Velázquez de Velasco divided Castilian poetry into four ages, the third of which, stretching from the time of Charles V to that of Philip IV, was "the golden century of Castilian poetry, a century in which it was inevitable that good poetry would flourish along with other good letters as they reached their zeniths."

With Velázquez de Velasco, whose scholarship is fundamental to the study of Hispanic epigraphy, the concept of a *Siglo de Oro* became firmly established, although *siglo* was understood not literally as a period of one hundred years but in the broader sense of the classical *saeculum*. This concept of the Golden Age was first applied to literature and also, though more loosely, to the fine arts. An early mention of the visual arts in this context appeared in a letter dated "Rome, October 20, 1765," from the neoclassical painter Francisco Preciado de la Vega (later established at the Madrid court) to fellow painter Giovanni Battista Ponfredi about the evolution of painting in Spain. Preciado de la Vega adheres closely to the words of Antonio Palomino, whose three-volume treatise on the art of painting (1715–24) included biographies of Spanish artists:

> Some days ago I promised you a brief account of the painters who have attained greatest renown in Spain, of whom little or nothing is known in Italy, as they are recognized only by those of their compatriots—and by those foreigners who happen by chance to be in that country—with some knowledge of Painting. Their works, as a rule, are preserved in churches, or hidden in palaces, or in private homes—which are not easily visited, unlike those of Italian princes—where they are interred, out of sight and inaccessible to potential purchasers; unlike [the works] of other esteemed painters from different countries, which usually reach Rome.
>
> I assure you that in that Kingdom there have been masters of such excellence that their works are worthy of standing alongside those of the most celebrated colorists displayed in the famous galleries of art-loving princes. . . . And going back to the beginning, in the remote past Spain was invaded and dominated by the Moors of Africa for almost eight centuries, as you will know from the histories, and in order to expel them completely we Spaniards were forced to undergo great hardship and sacrifice letters and the fine arts almost entirely. The more we were obliged to engage in warfare, the less opportunity we had to enjoy the delights of Painting.
>
> Nonetheless, it seems that the Moors tolerated a certain number of Christian painters, for in Seville, my native city, a confraternity was founded in a chapel of the parish church of San Andrés, where I was baptized, whose patron is Saint Luke the Evangelist. And this confraternity has its own statutes, granted by the glorious conqueror of that city, King Ferdinand, unless we are to believe that they were introduced from elsewhere or that they came into spontaneous existence.
>
> This righteous King lived in the mid-thirteenth century, which shows just how old this confraternity of painters is. The painters themselves, I imagine, would at that time have been little blessed with knowledge for, as in Italy, those that the *Siglo de Oro* was to produce much later had yet to emerge.
>
> At the time when the whole of Italy was enraptured by the works of Michelangelo and Raphael, in Spain there were some of such initiative that, when they heard the two heroes of our arts praised in such a manner, decided to cross the Alps to make their acquaintance and study with them in order to take back to their homeland, as they did, the teachings of that school and that manner of painting.

The *Siglo de Oro* was affirmed, with reservations and clear ideological connotations, by the Spanish statesman, philosopher, and author Gaspar Melchor de Jovellanos in a speech he delivered at the Academia de Bellas Artes de San Fernando on July 14, 1781, and published in 1782. In the nineteenth century the period of the Golden Age was defined, with regard to literature, as stretching from the time of the poet Jorge Manrique (1440?–78) until the death of the great dramatist Pedro Calderón de la Barca (1681). In the fine arts the Golden Age was determined to comprise the many years between Pedro Berruguete's return to Castile after his sojourn in Urbino (after 1482) and the death of the court painter Claudio Coello in 1692. "Great was the bleakness and prostration of our arts when Philip V [formerly the Duke of Anjou] acceded to the Spanish throne [in 1700]," wrote Menéndez y Pelayo in his *History of Aesthetic Ideas in Spain* (1882–91). The painters Juan Carreño de Miranda and Claudio Coello, he claimed:

> . . . had taken with them to the grave the last glorious traditions of Spanish painting, and it might be said that the admirable canvas *The Holy Form* [by Coello, in the sacristy of the Escorial, ill. 7] constituted the last will and testament of the national school. And to deliver the final death blow, in 1692 Luca Giordano came from Naples,

3. Pedro Berruguete
c. 1495
Saint Dominic Pardons a Heretic, oil on panel.
Museo Nacional del Prado, Madrid.

OVERLEAF:
4. The southern façade of the Real Monasterio de San Lorenzo de El Escorial, built by Juan Bautista de Toledo and Juan de Herrera, 1563–84.

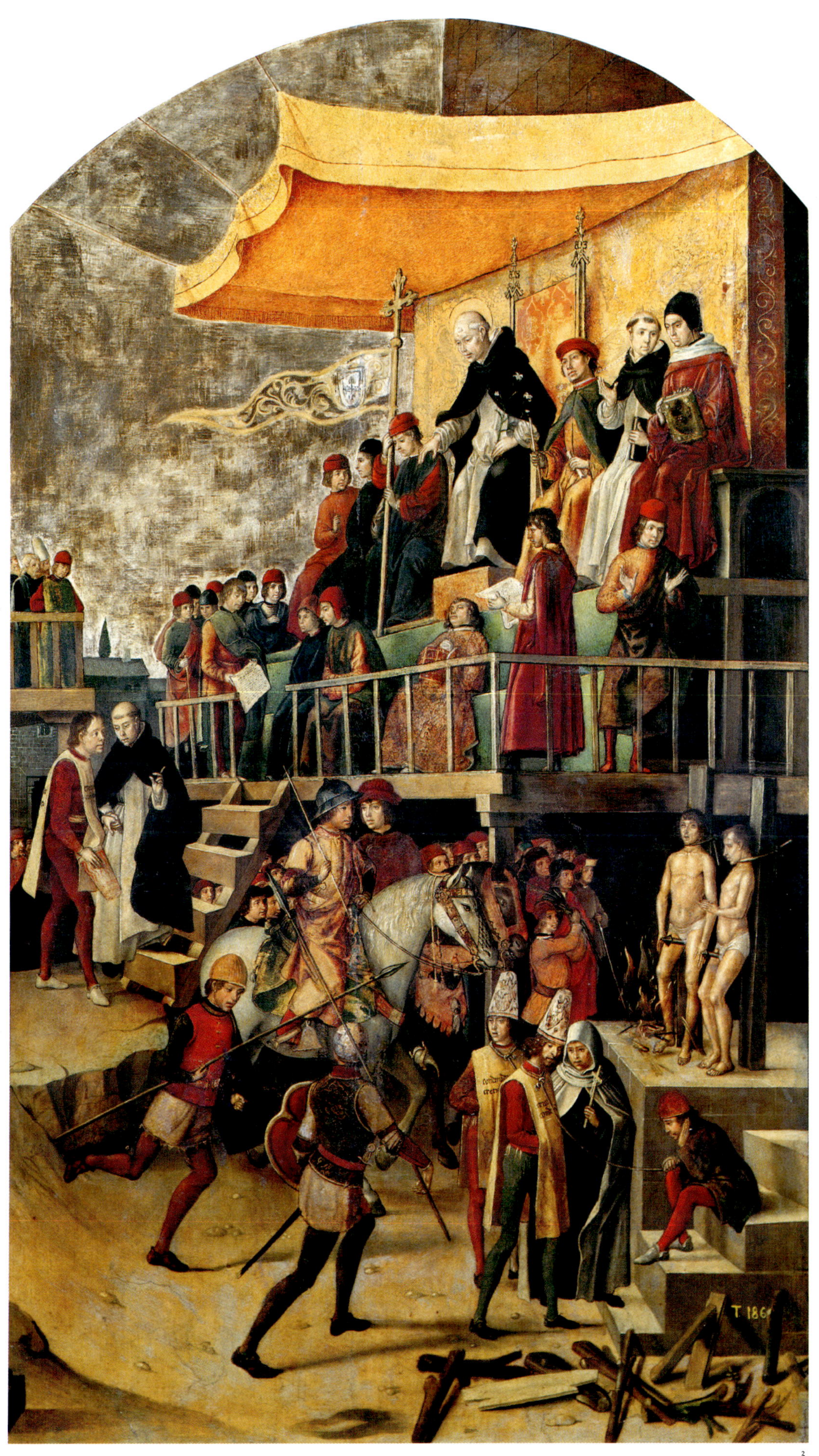

3

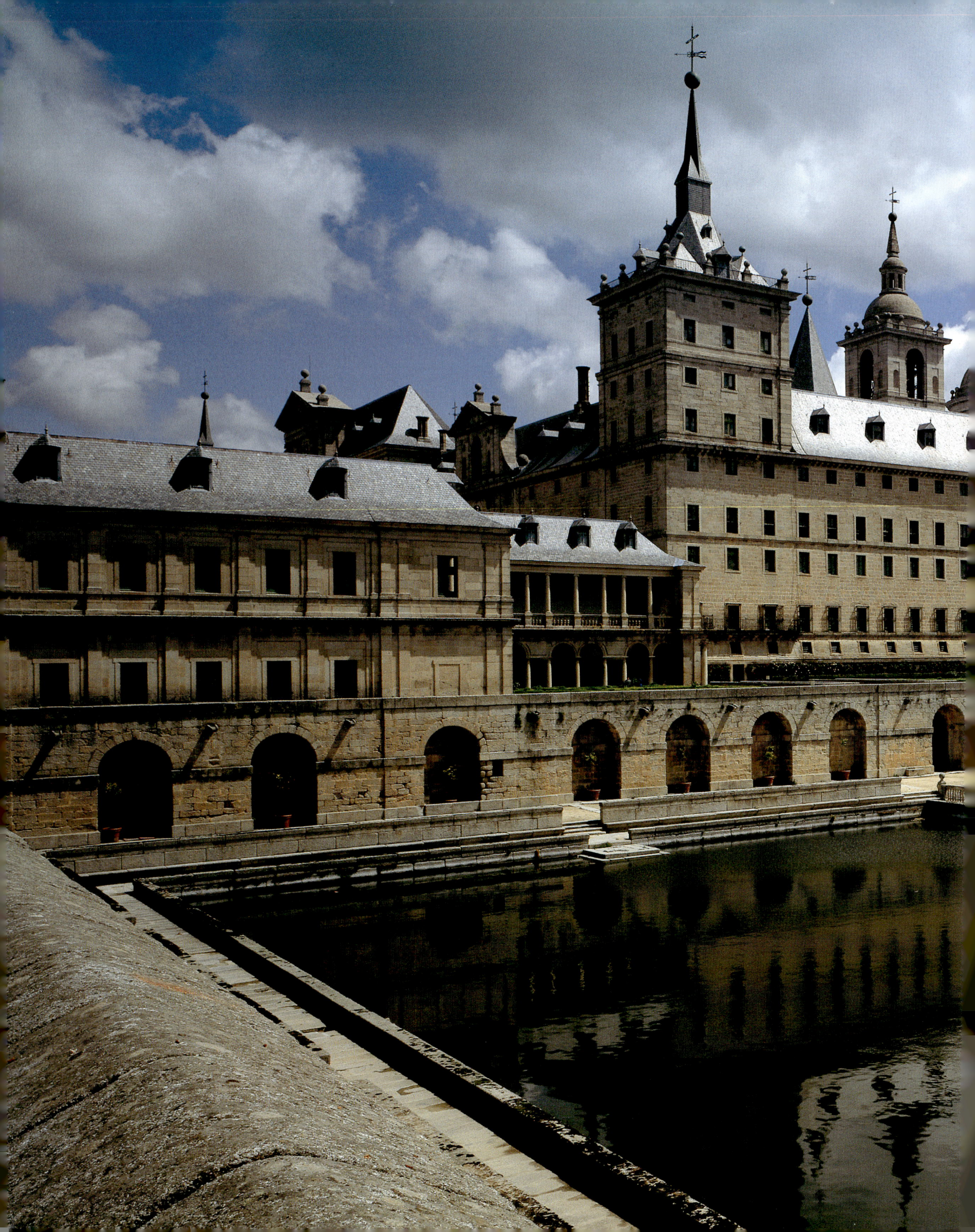

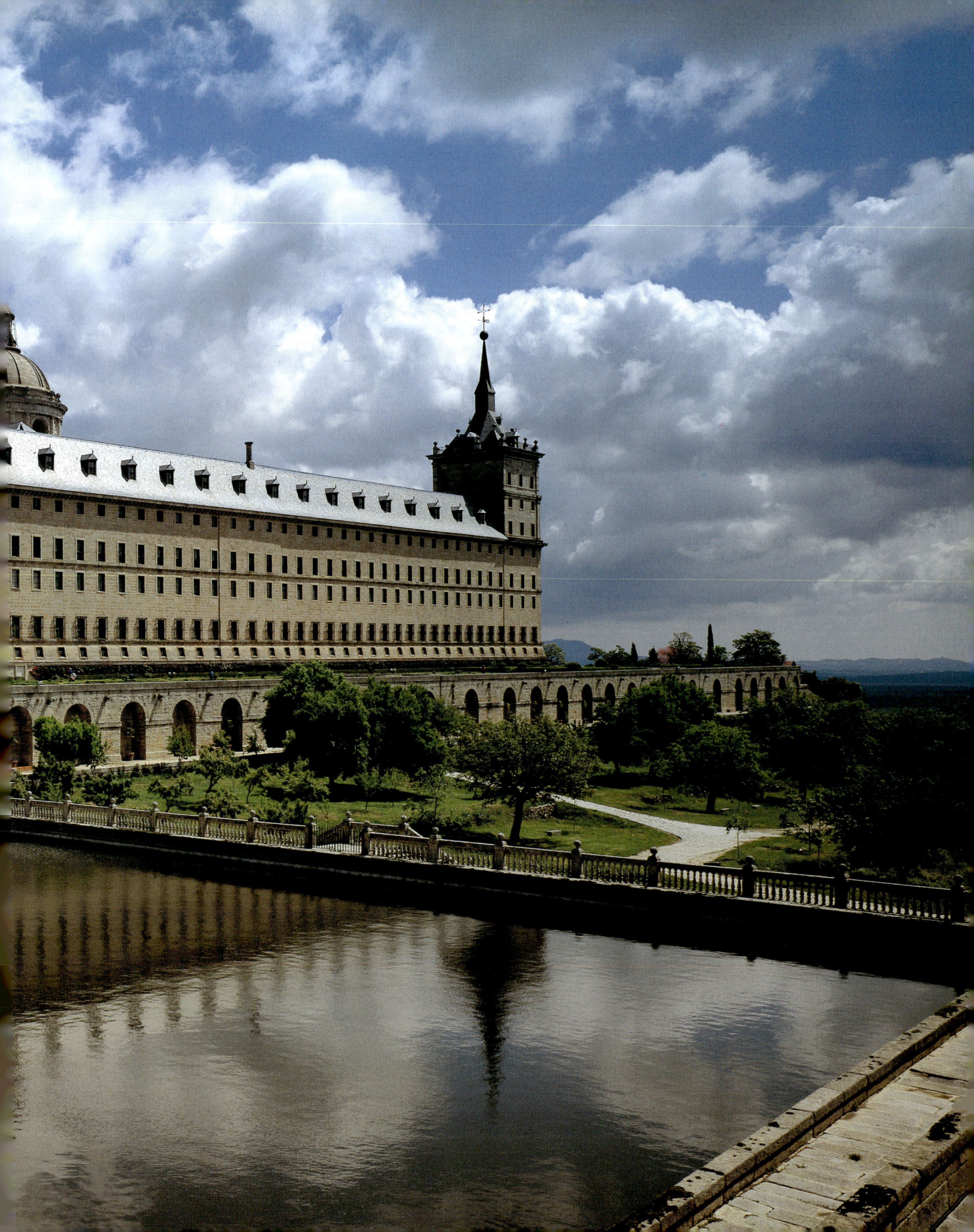

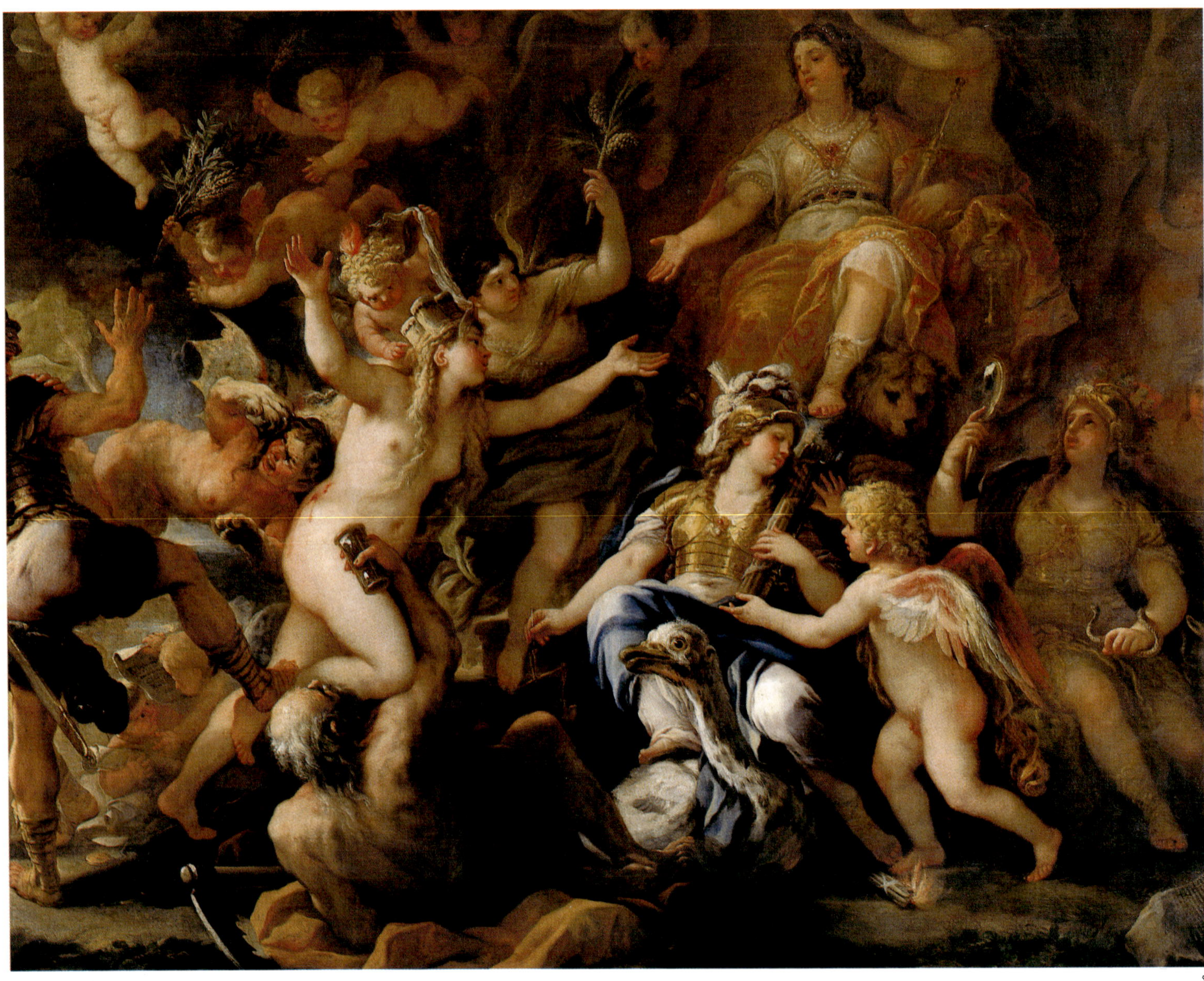

5

with all the prestige of his dramatic painting, with his admirable gift for adopting the styles of others, or rather for exaggerating or even surpassing them, and with his lax artistic conscience and distasteful thirst for money. The fire, the boldness, the bizarre intemperance, and the allegorical baroqueness of his huge frescos, which resemble stage sets, blinded the eyes and subdued the will of artists and patrons alike, so that for many years in Spain it was impossible to find precision in drawing or sobriety in composition.

That Golden Age, or those Golden Centuries, an era defined, as we have seen, more by historical tradition than by the nature of the period, witnessed the lives of great artists, ranging from Miguel de Cervantes Saavedra, the brilliant author of *Don Quixote,* to Diego Velázquez de Silva, the artist and courtier who transformed reality into painting and painting into reality with his brushes. It was the period of the reign of the Habsburgs, instituted by Emperor Charles V and brought to a close two centuries later with the death of Charles II. During this time the patronage of the arts reached two peaks, first under Philip II, who loved the

ABOVE:
5. Luca Giordano
c. 1678
Allegory of the Restitution of Messina to Spain.
Museo Nacional del Prado, Madrid.

RIGHT:
6. José de Ribera
1635
Detail of *The Virgin of the Immaculate Conception.*
High altarpiece, church of the Convento de las Agustinas Recoletas de Monterrey, Salamanca.

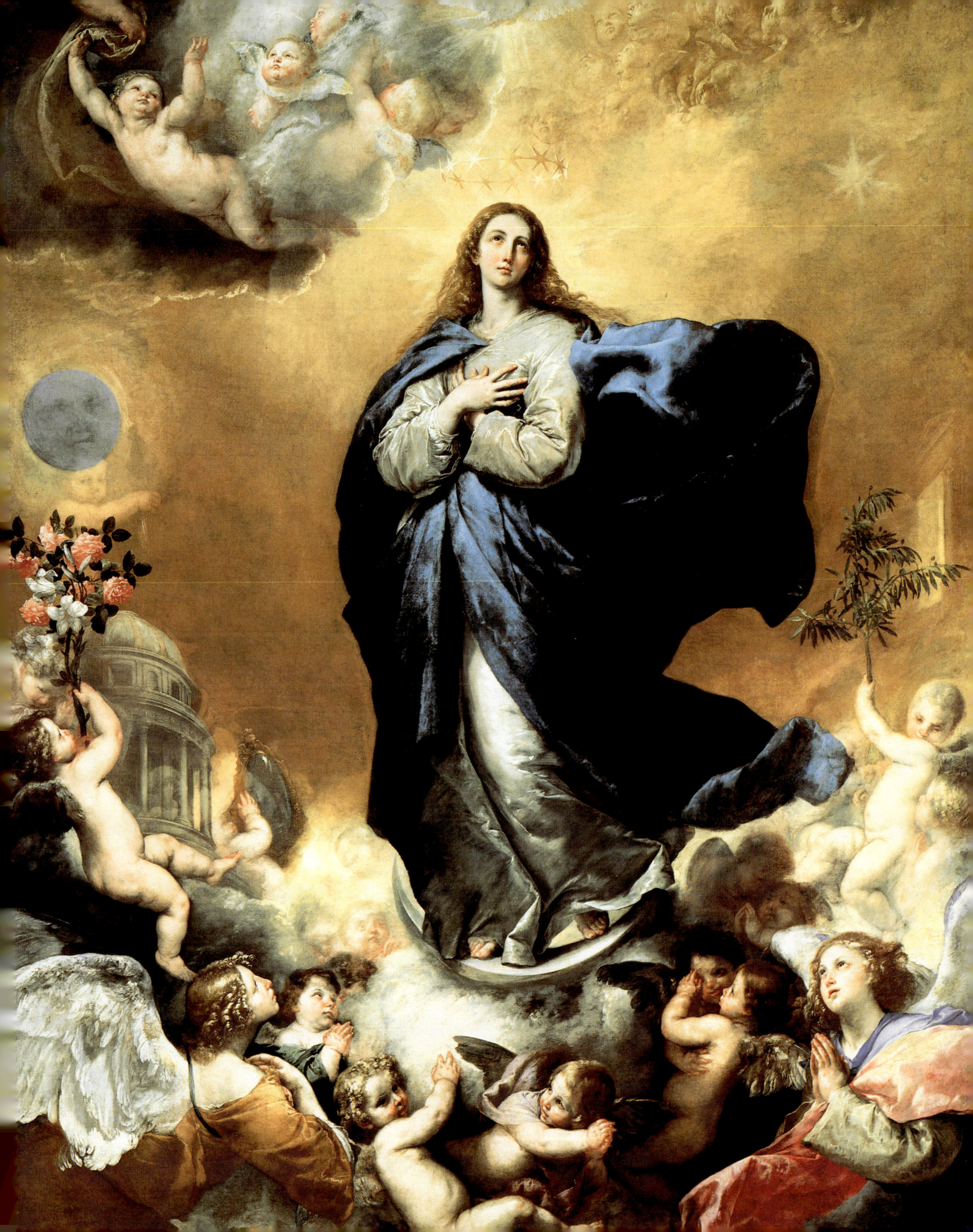

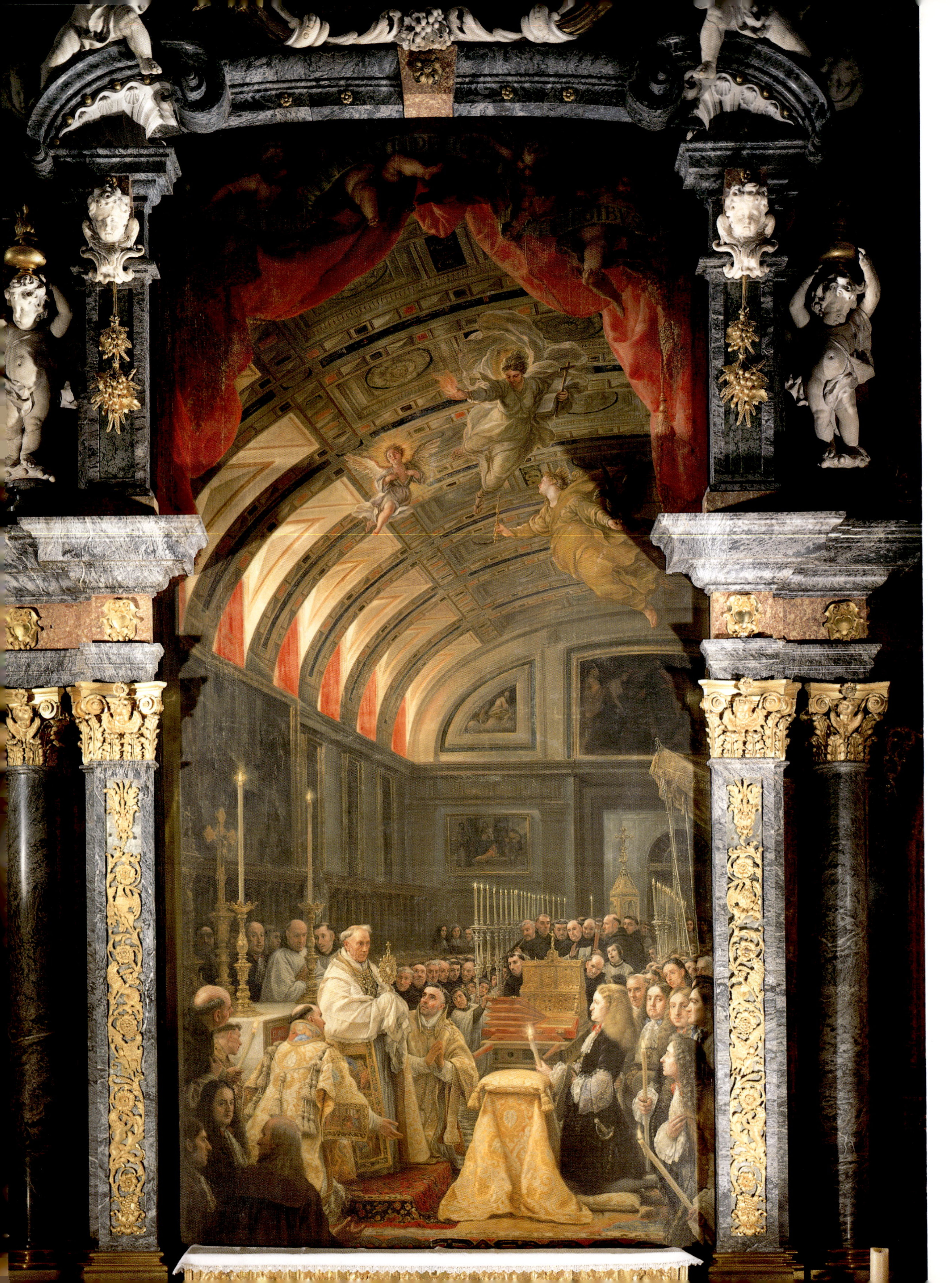

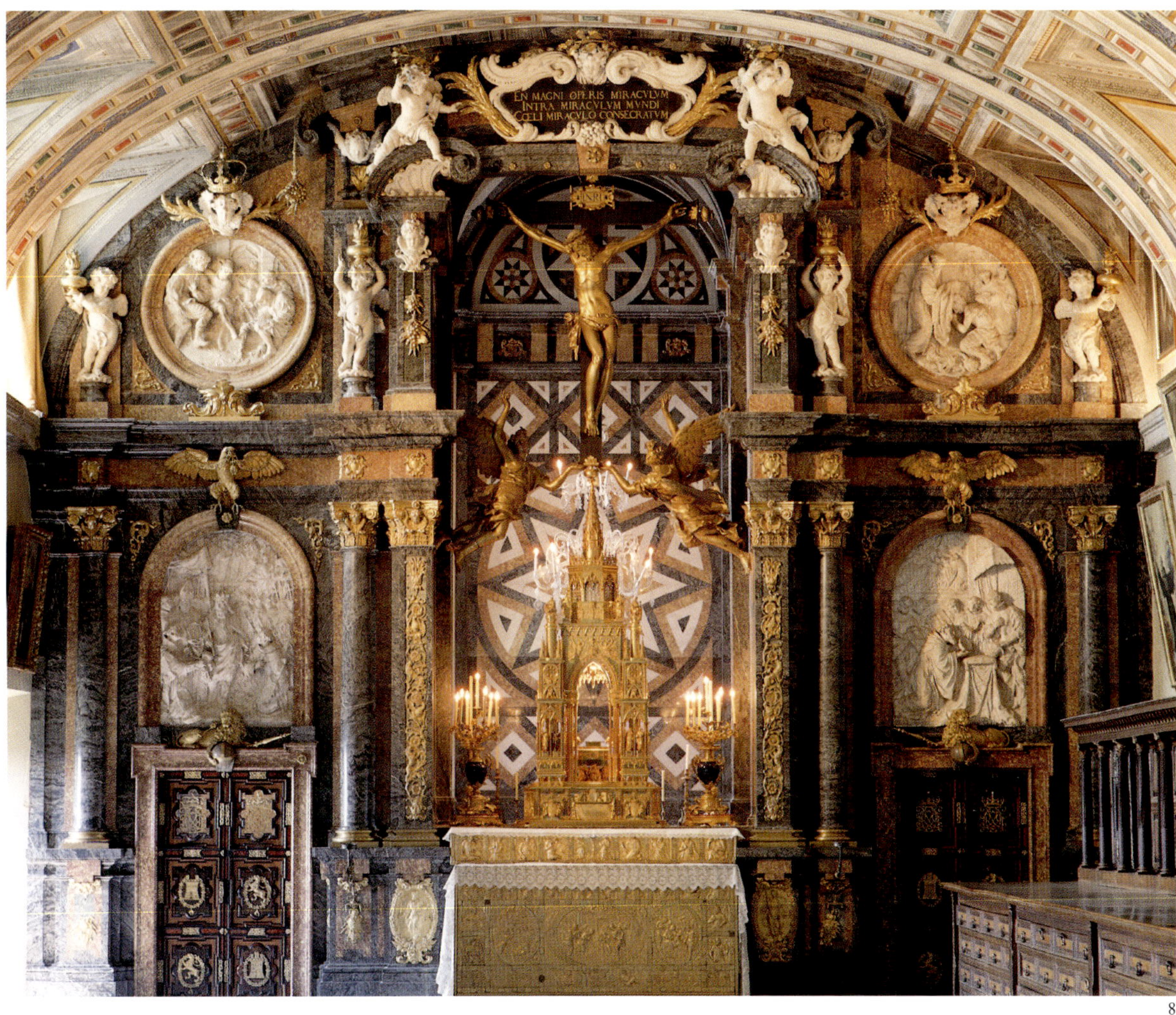

8

paintings of Hieronymus Bosch as much as those of Titian and who built the "eighth wonder of the world," the monastery/palace of the Escorial, and later under Philip IV, the monarch who entrusted Velázquez with the task of portraying the splendor of a period that was politically and socially in decline.

It was also the period of the discovery of the lands and civilizations of America—the latter destroyed by the cross and the sword—and East Asia, as well as the birth of the modern state, a state perpetually at war whose people were as much given to revelry and worldly pursuits as they feared for the salvation of their souls. It was a period in which the purity of geometrical reason was succeeded by the exaltation of the exuberant, yet also by a resonant, shattering quietude. It was a time in which the religious and cultural center of the West and, by extension, of the Christian world, was Rome, the city to which Spanish architects, sculptors, and painters who sought fame flocked: from Alonso Berruguete to Velázquez, with the extraordinary figure of El Greco in between.

From the second half of the sixteenth century on, some artists abandoned not only the Renaissance order mirrored in the canonical authority of antiquity but also the subjective, expressionist style called Mannerism. They were imbued with the spirit of the Counter-Reformation and exalted religious feeling against backdrops of all-embracing classical architecture with delirious, sensual forms, light, and materials; and with images both naturalistic and visionary that transformed carved, painted wood into "divine flesh."

This period of the construction, zenith, decline, and death of the Spanish empire of the House of Austria, this period of creation and destruction, provides us with the historical framework in which to examine from both the written and visual points of view specific aspects of the art of the time and of two of its main representatives—El Greco and Velázquez. We must not forget, however, that other "golden ages" have existed in the Hispanic domains of the Old and New worlds, during the medieval, modern, and contemporary eras.

LEFT:
7. Claudio Coello
1685–86
The Adoration of the Sacred Form.
Sacristy, Real Monasterio de San Lorenzo, El Escorial.

ABOVE:
8. The sacristy of the church of the Real Monasterio de San Lorenzo de El Escorial, showing the crucifix executed by the Italian sculptor Pietro Tacca (after 1635) and the altarpiece built by José del Olmo, 1684–92.

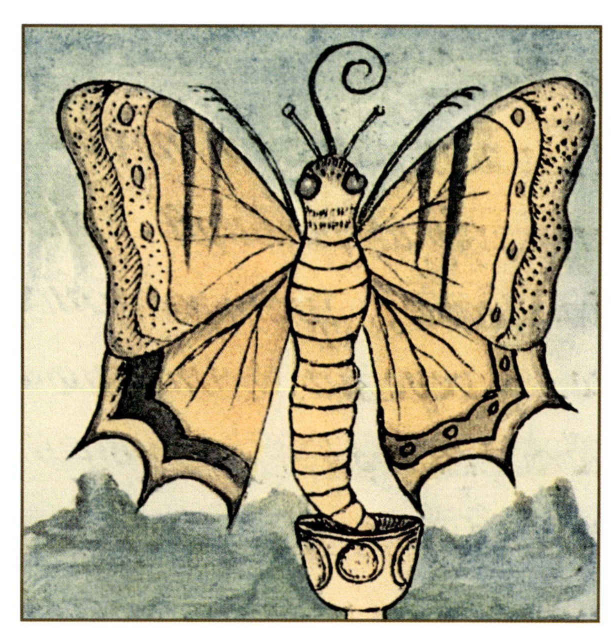

New Worlds and Natures

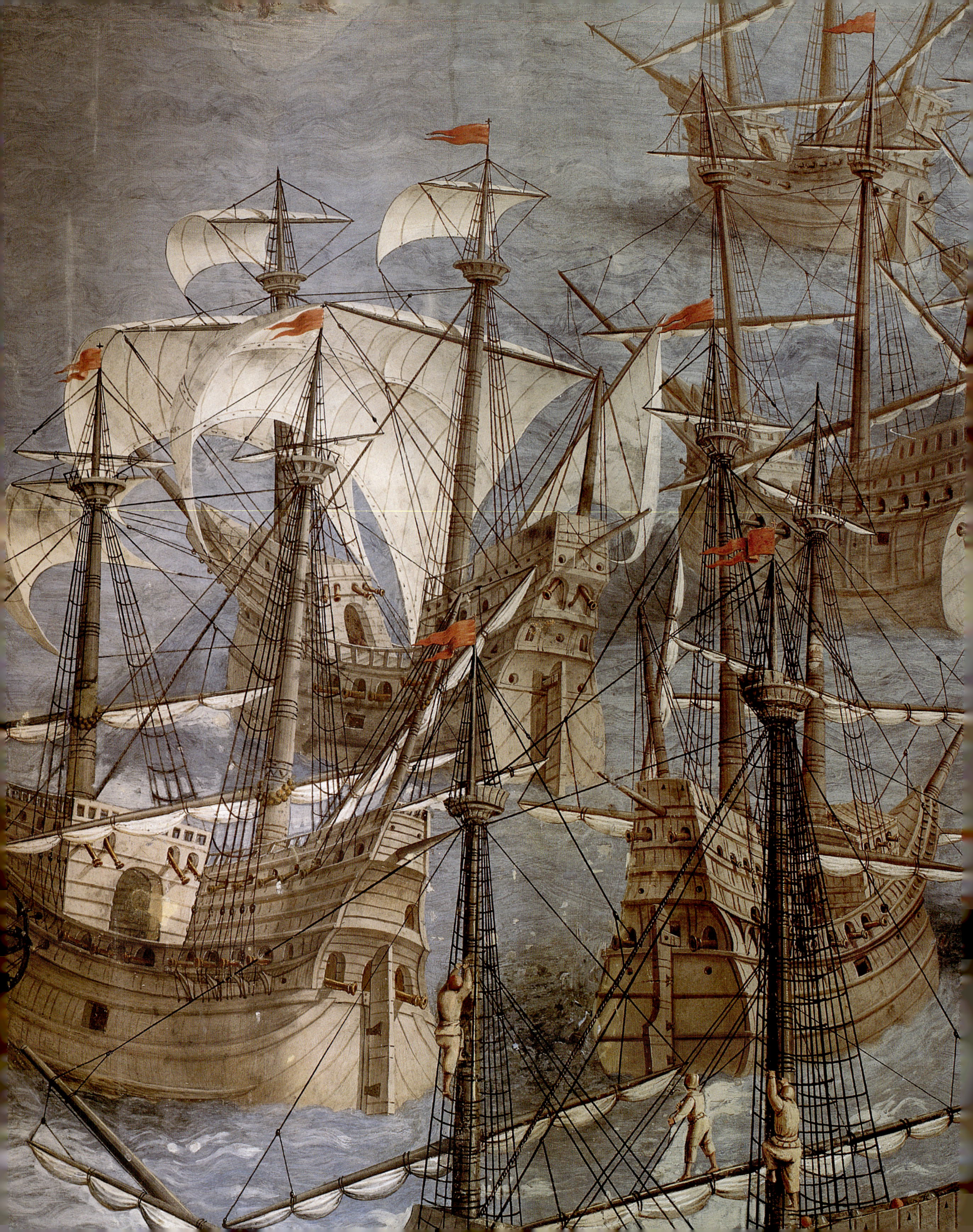

1

New Worlds and Natures

There is a wild tree called *tlacuilolcuáuitl,* which means that its wood is painted, because the wood is red with black veins that look is if they have been painted on the red. This tree is highly valued, for *teponaztles,* the drums and guitars that are made from its wood and produce a wonderful sound. The wood is greatly prized because it is very colorful and a delight to the eye.

—FRAY BERNARDINO DE SAHAGÚN, *General History of Things in New Spain,* Book Eleven (1576–77)

PRECEDING PAGE:
9. 1578
Butterfly *(xicalpapalotl), General History of Things in New Spain* (Florentine Codex) by Bernardino de Sahagún.
Laurentian Library, Florence.

LEFT:
10. Nicolás Granello, Fabrizio Castello and Lázaro Tavarone
1587
Detail of a fresco in the Hall of Battles.
Real Monasterio de San Lorenzo, El Escorial.

Grand Duchess Joan of Austria died in Florence in April 1578 and was buried in the Medici church of San Lorenzo. She had never been accepted by the Florentines, nor held in high regard by her husband, Francesco de' Medici, first Grand Duke of Tuscany. Throughout his marriage, Francesco had carried on a relationship with a Venetian woman, Bianca Capello, who was married to an obscure Florentine banker. When Joan died, the lovers—Bianca was by then a widow—were married, at first secretly, until the required period of mourning was past.

This was a time of crisis and decadence not only in Tuscany but throughout Italy, a time of bitter confrontations fought on land and sea among the European powers attempting to impose their religious beliefs while simultaneously conquering new territories in the Low Countries. Tuscany had not played a significant role in European affairs since the establishment of the Grand Duchy. However, the court of the Medici, which was admired and imitated by the court in Madrid, was the setting for continual entertainment and feasting, as well as for intrigue and conspiracy. Francesco showed no interest at all in public affairs, which he delegated to his subordinates. Yet like his ancestors, he was a great patron of the arts. Thanks to Francesco, the Uffizi (the offices) were organized as an art gallery, but his true passion and the objects of his greatest attention were the natural sciences and alchemy. The exquisite paintings that decorate Francesco's *studiolo* in the Palazzo Vecchio record his discovery of how to smelt rock crystal and how to imitate Chinese porcelain.

Francesco's enthusiasms and knowledge, coupled with the scant interest that Philip II showed in the cultures of the New World and the historical and ethnographical studies of them that were being conducted at the time, prompted the Spanish monarch to give the grand duke of Tuscany the codex written in Náhuatl, Castilian, and Latin that its author, the Franciscan friar Bernardino de Sahagún, referred to in a

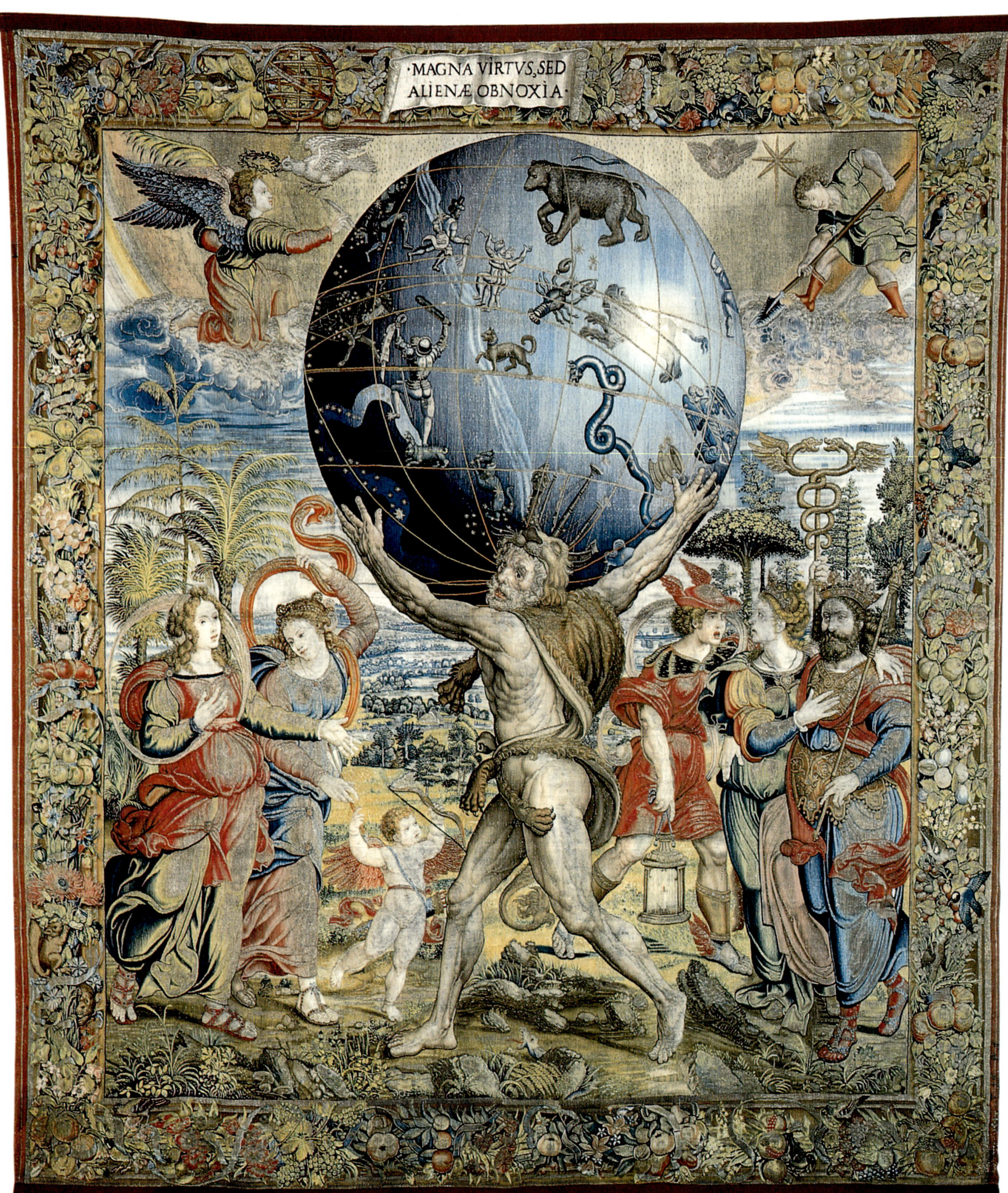
·MAGNA VIRTVS, SED
ALIENÆ OBNOXIA·

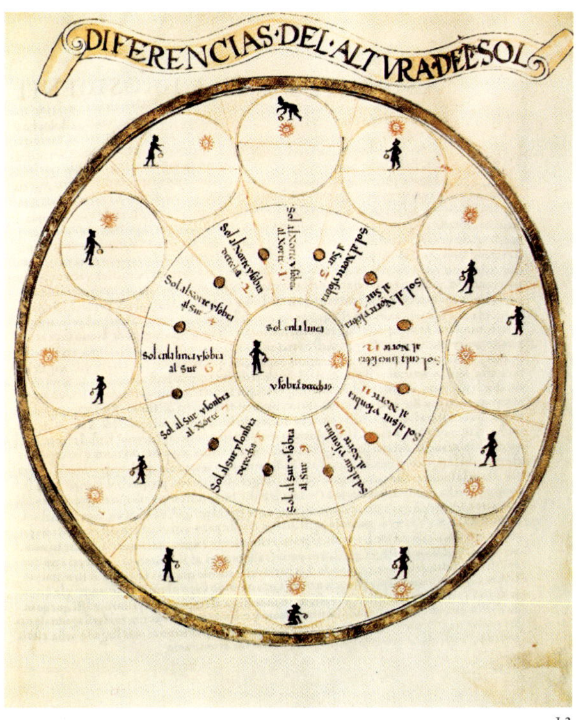

12

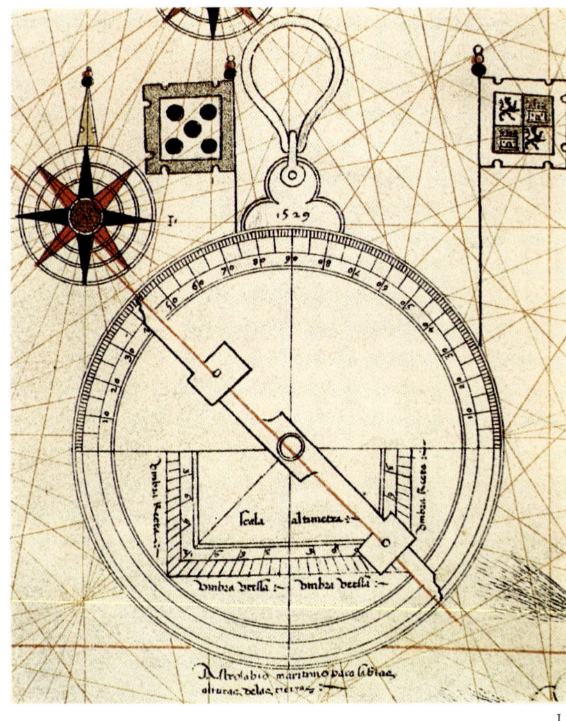

13

LEFT:
11. Georg Wezeler, after cartoons attributed to Bernard van Orley
c. 1530
Hercules Holding the Celestial Sphere,
from the series of tapestries called *The Spheres*.
Woven in gold, silver, silk and wool.
Throne room, Real Monasterio de San Lorenzo, El Escorial.

ABOVE LEFT:
12. Pedro de Medina
1538
Differences in the altitude of the sun,
Summa de Cosmographia.
Biblioteca Nacional, Madrid.

ABOVE RIGHT:
13. Diego Ribeiro
1529
Navigator's astrolabe,
Mapamundi.
Biblioteca Apostolica Vaticana, Vatican.

1578 letter addressed to the king: the manuscript entitled *General History of Things in New Spain* (ills. 14, 15), now preserved in the Laurentian Library in Florence. Philip sent it to Italy as a gift to celebrate Francesco's marriage to his Venetian lover, a woman as beautiful as a painting by Botticelli.

The Newly Discovered Lands Known as New Spain

Sahagún (1499–1590) studied at the University of Salamanca, an important Spanish center of humanist thought, and joined the Franciscan order. When he arrived in the Viceroyalty of New Spain (Mexico), he was made responsible for the religious and academic education of the sons of the indigenous nobility. To fulfill the first part of this mission—their conversion to Christianity and the eradication of the rites and superstitions of idolatry—he undertook the mammoth task of compiling everything he could find out about the lands, the customs, and the culture of the ancient Mexicans. Sahagún's studies resulted in the twelve books of his *General History*.

The first of these books deals with the "gods and goddesses that these natives worshipped"; the second, with the feasts by which they honored their deities; the third, with the immortality of the soul and funeral rites; the fourth, with the influence of the stars over human beings; the fifth, with omens that heralded the future; the sixth, with the natives' rhetoric and moral philosophy; the seventh, with natural philosophy; the eighth, with the manner and customs of governing; the ninth, with the mechanical trades; the tenth, with the virtues and vices of the Mexican peoples; the eleventh, with a description of the lands; and the twelfth and last, with how the Spaniards conquered Mexico City.

In Book Eleven Sahagún compiles a great lexicon of the "animals and fowl and fish, the generations that there are in this land, and the trees, herbs, and flowers and fruit, metals, and stones and other minerals," and provides us with a detailed description of the flora and fauna of the new territories at the antipodes of the "Isle of the Earth," lands blessed with great "diversity of mountains, woodland, and crags" in which there are "wild trees of all kinds, and savage beasts, and snakes." The Florentine Codex and the copy in Spanish, called the *Manuscrito de Tolosa*, are the only versions of Sahagún's codex from the period, for the *General History* was not actually published until the early nineteenth century. Sahagún paints a picture of Mexico as "a garden replete with fruit trees of all kinds and all manner of herbs, where there are fountains and rivers of different kinds"; a garden "full of wildfowl, animals, and fish of all kinds"; a place with fields, plains, and "pools and lagoons, where canes, rushes, and reeds, and a variety of water and land creatures breed."

For Christian Europe, the encounter with the New World, the *Novus Orbis* (ills. 12, 13)—with its somber, solitary, rain-drenched mountains, where the winds "roar and whirl," and with its crown-topped *cacaoacuáuitl* trees from whose fruit (cacao beans) a beverage is made that is "cooling and refreshing" when consumed in moderation, but can make one drunk when taken in excess—ended the notion of an "Isle of the Earth" consisting of Europe, Africa, and Asia, until then believed to be the only inhabitable lands on earth. No one had doubted that other lands (*orbis alterius*) might exist, but it was firmly believed that they could not be inhabited by the human race. When these "other lands" became "new lands" in fact inhabited by humans, Europeans undertook the task of converting the infidels into Christians, thereby civilizing them. Despite the supposition that all human beings are descended from Adam and Eve, the indigenous Americans were regarded as faithless and barbarous. So, too, were the inhabitants of farthest Asia. The governor of New Spain, Guido de Lavazares, wrote a letter to Philip II in late 1574, following the "discovery" of China by Juan de la Isla: "I trust to God that with this start Your Majesty will increase your domains in great number, bringing true knowledge of the Holy Catholic Faith to all the blind, barbarous people in these parts, including the great kingdom of China and many others, a task Your Majesty cannot fail to bring to a successful conclusion."

For Christian Europe—the "discoverers," colonizers, and evangelizers—America ("the fourth part of the world"), Asia, and Africa formed parts of a whole, the Earth. The new worlds were regarded as similar, even privileged, regions because of the exuberance and variety of their flora and fauna, the richness of their natural resources, and their inhabitants—"true men" able to comprehend the doctrine of the Faith, as Pope Paul III declared in his 1537 bull *Sublimis Deus,* which stated that God had endowed the people of the new worlds with the ability to reach heaven. Their lands, which were understood as manifestations of God's wisdom, power, and love for the human race, were, naturally, historically and culturally different from Europe. In the sixteenth and seventeenth centuries European civilization was the ideal: a Christian civilization, erected

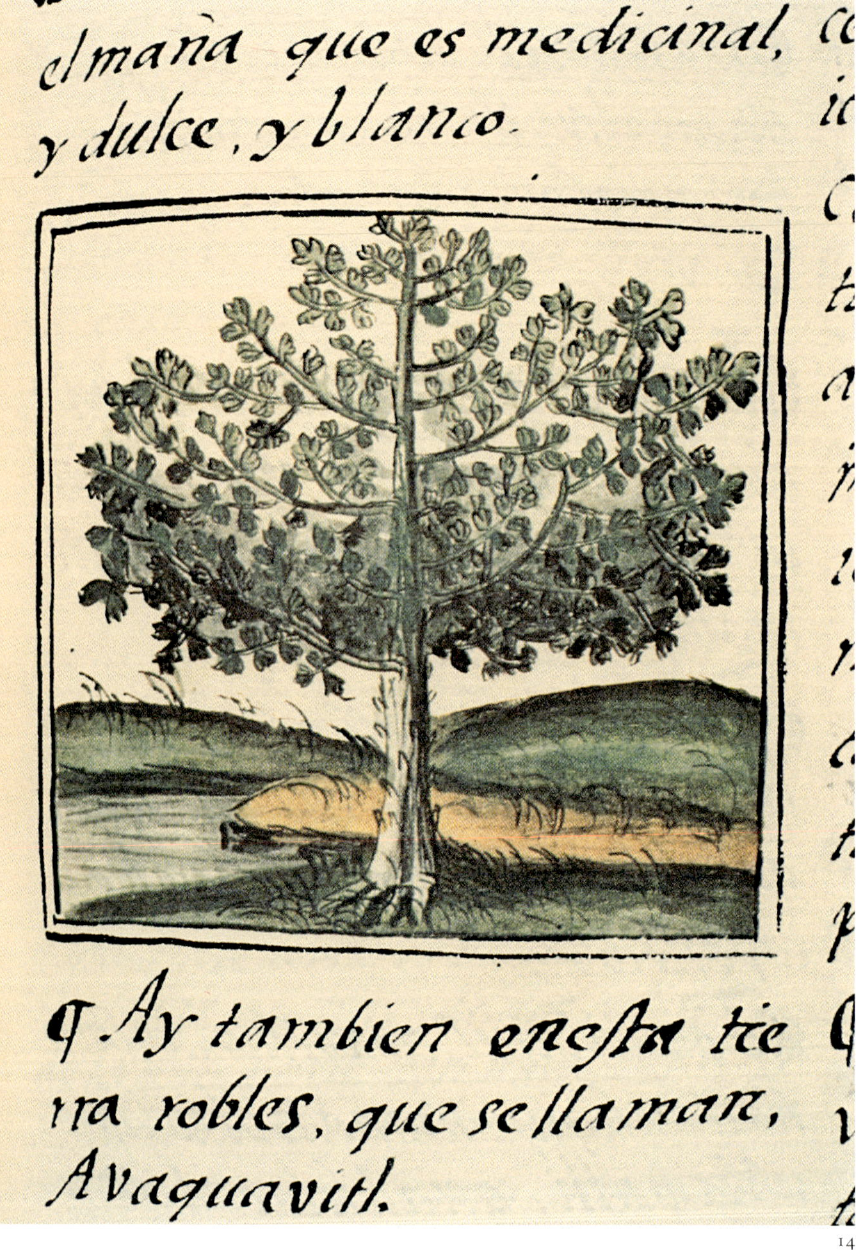

14. 1578
Oak tree *(avaquavitl), General History of Things in New Spain* (Florentine Codex) by Bernardino de Sahagún.
Laurentian Library, Florence.

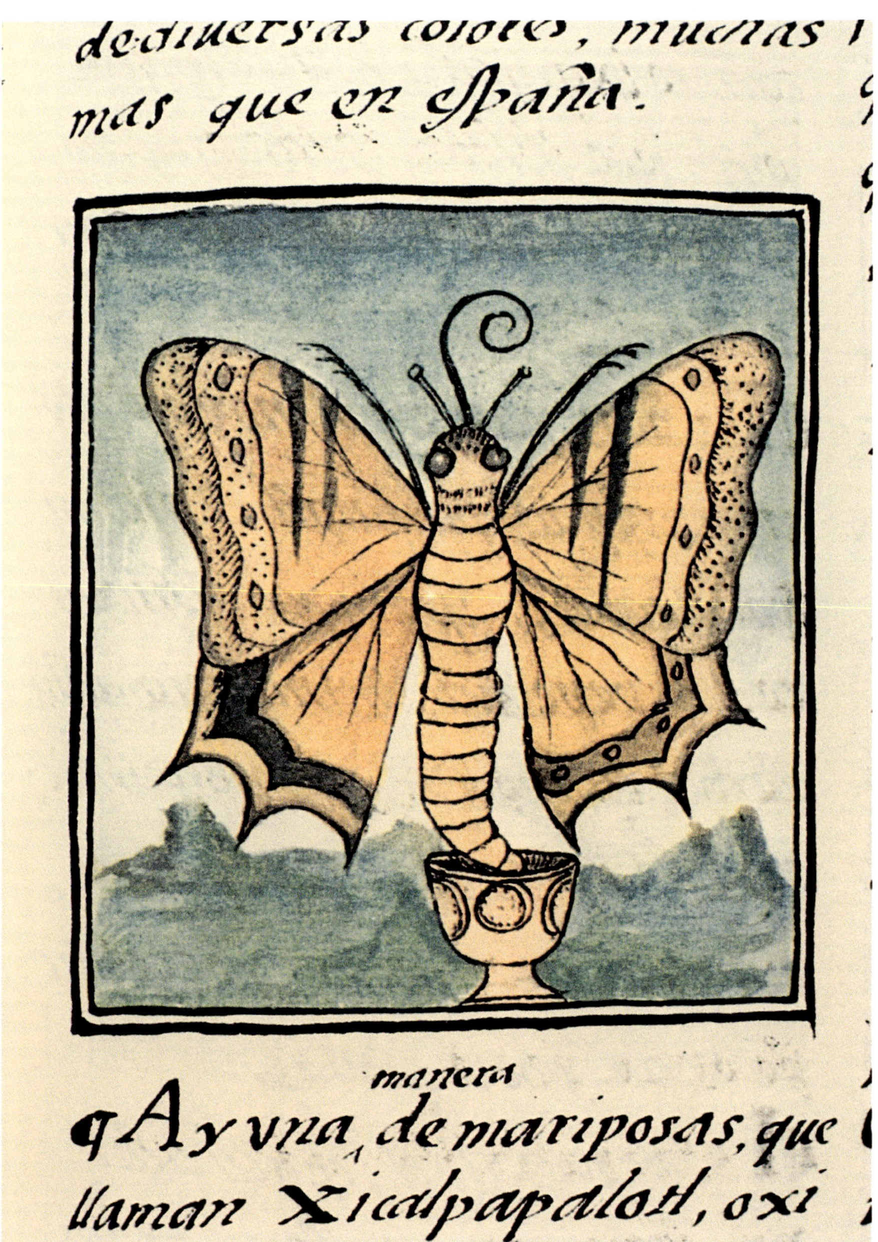

15

15. 1578
Butterfly *(xicalpapalotl)*, *General History of Things in New Spain* (Florentine Codex) by Bernardino de Sahagún.
Laurentian Library, Florence.

on the shoulders of the classical culture of antiquity. Europe appropriated the canon of world history, offered the criteria by which to judge and evaluate other civilizations, and regarded itself as the repository of the transcendent destiny of humanity, founded on the Christian mystery of redemption.

The "peoples of whom we have recent knowledge," as Paul III described them in *Sublimis Deus*, could not be treated as brutes created merely to serve the discoverers, nor could they be deprived of their property and freedom. That was the Christian ideal. However, the final article of the 1512 *Laws of Burgos*, which were in force until the enactment in Barcelona of the *New Laws* of 1542, established the number of Indians a single individual might possess (no more than one hundred fifty). These Indians, whose ability to become Christians was recognized in the *Laws*, were nonetheless regarded as inclined by nature toward idleness and vice. Pope Paul III, who commissioned Michelangelo to paint the *Last Judgment* in the Sistine Chapel and who convened the Council of Trent, asserted that the Indians could not be deprived of their property, but that they could and must be deprived of their spirit, of their own sense of the transcendent, and that their gods and sacred places must be destroyed. Fray Bernardino de Sahagún observed that the Mexicans perceived their gods in each and every one of nature's creatures: "This work will also be very timely," he writes in the prologue to Book Eleven of the *General History,* "in fostering a true understanding of these creatures, so that they might cease to ascribe divinity to them, for any creature they see as inherently good or evil they call *téutl,* meaning 'God.' So a creature might be called *téutl* by virtue of its beauty; the sea was so called for its vastness and ferocity; and many animals, on account of their terrifying disposition and savagery, were also called by this name, from which we infer that *téutl* applies equally to good and evil."

Deus Pictor

The discovery of the New World and the exploration of Asia completely invalidated the ideas about the Earth, its lands, and inhabitants that the Christian West had inherited from Strabo and Ptolemy (ills. 11–13). As Francisco López de Gomara, who had been Hernán Cortés's chaplain, states in his *General History of the Indies,* the world proved to be "so vast and beautiful and of such a great diversity of things so different from one another that it cannot fail to cause the admiration of those who ponder and contemplate it."

Strabo and Ptolemy knew nothing about this new world, a world that was not flat but round, not

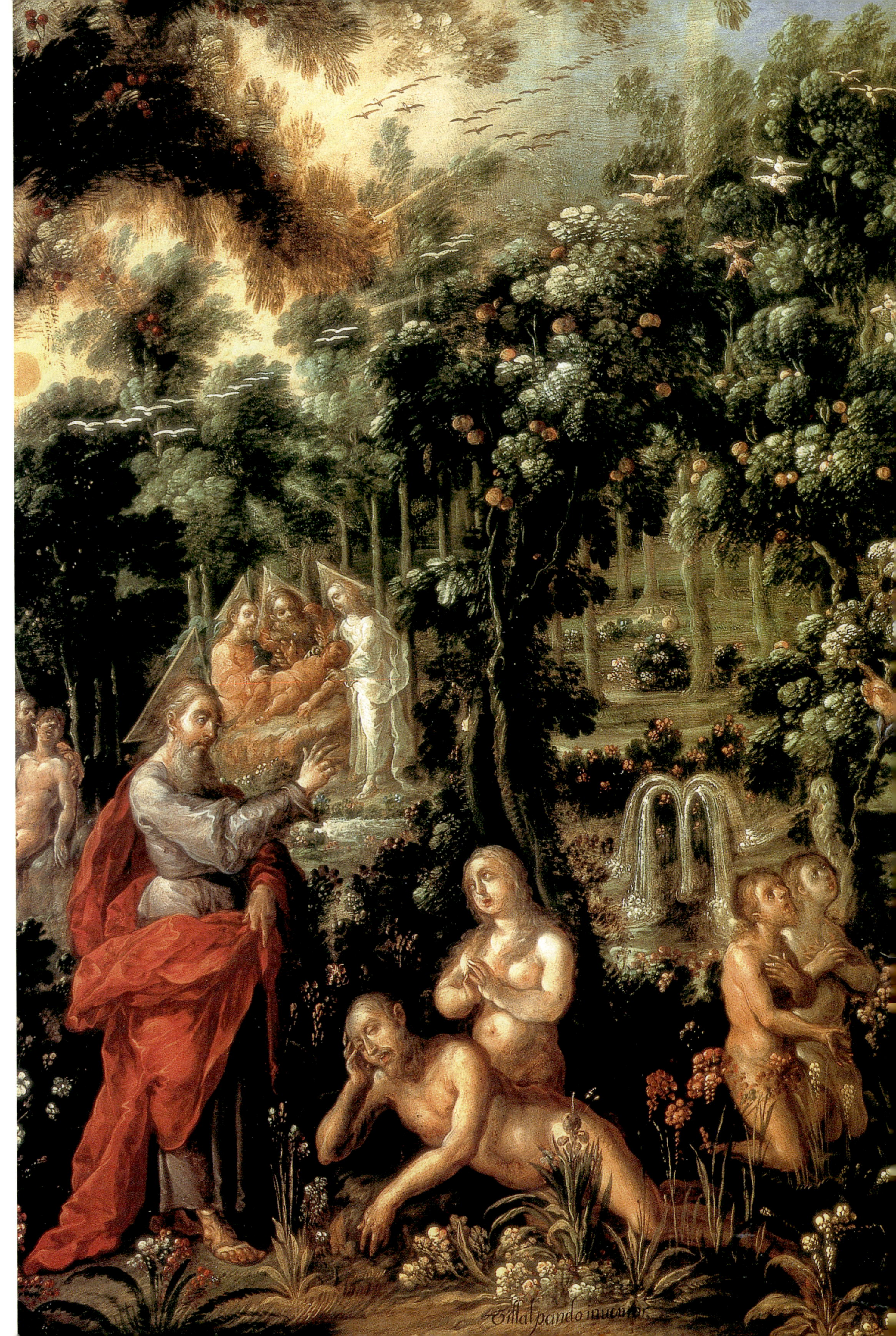

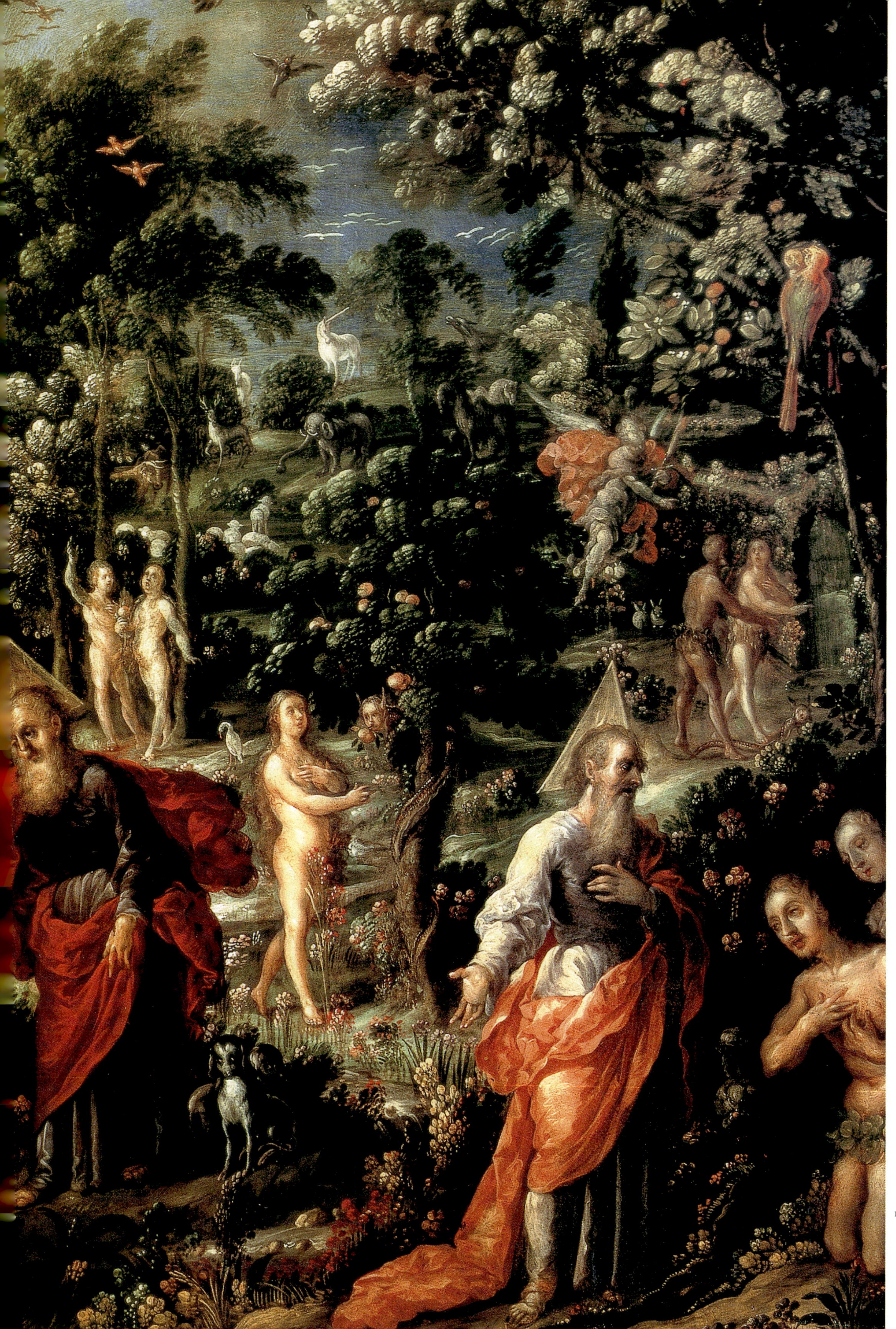

only habitable but inhabited, a world that differed considerably from the biblical accounts of the Creation. This new world transformed medieval concepts into a new reality in which God was represented as the supreme architect whose compass traced the absolute perfection of Earth as an ideal circle. However, at the time of the encounters and discoveries, at the dawn of the modern age, God no longer made His creatures with the self-assurance of a Platonic geometric instrument that imposes order on the trembling hand of the creator. God was no longer seen as the Great Demiurge, the architect of the Cosmos and arranger of nature; nor was he even the universal potter envisaged by Isaiah. He was certainly the *ideator mundi.* In the Petrarchan *Sacred Poems* that the great dramatist Lope de Vega wrote at the beginning of the seventeenth century, he asserted that God was "the painter," *Deus pictor,* who created light in the formless abyss, separating radiance from darkness, and hung two lamps from the heavens, two lanterns (the Sun and the Moon) that would eternally illuminate the whole Earth (ill. 16).

The Augustinian Tomás de Villanueva, who became Archbishop of Valencia in 1544 at the urging of Emperor Charles V, was famous for his acts of charity, which were painted in the seventeenth century by Bartolomé Esteban Murillo and Juan Carreño de Miranda. In his *Sermons of the Virgin Mary,* Villanueva describes God as the painter of the Virgin of the Immaculate Conception: "Come and see the works of God, the miracles He has worked on earth, the truly admirable work of the Sublime: the Supreme Celestial Artist has brought together the virtues of all the saints in the single soul of the Most Holy Virgin. . . . There is no beauty nor splendor that does not shine in the glorious Virgin" (ill. 17).

This was an era during which the figuration of the divine, the cult of images, and their use in the dissemination of faith were still under attack, when Protestants emptied churches of images in order to adapt the space to their own manifestations of faith. In the Catholic world, God, the Supreme Artist, took up with a vengeance the brushes of Saint Luke, the patron saint of artists, to paint the heavens, Virgins of the Immaculate Conception, and, in New Spain, the Virgin of Guadalupe. The Catholic church thus not only vigorously rejected the accusations of idolatry put forth by the Protestants, but also responded to the desire for images of the divine to have noble or miraculous origins. No work of art could be nobler or more miraculous than a work painted by *Deus pictor.* However, His painting is not always sweet and agreeable, like that of Saint Luke, the painter par excellence of the Virgin. *Deus pictor,* in Pedro Calderón de la Barca's play *The Painter of His Dishonor,* paints Human Nature as a perfect female portrait, the image of God: "Oh Human Nature . . . you are the image and likeness of your author." Human Nature, however, because of its freedom and ability to choose, is subject to the temptations of Lucero (Venus) and Culpa (Blame). With the Fall, the portrait of Human Nature loses its original perfection, which is reflected in the loss of its pictorial quality and in its metamorphosis from "oil painting"—the medium most highly regarded at the time—to "tempera painting," which was held in lesser regard, as the artist/theorist Francisco Pacheco tells us in *The Art of Painting,* published posthumously in 1649. Calderón de la Barca's *Deus pictor* expresses his disappointment in what has happened to his portrait of Human Nature:

> Who would believe that this
> was the image I painted?
> What light, what air has it
> other than that which I first gave it?
> I do not yet know it thus.

Pacheco regarded tempera painting as insipid and drab, its limited range of colors and tonal nuances insufficient for the imitation of nature. In his play *Give Him Everything and Nothing* Calderón described tempera as inadequate for the depiction of the beautiful and the good: "For fulfilling my duty as painter / and servant to laws / I shall paint your graces in oils / and my dejection in tempera," says the great artist Apelles to Hephaestion, the companion of Alexander the Great.

Hence the Flood, which God sent as punishment, because paintings in tempera are erased by

PRECEDING PAGES:
16. Cristóbal de Villalpando
1689
Adam and Eve in Paradise.
Octagon Chapel, Cathedral of Puebla (Mexico).

RIGHT:
17. Juan Bautista Maino
1612–13
The Adoration of the Magi.
Museo Nacional del Prado, Madrid.

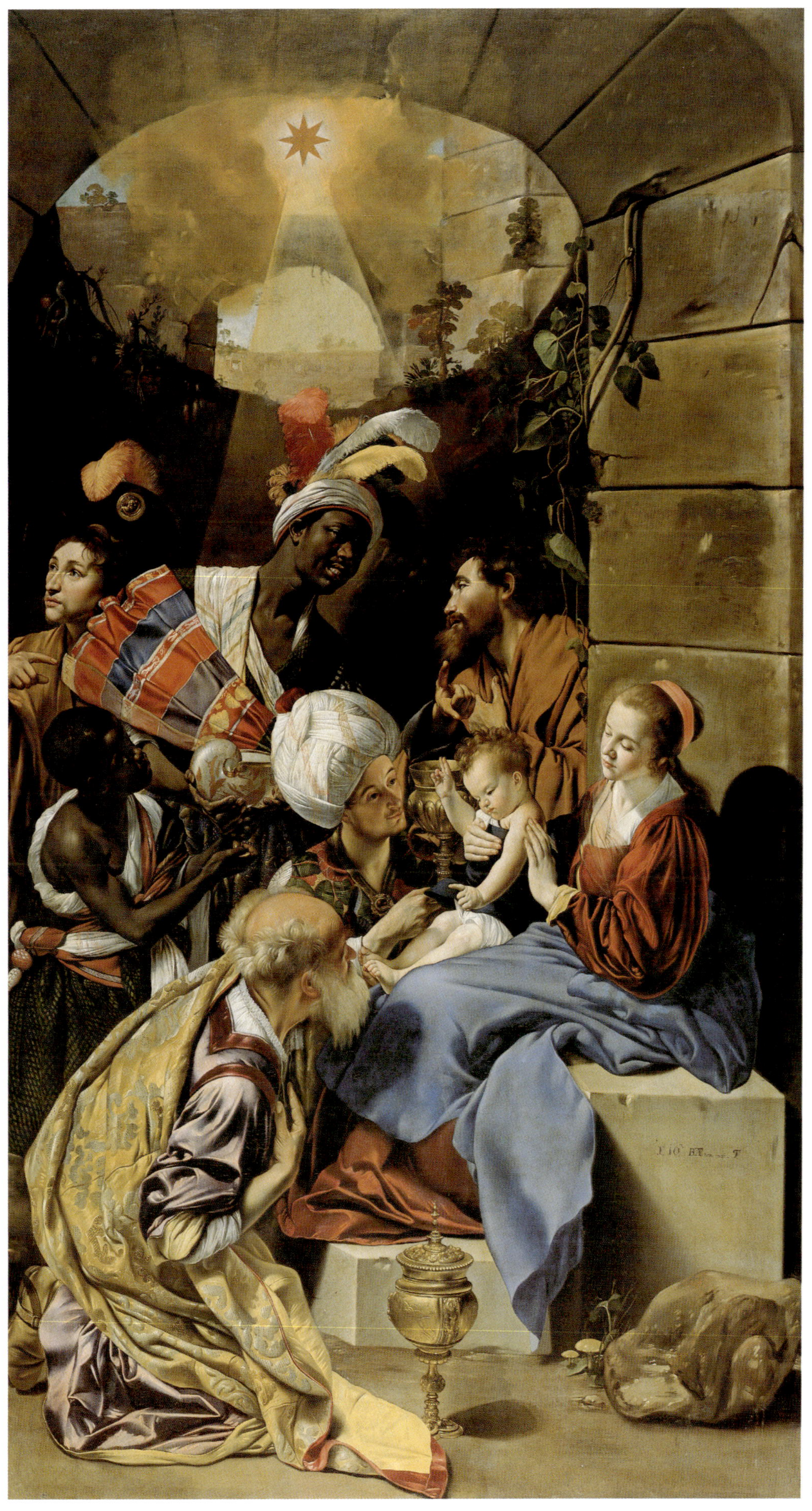

water, and hence the fact that when the Passion of Christ prepared the way for salvation, *Deus pictor* repainted Human Nature neither in tempera nor even in oil but in the red blood of Christ.

Sometimes God paints not only with His blood but with His nails. In a sermon preached on December 12, 1756, on the feast of the Immaculate Conception, Mario Antonio de la Vega celebrated the universal patronage of the Virgin of Guadalupe of New Spain:

> With wise arguments the orator denies men, angels, and even the Virgin herself the ability to portray our sovereign patroness, granting that gift only to the most powerful hand of the Almighty. In the smooth alabaster of the palms of my hands I described you, I embellished you, I painted you, I formed you, says Christ to the Church through Isaiah: *Ecce in manibus meis descripsi te* (49:16). And so that this portrait would be eternal, I took as my instrument not a brush but my hard, sharp nails that cut deep lines. And I did not use colors easily washed away, but my own blood, which is impossible to erase.

God is conceived not as an architect but as a painter, the divine Apelles who creates images with hard, sharp nails of pain, of suffering, with the blood of his Passion (ill. 18). This is not merely metaphorical, nor is it trivial. The idea of God as a painter meant that the Creation was something willed into being, something that might be affected by the uneven hand of the creator/painter, thanks to His skills, His genius, His vagaries. The world was no longer understood as immutable. It had become clear that old ideas must adapt to new events and phenomena.

Organic Nature

In the sixteenth century the earth, and nature along with it, came to be regarded as a living being, as something organic in an ongoing transformation governed by a *spiritus mundi*. That "spirit of the world" common to all living things was understood by some to be an actual physical substance, and by others as a symbol that centered on man as microcosm. Leonardo da Vinci reflected on this in his *Treatise on Painting*:

> Nothing is born in which there is no sensitive, vegetative and rational life. . . . We might say that nature has a vegetative soul and that its flesh is the ground; and its bones are the orders of rock aggregations that develop into mountains; and its tendons are tufa; its blood, the veins of water; the lake of blood that lies around the heart is the ocean; our breathing and the rise and fall of blood through our lungs, driven by the pulse, is the ebb and flow of the tides.

Leonardo da Vinci wrote about—and painted—clouds, the way water vapor rises so as to obscure the mountains, and the nature of leaves on trees in cold climates. Scientists began to describe and classify plants and animals. Poets like Garcilaso de la Vega transformed sunsets into verses. Painters like Pedro Fernández began to depict nature as seen through their own eyes and as suggested by their creative imagination (ills. 19–21). Fernández was a Spanish painter who was probably trained in the Flemish manner, but during his sojourn in Italy in the early sixteenth century he also learned from the art of Leonardo da Vinci and Bramante, and later from Michelangelo and Raphael. In one of his paintings, above a panoramic view of the lands of Subiaco, Blessed Amadeo Méndez de Silva rises to participate in the glory of his own celestial vision of the Last Judgment via a symbolic ladder that joins heaven and earth in bold foreshortening (ill. 20).

Pedro Fernández's landscape is of a grandeur then only rarely seen in the arts in the Hispanic world, except in the panoramic battlefields featured in Flemish tapestries; in the tormented view of Toledo by El Greco (see ill. 164), in which skies with their heavy gray clouds seem to threaten cities and fields; and in the distant blue vastness of the lands and skies painted by Velázquez. In his painting *The Surrender of Breda,* for instance, the smoke clouds of war; the distant, barely perceptible encampments and fortifications; the coming and going of troops;

18. Pedro de Mena
c. 1680
Detail of the *Ecce Homo*,
carved and polychromed wood.
Museo de Bellas Artes, Granada.

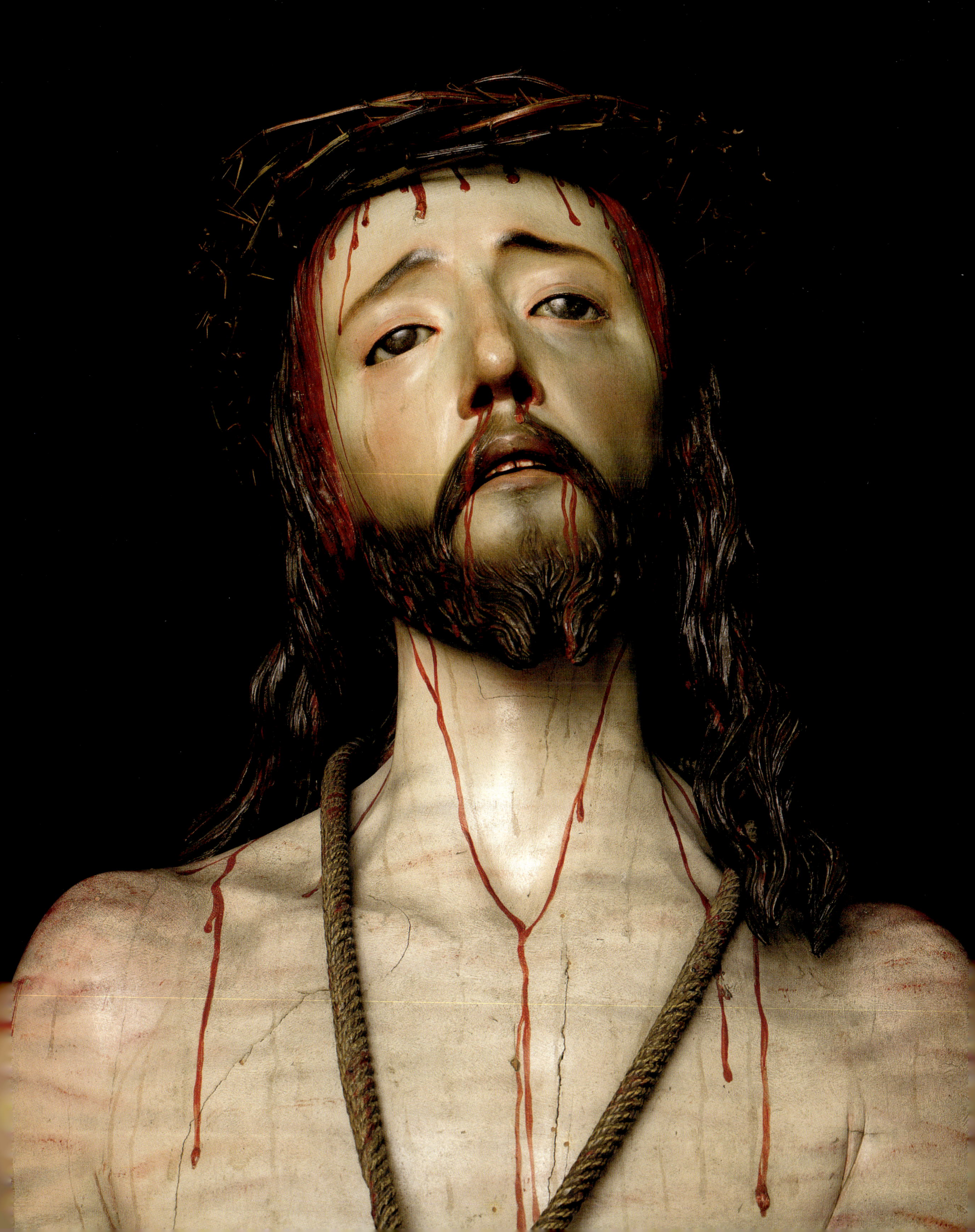

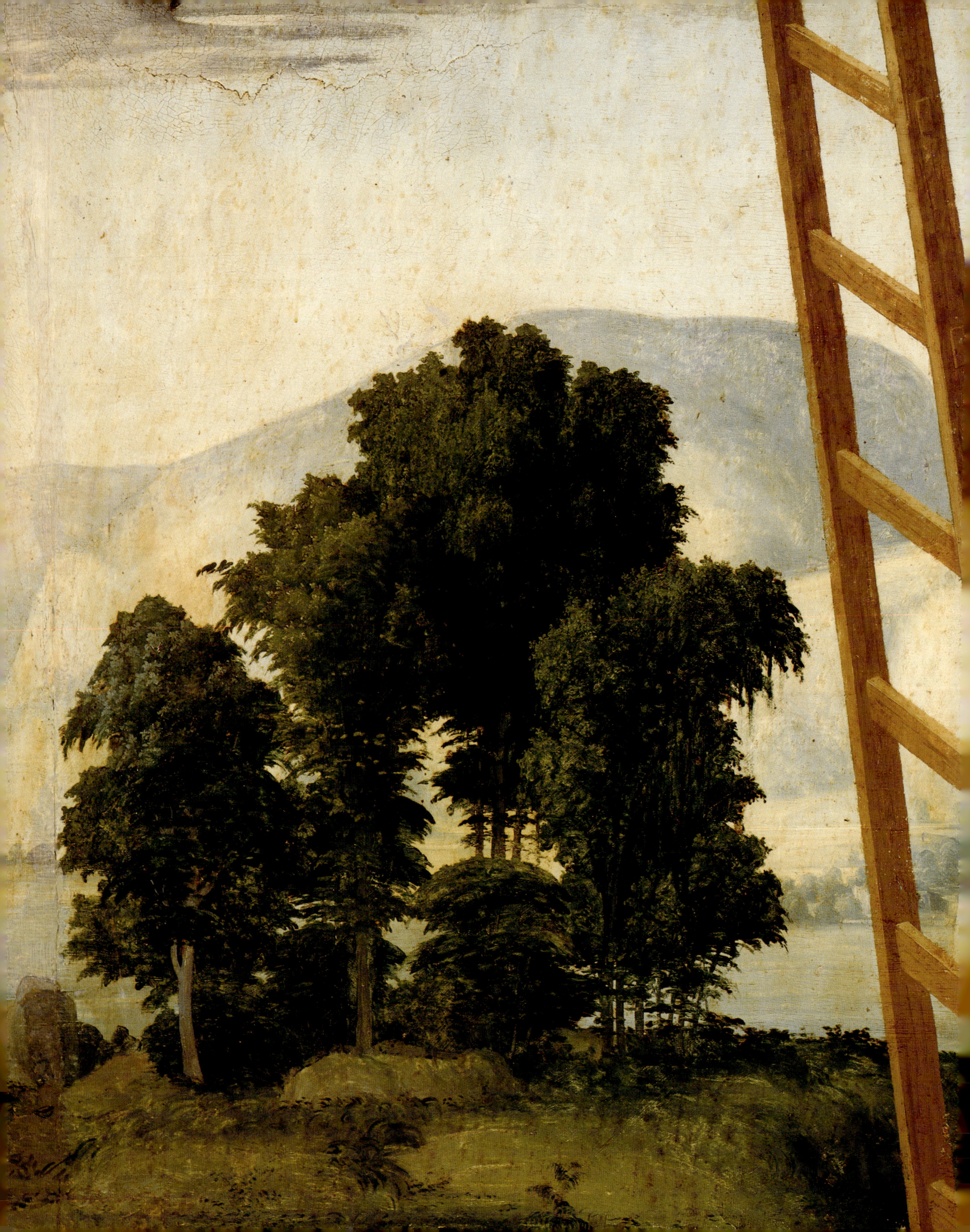

and the luminous cloudy sky confer truth on episodes in which the sublime finds the nobility, but also the cruelty, of human nature (ill. 22).

Bizarre Nature

Spanish artists like Pedro Fernández in the early sixteenth century, and later El Greco and Velázquez, traveled to Italy to familiarize themselves with the *maniera moderna,* and returned home. Bartolomé Ordóñez, Diego Siloé, Pedro Machuca, and Alonso Berruguete, among others, brought back with them open views of natural spaces, the details only barely sketched out but the whole composition shaped by the visual and intellectual organization of the painting. They also returned to Spain with a taste for the extravagant, bizarre classicism of the grotesque, which abandoned the natural world for a world of fantasy, freedom, and the irrational. This decorative style flourished in the mannerist culture of the first half of the sixteenth century, confusing the true with the false, the real with the fictive, the narrative with the symbolic, and the expressive with the subjective (ills. 26, 27).

Since the time of their invention in ancient Rome, grotesques—which Sebastián de Covarrubias defined in his dictionary of the Castilian language as "a certain way of painting that imitates the rough forms of grottoes and the sinister creatures that breed there and worms and night fowl" and that uses "ribbons and foliage, figures that are half-serpent, half-man, sirens, sphinxes, and minotaurs"—had been condemned not only for depicting unreal worlds beyond the sphere of the known and the unknown nature of human imagination, but also because they deformed the Platonic ideal of decorative geometry. In his *Ten Books of Architecture* (VII, 5), Vitruvius complained:

> But those subjects that were copied from actual realities are scorned in these days of bad taste. We now have fresco paintings of monstrosities, rather than truthful representations of definite things. For instance, reeds are put in the place of columns, fluted appendages with curly leaves and volutes instead of pediments, candelabra supporting representations of shrines, and on top of their pediments numerous tender stalks and volutes growing up from the roots and having human figures senselessly seated upon them; sometimes stalks having only half-length figures, some with human heads, others with the heads of animals. Such things do not exist and cannot exist and never have existed.

Despite these scruples on the part of Vitruvius—whose theories formed the canon of humanist architecture during the fifteenth-century Renaissance—by the end of that century the grotesques that had been discovered in Nero's *Domus Aurea* in the grottoes of antiquity beneath Rome had begun to take over both architectural and painted surfaces. Artists like Filippino Lippi, Signorelli, Perugino, Amico Aspertini, and Gaudenzio Ferrari used grotesque ornament to lend their works both classicism and novelty. Raphael and his workshop assistants, Giovanni da Udine in particular, raised the grotesque to the status of a recognized genre of painting in their great Roman mural decorations, mainly in the Vatican, such as the Stufetta of Cardinal Bibbiena and the Loggetta. In this complex world of flora, fauna, and human figures, architectural elements, foliage, the leaves of Corinthian capitals, volutes, monsters, satyrs, nymphs, small animals, chimeras, cupids, and a host of other elements are brought together in an apparently whimsical fashion, though in accordance with classical compositional order. Grotesque decoration came to Spain thanks to the artists who returned from Italy with their eyes and minds absorbed by the filigree of those fantastic natural forms, as well as through the engravings and the books of drawings of antiquities they brought back with them, such as the *Codex Escurialensis* 28-II-12. That volume, which includes some drawings attributed to Domenico Ghirlandaio and his workshop (ill. 26), was probably acquired on the 1502–03 trip to Italy of Rodrigo de Vivar y

19. Pedro Fernández
c. 1515
Detail of *The Vision of the Blessed Amadeo Méndez de Silva*, oil on panel.
Galleria Nazionale d'Arte Antica, Palazzo Barberini, Rome.

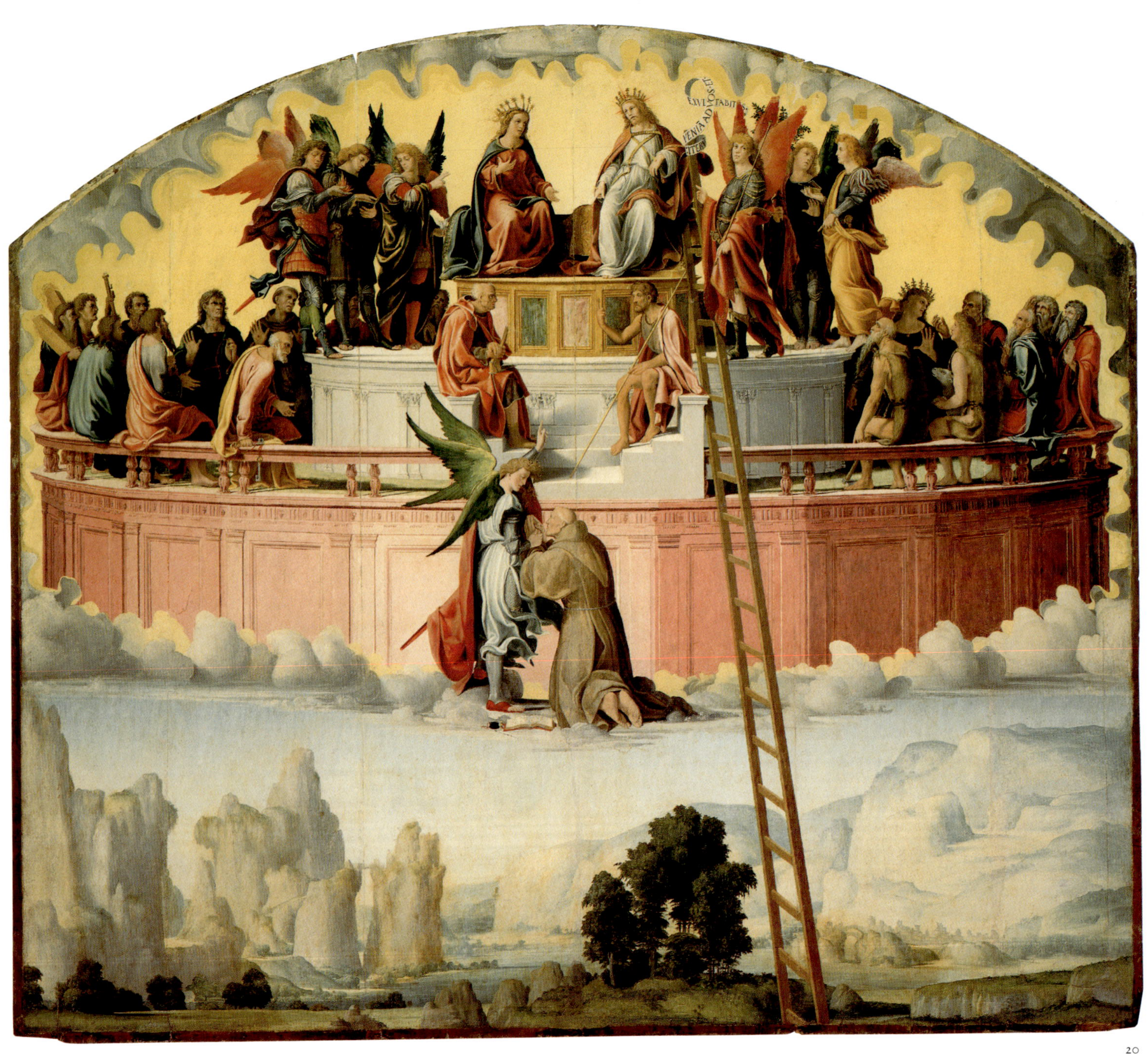

20

ABOVE:
20. Pedro Fernández
c. 1515
The Vision of the Blessed Amadeo Méndez de Silva,
oil on panel.
Galleria Nazionale d'Arte Antica, Palazzo Barberini, Rome.

RIGHT:
21. Pedro Fernández
c. 1515
Detail of *The Vision of the Blessed Amadeo Méndez de Silva*,
oil on panel.
Galleria Nazionale d'Arte Antica, Palazzo Barberini, Rome.

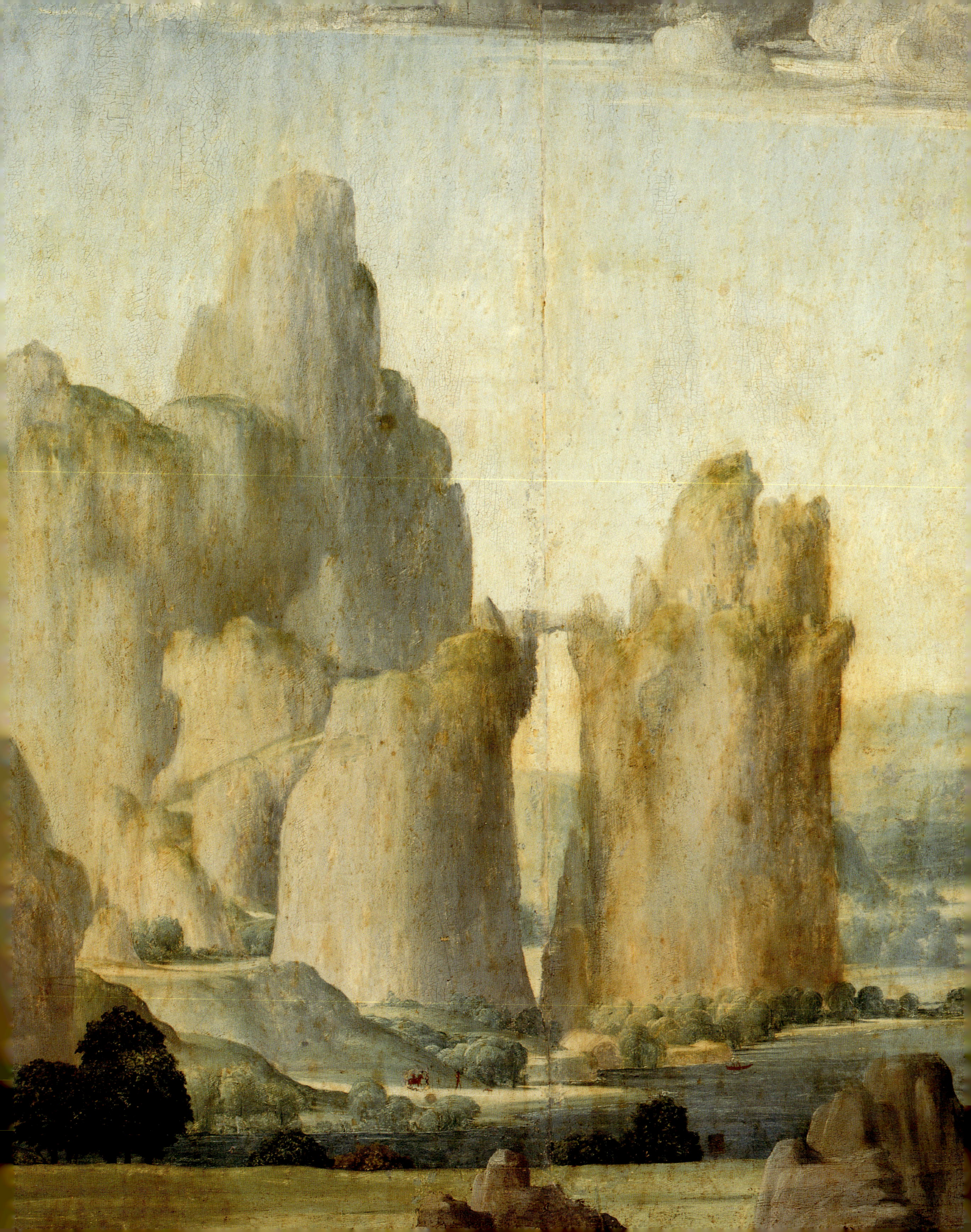

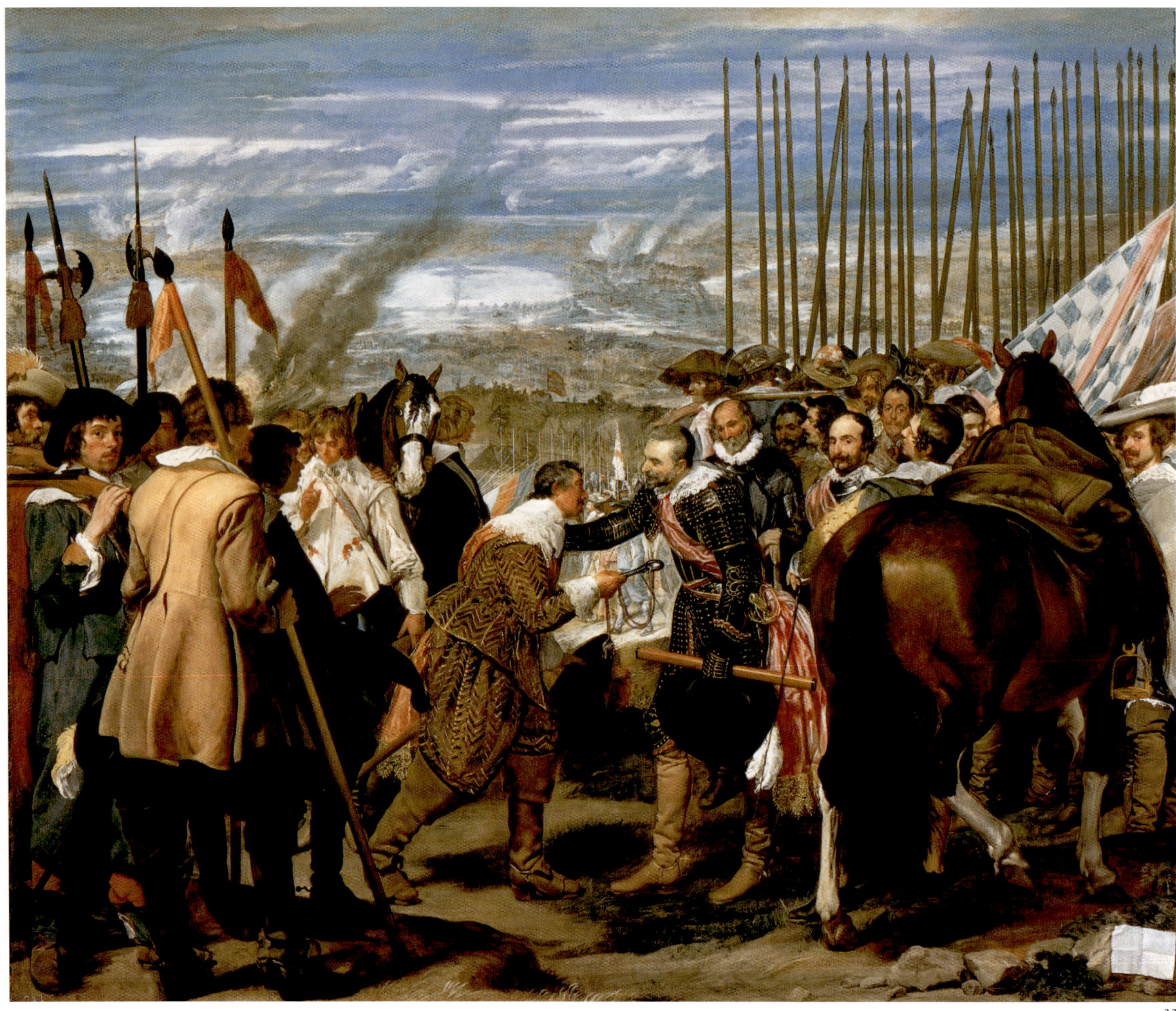

22

Mendoza, marquis of Zenete, and son (of a "lovely sin," as Queen Isabella indulgently called it) of Grand Cardinal Pedro González de Mendoza.

The Taste for a Certain Modern Manner

The Spanish nobility appreciated the Italian innovations as much as the artists did, and taste for the *maniera moderna* is reflected in the castle-palace of La Calahorra that the marquis of Zenete built on a rise on the north face of the port of La Ragua, with the wall of rock or snow (depending on the season) of the Sierra Nevada as backdrop (ills. 24, 25, 27). Though the structure is a castle by virtue of its robust, sober military geometry, the interior is a palace, dominated like its Italian models by a square *cortile* (courtyard). Two stories are linked by a three-level staircase of original design. On each side of the courtyard is an arcade of five semicircular arches resting on sturdy Corinthian columns. The castle-palace was begun in the late fifteenth century, but

ABOVE AND RIGHT:
22 and 23. Diego Velázquez
1634–35
The Surrender of Breda, or *The Lances*, and detail, from the Hall of Realms, the Buen Retiro palace, Madrid. Museo Nacional del Prado, Madrid.

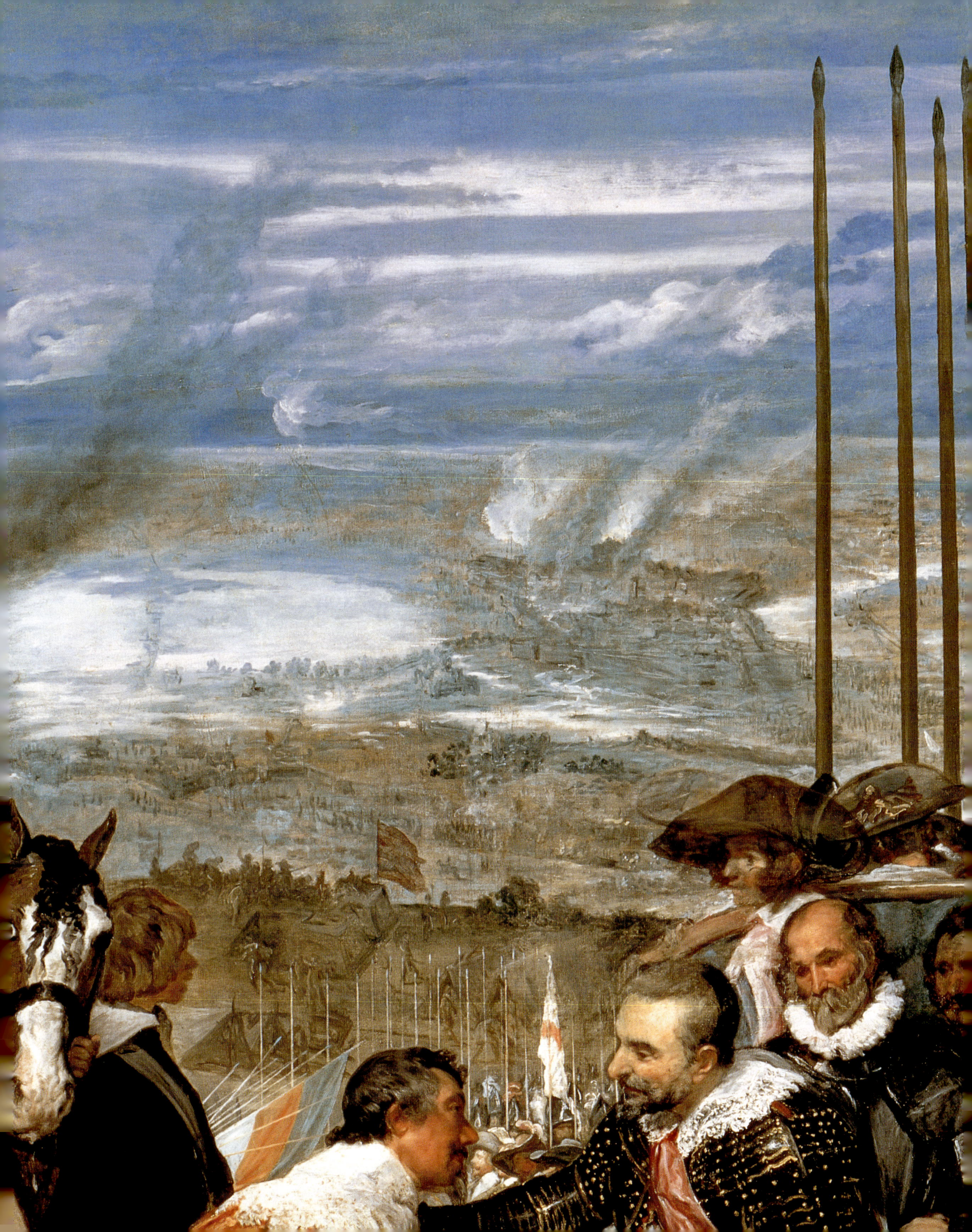

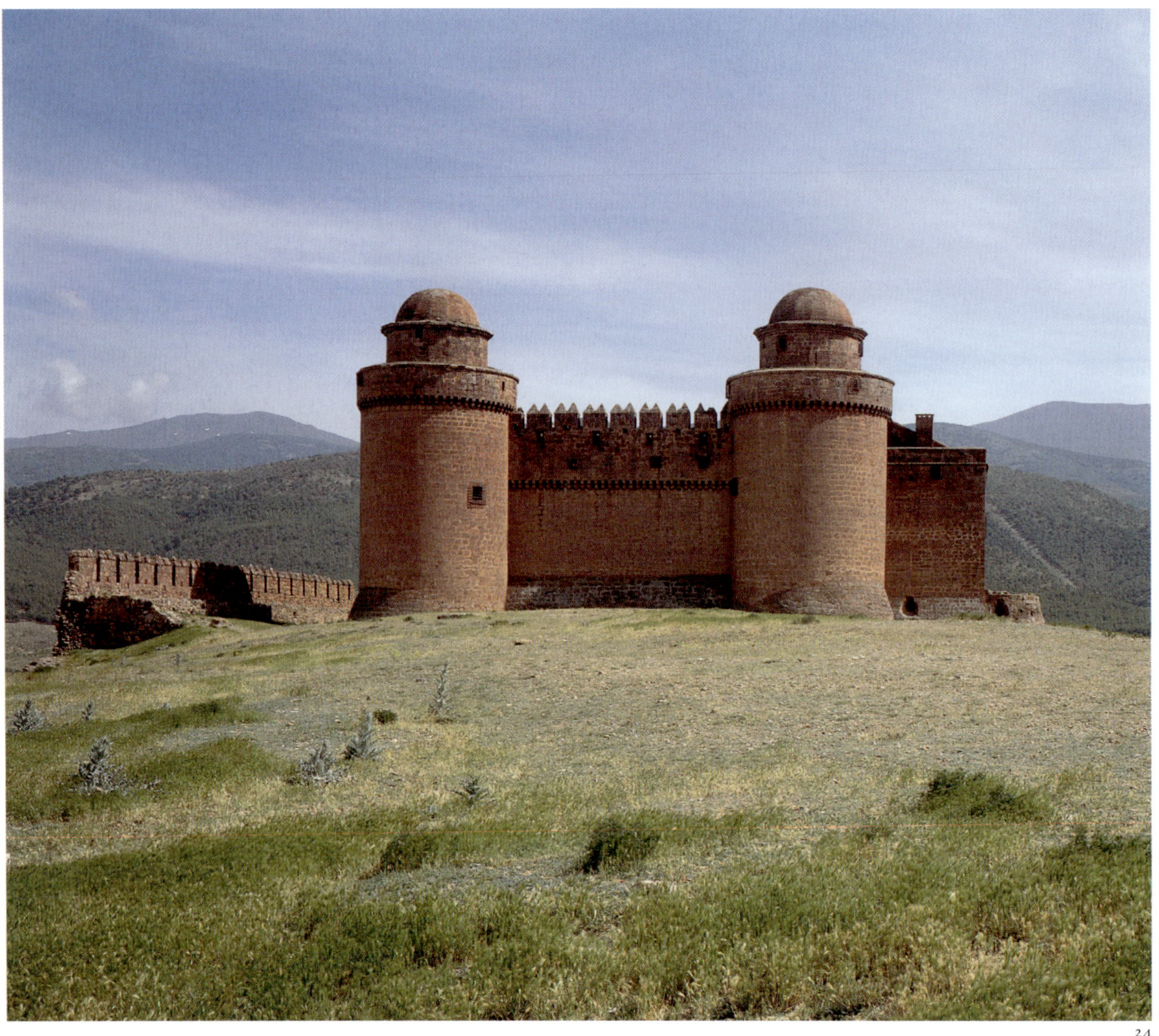

24

the pace of construction was speeded up in the early sixteenth century under the supervision of Lorenzo Vázquez, despite his tempestuous relationship with the marquis. Vásquez probably used the drawings in the *Codex Escurialensis* as models for the grotesques and other monstrous, fantastic, and mythological motifs that animate the surrounds of doors and windows, as well as the capitals on the ground floor.

The expressive though restrained chromatic dialogue between the whitewash, the reddish gold of the limestone, and the white Carrara marble is intensified on the doors, windows, balustrades, columns, and pedestals of the top floor, for the most part carved in Genoa by the sculptor Michele Cardone, who used both his own models and occasionally models taken from the *Codex Escurialensis*. Rodrigo de Vivar y Mendoza, banished from his marquisate in Granada in 1513 because of a conflict with King Ferdinand, returned to La Calahorra only sporadically from then until 1517, when he moved permanently to Valencia. The marquis left behind one of the first examples on the Iberian peninsula of the taste for fantastic nature and the pagan decoration reclaimed from ancient Rome.

This penchant for grotesques, which came to be imbued with hidden meanings, soon dominated the sculptural decoration on the façades of civic buildings (notably the University of Salamanca and the City Hall of Seville) and churches, choir stalls and tombs. Francisco Pacheco relates that both Spanish and Italian artists contributed to the revival of

ABOVE:
24. Lorenzo Vázquez and collaborators
1509–12
La Calahorra Palace.

RIGHT:
25. Michele Carlone
c. 1509
Doorway, marble.
Upper floor of the courtyard, La Calahorra Palace.

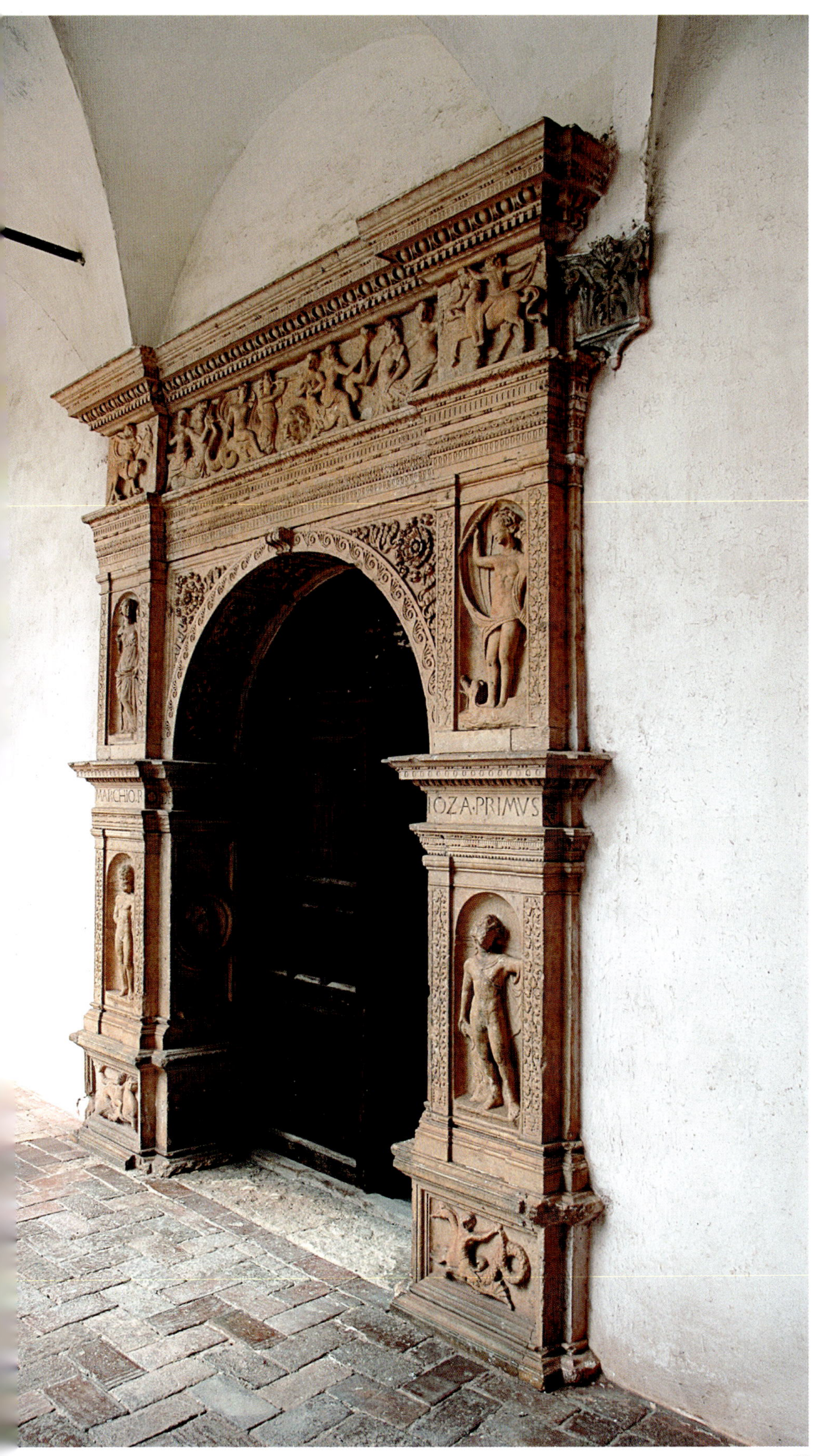

25

grotesques "in the time of Emperor Charles V, who fostered all the fine arts and restored [monuments] brought to ruin by the Goths, the enemies of the Roman Empire and of Roman genius."

Painting the Art of War

According to Pacheco, it was the "illustrious painters Giovanni of Udine and Raphael of Urbino" who entered the subterranean grottoes of San Pietro ad Vinculi eager to unearth the art of the ancient masters . . . and there they found some fragments of that manner of painting, and were greatly overcome with admiration for its strangeness and beauty." According to Pacheco, " . . . these discoveries also enriched Julio and Alexandro [Giulio de Aquilis and Alejandro Mayner], valiant men who came from Italy to paint frescoes for the house of Francisco de los Cobos, the emperor's secretary, in the city of Úbeda, and then the Royal House of the Alhambra of Granada, and whose painting lit the way for all the great Spanish masters to follow" (ills. 29, 31–34).

"Julio" was known by the nickname of Romano, like his father, Marcantonio, a painter active in Rieti, and his grandfather Antoniazzo, one of the foremost figures in late-fifteenth-century Roman painting. "Alexandro" was a painter probably of northern origin who trained in Italy and came to Castile in the third decade of the sixteenth century. We do not know for certain that they were summoned by the *comendador* Francisco de los Cobos, as Cristóbal de Villalón asserts in his comparison between the ancients and the moderns (1539). But we do know that four years after Giulio de Aquilis was documented in Valladolid (1533) he was in Granada, where he lived within the precincts of the Alhambra until at least 1540. Thereafter, he apparently worked in Úbeda for Los Cobos. In 1535 Alejandro Mayner was also in Granada, where he died prematurely in 1545.

Both artists, who trained in the Roman circles of Raphael, were most likely commissioned by the marquis of Mondéjar and supervised by the archi-

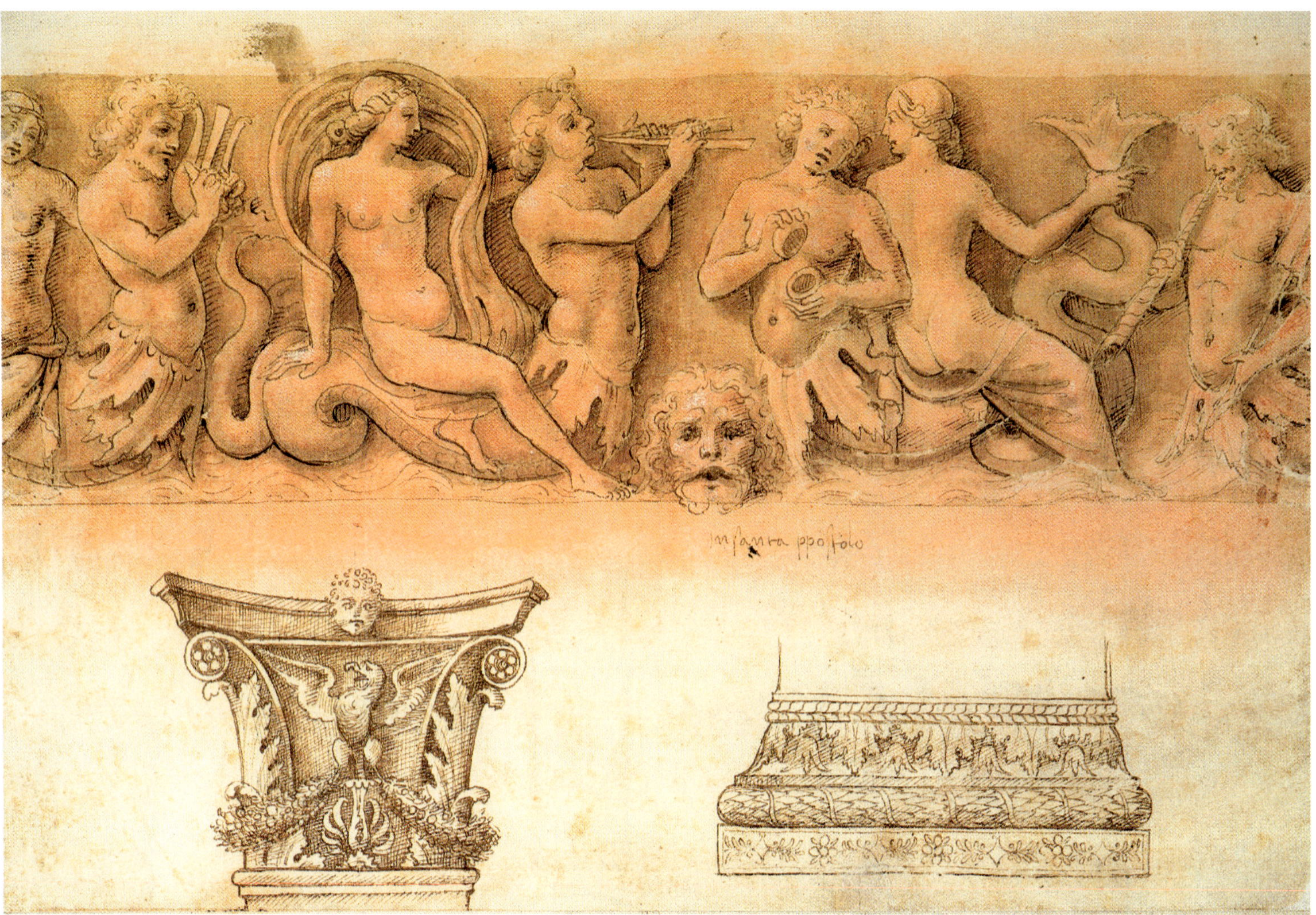

tect Pedro Machuca to create the best of the known series of painted grotesques during Charles V's reign: the murals that adorn what are known as the *cuartos nuevos* (new rooms) and the gallery that connects them, through the *Cuarto de Comares*, to what subsequently became known as the *Tocador* or *Peinador de la Reina* (Queen's Boudoir) in the Palace of Charles V, abutting the Alhambra in Granada.

The only murals that have survived in relatively good condition are in the two rooms (the antechamber and the boudoir itself) of the Tocador, originally the clerestory of the fourteenth-century Moorish tower of Abul Hayyay (ill. 28). This architectural alteration of the Alhambra was prepared to receive Charles V and Isabella of Portugal after their wedding in Seville. In the sixteenth century this small boudoir, circled by a narrow though splendid belvedere or loggia featuring depressed arches resting on Moorish capitals, was known as the *estufa de las Casas Reales* (stove of the Royal Houses). The antechamber received warm, aromatic vapors from the hearth in the room below, probably through a perforated marble slab. Today, after a renovation that changed the spatial relationship between the two spaces (in 1930 the tiled floor that separated them was removed), the room below is linked vertically to the antechamber.

The painted decoration of the loggia, which is outdoors, though originally protected by glass windows, is today in a very poor state of preservation. These frescoes featured full-length allegories of the Virtues, of which only the static but volumetric Temperance remains. Between these figures and the windows that provide the boudoir with light, grotesques in the Roman style (architecture, candelabra, curtains, garlands, putti, birds, winged beings, monsters and so on) transformed the three walls into leafy screens that enclose the garden of paradise that lies within the belvedere.

Before entering that fictive garden, however, either from the *cuartos nuevos* or from the exterior loggia, visitors were obliged to contemplate the

26. Domenico Ghirlandaio and his studio
c. 1490–1500
Frieze with tritons and sea gods (top) and column capital and base (bottom), *Codex Escurialensis* 28-II-12, fol. 15 v., ink drawing. Biblioteca, Real Monasterio de San Lorenzo, El Escorial.

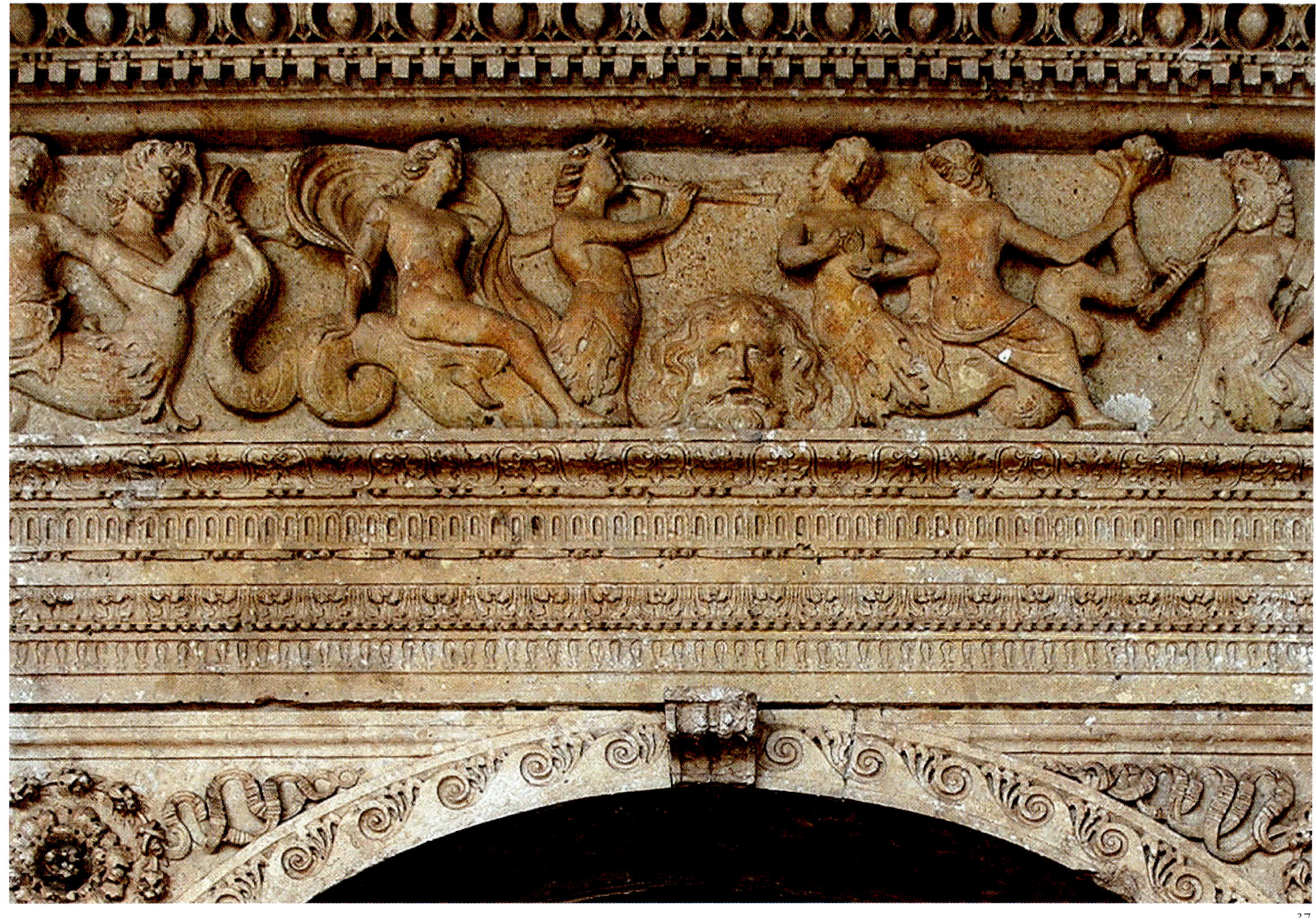

27

27. Michele Carlone
c. 1509
Detail of the frieze of tritons and sea gods, after the top drawing on folio 15 v. in the *Codex Escurialensis* 28-II-12 by Domenico Ghirlandaio and his studio, marble. Doorway on the top floor of the courtyard, La Calahorra Palace.

victories of Charles V's last crusade, the Tunis campaign (ills. 29, 31–34)—a triumphant military enterprise he personally commanded. The emperor faced the terrible Barbarroja (Redbeard), admiral of the armada of Sultan Suleiman, who had dethroned King Muley Hassan, thereby threatening Spanish possessions in the south of Italy. Charles V announced to his Castilian subjects on March 1, 1535:

> Considering the importance of this undertaking and what is at stake for the whole of Christendom, and primarily for our kingdoms and states, authority, and reputation, and in view of the great love we profess for these kingdoms and their inhabitants, and because of their greatness, nobility, and loyalty and the love they feel for us . . . I have resolved to depart for Barcelona to organize and equip our armada, as well as to give favor and encouragement and to be closer so that from there, and in response to the enterprises our enemies may intend to undertake, I may do what best befits the defense, safety, and peace of our kingdoms and of Christendom, and forestall any harm or damage that may otherwise befall, and myself embark, if need be, to fulfill this purpose or others that may arise.

This costly and perilous enterprise required the presence not only of the emperor, with his army of Germans, Italians, and Spaniards, but also the most illustrious knights of his court, including the dukes of Alba and Cardona, the counts of Benavente, Chinchón, Niebla, and Luna, and the marquises of Águilar, Astorga, Montesclaros, and Zenete, as well as the third count of Tendilla and second marquis of Mondéjar, Luis Hurtado de Mendoza y Pacheco, second warden of the Alhambra. During the rebellion of the *Comunidades* Luis Hurtado de Mendoza had secured Andalusia for Charles V and, following the emperor's visit to Granada after his betrothal to Isabella (1526), the marquis supervised the

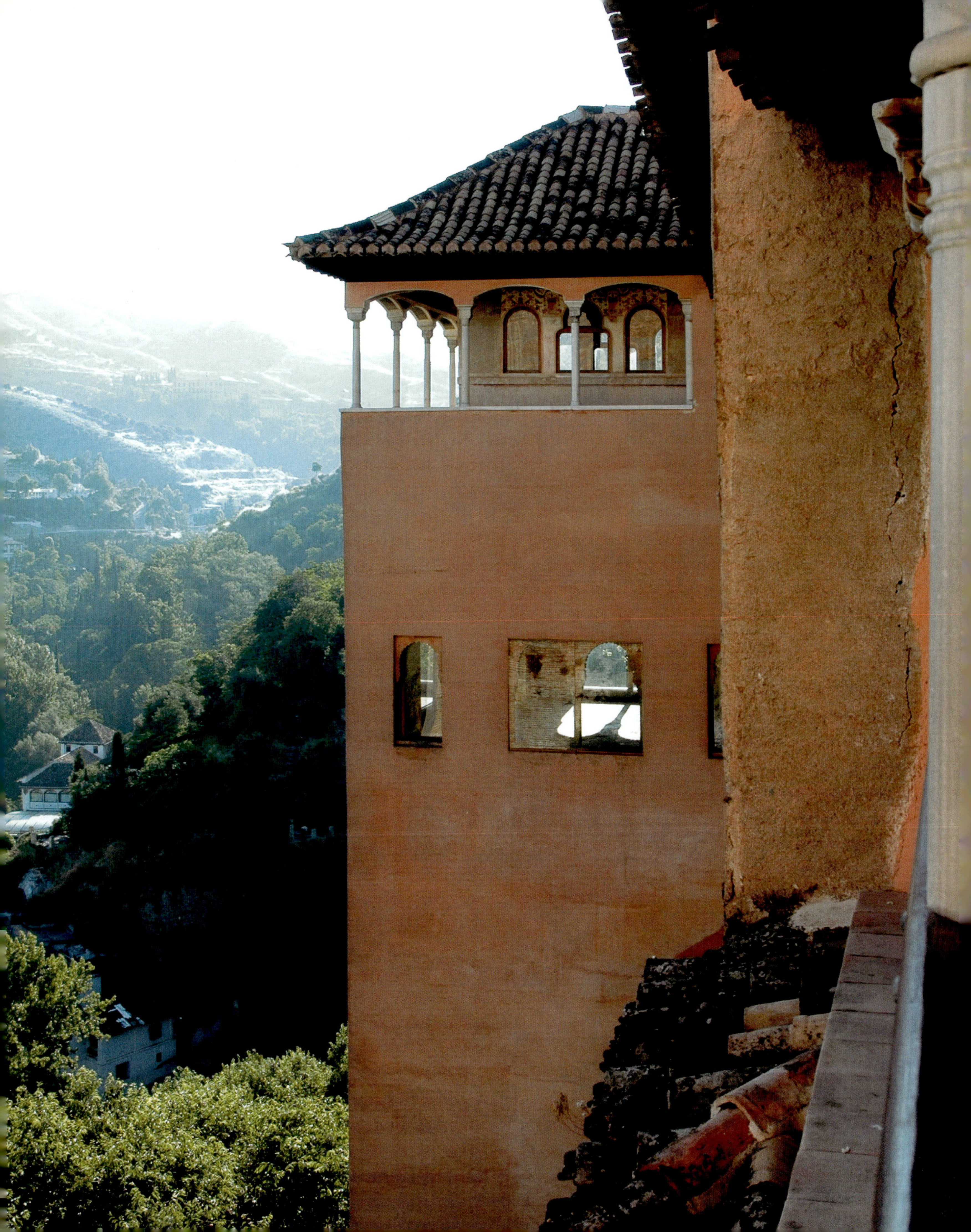

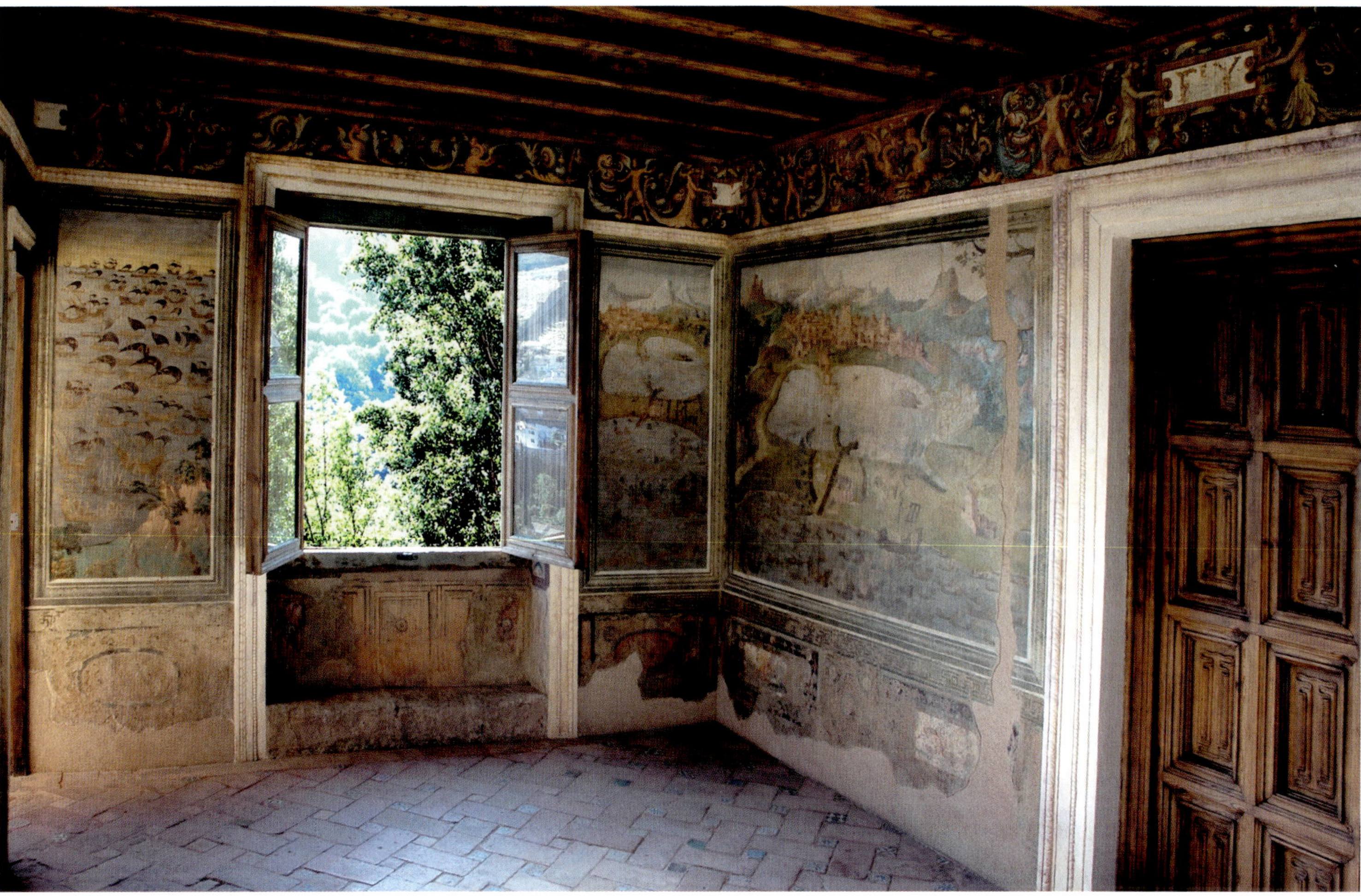

29

LEFT:
28. Fourteenth century
The ancient tower of Abul Hayyay at the Alhambra, Granada. At the top are the quarters called the Peinador de la Reina, prepared for Emperor Charles V.

ABOVE:
29. Alejandro Mayner
Begun in 1539
Murals depicting the Tunis campaign in the Antechamber to the Peinador de la Reina, the Alhambra, Granada.

construction of the cathedral of Granada and the imperial palace.

The Tunis campaign was so momentous that it required not only soldiers but also witnesses to provide firsthand literary and visual accounts. To this end, the emperor took with him the painters Jan Cornelizs Vermeyen and Pieter Coeck van Aelst. The former was entrusted with the task of making life sketches of the heroes and their feats, while the latter recorded the settings. A few years later Wilhelm Pannemaker used the sketches by the two artists to weave, with silk from Granada and fine wool yarn from Lyons, the twelve great tapestries representing the conquest of Tunis. The series begins with a general map of the operations, shown as a novel aerial view of an area stretching from the northern slopes of the Pyrenees to the coast of Africa (ill. 35), then proceeds to the review of the troops in Barcelona, followed by the taking of La Goleta and of the Tunisian capital.

The inscription at the top of the tapestry depicting the magnificent parade on the field of La Laguna in Barcelona (ill. 30), relates the planning of the conquest:

> All these things thus arranged, and enough time having passed to allow the armada to reach Barcelona, the emperor traveled from Madrid to that port city. There, having ascertained that all his orders had been duly carried out, he organized a display of the grandees and knights of his court. When the several fleets were gathered, he set sail on the last day of May, taking with him Don Luis, his brother-in-law, who had come to join the campaign with a host of Portuguese knights. The emperor made landfall in Mallorca and Minorca and in rather stormy weather proceeded via the Gulf

of León to Sardinia, to join the fleet that the marquis of El Gasto had brought from Italy, as depicted in the first tapestry, which is the navigational chart. With a combined fleet of over 350 sailing ships the emperor set off on his voyage to Africa.

The two armadas, Andrea Doria's commanded by Charles himself and the Italian fleet led by the marquis of El Vasto, mustered at Cagliari. On June 14 they set sail for the nearby coast of Africa, arriving two days later. The visual account of Charles's military campaign actually begins in the tapestry depicting the port of Cagliari.

Luis Hurtado de Mendosa, marquis of Mondéjar, was one of the heroes of the African expedition, during which he was seriously wounded. In 1539, four years after the conquest of Tunis and the year of Empress Isabella's death, Mendoza, who was warden of the Alhambra, commissioned Alessandro Mayner to paint eight murals narrating the events of that military campaign. The murals, which tell the story clockwise in the antechamber of the Peinador de la Reina, are now damaged by the passage of time.

Mayner would certainly have had the use of some of the sketches by Jan Cornelizs Vermeyen and Pieter Coeck van Aelst, which explains the similarities between the murals and the set of tapestries. However, whereas the tapestries are characterized by anecdotal aspects of the battles and by occasional views from land to sea, in the murals the view is from sea to land. In the murals, therefore, there is none of the suffering, heroism, or individual glory that may be seen both in the Tunis tapestries and in previous paintings celebrating military victories, such as those relating Cardinal Cisneros's conquest of Orán by Juan de Borgoña (1514), in the Mozarabic chapel of Toledo cathedral, as well as in later ones, like the frescoes in the Hall of Battles at the Escorial. In the murals in the Alhambra Moorish women anoint their headdresses with Christian blood, an act by which, according to Fray Prudencio de Sandoval, "they cleansed themselves of sin." Nor do we find depicted the thoughts expressed by Garcilaso de la Vega (who took part in the expedition) in his first elegy, dedicated to the brother of the duke of Alba, Bernardino de Toledo, who died in Tunis, exhausted by the heat and by the ordeal of hostilities, for which he can find no justification:

> Oh miserable fate, oh deplorable
> destiny that of man, and laborious
> the tasks he must undertake,
>
> and now much greater the misfortune
> of this age of ours that progresses
> in the guise of one evil to the next!
>
> Who among us has not been afflicted
> by the excess of wars, dangers and banishment,
> has not been tired out by the great trial?
> Whose blood has not been shed by the iron
> of the enemy? Who did not see his life lost
> a thousand times only to escape by chance?
>
> How many have lost and will lose
> their homes, their wives and their memory?
> And others seen their fortunes dissipated?
>
> What benefit is to be had from this? Glory?
> Rewards in abundance or tokens of gratitude?
> Those who read our history will know:
>
> There they will see that like dust in the wind
> all our efforts will come to nothing
> in the face of those who guide our intent.

The World in One's Hands

This sense of despair is absent from the antechamber frescoes, though they do give us a glimpse of an era in which Western man discovers new worlds not only in hitherto undiscovered lands, but also in the lands circumscribed by classical knowledge. These worlds, Baldassare de Castiglione reasons in *The Book of the Courtier,* must be "painted," because drawing and painting are skills that the courtier must cultivate to honor God, *Deus pictor.* Castiglione describes the earth as a "great and noble painting, traced by the

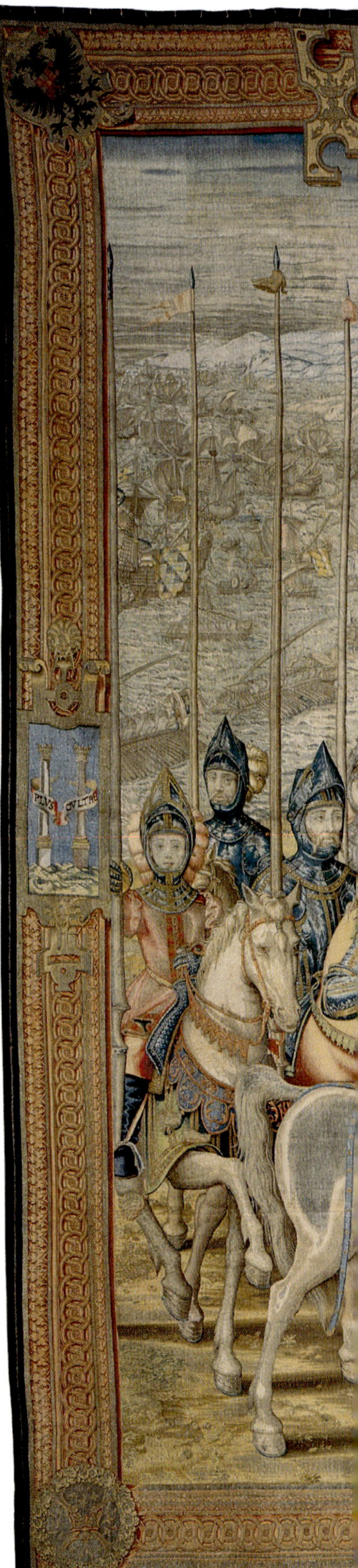

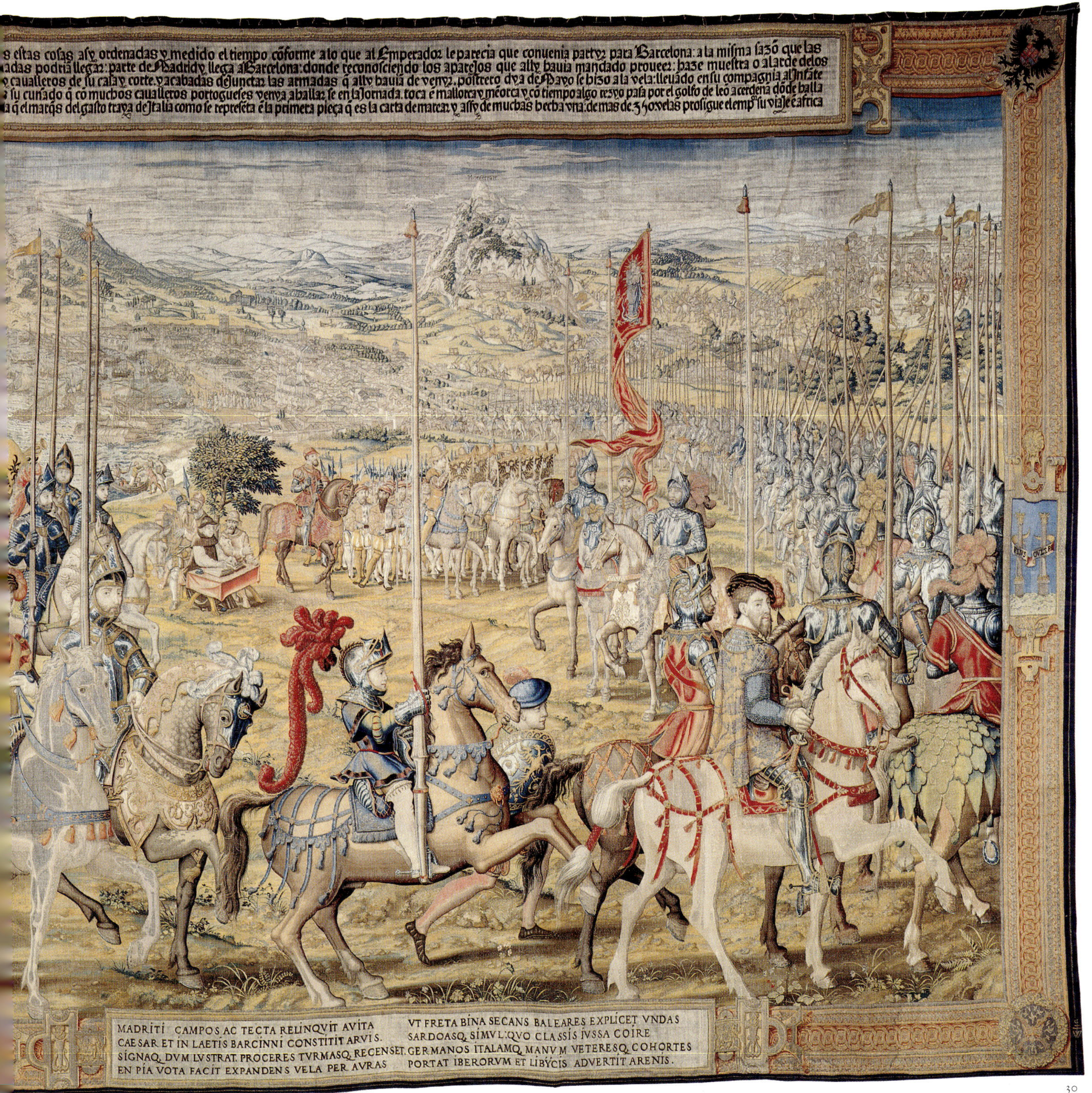
s estas cosas asy ordenadas y medido el tiempo coforme a lo que al Emperador le parecia que conuenia partyr para Barcelona: a la misma sazó que las
adas podriā llegar: parte de Madrid y llega a Barcelona: donde reconosciendo los aparesos que ally hauia mandado proueer: haze muestra o alarde delos
y caualleros de su casa y corte. y acabadas de junctar las armadas q ally hauia de venyr. postrero dya de Mayo se hizo a la vela: lleuado en su compagnia al Infāte
su cuñado q cō muchos caualleros portogueses venya a hallar se en la Jornada. toca é mallorca y méorca y cō tiempo algo rezyo pasa por el golfo de leō a cerdeña dōde halla
a q el marqs del gasto traya de Italia como se represēta ē la primera pieça q es la carta de marear y assy de muchas hecha vna: de mas de 350 velas prosigue el empor su viaje é africa
Montserrat
MADRITI CAMPOS AC TECTA RELINQVIT AVITA
CAESAR ET IN LAETIS BARCINNI CONSTITIT ARVIS.
SIGNAQ. DVM LVSTRAT. PROCERES TVRMASQ. RECENSET.
EN PIA VOTA FACIT EXPANDENS VELA PER AVRAS
VT FRETA BINA SECANS BALEARES EXPLICET VNDAS
SARDOASQ. SIMVL: QVO CLASSIS IVSSA COIRE
GERMANOS ITALAMQ. MANVM VETERESQ. COHORTES
PORTAT IBERORVM ET LIBYCIS ADVERTIT ARENIS.

30

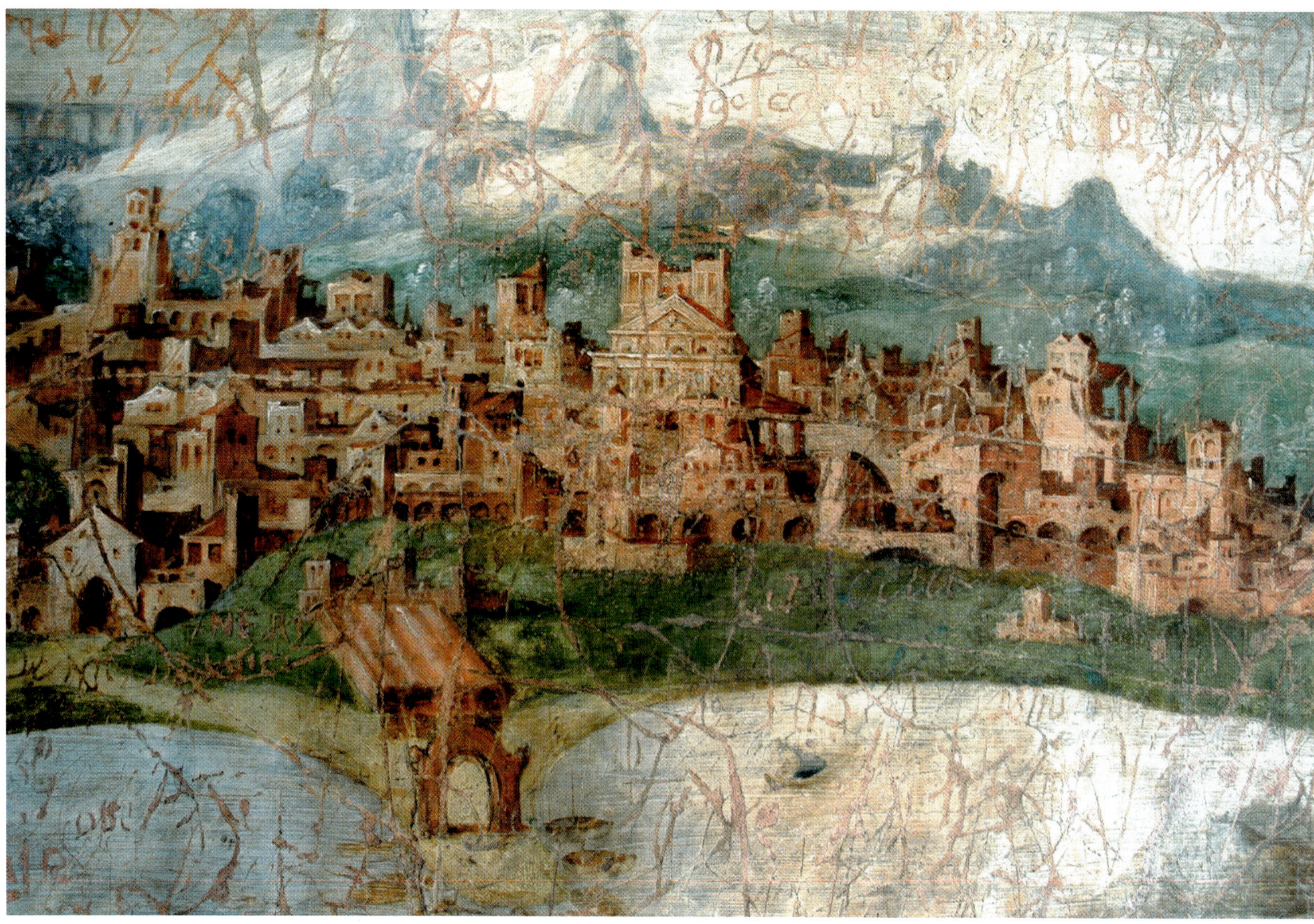

31

hand of nature and God." Such moral considerations aside, Castiglione recommends learning the art of drawing and painting lands, fortifications, rivers, bridges, and strongholds, a skill that is very useful for the art of war. In his *De tratendis disciplinaris* (IV, 1) the Spanish humanist Juan Luis Vives asserts that an understanding and interpretation of nature requires that its full rendering "be included as in a painting." Such complete descriptions increase human knowledge, serve as preparation for the art of war, and also offer financial benefits, since accurate maps of a ruler's dominions facilitate increased taxation. Charles V forcefully applied the latter principle in the Netherlands and in the Duchy of Milan, although his affinity for maps went beyond mere financial considerations. The map maker Alonso de Santa Cruz, who accompanied Charles V on his retreat to Toledo in 1539, recorded that Charles "derived much enjoyment and delight" from the study of astrology, the Earth, navigational charts, and terrestrial globes. Martin du Bellay related in his *Historical Memoirs* that when the emperor held maps in his hands he felt that he possessed the very places they represented. The emperor's sea was very different from those baroque seas transformed into a misty, distant view as described by Calderón de la Barca in Act One of his play *The Constant Prince:*

> I know it for on the sea
> one morning, at the hour
> when the sun, still half-asleep,
> sweeping away the shadows
> of twilight, unraveled
> tresses of blond hair
> over jasmine and roses,
> with cloth of gold wiped
> from the dawn tears of fire
> and snow which the sun

PRECEDING PAGE:
30. Wilhelm de Pannemaker, after cartoons by Jan Cornelisz Vermeyen and Pieter Coeck van Aelst
c. 1554
Parade on the Field of La Laguna, Barcelona, one of the *Conquest of Tunis* tapestries, woven in gold, silver, silk, and wool.
Palacio Real, Madrid.

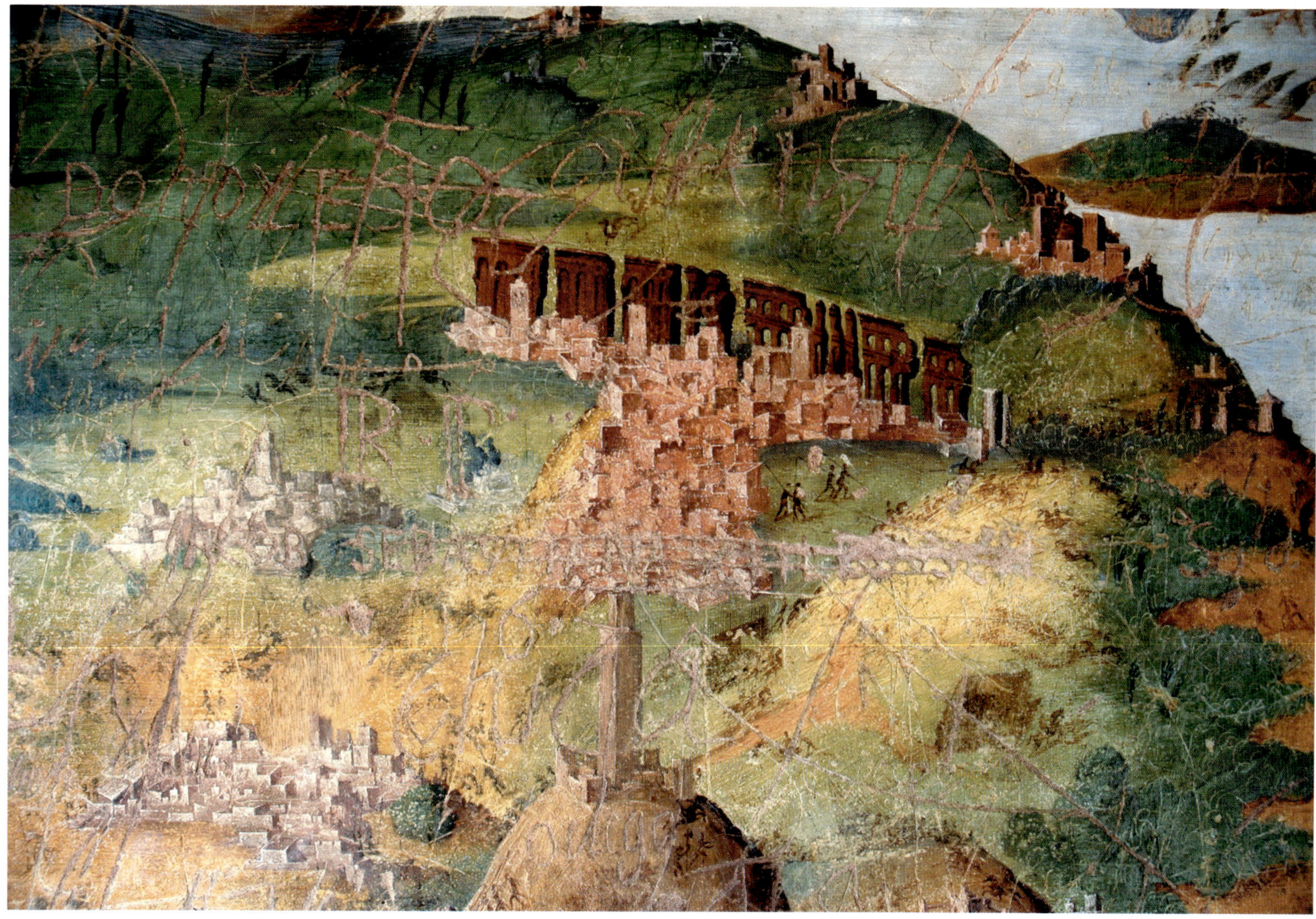

32

ABOVE LEFT AND RIGHT:
31 and 32. Alejandro Mayner
Begun in 1539
Details of the *View of Carthage,* fresco.
Antechamber to the Peinador de la Reina, the Alhambra, Granada.

transformed into seed pearl,
from far over the water
came a mighty fleet
of ships; although then
my riveted gaze could not
discern whether they were vessels
or whether they were rocks,
for as subtle brushstrokes
attain sheens, distances
that in illusory perspective
appear perhaps to be mountains
or even legendary cities,
for distance invariably forms
impossible monsters.

But the seas off the coast of Africa, whether the topographical renderings in the Alhambra or those depicted with the subtle brushstrokes of Calderón, did not belong solely to the emperor or Prince Ferdinand. In chapter XXXIX of *Don Quixote* Cervantes writes:

> We returned to Constantinople, and the following year, seventy-three, it became known that Don Juan had seized Tunis and taken the kingdom from the Turks, and placed Muley Hamet in possession, putting an end to the hopes which Muley Hamida, the cruelest and bravest Moor in the world, entertained of returning to reign there. The Grand Turk took the loss greatly to heart, and with the cunning which all his race possess, he made peace with the Venetians (who were much more eager for it than he was), and the following year, seventy-four, he attacked the Goletta and the fort which Don Juan had left half built near Tunis. While all these events were occurring, I was laboring at the oar without any hope of freedom; at least I had no hope of obtaining it by ransom, for

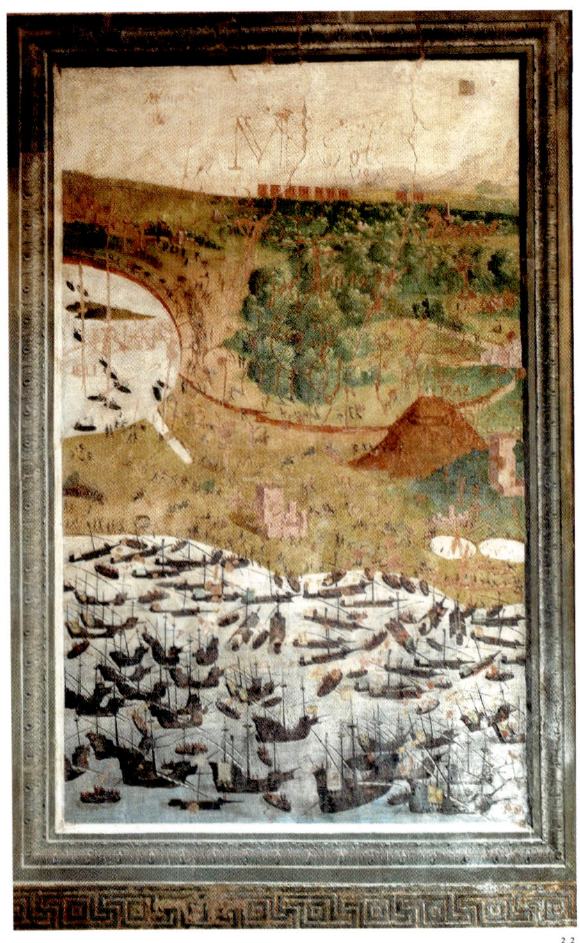
33

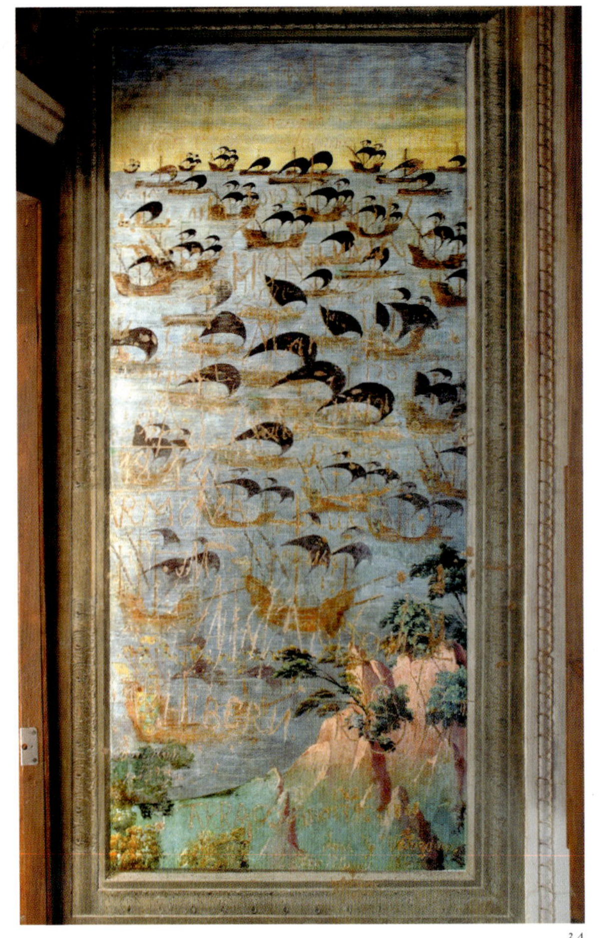
34

I was firmly resolved not to write to my father telling him of my misfortunes. At length the Goletta fell, . . . until then reckoned impregnable, and it fell, not by any fault of its defenders, who did all that they could and should have done, but because experiment proved how easily entrenchments could be made in the desert sand there.

The fortress island that guards the bay of Tunis and appears in the frescoes at the Alhambra (as do the ruins of Carthage, embodiment of the memory and the glory of ancient Rome) was indeed taken by the Turks in 1574. Thus ended the glorious victory of Charles V, the new Scipio, who, in the words of the Italian poet Pietro Aretino, had entered into the heart of Africa "sword in hand" to "free eighteen thousand Christians from their chains."

ABOVE LEFT AND RIGHT:
33 and 34. Alejandro Mayner
Begun in 1539
Details of the frescoes depicting the Tunis campaign.
Antechamber to the Peinador de la Reina, the Alhambra, Granada.

RIGHT:
35. Wilhelm de Pannemaker, after cartoons by Jan Cornelisz Vermeyen and Pieter Coeck van Aelst
c. 1554
Map on which Spanish lands are shown from the African coast (at the top), from the *Conquest of Tunis* tapestry series.
Woven in gold, silver, silk and wool.
Palacio Real, Madrid.

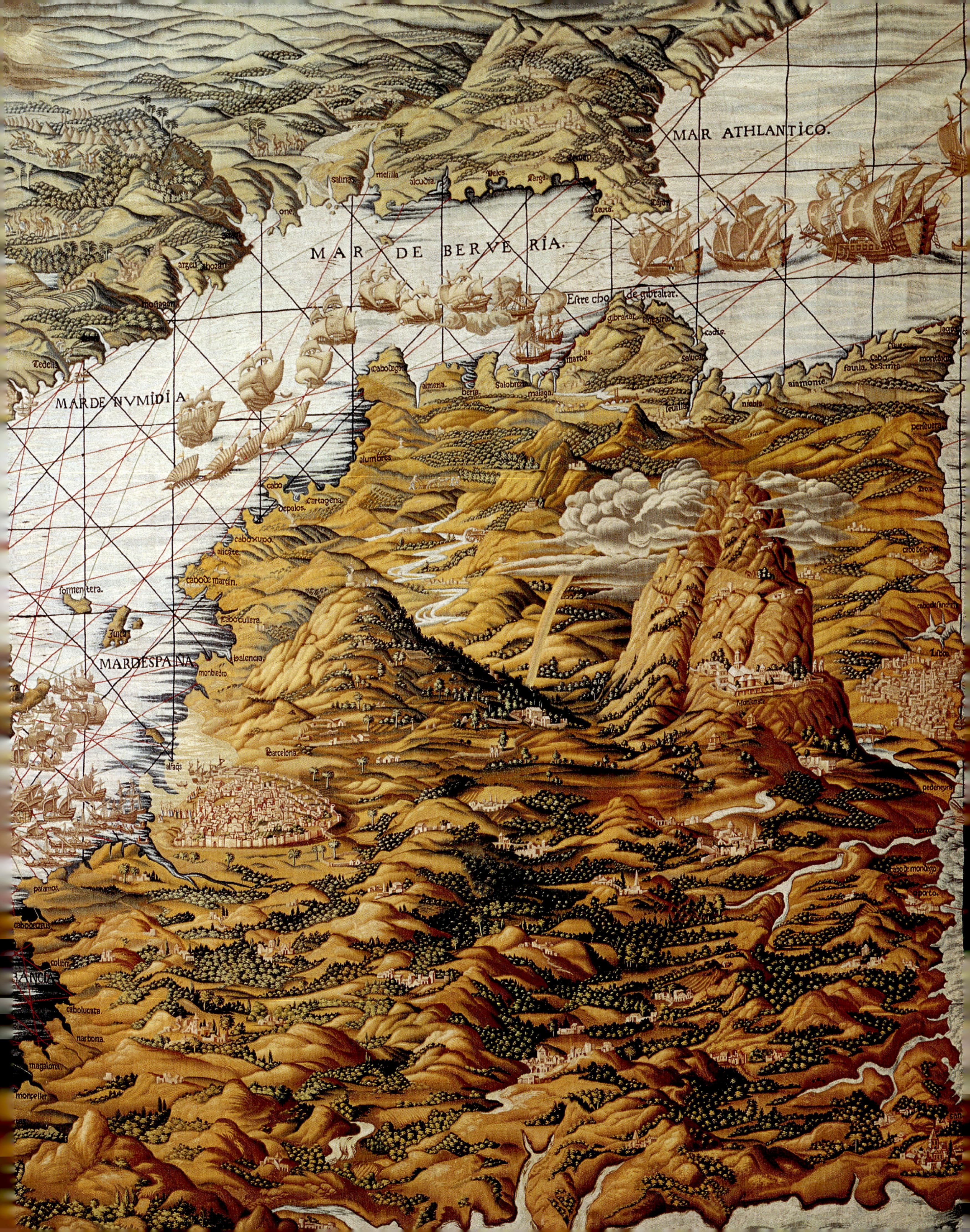

MAR ATHLANTICO.
MAR DE BERVE RIA.
MARDE NVMIDIA
MARDESPANA
Estre cho de gibraltar
melilla
ceuta
gibraltar
cadis
almeria
malaga
Cartagena
alicate
formentera
valencia
Barcelona
narbona
magalona
monpeller

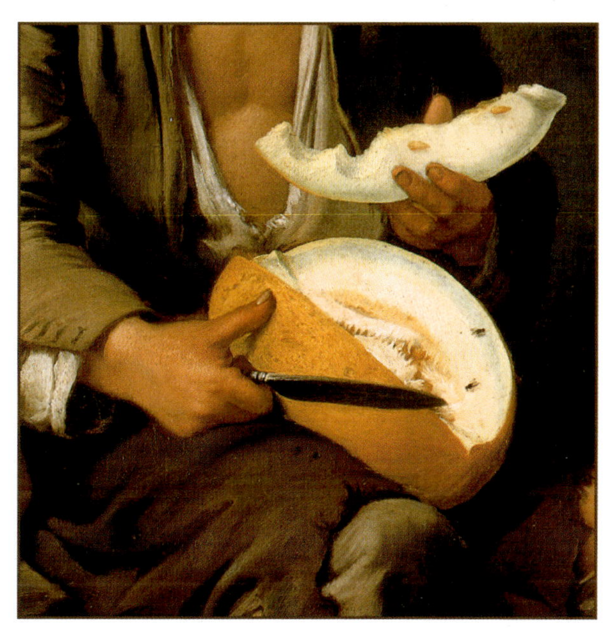

"The Haves and the Have Nots"

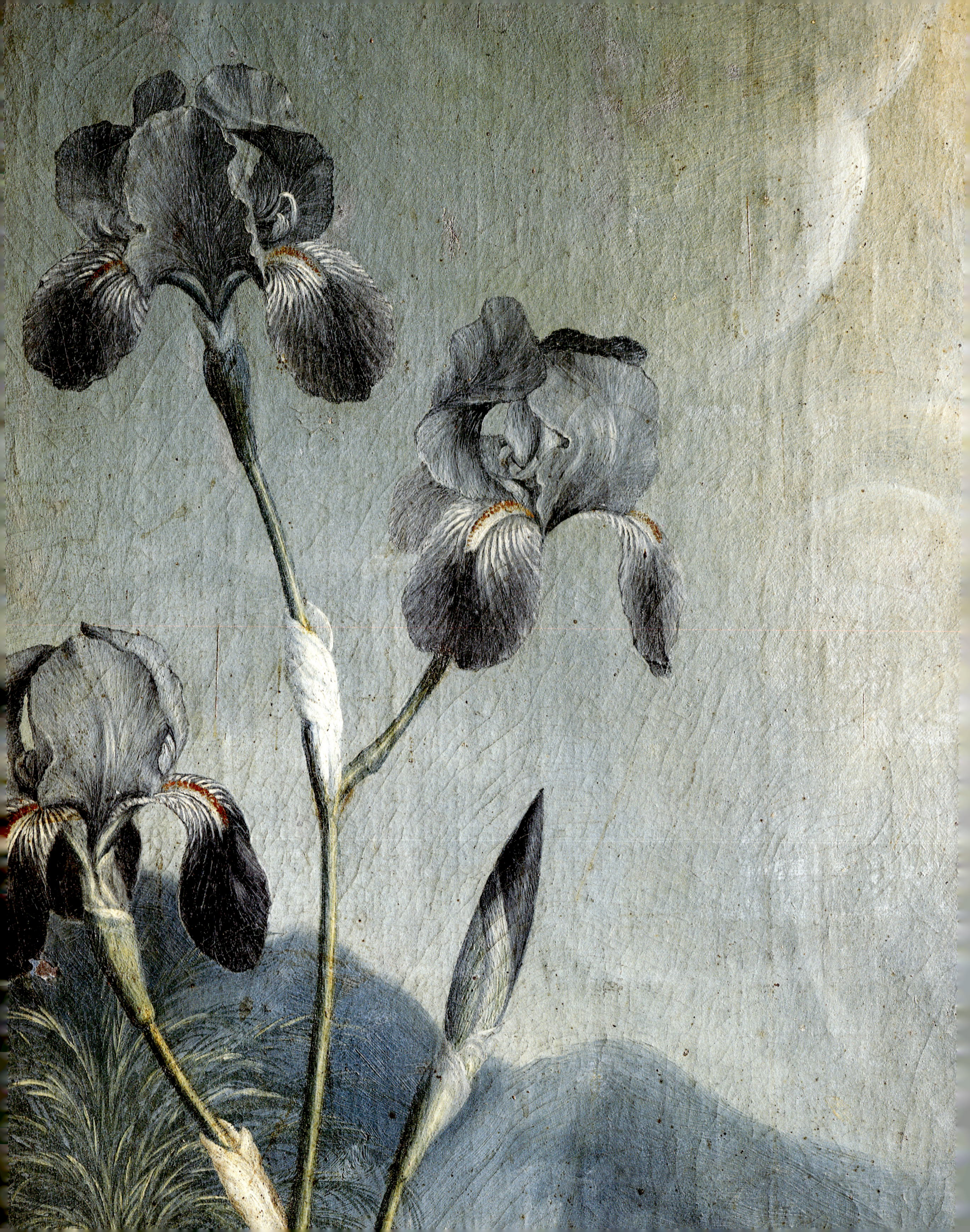

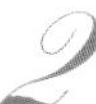

"The Haves and the Have Nots"

There went a publican anguished with doubts, who being tired fell by the way,
and it seemed to me a devil said to him:
"It is enough that you sweat water and do not sell it to us as wine."
One of the tailors, with a small body, a round face, a scruffy beard and even
worse deeds, said to the others:
"What could I possibly steal, if I was always near to starving to death?"
And the others said to him (seeing that he denied he was a thief), then why
show such disdain for his trade?

—FRANCISCO DE QUEVEDO Y VILLEGAS (1580–1645), *Vision of Justice,* 1605

The Palace of Charles V, which abuts the Moorish Alhambra in Granada, was designed by Pedro Machuca in 1526, though left unfinished at his death in 1550, and not completed until the twentieth century. The palace nonetheless embodied from its earliest beginnings the wishes of Charles V that it reflect a humanist vision of classical architecture and project an elaborate iconographical program about imperial power and grandeur. Laid out as a perfect square with a circular courtyard at its heart, the palace is designed as a complement to the private apartments in the Alhambra (the summer residence of the emperor) that would provide a setting appropriate for formal court ceremonies. Three of its exterior walls are soberly but elegantly decorated with Doric and Ionic pilasters, garlands, putti, and allegories celebrating the emperor's recent conquest of Tunis. The fourth wall is shared with the Alhambra itself, and above it rises the tower called the Peinador, which was decorated before the emperor first stayed there with frescoes on historical, mythological, and allegorical themes by the Italian artists Julio de Aquiles and Alejandro Mayner.

When the walls of the Peinador de la Reina were painted, the emperor was at the height of his power. He was like Caesar, like a sun god who, though accepting the transitory nature of human life, had his palace built in an ideal landscape of mountains, gardens, and fountains that can be viewed from the balcony of the Peinador. This view of nature is framed by an imaginary landscape that in turn frames the topographical scenes of the African campaign. The imagined and the real mingle with an unexpected richness.

The deep crimson of the background, like the red of the Alhambra itself, is perforated by the light (originally filtered through colored glass) from the windows and transformed into an intangible space where imaginary structures exist alongside fantastic beings. The decoration of the walls, painted with exquisite delicacy by Julio de Aquiles, reflects the re-

PRECEDING PAGE:
36. Bartolomé Esteban Murillo
c. 1650
Detail of *Beggar Boys Eating Grapes and Melon.*
Alte Pinakothek, Munich.

LEFT:
37. Juan Sánchez Cotán
c. 1617–18
Detail of *The Virgin of the Immaculate Conception,*
Carthusian monastery of La Asunción, Granada.
Museo de Bellas Artes, Granada.

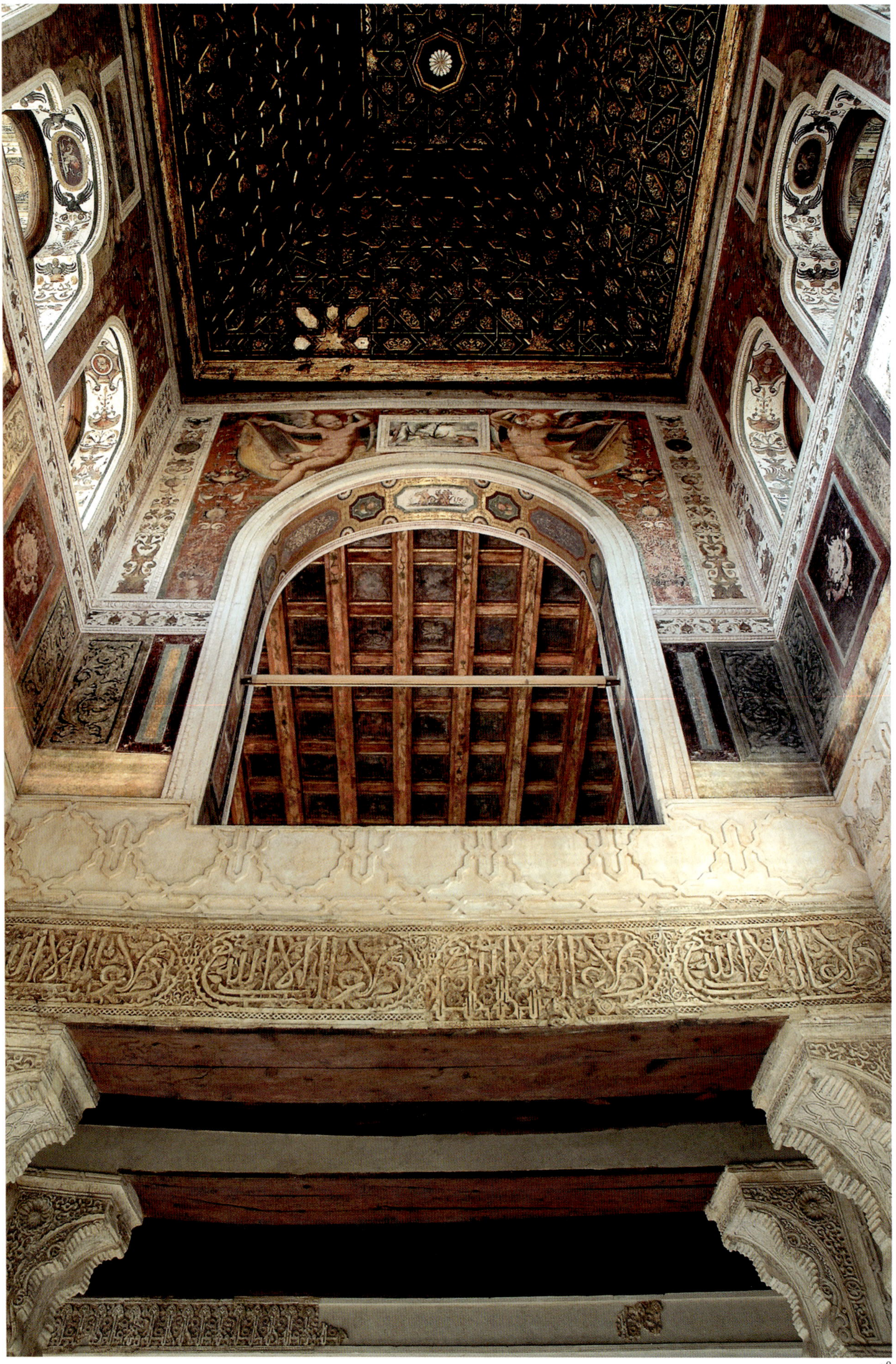

vival of the grotesques of antiquity in the visual arts—filigrees, putti, allegories, and gods frame the dramatic history of Phaeton, child of the sun god Helios and the Oceanid Clymene.

THE PALACE OF THE SUN

What is incorrectly called the Peinador de la Reina was thus actually conceived as a Granadan version of the mythological Palace of the Sun created by Vulcan and described by Ovid in his *Metamorphoses* (II, 1–18):

> The Sun's bright palace, on high columns rais'd,
> With burnish'd gold and flaming jewels blaz'd;
> The folding gates diffus'd a silver light,
> And with a milder gleam refresh'd the sight;
> Of polish'd iv'ry was the cov'ring wrought:
> The matter vied not with the sculptor's thought,
> For in the portal was display'd on high
> (The work of Vulcan) a fictitious sky;
> A waving sea th' inferiour Earth embrac'd,
> And Gods and Goddesses the waters grac'd.
> Aegeon here a mighty whale bestrode;
> Triton, and Proteus (the deceiving God)
> With Doris here were carv'd, and all her train,
> Some loosely swimming in the figur'd main,
> While some on rocks their dropping hair divide,
> And some on fishes through the waters glide:
> Tho' various features did the sisters grace,
> A sister's likeness was in ev'ry face.
> On Earth a diff'rent landskip courts the eyes,
> Men, towns, and beasts in distant prospects rise,
> And nymphs, and streams, and woods, and rural deities.
> O'er all, the Heav'n's refulgent image shines;
> On either gate were six engraven signs."

38. Julio de Aquiles and Alejandro Mayner
c. 1530–40
Frescoes in the Peinador de la Reina, the Alhambra, Granada.

The paintings on the walls of the Peinador narrate the story of young Phaeton. His pride and pretensions not only to be recognized as the child of the Sun but to actually drive the chariot of the sun on its daily course through the firmament led him to his death. Phaeton's story is told in four cartouches enclosed by stucco frames. On the western wall, two nymphs (who seem aware of the times of day that Michelangelo sculpted for the tombs of the young Medici dukes) bear, like Atlas, the image in which Phaeton, the key figure in Euripides' tragedy (of which there are only 327 verses extant), the "son whom a father could not renounce," begs the Sun, swearing on the Stygian waves, to let him drive Vulcan's fine chariot for just a day. In Ovid's verses this chariot of the sun is connected to the perpetual circular movement that attracts far-off constellations and whirls them into orbit.

The following episode, which is the heart of the mythological poem, is represented on the northern wall of the hall, in the visual axis that separates the scenes of the two key moments of the African campaign of Charles V: the departure of the Imperial Armada from the port of Cagliari, at the beginning of the daring adventure, and the triumphal arrival of the ships at the port of Trapani. The adventure of the ambitious Phaeton does not, cannot, end as well as that of the Sun, who with light reins in his hands guides the chariot of fire pulled by the swift horses Pyrois, Eos, Aethon, and Phlegon, something not even the great Jupiter could do. When Phaeton tries it, the horses break into a gallop and are propelled into the air by their wings, poorly guided steeds that quickly bolt out of control. They do not respond to the weak hand attempting to guide them. Then, as soon as they have reached the heights, as if tripping over rough terrain, they plunge back toward Earth.

The heat of the sun causes clouds to evaporate. The earth is engulfed in flames, great cities perish along with their powerful, and the people of entire nations are turned to ashes by fire. The ground crumbles. Some rivers burn beneath the heat, others dry up, and still others, like the Nile, flee in terror to the edge of the world. If Jupiter, the all-powerful father, does not come to the rescue, everything will be lost to a tragic destiny: "Then, aiming at the youth, with lifted hand / Full at his head he hurl'd the forky brand / In dreadful thund'rings. Thus th' almighty sire / Suppress'd the raging of the fires with fire." The horses and the chariot of the sun fall: "The breathless

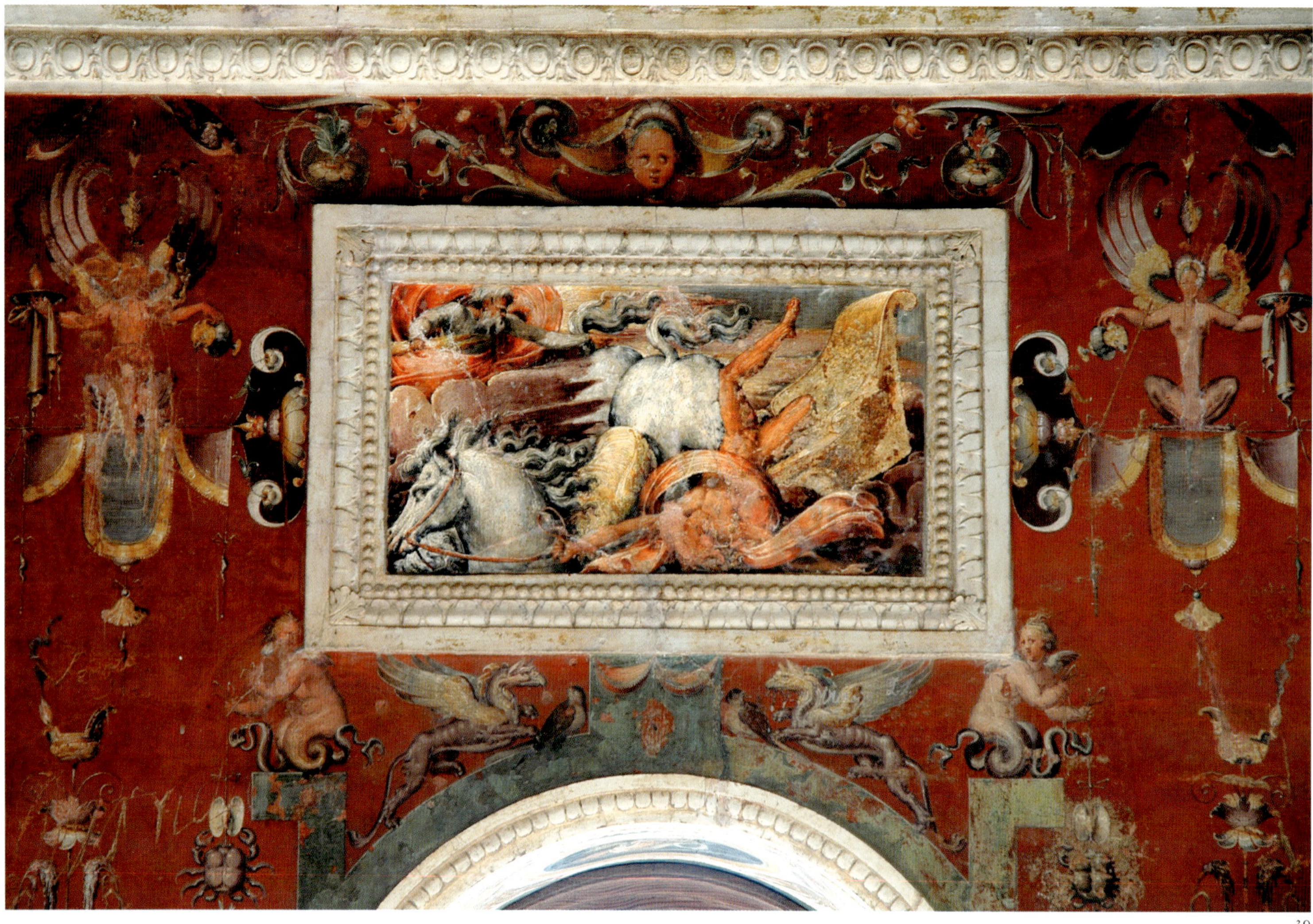

39

Phaeton, with flaming hair / Shot from the chariot, like a falling star / That in a summer's ev'ning from the top / Of Heav'n drops down, or seems at least to drop; / 'Till on the Po his blasted corps was hurl'd, / Far from his country, in the western world. / The Latian nymphs came round him, and, amaz'd, / On the dead youth, transfix'd with thunder, gaz'd; / And, whilst yet smoking from the bolt he lay, / His shatter'd body to a tomb convey."

Ovid narrates an end for Phaeton similar to the one in Euripides' tragedy, where the still-smoking cadaver of the young man is carried onto the stage. There seems to be no point to the universal disaster Phaeton has caused unless it is that the fires illuminated the Earth on the day that the Sun, aware of the tragedy that has befallen his son, is overwhelmed with grief and hides his face, recalling the epitaph that the Naiads inscribed on Phaeton's tombstone: HIC SITVS EST PHAETHON CVRRVS AVRIGA PATERNI QVEM SI NON TENVIT MAGNIS TAMEN EXCIDIT AVSIS. "Here lies Phaeton, driver of his father's chariot, who was not able to control it, but at least fell in grandeur."

In the Palace of the Sun in Granada, the fall of Phaeton (whom Francesco Colonna in *The Dream of Poliphilo* considers impious) is represented with full dramatic force. All-powerful Jupiter, lightning bolts in his right hand and the power of his left arm extended through the index finger (like that of the Creator on the ceiling of the Sistine Chapel), shoots down the beautiful chariot with its golden axle and wheel caps and silver spokes, while the frightened white horses free their necks from the yoke and, as Ovid tells it, escape the broken reins as Phaeton falls amid the flames that consume his blond locks (ill. 39).

Two other scenes complete the story of Phaeton. On the eastern wall is the weeping of the Heliades, who traveled the world over with Clymene, beating their breasts day and night in search of the remains of Phaeton. On the southern wall is the metamorphosis of Phaeton's sisters into poplar

39. Julio de Aquiles and Alejandro Mayner
c. 1530–40
The Fall of Phaeton,
fresco.
Peinador de la Reina, the Alhambra, Granada.

trees. These episodes reflect the literary and visual fortunes of the myth as interpreted in Franciscan friar Lucantonio's *Moralized Ovid,* in which Phaeton is portrayed as Lucifer, and his desire to guide the chariot of the sun symbolizes his rebellion against God. There were various editions of the *Metamorphoses* published in the late fifteenth century in Italy and later throughout Europe, beginning with the Latin versions and continuing with the 1497 version published in Italian: *Ovidio metamorfoseo vulgare . . . stampato in Venetia per Zoane Rosso vercellese ad istantia del nobil homo miser Lucantonio Zonta fiorentino.* This version was enhanced by fifty-two anonymous wood engravings that reflect Renaissance fascination with the ancient way of representing the classical myths. With minor variations the engravings also appear in later editions, such as those by Lucantonio (1501 and 1508) and Giorgio de Rusconi (published in Venice in 1517 and 1523), as well as the Milan editions of 1519 and 1520.

In the sixteenth century, thanks to Lucantonio's *Moralized Ovid,* the myths of the *Metamorphoses* took on a didactic function. In relation to the exercise of power, this meant that myths dealing with questions of insubordination, rebellion, and their punishments (primarily the myth of the giants rebelling against the gods of Olympus, and the myth of Phaeton) served an important role in the wall decorations of civic buildings, showing the tragic ends that await rebels and the inevitable triumph of God and of nearly divine men. Aside from the *Fall of Phaeton* that Sebastiano del Piombo painted in the Salon of Galatea in the Villa Farnesina in Rome (ca. 1511), the battle between the gods and the giants, as a visualization of a historical and political message, became especially important after the Sack of Rome in 1527. The representations of this myth reflected the self-interested will of the Italian nobility to praise the emperor who had gained control over them, especially after his coronation in Bologna. Among these princes were Andrea Doria, who in 1529 was named captain general of the Mediterranean and Adriatic fleet by Charles V (who had entered Genoa triumphantly on his way from Savona), and Federico Gonzaga, raised to the rank of duke by Charles V, who had been Gonzaga's guest in Mantua in 1530. The frescoes in their palaces are clear indications of their interest in the subject.

THE METAMORPHOSES OF RELIGION

The presence of the Gigantomachy and Phaeton in these murals is not exclusively a manifestation of Old World power struggles. When Spanish dominance was spreading over the New World, monks and artists arrived who knew and liked classical imagery for picturing both the real and the extraordinary. Copies of the *Metamorphoses* sent by Castilian booksellers helped to make the work better known, and the walls of the monasteries were covered with fantastic forms that united the visual traditions, rites, and myths of the indigenous people with those of the Europeans.

The best example of this is in the blend of images and ideas in the enormous, almost two-meter-high frieze of grotesques that runs along the two long walls of the nave of the Augustinian monastery at Ixmiquilpan, in the present-day state of Hidalgo in Mexico (ill. 40). In this mural tiger and jaguar knights symbolizing the conquistadors, civilization, and the Christian religion are engaged in a bloody battle against half-man, half-horse creatures representing the indigenous savagery and paganism of unconquered native populations like the Chichimec Indians during the second half of the sixteenth century.

The use of grotesque decoration in religious buildings both in Spain and in New Spain, where it was censored by the Third Mexican Council of 1585, began to decline in accord with the adoption of the strict rules concerning images dictated by the Council of Trent. However, grotesques continued to play an important role in the decoration of civic spaces by painters of Italian origin, like the ceiling of the Hall of Battles in the royal section of the Monastery of San Lorenzo of the Escorial (ill. 41).

PAINTING STILL LIFE

Still-life painting as an independent genre developed in Europe at the end of the sixteenth century, be-

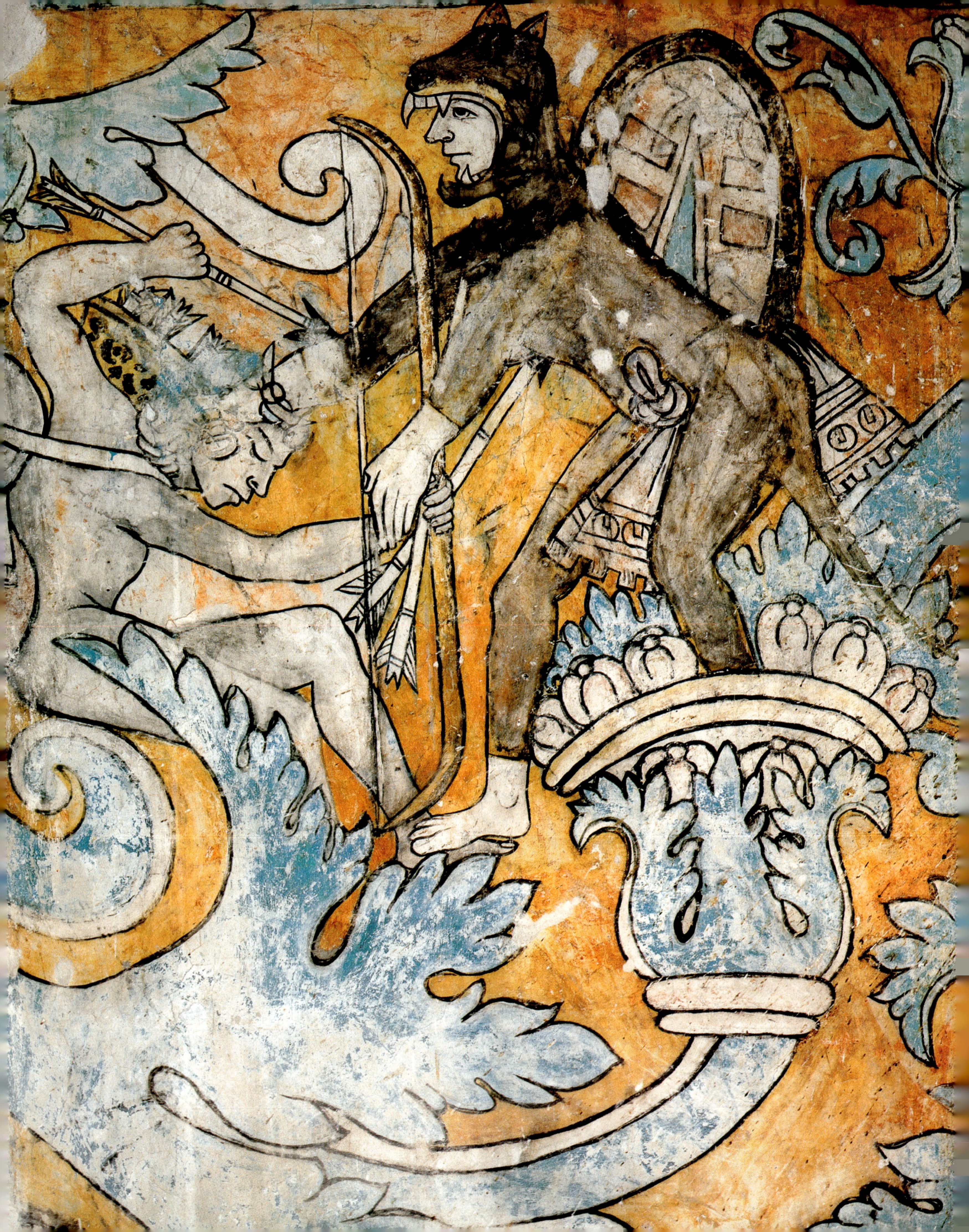

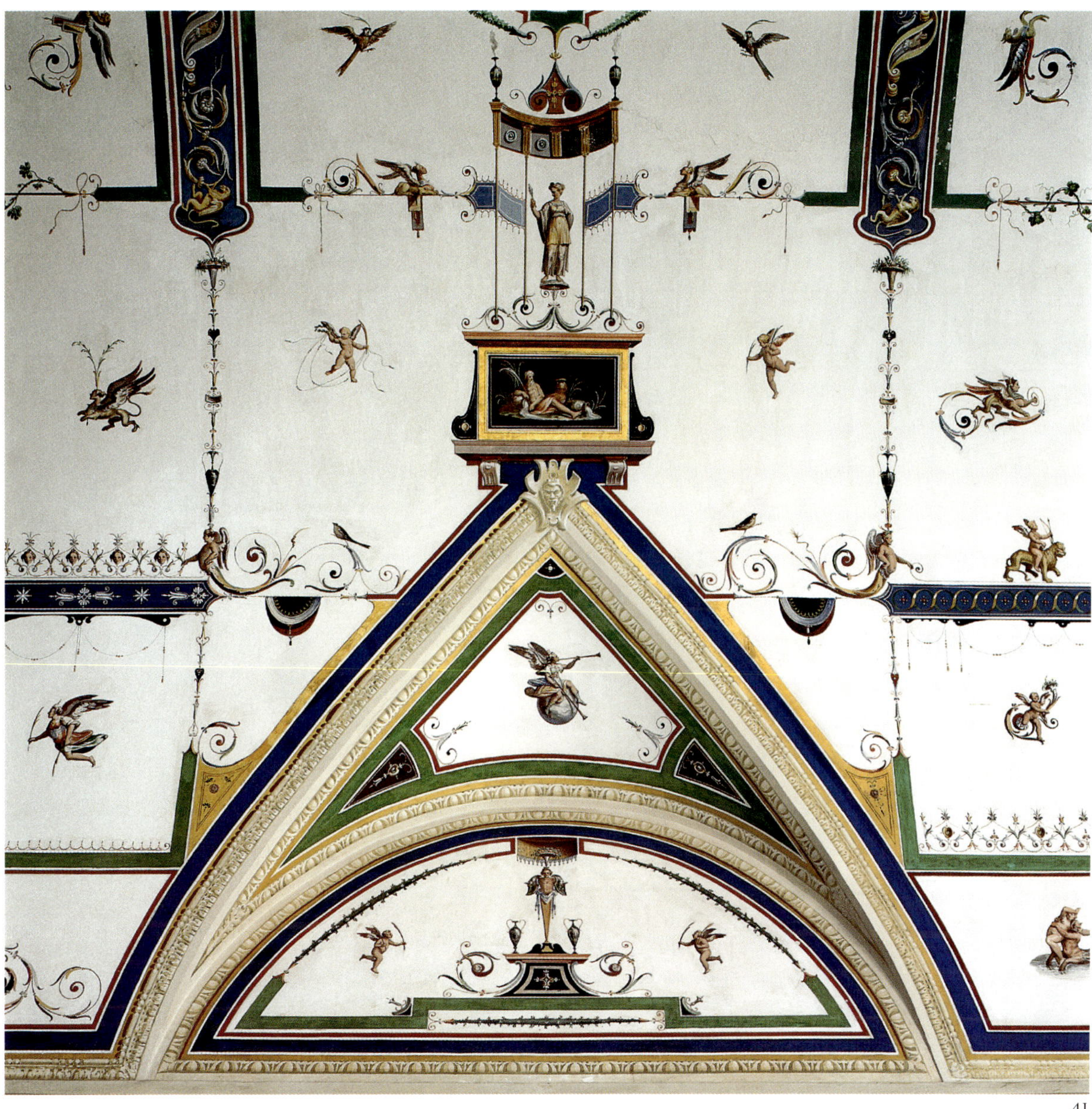

41

LEFT:
40. Late sixteenth century
Detail of the frieze of grotesques with scenes of combat, fresco.
Nave of the church of the Augustinian monastery at Ixmiquilpan (Mexico).

ABOVE:
41. Nicolás Granello, Fabrizio Castello, and Lázaro Tavarone
1587
Detail of a fresco in the Hall of Battles.
Real Monasterio de San Lorenzo, El Escorial.

ginning with allegories of the Five Senses, the Four Elements, the Four Seasons, or the Twelve Months in which plants and animals were important iconographical elements. Alongside this rise of new subject matter, the artist was increasingly expected to be able to describe accurately what his senses perceived. In a parallel development, Spanish poets, including the mystics Saint Teresa of Ávila and Friar Luis de Granada, associated concepts with objects, such as a skull, an hourglass, or a guttering candle, in still-life paintings.

Among the first artists to bring a very specific naturalism to the fore in their paintings were the northern painters Pieter Aertsen (1508–1575) and his nephew Joachim Beuckelaer (ca. 1530–1573). Their extraordinary technique was brought to bear on crinkly cabbage leaves and glistening fish scales, and that emphasis on naturalism remained a key element of still-life painting, whether applied to the skulls and crisp vellum covers of books in early Dutch still lifes, the resplendent table settings of seventeenth-century Flemish still lifes, the fruits and flowers by artists working in Naples, or the austere, carefully selected objects in Spanish still-life paintings, arranged with all the precision of liturgical vessels upon altars.

Just as still lifes froze ephemeral things in time, so did they serve as reminders of the fleeting nature of time and of life itself. They were called *vanitas* paintings because of the vanity, or futility, of human existence, or *mementi mori,* reminders that we all must die.

At the end of the sixteenth century and throughout the seventeenth, the human gaze and with it science, poetry, and painting homed in on the

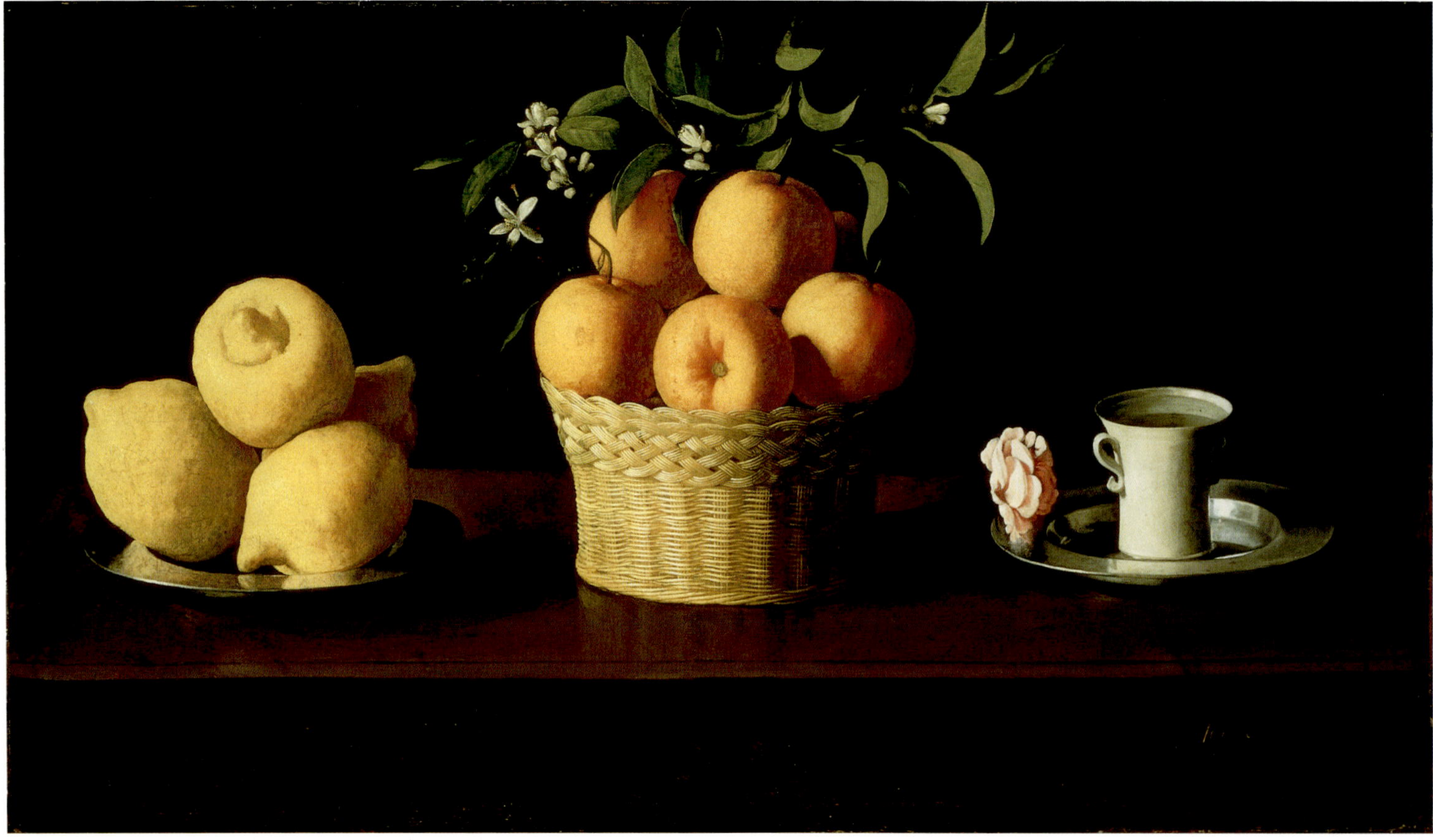

42

reality of nature, understanding it as a labyrinth that expresses the greatness of *Deus pictor,* its creator. Nature was seen as a machine obedient to a greater order that mankind cannot comprehend. Nature was also variously considered as a rational setting for a wild environment, as something fleeting bound to the passing of time, in which the beauty of color or the pleasure of an aroma is trapped between love and death, as expressed in the poem *To the Rose* by the Seville poet Francisco de Rioja (ca. 1583–1659), chief librarian of Philip IV, a friend of the count-duke of Olivares, and an advisor to the Tribunal of the Holy Inquisition:

> Pure, burning rose,
> rival to the flame
> opening with the day,
> how are you born with such joy
> knowing the time heaven has given you
> is a brief and fleeting flight?
> And the thorns on your stem
> and your beautiful purple
> will not be enough to detain for a moment
> the execution of your hasty fate.
> Steal in an hour,
> licentiously steal from your burning
> the color and the breath:
> you no longer spread out burning wings
> which now flutter faint to the floor:
> so close, so united
> your life is about to die,
> and I doubt if in your tears the musty
> dawn laments your birth or death.

Francisco de Rioja's rose is born and dies like all living things. It does not live in the world of fantasy, artifice, or myth as do the grotesques. It lives amid loves, yet it does not grow or die in the *loci amoeni,* the friendly places made especially for loving and being loved. The poet's rose praised by Cervantes and Lope

ABOVE AND RIGHT:
42 and 43. Francisco de Zurbarán
1633
Still Life with Lemons, Oranges, and a Rose and detail.
Norton Simon Foundation, Pasadena.

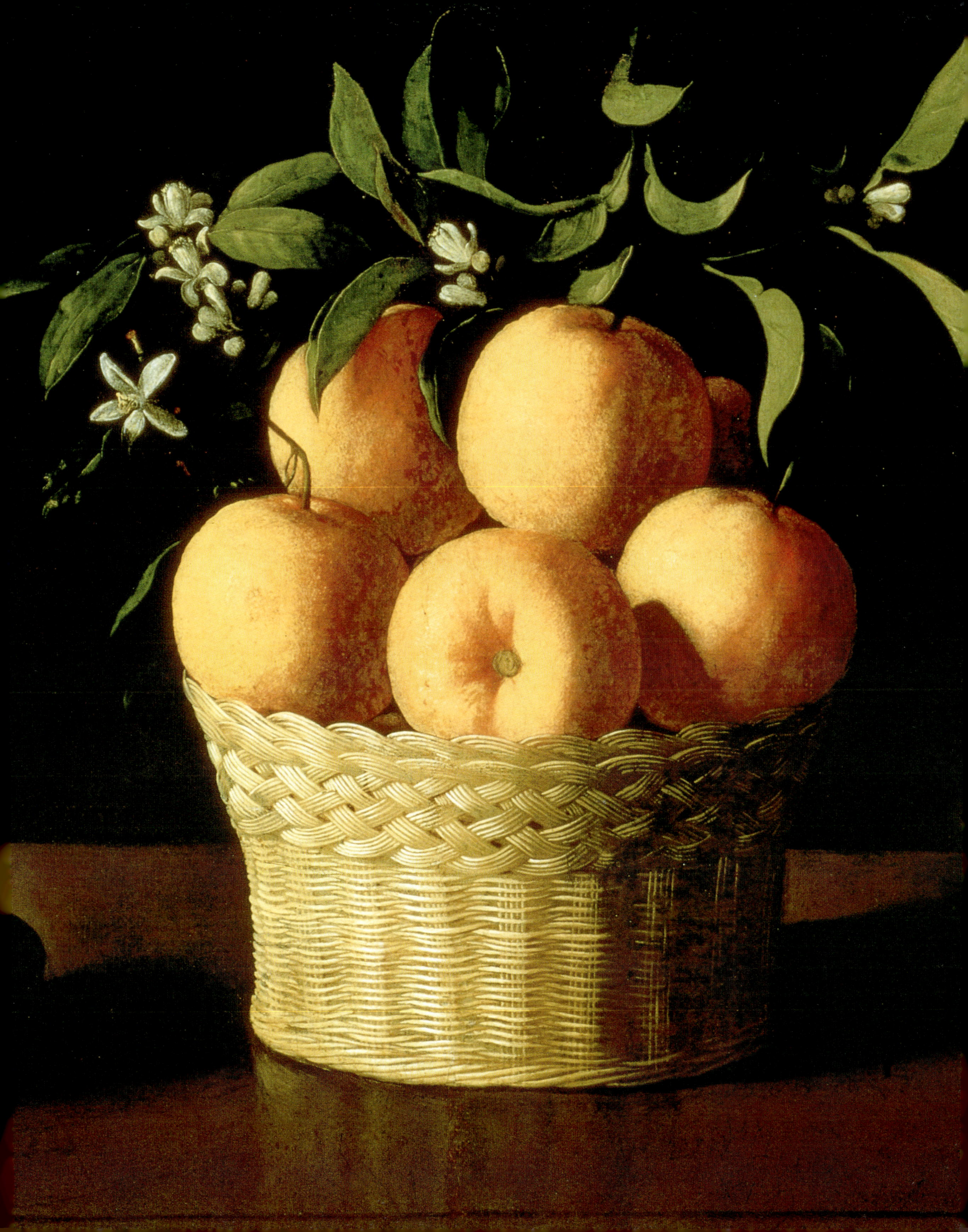

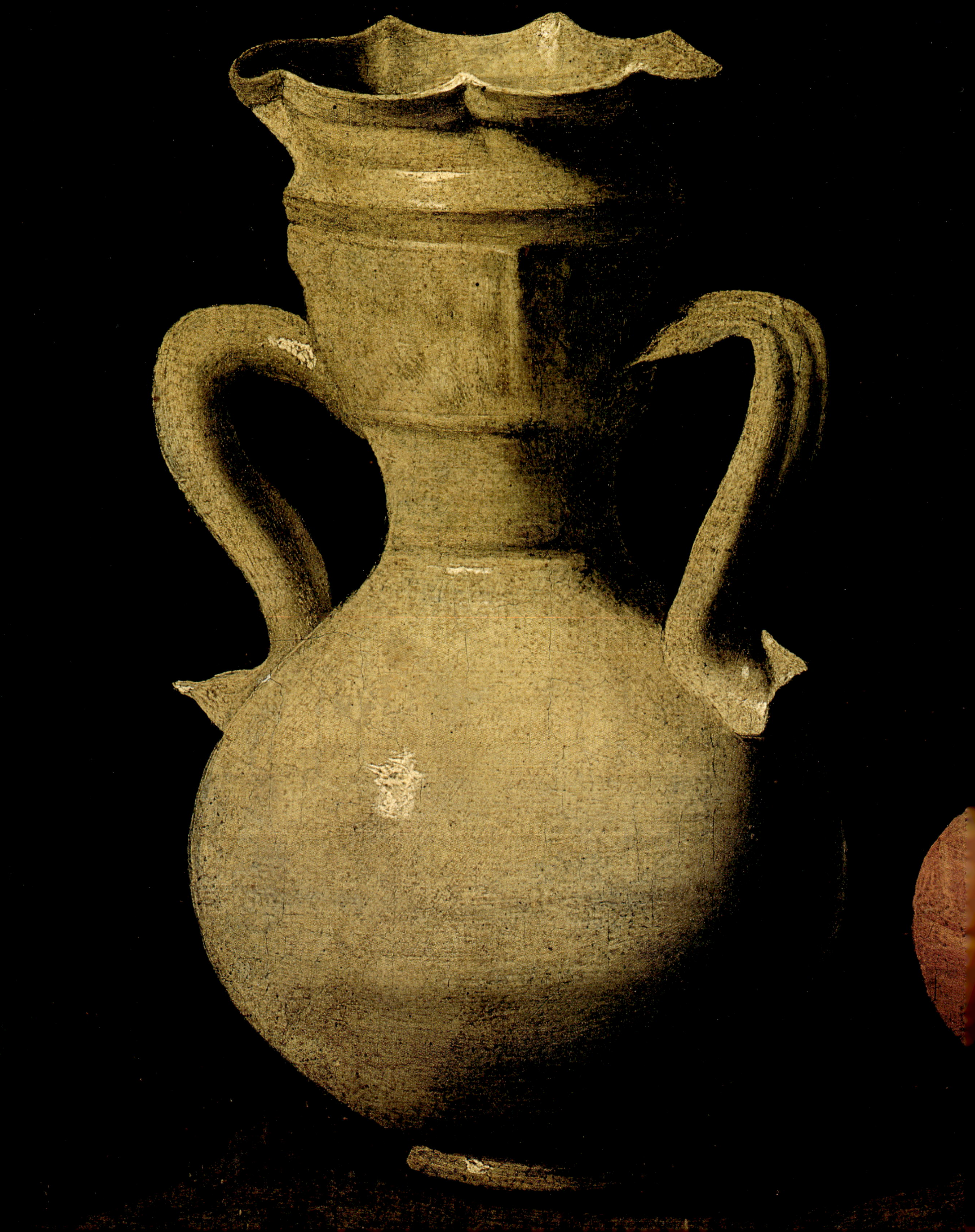

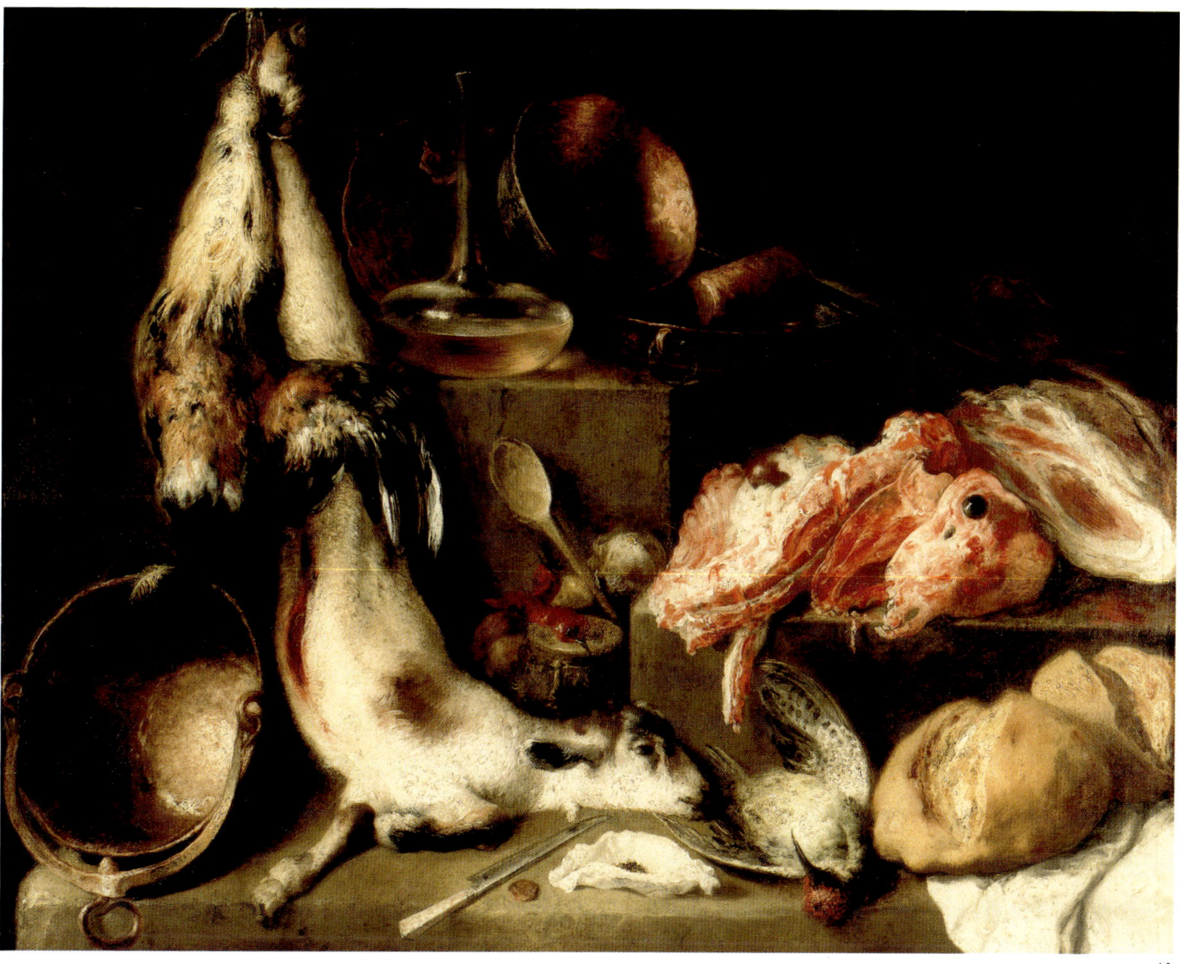

45

de Vega is the same Sevillian rose that Francisco Zurbarán painted in the spring and summer of 1633 in his studio-residence on the Callejón del Alcázar, which ran alongside the *alcázares,* the old, Moorish-style royal palace. Zurbarán captured this rose in a delicate painting (ill. 42) in which the oil paint tentatively describes a large table drawn out of the darkness by a tenuous light. On its bright surface, like a mirror, the painter from Extremadura (who at that time was producing large religious paintings like the altarpiece for one of the altars in the Church of the College of San Alberto, Seville, and had his mind set on trying his luck at the court in Madrid) places two pewter plates of different sizes alongside a small wicker basket, all in perfect order, as though for a ritual.

On the dish on the left are four or five lemons, which were thought to protect against poisons and the plague. In the basket are oranges, some of them with stems still in flower. In the plate on the right is a white cup containing water and a rose that refuses to let its red petals rest, the intense light turning them almost white against the edge of the underlying metal. The pewter plates, the basket, the fruits, and the flower are everyday objects that Zurbarán made his own. He signed the canvas "Franco de Zurbarán faciebat 1633," just as a year earlier he had signed a *Virgin of the Immaculate Conception,* painted for a group of clerics.

The fleeting quality that the poet exalts in his poem, the extremely thin line separating life and death, is what governs still-life painting and all of Baroque reality, since the only truth about anything is not its permanence but its passing. Reality is subject to change, to happenstance. The passing of time dominates everything; time is the world's great tyrant. The only thing that endures and lasts is what is fleeting, what flows, exactly what Francisco de Quevedo sings about the ruins of Rome:

LEFT:
44. Francisco de Zurbarán
c. 1635–40
Detail of *Still Life with Ceramic Pots.*
Museo Nacional del Prado, Madrid.

ABOVE:
45. Mateo Cerezo
c. 1660
Kitchen Still Life.
Museo Nacional del Prado, Madrid.

> You search in Rome for Rome, oh wanderer!
> and yet in Rome itself you don't find Rome
> the walls boasting its fame are now a corpse
> and the Aventine now serves as its own tomb. . . .
> Oh, Rome! of all your greatness, your allure
> what was firm has fled and nothing but
> what is elusive stays and will endure.

"What is elusive stays and will endure." Pictorial art, like poetry, paints cities and worlds as ruins, and paints the human being as a ruin. Under the mantle of the Sun, the sun around which Galileo discovered that the Earth moves—before humanists had discovered that blood also moves in the microcosm that is man, in the heart that is his sun—there is nothing new, nothing stable or perpetual or permanent because all things are always changing. The poet Rodrigo Caro (1573–1647), whose subjects are often archaeological ruins and ancient myths, wrote that not even life is certain because everything is mutable. Painters portray the fruit of the earth, and sometimes fish and fowl, in that instant when color and air have not yet run out, but when the wings of life have already been consumed, though they have yet to fall faintly to the ground.

The art of painting seems to come to the aid of nature. Trying to keep living things from moving along too quickly toward their end, artists resort to artifice in order to detain time. This is what Velázquez does with the spinning wheel in *Las Hilanderas* (*The Spinners,* or *The Fable of Arachne,* ill. 46), where the dynamism of the world is trapped. He extracts the very nature of transient reality and places it, with its color and breath intact, where the air grows thin, where silence is the only sound in the void, and the only light is that of life's happenstances. It is not reality that we see in a still life, but rather the appearance of something transitory that the painter seeks to make eternal. This is neither the fantasy world of the grotesques nor the world of reality, but rather a world of contradictions in which lies do not exist (though they are not denied) but where essential truth does not exist either (though it is not affirmed), since our eyes and those of the painter are deceived and represent quite different objects from those looked upon, as the dramatist Calderón de la Barca said in *Knowledge of Good and Evil.* There is no greater reason to think that the sky we look at and painters represent "is not the sky and is not blue," Calderón wrote. Others had also written of this deception, including Bartolomé Leonardo de Argensola (or perhaps his brother Lupercio), upon discovering that the deceptive tones of Doña Elvira's skin were the same as those found in nature:

> I wish to confess to you, Don Juan, first
> that the white and crimson of Doña Elvira
> is no more her, if we look right,
> than of having cost her money.
> What, then, with me quite lost
> through such a deceit, since we know
> that Nature deceives us in the same way?
> For this blue sky we all see
> is not the sky and is not blue; is so much beauty, then,
> that less great, for not being reality?

THE ORDER OF APELLES

The appearance of things—the metal of plates, the skin of lemons and oranges, a cup—and the sense of emptiness and silence, the phenomenon of light, would not be beautiful if order did not organize them. Nature must be ordered. Disorder would lead to chaos, and this would bring about death. In their still-life paintings Juan Sánchez Cotán (ills. 48, 49), Felipe Ramírez, Mateo Cerezo (ill. 45), Alejandro de Loarte, Juan van der Hamen y León, and Francisco de Zurbarán (ill. 44) first compose and organize their subjects through geometry. The balance between horizontal and vertical, symmetry and the perfect shapes of the circle, the square, the triangle, and the rectangle help the painters turn the void into a system, a system in which the weight, the presence of things, objects, or pieces of fruit are never lost. Quite the contrary: it is their physical presence, their shape, shininess or roughness, their weight that

46. Diego Velázquez
c. 1655
Detail of *The Spinners*, or *The Fable of Arachne.*
Museo Nacional del Prado, Madrid.

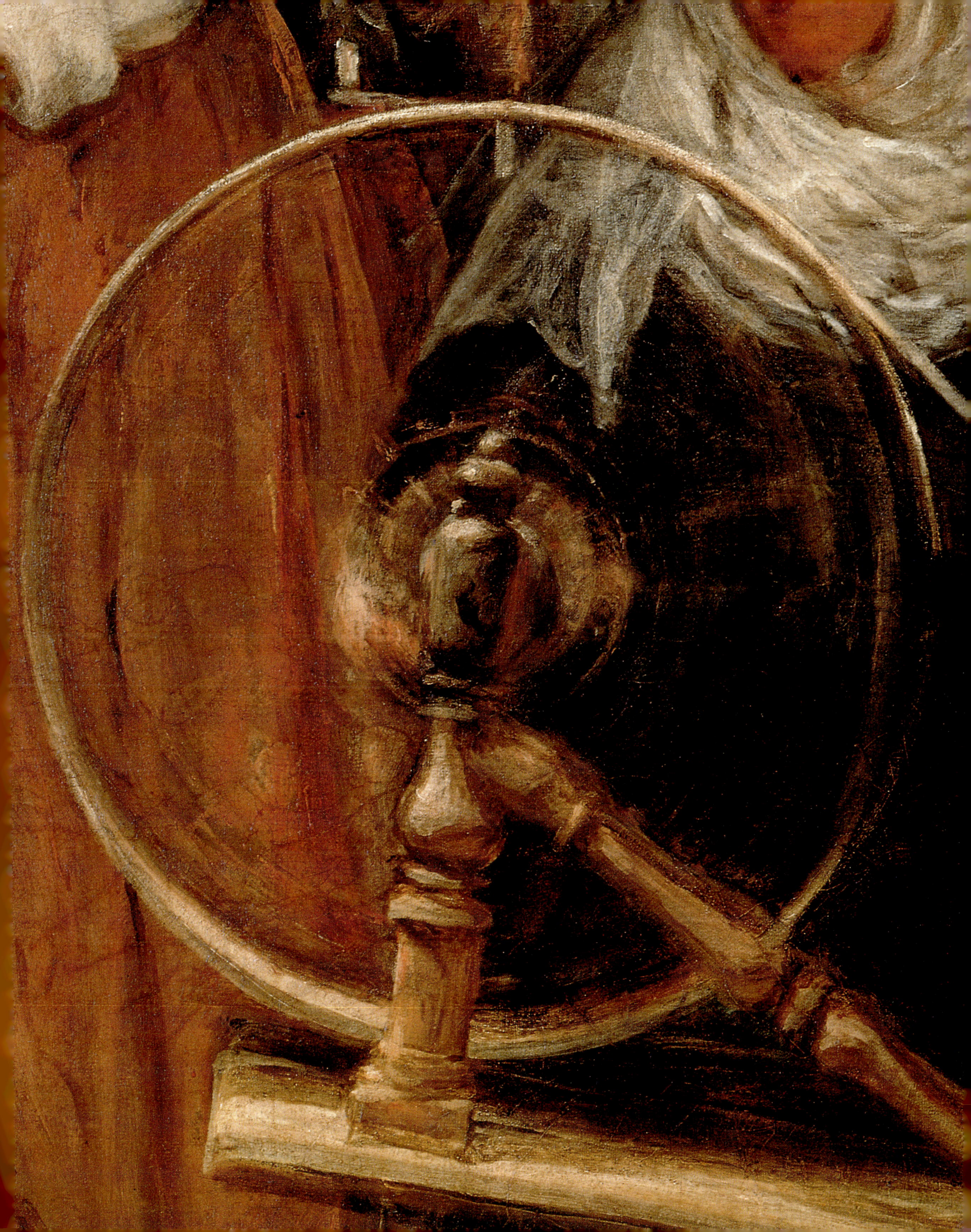

makes order possible. This is in apparent contradiction to the concept of mystical vision at that time, but it is the mystical vision that makes the geometrically precise order possible, especially in still-life paintings. This is accomplished above all through color, the color of the precious freedom that the prolific dramatist Lope Felix de Vega Carpio (1562–1635) sang about in his *Arcadia* when the century of humanism was coming to a close:

> Here the green pear
> with the ripe apple,
> in yellow and subtle blood red,
> and pink colored
> the fragrant *cermeña* pear fruit
> I have, and the deep purple sloe plum;
> here from the twisted
> vine the elm tree entwines,
> sweet grapes I pick;
> and in quantity I gather
> while the branches release
> in the warm summer,
> quince to end this river of delights.

Colors, like shapes and even flavors and aromas, can be charged with religious, secular, or philosophical symbolism, or simply entertain. In the still-life paintings one certainly sees Saint Teresa's idea that God is everywhere and His greatness can be perceived everywhere. However, those who wrote about still-life painting in the seventeenth century spoke above all of entertainment, and even more so of the capacity of the painter to imitate and describe what is visible, and of how even nature itself confuses painted reality with the reality it imitates. They suggest that the eye is deceived in the same way as the birds were fooled by the bunch of grapes painted by Zeuxis. This, for example, is how Lope de Vega summarized the artistic achievements of the court artist Juan van der Hamen y León (ill. 47):

> If with your crown of laurel,
> you copy, Vander, the friendly Spring,
> the blue iris, the candid lily,
> your brushes whisper ignorance:
> know of the envy, Castilian Apelles,
> before a table full of your flowers
> that Philomena sang in her deceit,
> and of bees that sipped your carnations.
> Yet if the conquering histories,
> of what is admired in unique painters,
> do not conquer destructive envies,
> and your favors silence your portraits;
> so many Dawns, Vander, return for you,
> to crown you with your own flowers.

The flowers Van der Hamen paints are so true, so much the fruit of observation and experimentation (values little esteemed during the Middle Ages, but revived during the Renaissance), that they become the glory of this Castilian Apelles. The relationship between art and nature has been altered, and what has become most admired in nature is its imitation of art. Baltasar Gracián (1601–1658), in his *Art of Prudence,* explained: "There is no beauty without assistance, nor perfection that is not almost barbaric without the aid of artifice, which saves the bad and perfects the good."

The rising respect for artifice, for capturing nature through a certain perspective, can be understood as a poetic and pictorial way of seeing and expressing nature that is not really so different from the method employed by Galileo Galilei and other scientists at that time. In 1633, the same year in which Zurbarán painted the *Still Life with Lemons, Oranges and a Rose* in Seville, Galileo was in Rome kneeling before the inquisitors and cardinals of the Holy Office, reneging on everything he had written in his *Dialogue Concerning the Two Chief World Systems.* He was persecuted for insisting that the sun was the center of the universe and that it did not move from east to west. However, he was above all persecuted for insisting on the separation of science from faith, the realm of the latter being salvation, while that of science is knowledge.

Faith gave man a way to reach heaven; science sought to find out what heaven was like, what reality was. This reality of things could be grasped only if their objective qualities, however fleeting, could be quantified and measured. Science thus sought to

47. Juan van der Hamen y León
1627
Offering to Flora.
Museo Nacional del Prado, Madrid.

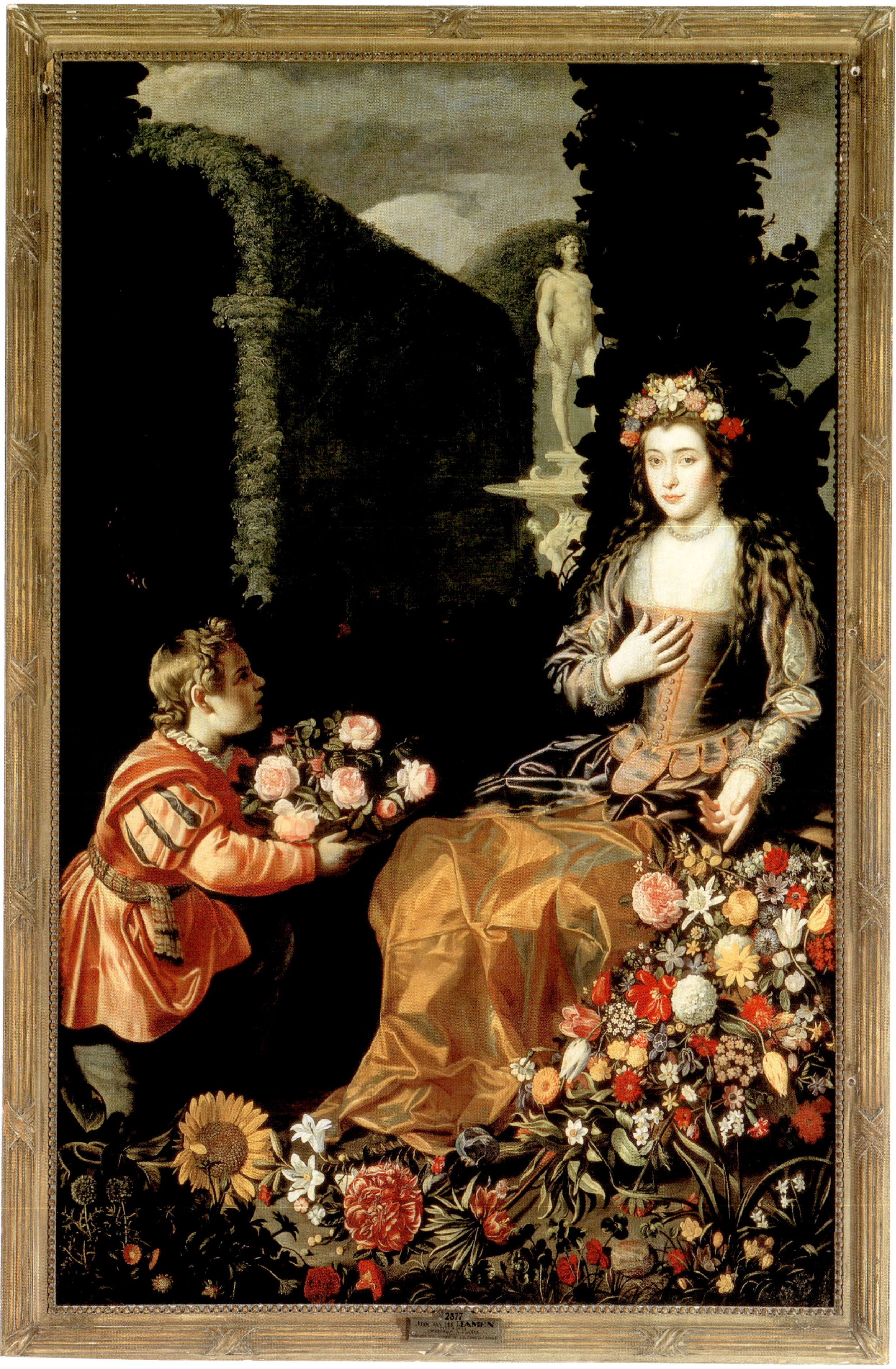
2877
JUAN VAN DER HAMEN

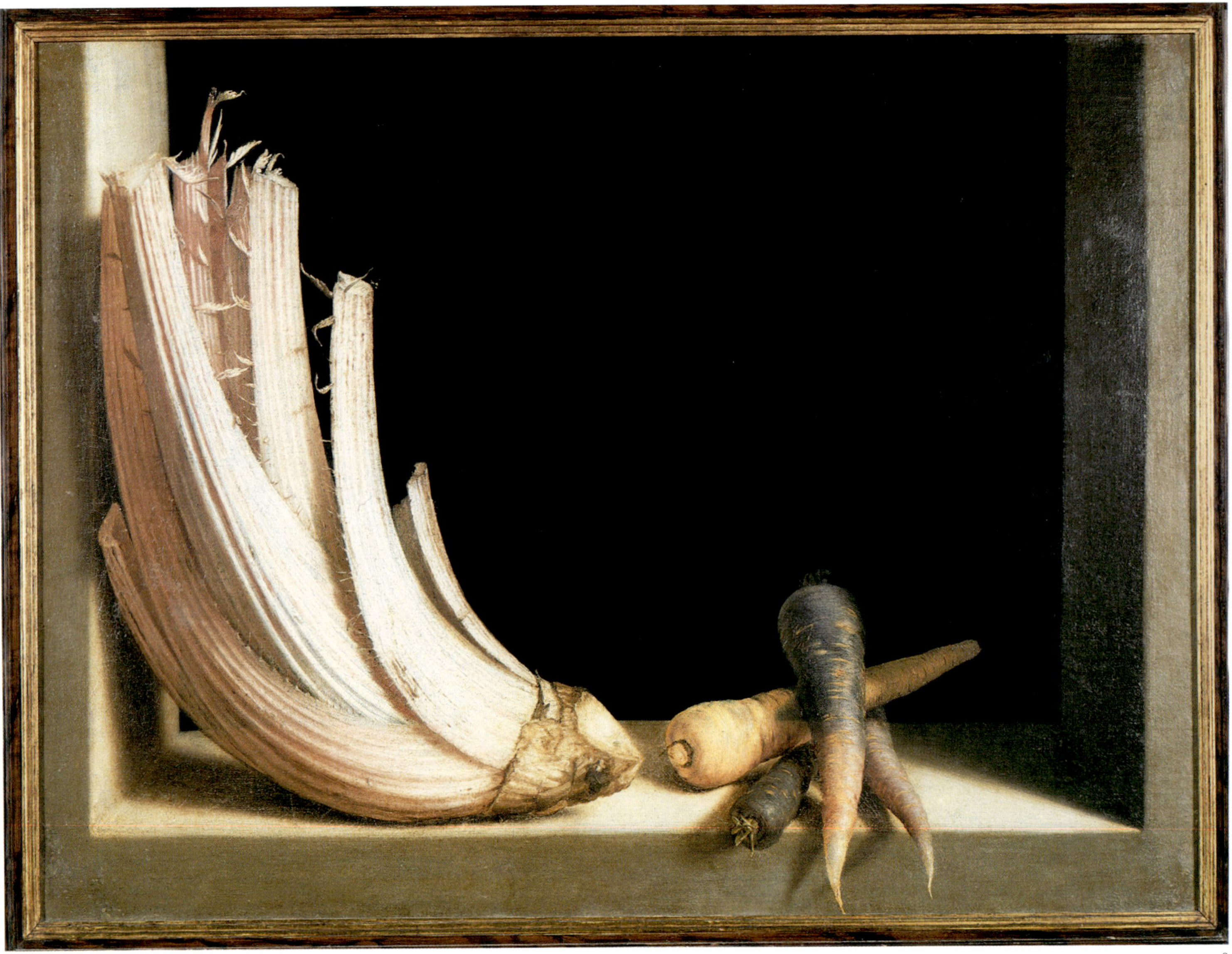

48

comprehend how things worked, but science could not pretend to know their true essence nor those qualities that depended on the eye of the observer. This could only be done through art and poetry, as the Jesuit priest Juan Eusebio Nieremberg (1595–1658), a theologian of German parentage who had come to the Madrid court with the entourage of Maria of Austria, daughter of Charles V, wrote in his *Treatises of Natural Philosophy*:

> Plotinus called the world "the Poetry of God." I add that this Poem is like a labyrinth in which everything one reads and senses is dictated by its Author. . . . Thus I imagine the world to be a Panegyric of God with a thousand labyrinths designed by him, uniting some natural things with others, proclaiming far and wide His greatness (at times defined generally, sometimes specifically, sometimes by His own doing, sometimes by chance). In all ways [these labyrinths] comprise His harmony, forming and composing a Divine Hymn.

FREEDOM AND FOOD

The art of painting brought lemons, apples, grapes, sweets, partridges, chard, vegetables, and game closer to people's eyes and did so better than nature itself could do. Yet these foodstuffs, presented boldly and with false humility, accompanied only by a silent but ostentatious emptiness, underscored the paradox that foodstuffs and trifles were more fantasy than reality for a good part of the population of the time. This was not the case for the aristocratic clients who could purchase quince and pastries

48. Juan Sánchez Cotán
After 1603
Still Life with Cardoon.
Museo de Bellas Artes,
Granada.

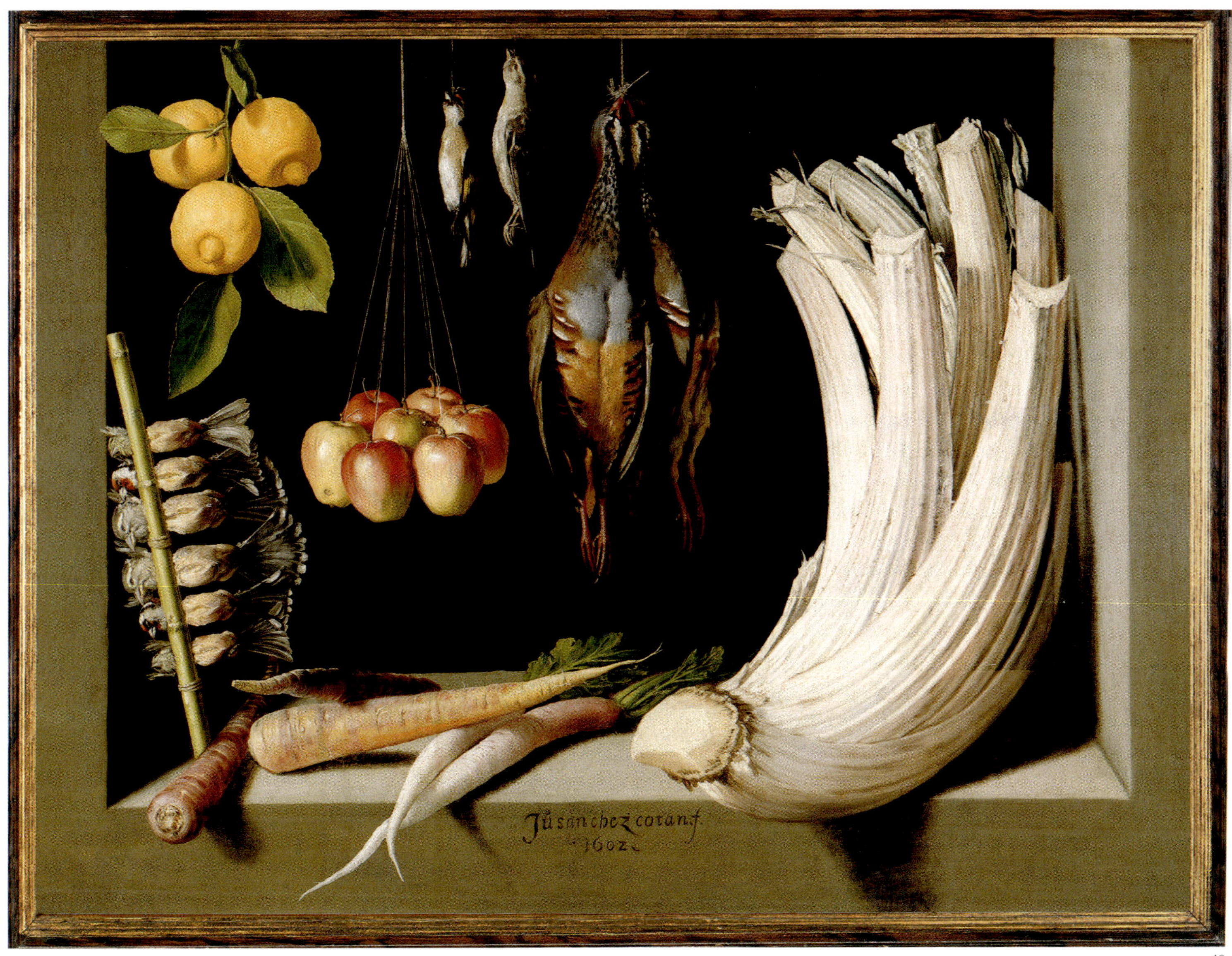

49

alongside the master Van der Hamen on Madrid's Calle Mayor (the painter's studio was nearby, on the affluent Calle de Tintoreros). But it was indeed the situation for others who moved from one end of the city to the other, lowering their heads when they caught the scent of human vanity in the form of trays of sweets, hanging partridges, and stalks of vegetables displayed in stall windows. Their story was quite different: "History, poetry, and painting are mutually symbolic, and are so similar that when you write history you are painting, and when you paint you are composing poetry," wrote Cervantes in his 1617 novel *The Trials of Persiles and Sigismunda*. "History does not always have the same weight, painting does not always portray great, magnificent subjects, and poetry is not always in dialogue with the heavens. History allows for low points, painting can depict grass and broom, and poetry can even be elevated by singing of humble things." Yet still-life painting was not admired by those who had to sell their personal freedom in order to feed their children, as Cervantes continues:

49. Juan Sánchez Cotán
1602
Still Life with Game, Fruits and Vegetables.
Museo Nacional del Prado, Madrid.

> This truth is ably demonstrated by Bartolomé, baggage carrier of the pilgrims. . . . This man, turning over in his imagination the tale of the man who sold his freedom to feed his children, once said, in conversation with Periandro:
>
> "It must be great, sir, the force that obliges parents to give sustenance to their children; and if that were not the case, tell the man who didn't want to take a chance for fear of losing, and sold his freedom so as to sustain his poor family. Freedom, I have heard said, should not be sold for any

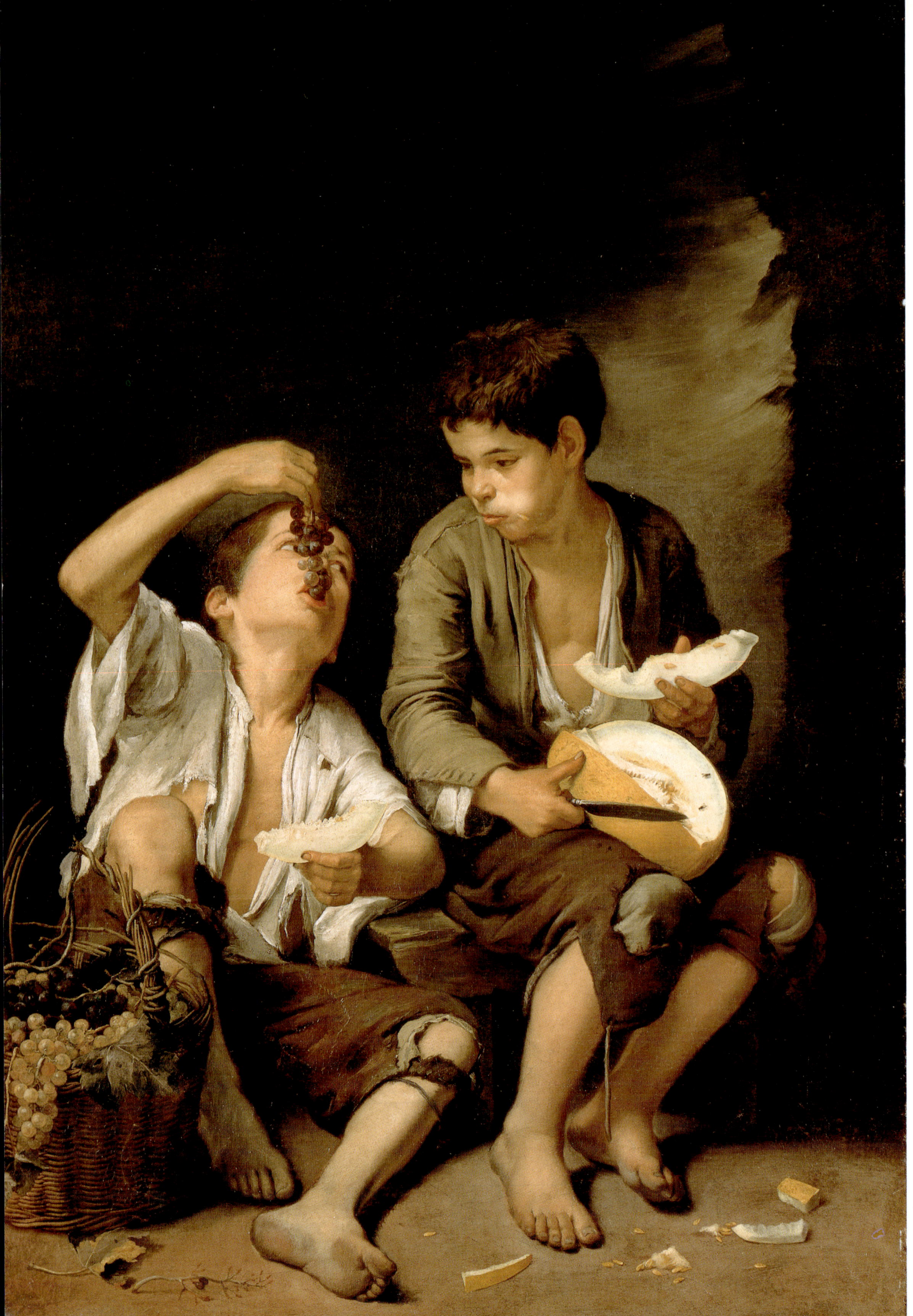

sum, and this man sold his for so little that his wife was able to carry it away in her hands."

I also recall having heard my elders say that, as an old man was being taken to the gallows, accompanied by priests who were assisting him to die well, he said to them:

"Do not worry, sirs, and let me die slowly, for even though this step I am about to take is terrible, many times I have seen myself in more terrible straits."

They asked him what they were. He answered that once, at the break of dawn, when his six small children surrounded him, clamoring for bread, but not having any to give them, "this necessity made me put a hook in my hand and felt cloths on my feet, so as to assist me in my thefts, which were born not of vice but of necessity."

Until the seventeenth century, painters did not bother to represent people who had sacrificed their freedom in order to feed their children, nor did they paint anyone at the margins of society except to express through them divine munificence, the practice of charity, or the need to pass through suffering to attain the light of Truth. In the painting of the time, and even more often in the literature, we see the emergence of that heretofore submerged world of common people who did not have bread to eat—child beggars and vagabonds, rogues, the crippled and importunate, actors, fools, and jesters, people who for whatever reason suffered social marginalization and disdain (ill. 50). Yet there were also others, like the philosophers who, though they were not common folk or manual laborers, were depicted by seventeenth-century writers and painters wearing tattered rags. They were shown in tatters not because they were poor, but because they spurned outward appearances. The philosopher Democritus laughed at such pretensions, and Heraclites wept at the vain errors of the world, a great theater in which everyone played his God-given role, as Quevedo put into verse:

50. Bartolomé Esteban Murillo
c. 1650
Beggar Boys Eating Grapes and Melon.
Alte Pinakothek, Munich.

> The one to whom [the supreme creator] gives
> a modest role
> only has to do it as he should;
> and to whom a larger one is given
> only in doing it well fulfills his charge.
> If I order you to play
> the part of a poor person or a slave
> of a king or a cripple,
> play the part God has handed you,
> for it is your only commission
> to play your part with perfection
> in works, actions and language;
> while the distribution of speeches and roles,
> in performance, whether much or little
> is the sole responsibility of the author of the play.

For those who cried, the world was a tragedy, while for those who laughed it was a brief theatrical interlude. When Zurbarán painted his still lifes, there was no middle ground: you were either very poor or very rich, a cripple or a king, and the poor were treated with disdain even by the poor, as Sancho Panza does with Basilio in Chapter 20 of *Don Quixote*:

> "A fig for the accomplishments of Basilio! As much as thou hast so much art thou worth, and as much as thou art worth so much hast thou. As a grandmother of mine used to say, there are only two families in the world, the Haves and the Have Nots; and she stuck to the Haves; and to this day, Señor Don Quixote, people would sooner feel the pulse of 'Have' than of 'Know'; an ass covered with gold looks better than a horse with a pack-saddle. So once more I say I stick to Camacho, the bountiful skimmings of whose pots are geese and hens, hares and rabbits; but of Basilio's, if any ever come to hand, or even to foot, they'll be only rinsings." "Hast thou finished thy harangue, Sancho?" said Don Quixote. "Of course I have finished it," replied Sancho, "because I see your worship takes offense at it; but if it was not for that, there was work enough cut out for three days."

Food was an obsession for the poor; for them hunger ruled the day, every day. The little they had was spent on surviving in a society where basic foodstuffs such as meat, olive oil, and wine were taxed so steeply that they were prohibitive for the poor. In contrast, the tables of the wealthy were

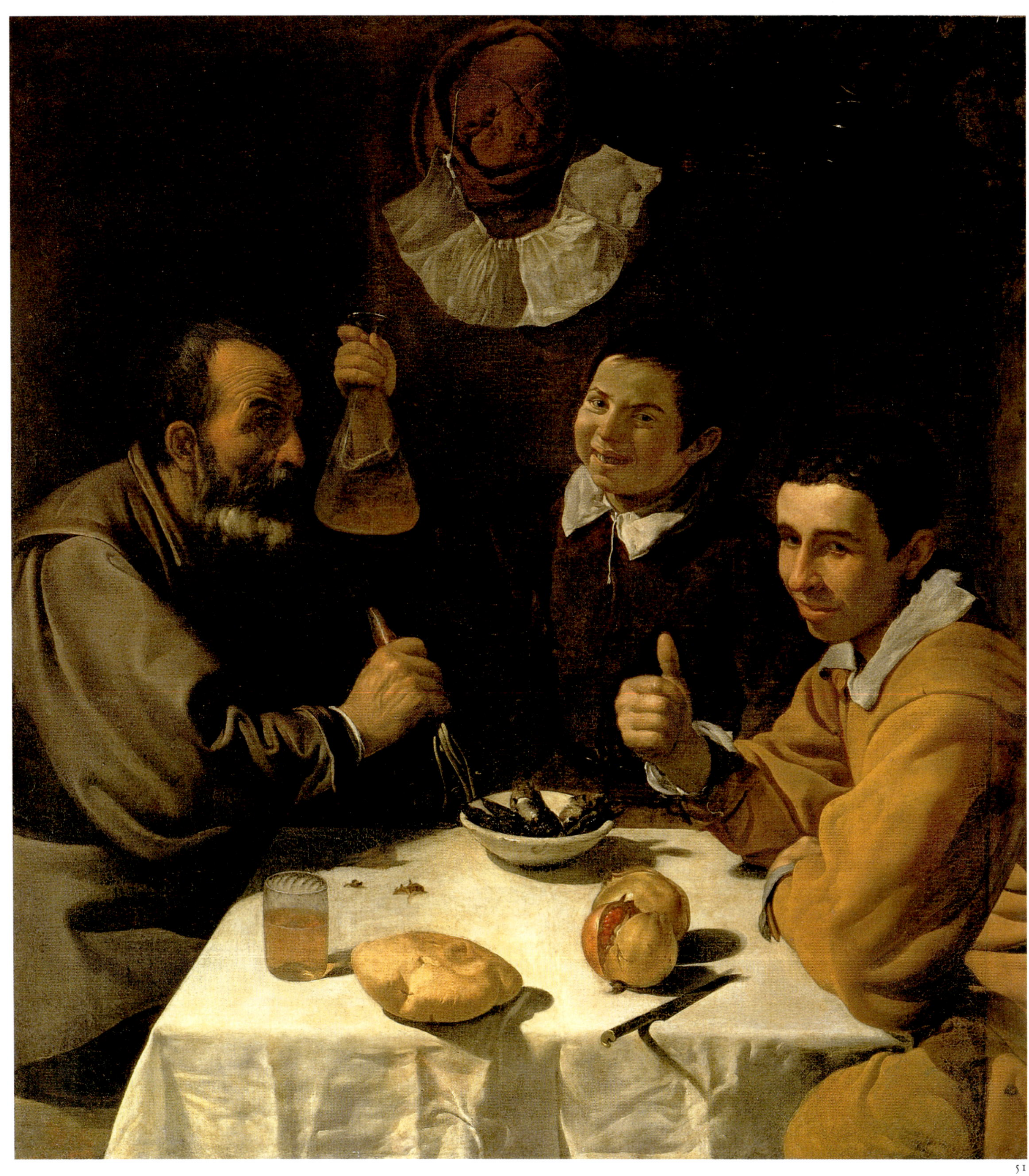

51

51. Diego Velázquez
c.1615–17
The Luncheon.
Hermitage Museum, St. Petersburg.

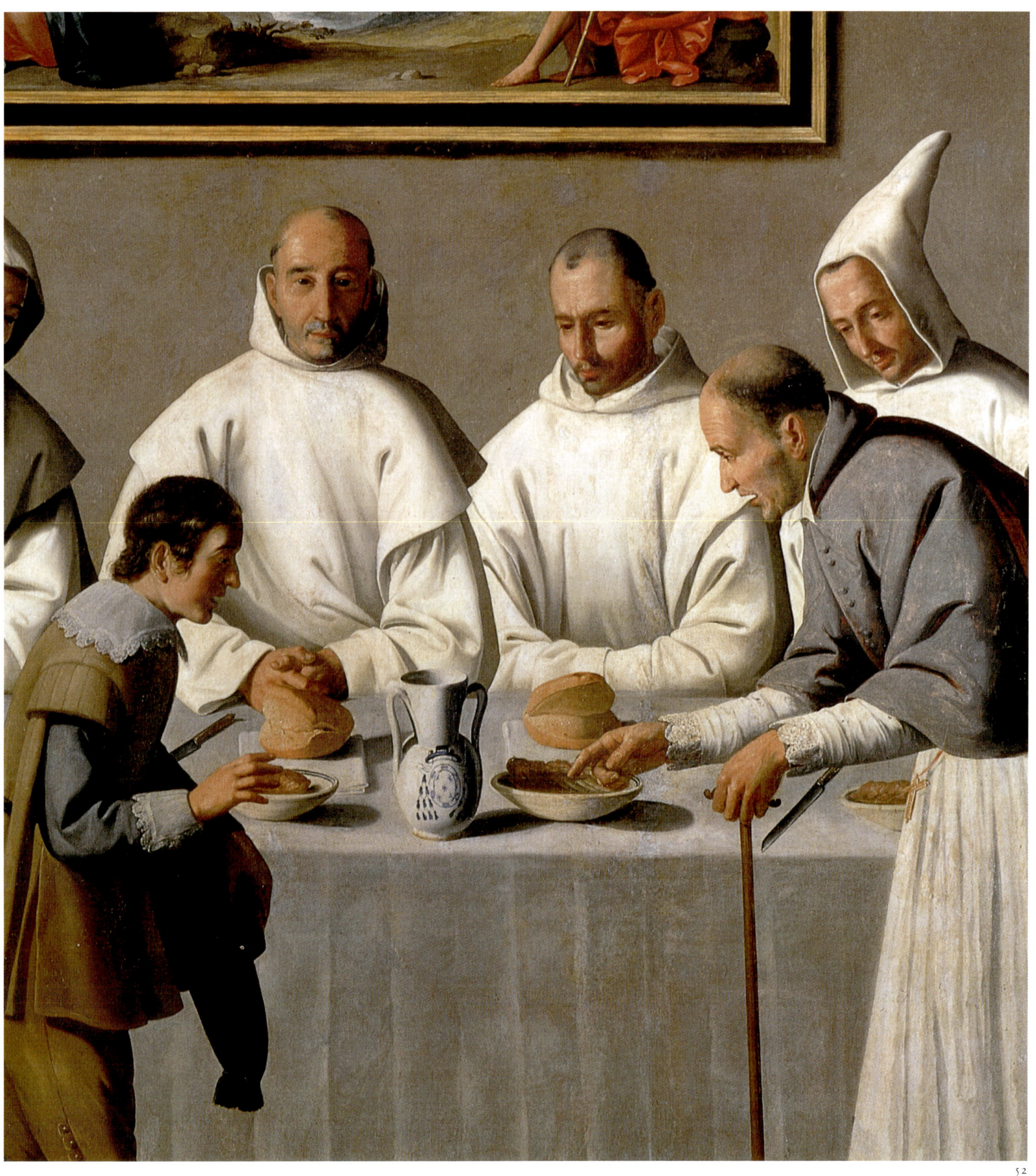

52

52. Francisco de Zurbarán
1630–35
Detail from *Saint Hugh in the Refectory*, Carthusian Monastery of Nuestra Señora de las Cuevas, Seville.
Museo de Bellas Artes, Seville.

abundant and excessive, if not simply insulting. As an example, there is Camacho's table in *Don Quixote:*

> The first thing that presented itself to Sancho's eyes was a whole ox spitted on a whole elm tree, and in the fire at which it was to be roasted there was burning a middling-sized mountain of faggots, and six stewpots that stood round the blaze had not been made in the ordinary mould of common pots, for they were six half wine-jars, each fit to hold the contents of a slaughter-house; they swallowed up whole sheep and hid them away in their insides without showing any more sign of them than if they were pigeons. Countless were the hares ready skinned and the plucked fowls that hung on the trees for burial in the pots, numberless the wildfowl and game of various sorts suspended from the branches that the air might keep them cool.
>
> Sancho counted more than sixty wine skins of over six gallons each, and all filled, as it proved afterwards, with generous wines. There were, besides, piles of the whitest bread, like the heaps of corn one sees on the threshing-floors. There was a wall made of cheeses arranged like open brick-work, and two cauldrons full of oil, bigger than those of a dyer's shop, served for cooking fritters, which when fried were taken out with two mighty shovels, and plunged into another cauldron of prepared honey that stood close by.
>
> Of cooks and cook-maids there were over fifty, all clean, brisk, and blithe. In the capacious belly of the ox were a dozen soft little suckling pigs, which, sewn up there, served to give it tenderness and flavor. The spices of different kinds did not seem to have been bought by the pound but by the quarter, and all lay open to view in a great chest. In short, all the preparations made for the wedding were in rustic style, but abundant enough to feed an army.

Sancho ate from the pots, cauldrons, and earthen jars of Camacho, but his case was exceptional. The Counter-Reformation institutionalized poverty, and numerous hospitals were created to aid beggars,

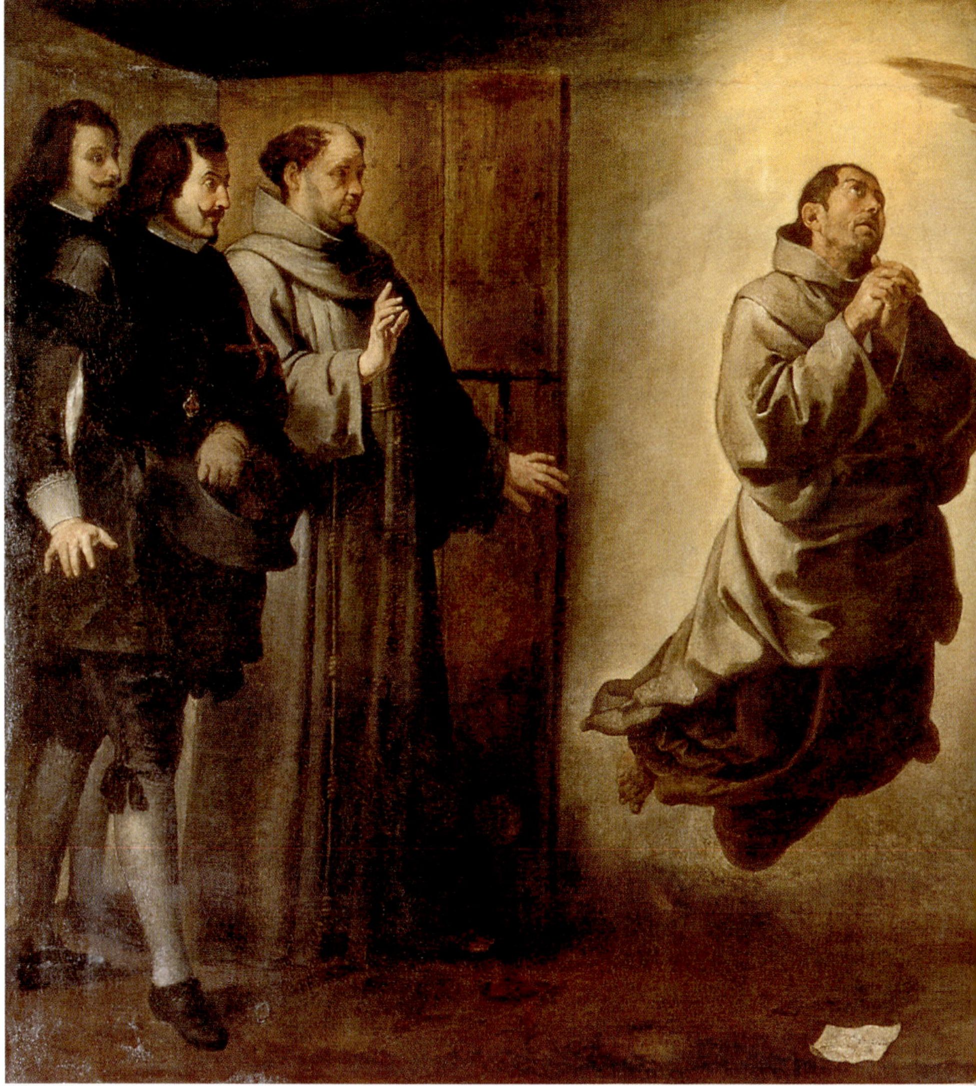

the elderly, orphans, and the ill, as Murillo shows in *San Diego Feeding the Poor* (ca. 1645–46, Madrid, Academia de San Fernando) which, like the other paintings in the series such as *The Angels' Kitchen* (ill. 53), was painted for the small cloister of a Franciscan monastery in Seville with the sole objective of exalting the virtues of the order.

Hunger and the need to obtain sustenance were not the sole province of the seventeenth century. However, in the sixteenth century it was still possible at least to find a master to serve, as was the case of Lazarillo de Tormes, the urchin who is the hero of a novel published in 1554, though such a master was usually found with great difficulty and to little avail: "I thought many times to leave that miserly

53. Bartolomé Esteban Murillo
1646
The Angels' Kitchen.
Musée du Louvre, Paris.

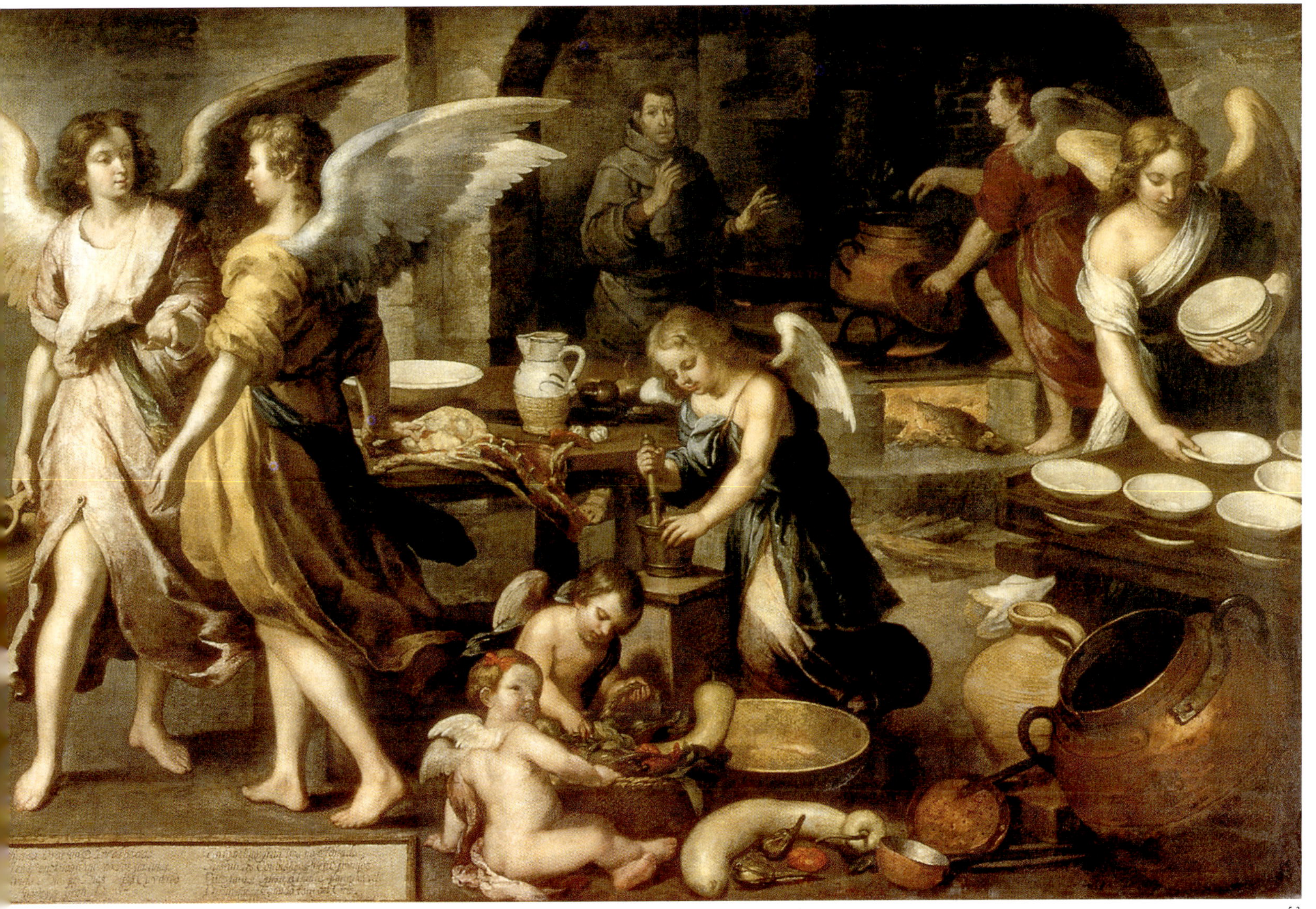

53

master," Lazarillo tells us, "though for two reasons I did not do so: first, so as not to push my legs, for fear of my own weakness, which came upon me out of pure hunger." The other he came to after thinking for a moment: "I have had two masters, the first left me starving to death, and upon leaving him, I came upon another, who had me with him in the tomb; so if I reject this one and chose another even lower in rank, what will that be if not death?"

Then there was no one left to serve, not even of the sort who toyed with the hunger of his servants so that they would not abandon him. The nameless street child had to search for sustenance by other means in a society that was in ruins. Witness the response of the Council of Castile to a question that Philip III had raised in 1618 concerning the problems of his realm and their possible remedy:

> First, I affirm that depopulation and the lack of people is the worst we have seen or heard in these dominions since the ancestors of His Majesty began to reign, for this crown is becoming totally finished and ruined, without any doubt, with our Lord not providing the remedy we need, despite the piety and grandeur of His Majesty; and that the cause of this arises out of the excessive charges and taxes imposed on His Majesty's subjects, who, seeing that they cannot bear them, are obliged to leave their children and wives and homes so as not to die of starvation in them, and

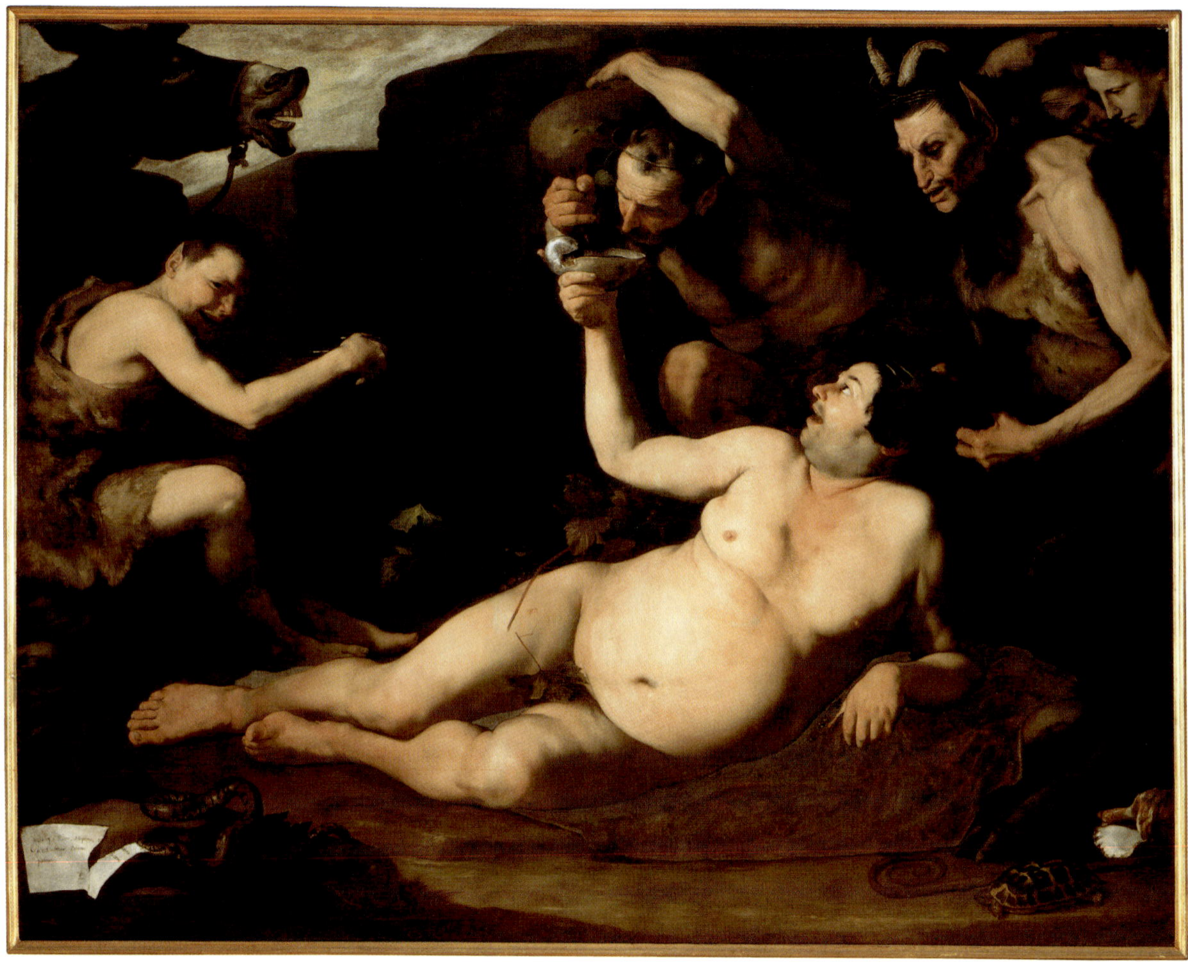

54

go to lands where they hope to find sustenance, thus being absent from working their own lands, and from control over the little property they possessed and that remained to them.

The rascal who is the hero of Mateo Alemán's novel *Guzmán de Alfarache* (1599) did not want the bread of charity, which he considered the "bread of pain" and the "bread of blood." He sought instead the "glorious freedom" of eating something found or stolen. That version of freedom characterizes the lives of the vagabond children that Murillo painted, children with eyes tired of life, in a Seville that had long since forgotten what it was to be the cornerstone of Spain. In his early paintings in this genre, Murillo portrayed the sordid side of this lifestyle. Though there is food for the beggar, he is pictured as imprisoned in the dungeon of his own poverty, infested with lice, and with nostalgia and sadness. Murillo's portrait of poverty may have been too true to life for the collectors of this kind of painting, primarily Flemish and English merchants residing in Seville. For this reason, Murillo soon transformed the portrayal of poverty into praise for a life that was simple and free, and the vagabond children became children who seem to enjoy their impoverished existence (ill. 50).

Murillo's children would never become the Phaetons of power; they would never aspire to drive, even for a single day, the chariot of the sun. Perhaps beggars would not aspire either to play with a god as the satyrs do in *The Triumph of Bacchus* (ill. 56), painted by Velázquez in 1628–29, only a few years before Zurbarán gave life to the dead rose that rests its petals on the pewter plate. The satyrs portrayed by Velázquez are quite different from the image of the *Drunken Silenus* (ills. 54, 55) that flowed from the brush of José de Ribera. In this painting Ribera (called in Italy "Lo Spagnoletto") displays his status as a member of the

ABOVE AND RIGHT:
54 and 55. José de Ribera
1626
Drunken Silenus and detail.
Museo di Capodimonte,
Naples.

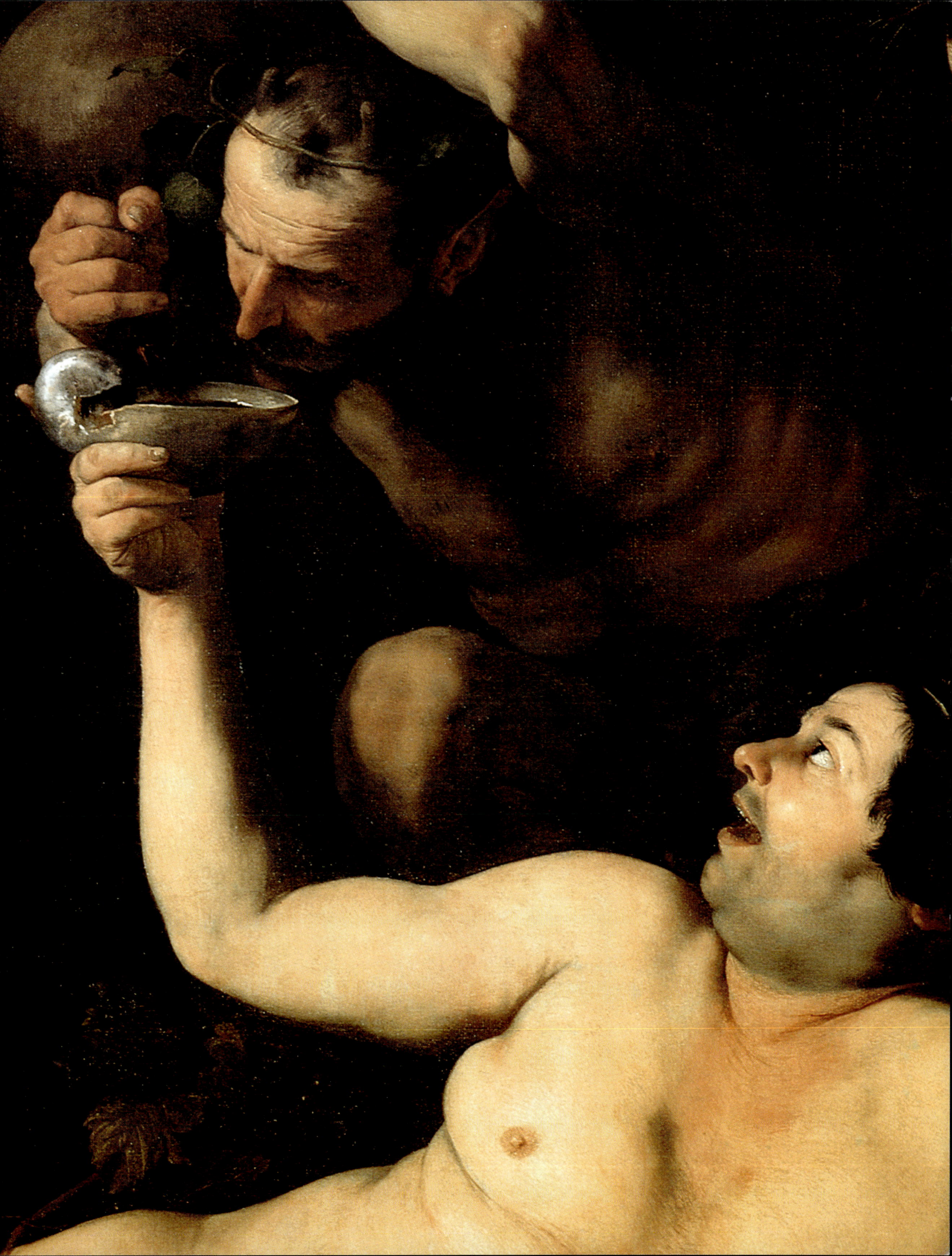

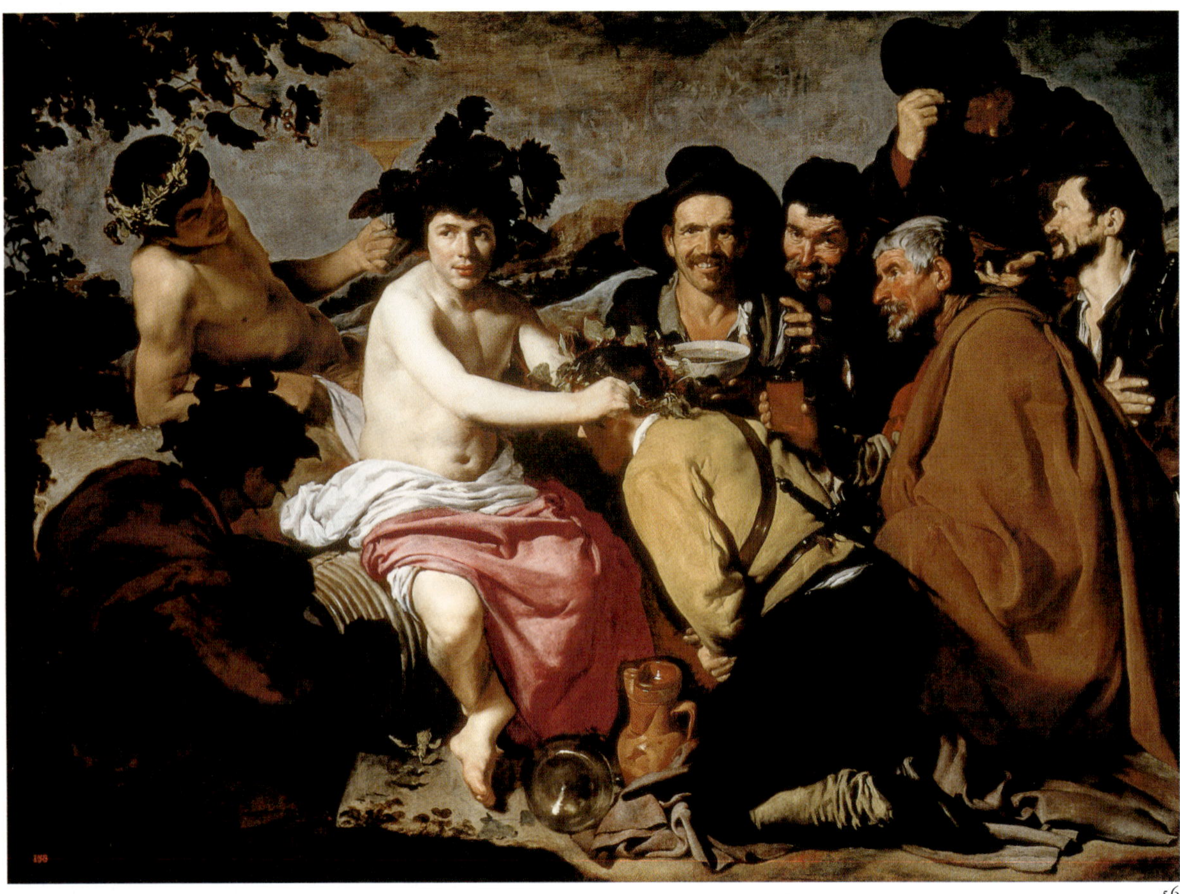

56

painting academy in Rome by including allegorical details, some of them with a variety of scholarly interpretations. There is the serpent carrying the torn slip of paper in its mouth with the date and the signature of the artist on it (a serpent that could also be an allegory of death or an allegory of good health, fame, or wisdom); the donkey that Silenus rides; or the shepherd's staff he often uses when walking. We also see a shell and a tortoise in the lower right-hand corner: the former is an emblem of death; the latter, an emblem of the laziness of Pan, Silenus's father, probably the ancient satyr with goat-like features who seems to be crowning his pot-bellied son.

In spite of these academic references, Ribera pictures the fable in burlesque fashion. Silenus, son of Pan and a nymph, was the keeper of young Bacchus and the inseparable companion of the god in his travels. Ribera's Silenus is shown reclining on the ground like an indiscreet Venus, though a Venus whose soft, feminine beauty has been transformed into the fleshy corpulence of a drunken man. He is a joyful, humorous Silenus, the easy butt of practical jokes who delights the banquets of the gods with his presence. Here he seems to delight the child, a scamp not as hungry as Murillo's street children, who invites our presence at this festive, amusing event.

In Velázquez's *Triumph of Bacchus*, painted "in the service of the king," as noted in the 1629 document recording payment for it, there are no scholarly references nor any ridicule of the mythological. Velázquez paints a sort of secular act of charity in which wine takes the place of bread and the usual benevolent saint is replaced by Bacchus, whose gaze seems drawn either to the light or to the supernatural. Neither Bacchus nor his companions appear to be drunk. Those crowned by bunches of grapes and leaves turn sensually toward the illuminated figure or observe him attentively, while others, some joyful and others more anxious, look out at the viewer defiantly, speak to each other, bend down to receive the crown, or wait nervously for Bacchus to satiate their thirst. The wine has replaced water, as life replaces death.

ABOVE AND RIGHT:
56 and 57. Diego Velázquez
1628–29
The Triumph of Bacchus,
or *The Drunkards* and detail.
Museo Nacional del Prado,
Madrid.

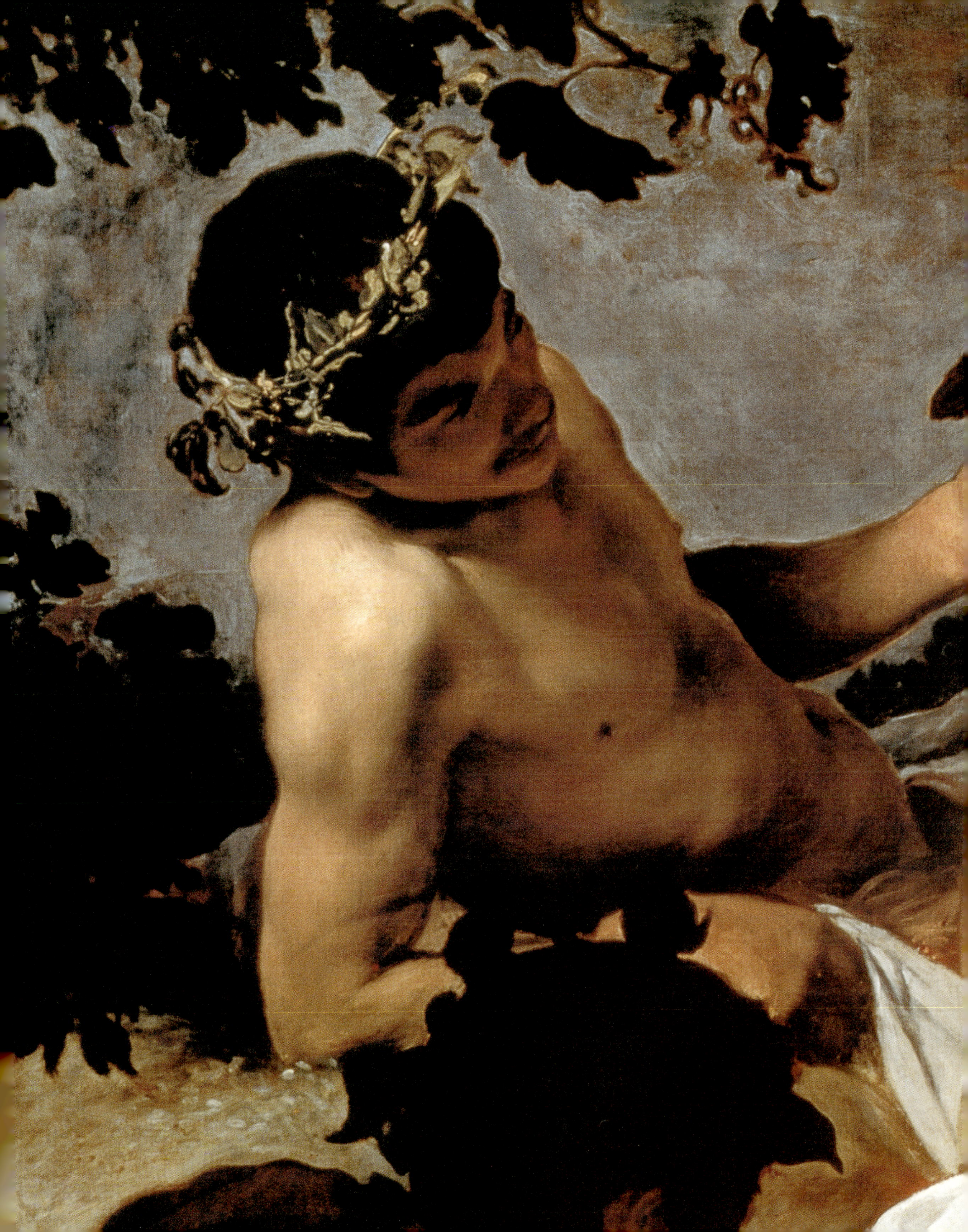

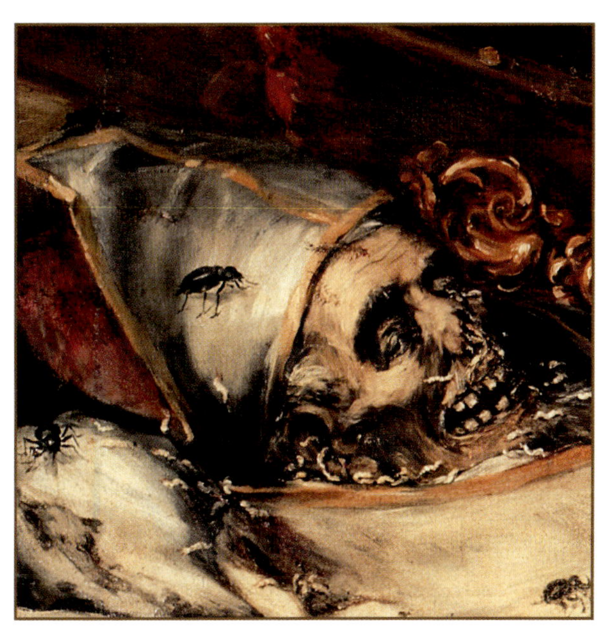

HUMAN VANITY

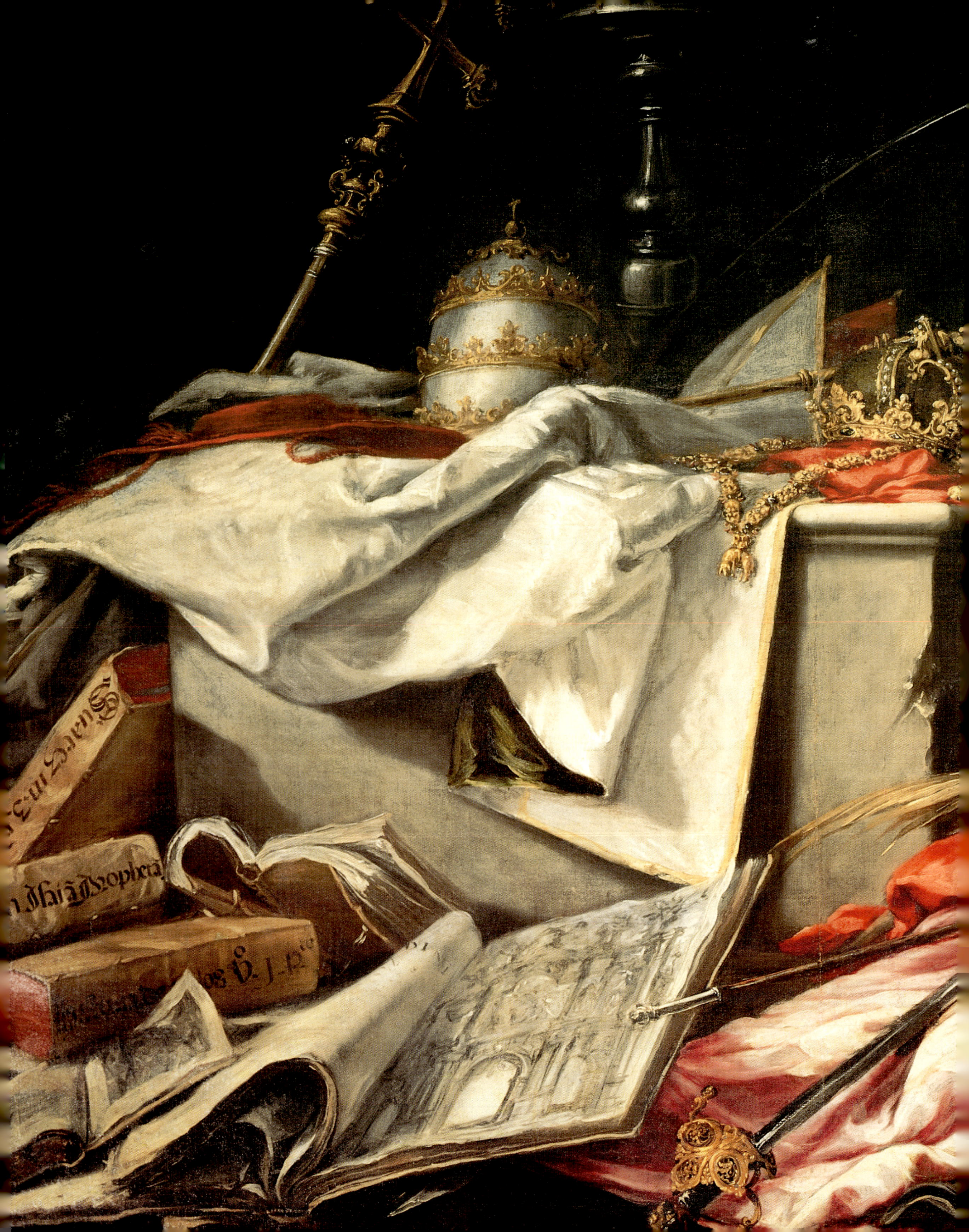

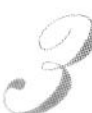

Human Vanity

And digging into her bag, she gave him another coin, and ordered him to place two candles before the saints that she considered to be most beneficial and appreciative. With this La Pipota left, saying to them
"Enjoy life, children, while you have time: old age will come, and in it you will cry for the times you lost when you were young, as I weep for them: and pray to God for me, as I will do the same for myself and for you, for He frees us and protects us from harm without suffering the ups and downs of justice."
And with this, she went away.

—MIGUEL DE CERVANTES, *Rinconete and Cortadillo*, before 1604

PRECEDING PAGE:
58. Juan de Valdés Leal
1671–72
Detail of *Finis Gloriae Mundi, Hieroglyphs of the Four Last Things.*
Church of the Hospital de la Caridad, Seville.

LEFT:
59. Juan de Valdés Leal
1671–72
Detail of *In Ictu Oculi, Hieroglyphs of the Four Last Things.*
Church of the Hospital de la Caridad, Seville.

The Spaniard who became Saint Ignatius of Loyola, the founder of the Jesuit order in 1540, composed his *Spiritual Exercises* during a retreat in 1522 and 1523. This guide to the practice of meditation, published in 1548, inspired many other versions during the sixteenth and seventeenth centuries. Ignatius recommended a highly structured system of contemplation, in which considerations of the wages of sin and their punishments in hell were primary stimuli. However, Ignatius was not alone in his emphasis on reminders of death. Such mementi mori are widely found in Dutch seventeenth-century paintings as well as in Spanish sermons and art. Missionaries in both Europe and the Americas, especially following the Council of Trent (1545–63), disseminated what has been called a "pedagogy of fear" that influenced spirituality in the western world until the Enlightenment. It was a spirituality that drew the faithful to focus on concerns with death and dying and the future of their souls, as well as on the disposition of their earthly bodies and the placement and design of their tombs and mausoleums.

The church synod held in Plasencia in early 1499 forbade cooking, eating, banquets, or receptions, whether organized as "charitable acts for the deceased" or for weddings, in churches, hermitages, or cemeteries. The synod of Salamanca had adopted similar injunctions in 1497, as did later synods at Badajoz in 1501 and Tuy in 1528. These synods ruled that on the days of funerals the clergy should not "eat and drink with the heirs or executors of wills" under threat of fining those attending such a *refrigerium*—the Latin name of banquets held for the dead—with a ducat each "for construction work on the church."

These were not new rules. As early as the Second Council held in Braga, Portugal, in 572 the presence of food at funerals and the practice of sacrifices at tombs were prohibited. Yet for the next thousand years the Catholic Church had been unable to put an end to these rituals, which were intended to assist the souls of the deceased in purgatory, understood as a necessary stopping place in

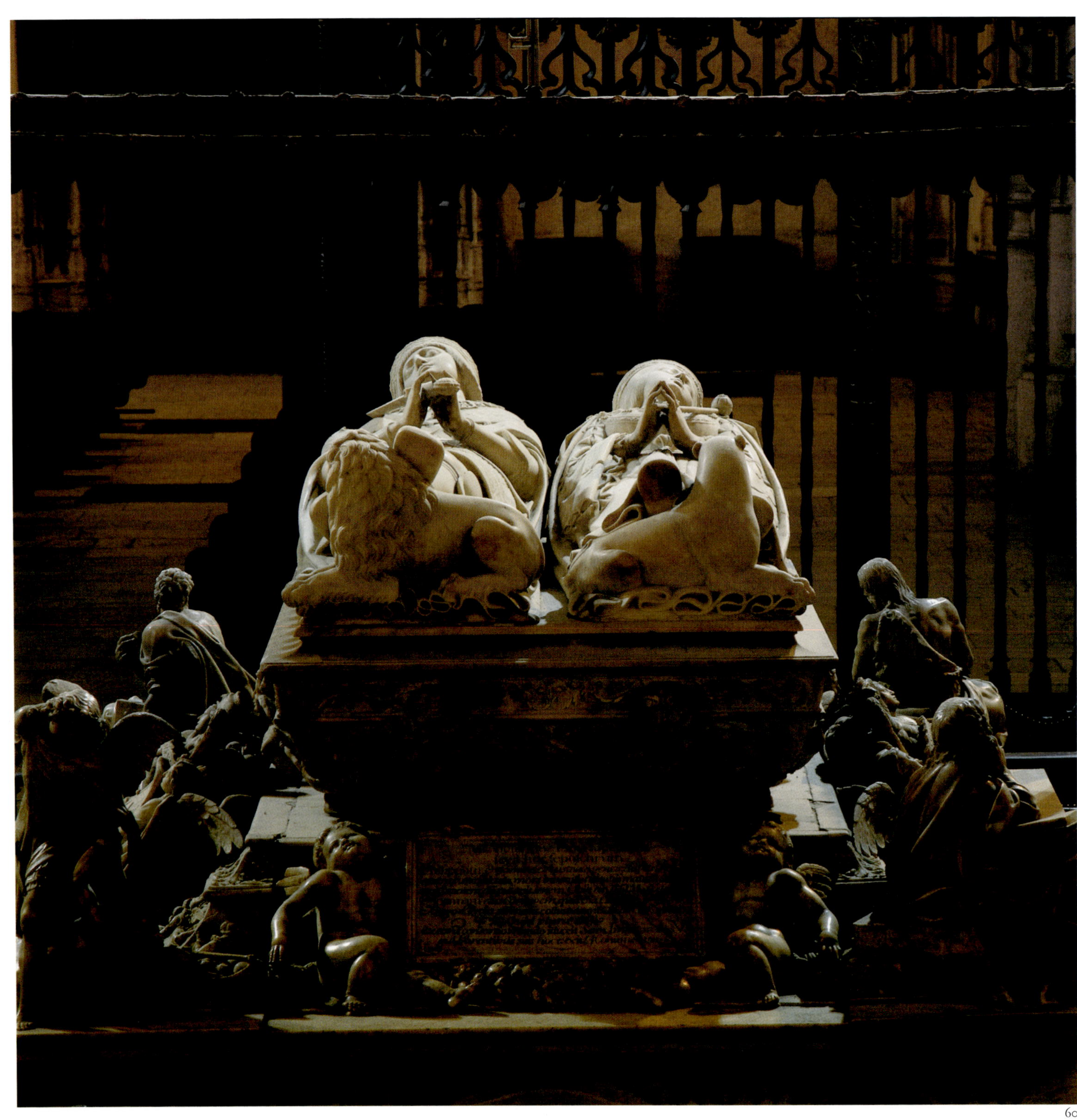

60

60. Bartolomé Ordóñez
1519
Funeral monument of Philip the Fair and Joan the Mad,
marble.
Capilla Real, Granada Cathedral.

the voyage toward salvation from the twelfth century on. The funeral feast assisted the departed soul directly with food and drink, or a friend or relative could indirectly shorten the deceased's time in purgatory through gifts of food to the poor and the sick. At the beginning of the sixteenth century, the Church was still trying to suppress these funeral rituals, lessen their excessive and exaggerated expressions of mourning, and at the very least remove them from the sacred precinct of the church. The clergy recognized that the feasts did not celebrate the transcendence of death, the moment when the soul of the deceased gained access to eternal life, but were rather in the tradition of the pagan *refrigerium,* which celebrated life over death, a triumph of the well-lived course of life itself.

CARPE DIEM

In the sixteenth century some people regarded the ephemeral nature of earthly things as corrupting and incompatible with the yearning for eternal life. One could seek, as did Saint Teresa of Ávila (1515–82), to live a more elevated existence in which death did not mean dying, but rather living a better life in heaven. However, Saint Teresa's search for a divine death—"I live without living in me"—was not the personal goal of most people. Everyone knew that death awaited them; it would come eventually and perhaps unexpectedly. Everyone—kings, poets, thieves, and prostitutes—would die, yet everyone, as Horace pronounced at the tomb of Archytas (*Odes,* I, 11), could take advantage of life before time ran out: ". . . dum loquimur, fugerit invida aetas: carpe diem, quam minimum credula postero"; that is: ". . . even as we speak, envious time is running away from us. Seize the day, trusting little in tomorrow."

Carpe diem, "seize the day," is the song of everyday life, of the here and now rather than the beyond. It was the motto of many sixteenth- and seventeenth-century writers, such as the soldier and lyrical poet Garcilaso de la Vega (ca. 1501–36) in his "Sonnet XXIII." He praises a girl's beauty while reminding us how fleeting time will destroy it:

> While of red rose and lily white
> the colors of your face now show
> and your impassioned, honest glance
> the heart inflames and holds in tow;
>
> And while your hair, which in a vein
> of gold was mined, with rapid flight
> around your white and haughty throat
> the wind moves, scatters, and uncombs;
>
> go, pluck now from your happy spring
> the sweetest fruit, ere angry time
> covers with snow the lovely peak.
>
> The icy wind will wilt the rose;
> to make no change in its routine
> age, fickle, alters everything.

De la Vega served Charles V in several military campaigns, including the Battle of Pavia. He temporarily lost the emperor's favor over a bit of court intrigue and was imprisoned for a few months on an island in the Danube. He was soon back in the service of the emperor, but was mortally wounded in battle. Garcilaso's poem suggests that death's inevitability is a good reason to seek pleasure in life. This understanding of life (familiarly reflected in the English poem that starts "Gather ye rosebuds while ye may . . .") would, decades after Garcilaso wrote his poem, be reflected in a sonnet by Luis de Góngora y Argote (1561–1627)—priest, poet, and courtier:

> While trying with your tresses to compete
> in vain the sun's rays shine on burnished gold;
> while with abundant scorn across the plain
> does your white brow the lily's hue behold;
>
> while to each of your lips, to catch and keep,
> are drawn more eyes than to carnations bright;
> and while with graceful scorn your lovely throat
> transparently still bests all crystal's light,
>
> take your delight in throat, locks, lips, and brow,
> before what in your golden years was gold,
> carnation, lily, crystal luminous,
>
> not just to silver or limp violets will turn,
> but you and all of it as well
> to earth, decay, dust, gloom, and nothingness.

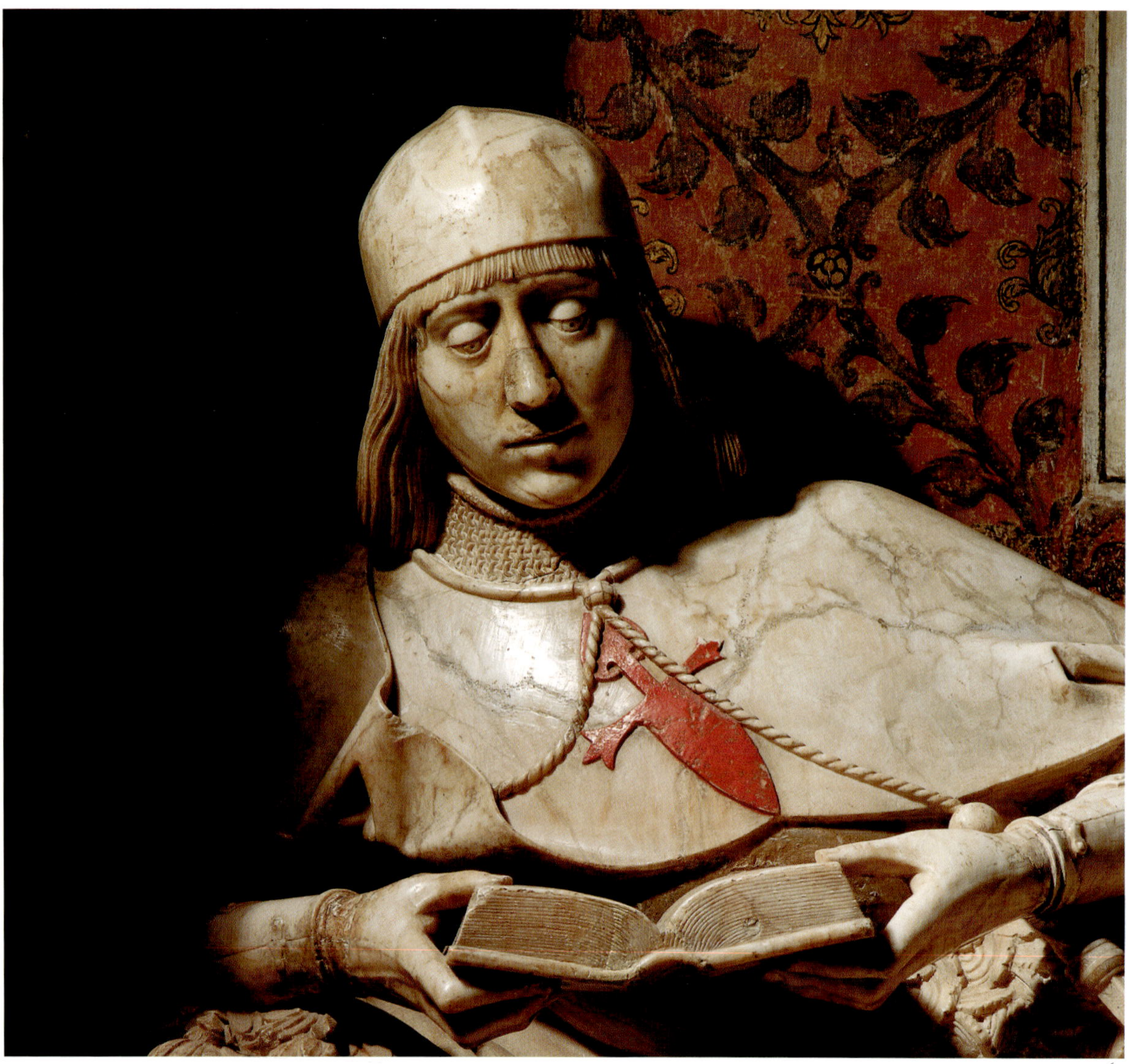

61

PREPARING FOR A GOOD DEATH

For some, then, it was imperative to seize the day, to take full advantage of youth and of life itself before the inevitable passage of time and death. For others, life was only the journey toward a liberating death for which one had to prepare and keep vigil. Fifteenth-century engravings and paintings had pictured Death as a skeleton, standing or on horseback, triumphantly wielding a lance or a sickle, waiting to snatch life from one who was then on the path to heaven. Illustrated treatises about the preparation for death published around the end of the fifteenth century offer various versions of the *ars moriendi*, the art of dying, such as the *Brief Treatise on the Very Good and Beneficial Art and Form of Dying Well* in the library of the Escorial. In these guidebooks a "Good Death" presupposes the triumph of the saints and angels who intervene against the forces of evil—the victory, in effect, of the Archangel Michael over the Antichrist. However, the treatises about the art of dying well advised not only how to prepare the soul through prayer, but also how to purchase indulgences and establish suitable bequests for the church and clergy.

Such abuses were denounced by sixteenth-century reformers influenced by the zealous Italian reformer Girolamo Savonarola (1452–98), and promoted by Spanish intellectuals such as Cardinal Jiménez de Cisneros (1436–1517) at the Complutense University in Alcalá de Henares near Madrid. These reformers interpreted the "Good Death" not as the fruit of last-minute preparation, but as the reward for a continuous Christian life. Erasmus of Rotterdam expressed this opinion in his *Praeparatione ad mortem,* a small volume widely known in Spain through translations and variations. Among the latter are the anonymous *Book of What One Must*

61. 1475–1500
Detail of the *Tomb of Martín Vázquez de Arce,*
alabaster.
Cathedral chapel, Sigüenza.

Do to Die Well, published in Burgos in 1536; Bernardo Pérez de Chinchón's *Preparation and Arrangements for a Good Death,* published in Valencia; and the *Final Stages of the Passage to Death,* published in 1537 by the Toledan writer Alejo Venegas.

Erasmus of Rotterdam and like-minded thinkers believed that one ought not await the moment of death to hope for a "good death," but rather live in continuous fear of death, a death that awaits everyone everywhere, at any moment. One should not put one's trust in a deathbed test of conscience and full confession of sins; instead, one ought to confess daily and frequently partake of holy communion. "So that in various ways God purges his own," Bernardo Pérez asserts in his *Preparations and Arrangements for a Good Death:*

> . . . no death is bad if the life preceding it has been good. Some who die without any pain whatsoever go to Hell; others die with a thousand sufferings and go straight to Heaven. Some, when dying, want full confession, extreme unction, the eucharist, and in ancient times even baptism; yet I do not know why we desire to do all at once what we can and should do every day. The best piece of advice is for everyone, each day, before going to bed, to diligently examine his conscience and, if he finds that on that day he has committed some sin, he should strike his breast and with tears in his eyes ask forgiveness from the Lord and, invoking divine favor, promise to improve himself.

Confession and the other sacraments were understood as insufficient in and of themselves to assure access to heaven—the only guarantee in the face of death was Christ, who suffered and died on the cross, Christ "the triumphant banner, the banner of victory, the banner of eternal glory."

TO LIVE ON, AFTER DEATH, IN THE HERE AND NOW

Man lived to prepare for death, and also to prepare his eternal resting place, a place that would suitably reflect his possessions and his fame. Cardinals, archbishops, bishops, abbots, archdeacons, and nobles all fought to have their tombs located in the most privileged parts of the church. They wanted to erect their mausoleums not only as resting places for their souls, which would not be trapped within the marble anyway, but out of vanity for their bodies, bodies that paradoxically do not seem, in these monuments, to be affected by death. The nobler the people laid within them, the nobler the materials used for the mausoleums. Stone and metal, or, more cheaply, plaster and wood, represent the bodies of those whose souls have already escaped. In these sculpted effigies, the faces of the deceased—whether they are shown reclining, kneeling in adoration, seated, or propped up on their elbows on their eternal beds—remain serene, as if neither pain nor the passing of time has left a mark on them. Some seem to be in the midst of a sweet dream, others pray, others read, and others simply gaze with open eyes toward infinity, toward a resurrected Christ, from whom emanates the eternal light that comforts them and illuminates their path toward eternal glory.

Christ was the guarantee both for simple folk and for the kings and emperors who sought to reach heaven. Yet another soldier-poet, Hernando de Acuña (1518–80), served Charles V in a number of military campaigns in Italian territory and participated in his victories. Acuña described heaven as the "greater empire," and boldly set out his political ideal—"A Monarch, an Empire, and a Sword"—in his poem "To the King Our Lord" (v. 8). Acuña exalted the victory of "the human condition" in an epigram dedicated to the tomb of Charles V. Fame sings of her worldly glories and of the victory that silences all others:

> I, the one who raises
> man from the tomb
> and with my voice can do so,
> making immortal the name
> of the famous man I sing of,
> with a thousand tongues and cries
> I will sing of the greatest
> the most famous and supreme

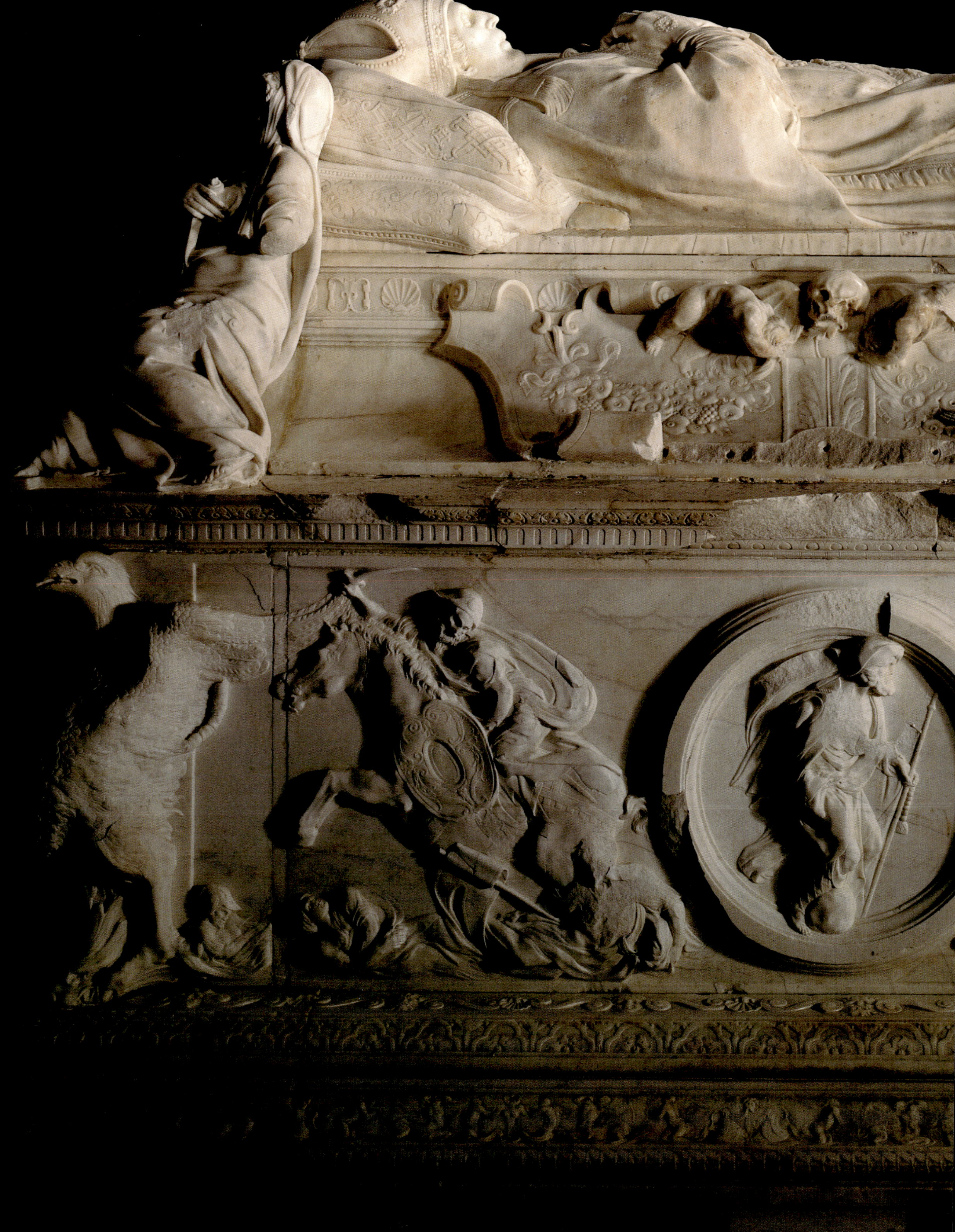

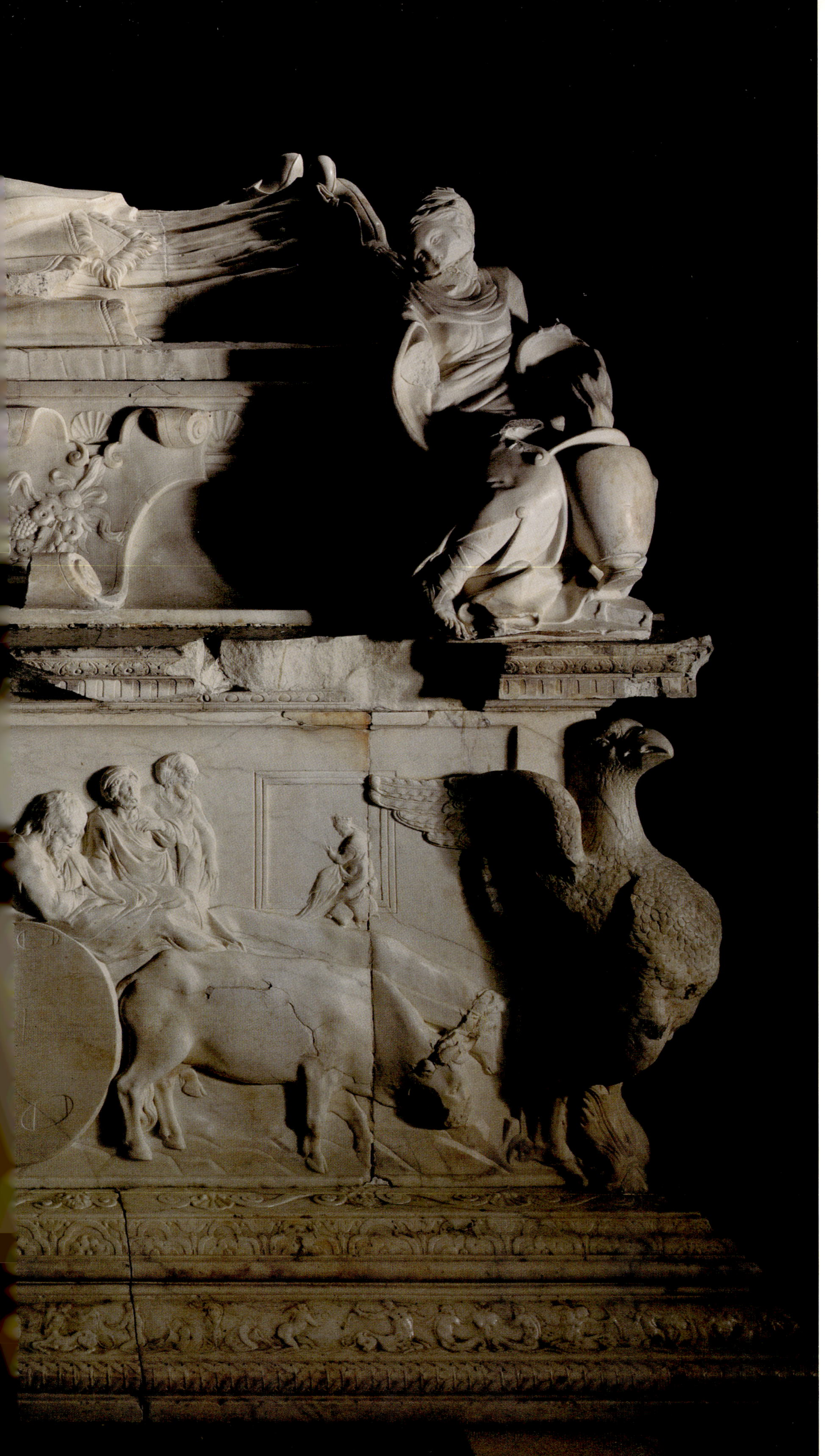

62. Alonso Berruguete
1554–61
Tomb of Cardinal Tavera,
marble.
Hospital de San Juan
Bautista, or Hospital de
Afuera ("outside the
walls"), Tavera, Toledo.

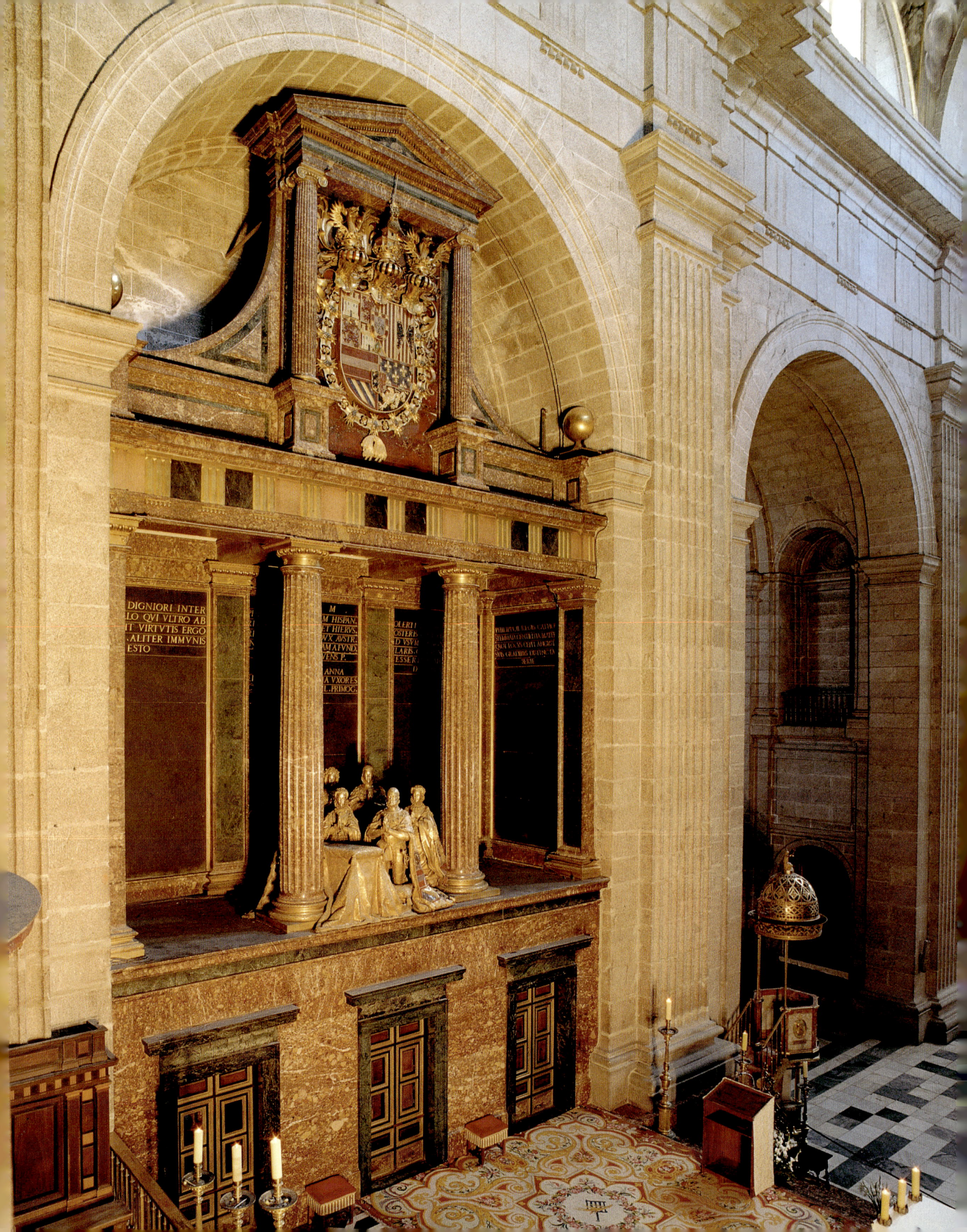
DIGNIORI INTER
LO QVI VLTRO AB
IT VIRTVTIS ERGO
ALITER IMMVNIS
ESTO

and the imperial monarch
of kings and emperors.
And in the end there was another victory
darkening the light,
and it is worthy of such memory,
that for itself deserves
a divine, and not a human history;
for only he was the conqueror
of his greatness and valor,
when the human state
shunning the highest degree,
won the greater Empire.

Thinking about that "eternal victory" well before it was in sight, Charles V planned for his body to be buried alongside those of his wife, his parents, and his grandparents, the Catholic monarchs Isabella and Ferdinand, in the Royal Chapel of Granada. Just after ascending to the throne in 1518 he had ordered tombs built there for Isabella and Ferdinand and for their daughter Joanna the Mad and her husband, Philip the Handsome (ill. 60). Yet, when Charles lay dying in the Hieronymite monastery at Yuste he added a codicil to his will, dated September 7, 1558, expressing his wish to rest not in Granada but temporarily in Yuste, beneath the high altar of the monastic church, where the friars would offer constant prayers for his soul. Charles wanted sculptures of himself and his wife in perpetual adoration of the Eucharist placed on the right side of the altar, like the painted wood sculptures of Ferdinand and Isabella by Diego de Siloé that were placed on either side of the high altar in the Royal Chapel of Granada.

THE LIFE THAT MUST LAST FOREVER

The death of Charles V in 1558 was described by an eyewitness in a letter:

> On the brink of death, he asked the Archbishop of Toledo to recite for him a few verses of the psalm "De Profundis," and the Archbishop recited the first three for him, and, while reciting the fourth, which begins *quia apud te propitiatio est,* the final death throe came upon [the Emperor] and the Archbishop put in his hands the cross, which he grasped so tightly and with such devotion that it was deeply moving to see. And, being unable to speak, struggling with death, he suddenly, as if responding to someone, called out, "I am calling, Lord" . . . and when his soul was being taken from him his whole body trembled, and he said with such a strong voice that he seemed well, "Jesus!" and with this holy word his life ended and he began the life that must last forever.

63. Pompeo Leoni
1590–1600
Cenotaph of Philip II,
marble and gilt bronze.
The epistle side (on the congregation's right) of the church at the Real Monasterio de San Lorenzo, El Escorial.

The highly influential *Imitation of Christ* by Thomas à Kempis (d. 1471) had inspired this need to possess Jesus Christ and to have a clear vision of the divine. The *Imitation of Christ* was followed in Spain by the popular *Book of Prayer and Meditation* by the Dominican friar Luis de Granada (1505–88). No one could attain this vision of the divine until the moment of death. The desire to see God face to face guided the funerary rites of Charles V in the monastery at Yuste, and the burial of his body in a leaden coffin beneath the high altar. It was, nonetheless, a temporary sepulcher, since during his lifetime Charles had expressed his desire to leave the decision about his final resting place to his son Phillip.

King Philip II established a dynastic mausoleum at the Hieronymite monastery/palace of San Lorenzo de El Escorial. Along the roadways of Spain people—some idly, some deeply moved, watched the funerary processions that brought the remains of kings and princes to the Escorial: those of Charles V and his wife Isabella, the melancholy empress; the emperor's sisters Maria of Hungary, the energetic governor of the Netherlands, and Leonora of Austria, who was crowned queen of France in Saint Denis; the first wife of Philip II, Maria Manuela of Portugal, and her brothers Don Juan and Don Fernando. Later, the mortal remains of Philip II 's third wife, Isabel de Valois, along with those of his son the unfortunate Carlos, as well as those of the crown princes born of the marriage between Philip II and the light-hearted Ana de Austria, were also taken to the Escorial. When these people were still alive and even before some of them were born, the preacher Antonio de Guevara had written in his *Reloj de príncipes* (1529), which was

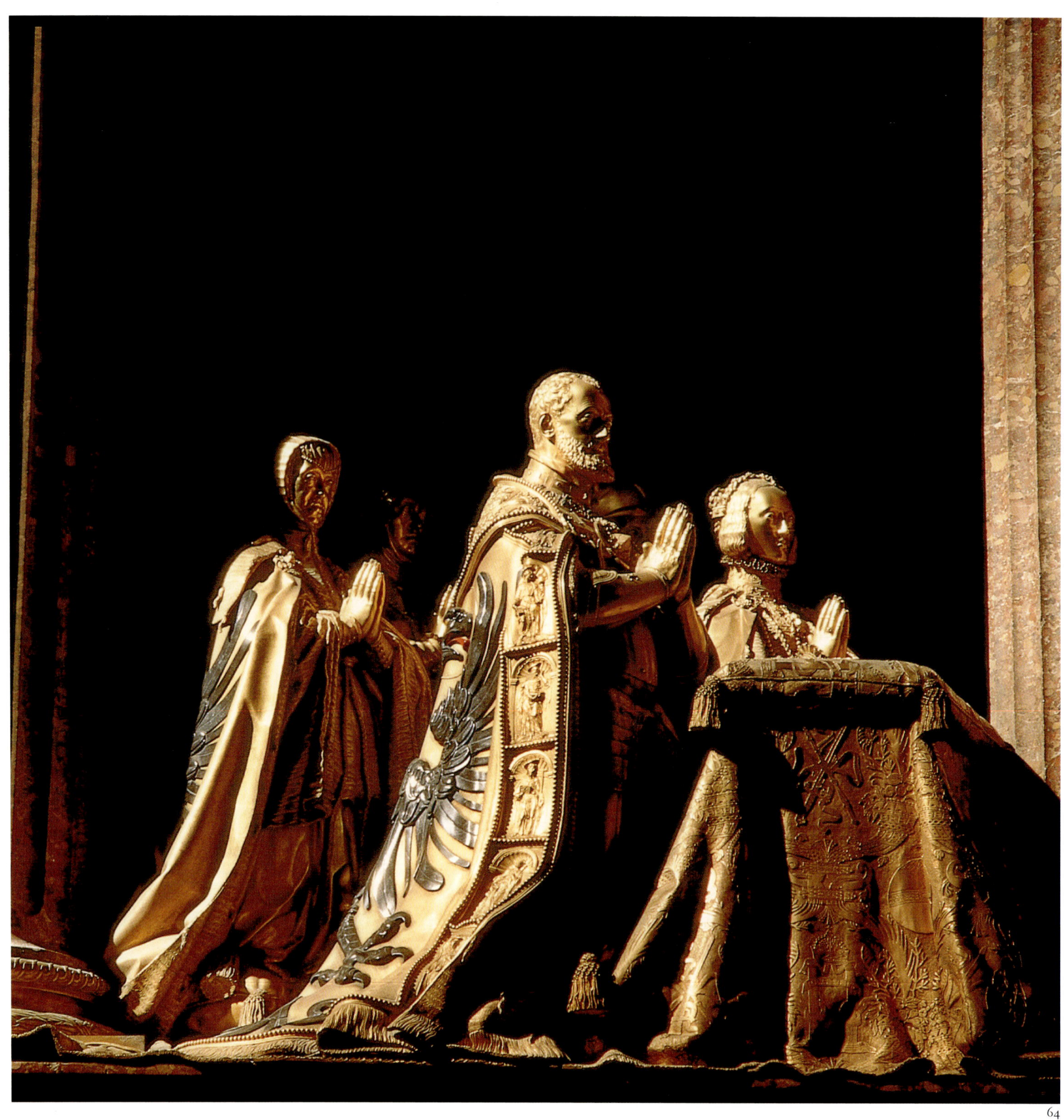

64

64. Pompeo Leoni
1590–97
The Family of Charles V,
gilt bronze.
The gospel side (on the congregation's left) of the church
at the Real Monasterio de San Lorenzo, El Escorial.

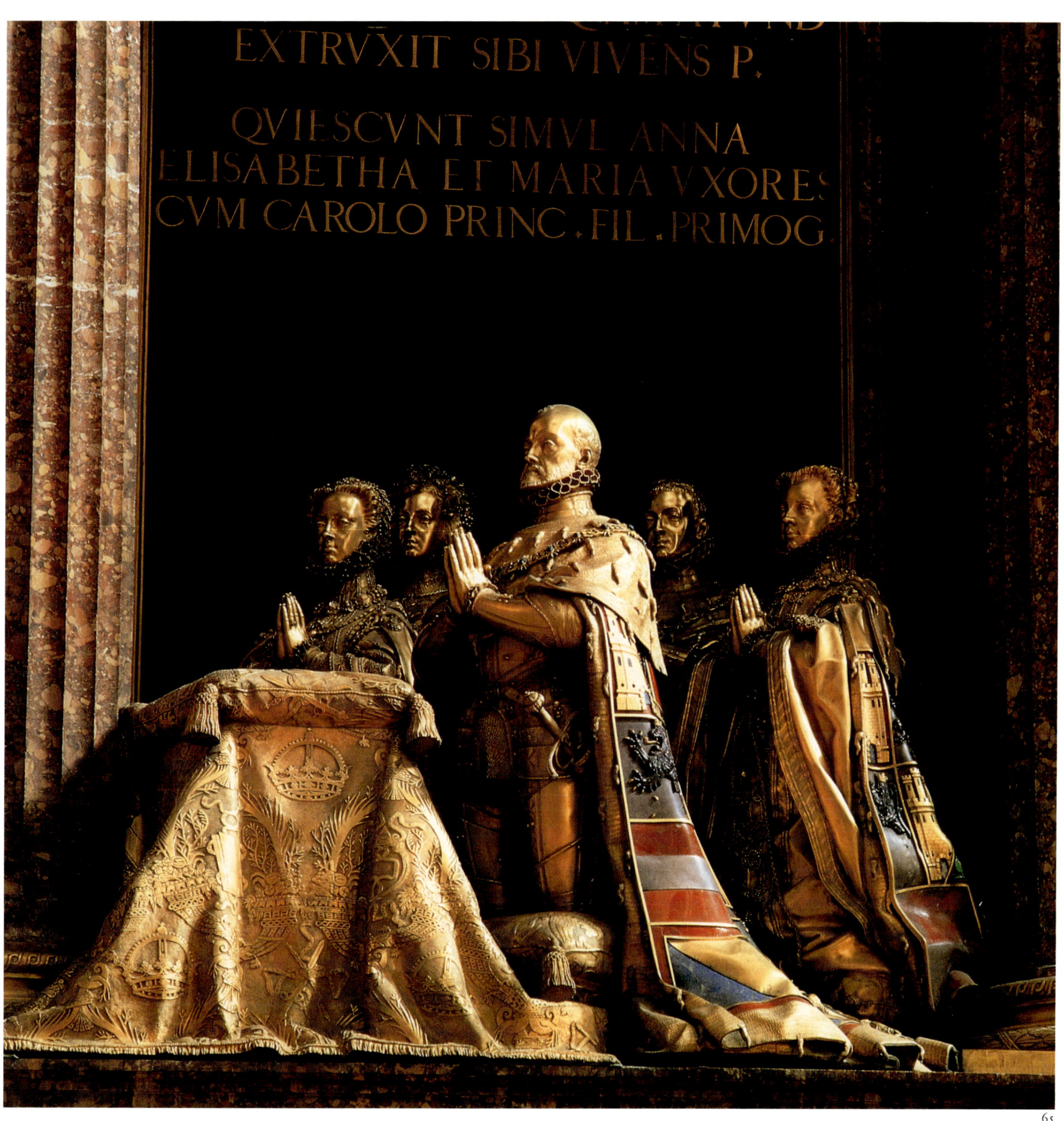

65

65. Pompeo Leoni
1590–1600
The Family of Philip II,
gilt bronze.
The epistle side of the church at the Real Monasterio de San Lorenzo, El Escorial.

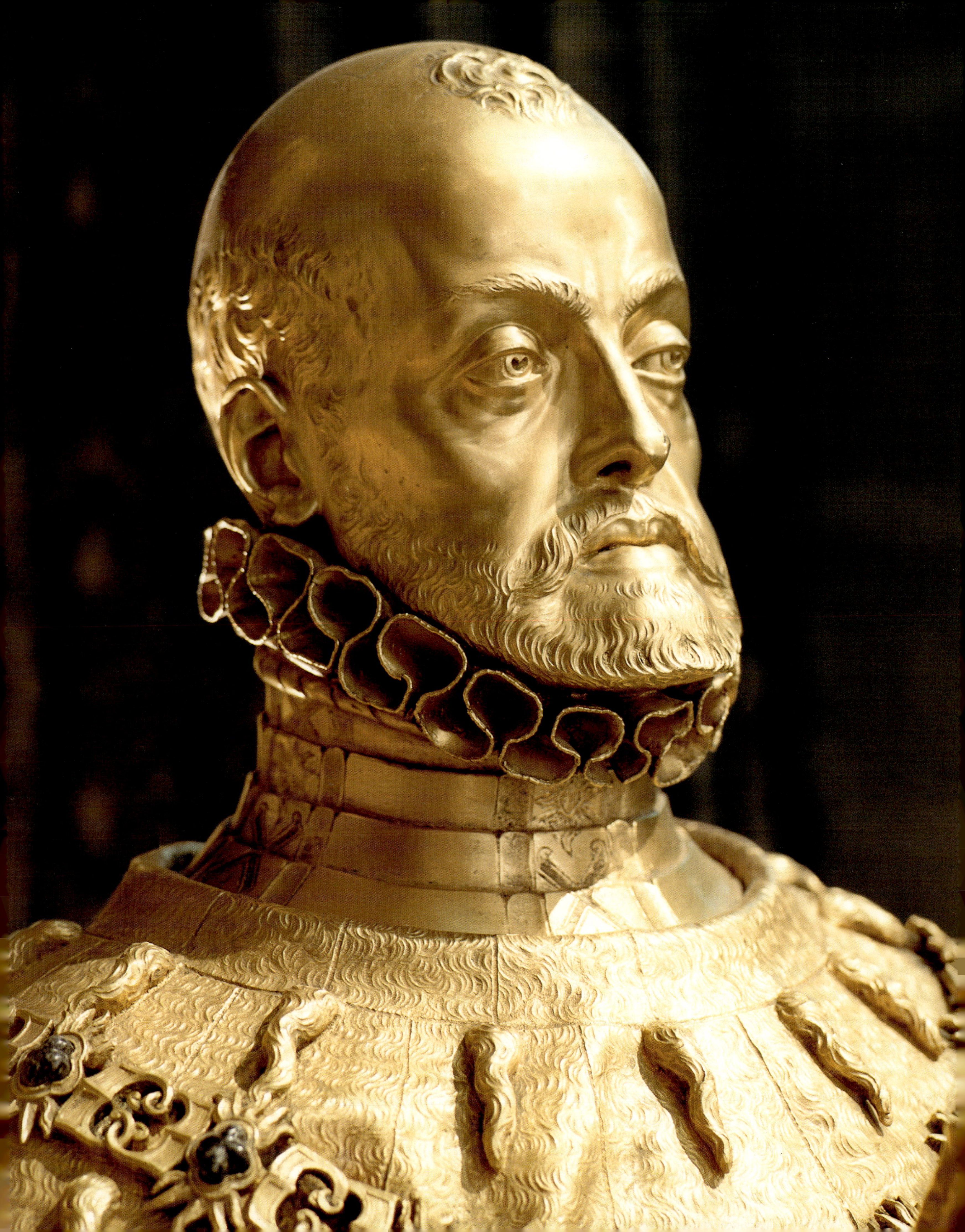

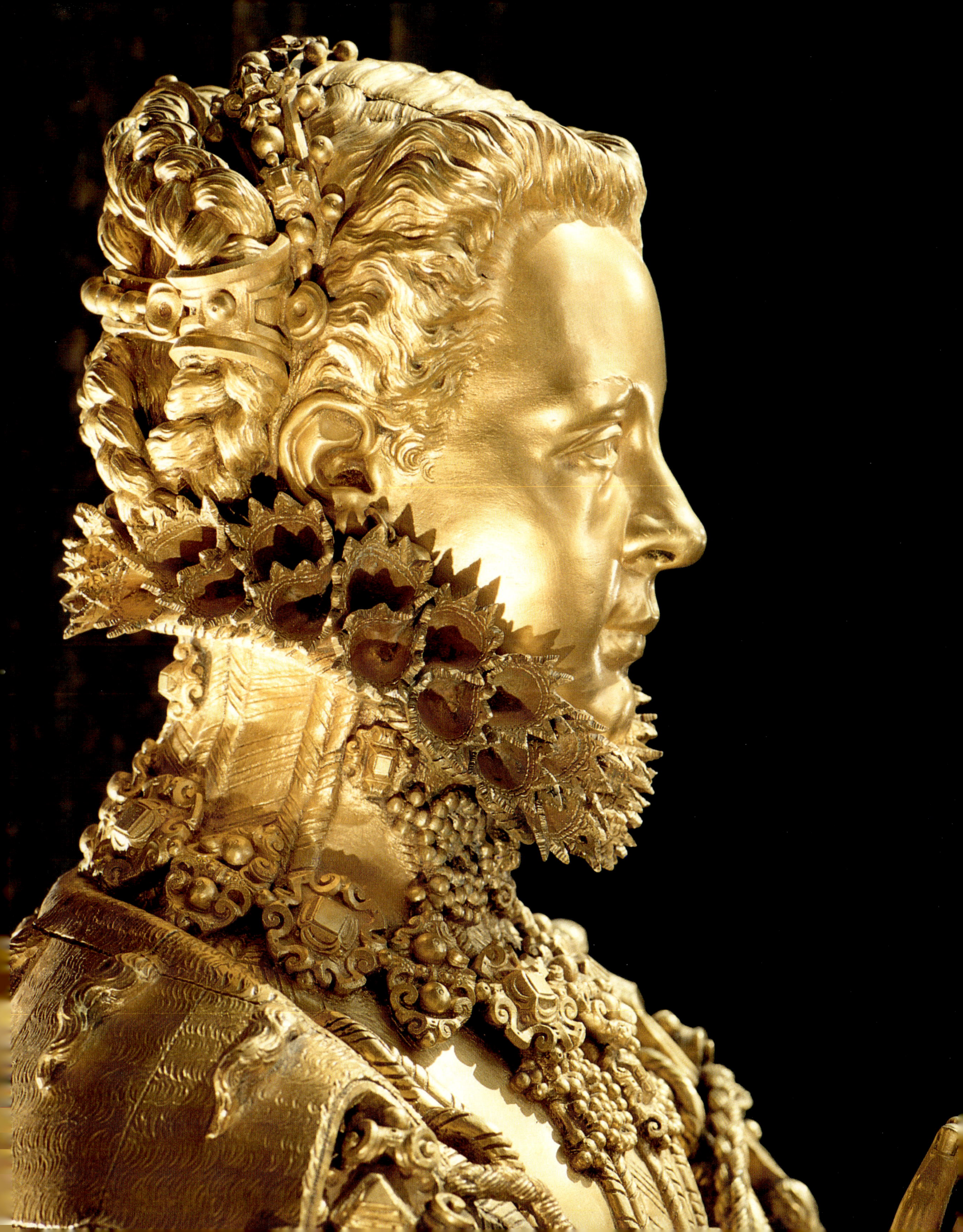

quickly translated into English as *The Golden Book of Marcus Aurelius:*

> Why do you think, Serene Prince, that I remind you of all these things, if not to ask you how it is possible that, having seen you boasting about death so openly, you are now so unwilling to leave this life? Well the gods so require it, your age desires it, your illness causes it, your weak nature permits it, sad Rome deserves it, your deceptive fortune consents to it . . . so why are you starting to sigh that way, just because of death?

After their bodies rested for a certain time in the so-called putrefaction hole, the members of the families of Charles and of Philip were deposited in a chapel set beneath the altar until they were finally entombed in the Royal Pantheon of the Escorial. Sculptures of them kneeling in perpetual prayer were placed in monumental architectural tribunes on either side of the high altar of the basilica within enormous stone niches capped by semicircular arches set above the doors of the royal oratories at the same height as the tabernacles (ills. 63, 64, 65). Above the figures two porphyry columns bear a grand Doric entablature surmounted by the heraldic coat of arms of the House of Austria.

The bronze rendering of the emperor was described by the Hieronymite friar José de Sigüenza in *The Foundation of the Monastery of the Escorial:* ". . . as pious as it was strong, armed with a girded sword, his head uncovered, his cloak adorned with the two-headed eagle [emblem of the Habsburg dynasty], carved in jasper, whose color is that of the royal bird." In front of the sculpture is a ceremonial seat covered with brocade, "all so natural . . . that the cloak could be taken off and could almost be folded up and placed in a box." Next to the figure of Charles V is the portrait of the Empress Isabella, as exquisite as all of the other bronze portraits by the great Italian sculptor Pompeo Leoni. Behind the Holy Roman Emperor, from left to right, are images of his sisters Maria and Leonora, and his daughter Maria, wife of Maximilian II of Austria.

Opposite the family of Charles V is the group of praying figures headed up by Philip II, "with armor and royal cloak or cape entirely covered by the royal coat of arms, in blues, reds, whites, and other colors that look like precious stones," writes friar José de Sigüenza, "expensively, richly, and skillfully worked, so that all of its pieces could be put on and taken off, being of bronze and stone, of extraordinary beauty." Next to the king are his first wife, Maria of Portugal, and his fourth wife, Ana. Behind the monarch is his third wife, Isabel de Valois. Completing this gathering of worshippers is the sculpture of the unfortunate prince Carlos, all arranged so that, as Sigüenza explains, "without disturbing each other they can all look upon the cross in the center of the altar, and from it their five faces can be clearly seen."

These bronze worshippers have parallels in the wise men and shepherds of the Gospels that appear in two paintings by Pellegrino Tibaldi on the main altarpiece. Like Leoni's bronze royals, Tibaldi's figures seem to pray to the Holy Sacrament placed in the monstrance in the tabernacle that Leoni also created. The Nativity, picturing the adoration of the Son of God, and the Epiphany, in which He is recognized by the three kings, are common themes in the decoration of funerary chapels and monumental tombs in sixteenth-century Spain. A fine example is found carved on the monumental wall tomb of the writer and theologian Alonso de Madrigal, known as El Tostado (ill. 68), located in the retrochoir of the Cathedral of Ávila. He is represented as a man of letters in the act of writing, but also as a bishop. He had died in 1455 without having left plans for his own tomb; it was created in 1511 by the sculptor Vasco de la Zarza, who carved a profusion of classical motifs in great detail.

In the marble image of El Tostado or in the bronzes of Charles V and Philip II and their families, death is commemorated through life, which is perceived as a journey between "lives": between the mortal and the immortal, between birth and resurrection. The men who lead a "good life" have no

PRECEDING PAGES, LEFT:
66. Pompeo Leoni
1590–1600
Philip II, from
The Family of Philip II,
gilt bronze.
The epistle side of the church at the Real Monasterio de San Lorenzo, El Escorial.

PRECEDING PAGES, RIGHT:
67. Pompeo Leoni
1590–1600
Ana of Austria, from
The Family of Philip II,
gilt bronze.
The epistle side of the church at the Real Monasterio de San Lorenzo, El Escorial.

RIGHT:
68. Vasco de la Zarza
c. 1511
Funeral monument of Bishop Alonso de Madrigal, called "El Tostado,"
marble.
Retrochoir at Ávila Cathedral.

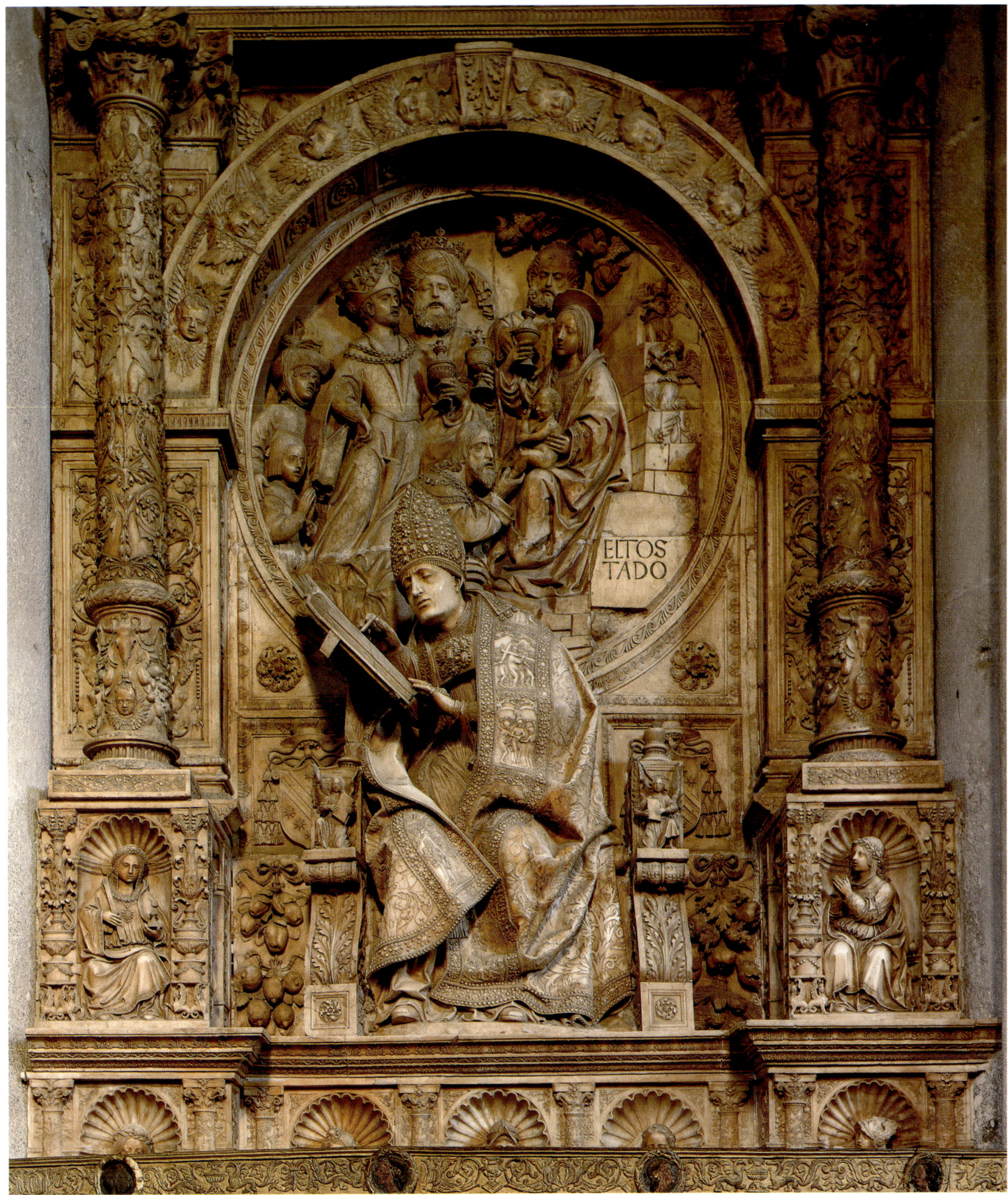
ELTOS
TADO

reason to fear death, and only have to "happily await" it, as Francisco de Ávila argues in the prologue of his *Beneficial Advice to Live in All Conditions without Disillusion* (1565). Yet this optimistic vision of the "good life" and of death dissipates after the Council of Trent pitches mankind into a dark world governed by fatalism, calamity, fear, and guilt. Even the treatises dedicated to the preparation for death that had been inspired by Erasmus were relegated to the Index of Prohibited Books.

DEATH IS A SKULL

The seventeenth century, more than any other period, recognized the inevitability of change, the ephemeral nature of life, and eventual decrepitude. The pious individual who regularly, even daily, practiced confession, penitence, communion, prayer, fasting, and even self-flagellation lived in an eternal war with himself and against humanity. A man battling his own humanity was reduced to the status of an animal (*homo hominis lupus*). Death was no longer a journey to another life but a force against life that kept men obsessed, terrorized, and confused. "You do not know death," says Death to the narrator, none other than the author Francisco de Quevedo in *The Dream of Death* (1622):

> . . . and you are your own death: it has the face of each and every one of you, and you are all dead to each other. The skull is death and the face is death, and what you call death is to finally die, and what you call birth is the beginning of death, and what you call life is a living death, what your death leaves behind are your bones, and what is left over is for the tomb.

In the homes there are as many dead people as there are living ones. Houses are full of the dead, beings that are skulls and bones even before they are born. In the seventeenth century, the century of the Baroque, death is a skull, a skeleton. Seventeenth-century tombs do not reveal, exalt, or render tribute to the virtues of the deceased, but instead show that life is but death itself, revealed in the quiet efficiency with which a cadaver is devoured by life forms. A cadaver (in this case the inert body of his deceased wife) led the licentious, womanizing, and brawling Miguel de Mañara Vicentelo de Leca to burn with a desire to join the pious Seville confraternity of La Caridad, or Charity, dedicated to the Christian burial of the dead.

The famously arrogant and disorderly Mañara, a knight of the order of Calatrava, had for years been the "mad and blind servant of the Great Babylon, mother of fornication and of the abomination of the earth, drunken on the blood of the martyrs of Jesus Christ," and had imbibed from "the dirty chalice of delight, golden on the outside and poisonous within." All this led the brothers of the congregation to initially deny him membership. However, his new but sincere disavowal of worldly things eventually convinced them to accept him. Miguel de Mañara abandoned the comforts of his palace and went to live in an austere cell in the Hospital de la Caridad. According to his biographer, the Jesuit Juan de Cárdenas, the brotherhood "set him the task of asking for charity for burials, accompanying the bodies of the dead as he begged for donations in the streets of the city." At first he loathed this task, but he soon accepted that there was only one truth in life, "that of the death shroud we must wear," a shroud that must be seen every single day in order to forget the honors and estates of the present, and that must reign in our hearts as "dust and ash, corruption and worms, the tomb and oblivion."

In the church of the Hospital de la Caridad, which was completed soon after Miguel de Mañara entered the confraternity, worship was reserved exclusively for the brothers—aristocrats who had enough time and money to dedicate their lives to caring for the poor and the sick and burying the dead. When Mañara was elected senior brother of the congregation in 1663, a post he held until his death, he dedicated his efforts to maintaining a hospital to care for the poor and the sick. He reminded them, as he constantly reminded himself, that death does not distinguish between great and small, rich and poor, wise and foolish—in short, that all humans are bones and skulls when faced with death, and that there is only one path to salvation.

69. Bernardo Simón Pineda (ensemble), Pedro Roldán (sculptures) and Juan de Valdes Leal (polychrome)
1670–73
Main Altarpiece with *The Internment of Christ*, carved, quilted, and polychromed wood.
Church of the Hospital de la Caridad, Seville.

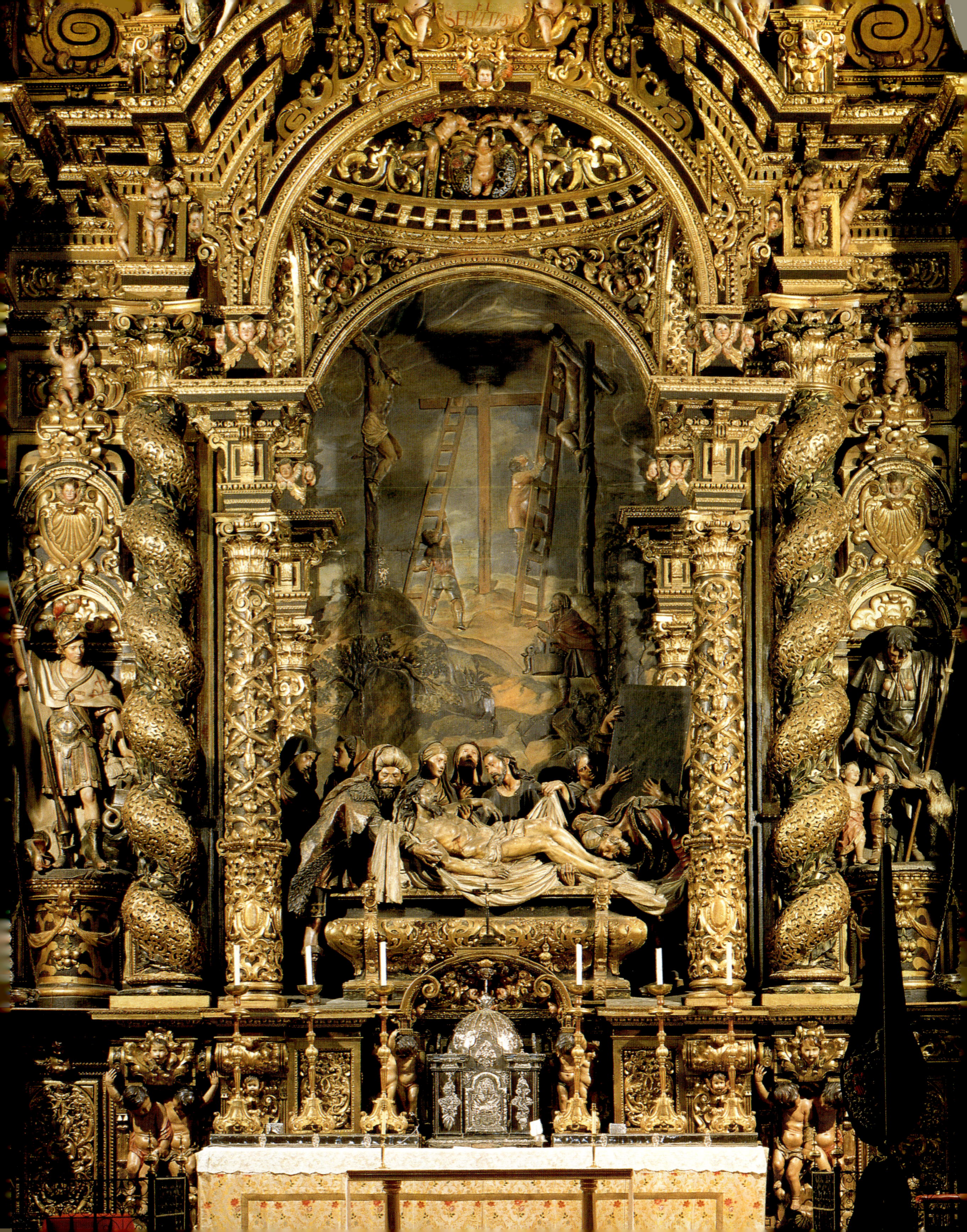

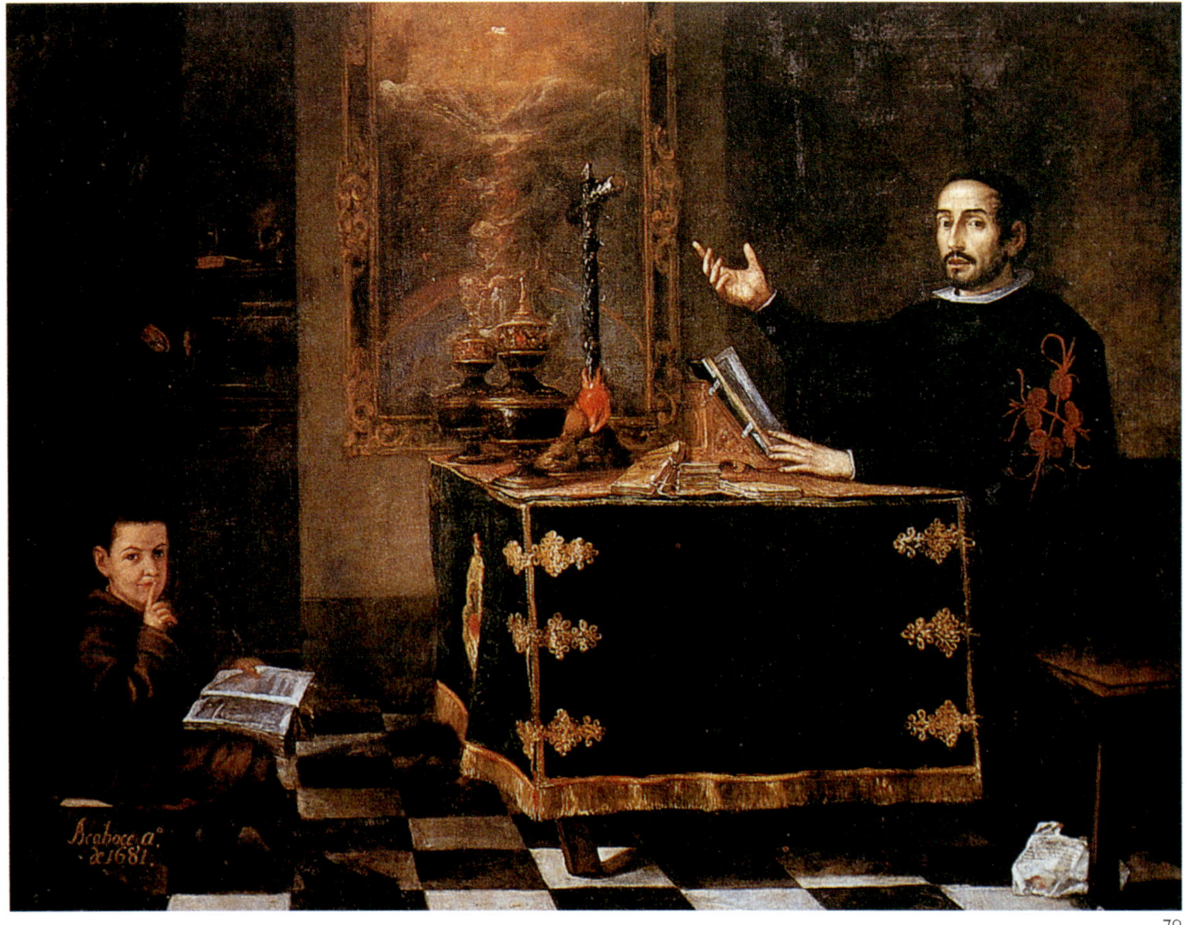

70

He ordered an inscription to be placed in the public area of the hospital: "This house will endure / while God is feared / and while the poor of Jesus Christ are served / and entering into it / greed and vanity / will be lost." Through the talents of artists Juan de Valdés Leal (ills. 70, 72, 73), Bartolomé Esteban Murillo (ill. 71), and Pedro Roldán (ill. 69), Mañara sought to express in the decoration of the church of the hospital the emptiness of fame and of human vanity, of earthly goods and worldly power. On canvases of various formats and sizes, Murillo represented the seven acts of mercy through which men could save their souls. Some of these masterpieces can still be seen in the church for which they were painted. Others, following French Marshal Soult's sack of the artistic treasures of Seville in 1810, are now held in various museums. On the main altarpiece, the tormented, anxious Baroque architecture by Bernardo Simón de Pineda frames sculptor Pedro Roldán's expressive sculpture representing the burial of Christ. The lateral walls of the lower choir are hung with Juan de Valdés Leal's paintings called *Hieroglyphs of the Four Last Things* (ills. 72–74).

DEATH OF WORLDLY THINGS

Miguel de Mañara's *Discourse on Truth* (1672) undoubtedly inspired the most macabre vision of death and human vanity: "What does it matter that you are great in the world if death will make you the same as the small?" The *Discourse* continues:

> Go to an ossuary full of the bones of the dead, and try to distinguish between the rich and the poor, the wise and the foolish, the great and the small. They are all bones, all skulls, and all of them look alike. The lady who was surrounded by drapery and brocades in her drawing room, whose head was adorned with diamonds, now accompanies the heads of beggars; the heads that wore plumed headdresses at court festivals now rest alongside the skulls of those who wore cowls in the countryside. Oh, justice of God, how you equalize, in death, the inequalities of life!

Mañara conceived the world as a holy mountain that required those who sought to reach the summit to leave behind everything that might impede their

ABOVE:
70. Juan de Valdés Leal
1681
Miguel de Mañara Reading the Rule of the Confraternity of Charity.
Hospital de la Caridad, Seville.

RIGHT:
71. Bartolomé Esteban Murillo
1670–74
Saint Elizabeth of Hungary Washing Scabs from a Boy's Head.
Church of the Hospital de la Caridad, Seville.

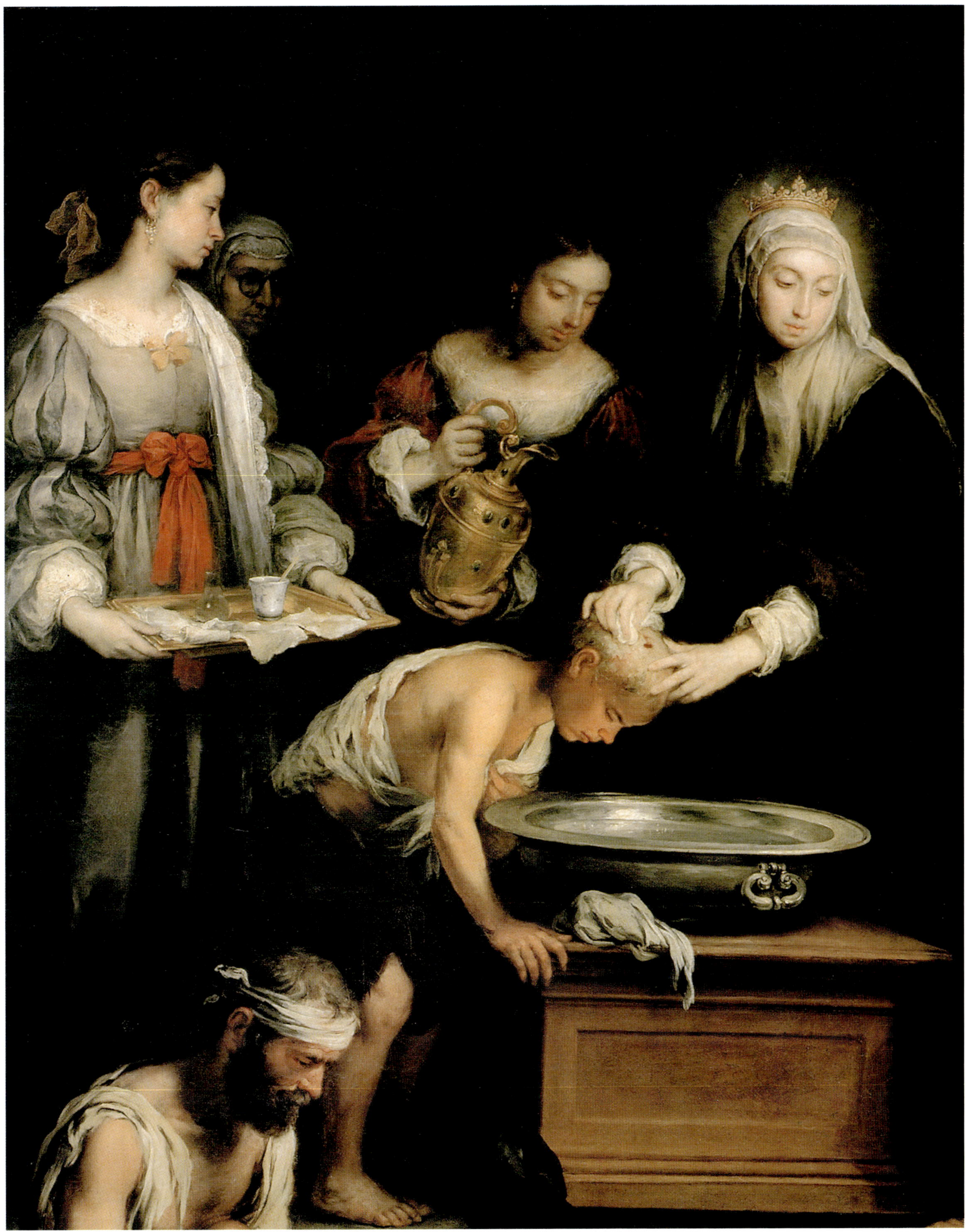

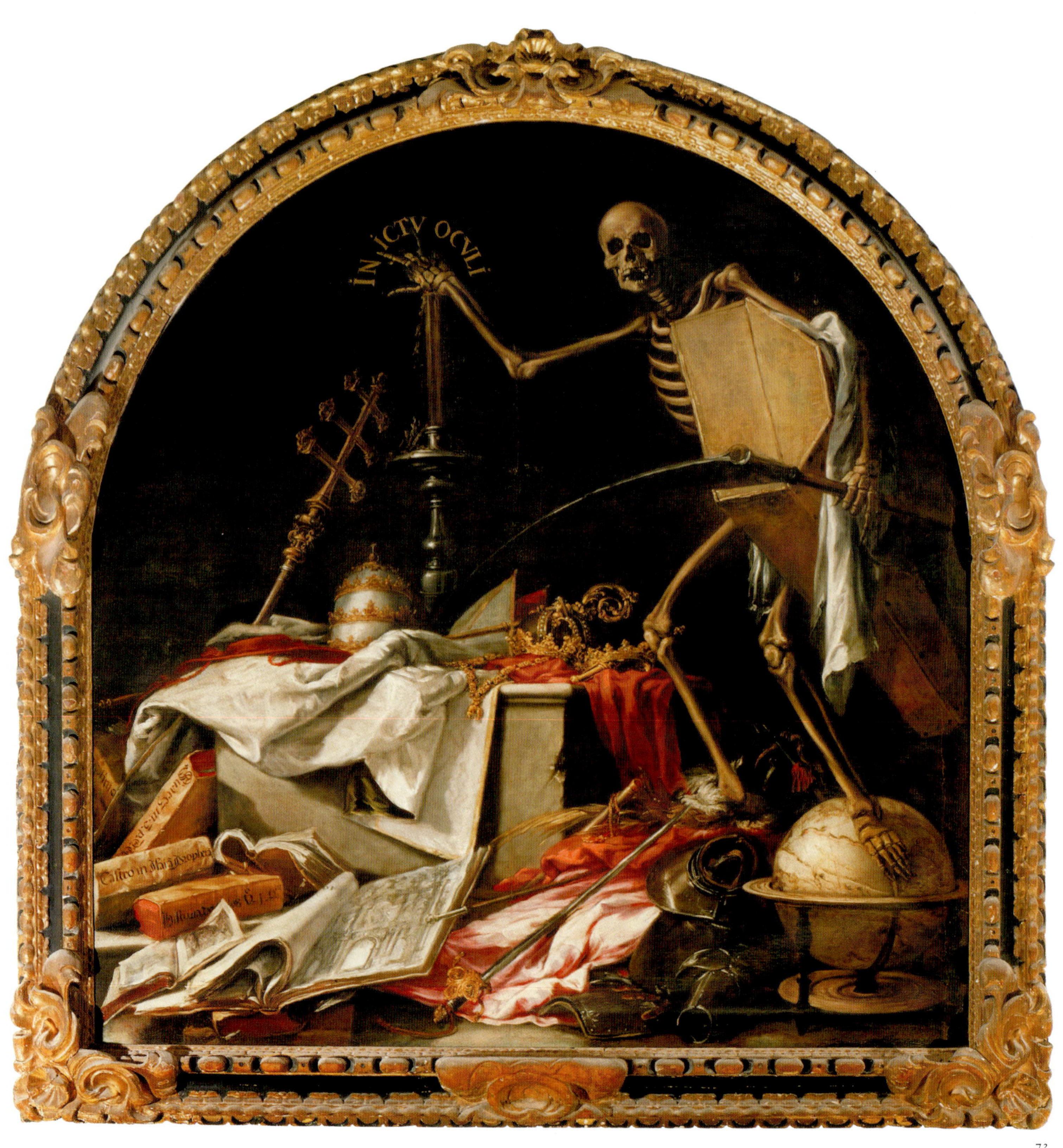

72

72. Juan de Valdés Leal
1671–72
In Ictu Oculi, Hieroglyphs of the Four Last Things.
Church of the Hospital de la Caridad, Seville.

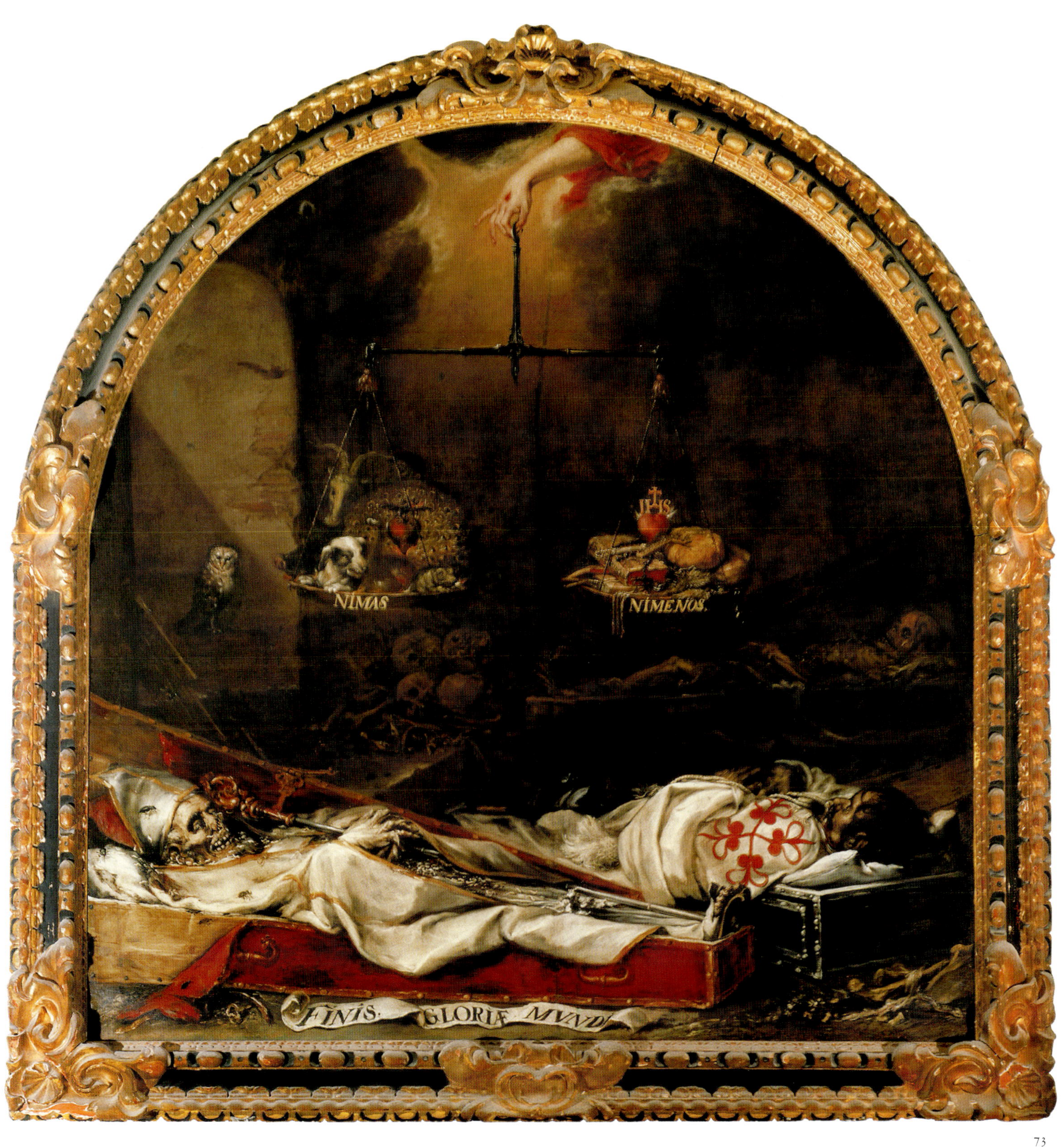

73

73. Juan de Valdés Leal
1671–72
Finis Gloriae Mundi, Hieroglyphs of the Four Last Things.
Church of the Hospital de la Caridad, Seville.

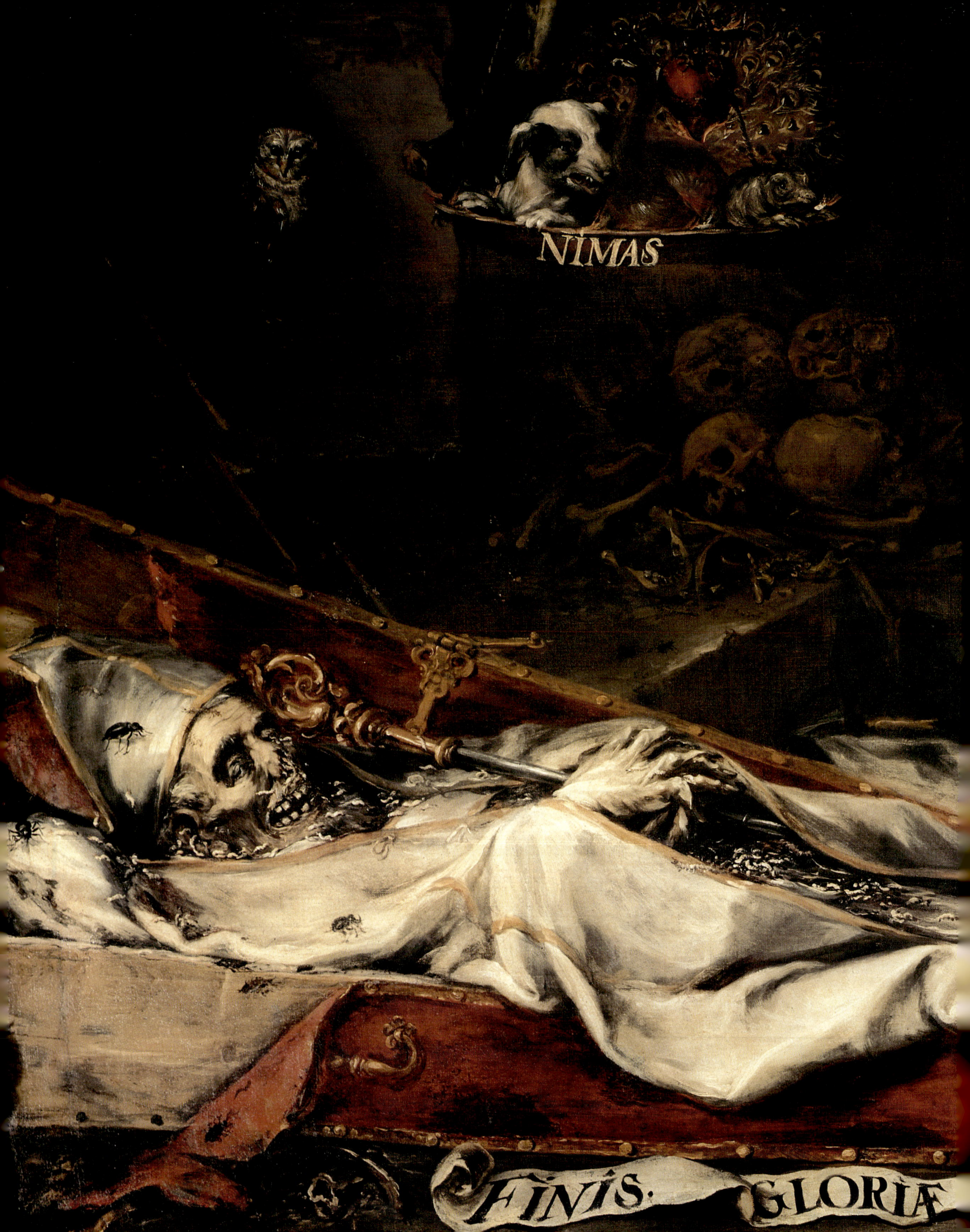
NIMAS
FINIS. GLORIÆ

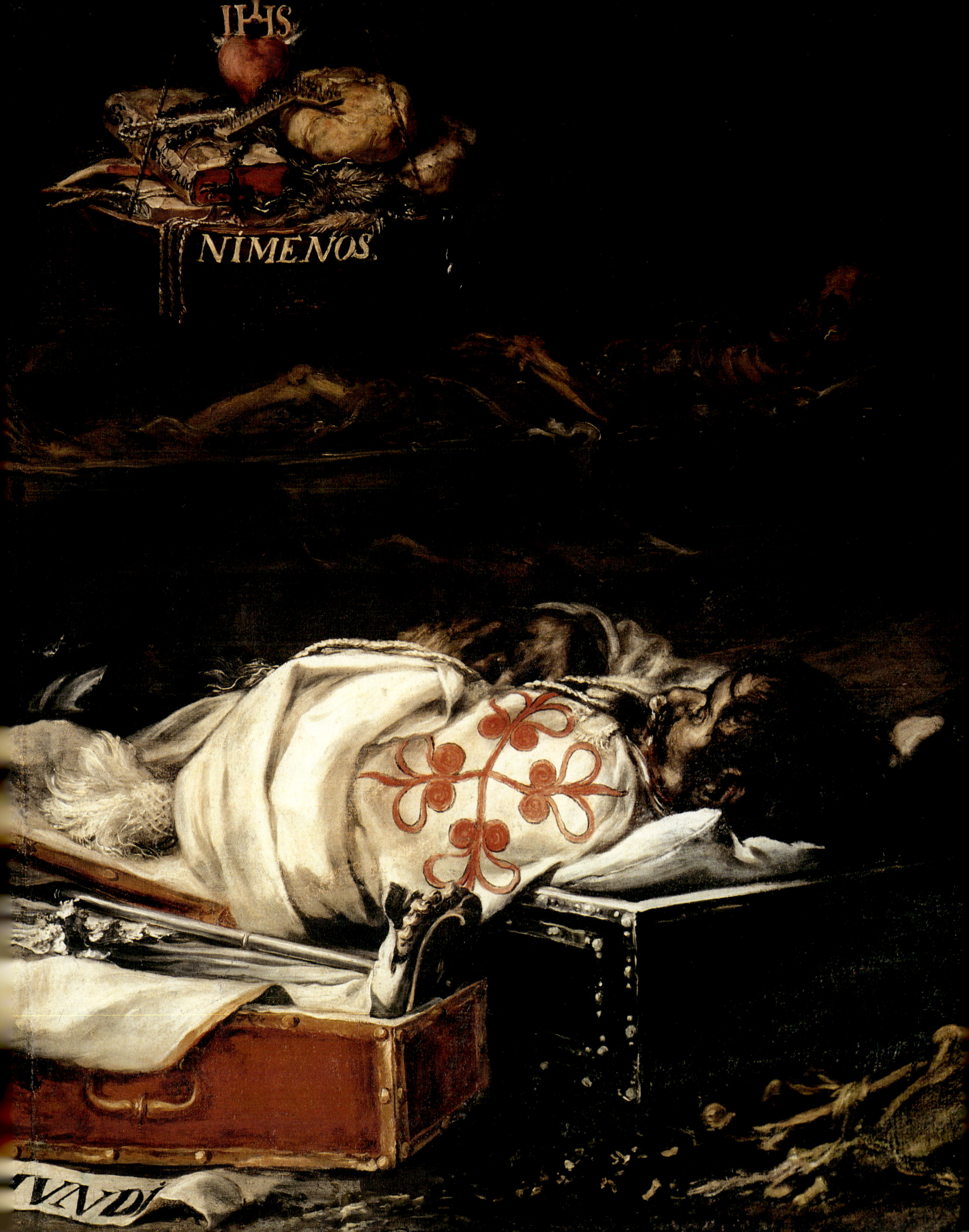
IHS
NIMENOS.
VNDI

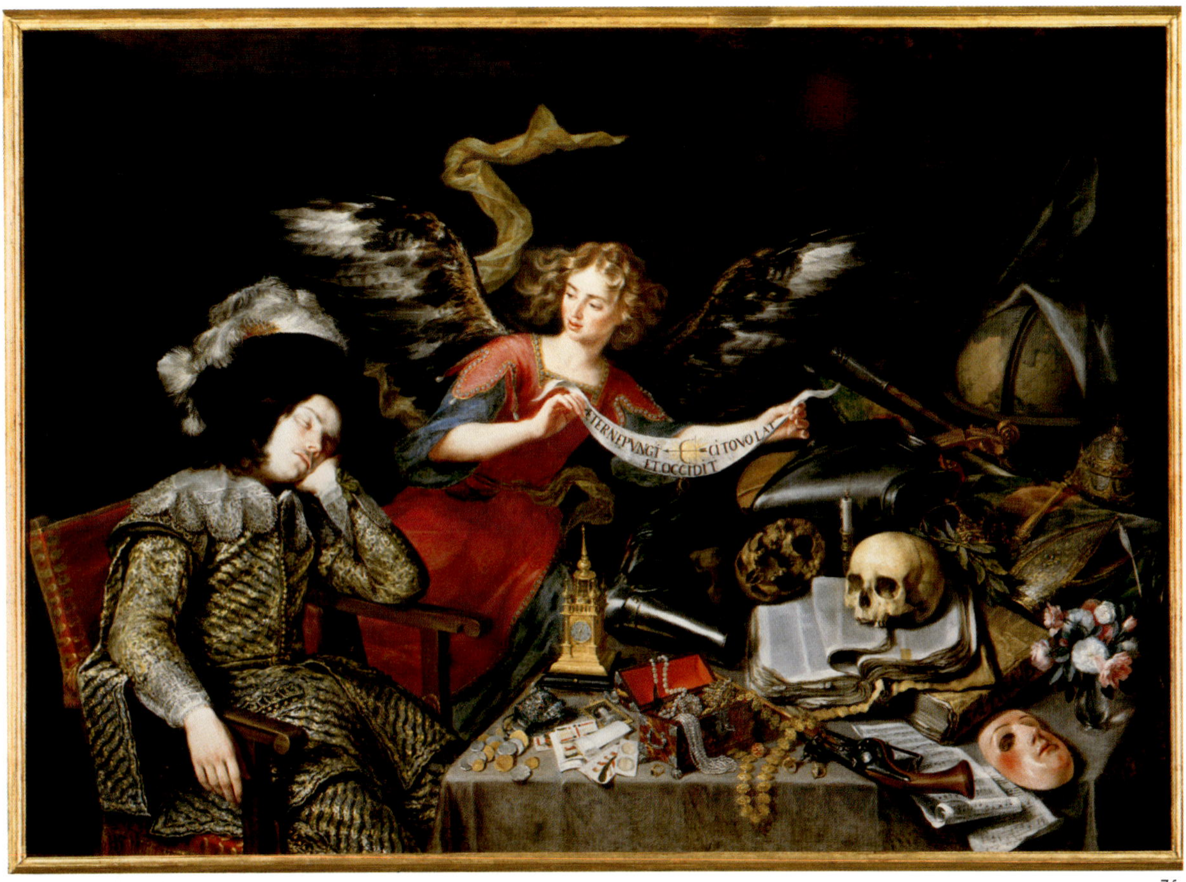

75

ascent. The king had to leave his crown; the powerful, his riches; the learned man, his books; and the soldier, his weapons. Thus, he wrote: "... as they go up along the path, the fatigue and strain that one's position or dignity might endure at first is quickly left behind; soon even their cloaks weigh them down, and then even their shirts are too heavy...."

To reach the summit of this holy mountain—as expressed by Valdés Leal in the first of the *Hieroglyphs*—we have to leave behind their majesties, grandees, coddlers, pages, and lackeys, their meals and drinks and the aromas of their gluttony. We must walk alone and barefoot. Otherwise, it will be only bones, the night of death that always arrives unexpectedly with the coffin and shroud under its arm, brandishing a scythe, the night that will put out the solitary flame of our life in the blink of an eye: IN ICTV OCVLI. Death tramples and destroys all worldly things: the mountains that stain the face of the earth with their vanities; the purple ecclesiastical and civil robes; the cross of the patriarchs; the miters, tiaras, staffs, scepters, and hats of cardinals; members of the religious orders; the most highly regarded of men, along with their scepters, crowns, weapons, swords, luxurious fabrics, and books of knowledge. All will end up in the ephemeral Babylon of worldly glory.

FINIS GLORIAE MUNDI reads the banderole casually lying on the floor of the second of Valdés Leal's *Hieroglyphs* (ill. 73). We have been defeated by death; our bodies, whether of bishops or knights of Calatrava, lie in eternal darkness, in the horrifying realm of owls and bats, the food of worms and cockroaches, dust and ashes, the tomb and oblivion: "If you remember that you are to be covered with earth and trampled by everyone, you will easily forget the honors and estates of this century," Mañara remarks in the *Discourse on Truth*.

> And if you think of the vile worms that will eat away at this body, and how ugly and abominable it must be in the tomb, and how these eyes, the

PRECEDING PAGES:
74. Juan de Valdés Leal
1671–72
Detail of
Finis Gloriae Mundi.
Church of the Hospital de la Caridad, Seville.

ABOVE AND RIGHT:
75 and 76. Antonio de Pereda
c. 1660
The Knight's Dream, or *Disillusion of Life*, and detail.
Real Academia de Bellas Artes de San Fernando, Madrid.

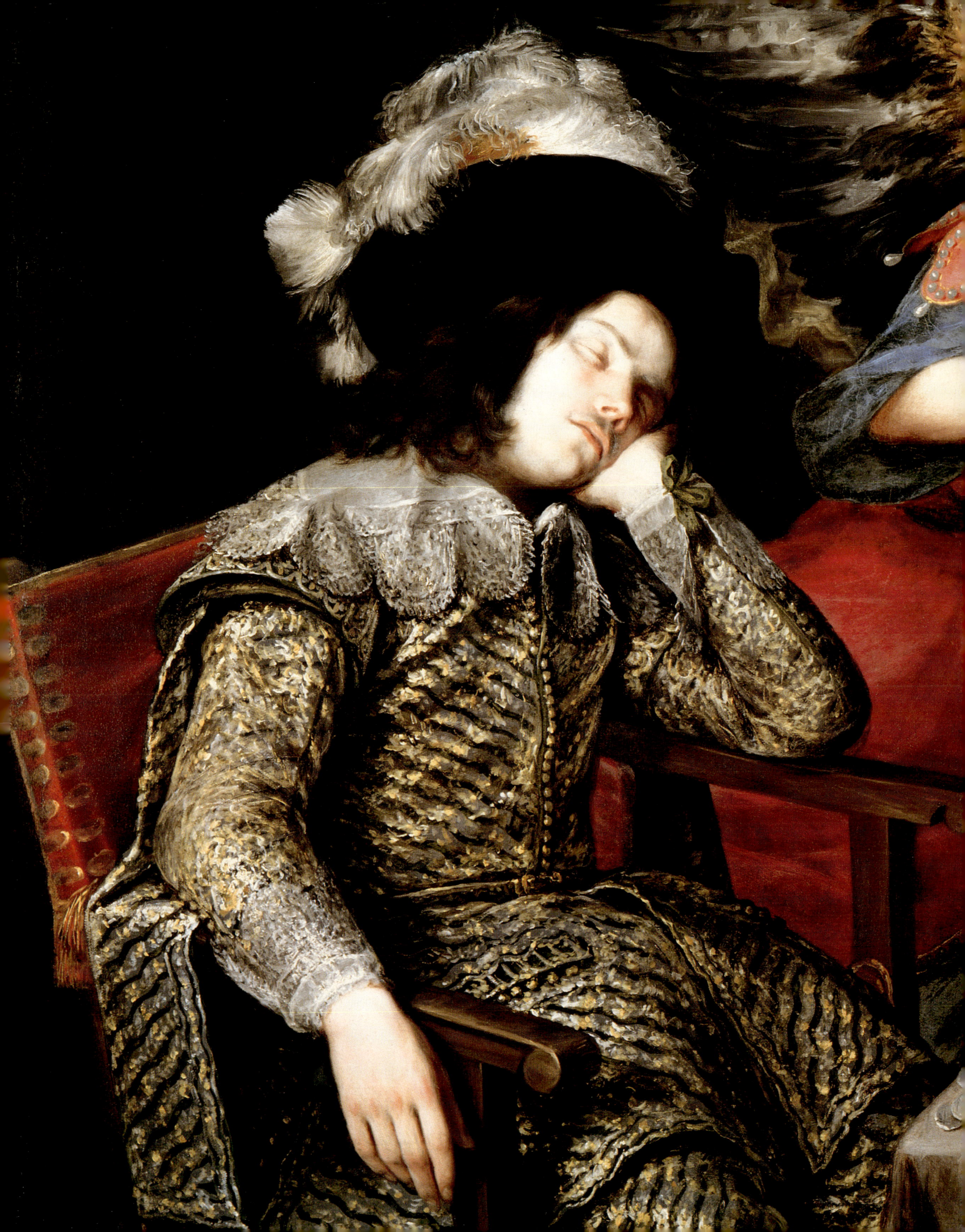

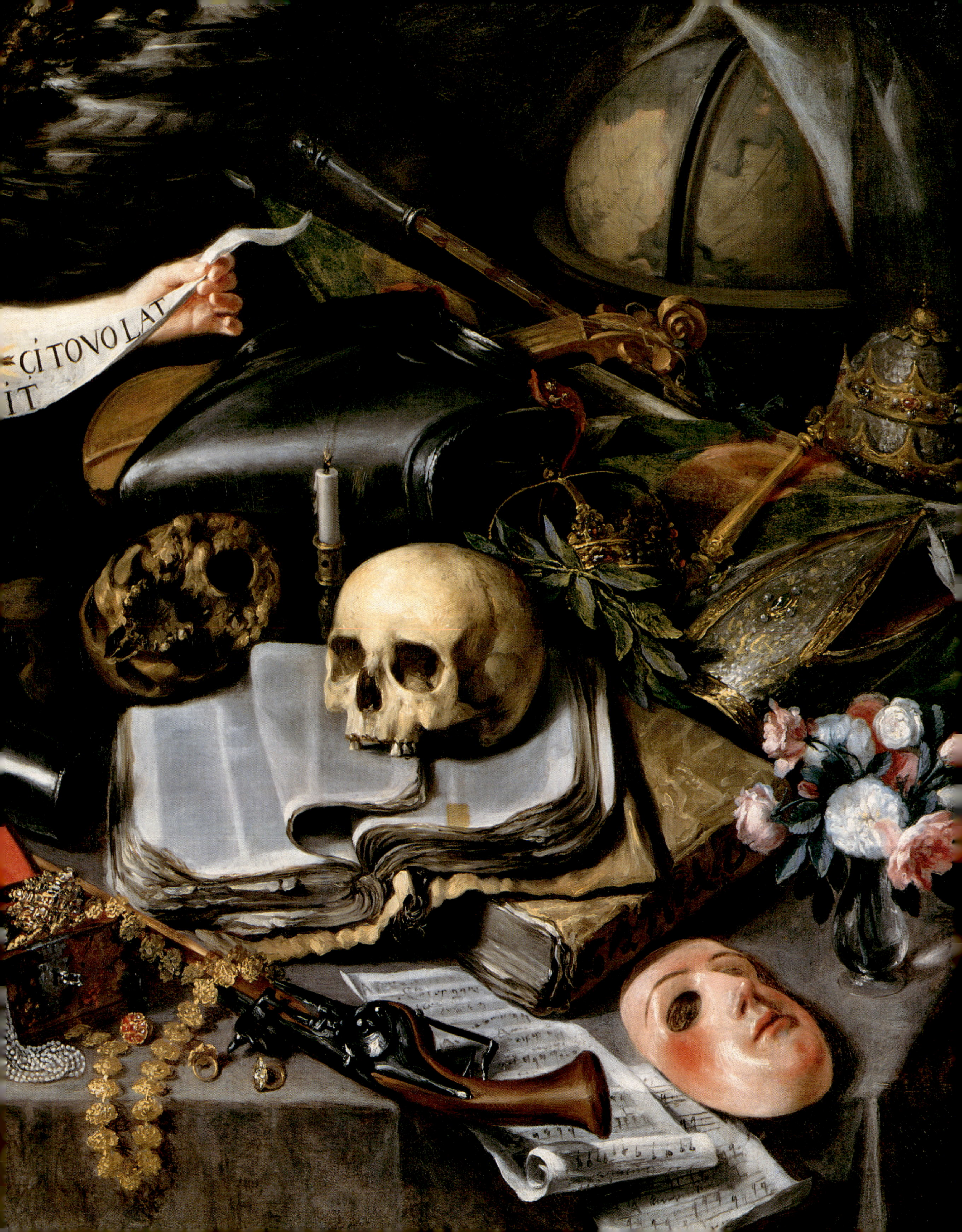
CITO VOLAT
IT

ones reading these words, will be eaten in the earth, and how these hands will be eaten and will dry up, and the silks and raiment that you wore today will become a rotting death shroud, the scent of ambergris become stench, beauty and kindness become worms, family and greatness yield to the deepest loneliness you can imagine . . . What silence! No sound is heard but the chewing of woodworms and insects. What happened to the noise of pages and lackeys? . . . Consider, my brother, that this will surely happen to you, and all your composure will collapse into brittle, horrible, frightening bones, so much so that the person you are sure loves you the most, whether your wife or a son, will be shocked to see you.

In Valdés Leal's painting the wounded hand of the resurrected Christ, in His great mercy and paternal piety, holds the balance—the NO MORE (NI MAS) of the sins and the NO LESS (NI MENOS) of the virtues—and guides the soul toward its resting place." Pray now, my brother," concludes the *Discourse on Truth,* "that with mature judgment you might find yourself between these two very different mountains. Gaze upon the one crowned by God your Father, and the other by your enemy the devil. One is full of the blessings of His paternal hand, the other full of the damnations of his fury; one is a mountain of truth, whose end is an eternal realm, eternal life, eternal rest, and the other is a mountain of vanity, whose end is eternal hell, eternal horror, eternal torment, and eternal blasphemy. . . . You have free will, so choose to crown God with your good works so that they earn your freedom."

In the residue of death ("dust and ash, corruption and worms, the tomb and oblivion") Valdés Leal "portrayed" Miguel de Mañara more truthfully than when he painted his posthumous portrait in 1681 (ill. 70). Mañara is shown conventionally seated, reading the book of rules of the Santa Caridad, accompanied by a child wearing the habit of a nurse of the brotherhood. This artificial composition does not show us the Miguel de Mañara who asked to be buried at the door of the church so that everyone who entered would tread upon his bones. His grave was to be commemorated with a stone inscribed: "Here lie the bones and ashes of the worst man ever to walk the earth. Pray to God for him."

77. Antonio de Pereda
c. 1660
Detail of T*he Knight's Dream*, or *Disillusion of Life.*
Real Academia de Bellas Artes de San Fernando, Madrid.

The dreams of men, the dreams of life, the dreams of the nobleman painted by Antonio de Pereda in *The Knight's Dream,* or *Disillusion of Life* (ills. 75–77), all slip away, as do the flowers, fruit, jewels, books, plumes, weapons, coins, playing cards, precious stones, crowns, tiaras, miters, and the love recalled by the portrait of a woman, and with them all earthly pleasures, powers, and triumphs (symbolized by the laurel). Everything human, all these worldly things are displayed on this table of vanities, all as fleeting as a dream. As in the title of the famous drama by Pedro Calderón de la Barca (1600–81), "Life is a dream." Like the arrow on the banner borne by the handsome admonishing angel, who both watches over the knight and uselessly troubles his sleep, the relentless passing of time "eternally threatens, flies quickly, and kills" (AETERNA PVNGIT, CITO VOLAT ET OCCIDIT). Time ruins everything, turning everything into a skull that, like the one in the painting, symbolizes the triumph of death even over knowledge.

The rosy mask of a life of merriment and vice is useless to the elegant and vain young knight, as is the mask of dreams and of the night that fades with the dawn. Rich fabrics and weak flesh will succumb equally: "Sit yourself down, then, on that throne of cadavers," writes the Jesuit scholar Baltasar Gracián (1601-58) in *The Critic,* "on a chair of peeling ribs, with arms of dry, fleshless shinbones, the ceremonial chair of skeletons, and on cushions and skulls beneath a sagging canopy of three or four death shrouds dripping with tears, the air filled with sighs, as if triumphing over your sovereignties, beauties, bravery, wealth, prudence, and everything that is valued and loved."

Man does not live. It is only time that lives, a time that blossoms in spring, bears fruit in summer, is saddened in autumn, and sleeps in winter only to be born again in the spring: "You are the time that remains," writes Góngora, "and I am the one who goes."

THE FASCINATION OF THE GAZE

I

THE ESCORIAL

II

THE ESCORIAL LIBRARY

III

FROM MANNERISM TO BAROQUE

IV

THE ART OF WAR

V

FLESH SUBLIMATED BY PRAYER

VI

SAINTS AND SINNERS

VII

BEGGARS, JESTERS, AND PRODIGIES

VIII

WOMEN

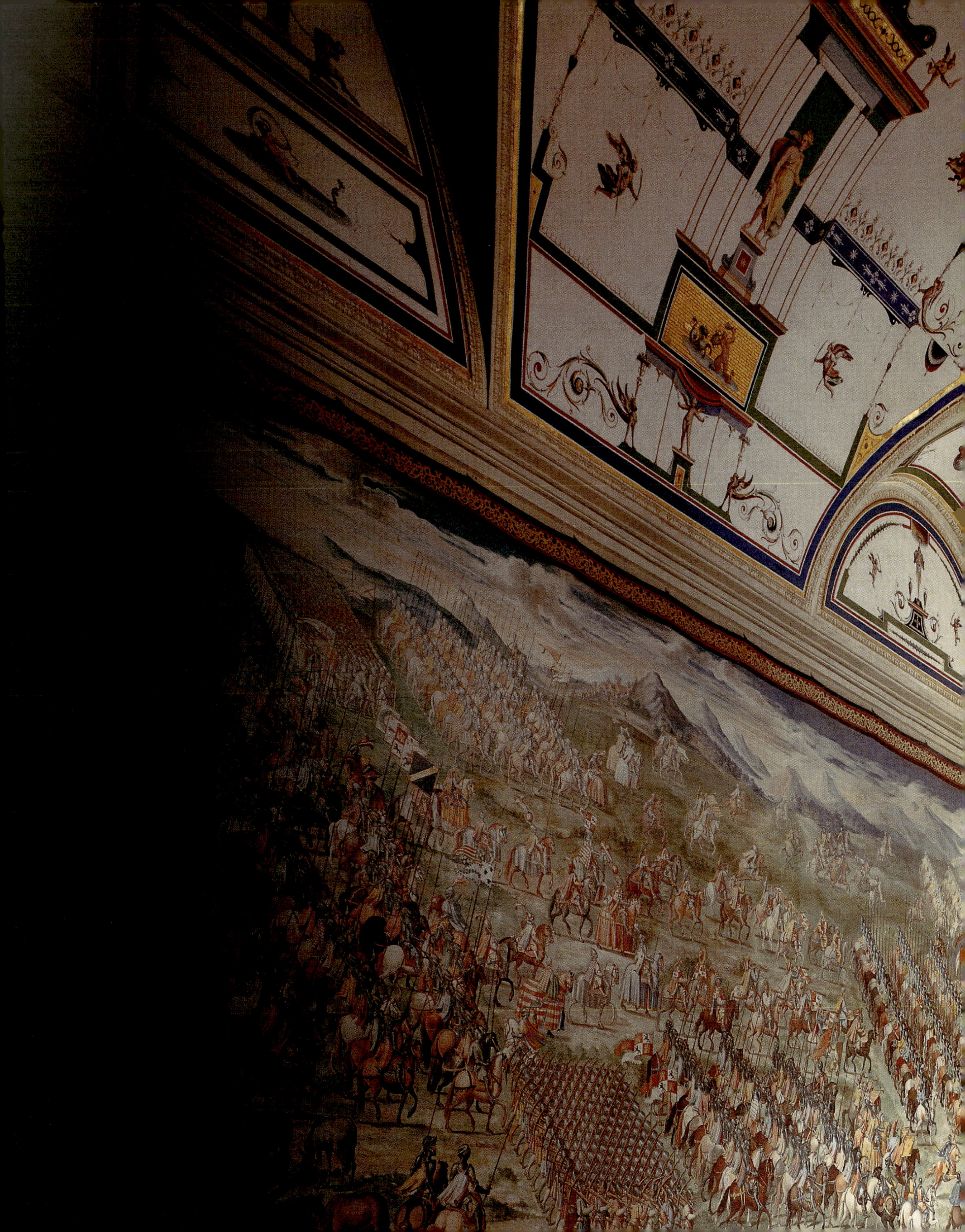

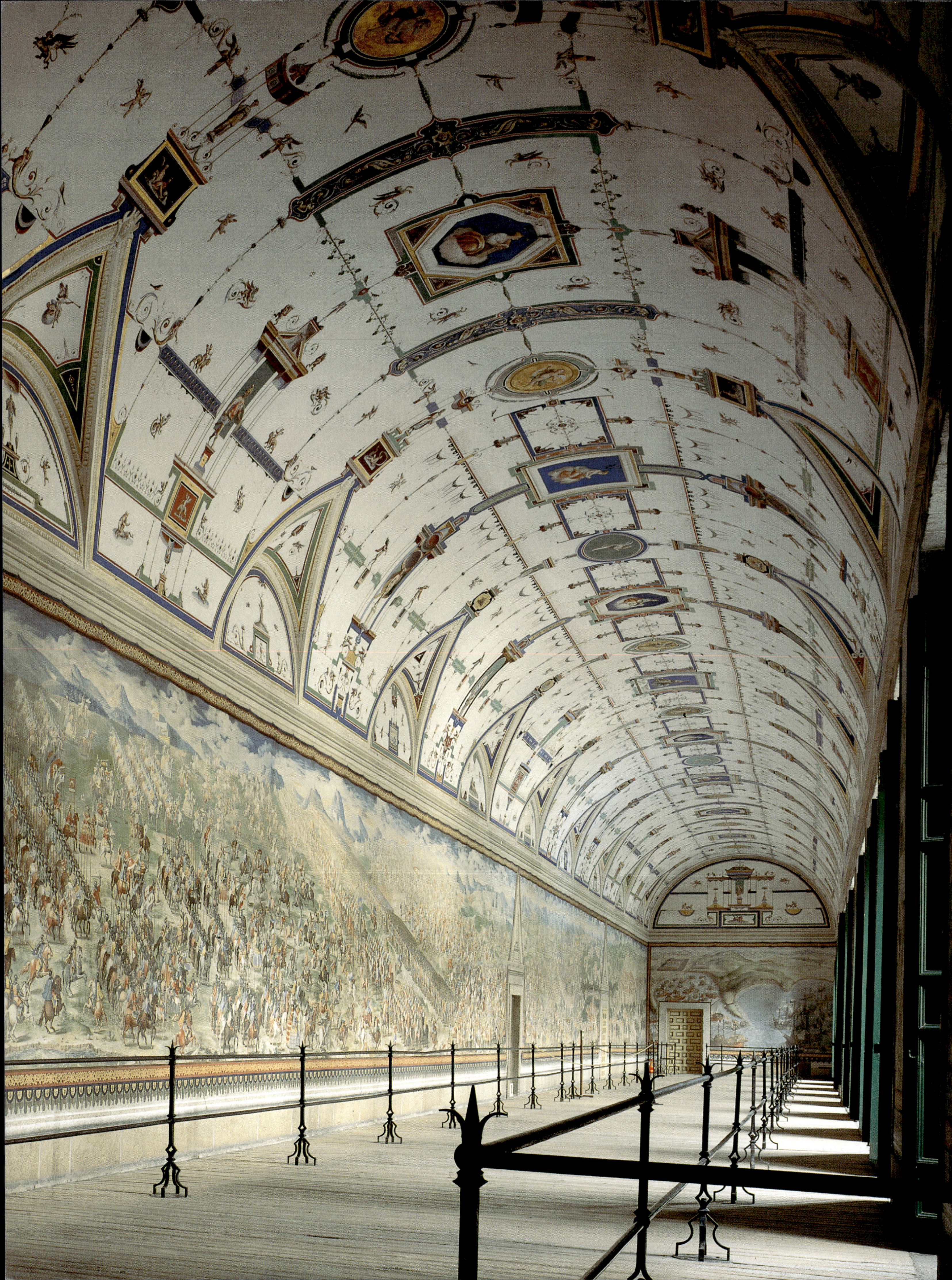

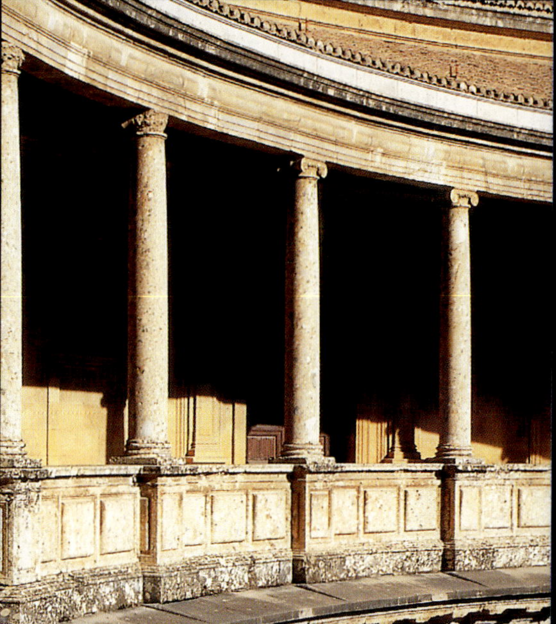

I

THE ESCORIAL

IN 1492 THE VANQUISHED Nasrids handed over Granada, the last bastion of Moorish rule on the Iberian peninsula, to the "Catholic Monarchs," Isabella of Castile and Ferdinand of Aragon. They sought to turn that Andalusian city into the symbol of the new Christian nation, a "kingdom of kingdoms," by undertaking the preservation and "Christianization" of the Alhambra, the Moorish palace that Spaniards and foreigners alike regarded as unique in the world. They invested considerable sums of money in the project, but in 1526, when their grandson Charles V lived temporarily in Granada on the occasion of his wedding to Isabella of Portugal, the city still seemed "Moorish" to him. He thus decided to build the finest and most modern of sixteenth-century palaces adjacent to the Moorish one. It was designed to serve not only as a permanent symbol of his personal glory, but also as the symbol of an empire and a dynasty.

With this aim in mind, Charles V commissioned the great artist Giulio Romano (friend and protégé of Baldassare Castiglione and the dukes of Mantua), Pedro Machuca, and Luis de Vega to design and build it. However, the palace, an austere, perfect balance of the circle and the square, the ideal geometrical forms of the Renaissance, was neither completed nor inhabited (ills 80–83).

Charles V died in 1558 at the secluded monastery of Yuste, in Cáceres, in despair over the political and religious fragmentation that was tearing apart the Holy Roman Empire of Europe. When his son Philip II took charge of the Spanish and American territories of the monarchy, he decided to build a monastery to commemorate his triumph over the French at the Battle of Saint Quentin, on the feast day of Saint Lawrence, and to establish a permanent seat for his court. For his court he chose Madrid; for the monastery, a plain near the small village of El Escorial. Owing to its grandeur, the monastery—which houses the mortal remains of Philip II, his ancestors, and descendants—has sometimes been compared to the Temple of Solomon (ills 78, 79, 84–87). Its architecture, however, in which geometry entirely dominates form, has less to do with Biblical associations than with the architectural traditions established by Bramante and Michelangelo, as expressed by the architect Juan de Herrera in his *Discourse on the Cube.* The cube and the square certainly dominate both the plan and elevation of the monastery, whose foundation stone was laid at the close the Council of Trent, when Europe witnessed the beginning of a new era of politics and religion.

PRECEDING PAGES:
78 and 79. Nicolás Granello, Fabrizio Castello, and Lázaro Tavarone
1587
Details of the frescoes in the Hall of Battles.
Real Monasterio de San Lorenzo, El Escorial.

80. Giulio Pippi, called Giulio Romano(?), Pedro Machuca, and Luis de Vega
After 1527
Detail of the colonnaded gallery in the courtyard of the Palace of Charles V, Granada.

RIGHT:
81. Juan de Orea
1550
The Battle of Mülhberg.
Center-left column base, west portal,
Palace of Charles V, Granada.

FOLLOWING PAGES:
82. Giulio Pippi, called Giulio Romano(?), Pedro Machuca, and Luis de Vega
After 1527
South façade of the Palace of Charles V, Granada.

83. Giulio Pippi, called Giulio Romano(?), Pedro Machuca, and Luis de Vega
After 1527
Colonnaded gallery in the courtyard of the Palace of Charles V, Granada.

84. Aerial view of the Real Monasterio de San Lorenzo de El Escorial, built by Juan Bautista de Toledo and Juan de Herrera, 1563–84.

85. Juan de Herrera
1574–84
Façade of the royal chapel with sculptures executed by Juan Bautista Monegro, 1583–93.
Basilica of the Real Monasterio de San Lorenzo, El Escorial.

86. Nicolás Granello, Fabrizio Castello, and Lázaro Tavarone
1587
Detail of a fresco in the Hall of Battles.
Real Monasterio de San Lorenzo, El Escorial.

87. Leone Leoni and Pompeo Leoni
c. 1579–99
Detail of *Saint Ambrose*, gilt bronze.
High altar, Basilica of the Real Monasterio de San Lorenzo, El Escorial.

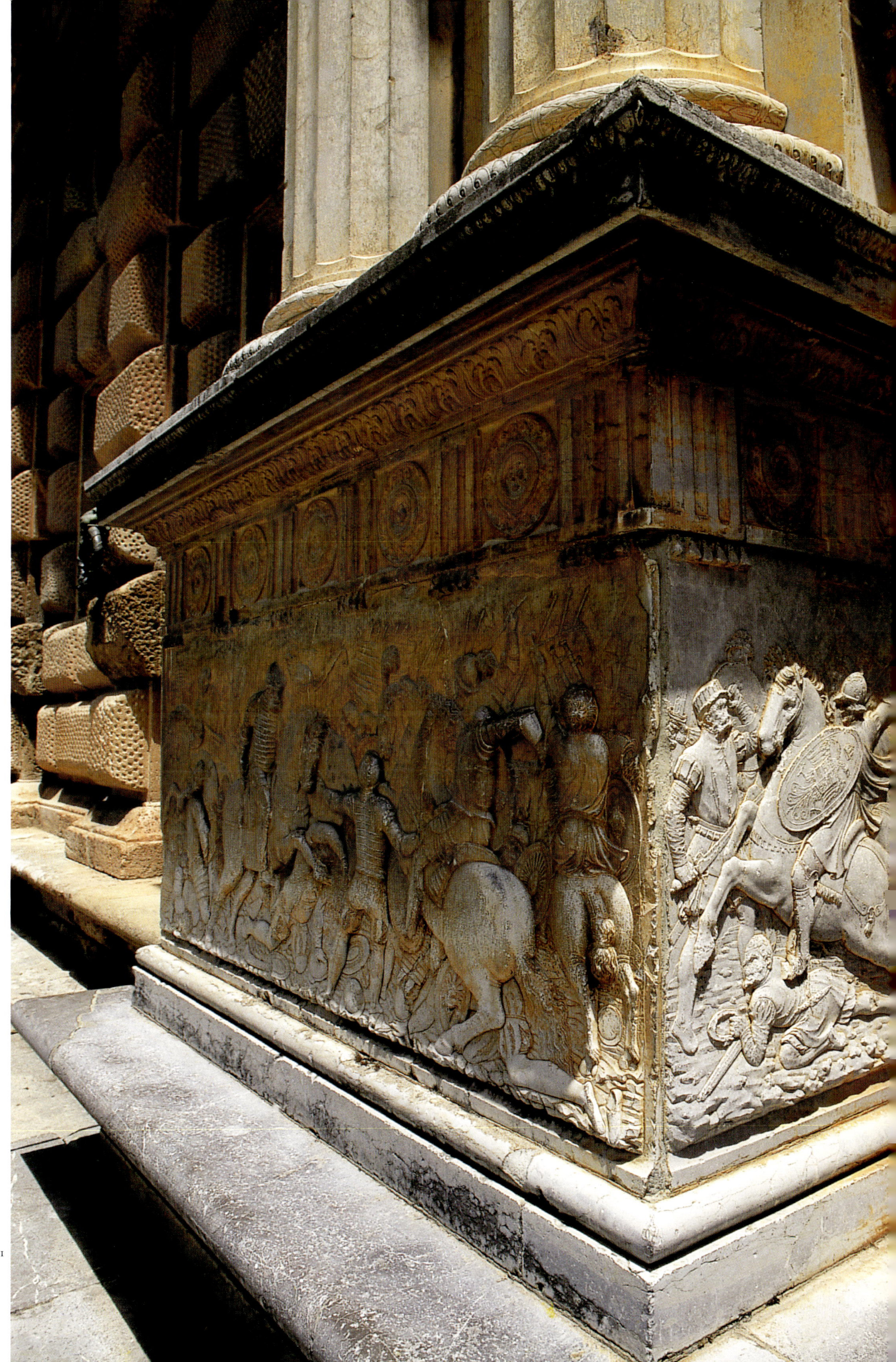

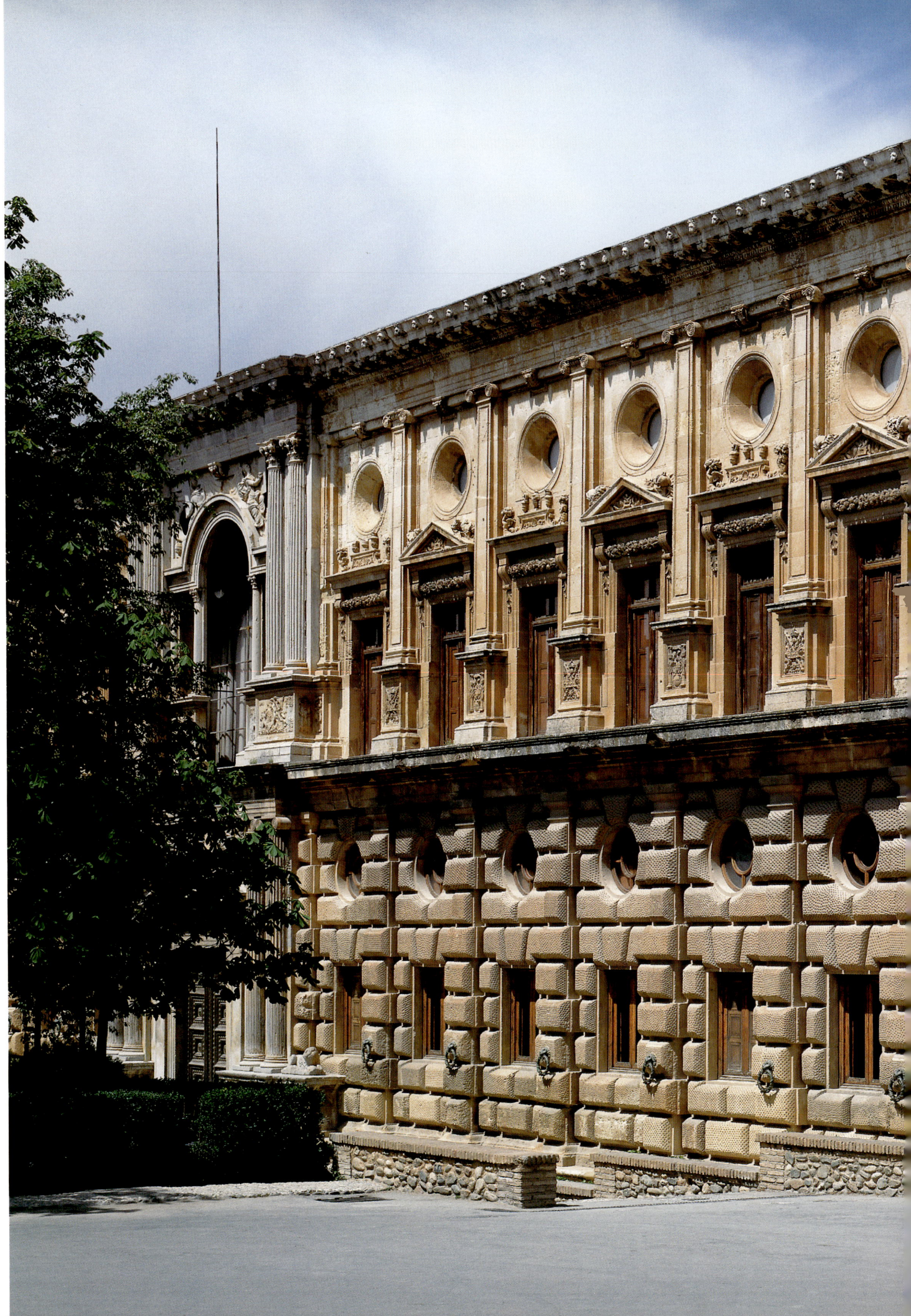

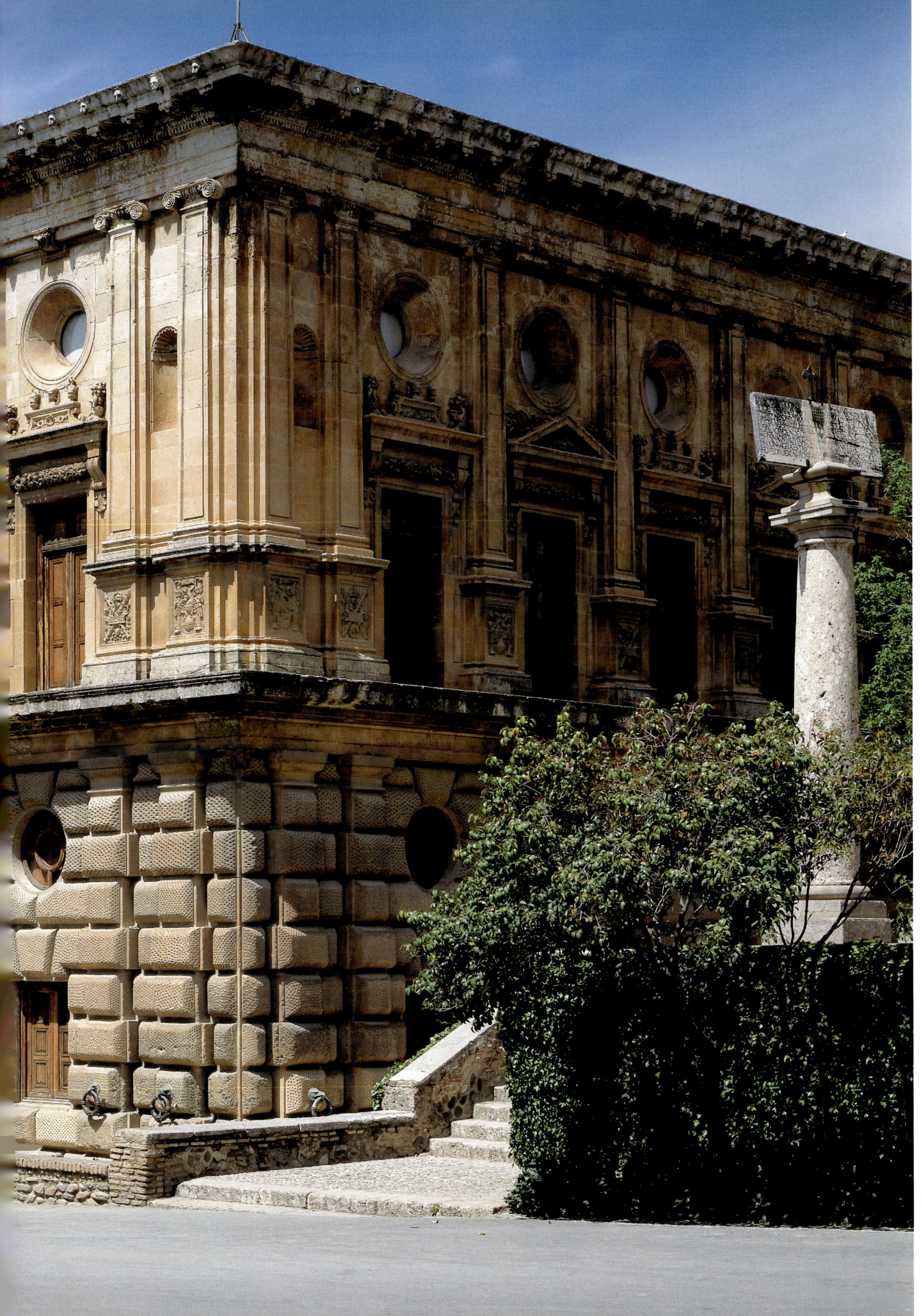

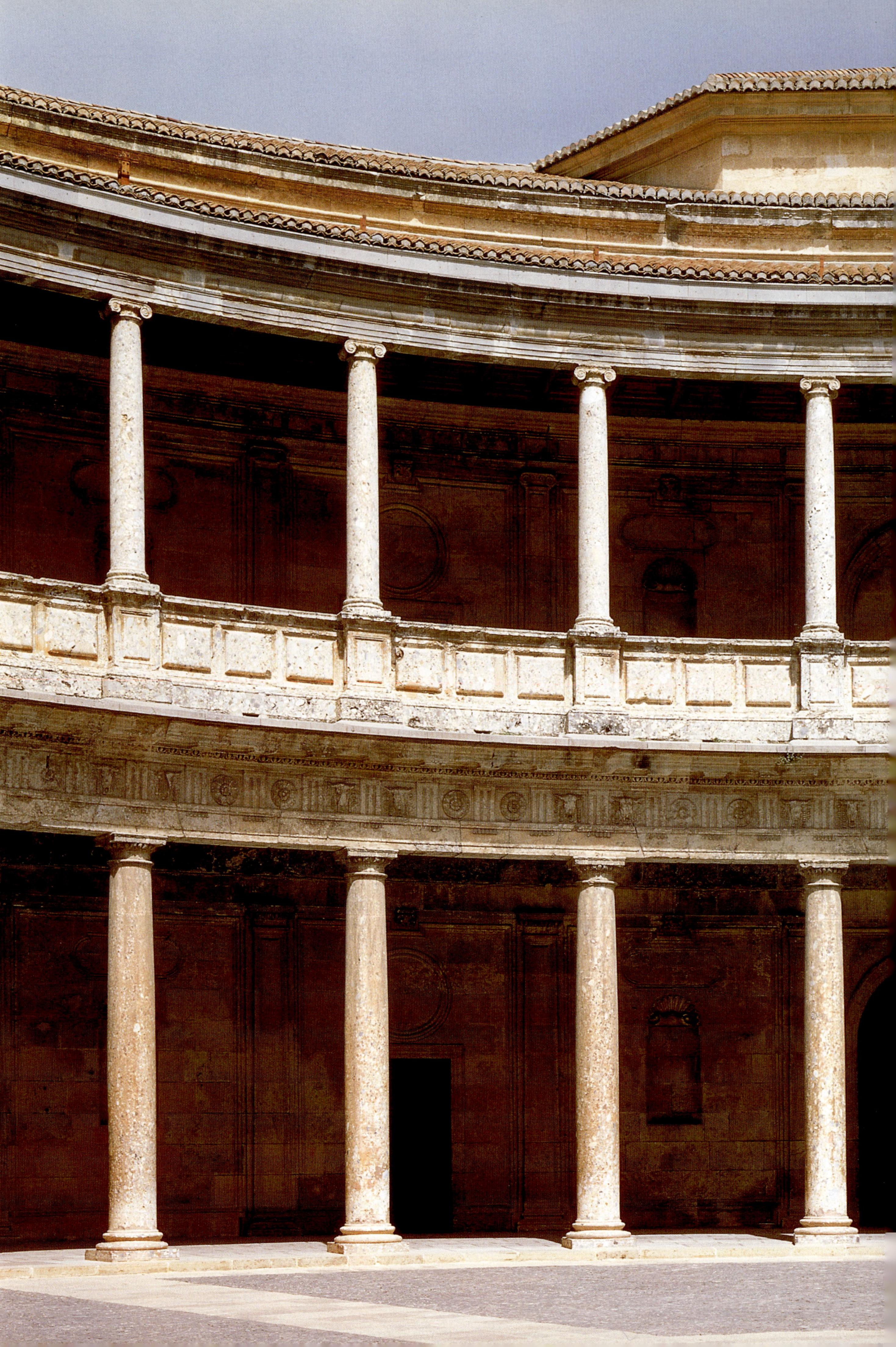

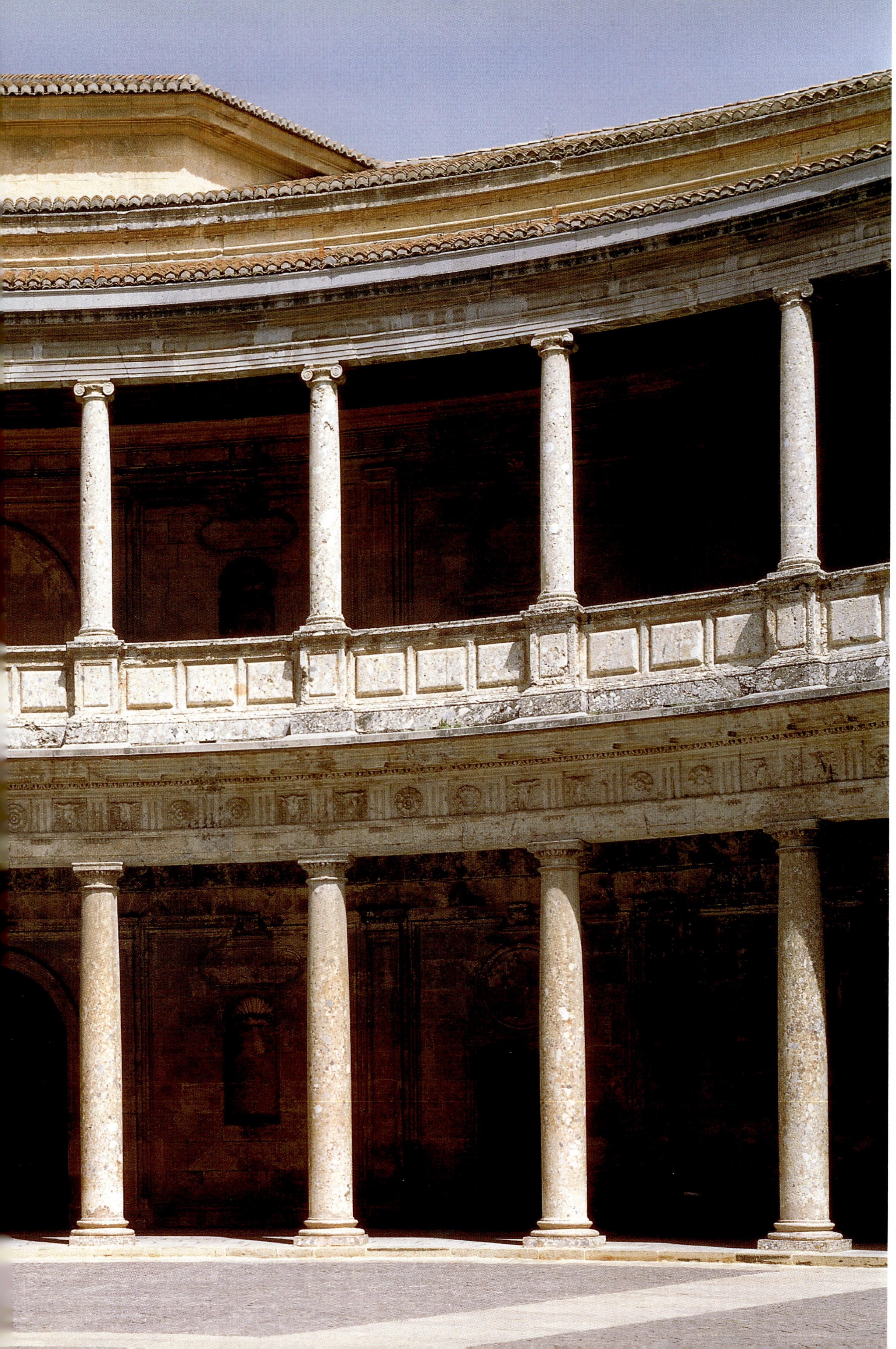

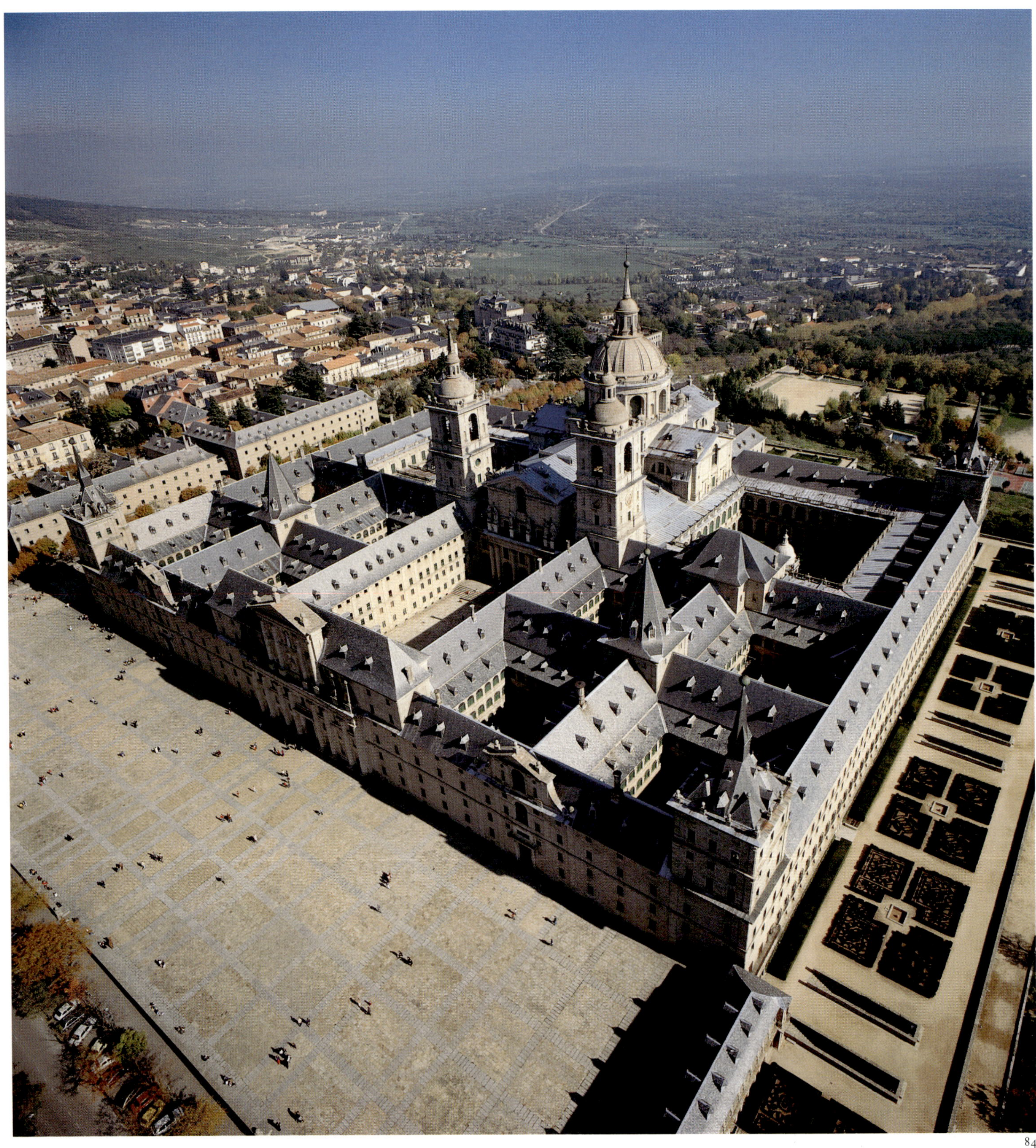
84

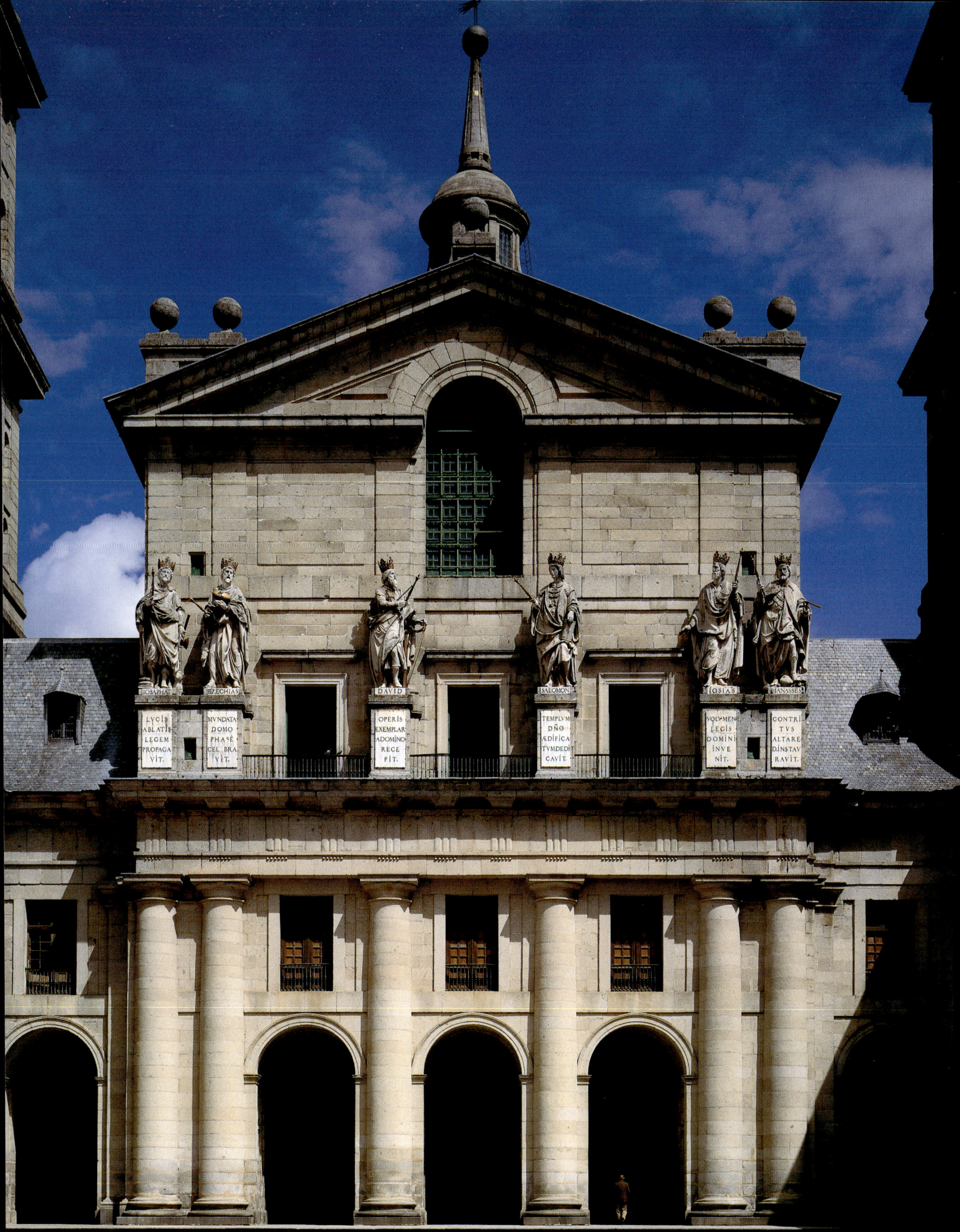
IOSAPHAT
LVCIS ABLATIS LEGEM PROPAGAVIT.
EZECHIAS
MVNDATA DOMO PHASE CELEBRAVIT.
DAVID
OPERIS EXEMPLAR A DOMINO RECEPIT.
SALOMON
TEMPLVM DÑO ÆDIFICATVM DEDICAVIT.
IOSIAS
VOLVMEN LEGIS DOMINI INVENIT.
MANASSES
CONTRITVS ALTARE D. INSTAVRAVIT.

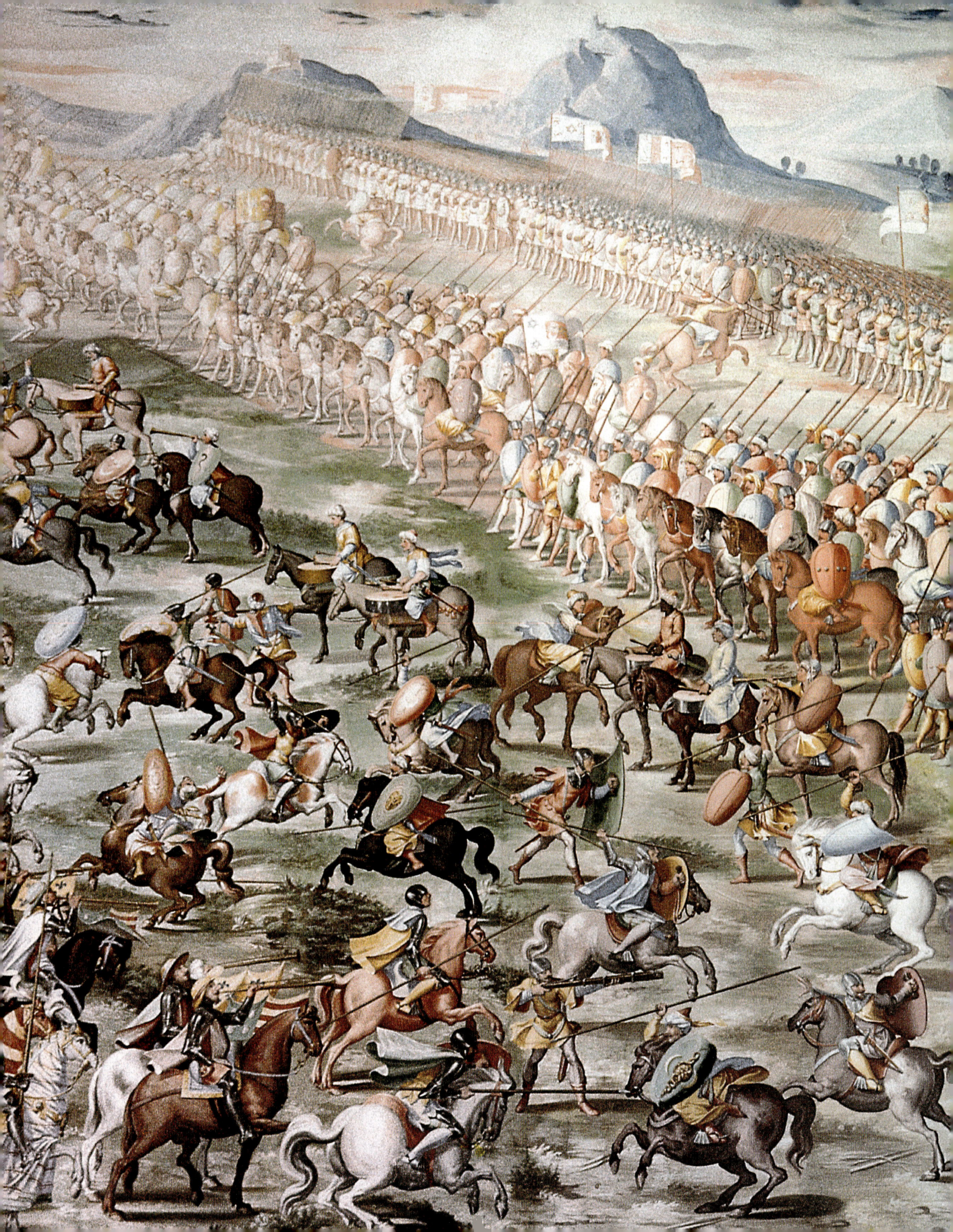

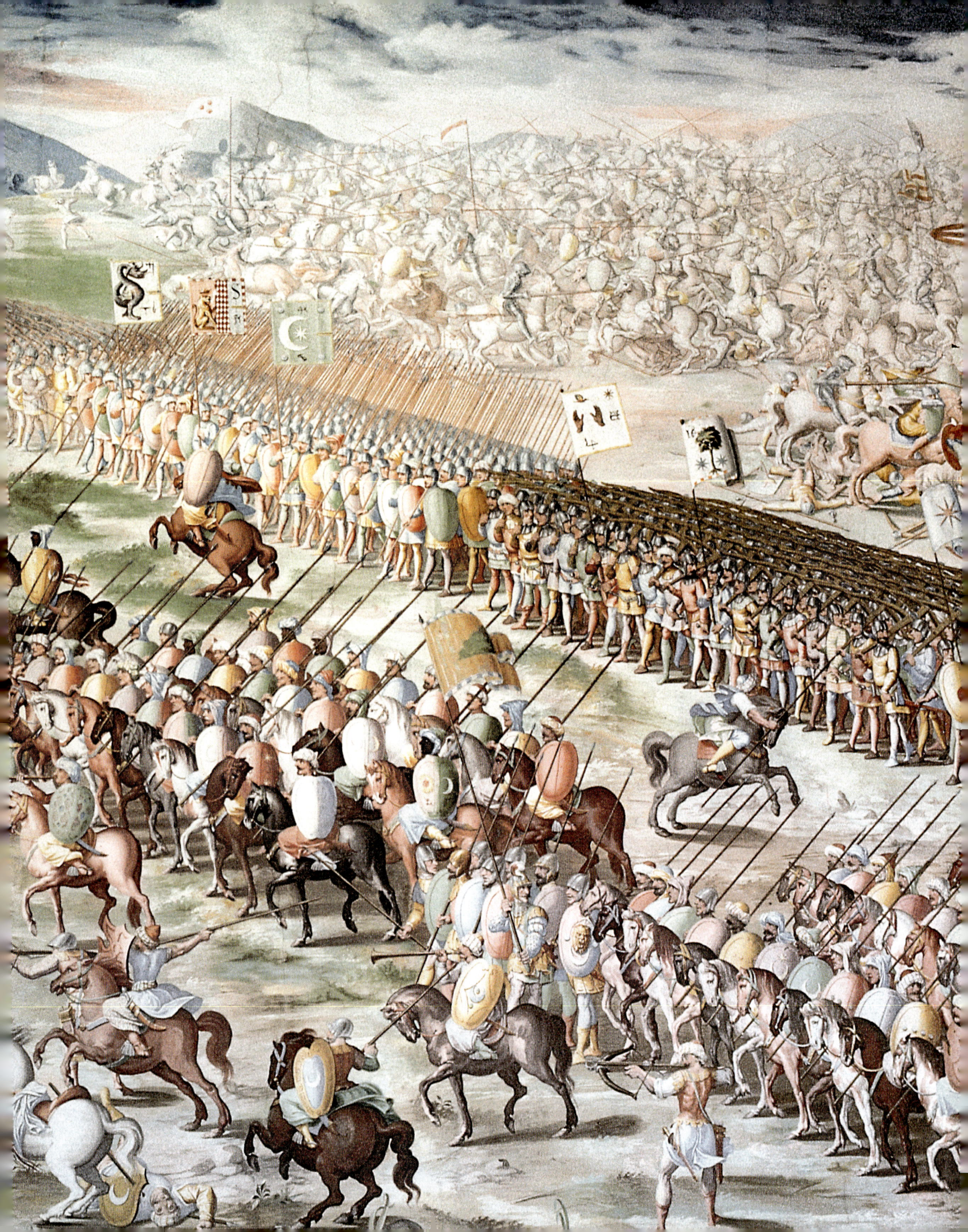

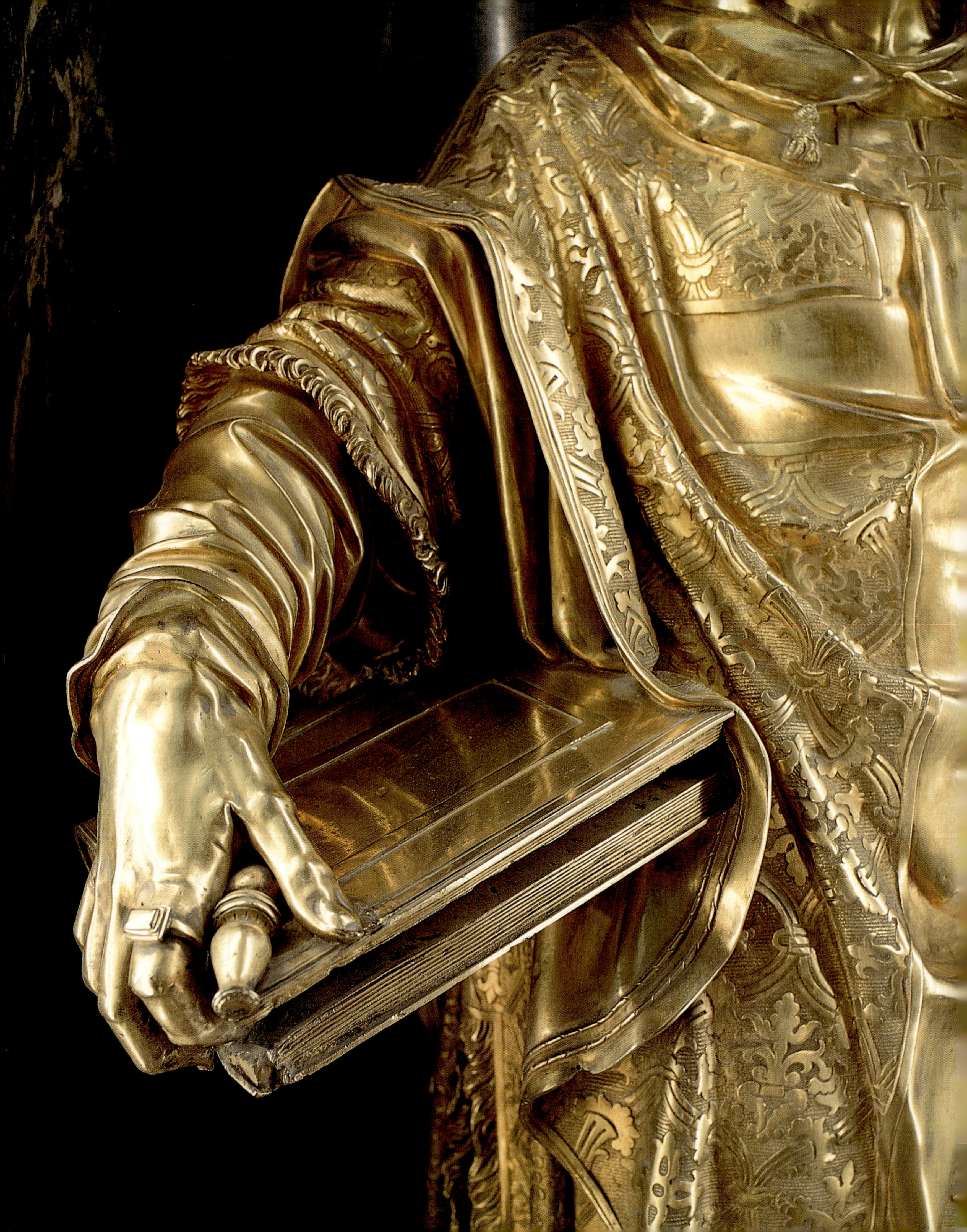

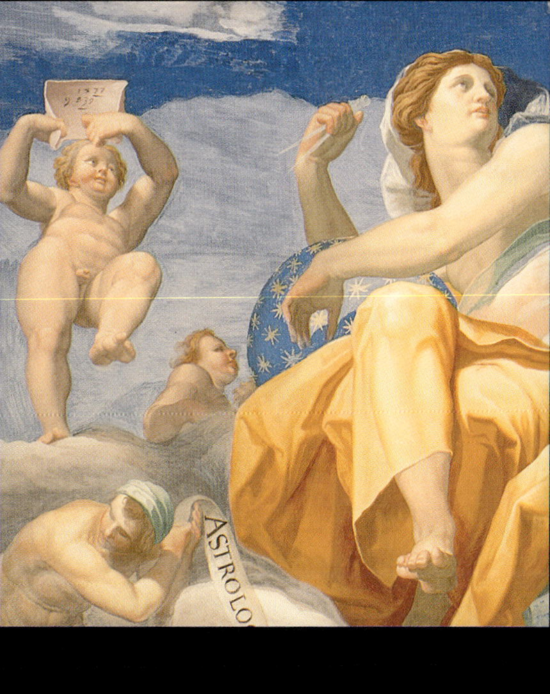

THE ESCORIAL LIBRARY

II

THE ESCORIAL LIBRARY

PRECEDING PAGE:
88. Pellegrino Tibaldi and Bartolomé Carducho
1588–93
Detail of *Astrology*, fresco.
Ceiling of the library, Real Monasterio de San Lorenzo, El Escorial.

RIGHT:
89. Francisco de Zurbarán
1639
Friar Gonzalo de Illescas.
Sacristy of the Monastery, Guadalupe.

FOLLOWING PAGES:
90. Pellegrino Tibaldi and Bartolomé Carducho
1588–93
Frescoes on the ceiling of the library.
Real Monasterio de San Lorenzo, El Escorial.

91 and 92. Pellegrino Tibaldi and Bartolomé Carducho
1588–93
Details of the frescoes on the ceiling of the library.
Real Monasterio de San Lorenzo, El Escorial.

93. Pellegrino Tibaldi and Bartolomé Carducho
1588–93
Astrology, fresco.
Ceiling of the library, Real Monasterio de San Lorenzo, El Escorial.

94. Pellegrino Tibaldi and Bartolomé Carducho
1588–93
Dialectics, fresco.
Ceiling of the library, Real Monasterio de San Lorenzo, El Escorial.

95. Pellegrino Tibaldi and Bartolomé Carducho
1588–93
Detail of the frescoes on the ceiling of the library.
Real Monasterio de San Lorenzo, El Escorial.

MEN OF LETTERS such as Hernando Colón in Seville, the *comendador* Fernán Núñez in Salamanca, and Cardinal Francisco de Mendoza in Burgos all collected books, and Mencía de Mendoza, who loved both classical literature and the pictorial arts, established a library in Valencia. However, libraries were largely neglected in the Imperial Spain that emerged from its medieval kingdoms and entered the modern era as discoverer of a New World. Hence, encouraged by humanists at the royal court such as Honorato Juan, Páez de Castro, Antonio Agustín, Ambrosio de Morales, and Benito Arias Montano, Philip II, the "Prudent King," endowed his monastery at the Escorial (and the school he founded there), which was already regarded as the eighth wonder of the world, with his own collection of books. Philip's library was partially inherited from his father and partially gathered by the envoys he sent all over Europe, especially to Italy, to find books by learned men, and to make copies of incunabulae and manuscripts.

Situated above the hallway that leads to the Patio de los Reyes, the library is a masterpiece by the architect Juan de Herrera (ills 88, 90–95). Herrera also designed the exquisitely refined furnishings of the library, as Michelangelo had done for the library of the Medici at San Lorenzo in Florence. According to Antonio Gracián, the chaplain of San Juan de los Reyes in Toledo, Philip's achievement was blessed "by the grace of the glorious saints Lawrence and Jerome, his inspiration for the most subtle and most necessary work for these kingdoms." By virtue of his creation of the Escorial library, Philip II was compared to the monarchs of antiquity; to the powerful Renaissance princes whose building programs benefited not only those in power but also "remote nations"; to the Ptolemies of Egypt; to the kings of Cilicia; and to Attalus of Pergamon, who "to better preserve the writings of wise men had them inscribed on the hides of animals." The barrel vault of the main room of the library (ill. 91), over fifty meters long by nine wide, on which Pellegrino Tibaldi painted alfresco the greatest of Imperial Spain's contributions to the sciences and the liberal arts, placed him on a par with Caius Asinus Pollio, the mentor of Virgil and Horace; the emperors of Constantinople; King Matthias Corvin of Hungary; Lorenzo de' Medici; popes Leo and Clement; and Francis I, king of France.

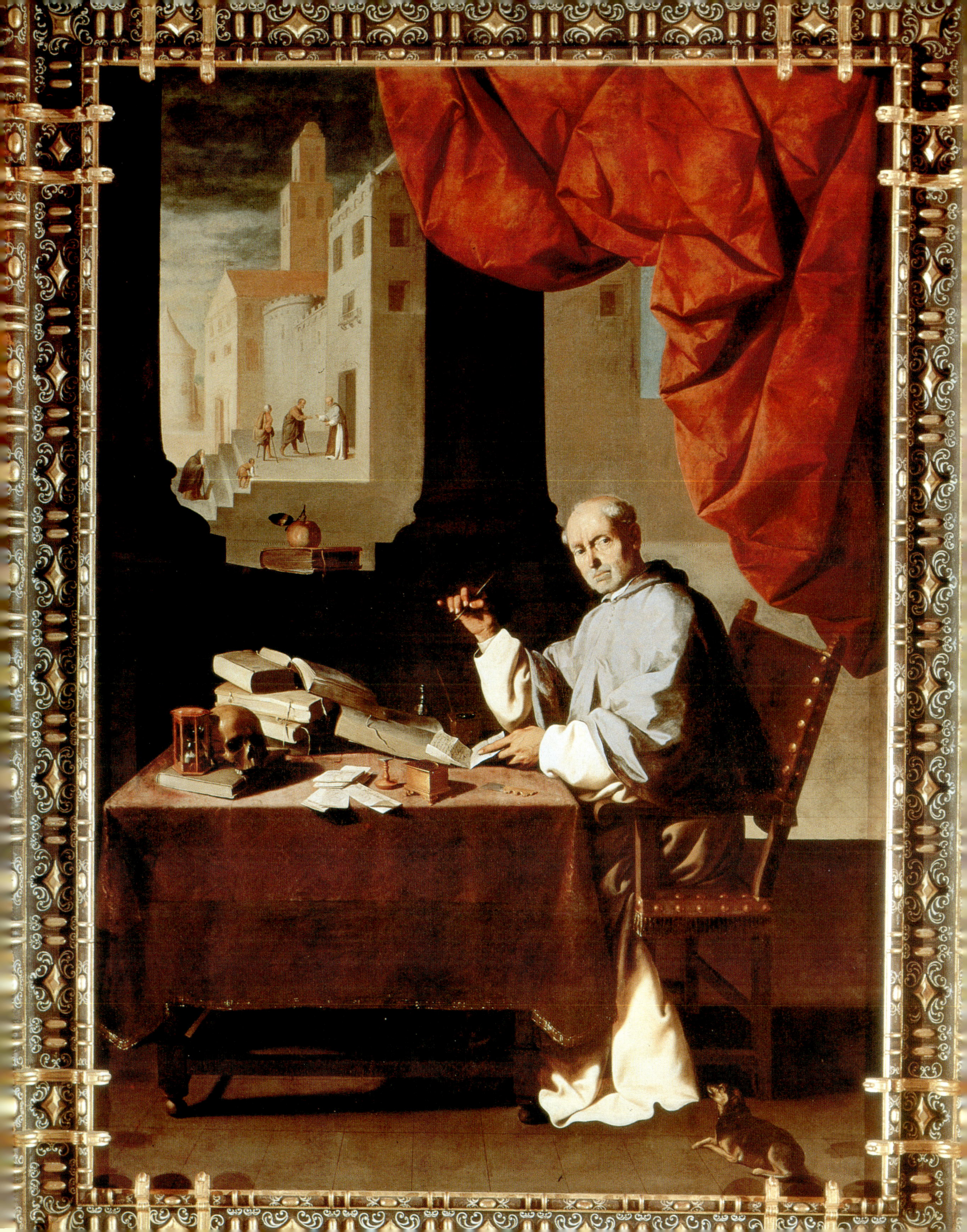

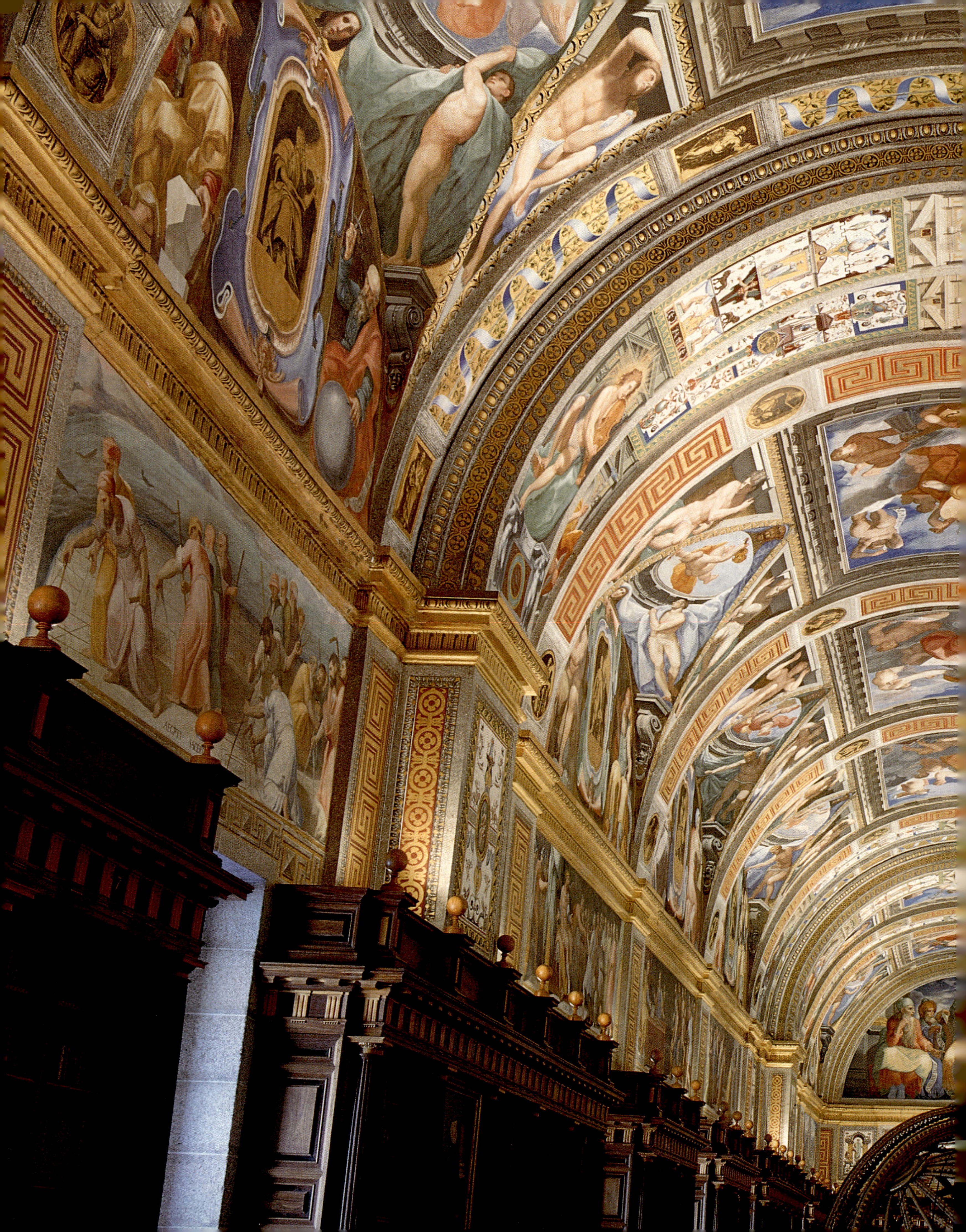

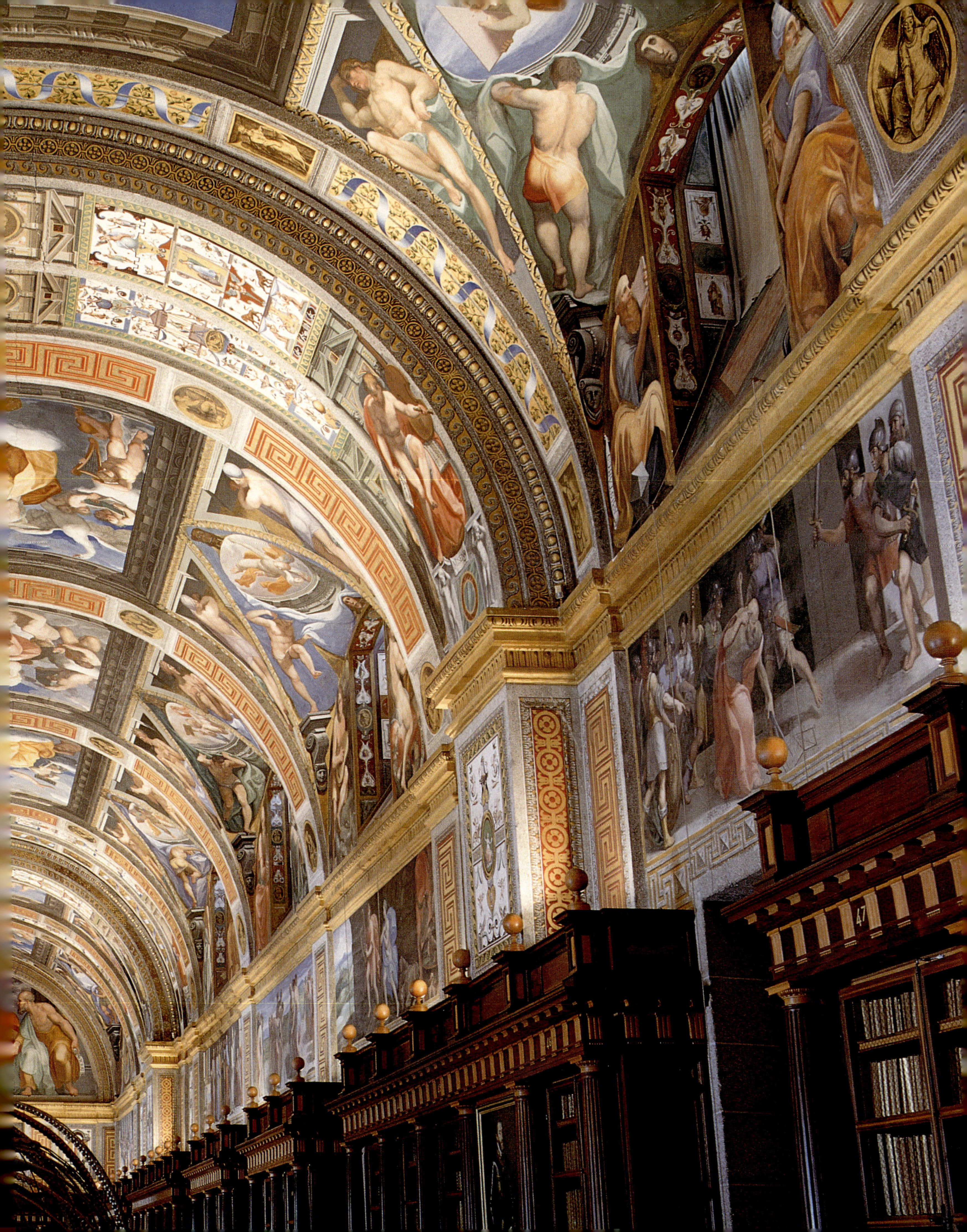

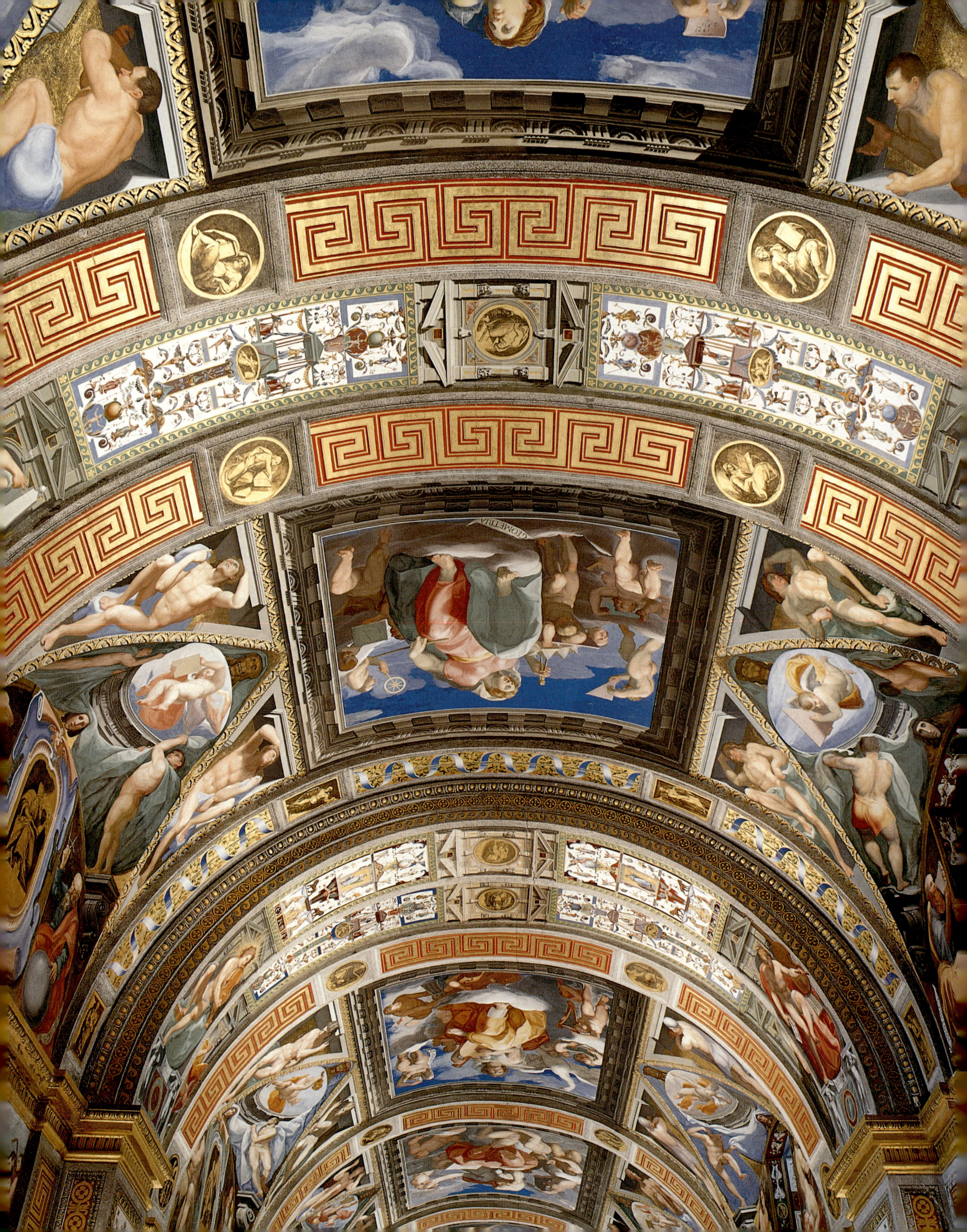

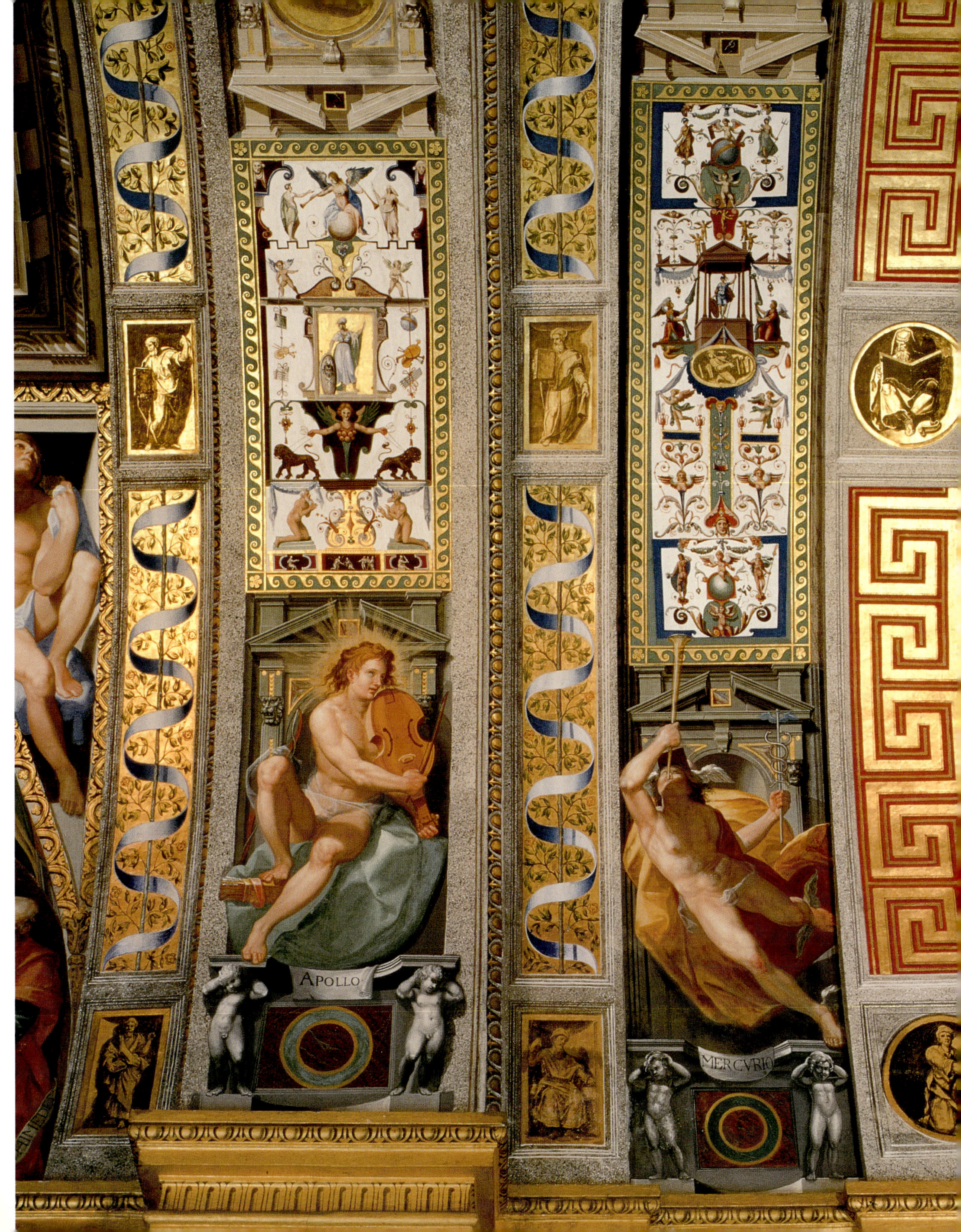
APOLLO
MERCVRIO

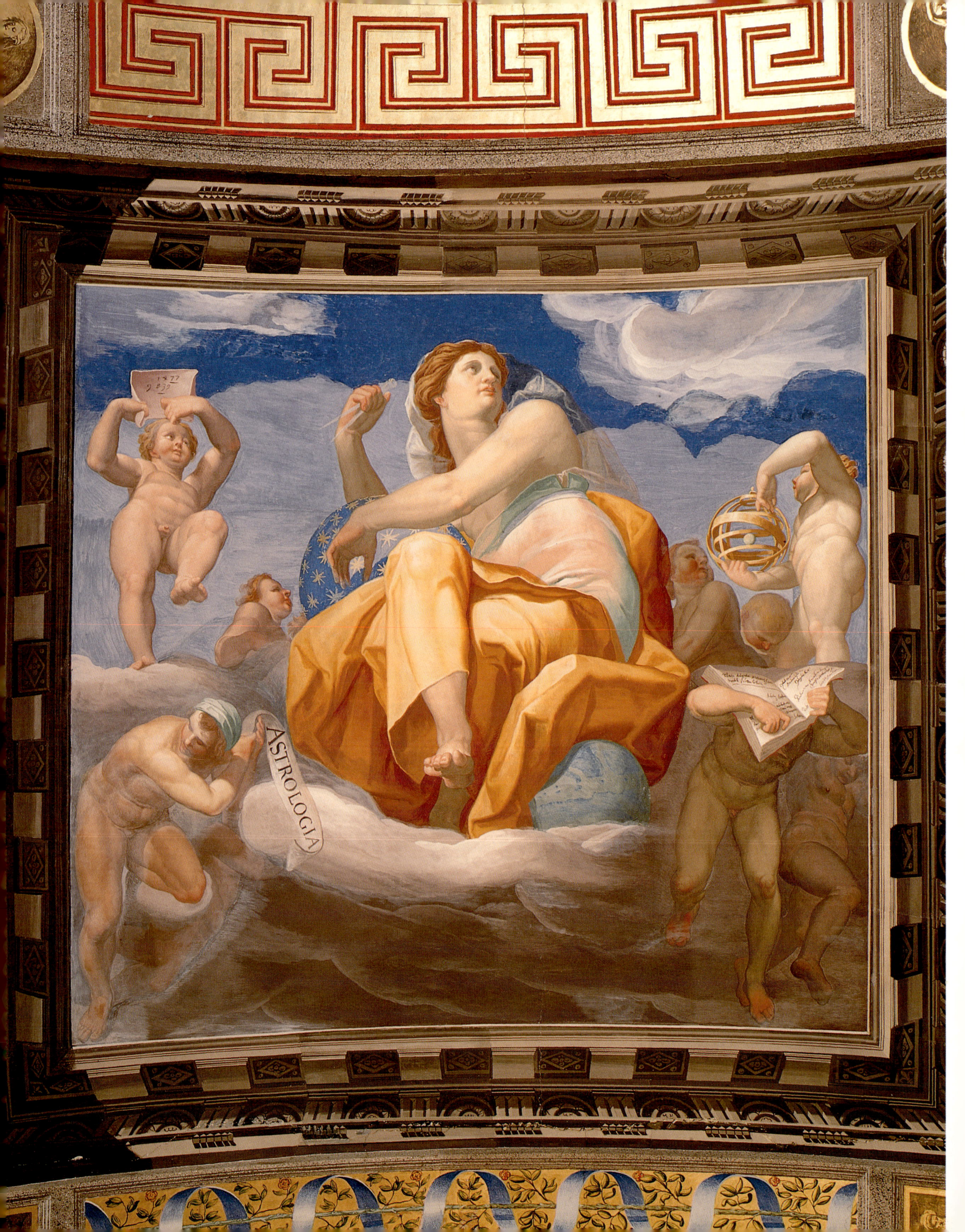
ASTROLOGIA

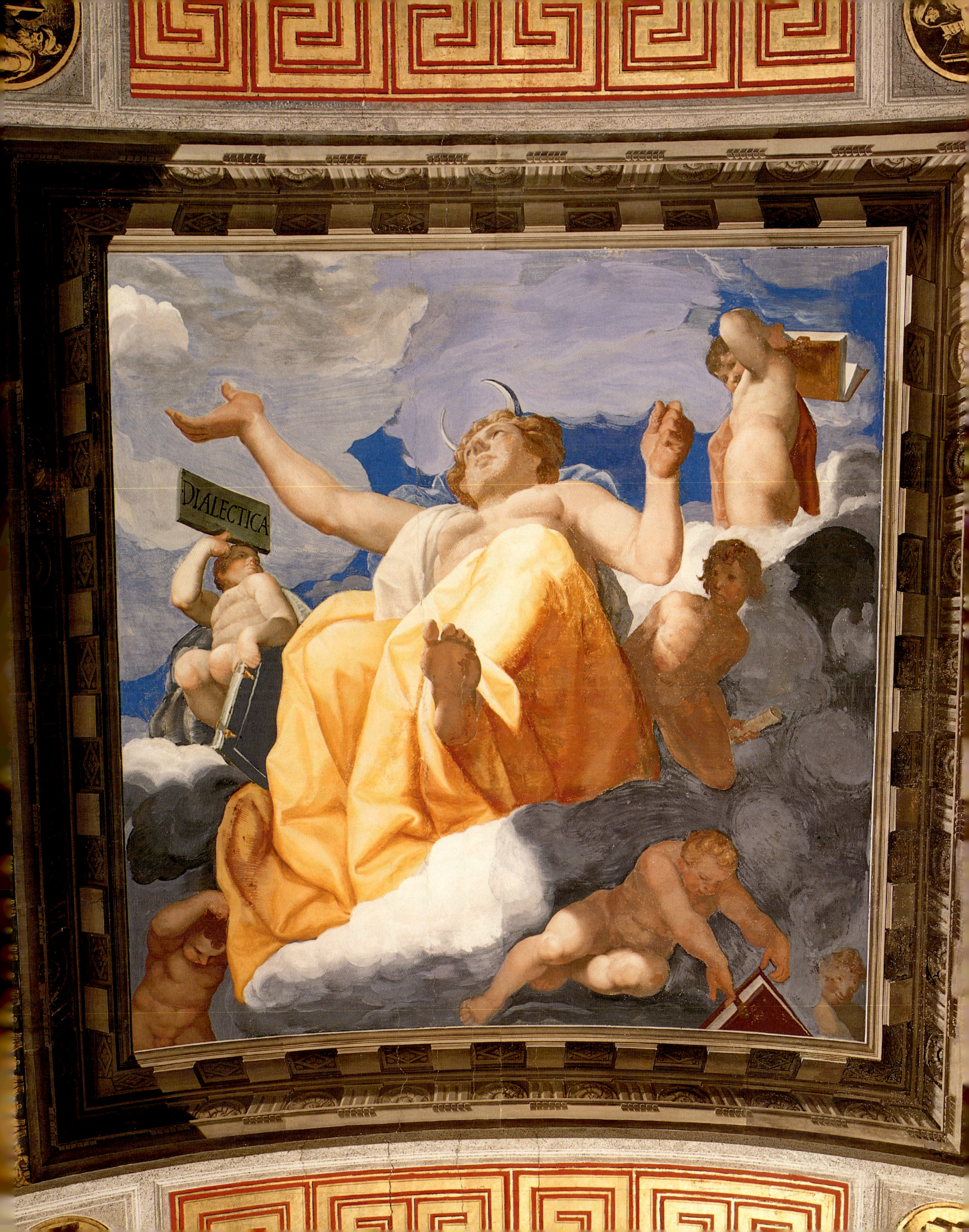
DIALECTICA

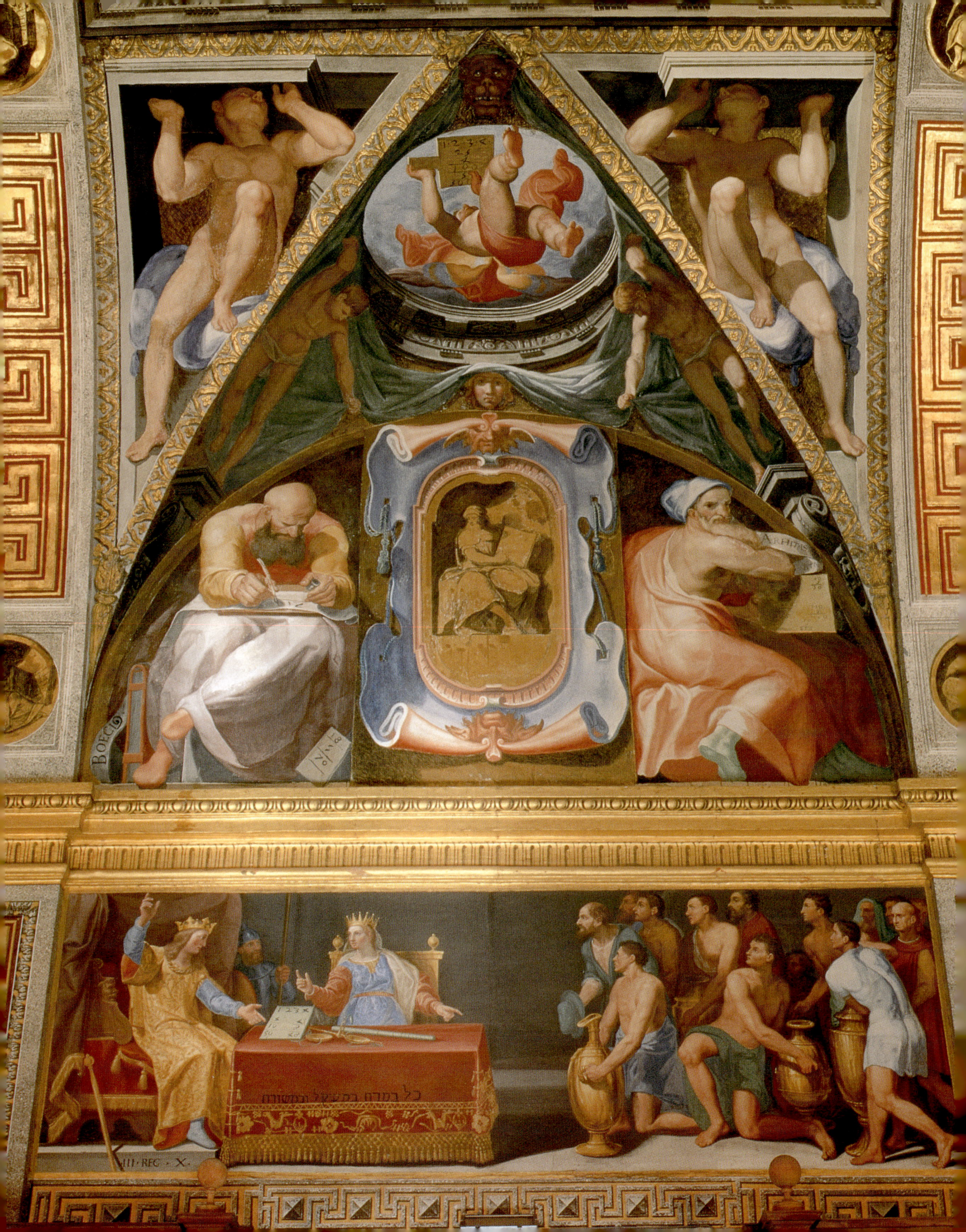
BOECIO
III·REG·X·

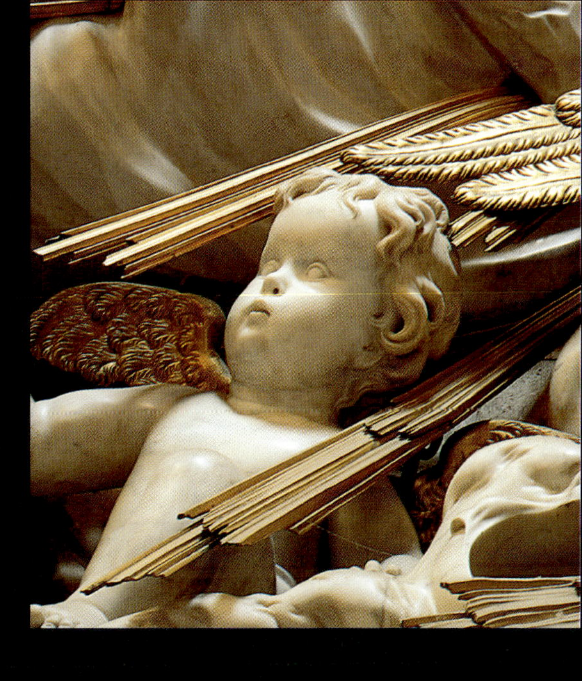

FROM MANNERISM TO BAROQUE

III

FROM MANNERISM TO BAROQUE

ECHOES OF THE SOBER, if grand, architecture of the Escorial—all geometry with only occasional expression of the sensual luxuries of painting and sculpture—were very influential in Spanish architecture of the first decades of the seventeenth century. However, that solemn classicism was soon invaded not only by the stylistic extremes of Mannerism, but also by the expressive and agitated Baroque.

These were the years when the young Diego Velázquez left Seville to seek his fortune in Madrid, and when Luis de Góngora eked out a living at court as chaplain to Philip III. Góngora may have been a cleric, but he was above all a poet who brought poetry, and with it art, into an artificial and artful world in which nature vanished into intricate labyrinths of words and forms that demanded freedom, disorder, even incoherence. This was the era when architecture and the other arts created cascades of apparently discordant parts that together comprised a harmonious ensemble. This "ensemble," as the wise Critilo announced in Baltasar Gracián's *The Critic,* is "composed of opposites and arrayed in disarray." Finding its inspiration both in the present and in medieval Christian and Islamic manifestations, art became dark, hermetic, complex; its forms became delirious, fatuous, antithetical, unstable, estranged from reason, and tied to emotion.

As a result of this mixing of forms and cultures throughout the Hispanic world during the seventeenth and even the eighteenth centuries, creativity ranged from the austerity of the Escorial to the exuberant, theatrical Churrigueresque style (ills. 96–103), and from the eloquent painting of Murillo to that of Zurbarán, which seems suspended in silence. However, if we carefully study this apparent dispute between forms (which was not as explicit as the literary conflict between Góngora's *culteranismo* (high-flown style) and Quevedo's *conceptismo* (direct, concise style), we can see that both the delirious, absurd forms of the Baroque and those that seem caught in the breath of classical orthodoxy actually respond to the same system, structure, and order, to the same coherence and understanding of light. For without structure there is no freedom; without order there is disorder; without coherence there is incoherence; and without light there is only darkness.

PRECEDING PAGE:
96. Narciso Tomé
1721–32
Detail of the Glory on the altarpiece called the *Transparente*, marble and bronze.
Toledo Cathedral.

RIGHT:
97. Juan de Badajoz
1549
Vault decoration.
Sacristy of San Marcos Monastery, León.

FOLLOWING PAGES:
98. José Benito de Churriguera (sculpture) and Claudio Coello (painting)
1692
High altar.
Church of San Esteban Monastery, Salamanca.

99. Narciso Tomé
1721–32
The *Transparente* altarpiece, marble and bronze.
Toledo Cathedral.

100. Narciso Tomé
1721–32
Detail of the Glory on the *Transparente* altarpiece. marble and bronze.
Toledo Cathedral.

101 and 102. José Risueño
1702–20
Details of the tabernacle.
Sacrarium at the Carthusian monastery of La Asunción, Granada.

103. Pedro Borja and Miguel Borja
1659
Vault decoration.
Church of Santa María la Blanca, Seville.

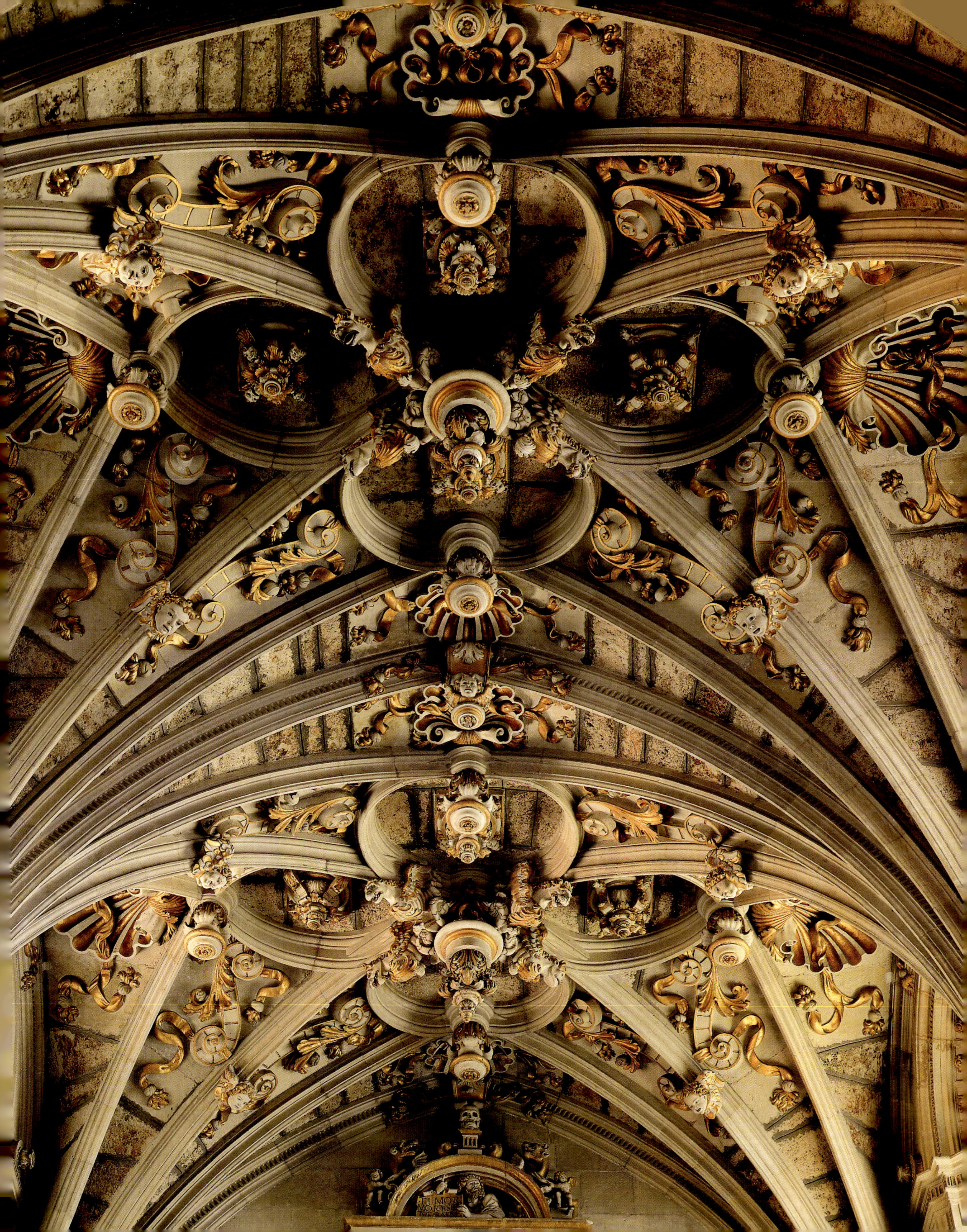

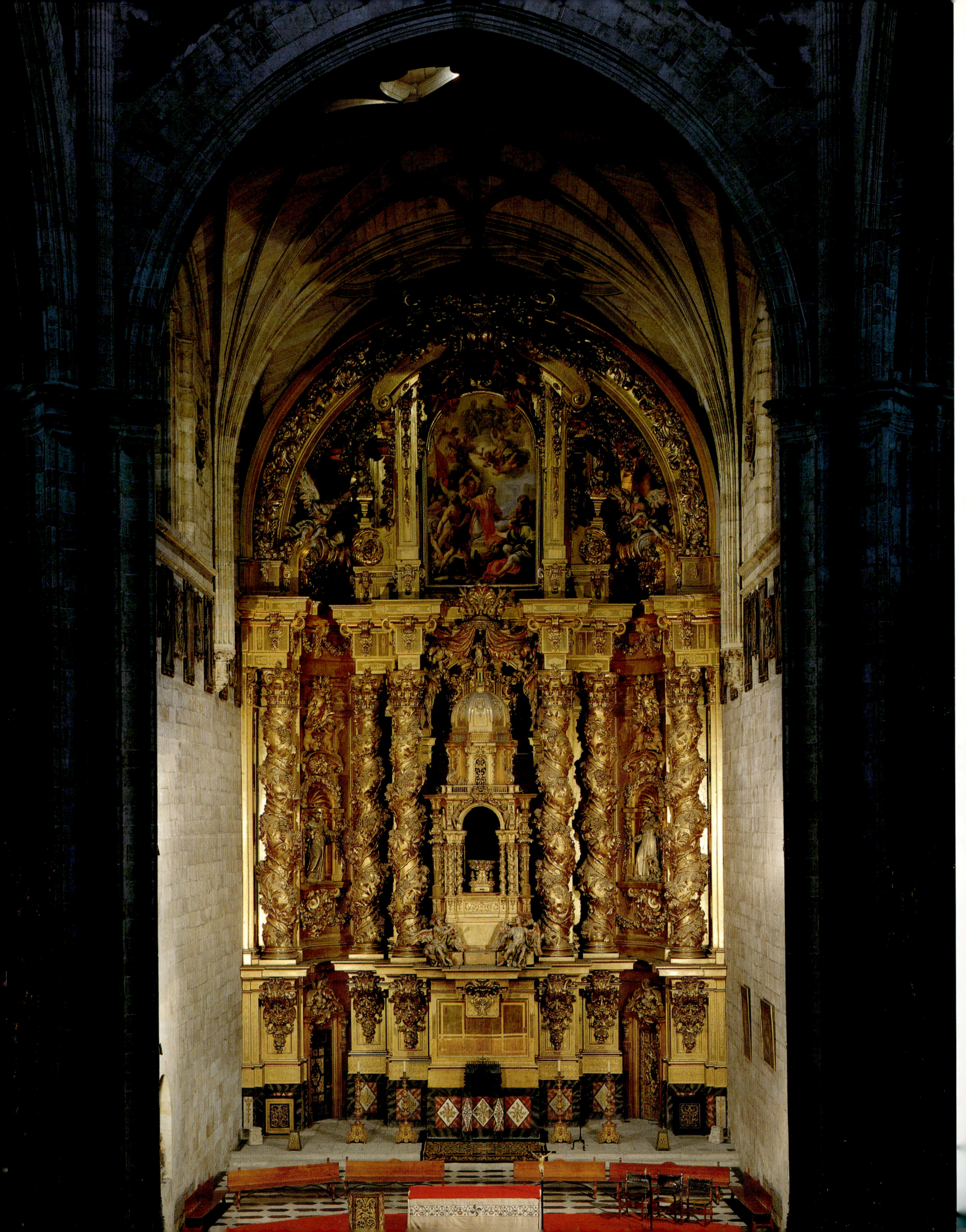

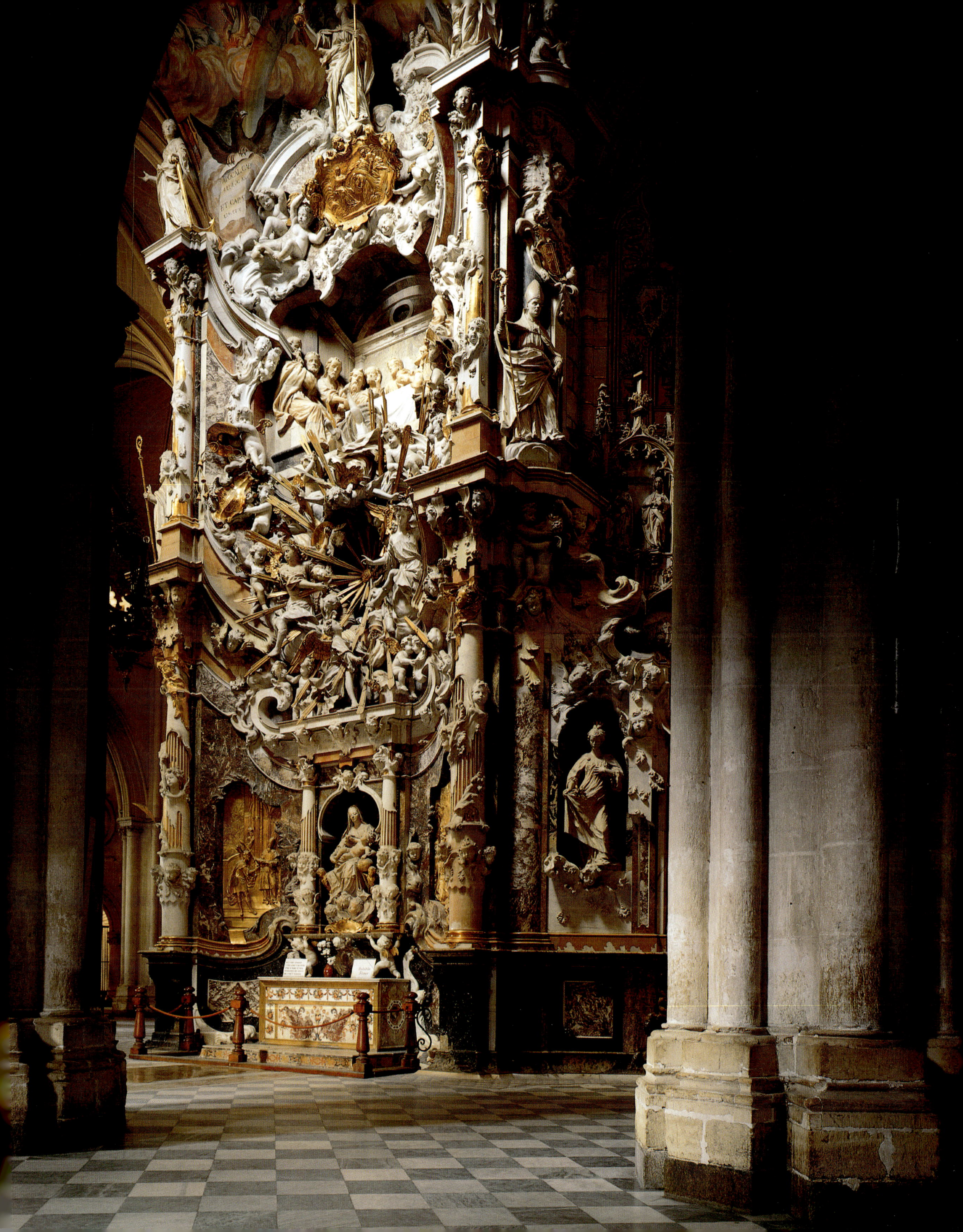

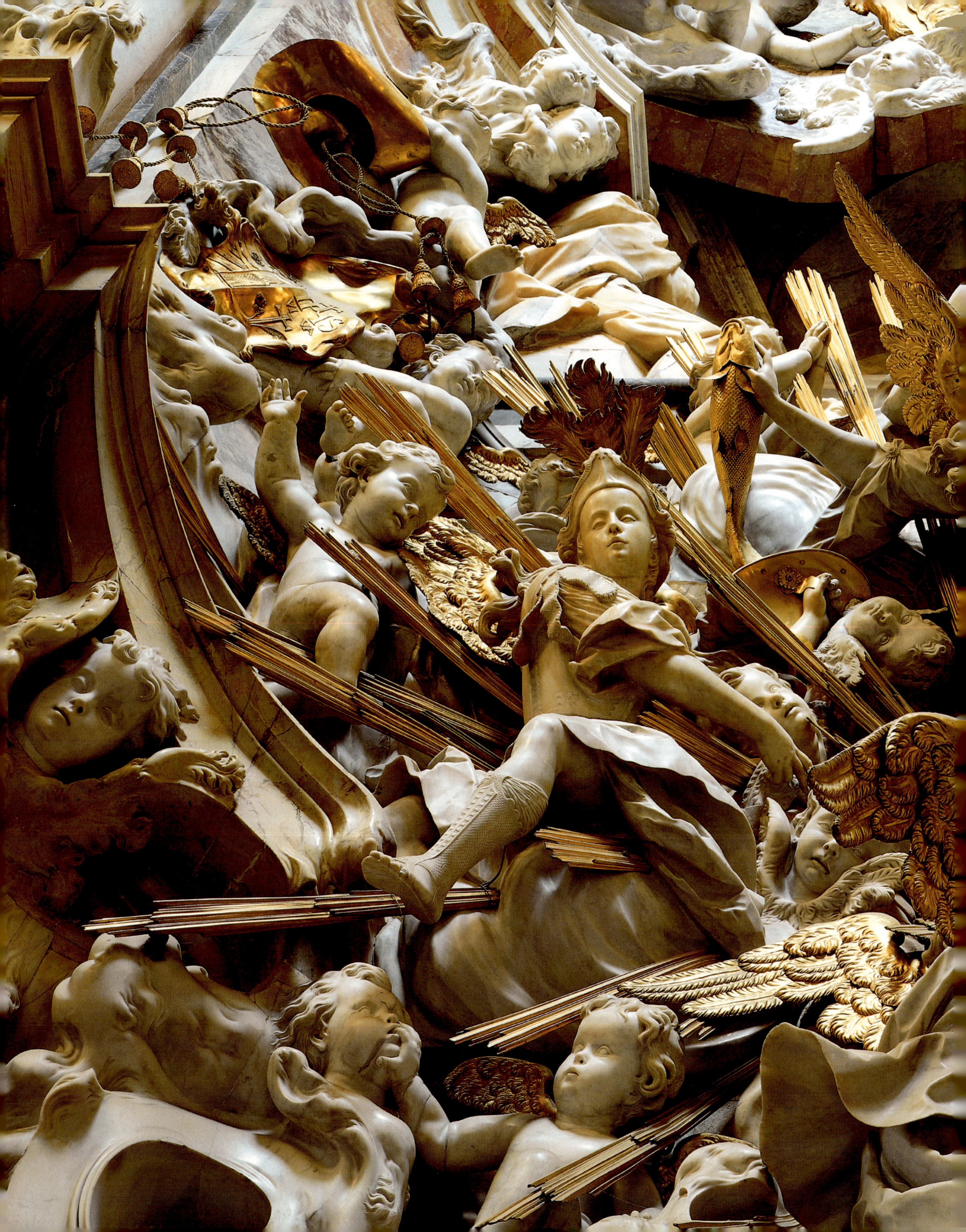

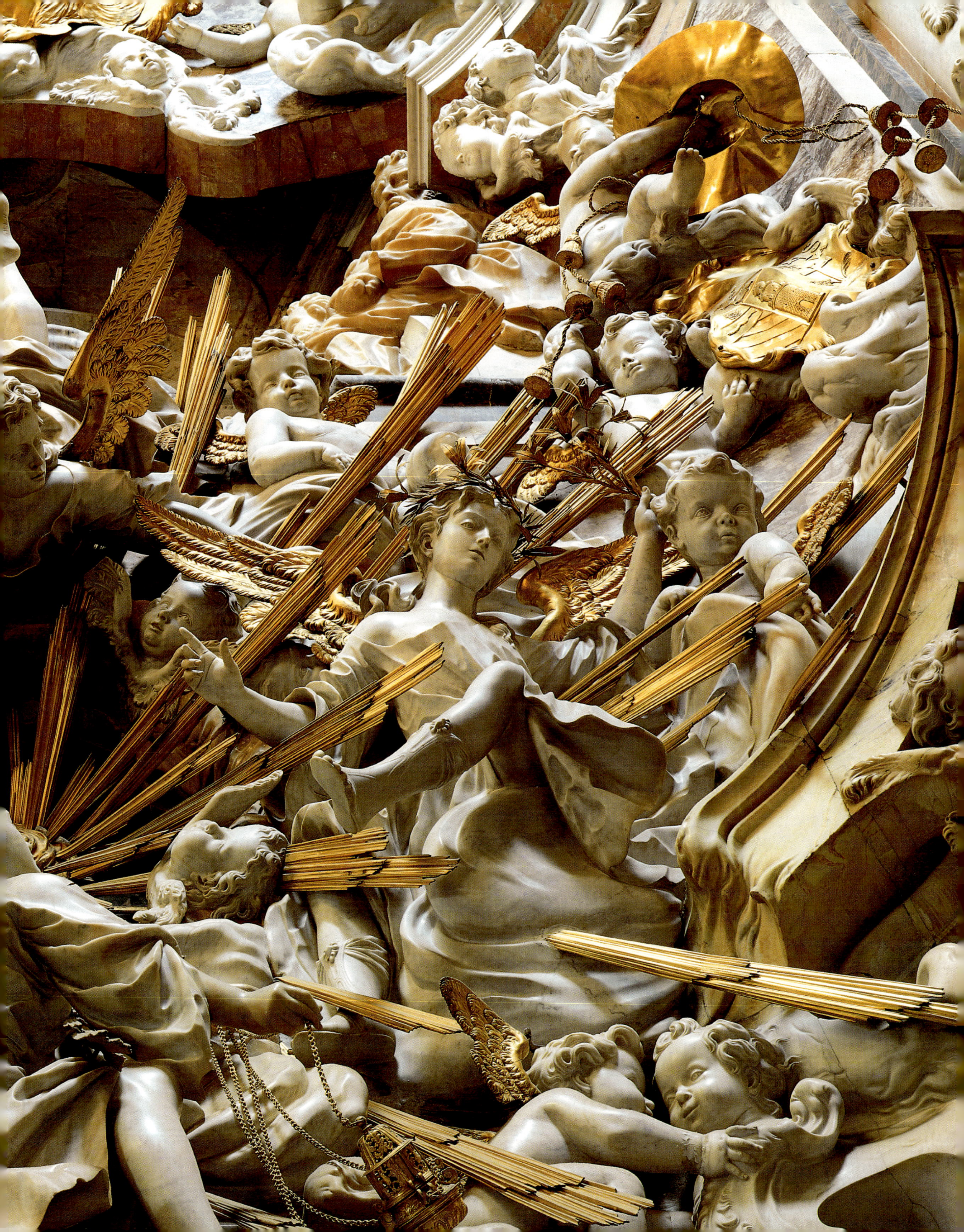

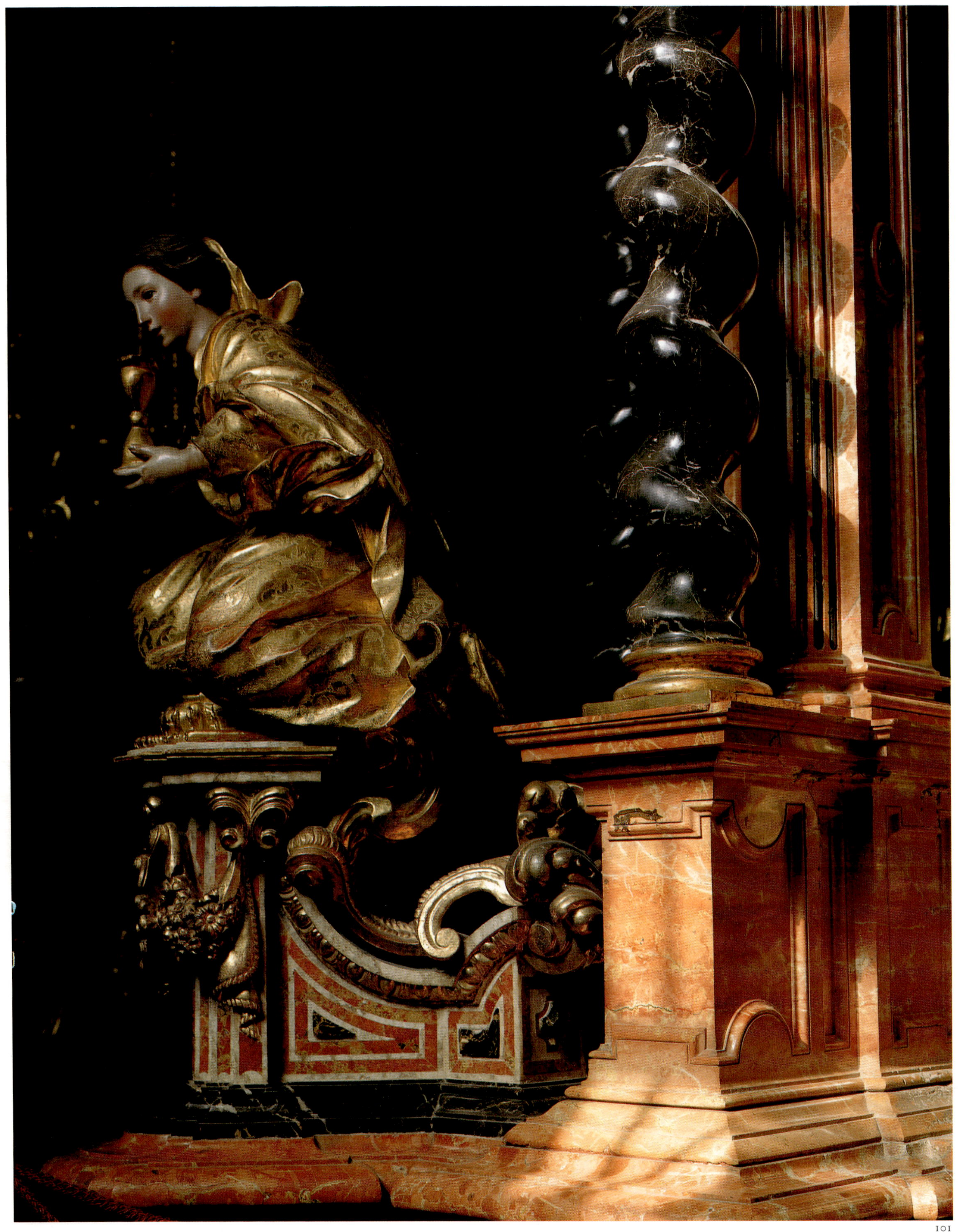

101

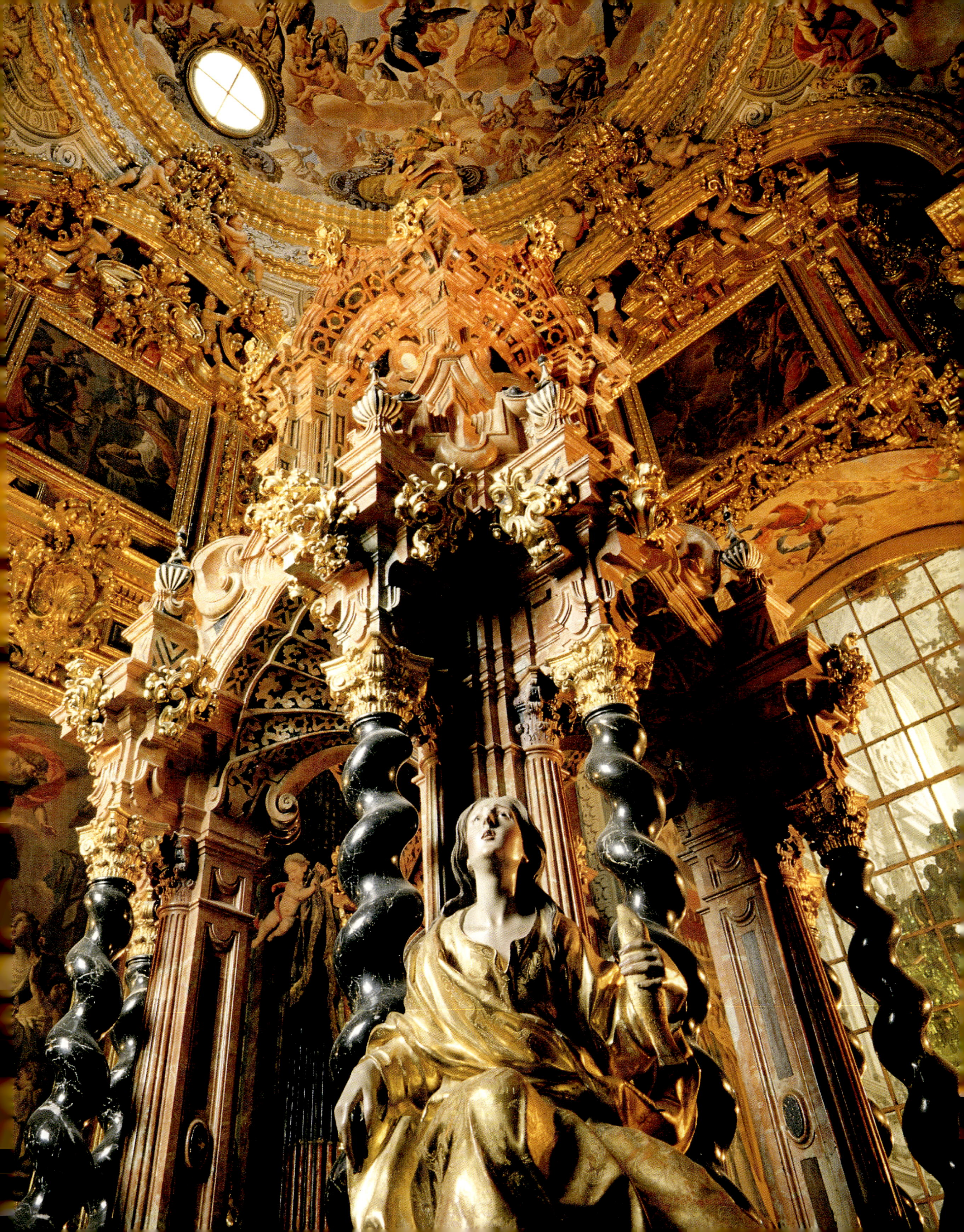

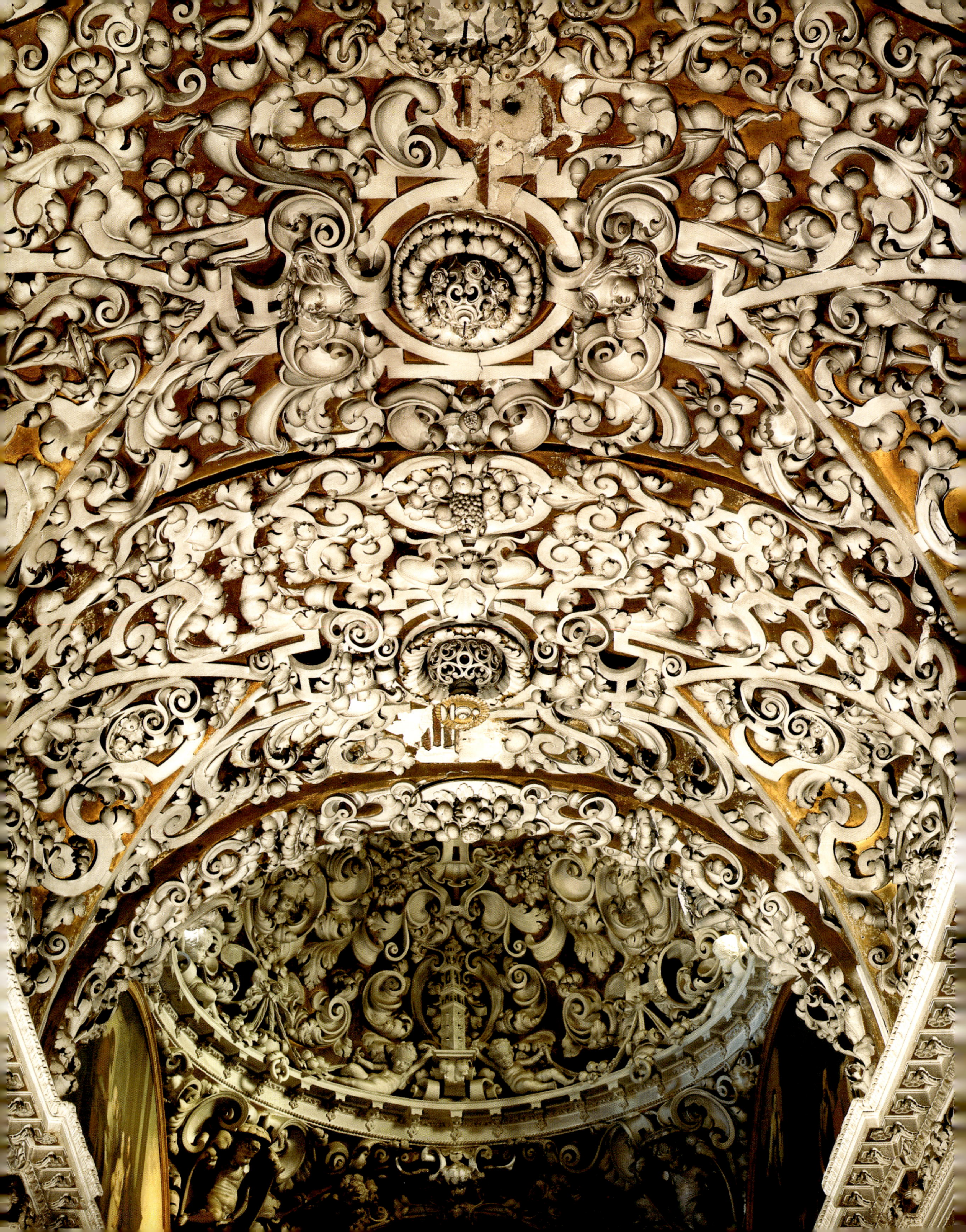

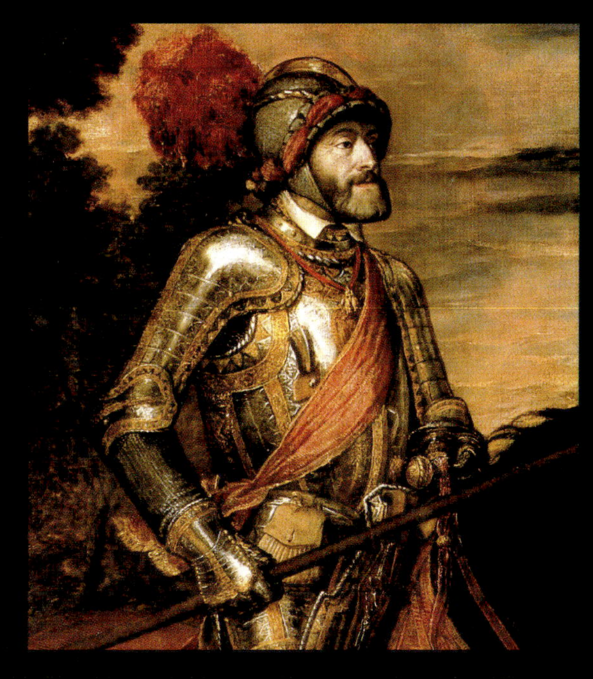

THE ART OF WAR

IV

THE ART OF WAR

PRECEDING PAGE:
104. Titian
1548
Detail of *Charles V at the Battle of Mülhberg.*
Museo Nacional del Prado, Madrid.

RIGHT:
105. Diego Velázquez
1630
Detail of *The Forge of Vulcan.*
Museo Nacional del Prado, Madrid.

FOLLOWING PAGES:
106. Titian
1548
Charles V at the Battle of Mülhberg.
Museo Nacional del Prado, Madrid.

107. Desiderius Helmschmid
1544
Armor of Charles V, called the armor of Mülhberg, steel and gold.
Real Armería, Palacio Real, Madrid.

108 and 109. Kolman Helmschmid
1517–18
Hercules and the Hydra of Lerna, armor of Charles V, steel and silver.
Real Armería, Palacio Real, Madrid.

110 and 111. Diego Velázquez
1634–35
Details of *The Surrender of Breda*, or *The Lances*, from the Hall of Realms, the Buen Retiro palace, Madrid.
Museo Nacional del Prado, Madrid.

112. Kolman Helmschmid
c. 1530
Armor of Charles V, steel and gold.
Real Armería, Palacio Real, Madrid.

113. Desiderius Helmschmid
1535–40
Armor of Charles V, steel and gold.
Real Armería, Palacio Real, Madrid.

114. Diego Velázquez
c. 1639–41
Detail of *Mars.*
Museo Nacional del Prado, Madrid.

LUIS CABRERA DE CÓRDOBA, historian and biographer of Philip II, was involved in the preparation of the so-called Invincible Armada, whose 1588 mission was to invade Britain. He wrote that the ancient empires, both Eastern and Western, began to decline when their "wars ceased being offensive and became defensive." Like those empires, Imperial Spain began to decline when its wars ceased to be wars of conquest and its triumphs symbols of its power. Instead, Spain's battles, although victorious, were limited to the defense of its territories and to the suppression of notions of independence that had begun to germinate throughout its European possessions.

The distance between glory and decadence, between ecstasy and agony, lies between the heroic, resolved, proud, dominant, and tireless image of Charles V on horseback at the Battle of Mühlberg, painted by Titian to celebrate the imperial triumph over the Protestant princes of Germany and the Netherlands (ills. 104, 106), and the noble, though stooping and excessively magnanimous figure of Ambrogio Spinola, the Genoese general whom Velázquez depicted receiving the keys of Breda from the defeated Justin of Nassau. (Spinola receives the keys in place of Philip IV, who was no lover of military exploits. With few exceptions, it was military strategists, not monarchs, who led troops on the battlefield.) In Velázquez's *The Surrender of Breda,* also called *The Lances* after the bristling weapons held by the Spanish soldiers (ills. 110, 111; see also 22, 23), a painting the artist probably intended to sign but never did, magnanimity is not so extreme as to depict the two strategists equally costumed. Justin of Nassau wears a brown leather doublet and trousers flecked with gold, his neck is encircled by a lace collar, and he holds a broad-brimmed black hat in his left hand. Spinola, in contrast, is decked out in armor with gold adornments, leather boots, and a crimson sash, while in his gloved left hand he holds the baton that symbolizes his authority. Dressing Spinola in a suit of armor reflects a visual tradition established early in the sixteenth century. By the time of Velázquez's painting, suits of armor had disappeared from the battlefield, becoming instead objects of great artistic merit reserved for parades and tournaments (ills. 107–109, 112, 113). This change of purpose is reflected not only in the forms of the different parts of the armor (helmet, buckler, breastplate, backplate, etc.), but also in their ornamentation.

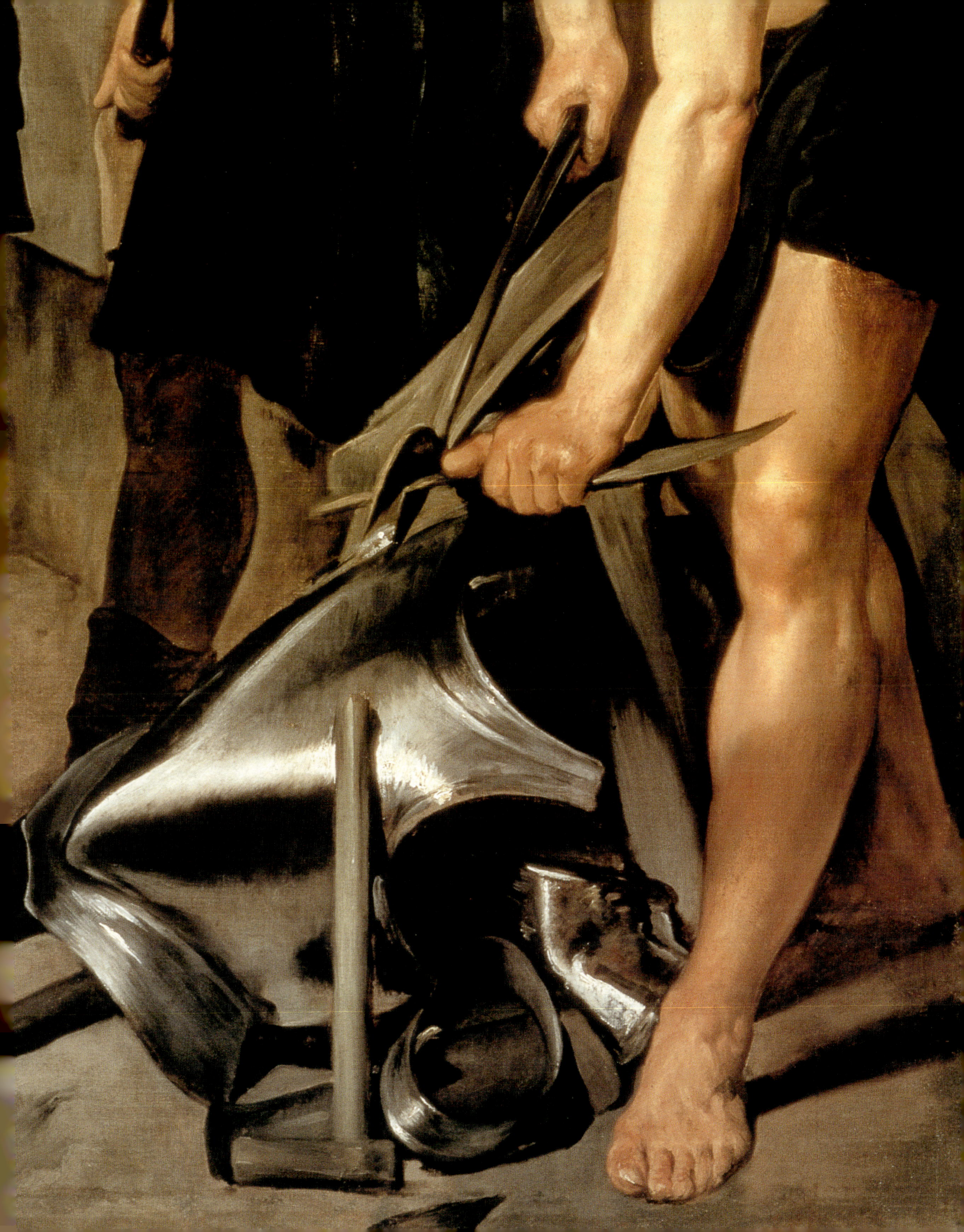

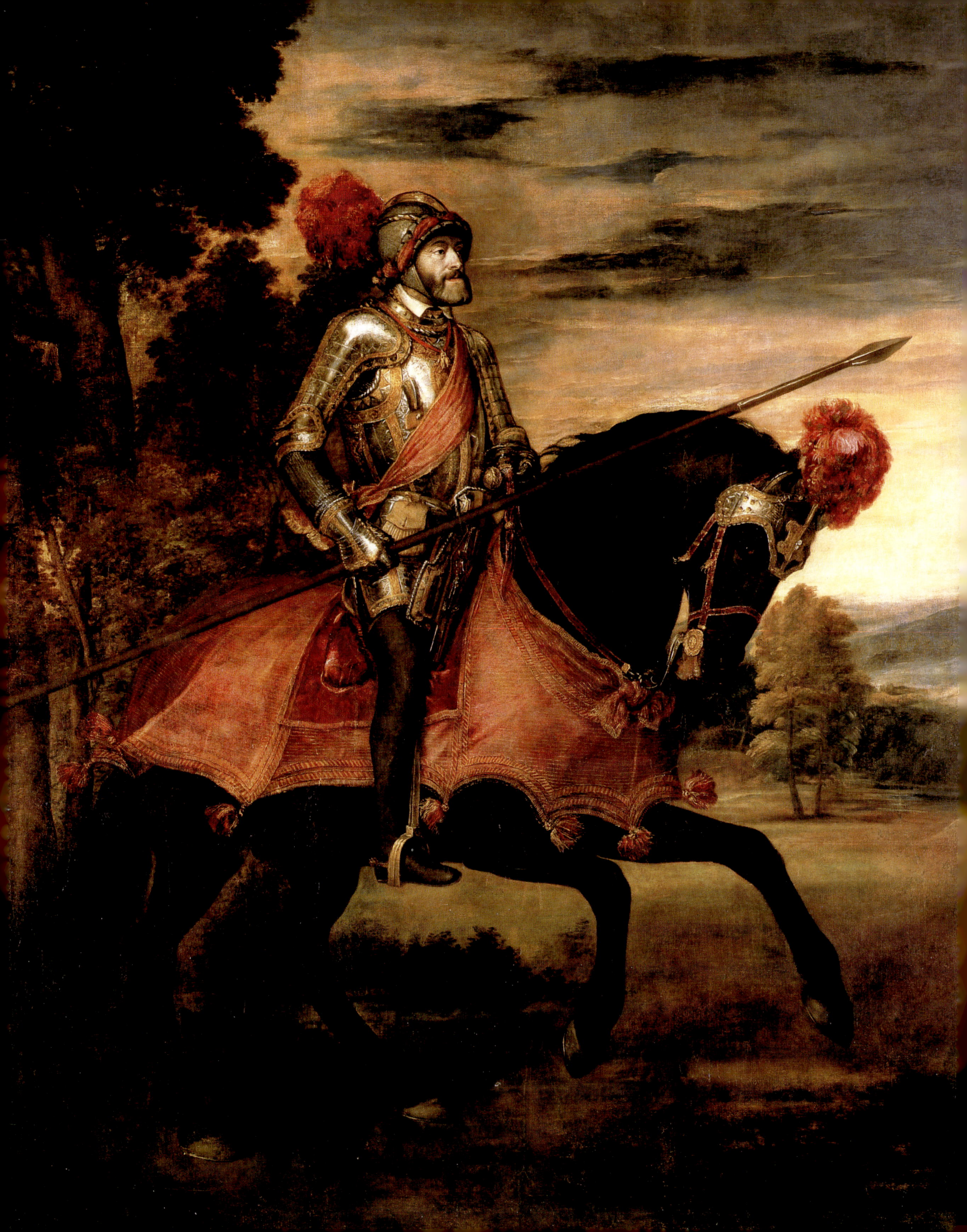

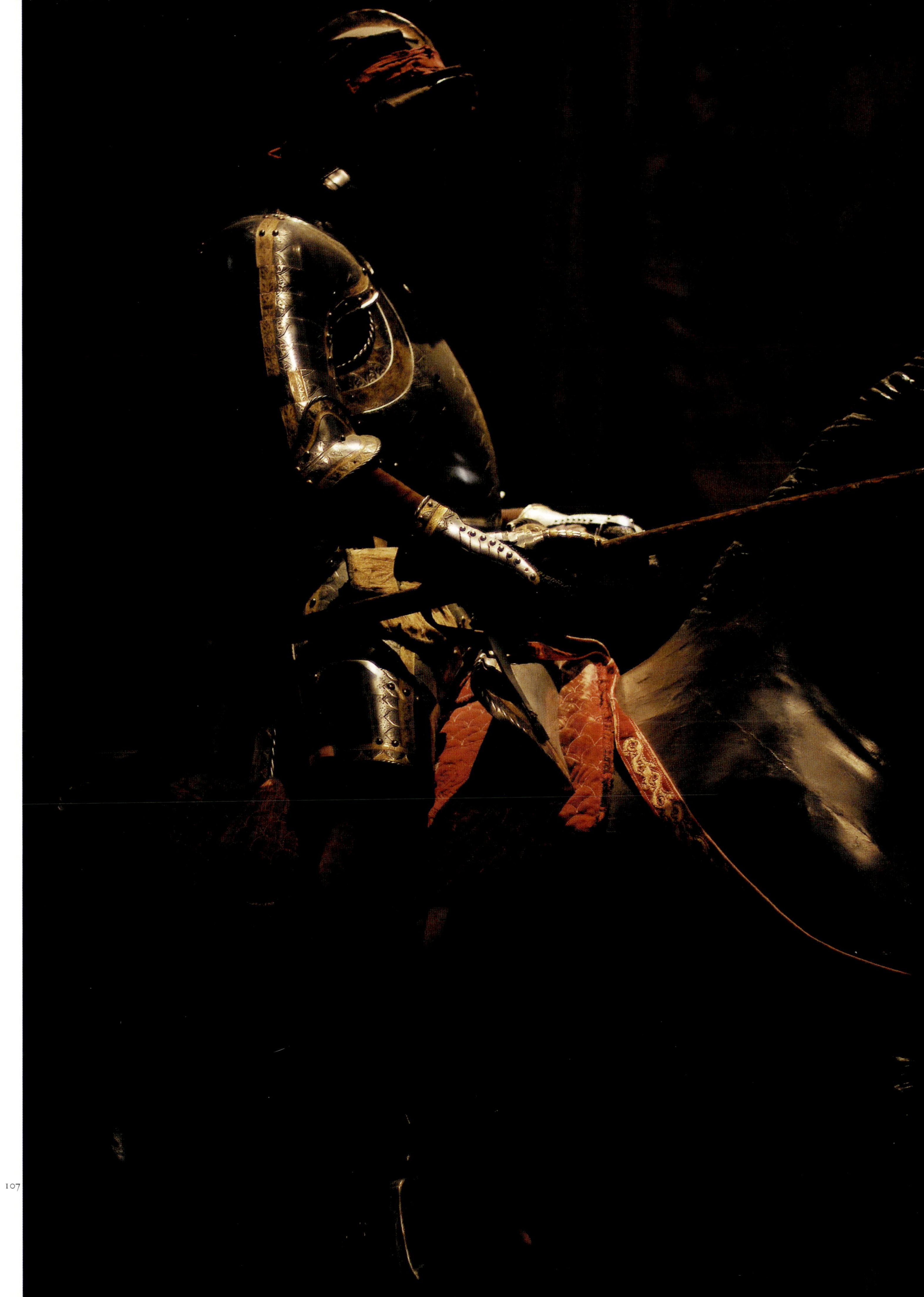

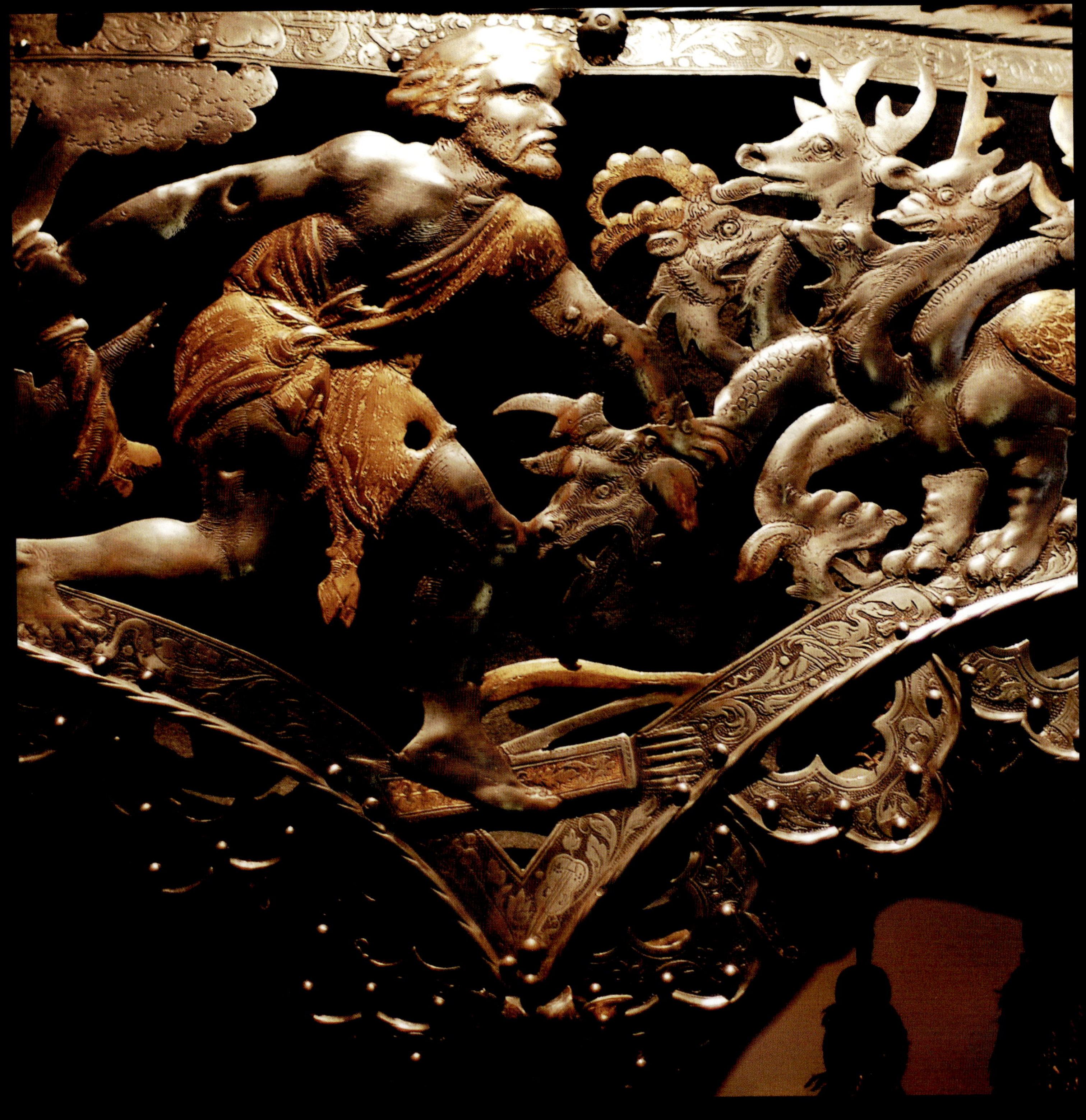

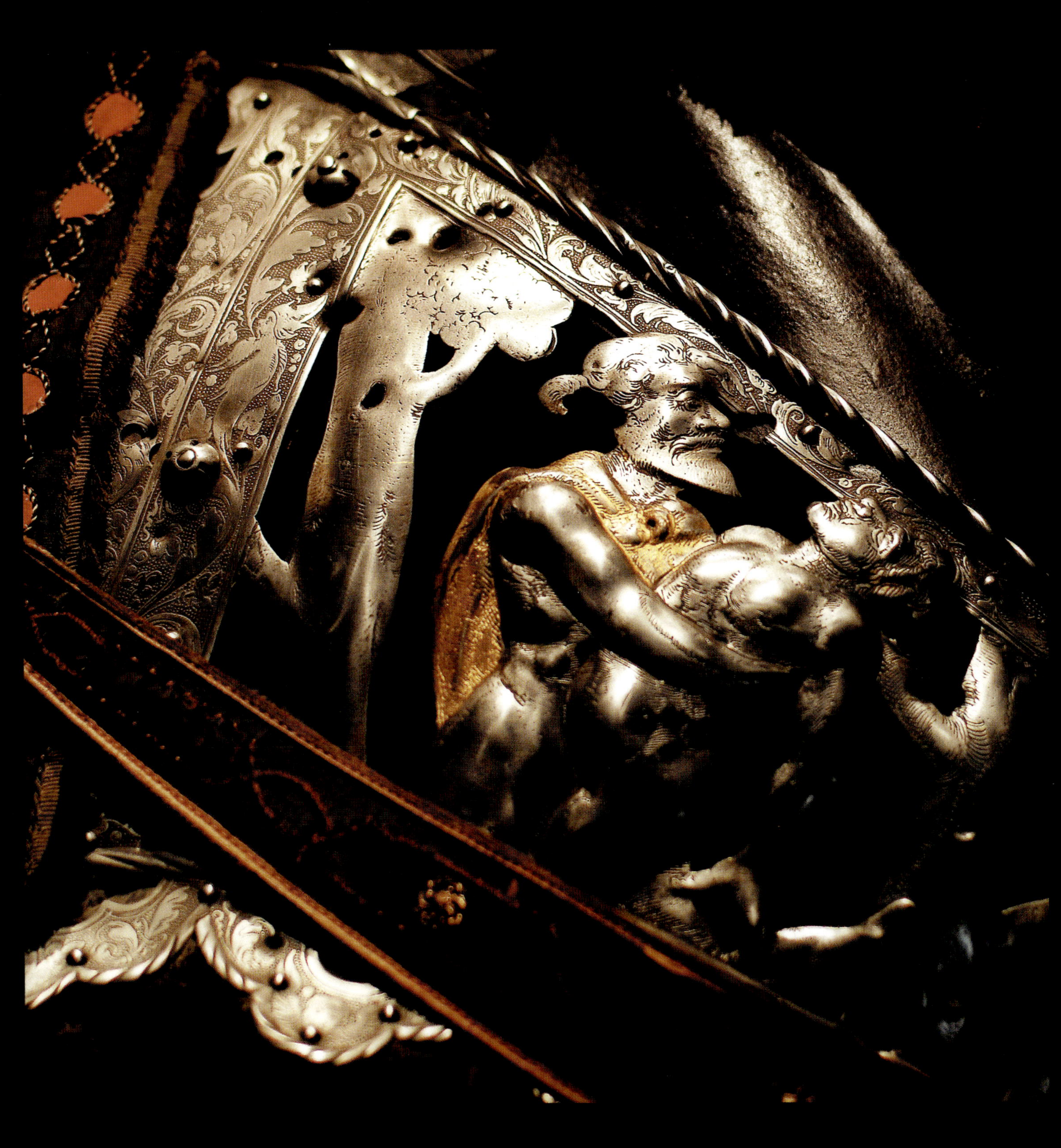

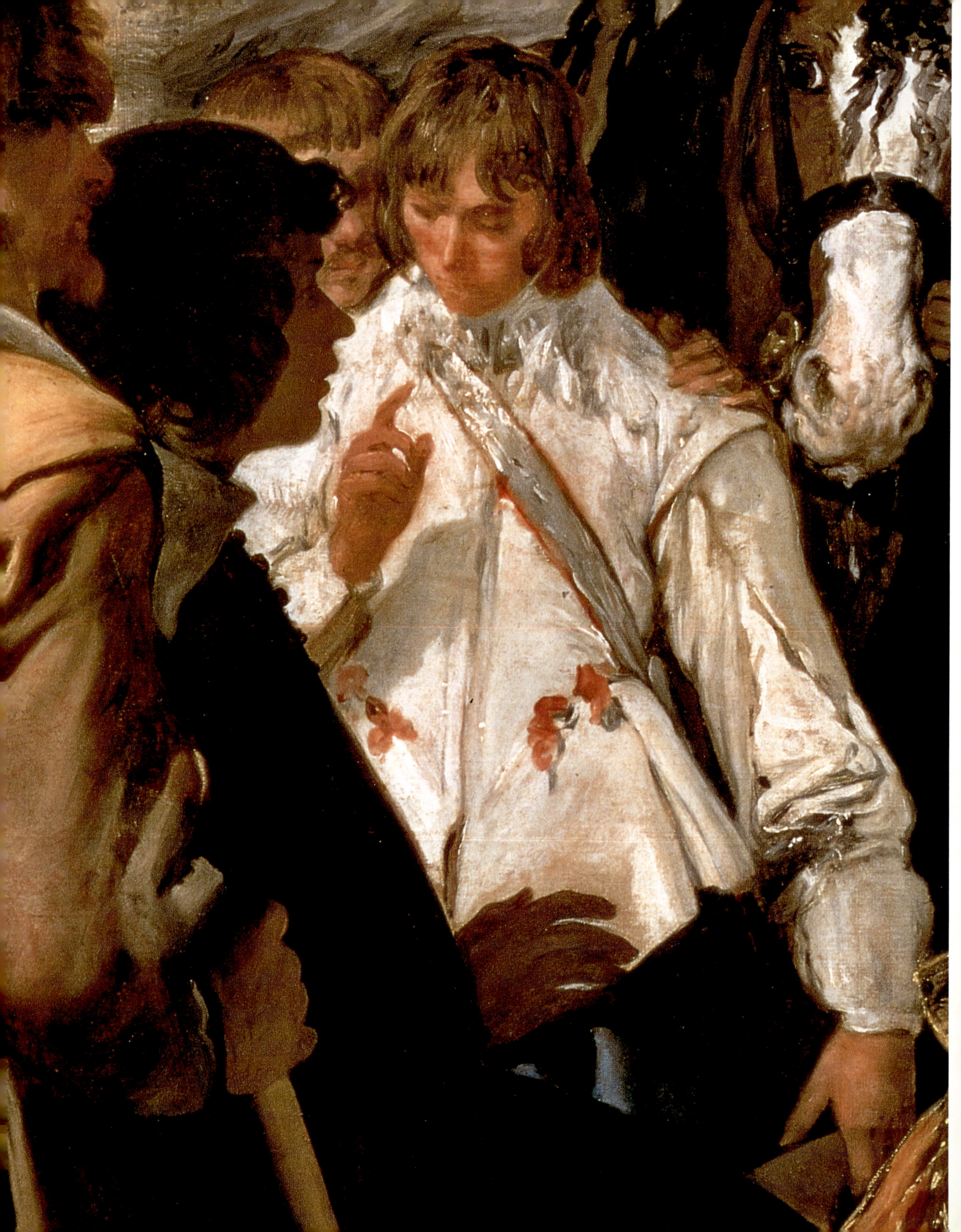

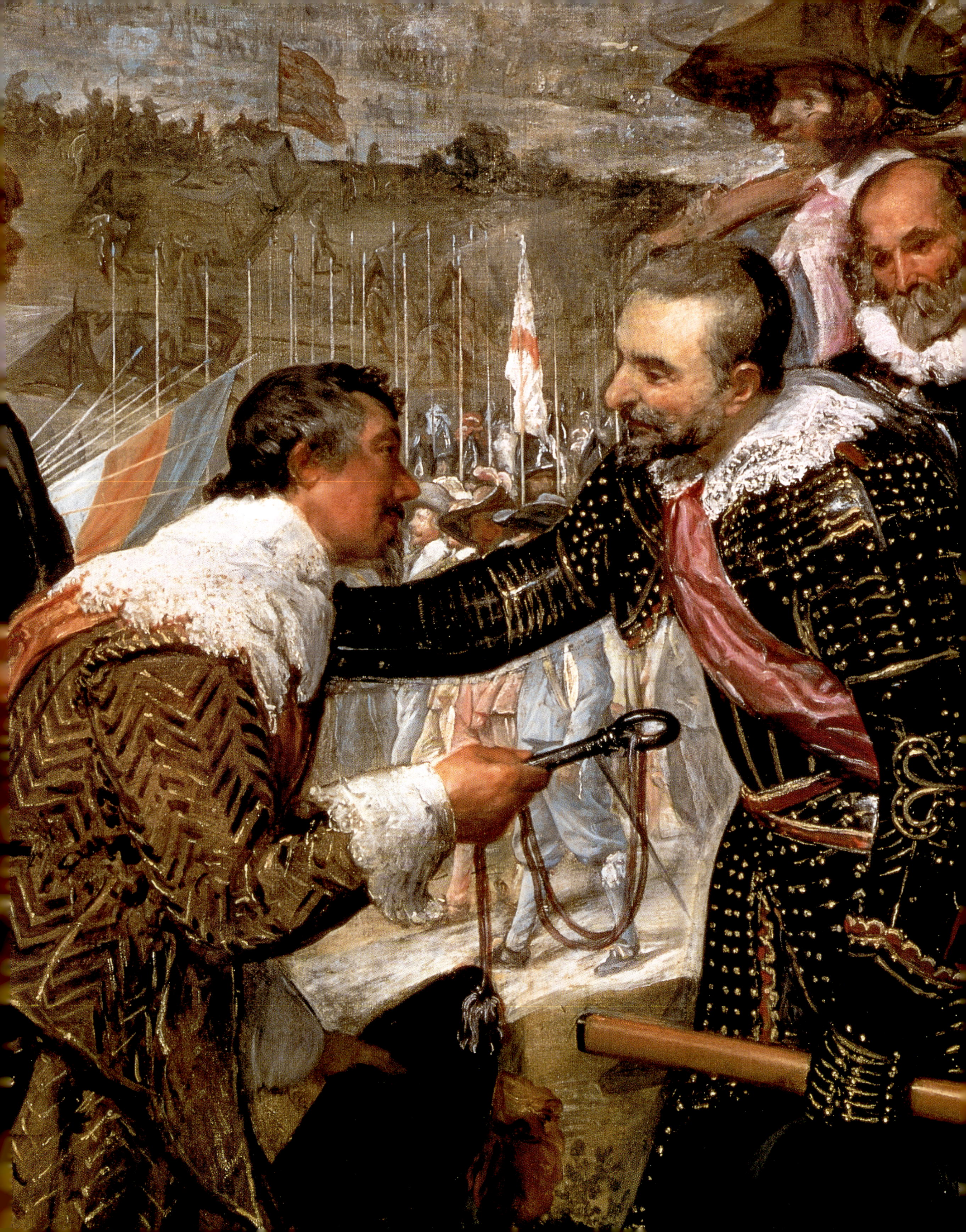

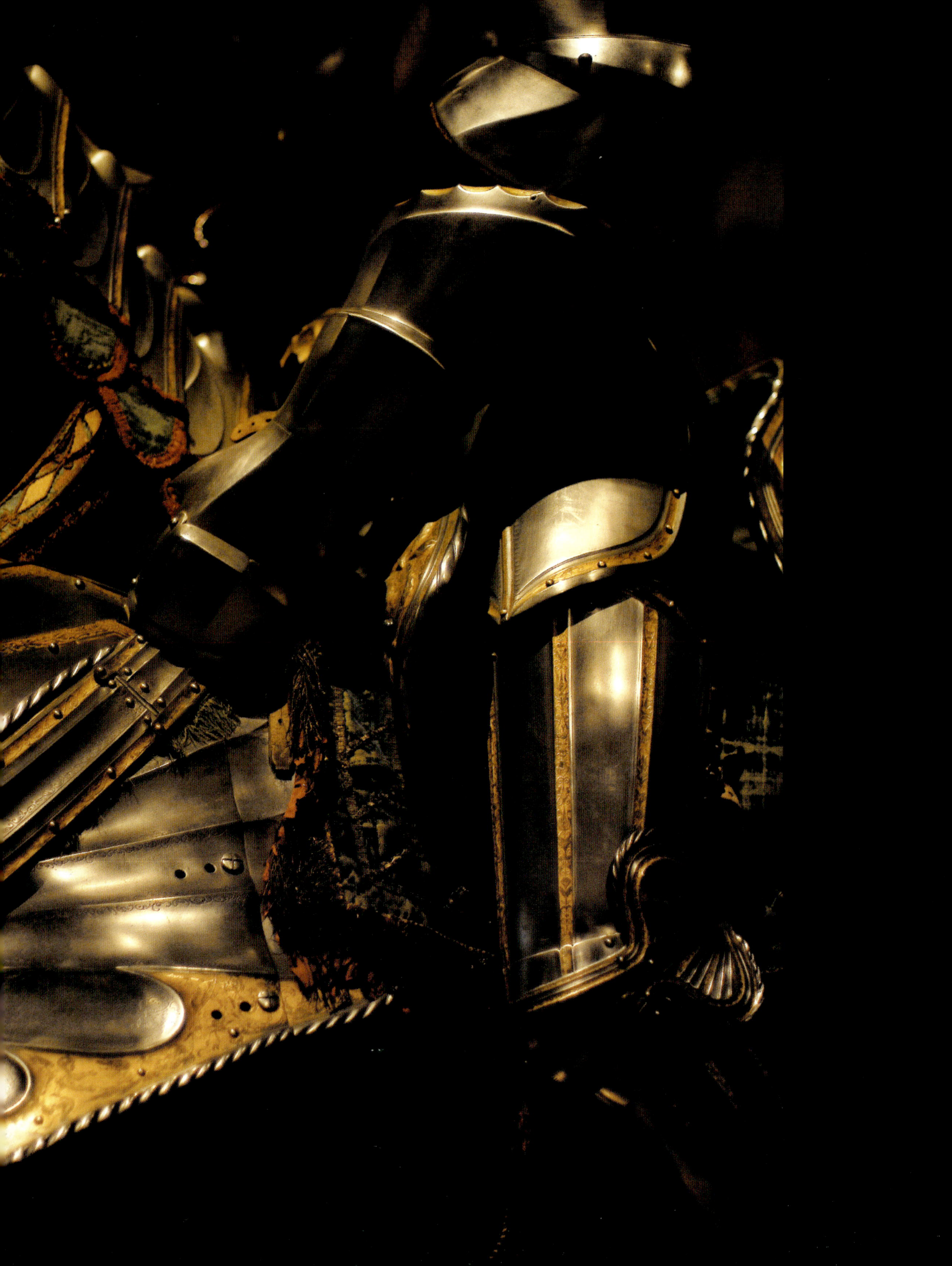

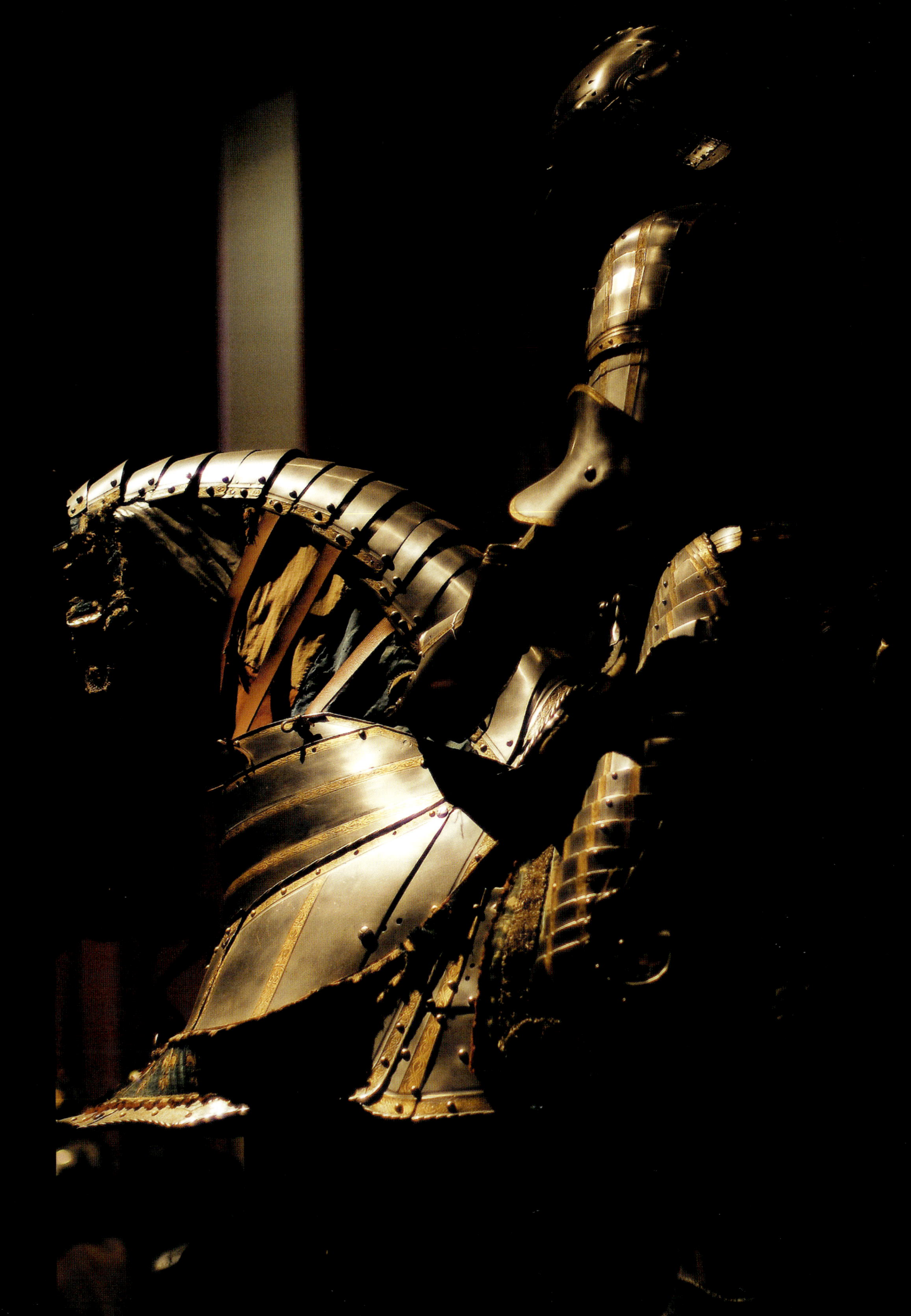

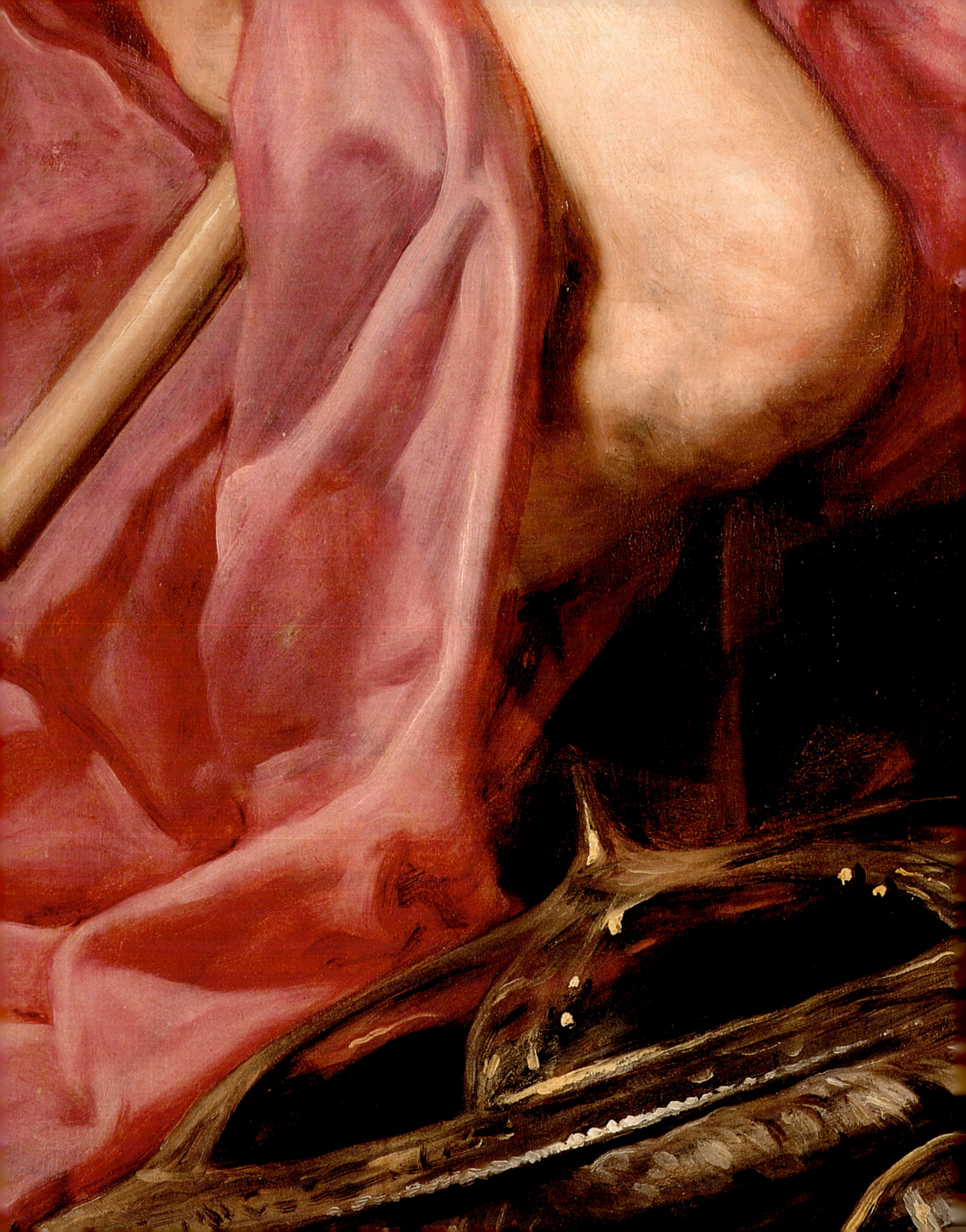

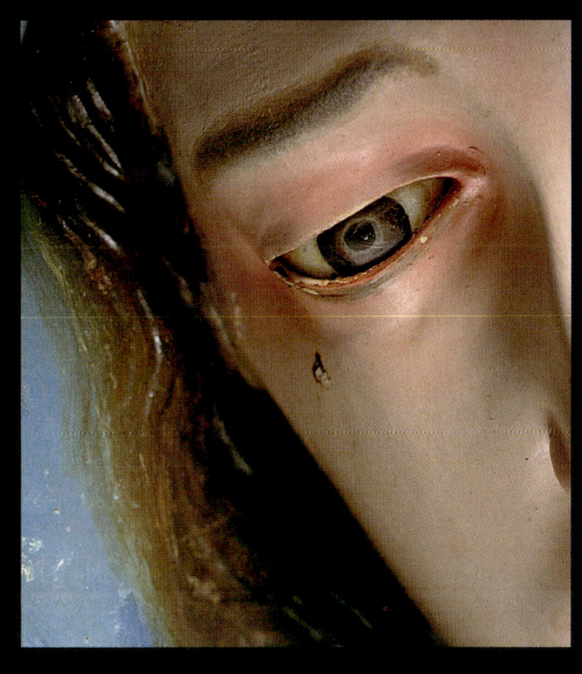

FLESH SUBLIMATED BY PRAYER

V

FLESH SUBLIMATED BY PRAYER

PRECEDING PAGE:
115. Attributed to Pedro de Mena
c. 1680
Detail of *The Sorrowing Virgin*,
carved and polychromed wood.
Museo de Bellas Artes, Granada.

RIGHT:
116. Alonso Cano
c. 1655
Detail of *Saint John of God*,
carved and polychromed wood.
Museo de Bellas Artes, Granada.

FOLLOWING PAGES:
117 and 118. José de Ribera
1639
Details of *The Martyrdom of Saint Philip*.
Museo Nacional del Prado, Madrid.

119. José de Mora
c. 1675–1700
Detail of *The Sorrowing Virgin*,
carved and polychromed wood.
Museo de Bellas Artes, Granada.

120. Attributed to Pedro de Mena
c. 1680
Detail of *The Sorrowing Virgin*,
carved and polychromed wood.
Museo de Bellas Artes, Granada.

121. Pedro de Mena
1663
Detail of *Saint Francis of Assisi*,
carved and polychromed wood.
Treasury of Toledo Cathedral.

122. Francisco de Zurbarán
c. 1630
Detail of *Saint Francis in Ecstasy*,
carved and polychromed wood.
National Gallery, London.

123. Francisco de Zurbarán
1639
The Appearance of Christ to Friar Andrés Salmerón.
Sacristy of the monastery, Guadalupe.

THE COUNTER-REFORMATION encouraged Catholics to experience their faith by sharing Christ's suffering on the cross, as did the holy women who washed the blood and wept over the lacerated body of the Savior who died to redeem our sins. The faithful ardently sought union with God through the shared pain and suffering of daily life, through contemplation and love, as did Saint Teresa of Ávila and Saint John of the Cross. The latter lamented in his *Spiritual Canticle:*

> Where have You hidden Yourself,
> And abandoned me to my sorrow, O my Beloved!
> You have fled like the hart,
> Having wounded me.

Until the Council of Trent, indulgence of the flesh was sublimated by the ladder of prayer. On the tenth and topmost rung of that ladder the soul, abandoning flesh, becomes one with and fully possesses God, quenching its thirst with the light and fire of the lamps of the Almighty. After the Council, martyrdom of the flesh was newly sought after, echoing as it did the sufferings of the early Christians. The Church's exemplars were martyrs and hermits like Saint Teresa, who, unable to find martyrdom, wished to be a hermit. Martyrdom and mortification of the flesh served as weapons in the crusade against the reformers Martin Luther and John Calvin, and against those who persisted in ridiculing the power of holy relics, arguing that they were just dry bones, like those of all the dead, destined to become dust and ashes. And examples of martyrdom also brought pagans of the New World and the Far East into the fold of the Cross.

Images of tormented flesh and visions of the soul alluded to the salvation of mankind and comforted the human spirit. The brushes and chisels of painters and sculptors became stained with the blood of flayed, decapitated bodies, raised up to be crucified and transfixed by arrows. The artists expressed on canvas and in wood the suffering and pain of those who, by turning their eyes to the heavens, toward God, saw the path to light through the tenebrous death they embraced like a skull in their hands.

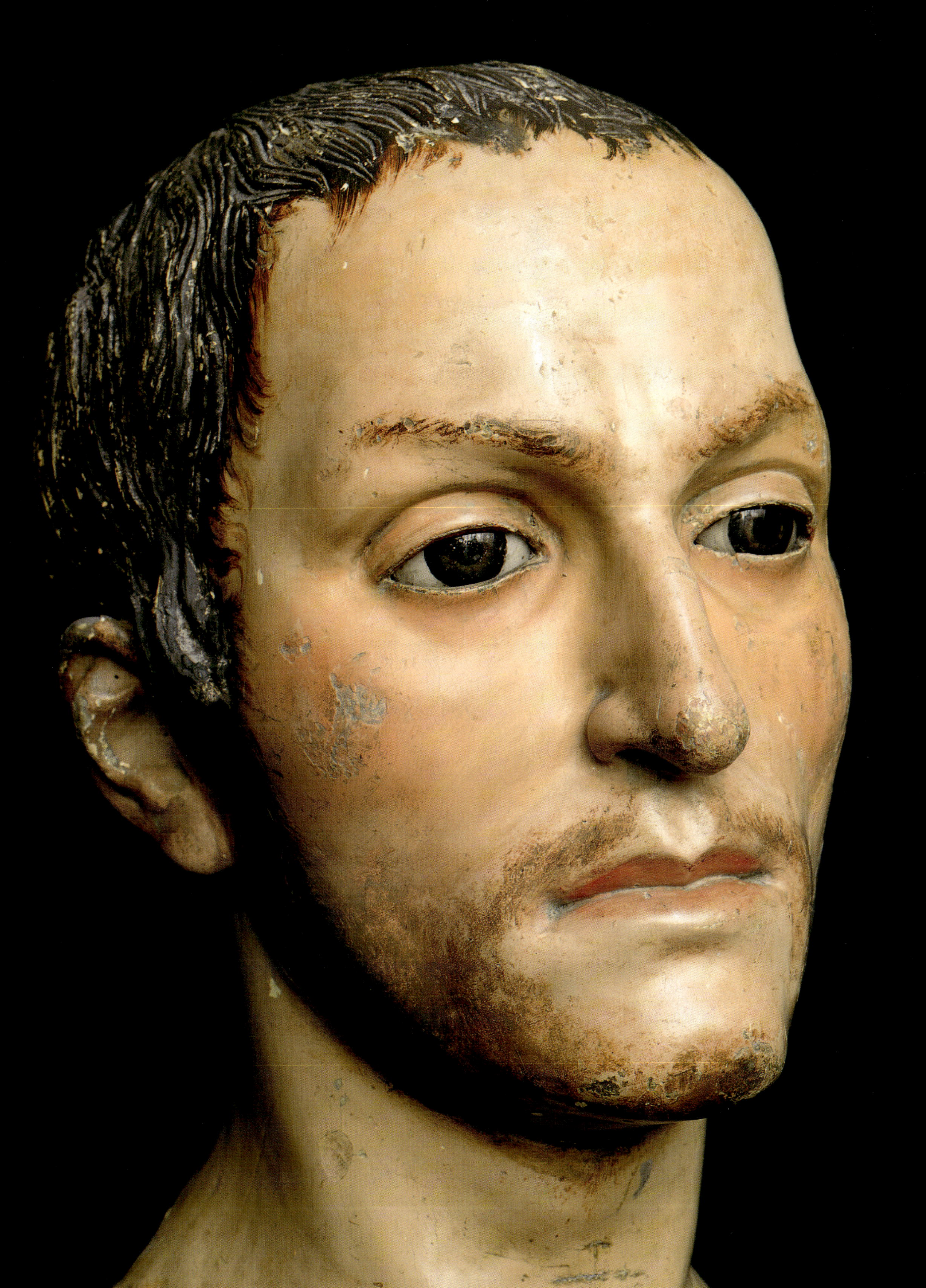

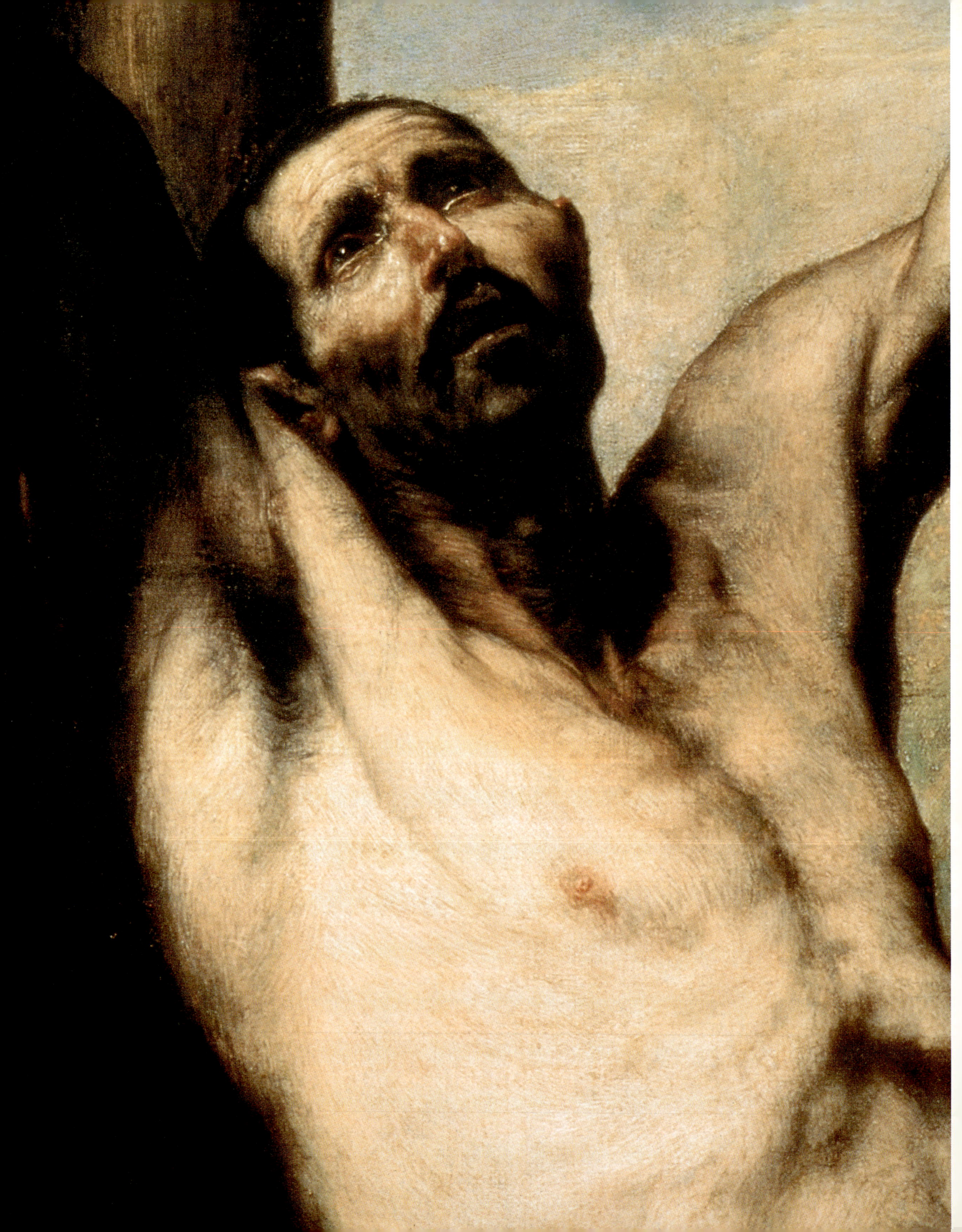

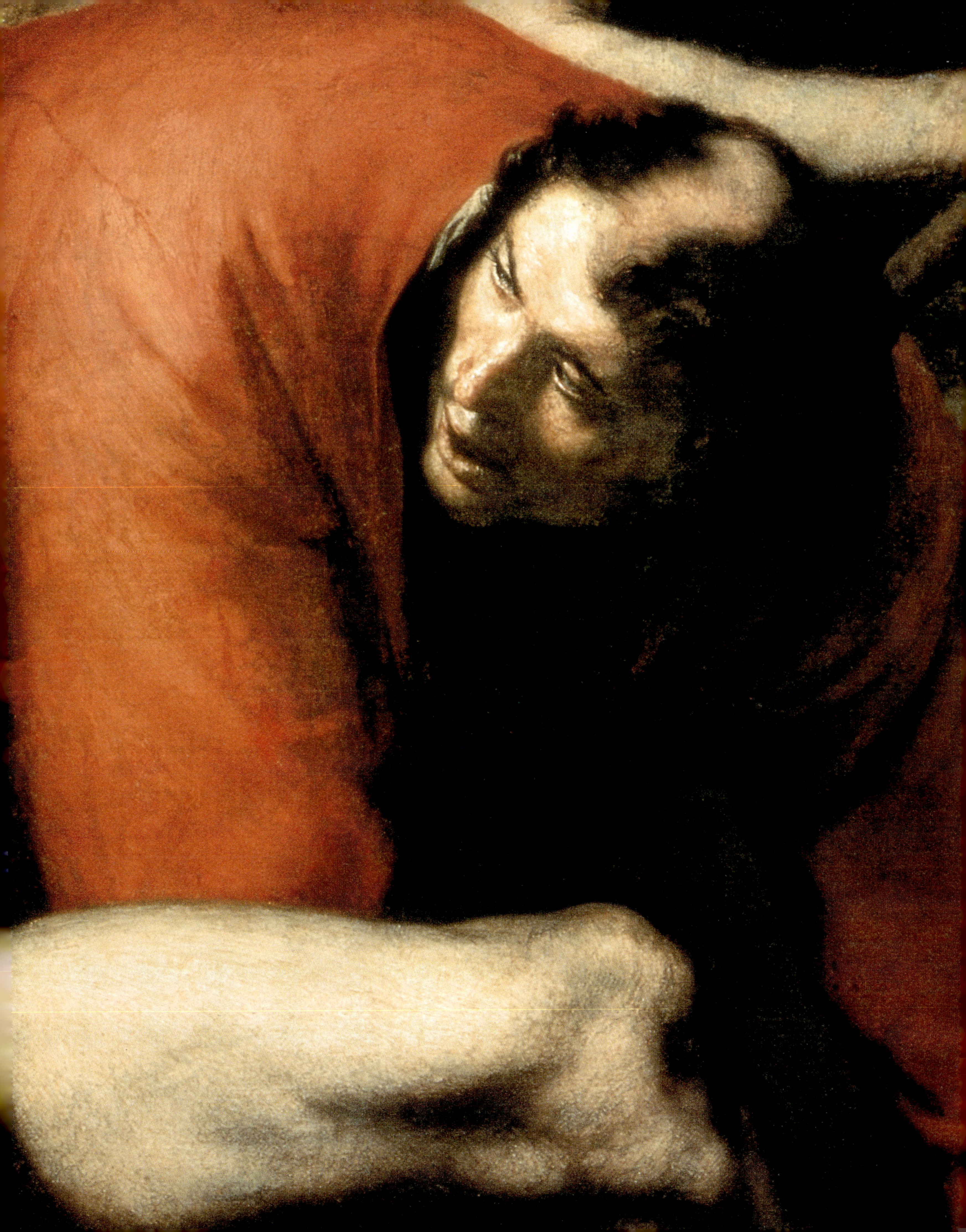

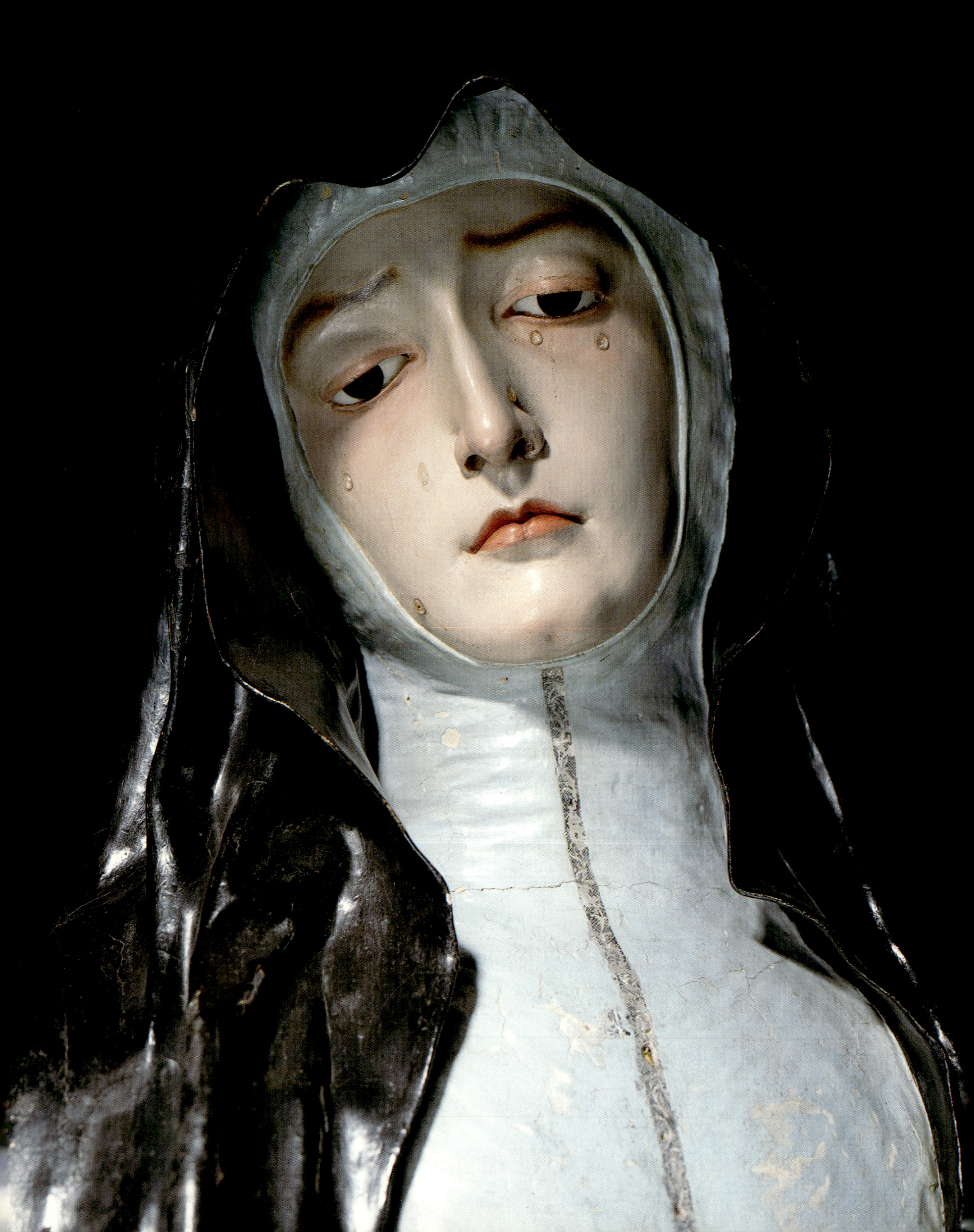

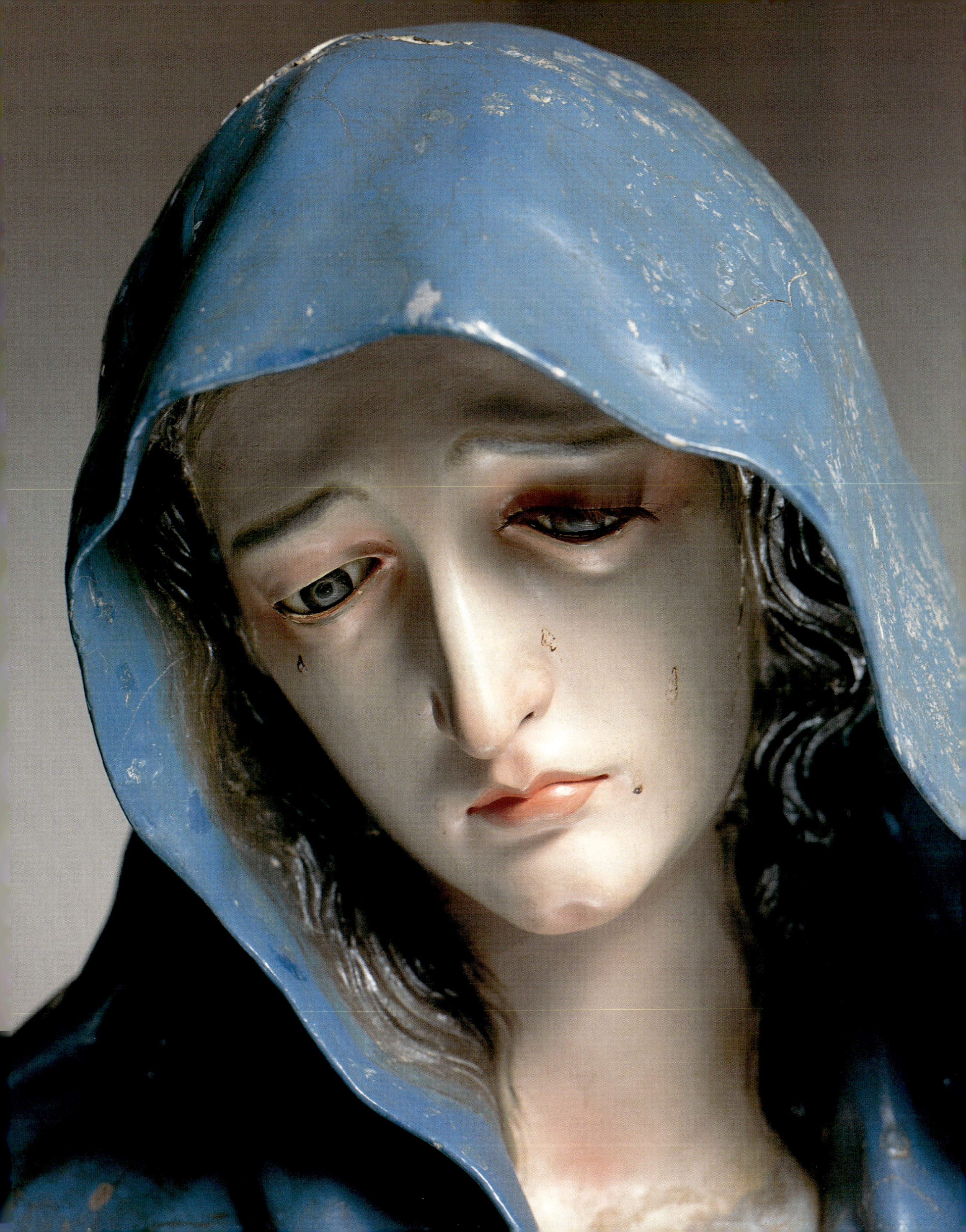

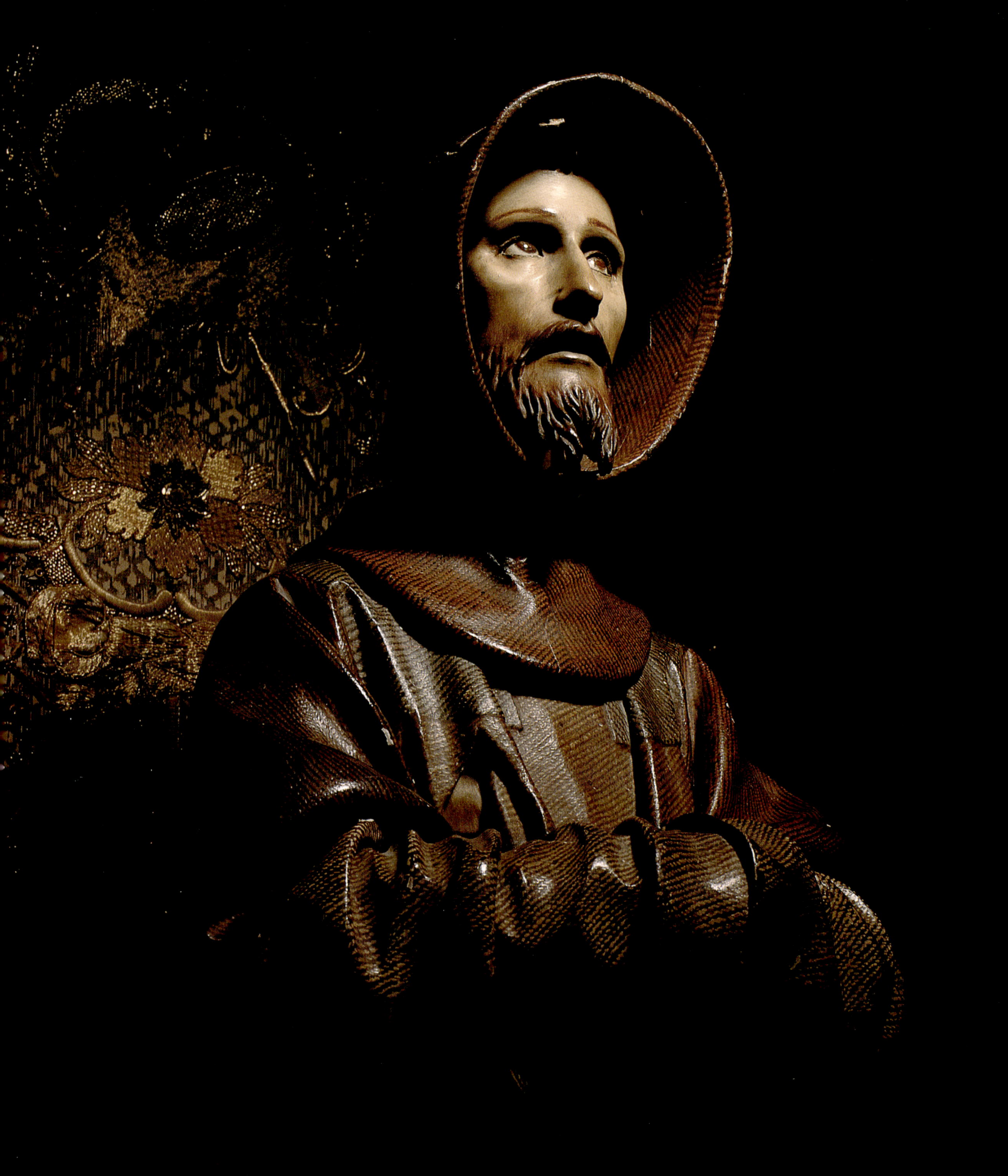

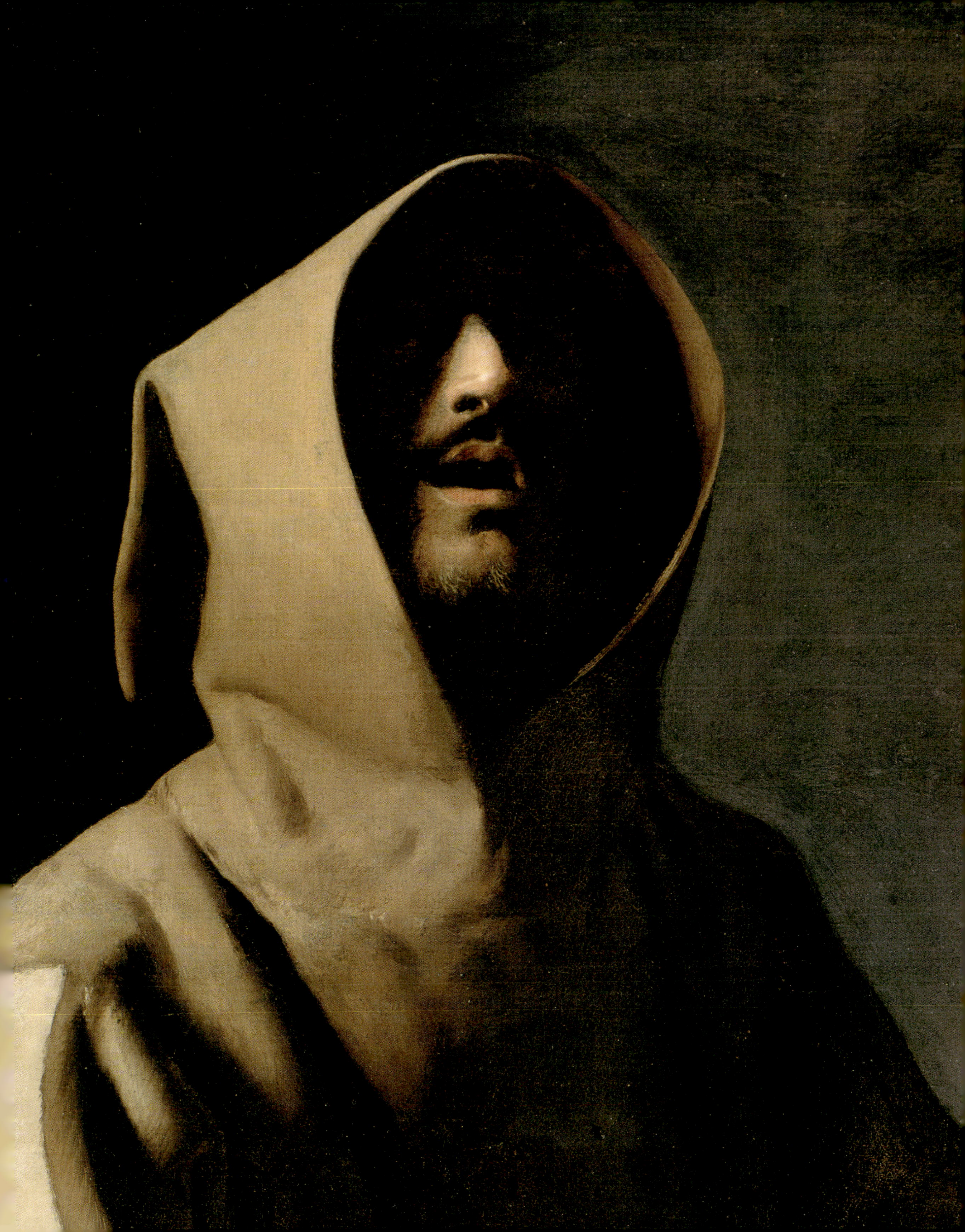

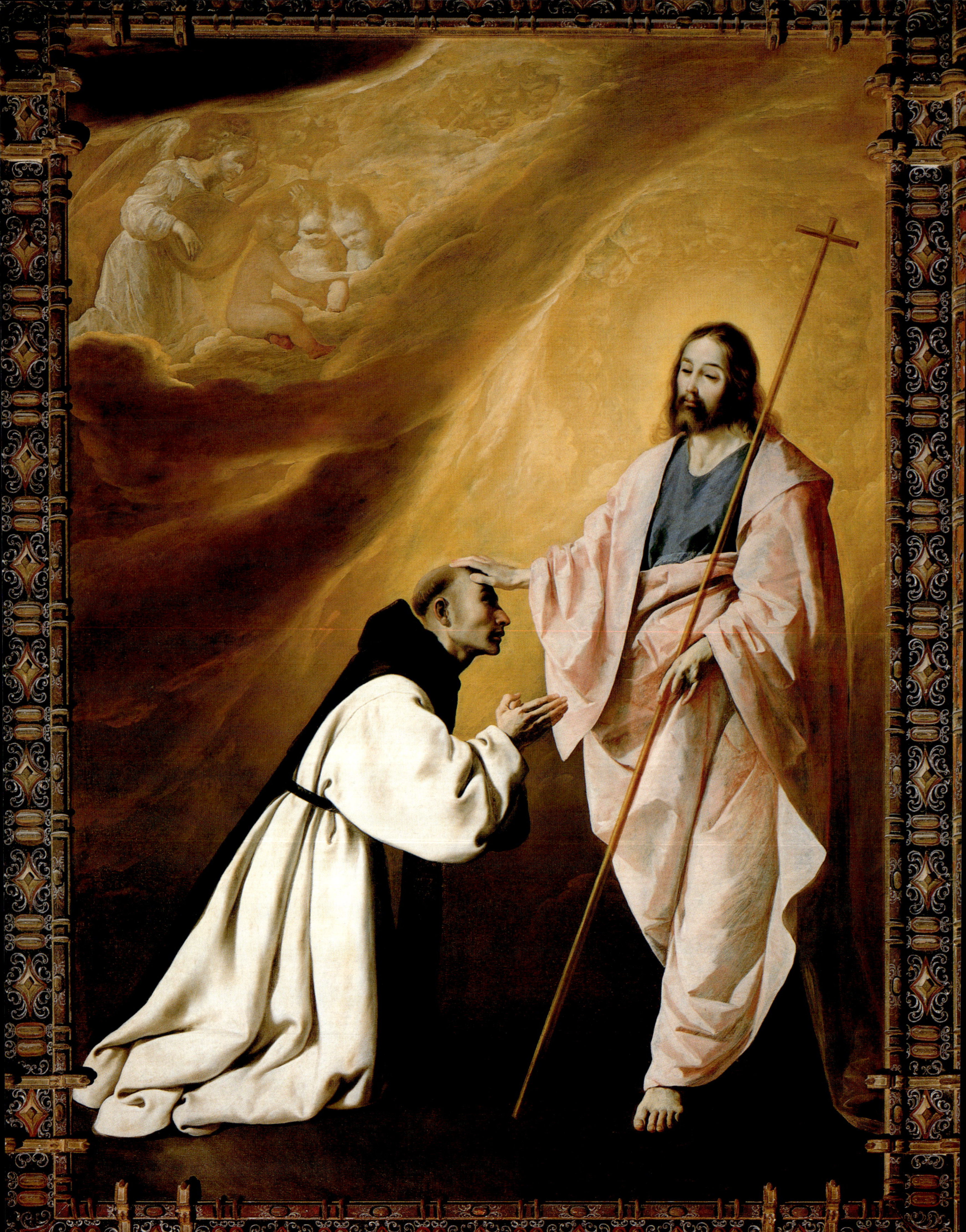

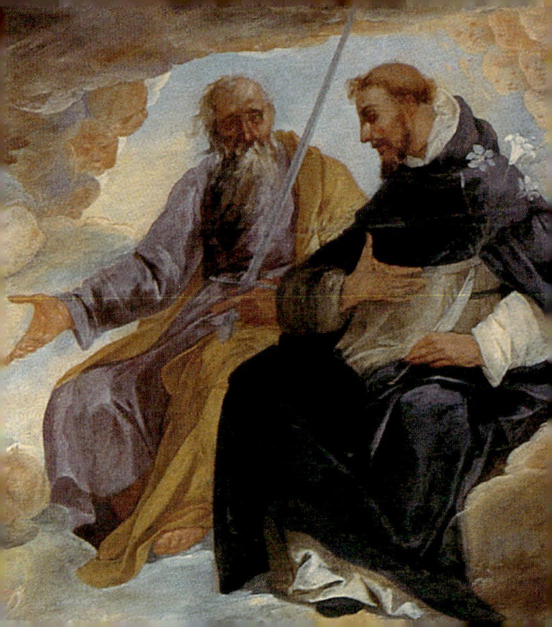

VI

SAINTS AND SINNERS

ACCORDING TO THE Counter-Reformation thought that informed the Spanish Golden Age, a man's encounter with Christ was the greatest moment of his life. This was as true for the humblest of men as it was for God's chosen ones who became saints. The many individuals who were granted sainthood during this period were both symbols and instruments of the renewal of the Church and its splendor. Some of the saints sought grace, like Saint Francis and Saint Catherine of Siena, both of whom bore the stigmata of Christ. Others, like Saint Anthony of Padua, longed to hold the Christ Child in their arms. And others sought an ecstatic vision of God himself. More than any other episode in their lives or any miracle they may have performed, the vision of God granted the highest degree of saintliness and the immeasurable joy described by the sixteenth-century mystic Saint John of the Cross.

The churches, chapels, and colleges of Jesuits, Dominicans, Franciscans, Carmelites, Augustinians, Mercedarians, and Carthusians—all the religious institutions that strove to make Catholicism flourish—saw their walls gradually covered with visionary saints struck by the love of God. In some cases, the saints had not only seen God, but had themselves appeared as visions to the faithful and had served as guides to salvation. With a rhetorical and dramatic appearance as intense as the language of the sermons of the era, the apotheoses and triumphs of the saints no longer featured men and women with agonized expressions beseeching God to hear their pleas. The saints were no longer pictured as men and women desperate to be freed from the prison of earthly life in order to finally reach heaven. These saints shrug off their worldly existence, thanks to their blessed state, to appear before us in timeless spaces as intermediaries, as powerful advocates for those who, despite their humble condition, may also attain celestial glory.

PRECEDING PAGE:
124. Francisco de Zurbarán
1631
Saints Paul and Dominic, detail of
Apotheosis of Saint Thomas Aquinas,
Colegio de Santo Tomás de Aquino, Seville.
Museo de Bellas Artes, Seville.

RIGHT:
125. Francisco de Zurbarán
1639
The Glory of Saint Jerome.
Chapel of San Jerónimo, sacristy of the monastery, Guadalupe.

FOLLOWING PAGES:
126. Francisco de Zurbarán
1631
The Apotheosis of Saint Thomas Aquinas,
Colegio de Santo Tomás de Aquino, Seville.
Museo de Bellas Artes, Seville.

127. Francisco de Zurbarán
1631
Detail of Charles V kneeling in
The Apotheosis of Saint Thomas Aquinas,
Colegio de Santo Tomás de Aquino, Seville.
Museo de Bellas Artes, Seville.

128. Claudio Coello
1664
Detail of *The Triumph of Saint Augustine*, Convento de los Agustinos Recoletos de Alcalá de Henares.
Museo del Prado, Madrid.

129. Claudio Coello
1664
The Triumph of Saint Augustine, Convento de los Agustinos Recoletos de Alcalá de Henares.
Museo del Prado, Madrid.

130. Luca Giordano
1692–93
Fresco above the main staircase.
Real Monasterio de San Lorenzo, El Escorial.

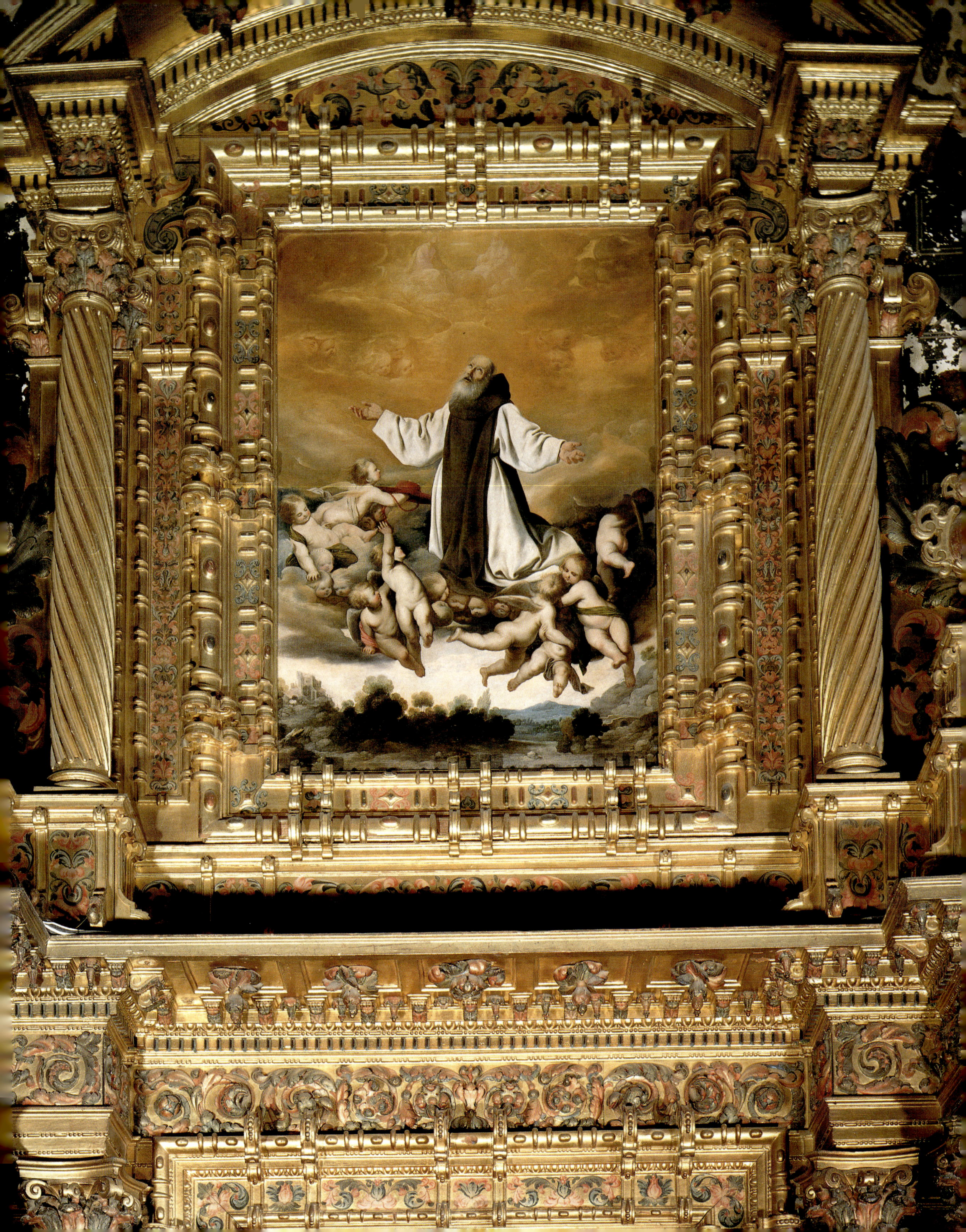

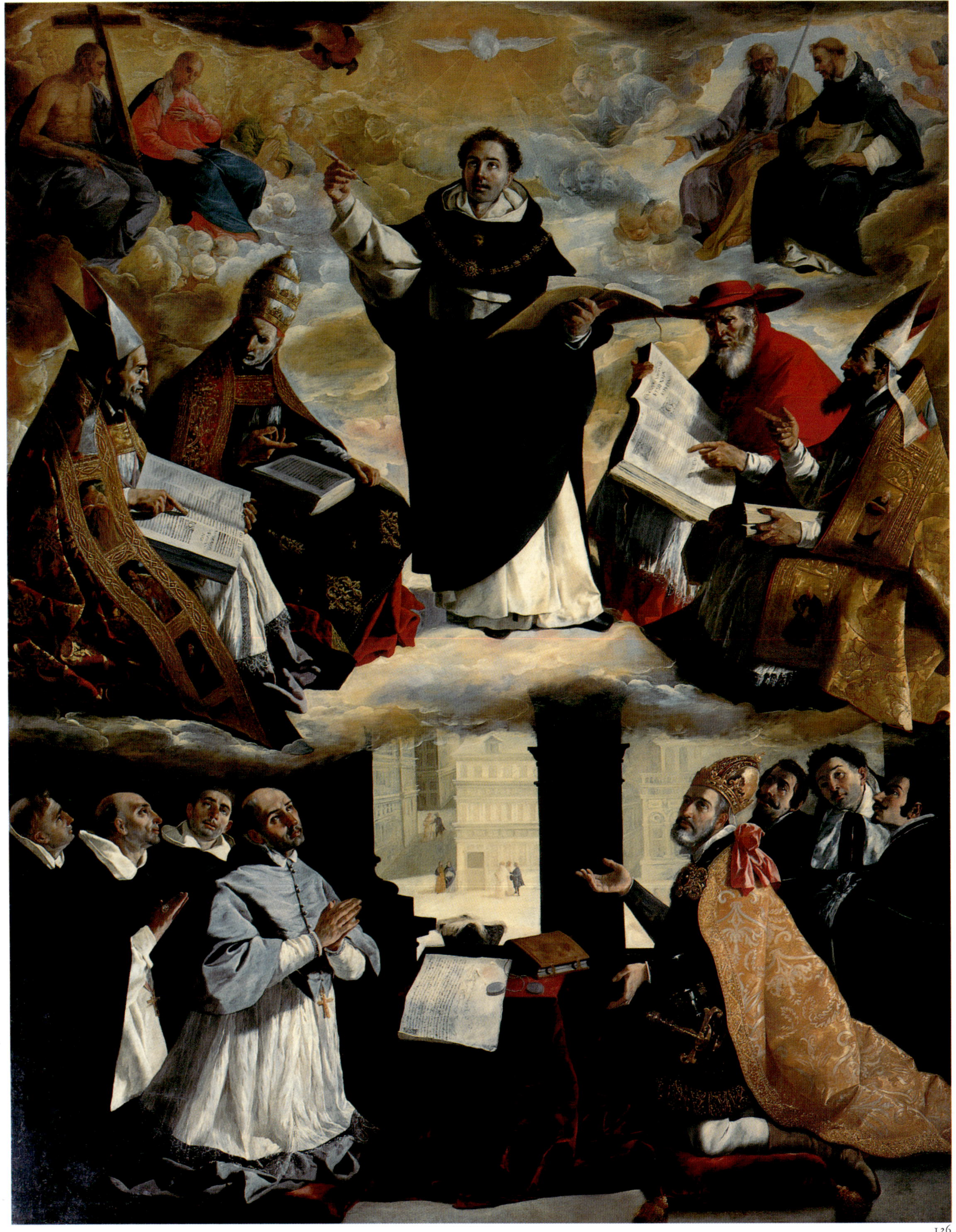

126

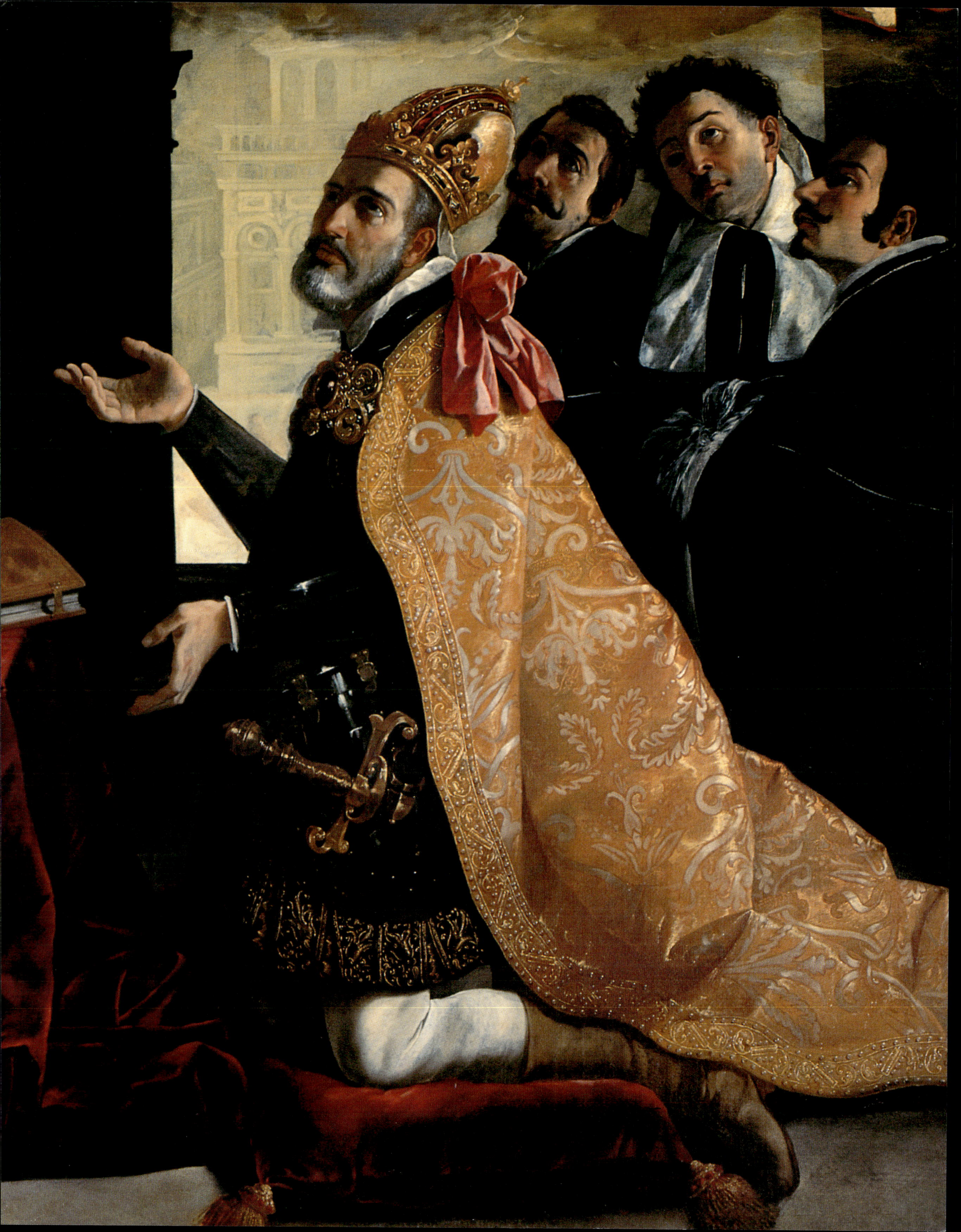

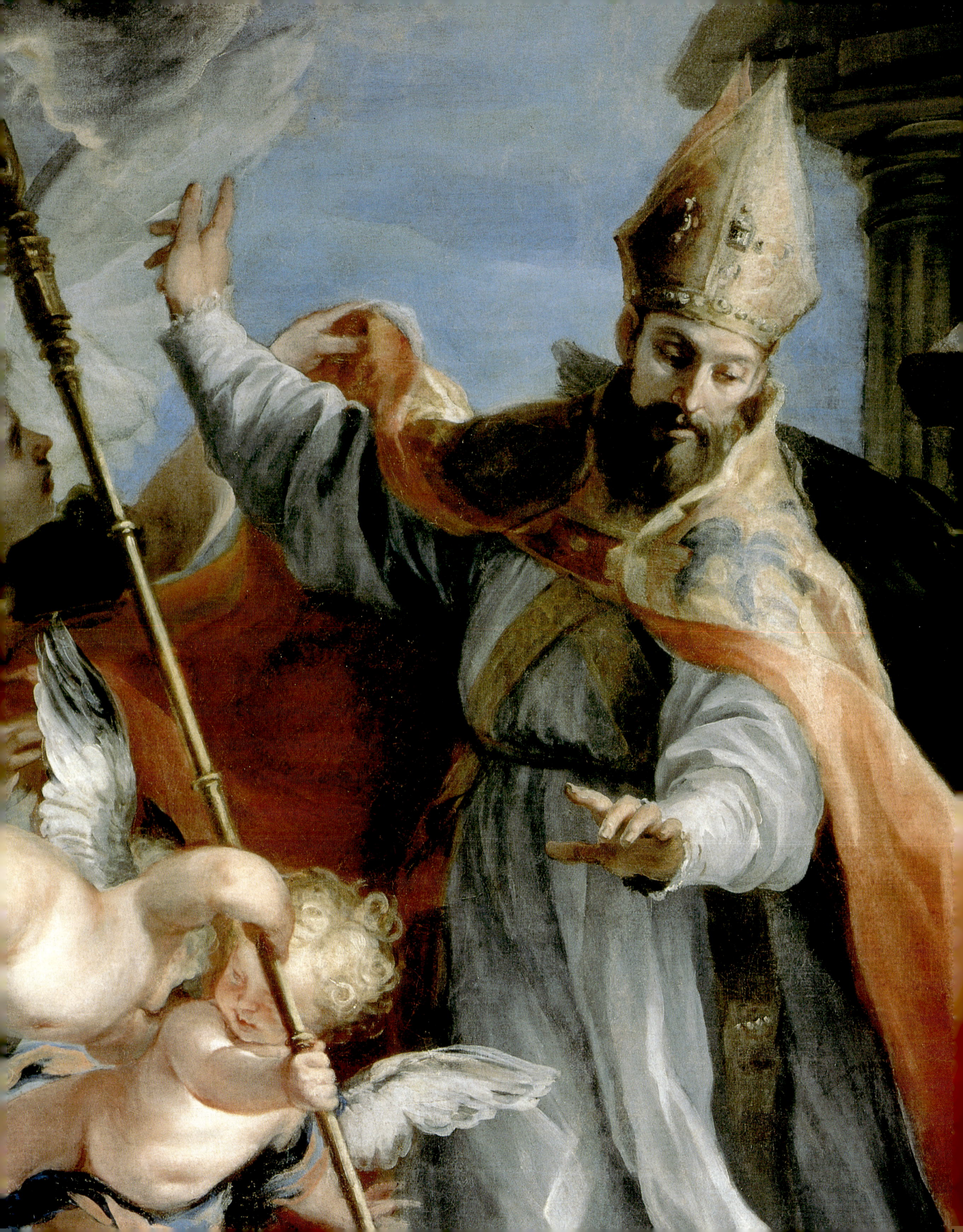

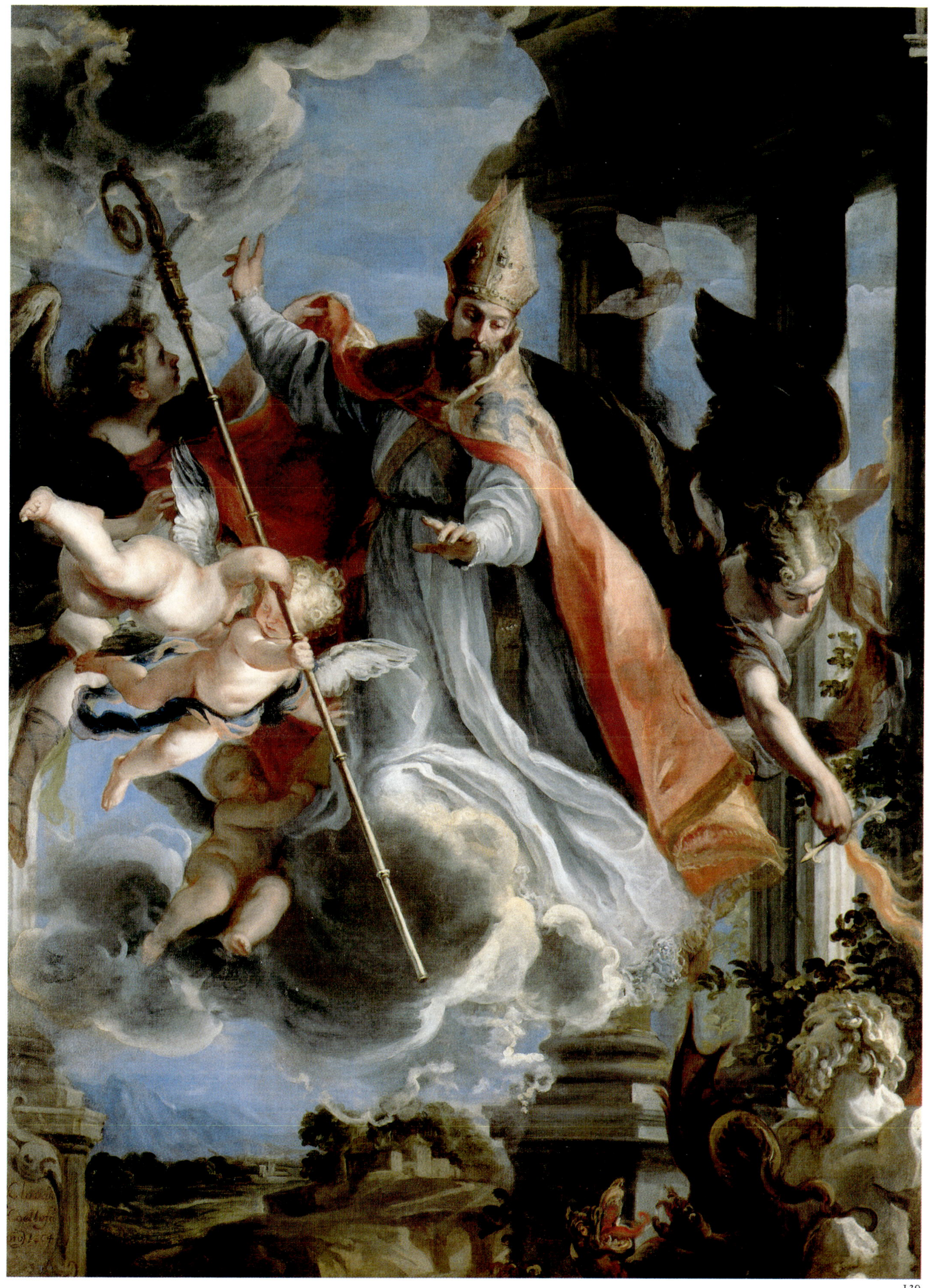

129

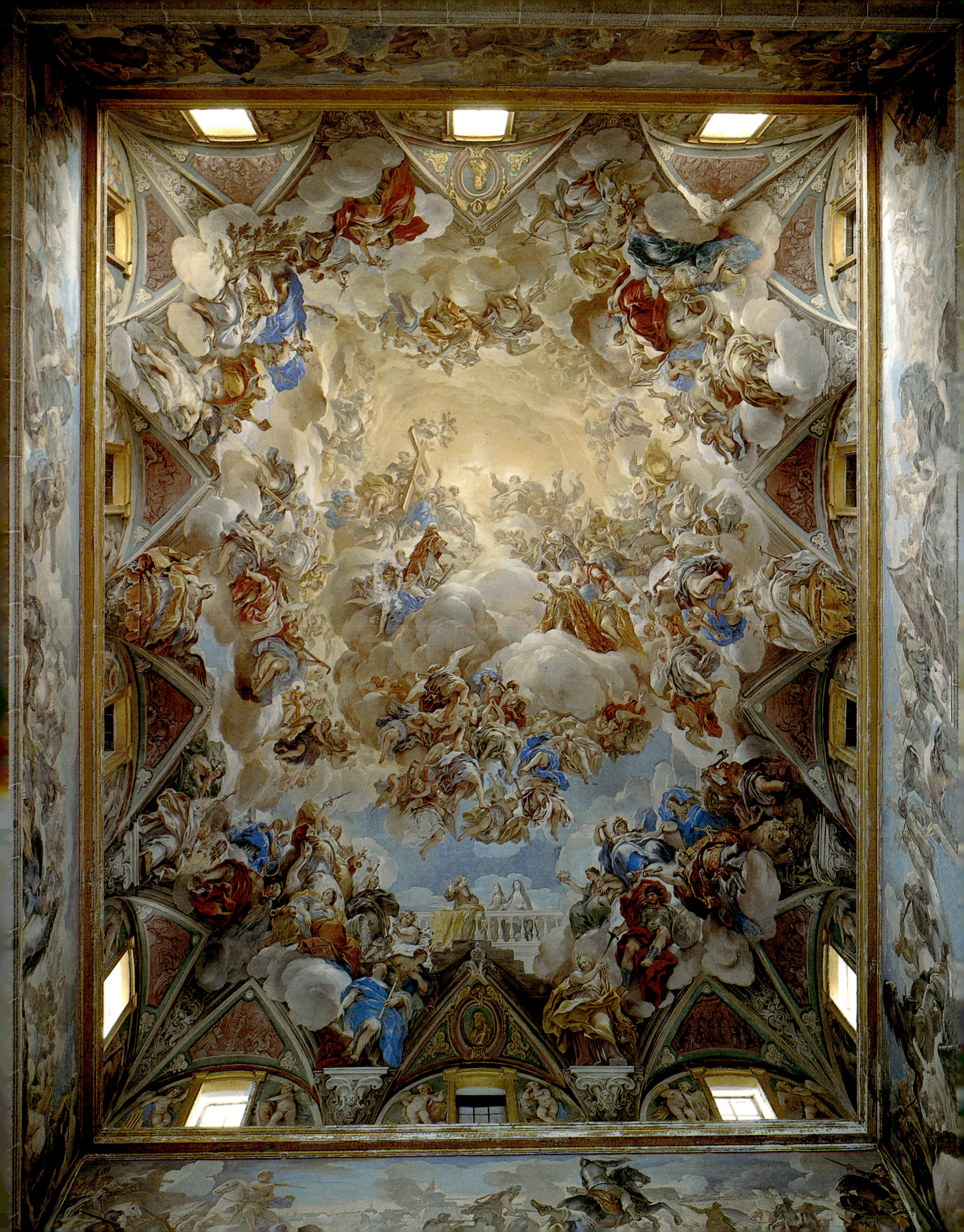

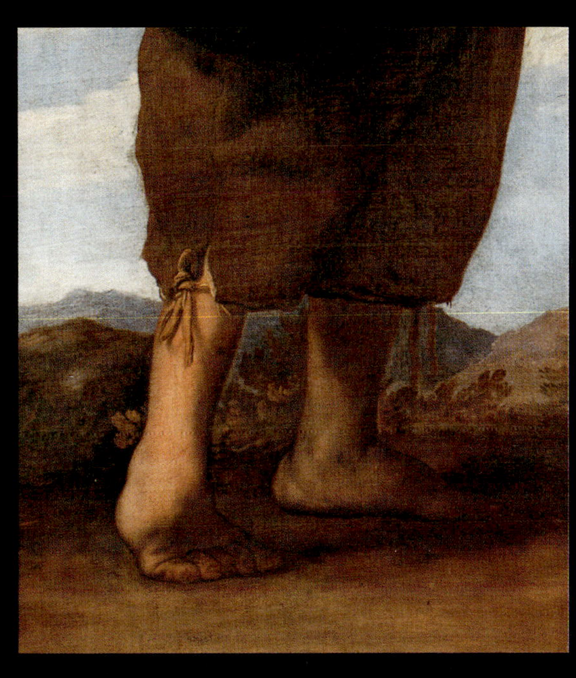

BEGGARS, JESTERS, AND PRODIGIES

VII

BEGGARS, JESTERS, AND PRODIGIES

THE CROPS AND LIVESTOCK produced in rural Spain continued to be the driving forces behind the economy of the country, but life in the Golden Age was dominated by the cities—Seville (which even in decline was still a center of trade), Valencia, Alicante, Barcelona, Toledo, Segovia, Salamanca, Zaragoza, Santiago de Compostela, Valladolid (for five years during the reign of Philip III the capital of Spain), and, above all, Madrid. Home to the royal court, Madrid had no more than 15,000 inhabitants at the beginning of the sixteenth century, yet by the early decades of the seventeenth its population topped 150,000. At least until the mid-seventeenth century, cities continued to grow at a rapid pace. City dwellers lived in either palaces or hovels, and the ostentation of the few did not cover up the poverty of the rest.

In the cities, and especially at court, there was plenty of food, drink, fine clothes, adornments, whims, amusements, spellbinding plays, and jesters, those comic characters immortalized by the brushes of Ribera (ill. 135), Velázquez (ill. 132), and the other artists who portrayed them. Most were men, although there were also some women; they entertained kings, queens, and courtiers with their clowning and grotesque and extravagant gestures, emphasized by their physical abnormalities, their subtle intelligence, or, more rarely, their mental retardation.

The court city of Madrid—regarded at the time as a deceptive entrancement, an alluring falsehood, and a labyrinth of intrigues—also numbered among its inhabitants a swarm of poverty-stricken though quick-witted people: cadgers, cajolers, intriguers, thieves, scoundrels, hypocrites, and idlers who lived in the shadow of the rich and set out to live off the work of others, and slaves (black from sub-Saharan Africa or white from the Magreb), who were ruthlessly exploited. All these people played the role of extras in a city in which foreigners, as they were warned in the *Guide and Warnings for Foreigners Who Come to Madrid,* written in 1621 by Antonio Liñan y Verdugo, needed to be alert to the risks of taking lodging in low-class districts, choosing their friends, strolling through the streets, engaging in conversation, or amusing themselves with empty pleasures.

PRECEDING PAGE:
131. José de Ribera
1642
Detail of *The Clubfooted Boy.*
Musée du Louvre, Paris.

RIGHT:
132. Diego Velázquez
1644
The Dwarf Don Diego de Acedo (El Primo).
Museo Nacional del Prado, Madrid.

133. Bartolomé Esteban Murillo
c. 1645–50
Beggar Boy Picking Lice.
Musée du Louvre, Paris.

134. Bartolomé Esteban Murillo
c. 1668
Saint Thomas of Villanueva Distributing Alms,
side chapel of the church of the Capuchin Monastery, Seville.
Museo de Bellas Artes, Seville.

135. José de Ribera
1642
The Clubfooted Boy.
Musée du Louvre, Paris.

136. Diego Velázquez
c. 1643–45
Detail of *Portrait of Francisco Lezcano (el Niño de Vallecas).*
Museo Nacional del Prado, Madrid.

137. Diego Velázquez
c. 1645
Sebastián de Morra.
Museo Nacional del Prado, Madrid.

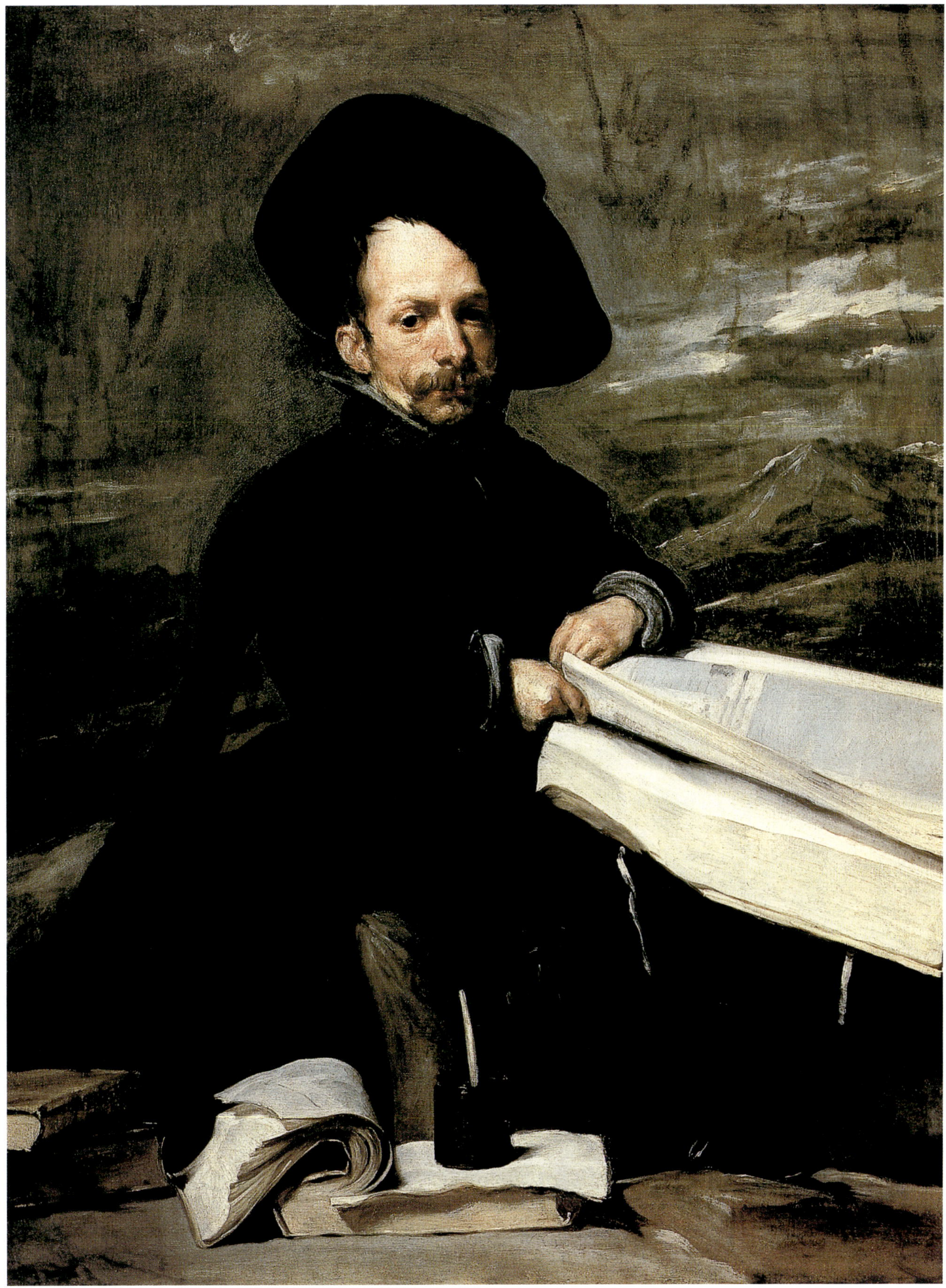

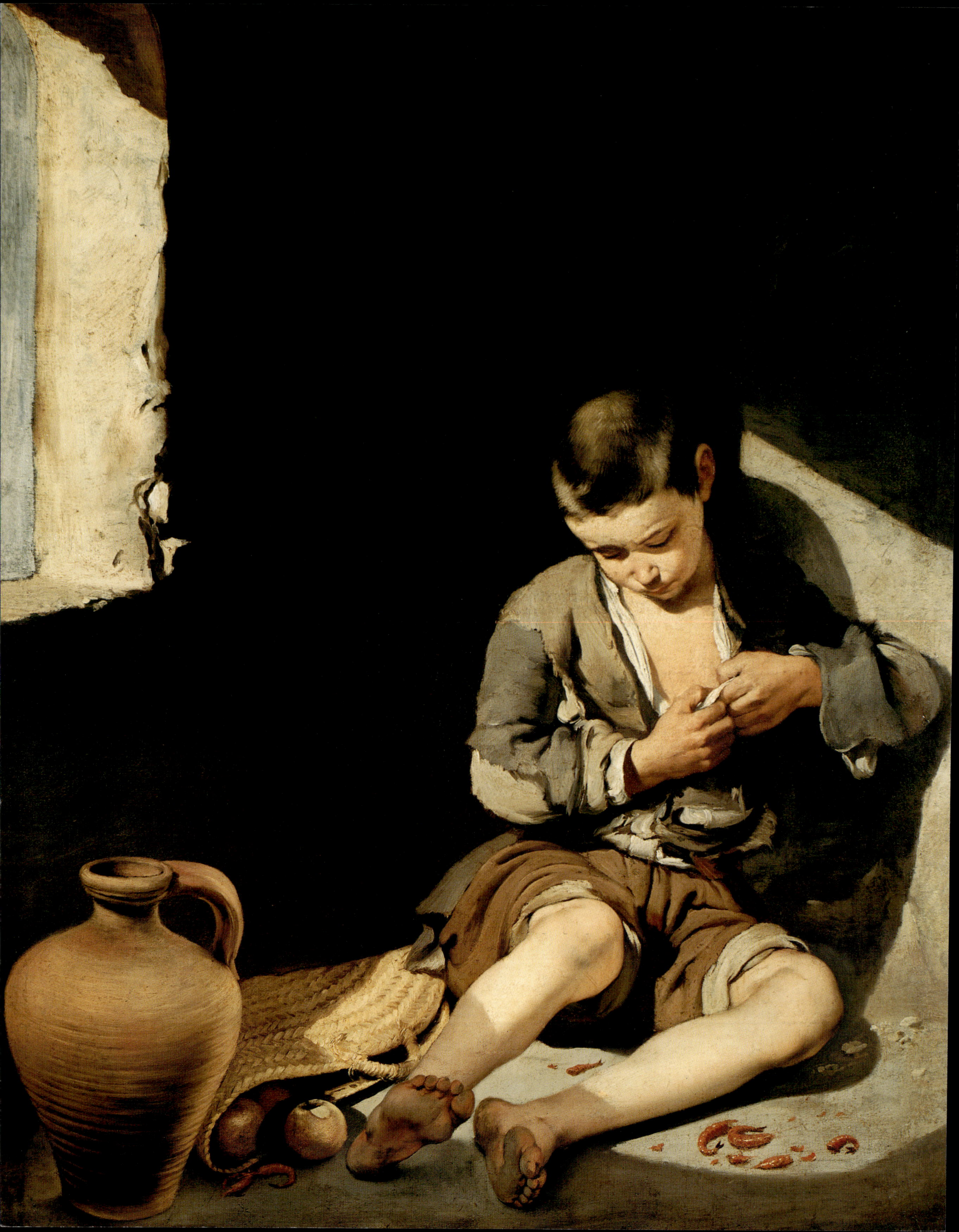

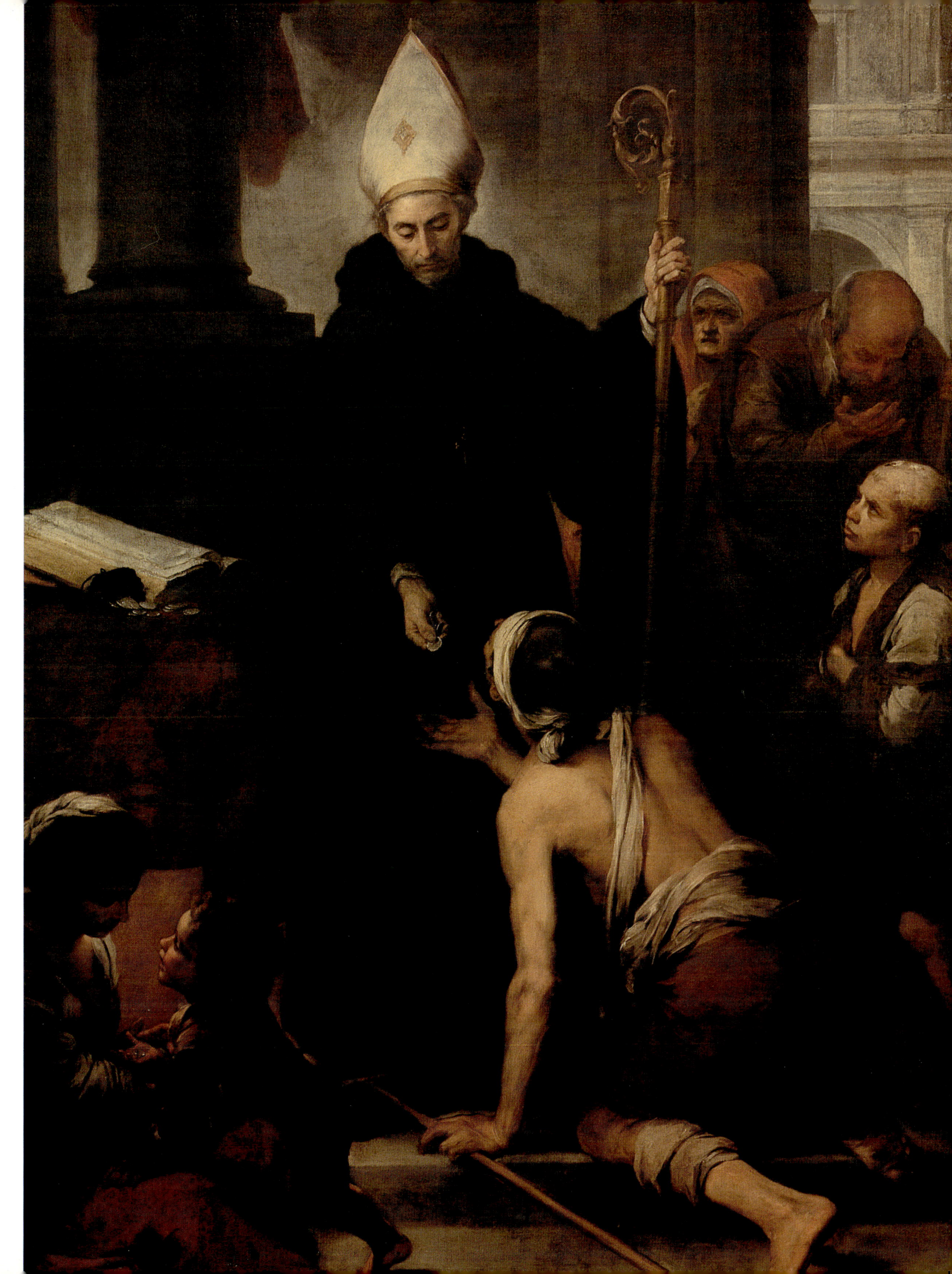

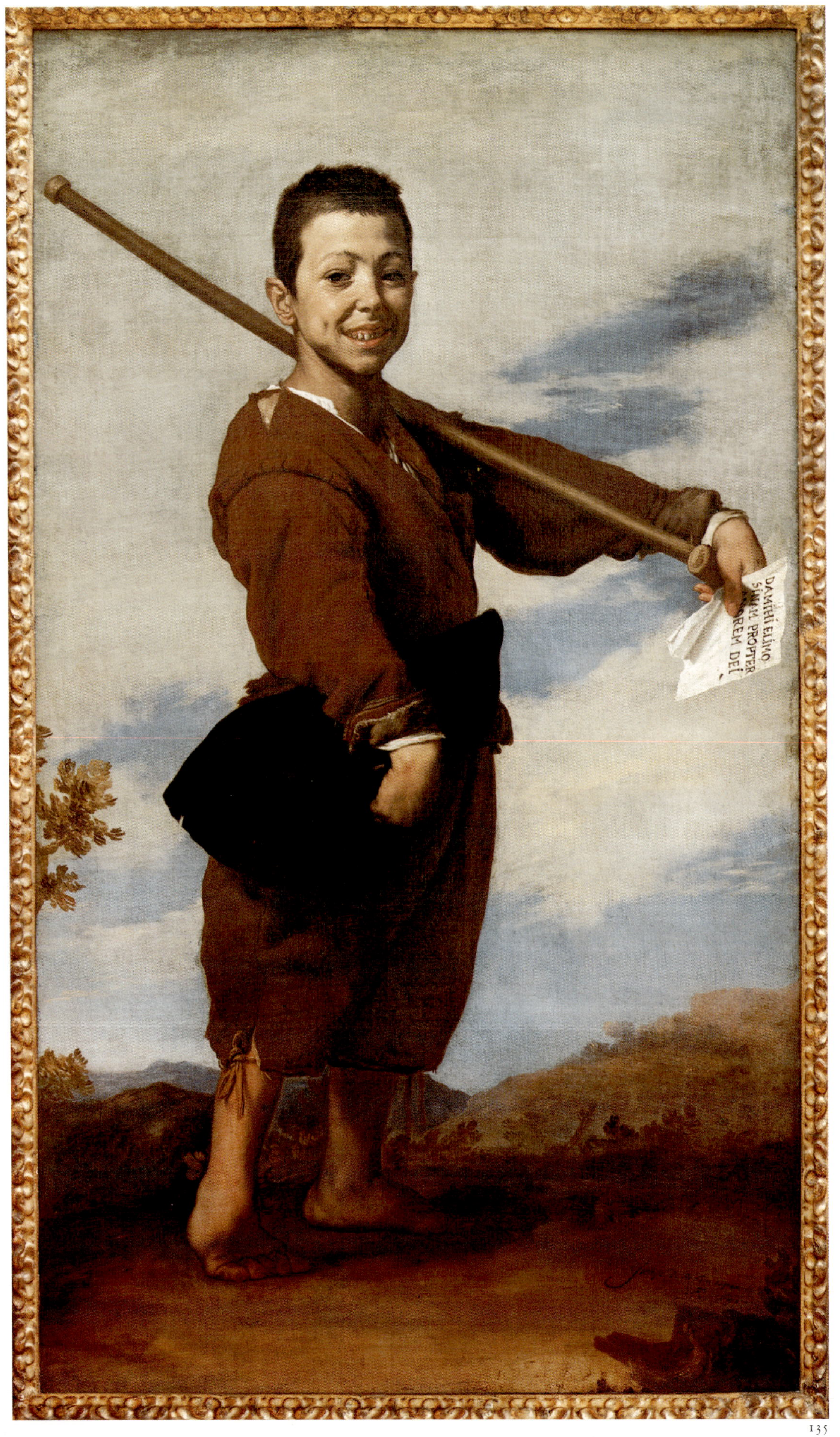

135

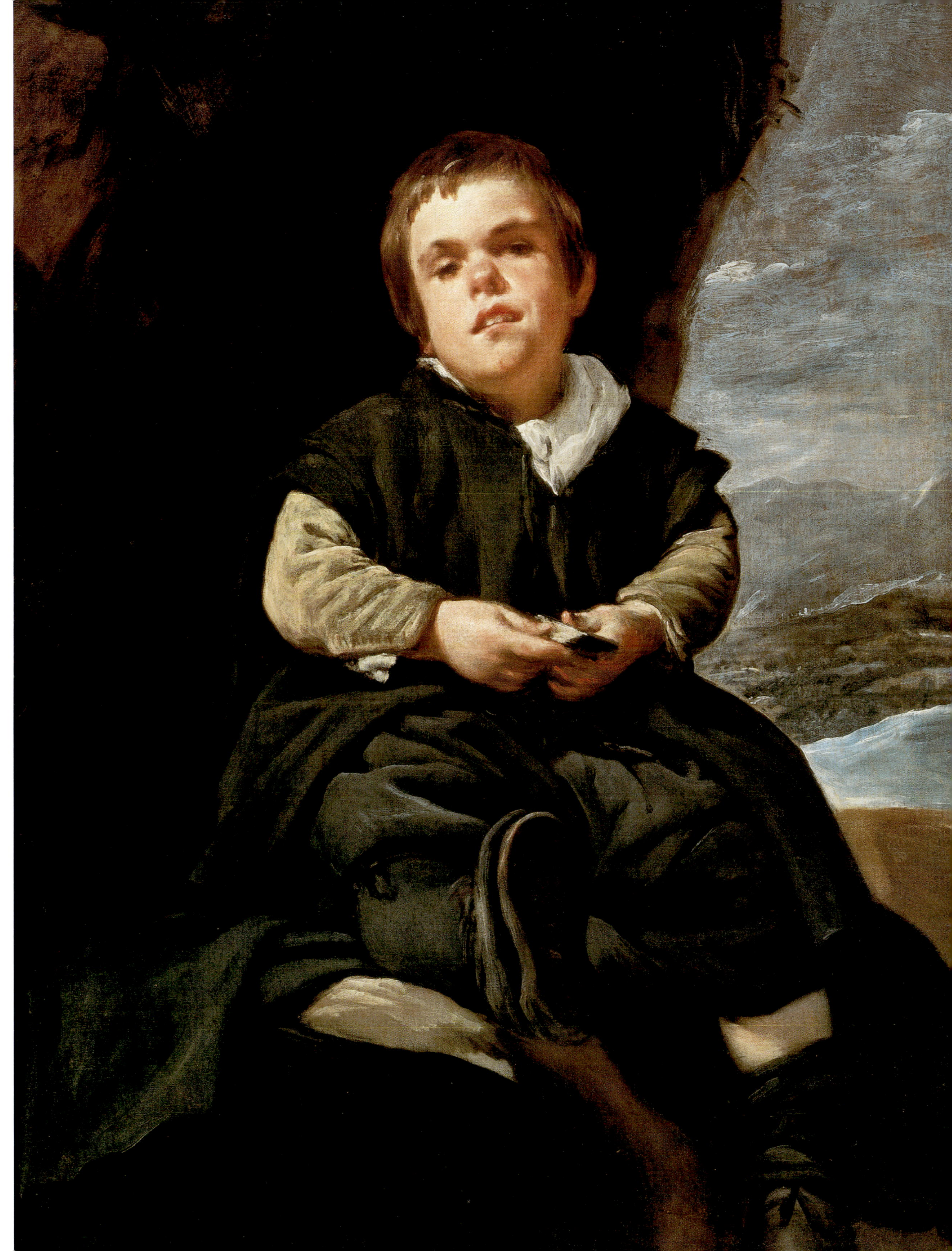

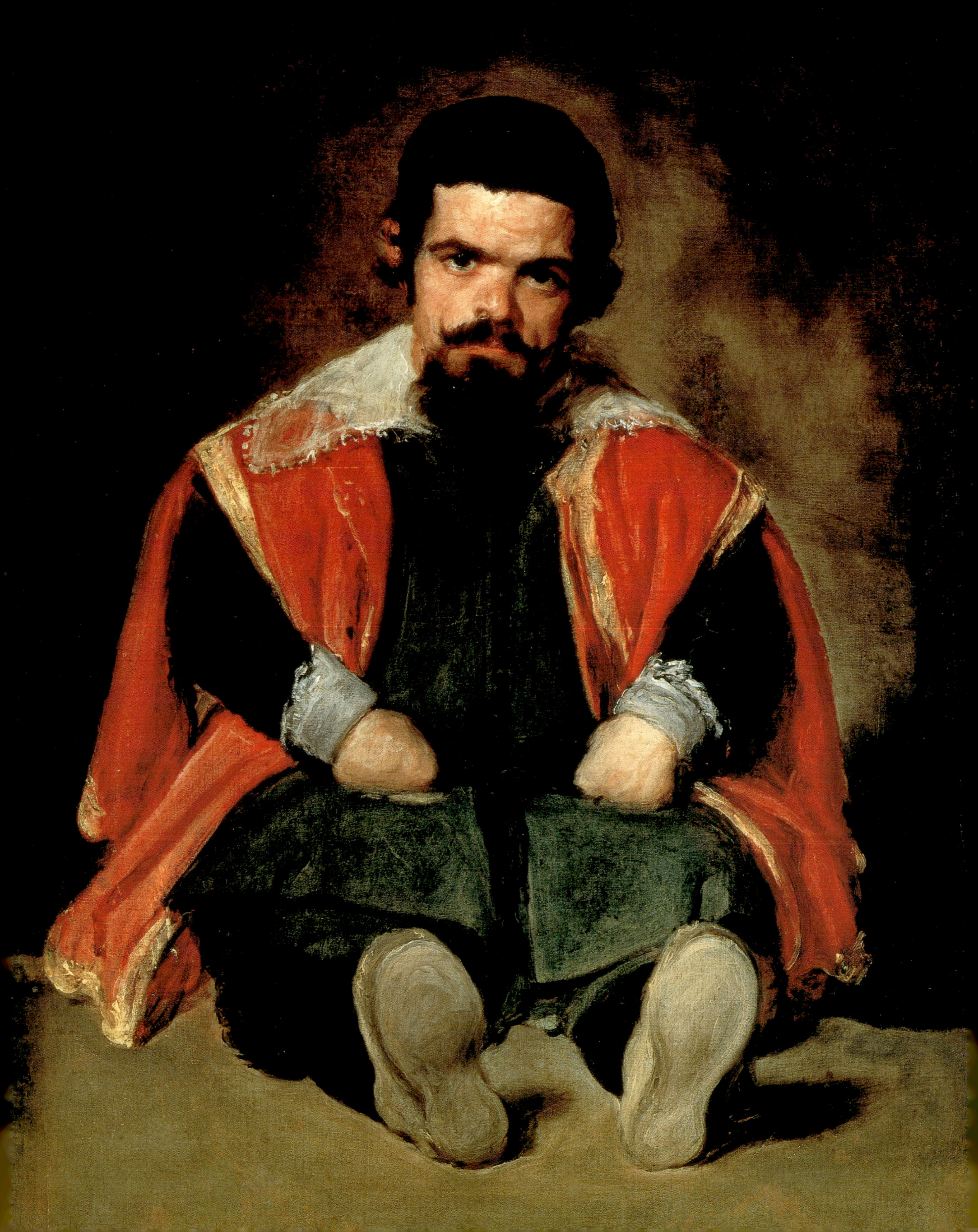

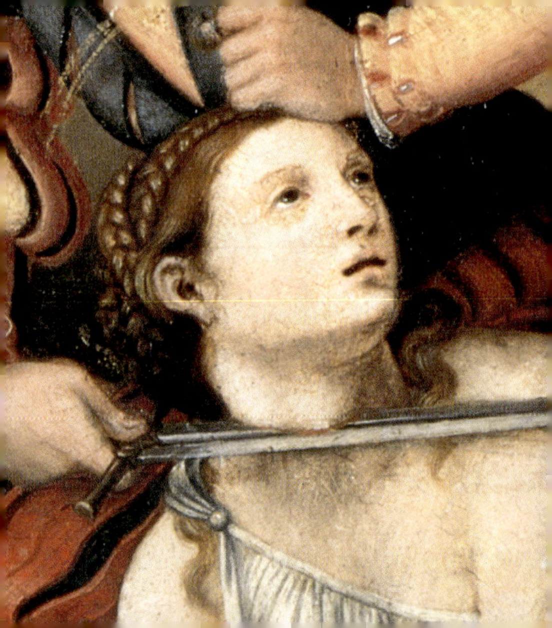

VIII

WOMEN

FOR THE AUGUSTINIAN friar Luis de León, a follower of Erasmus who was persecuted and jailed by the Inquisition, the "courageous woman" or *mujer varonil* (manly woman, ill. 142), or the *perfecta casada* (perfect wife) was as rare and hard to find as an oriental pearl, a flawless diamond, an emerald, or any precious jewel of inestimable value. According to Luis de León, many women believed that to marry was just a matter of leaving the father's house and entering the husband's, "exchanging servitude for freedom and an easy life," seeing their obligations as only to serve their husbands, run the family, and raise the children, show their fear of God, and possess a clear conscience. In a society governed by a few learned nobles and clergymen, a woman, in the words of Luis de León, was regarded as "more weak-willed than any other creature, fragile and affected in her ways." For Luis Vives, another Erasmist, women, epitomized by Eve, were much more easily deceived and much more given to pleasure than men. As a consequence, he wrote, they should not be allowed to leave the house, and under no circumstances be allowed to teach, since by doing so they would inevitably lead their listeners to error.

Thus marginalized, women, with the exception of royalty or members of the powerful nobility, who could handle their apparent marginalization differently (ill. 143), could be only wives or nuns. In either case they needed dowries, which might consist of money, material goods, or land, which their families had to deliver to the groom or the convent for their future keep. Less fortunate women had to rely on the few remaining roles that society assigned to them so they might eke out a living: servants, washerwomen, spinners, and prostitutes. A few women, and some men, were considered wonders of nature, like the bearded Magdalena Ventura, compassionately depicted with her husband and infant son by José de Ribera in 1631 (ill. 146), a painting commissioned by Don Fernando Afán de Ribera y Enríquez, duke of Alcalá and viceroy of Naples.

PRECEDING PAGE:
138. Vicente Macip
c. 1540
Detail of *The Martyrdom of Saint Ines*, convento de Santo Tomás de Villanueva, Valencia, oil on panel.
Museo Nacional del Prado, Madrid.

RIGHT:
139. Diego Velázquez
ca. 1650
Detail of *Venus at Her Mirror.*
National Gallery, London.

FOLLOWING PAGES:
140. Domenikos Theotokopoulos, called El Greco
c. 1600–10
Epimetheus and Pandora (as Adam and Eve),
carved and polychromed wood.
Museo Nacional del Prado, Madrid.

141. Alonso Cano
c. 1660–67
Virgin of the Immaculate Conception,
carved and polychromed wood.
Oratory of the sacristy, Granada Cathedral.

142. Vicente Macip
c. 1540
Detail of *The Martyrdom of Saint Ines*, convento de Santo Tomás de Villanueva, Valencia, oil on panel.
Museo Nacional del Prado, Madrid.

143. Antonio Moro
1552
Catherine of Austria.
Museo Nacional del Prado, Madrid.

144. Diego Velázquez
c. 1615–17
Christ in the House of Martha and Mary.
National Gallery, London.

145. Francisco de Zurbarán
1640
Saint Casilda.
Museo Nacional del Prado, Madrid.

146. José de Ribera
1631
The Bearded Woman (Magdalena Venturi with Her Husband), Palacio Lerma, Fundación Casa Ducal de Medinaceli, Toledo.
Museo Nacional del Prado, Madrid.

147. Diego Velázquez
c. 1635–40
The Seamstress.
National Gallery of Art, Washington, D.C.

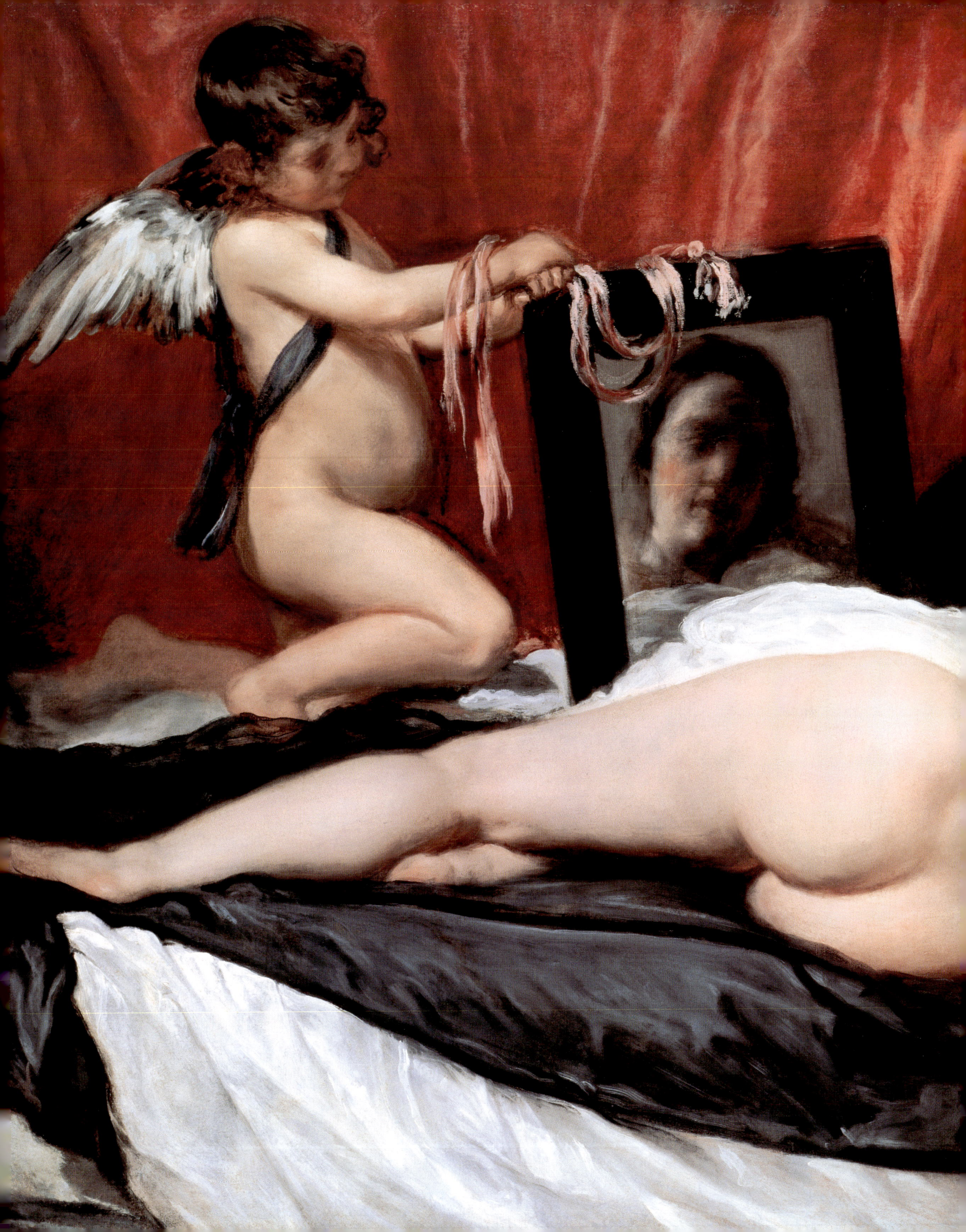

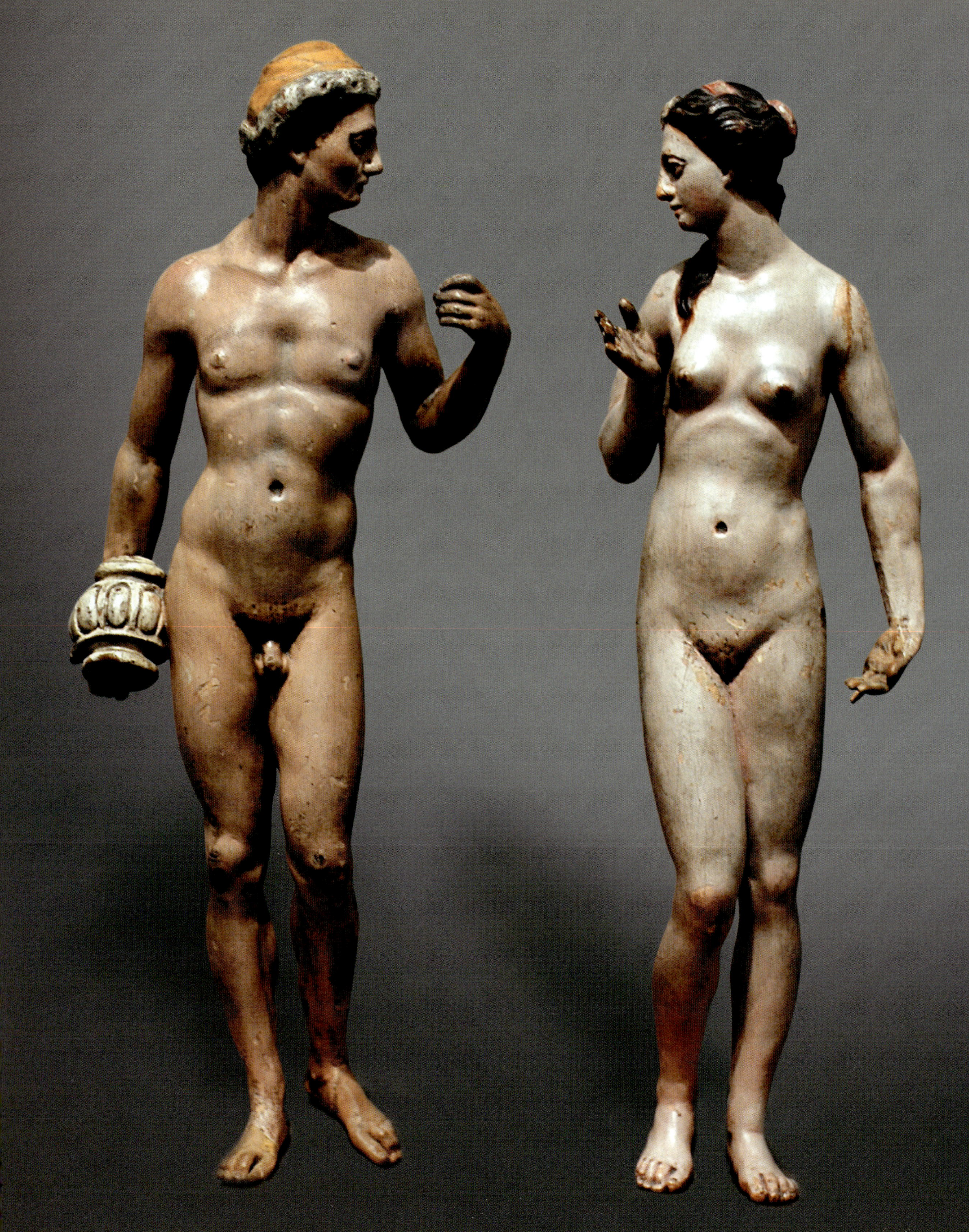

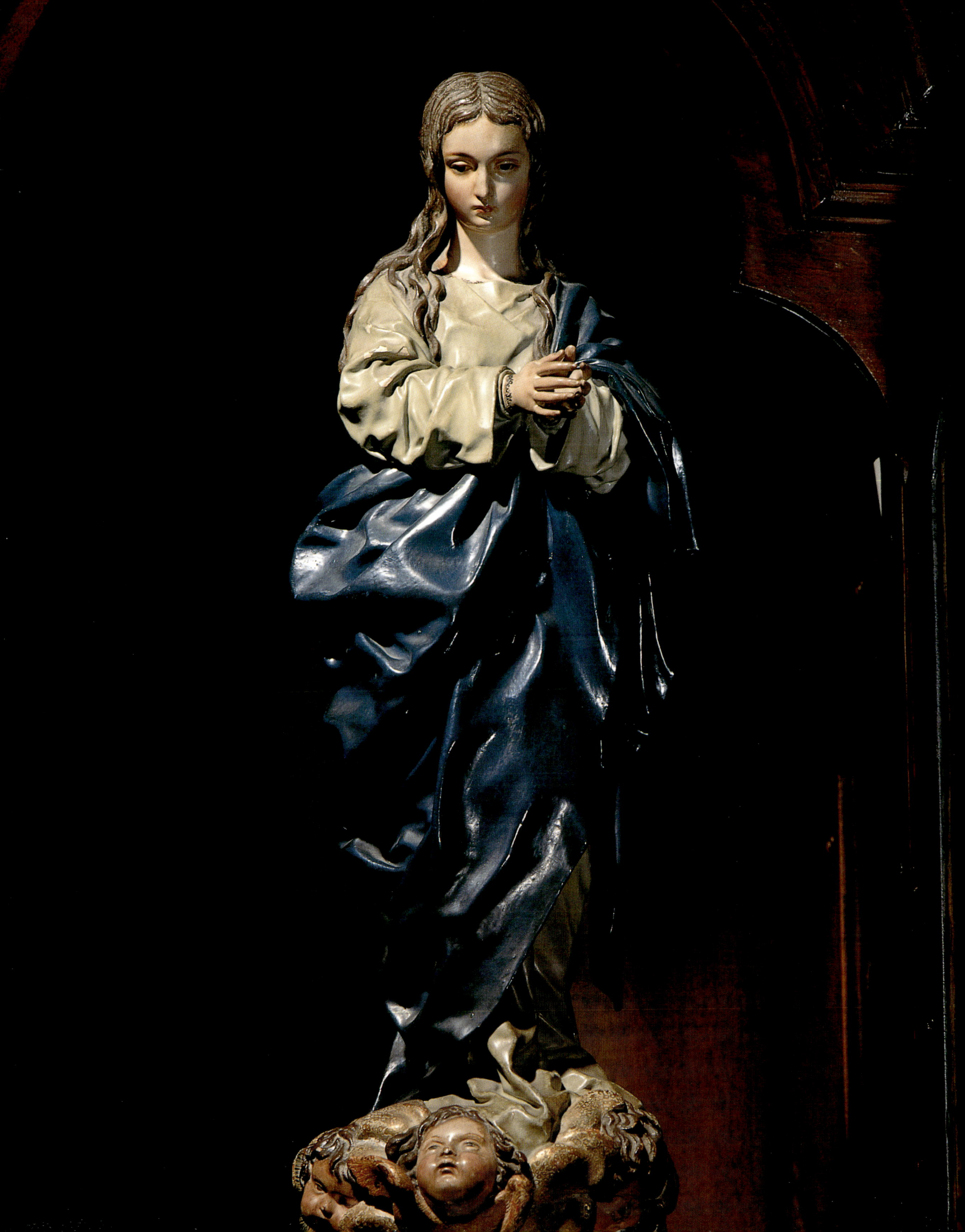

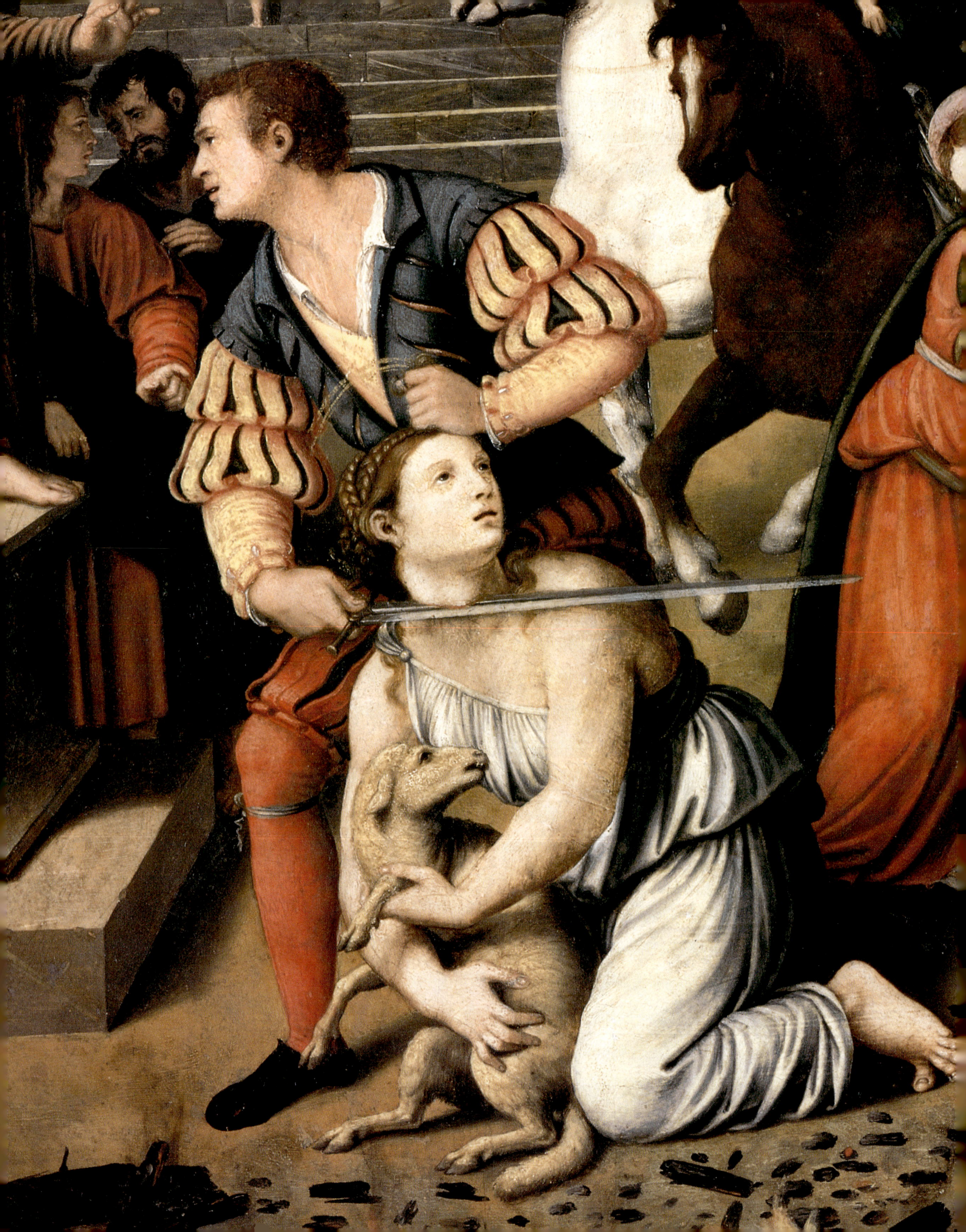

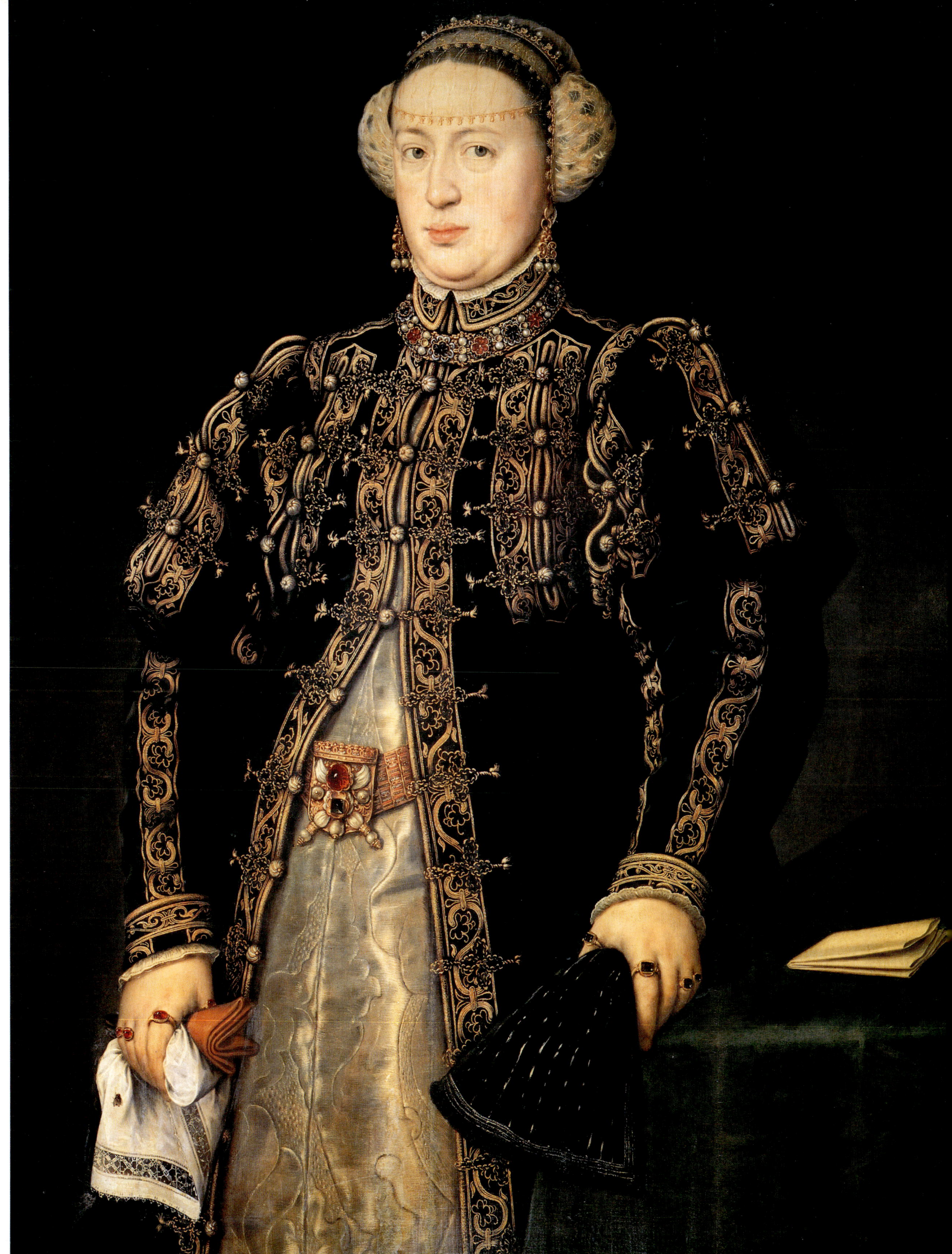

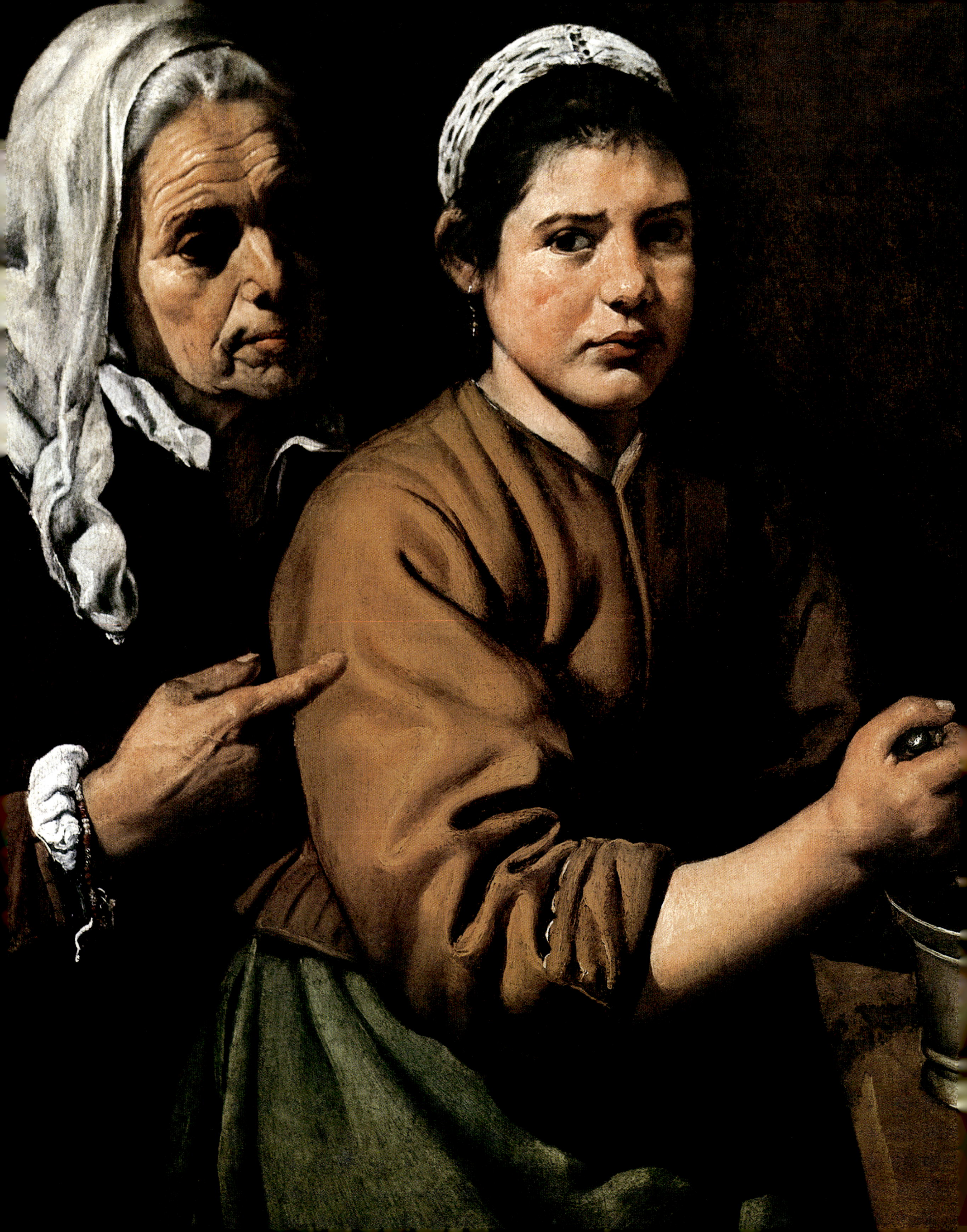

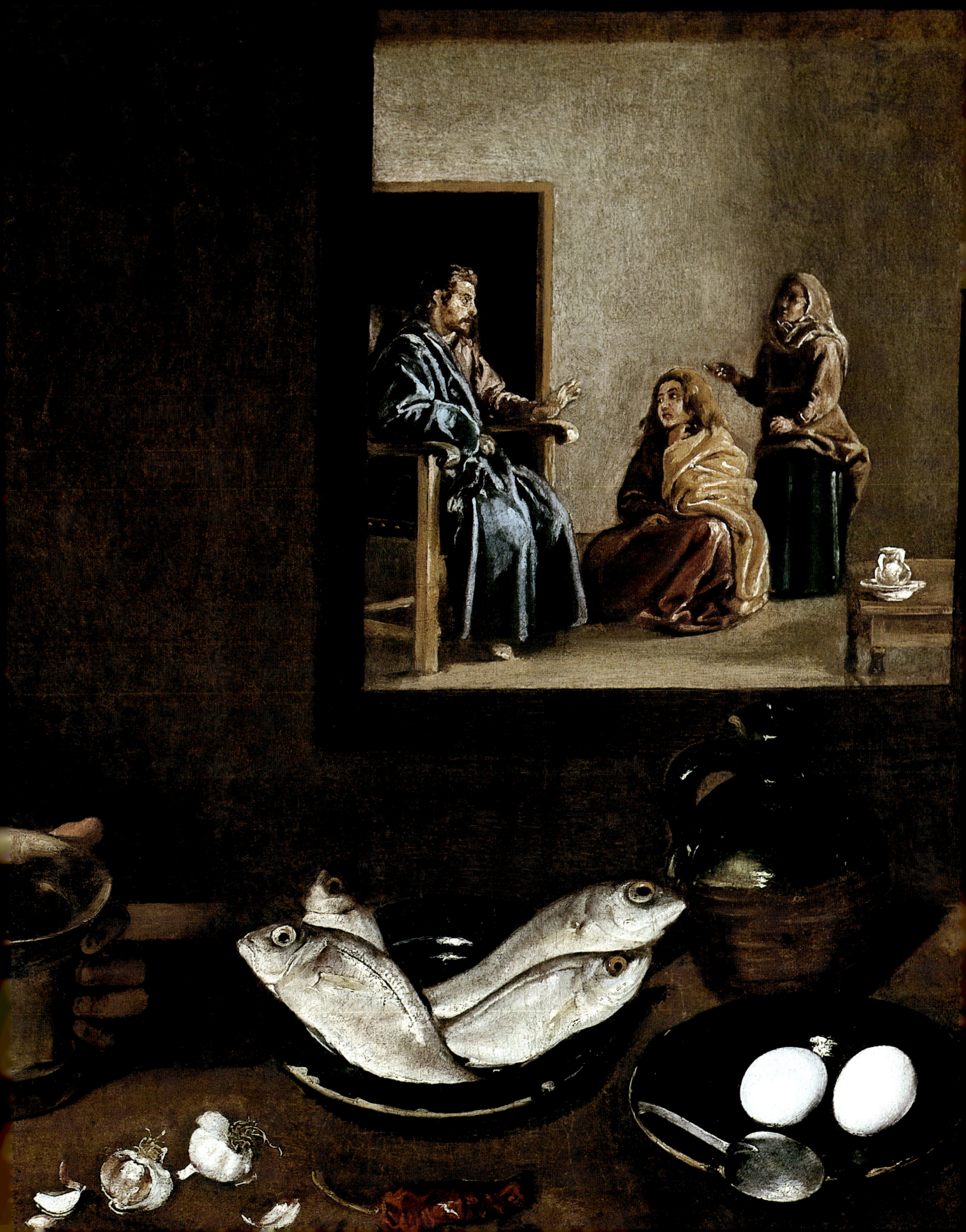

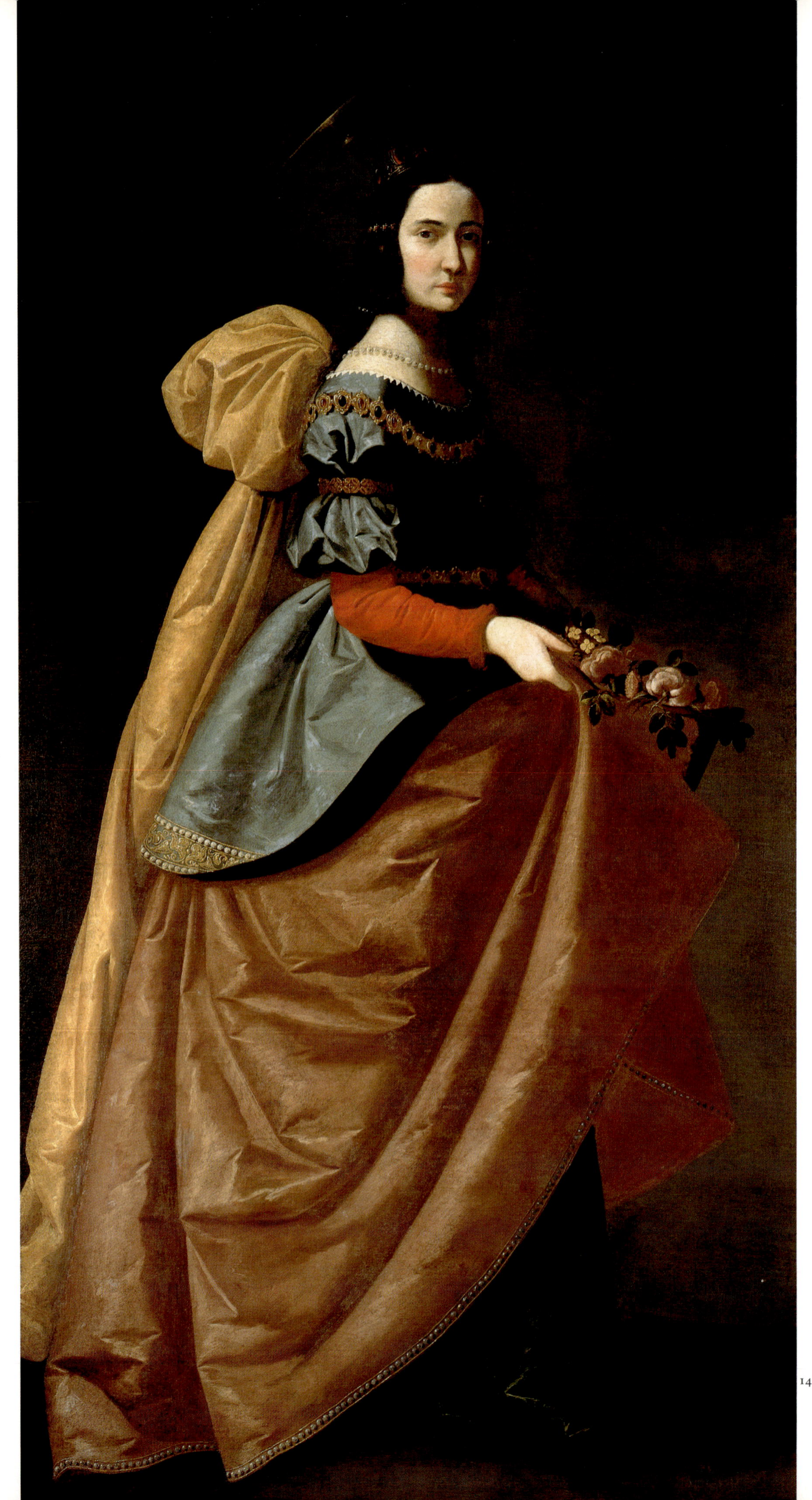

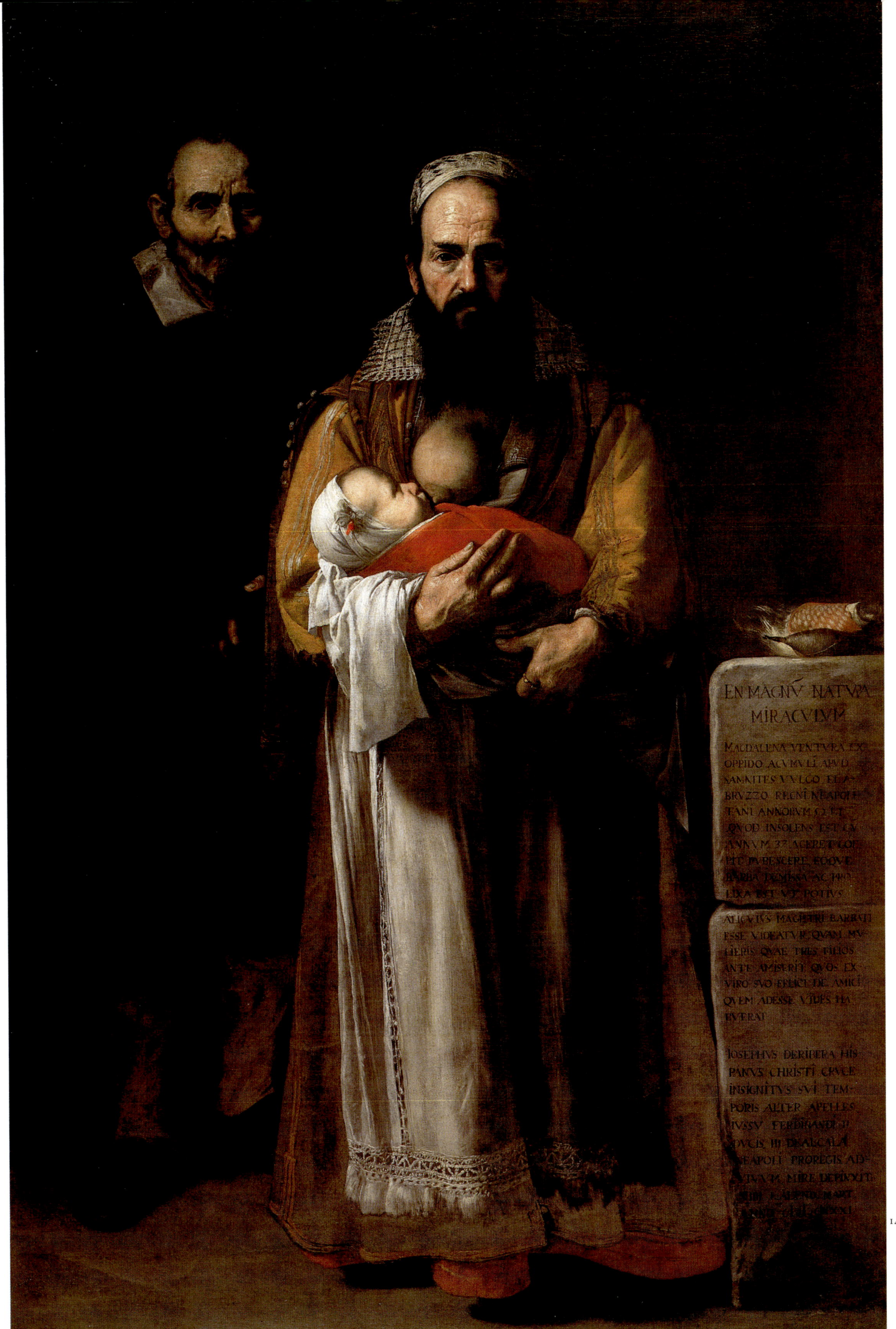
EN MAGNV NATVRA
MIRACVLVM
MAGDALENA VENTVRA EX
OPPIDO ACVMVLI APVD
SAMNITES VVLGO EL A-
BRVZZO REGNI NEAPOLI-
TANI ANNORVM 52 ET
QVOD INSOLENS EST CV
ANNVM 37 AGERET COE-
PIT PVBESCERE EOQVE
BARBA DEMISSA AC PRO-
LIXA EST VT POTIVS
ALICVIVS MAGISTRI BARBATI
ESSE VIDEATVR QVAM MV-
LIERIS QVAE TRES FILIOS
ANTE AMISERIT QVOS EX
VIRO SVO FELICI DE AMICI
QVEM ADESSE VIDES HA-
BVERAT
IOSEPHVS DE RIBERA HIS-
PANVS CHRISTI CRVCE
INSIGNITVS SVI TEM-
PORIS ALTER APELLES
IVSSV FERDINANDI II
DVCIS III DE ALCALA
NEAPOLI PROREGIS AD-
VIVVM MIRE DEPINXIT

146

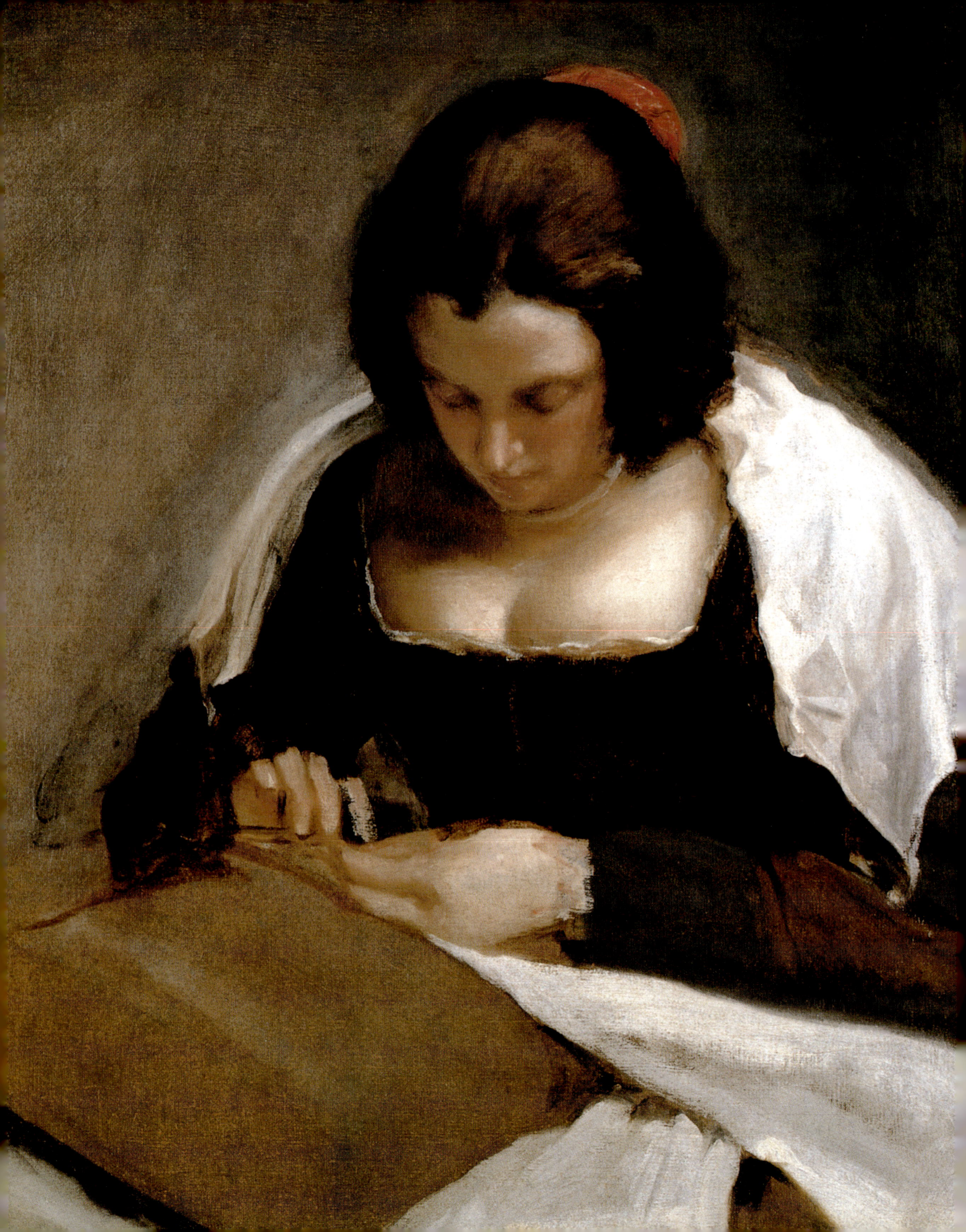

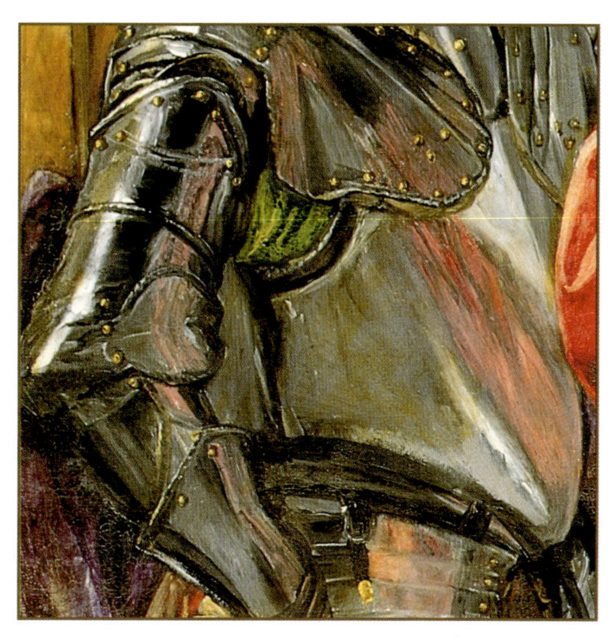

EL GRECO,
DIVINE PAINTER

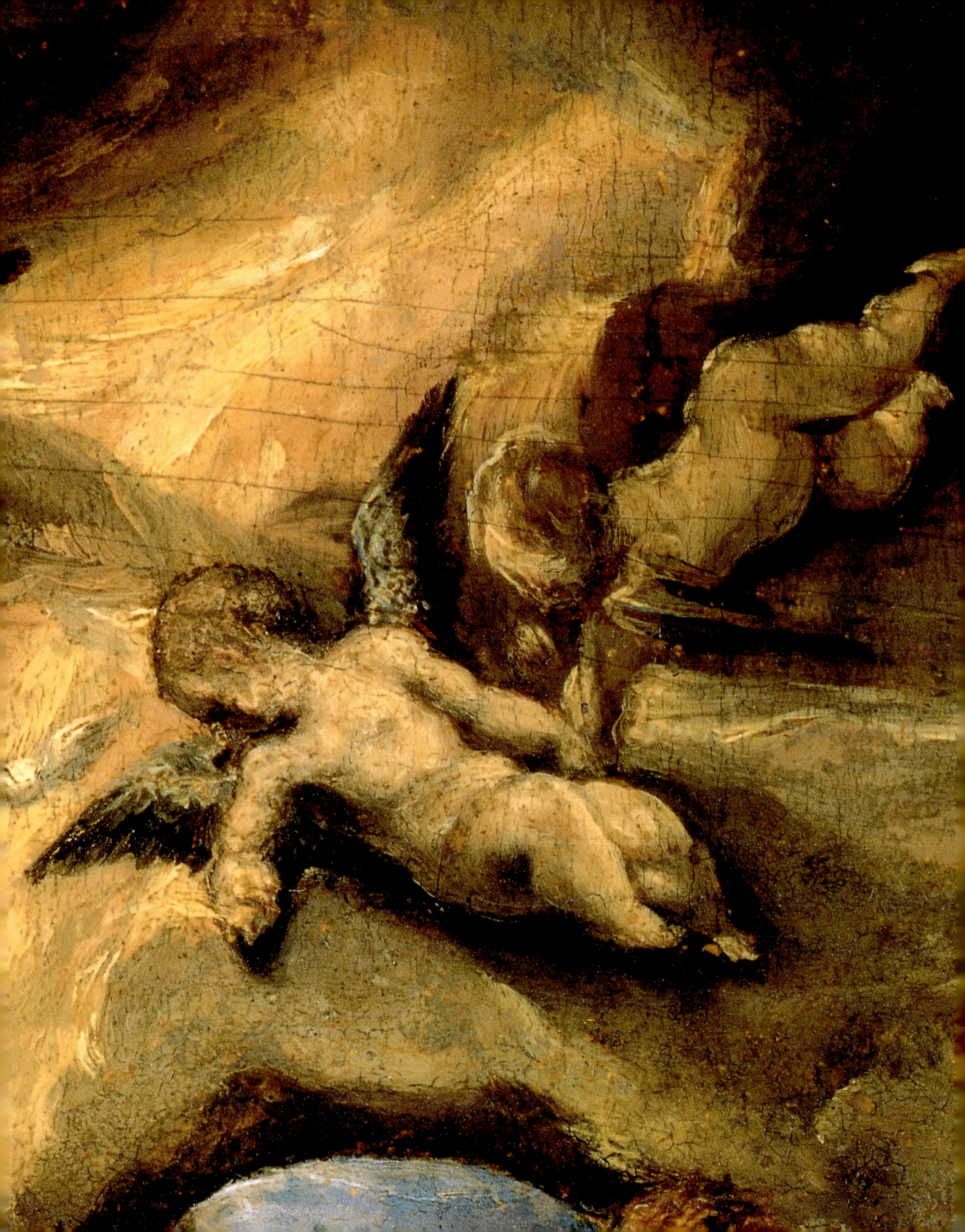

4

El Greco, Divine Painter

Two panels painted
that unwise painter;
one of Deukalion
while in the other he depicted Phaeton.
The work was beautifully done.
He asked what a right and dignified price
would be for his draughtsmanship.
And jokingly the Oracle responded to him:
One deserves water and the other fire.

—G. B. MARINO, *Dipintura Goffa: Del Greco,* 1620

Some twentieth-century artists considered El Greco "the god of painting," a divinity who in his time altered the visual order of the universe, turned the world upside down, and fulfilled a dream once thought to be unattainable. That dream was to reunite the artistic ideals and religious sentiment of Catholic Europe and the Greek Orthodox east, creating an empire with its lands on the shores of the Mediterranean and capitals in Rome and Byzantium.

El Greco's beginnings in painting were in the spiritual, transcendent Byzantine tradition of his birthplace in Crete, a style in which bodies typically lacked weighty materiality and space was not governed by the rational coordinates of vision. He left Crete to study painting in Venice, which was then dominated by the dense, expressive, and intense forms of Titian (who served as painter to Charles V and Philip II). El Greco then spent time in Rome, a city shaken by the stern Counter-Reformation constraints placed on artists by Pius V, the pope who led the crusade against the Turks at the Battle of Lepanto. Despite these restrictions, El Greco was able to adopt the "modern manner" of conceiving reality and the mannerist style of painting. He brought that exaggerated, expressive style to Toledo, then a city of little or no importance to the Spanish monarchy but still vital to the Catholic church and boasting many important religious institutions.

Art in Toledo had been dominated by secondary painters such as Luis de Carvajal, Blas de Prado, and Luis de Velasco, so El Greco was quickly able to obtain important commissions. He worked in the city for thirty-six years, creating altarpieces, devotional images, and portraits for a clientele with a limited interest in innovation, and, according to Francisco Pacheco, writing about "painting, sculpture, and architecture."

El Greco died in Toledo, the "new" Troy, with its intensely blue skies tinged with dense gray tones and its clouds streaked with bright, white light, on April 7, 1614. His remains were buried in a chapel

PRECEDING PAGE:
148. Domenikos Theotokopoulos, called El Greco
1577–79
Detail of *The Disrobing of Christ.*
Sacristy of Toledo Cathedral.

LEFT:
149. Domenikos Theotokopoulos, called El Greco
c. 1575
Detail of *The Annunciation,* oil on panel.
Museo Nacional del Prado, Madrid.

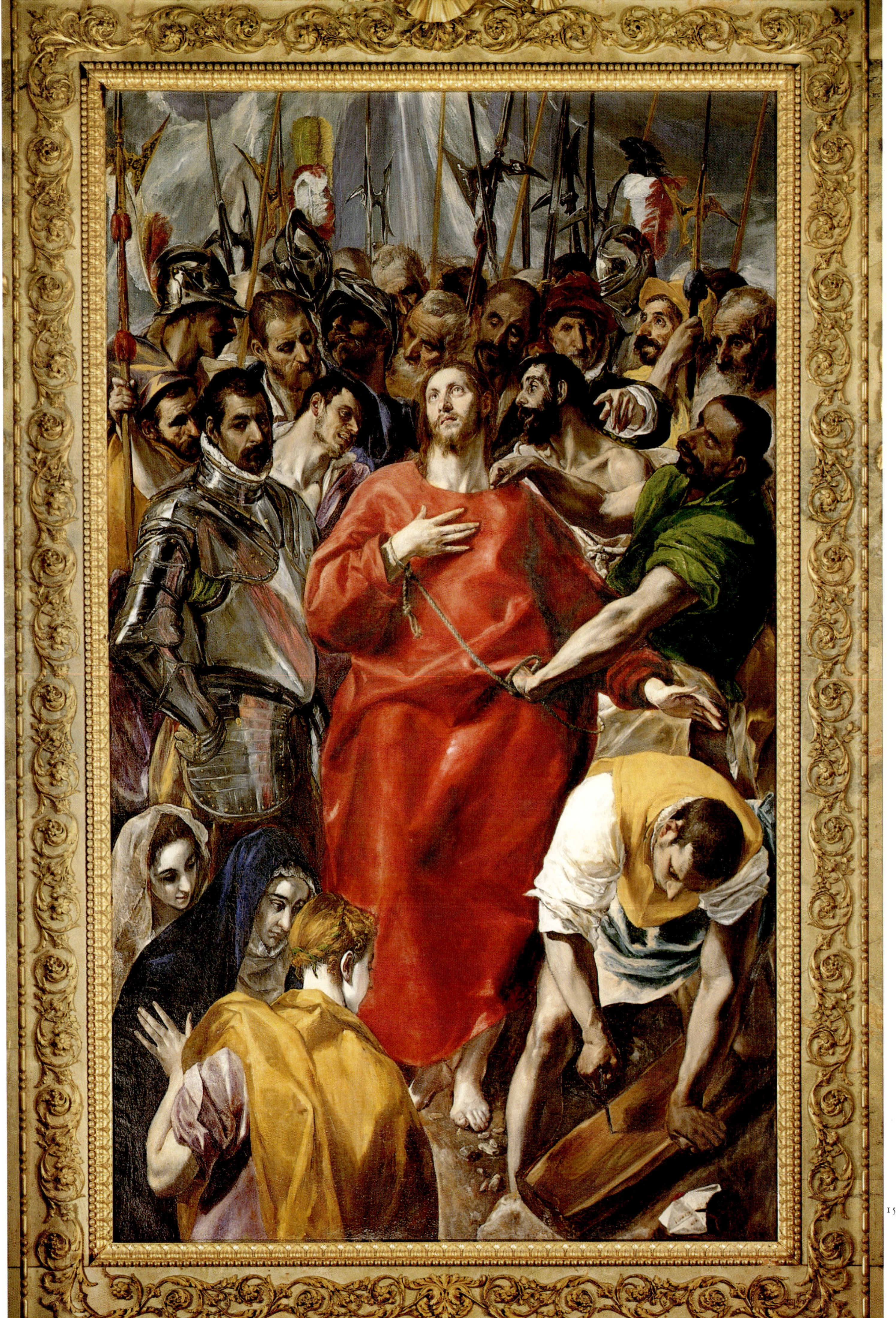

in the Church of Santo Domingo el Antiguo, but five years later they were moved to a site presently unknown. When El Greco died, the poet Luis de Góngora evoked his memory in a sonnet, "Inscription for the tomb of Domenico Greco":

> Pilgrim, behold this cold slab's elegance,
> this pediment of gleaming porphyry,
> that to the world denies the sweetest brush
> ever to give wood spirit, canvas life.
>
> The name, worthy to be bruited with more breath
> than Fame's trumpets could ever exercise,
> makes this grave marble's face illustrious.
> Pay tribute, and proceed along your path.
>
> Here lies the Greek. Nature has thus acquired
> Art, while Art acquires example, Iris
> color, Phoebus light, and Morpheus shade.
>
> May this great tomb, though in hard stone attired,
> soak up wet tears and fragrances exhaled
> by the costly bark that's from the East conveyed.

CRITICISM AND PRAISE

Even before this eulogy, El Greco had been praised in verse by Friar Hortensio Félix de Paravicino, who called him the "divine Greek," and by Cristóbal de Mesa, who wrote, "How like an ancient painter a modern painter would be / who with art makes man eternal." Most critics and theorists of the time, however, did not understand his work. Francisco Pacheco said that he painted "cruel sketches," and the Hieronymite friar José de Sigüenza, in his book about the building and decoration of the Escorial (1605), offered only a cautious compliment to El Greco's *Martyrdom of Saint Maurice and the Theban Legions,* which was painted for Philip II: "They say it is very artful." Years after El Greco's death he was criticized by Jusepe Martínez in his *Practical Discourses about the Very Noble Art of Painting,* c. 1675), as an extravagant painter who followed capricious rules.

The art theorists of the purist, neoclassical eighteenth century were no more gracious toward El Greco. While recognizing his talent for drawing, they considered his use of color tasteless, harsh, and strange, so much so that Antonio Palomino described El Greco's paintings as "contemptible and ridiculous." Due recognition of El Greco's work finally came with the swell of romanticism in the nineteenth century, a recognition greatly influenced by the presence of many of the painter's canvases in Louis-Philippe's Spanish Gallery at the Louvre, which opened in 1838. There El Greco's work was seen and admired by painters like Delacroix and Millet and soon thereafter by Manet and Degas, as well as by writers such as Baudelaire (who was equally able to appreciate the sharp coldness of Bronzino) and the critic Théophile Gautier. The latter traveled across the Pyrenees to submerge himself in Hispanic exoticism; there he found in El Greco's painting depraved energy, unhealthy power, and signs of a "brilliant madness."

This madness, without the modifier "brilliant," was cited by others to explain the distortions and strange color that gave El Greco's self-absorbed figures their presence. The Scottish historian William Stirling-Maxwell found madness in the artist's oeuvre, as did Baron Charles Davillier and Gustave Doré, who published a series of articles (1862–73) documenting their travels through Spain. About El Greco's *Expolio* (The Disrobing of Christ) in the sacristy of the cathedral of Toledo (ills. 148. 150, 151) they wrote:

> . . . these strange compositions, in which the most violent tones and the most extreme opposites struggle against each other in unique fashion, have clearly been conceived outside the realm of reality and reveal a diseased imagination, with the hand of the painter clearly not that of a person in his right mind.

While El Greco earned both admirers and detractors in France, his recognition in Spain at the close of the nineteenth century had much to do with the grave identity crisis generated by the end of its colonial empire and an anxious search for a national soul. For the writers and intellectuals known as the Generation of '98, this "national" soul endures in the austere Castilian landscape, in the

LEFT AND OVERLEAF:
150 and 151. Domenikos Theotokopoulos, called El Greco
1577–79
The Disrobing of Christ and detail.
Sacristy of Toledo Cathedral.

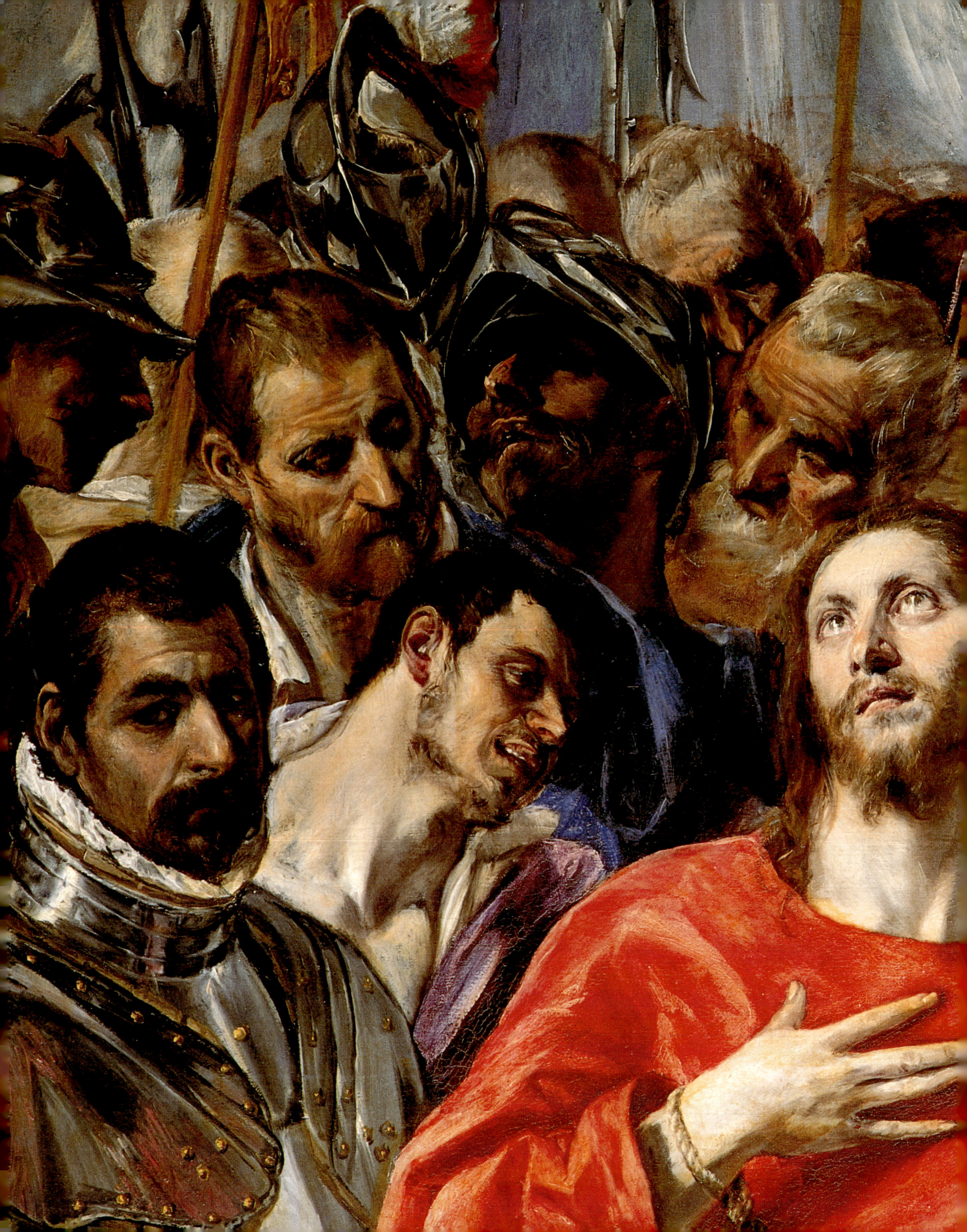

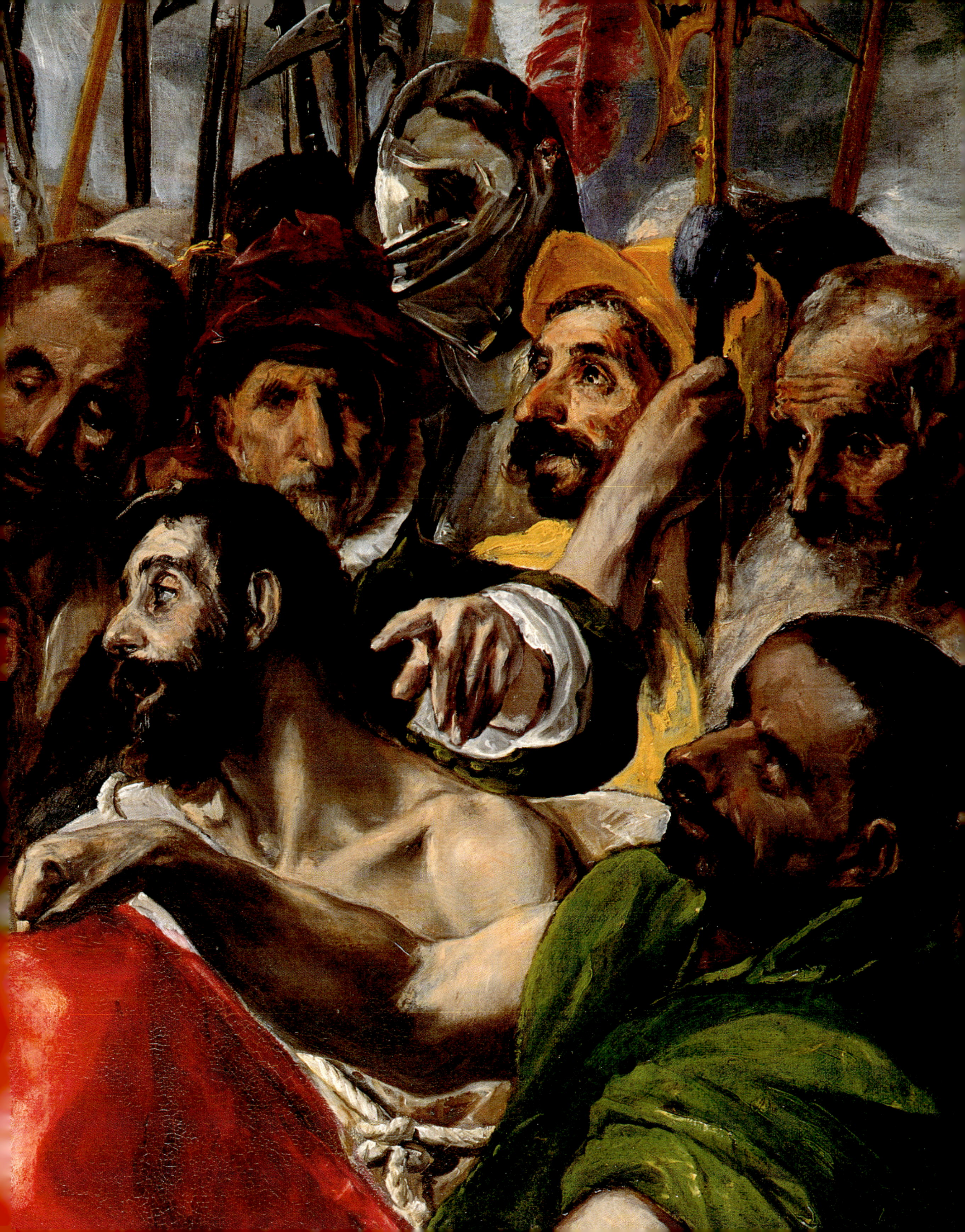

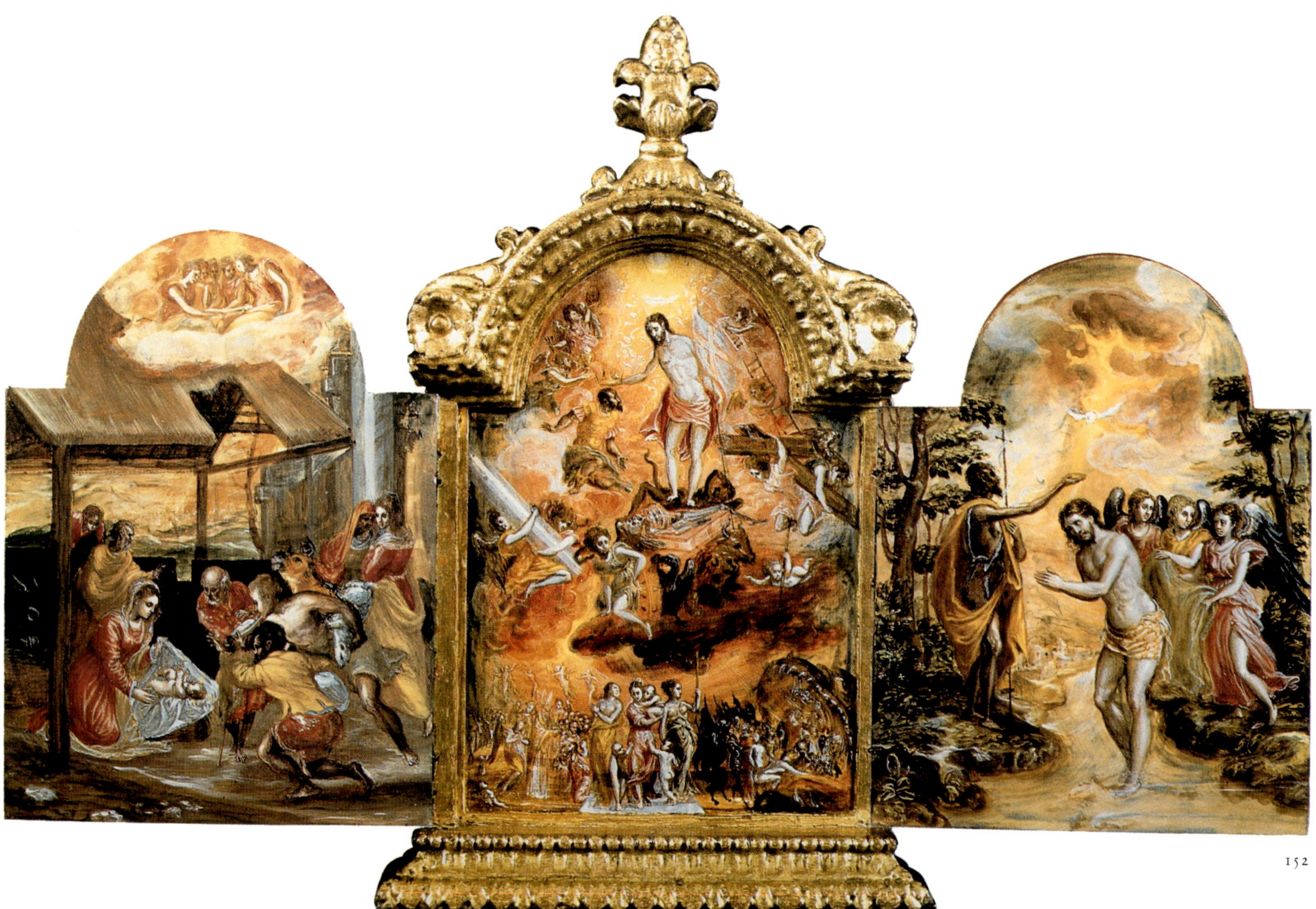

poverty and simplicity of its people, and in the extremes of its climate. It flourishes in the writings of Gonzalo de Berceo, Jorge Manrique, Cervantes, and Quevedo, and breathes in El Greco's expressive forms and intense stains of color infused with a particularly Spanish mysticism. This is what Manuel Bartolomé Cossío wrote in 1908 in reference to *The Burial of the Count of Orgaz* (ill. 162):

> The idealist and apocalyptic—rather than evangelical—humanism that nourished El Greco in Italy . . . enabled him, when he arrived in Castile, to quickly grasp not only that other more Horatian, friendly, and familiar humanism found in the writings of Luis de León, but also the characteristic Spanish mysticism of Saint John of Ávila, Saint Teresa, and Saint John of the Cross: arduous, subtle, and intellectual on the one hand, contemplative and restrained on the other, with the realist intimacy of his subjects in genre painting and his constant, sober preoccupation with eternal judgment. This new note, born out of El Greco's assimilation of a mysticism that is both naturalist and ascetic, united with prior elements, comprises the essential background of the *Burial*, and makes it an exceptionally emblematic product, whether spontaneous or reflexive, of the spirit of the time and of the race.

In the twentieth century scholars delved more deeply into the personal and artistic trajectory of El Greco, cataloguing his works and constructing his position as both a representative of Byzantine art and as a precursor of modernity. Above all, critics and theorists of the twentieth century were interested in interpreting his art, in discovering its true meaning. El Greco's paintings cannot be understood without considering them expressions of both mysticism and the religious and spiritual precepts of the Counter-Reformation. The meaning

152. Domenikos Theotokopoulos, called El Greco
c. 1567–68
The Modena Triptych: The Adoration of the Shepherds (left), *Allegory of the Christian Knight* (center), and *The Baptism of Christ* (right),
oil on panel.
Galleria Estense, Modena.

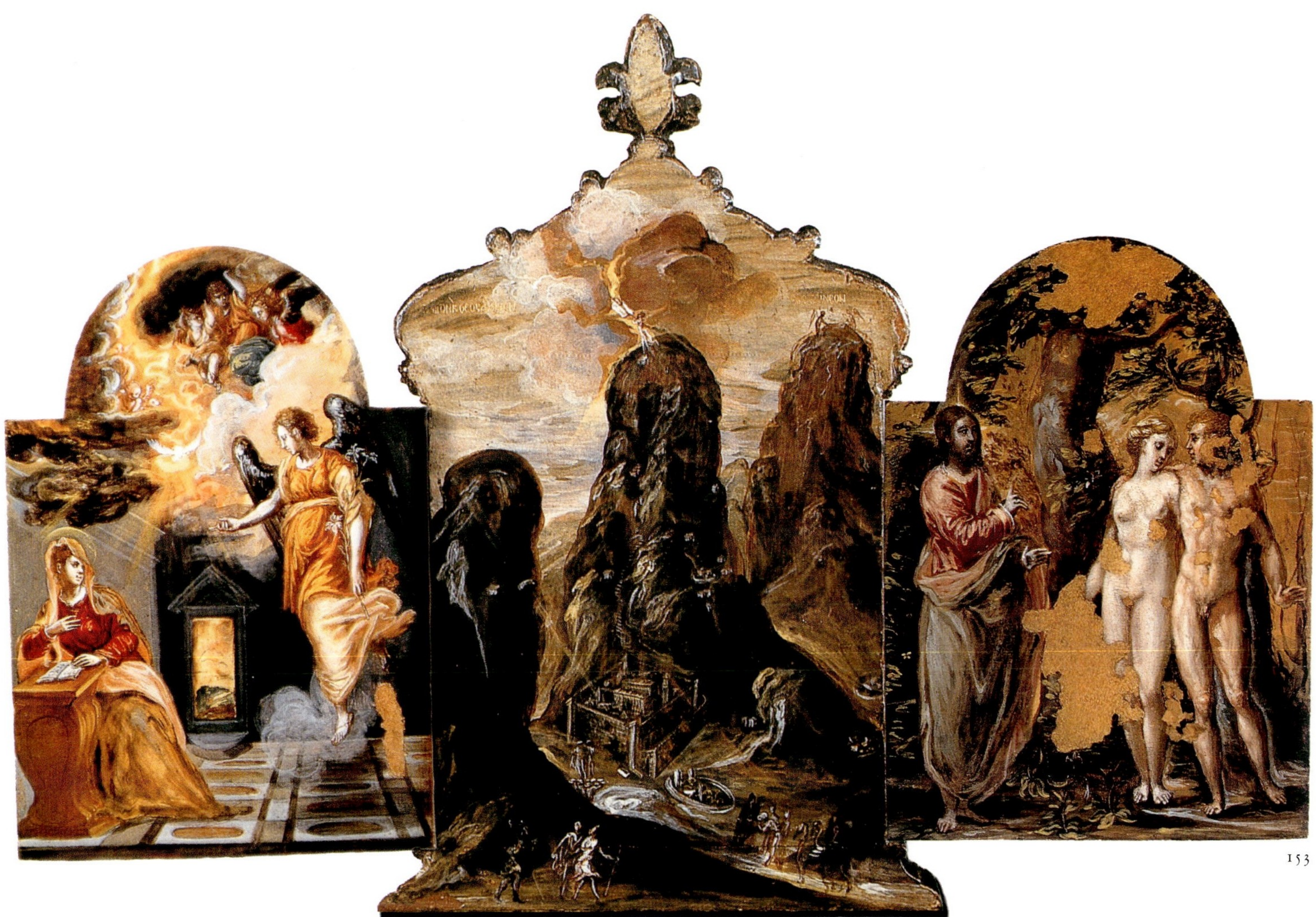

153

153. Domenikos Theotokopoulos, called El Greco
c. 1567–68
The Modena Triptych (reverse side): *The Annunciation* (left), *View of Mount Sinai* (center) and *Adam and Eve in the Presence of the Almighty (right),* oil on panel.
Galleria Estense, Modena.

of the paintings does not lie only in the artist's personal beliefs, but in the beliefs of his clients as well. El Greco's art synthesized Byzantine abstraction, Venetian color, and the expressive power of Roman Mannerism, a style ultimately indebted to the Hellenistic world of ancient Greece.

CRETE, VENICE, AND ROME

Some of what we know about El Greco's early life was recorded by him over the years in various documents. Domenikos Theotokopoulos was born in late 1540 or early 1541 on the island of Crete into a family working in maritime trade and tax collection, with bases in present-day Heraklion, formerly Muslim Khandak and Venetian Candia. He was trained as an icon painter within the local Byzantine tradition, a tradition aware of the new style brought about by the Italian Renaissance but nonetheless bound by medieval conventions. El Greco was already considered a master in 1563 and more explicitly called a master painter by 1566, the year he painted a panel representing the Passion of Christ. That work, which has been lost, was intended to be sold through a lottery system. It was likely painted in a style close to that of the *Dormition of the Virgin,* now in Ermoupolis (Syros), and to other similar paintings by him or attributed to him.

A desire to improve his skills, mixed, perhaps, with a degree of restlessness, and possibly fueled by the encouragement of a client, motivated El Greco's move to Venice, a move also made by other artists from Candia, some of whose panel paintings have occasionally been mistaken for works by the young El Greco. He arrived in Venice in early 1567 and remained in the city until October 1570. Venice was not then at its peak of splendor in either economic or political terms. Attacks by the Turks against Malta, Cyprus, and Crete were feared, and in only three years the Venetian government passed

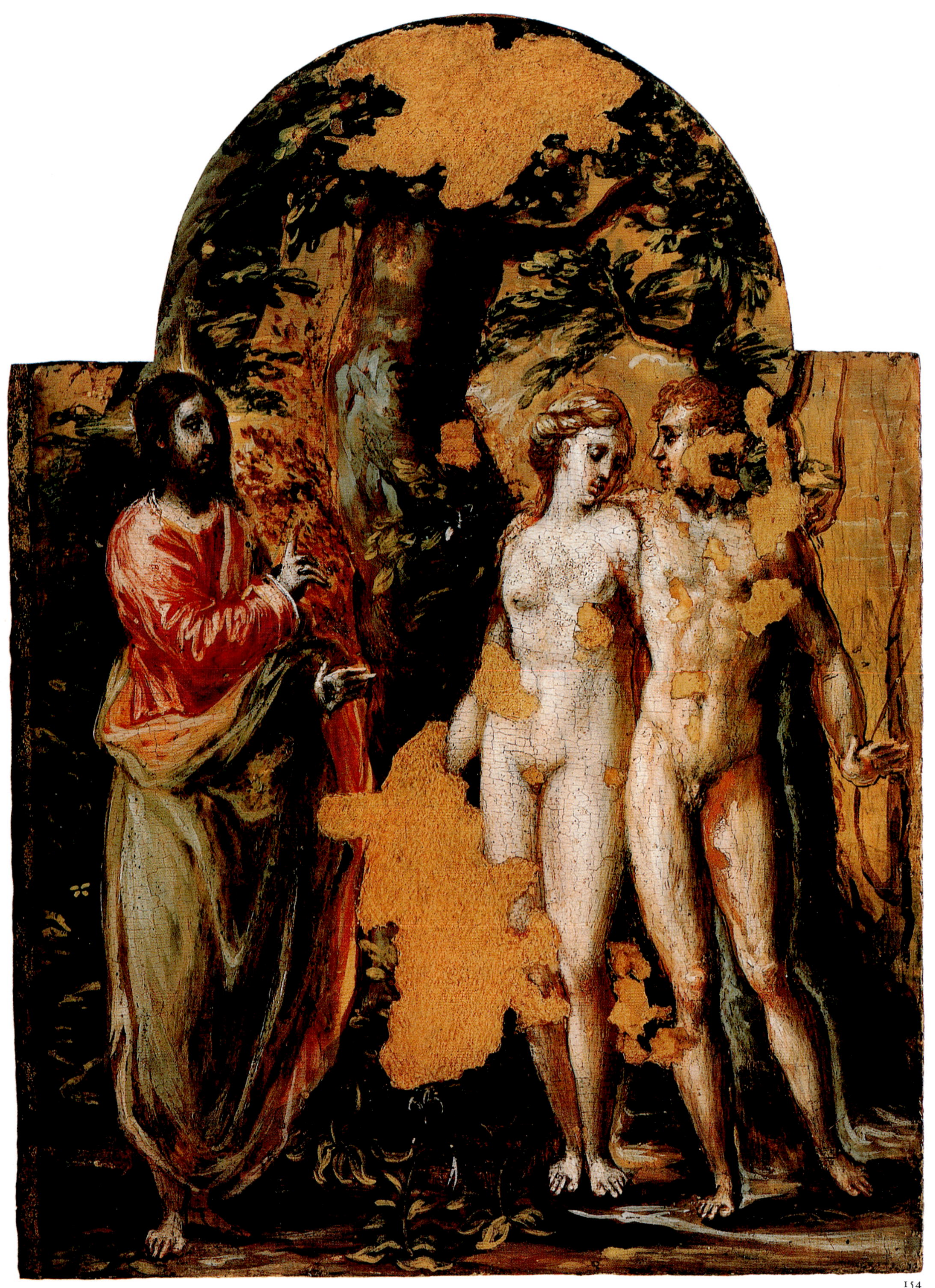

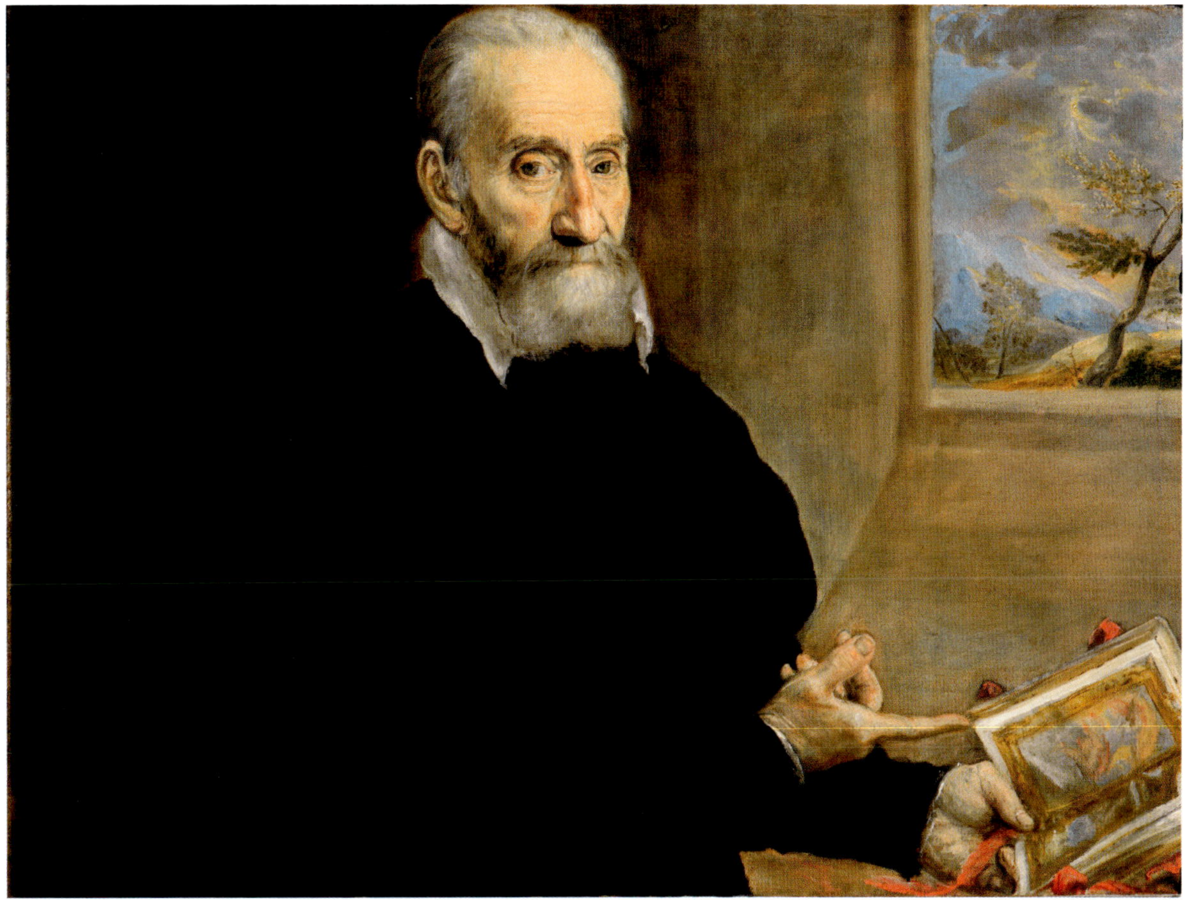

155

LEFT:
154. Domenikos Theotokopoulos, called El Greco
c. 1567–68
Adam and Eve in the Presence of the Almighty, reverse side of *The Modena Triptych,* right, oil on panel.
Galleria Estense, Modena.

ABOVE:
155. Domenikos Theotokopoulos, called El Greco
1572
Portrait of Giulio Clovio.
Museo di Capodimonte, Naples.

PAGE 208:
156. Michelangelo Buonarroti
1537–41
Christ the Judge and the Virgin, detail of *The Last Judgment*, fresco.
Sistine Chapel, Vatican.

through the hands of three doges: Girolamo Priuli, Pietro Loredan, and Alvise Mocenigo, the latter under the protection of Charles V.

Though Venice was in some respects in decline, it was still the city of Andrea Palladio (El Greco could watch the construction of San Giorgio Maggiore), Veronese, Jacopo Bassano, the aging Titian—"who had the greatest knowledge of nature and was its most able imitator," El Greco wrote—and Tintoretto, creator, according to El Greco, of "the finest painting to be found now in the world." The young artist from Crete could admire and study the works of these painters in churches and palaces (where he also appreciated paintings by Giovanni Bellini), and perhaps he even spent some time in the studio of Tintoretto himself.

Despite all of this, El Greco continued to conceive of pictorial reality in a fundamentally Byzantine way. He increasingly understood landscape as truth, though a truth sometimes touched by fantasy and even torment: he depicted natural phenomena while imbuing them with his own feeling. He constructed space according to the principles of Alberti's perspective, created bodies with naturalistic anatomy, worked with light so as to mold and give volume to form, conceived the world and even the realm of the divine in a dynamic way, and described nature and objects in minute detail. Yet above all, Venice, the most eastern of western cities, taught him, as we can see in the so-called *Modena Triptych* (c. 1569, ills. 152–54), that in art mankind is not only the visible representation of invisible eternity (which it would always remain for El Greco), but the living, changeable material of the everyday. Beyond that, he learned that the intense life that dwells in a body is not best expressed through forms, however pliant they may be, but through light and color.

Though El Greco did not obtain commissions in Venice, the city provided him with great depth of understanding and more. Both his personal situation and the overall political situation precluded a return to Crete, so he decided to make his way to Rome, then still the *caput mundi,* or "head of the world." The trip was slow but educational, as he traveled through Padua, Vicenza, Mantua, Parma, Bologna, and the Florence of the Medicis before finally reaching his destination. His journey could also be described as a journey through the history of

Italian painting, for along the way he became familiar with the work of Giotto, Mantegna, Giulio Romano, Correggio, Parmigianino, Pontormo, and Michelangelo. Each of these artists played a role in his new visual culture, even though he criticized nearly all of them for one defect or another.

What was his calling card when he arrived in Rome? The answer is found in a letter written on November 16, 1570, by Giorgio Giulio Clovio, the miniaturist from Croatia, to Cardinal Alessandro Farnese, his protector and one of the outstanding art patrons of the time. Clovio asked for the cardinal's support for a young Cretan lately arrived in Rome, a disciple of Titian, with a unique gift for painting. Clovio added that El Greco had created a portrait that would amaze the painters of Rome, so ably had he captured the identity of the sitter. But the Cretan apparently did not garner any commissions from the cardinal, though he probably painted the occasional small work for him, such as the *Healing of the Blind Man* now in the Galleria Nazionale, Parma. Much more important for El Greco was his contact with the illustrious men in the cardinal's circle. One of them was the humanist Fulvio Orsini, who maintained important relationships with erudite men, artists, politicians, and ecclesiastical authorities, some of whom had come from Spain in the service of the Spanish court. Orsini's friendship with Antonio Agustín, the archbishop of Tarragona, Spain, is a case in point.

However, El Greco's contacts with Roman society and with artists such as Giorgio Vasari who were favored by art lovers did not prove very fruitful. Two years after his arrival in Rome El Greco appeared on the lists of the Academy of Saint Luke, which meant that he was allowed to open his own studio in the city. He did so, dedicating himself primarily to portrait paintings like the one of his mentor, Giorgio Giulio Clovio (ill. 155), and devotional images, all without much success.

He continued to paint without abandoning his Byzantine and Venetian background, though incorporating stylistic elements and motifs from the work of the painters he particularly appreciated in Rome,

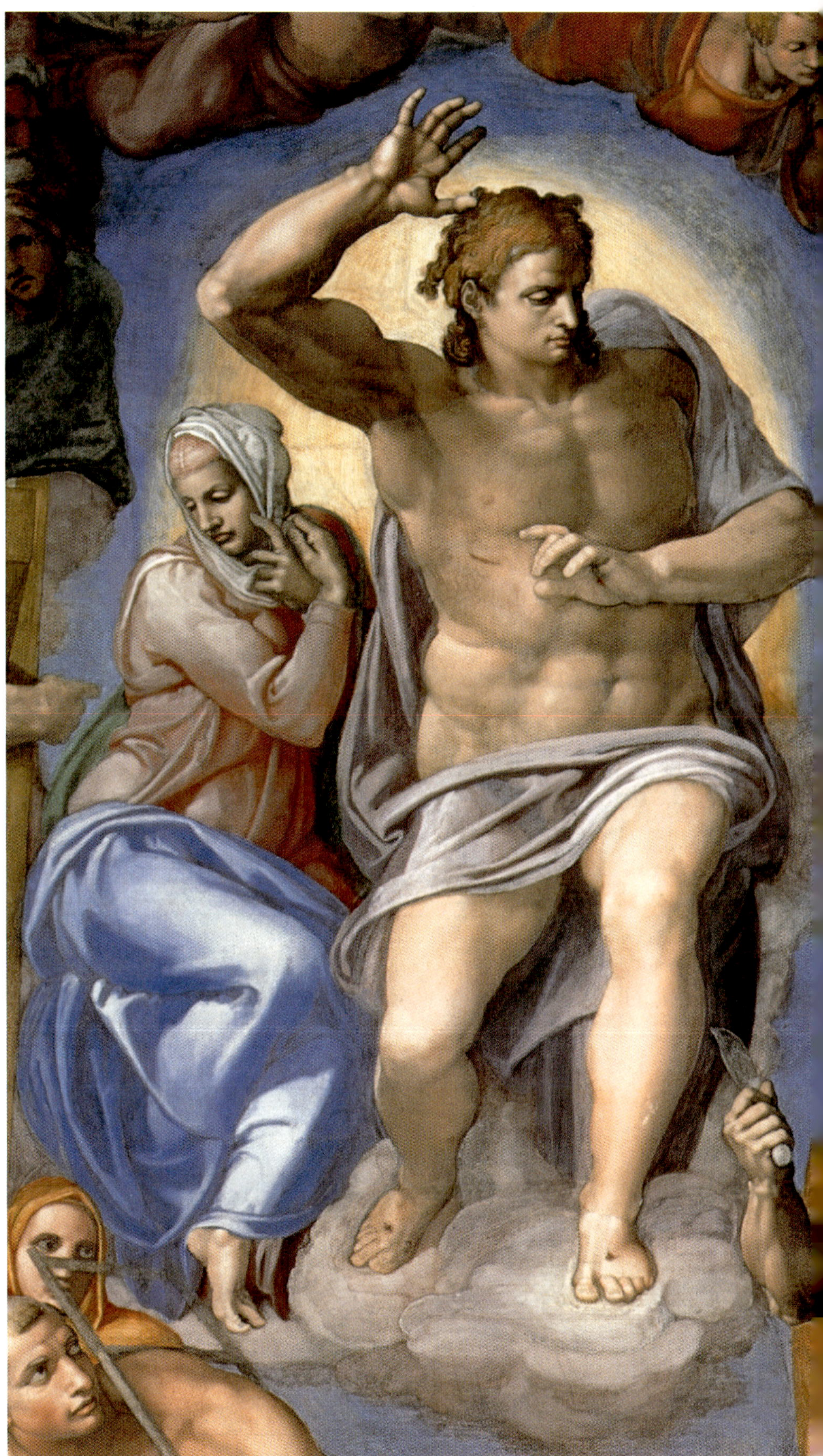

156

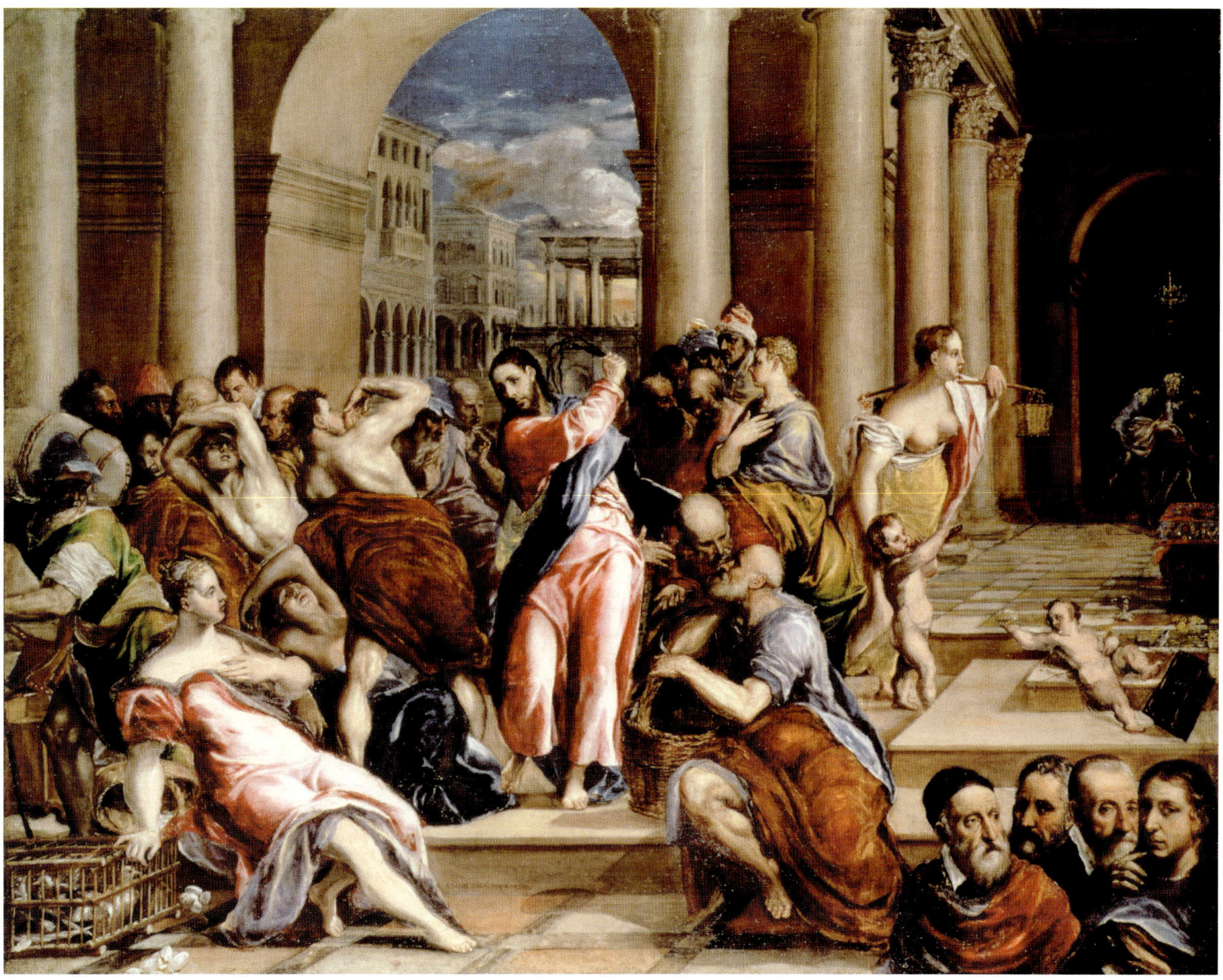

157

157. Domenikos Theotokopoulos, called El Greco c. 1570–72 *The Purification of the Temple.* Minneapolis Institute of Arts, Minneapolis.

including Michelangelo. He was especially influenced by the Michelangelo who loved classical sculpture, though El Greco would eventually express disdain for Michelangelo as a painter. Giulio Mancini, a Sienese physician, art lover, and art theorist wrote the first laudatory biography about El Greco that we have. It was based on information given to him by Lattanzio Bonastri, who had worked in El Greco's studio in Rome. Mancini wrote:

> They were preparing at that time to cover up certain [nude] figures of Michelangelo's *Last Judgment,* considered by Pius to be indecent, and [El Greco] broke in to say that if they tore down that work he could redo it with honesty and decency in a manner that was not inferior to [Michelangelo's] in terms of good, pictorial execution. Faced with the indignation of all the painters and lovers of painting, he was forced to leave for Spain, where under Philip II he painted many works in good taste.

While he was in Rome El Greco arranged the figures in his paintings in the tormented poses characteristic of Michelangelo's sculptures (though not always of his painted figures). The figures in El Greco's earlier works had never really acquired a convincing physical presence, despite his efforts as exemplified by the Adam and Eve of the *Modena Triptych.* In

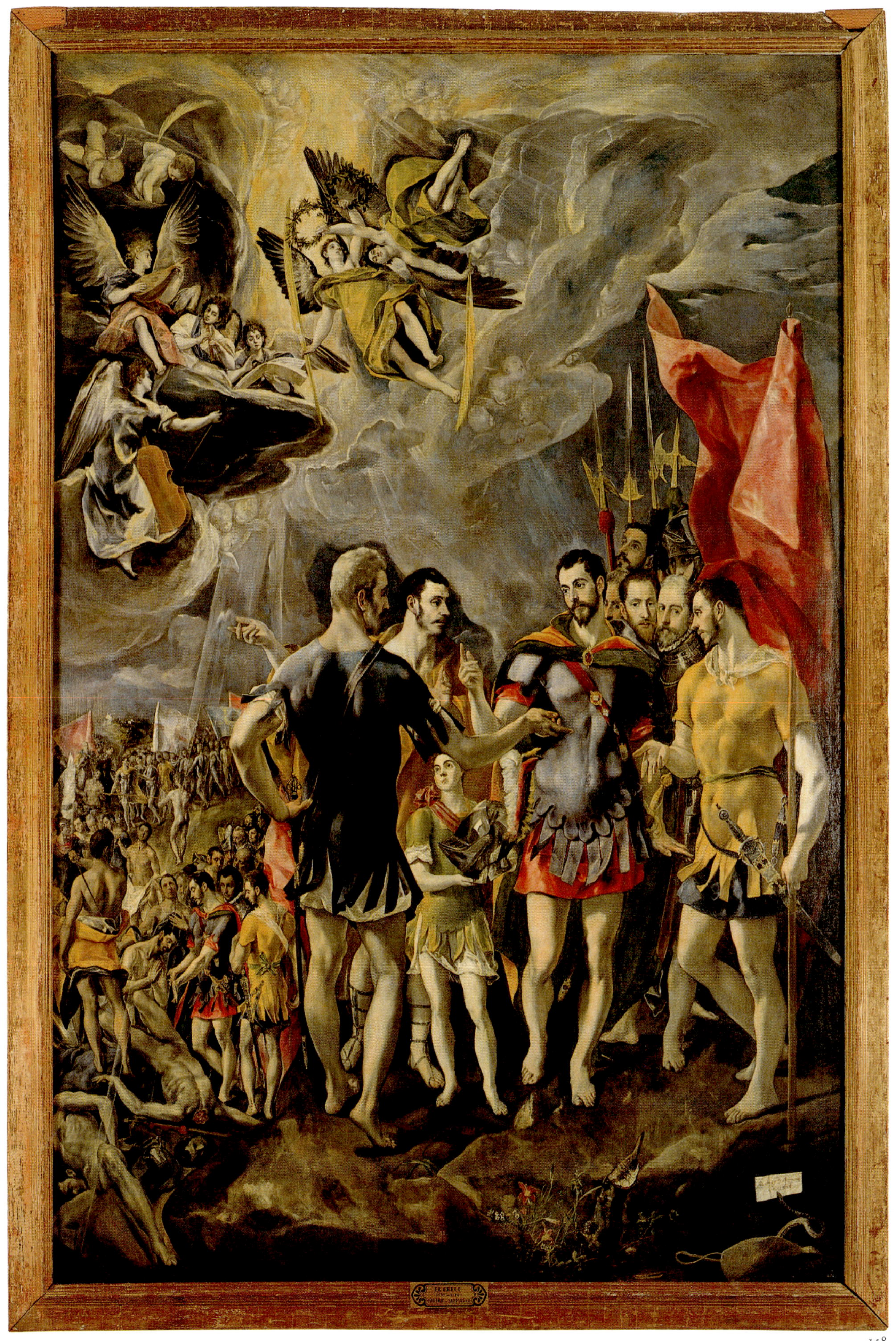

Rome, the artist began to endow his figures with a dynamic described as *terribilità* in the work of Michelangelo that makes them move and rise with an internal, unquiet, hallucinatory expressiveness. This development in El Greco's art can be seen in his first—and last—staged compositions. Two versions of the *Purification of the Temple* painted in Rome are today in the National Gallery of Art in Washington, D.C., and in the Minneapolis Institute of Arts (ill. 157). In the latter, El Greco includes portraits of Titian, Michelangelo, Giulio Clovio, and, probably, Raphael. El Greco places the enraged figure of Christ, whose pose reflects that of Christ in Michelangelo's *Last Judgment* in the Sistine Chapel (ill. 156), in an architectural setting filled with Venetian memories and Roman presences, with spaces inspired by Tintoretto and geometric constructions derived from Bramante. Christ wields a whip as he furiously expels the merchants and prostitutes who had turned the temple into a den of thieves. Jacopo Bassano's paintings of the subject treat it as an everyday market scene, and El Greco, who would have known Bassano's work in Venice, retains those anecdotal aspects of the scene while transforming it into a confrontation between the reason of law and passion. He borrows the expressive force of the figures in the *Laocoön* sculptural group (ill. 168), which had been excavated in 1506, as well as other antique sculptures, like the one then thought to represent Cleopatra.

Yet Rome, like Venice, was not the ideal place for El Greco's art, which was bizarre both in formal and conceptual terms. In 1576, after six years in Rome, with another short stay in Venice toward the end, El Greco left Italy for good. In 1577 he was in Toledo, where he lived until his death.

158. Domenikos Theotokopoulos, called El Greco
1580–83
The Martyrdom of Saint Maurice and the Theban Legion.
Real monasterio de San Lorenzo, El Escorial.

FOLLOWING PAGES:
159 and 160. Domenikos Theotokopoulos, called El Greco
c. 1577
Allegory of the Holy League, or *The Adoration of the Name of Jesus* and detail.
Real Monasterio de San Lorenzo, El Escorial.

161. View of Toledo.

"LOSING THE DESIRE TO PRAY"

Although what inspired El Greco to travel to Spain was probably the possibility of working for Philip II on the decoration of the Escorial, we know that on July 2, 1577, after a brief stay in Madrid, he received an advance payment for the painting *The Disrobing of Christ.* That commission was probably granted by the dean of the bishopric, Diego de Castilla, and, two months later Castilla also commissioned El Greco to design the main altarpiece and two side altars for the new church of the Monastery of Santo Domingo el Antiguo.

Not long after El Greco arrived in Spain, either by way of introducing himself to Philip II or perhaps on commission from the king himself, the artist painted the visionary *Allegory of the Holy League* (also called *The Adoration of the Name of Jesus*, ills. 159, 160). The painting seems to have met with the monarch's approval, as shortly afterward El Greco was asked to paint *Saint Maurice and the Theban Legions* (ill. 158) for one of the altars of the royal chapel of the Escorial. The painting is one of the artist's finest achievements. Yet, as Fray José de Sigüenza relates in his history of the building and decoration of the Escorial, the work "did not please His Majesty, which is not saying much, for it pleased few observers, although they say that it is very artistic and that its creator is learned, as can be seen in excellent works by his hand. . . . As our Mudo [the mute Spanish painter Juan Fernández de Navarrete] observed, in his way of speaking . . . 'saints should be painted so that we do not lose our desire to pray to them, putting devotion first, for this must be the main effect and goal of painting.'" By not considering the orthodoxy of the time when he created the painting, El Greco had breached decorum. King Philip surely did not like the mannerist composition of this innovative work, which ignored the Counter-Reformation requirements of clarity and propriety that the decoration of the royal chapel was intended to promote. Nevertheless, El Greco was generously paid 800 ducats for the painting at a time when paintings by Navarrete el Mudo, the most outstanding Spanish painter working at the Escorial, usually cost between 150 and 300 ducats each. Philip II consigned *The Martyrdom of Saint Maurice and the Theban Legions* to the upper cloister *(Sacristía de las Capas)* and commissioned Rómulo Cincinato to paint another version (which in fact turned out to be much indebted to El Greco) for the corresponding altar in the basilica. This incident led to El Greco's loss of any further royal commissions and the end of his dream of significant participation in the decoration of the

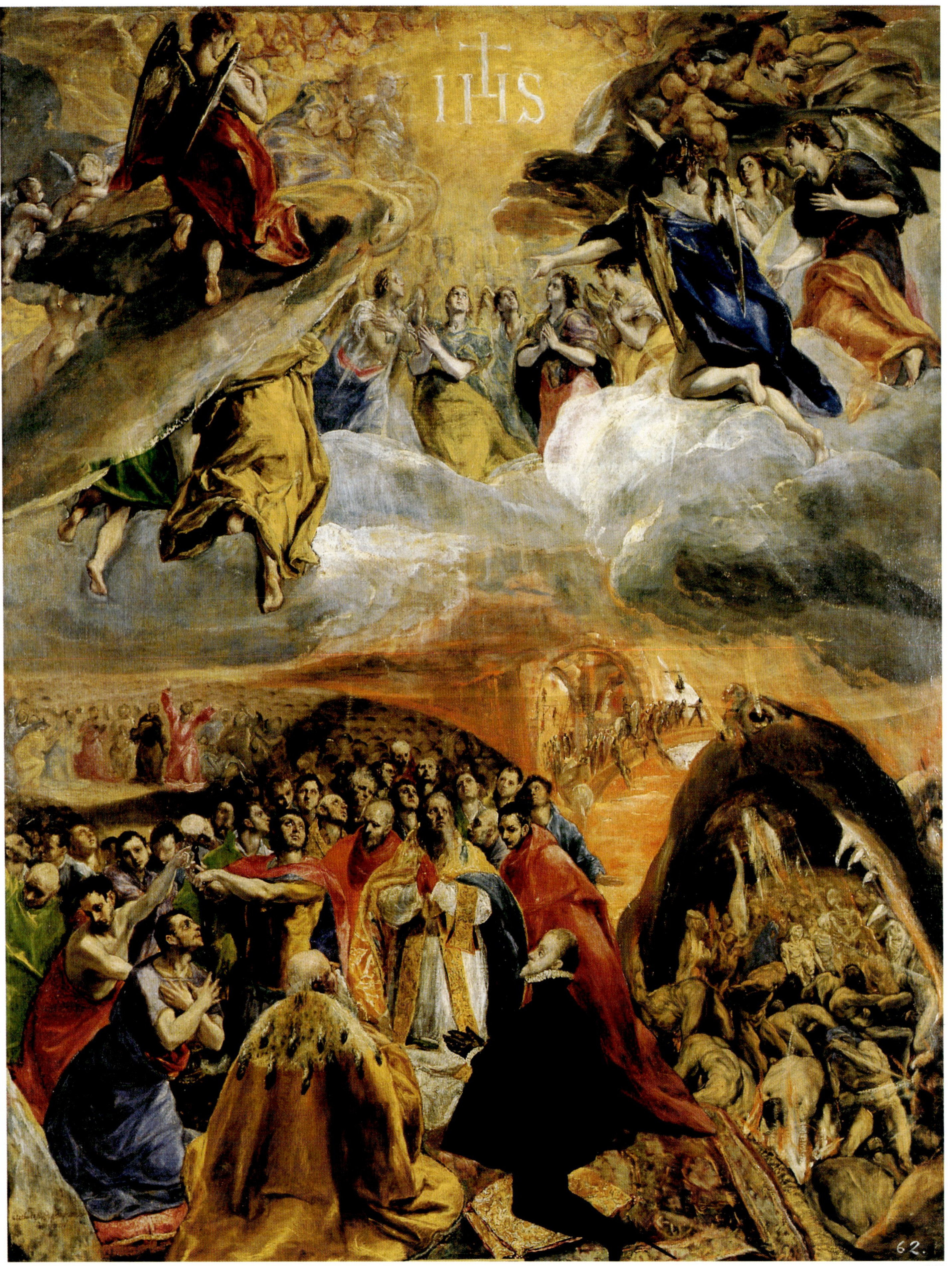
IHS
62.

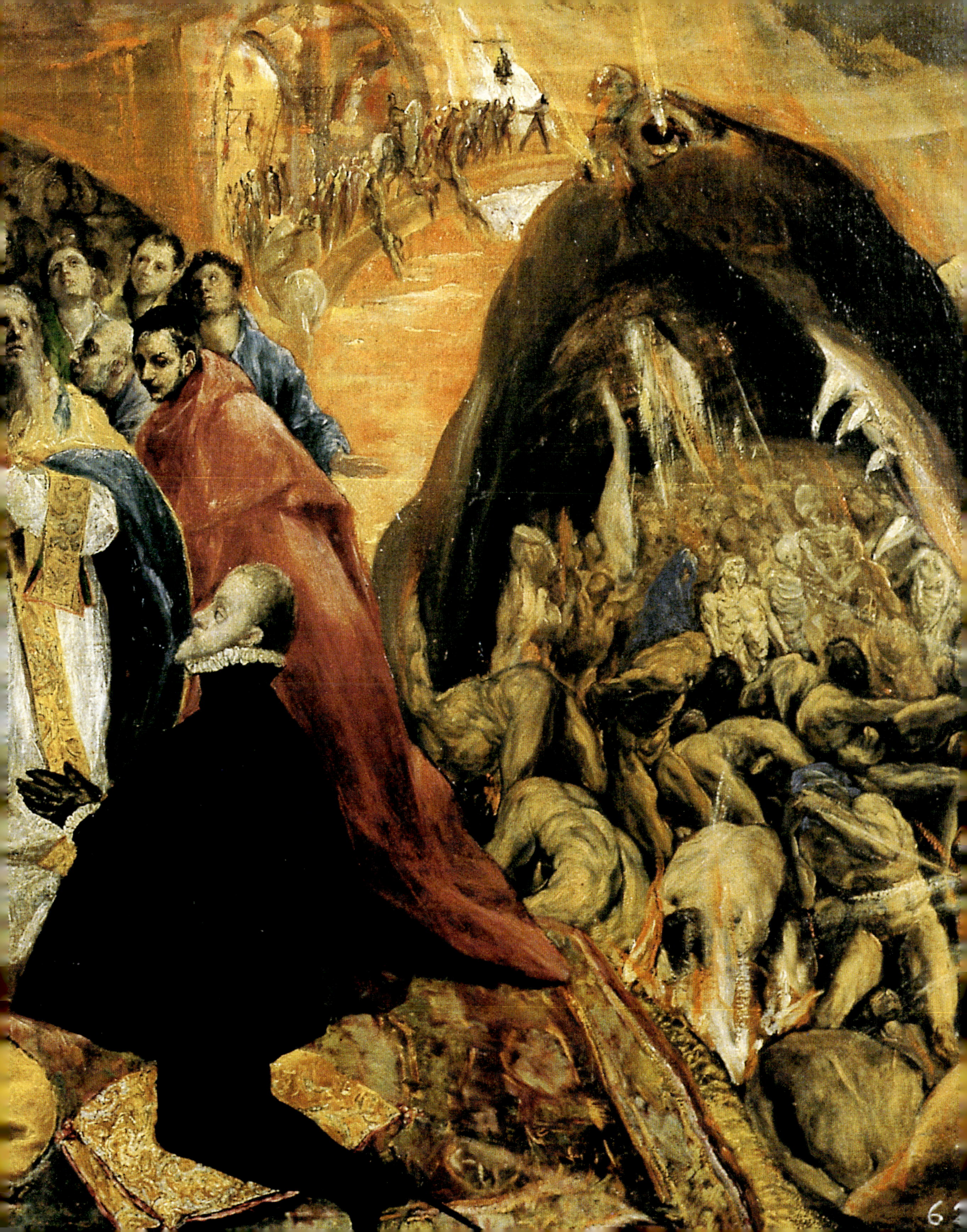

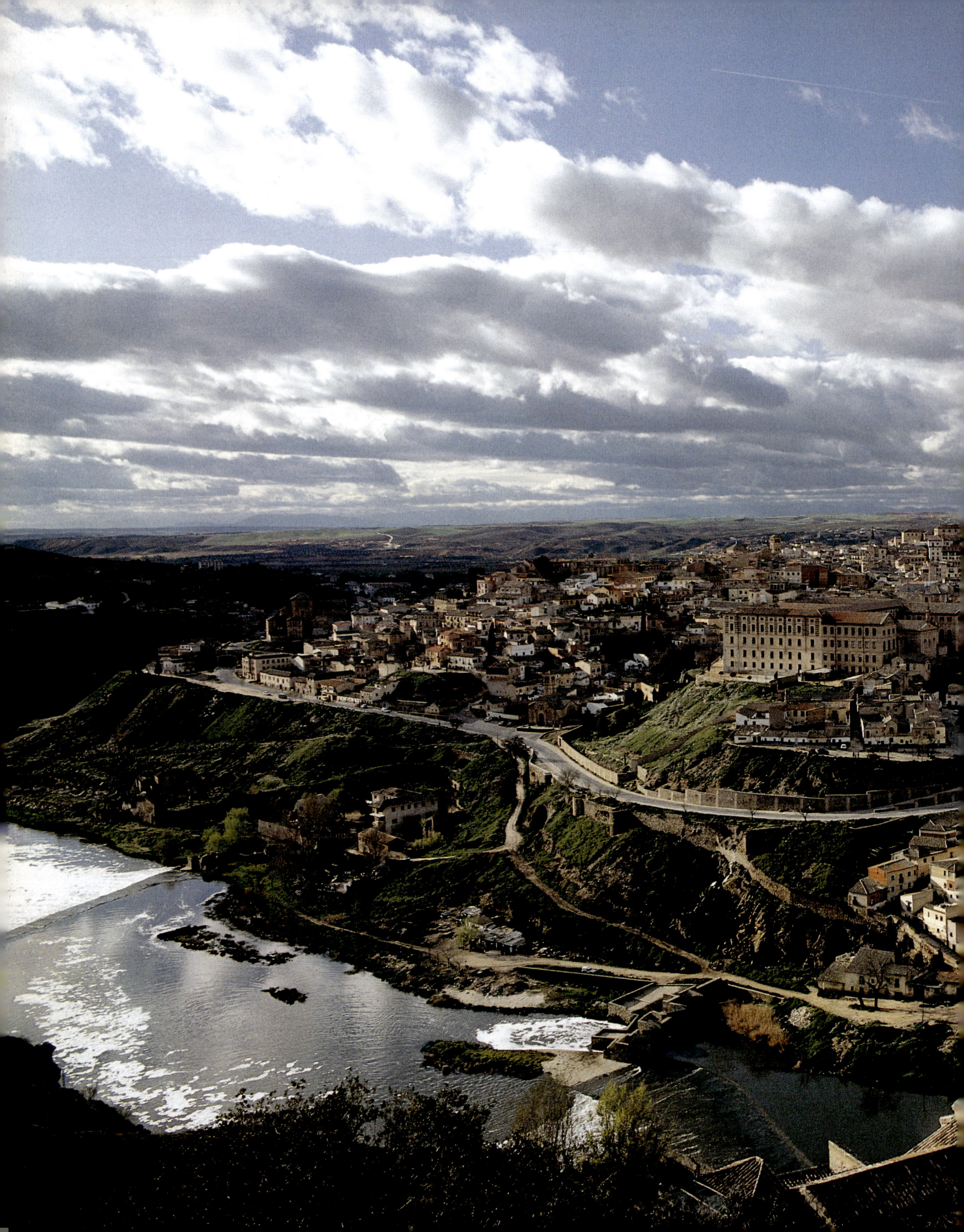

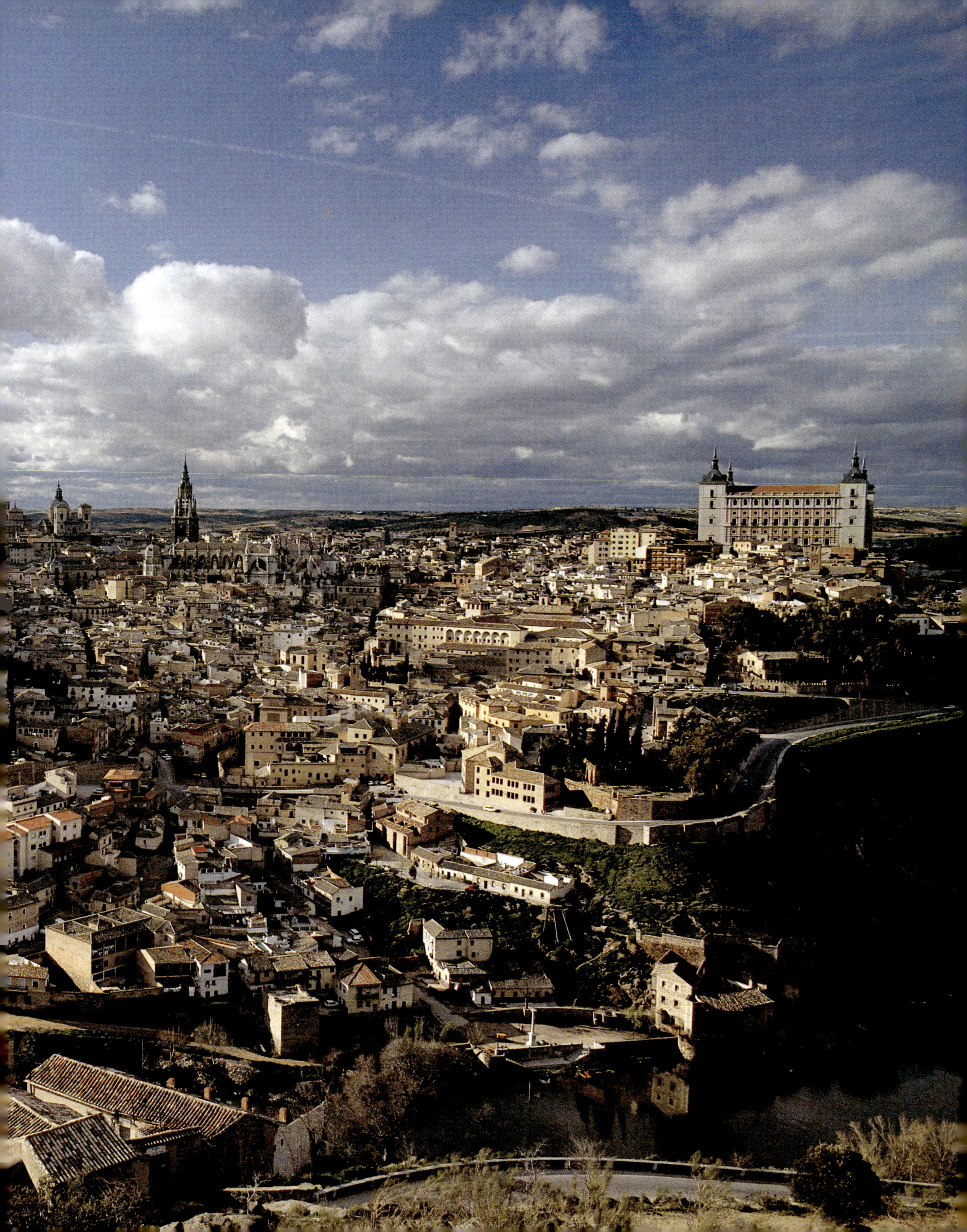

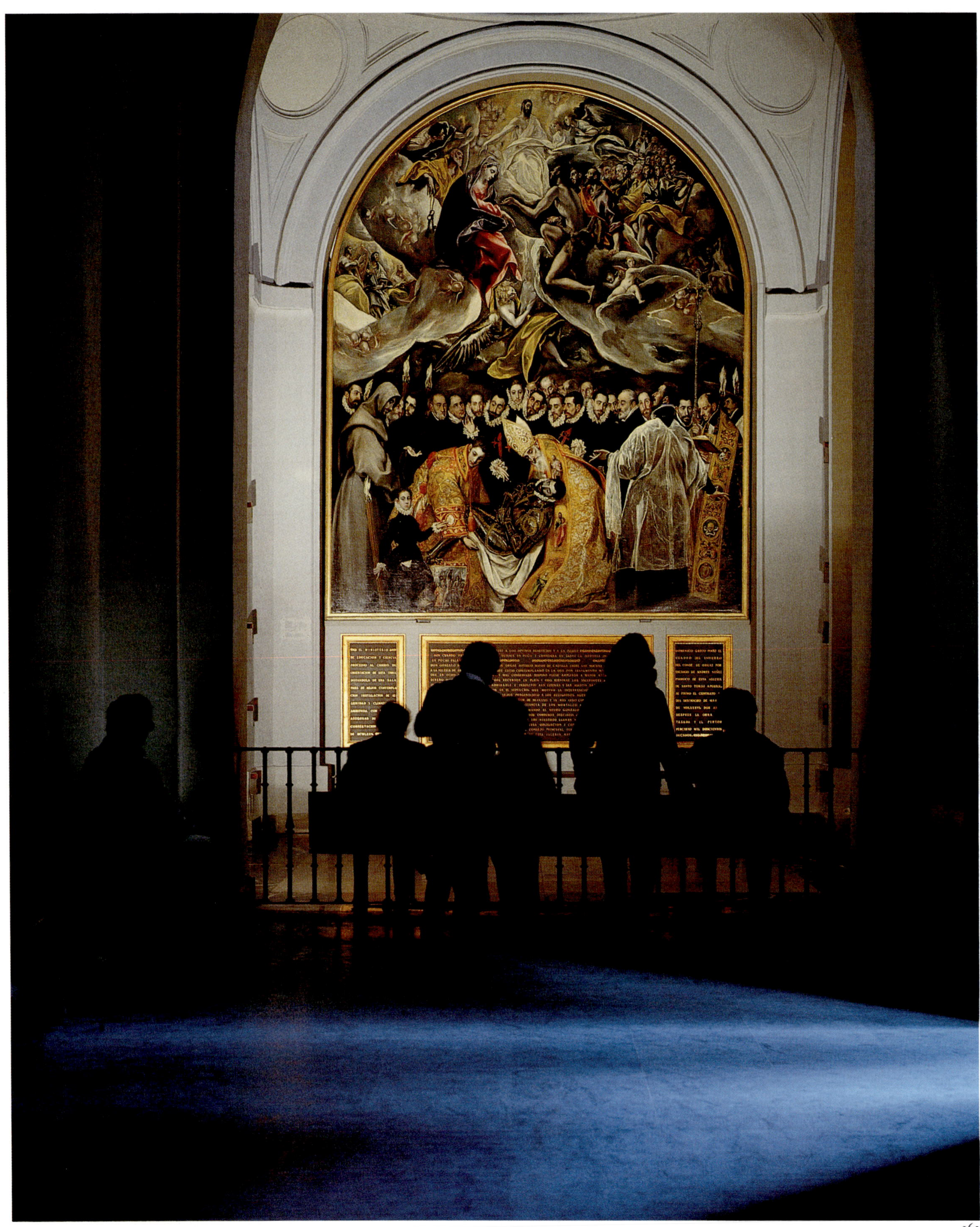

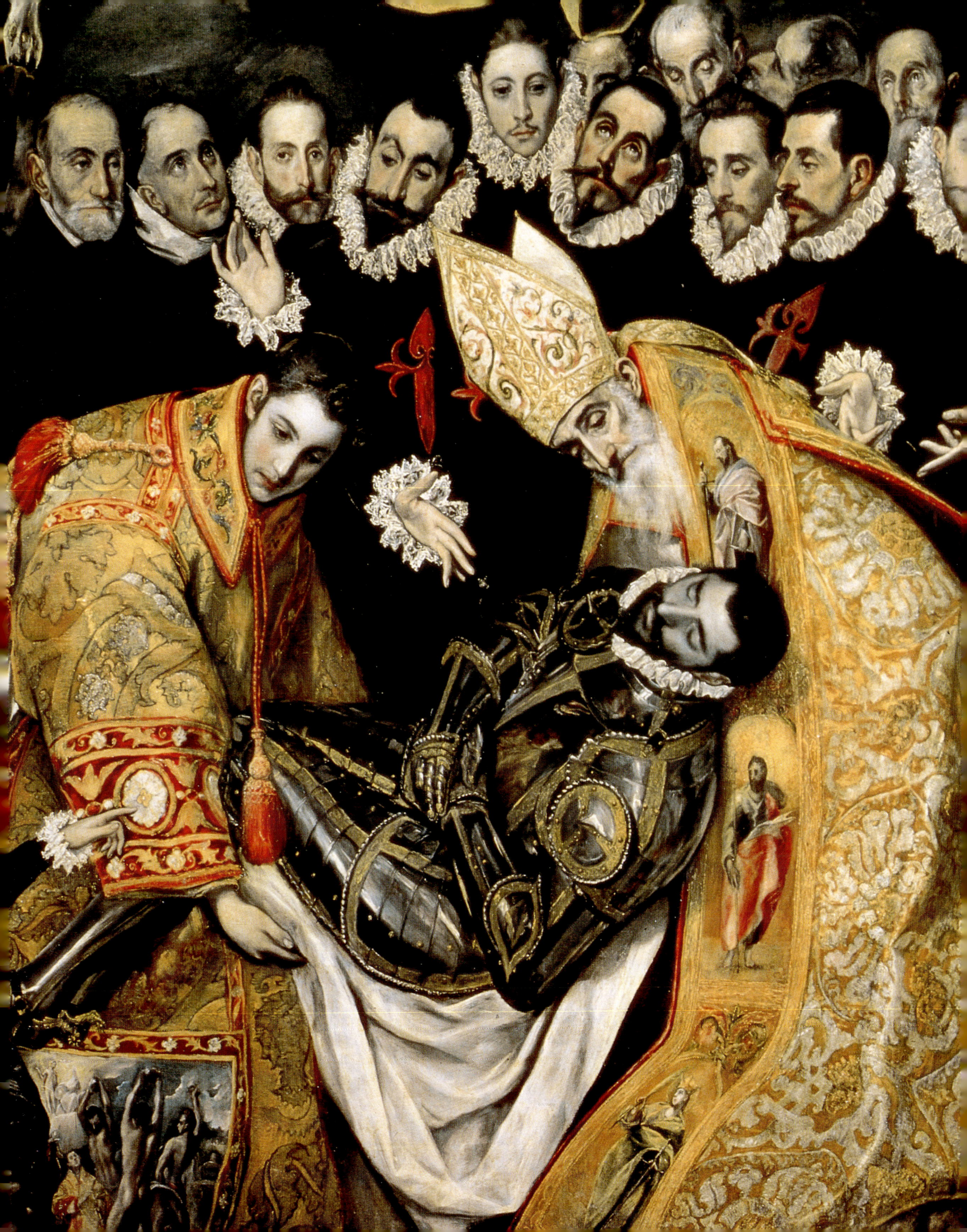

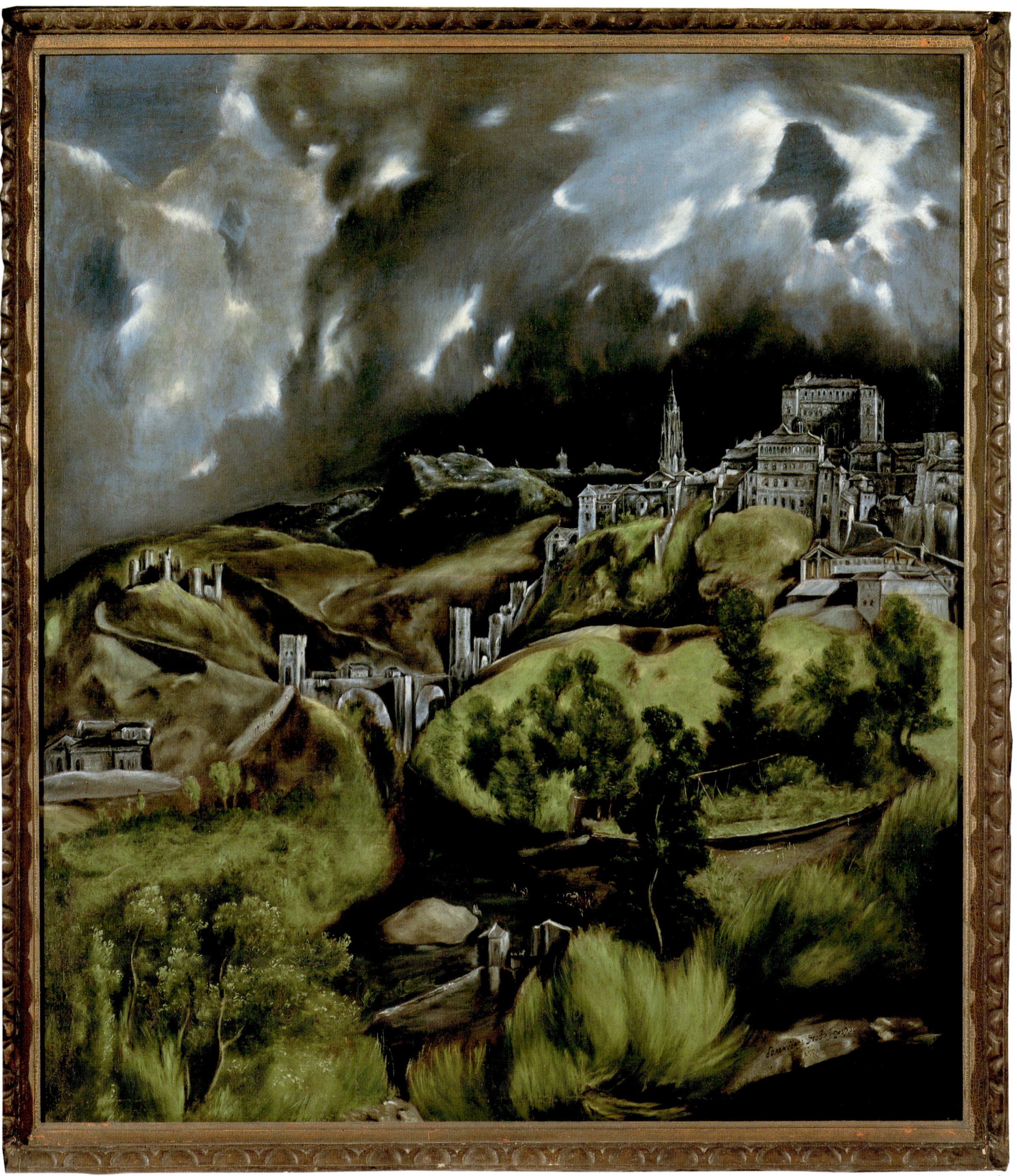

Escorial, which, he may have hoped, would be on the scale of Michelangelo's contributions to the Sistine Chapel in the Vatican.

TOLEDO

Thus disappointed, El Greco settled in Toledo for good (ill. 161). In 1578 Jorge Manuel Theotokopoulos was born to El Greco and Jerónima de las Cuevas. We know that in 1585 the painter rented a home from Juan Antonio de Cetina, in the houses of the Marquis of Villena (a renowned Toledan residence no longer extant), where he evidently lived in a fair amount of luxury until 1590, and again from 1600 to 1604. If we are to believe Jusepe Martínez's biography of the artist, "he earned many ducats, spending them in excessive ostentation on his home, even hiring musicians so as to enjoy their talents while he ate." It is possible that this rise in status began with the commission by the parish of Santo Tomé to paint one of his masterpieces, *The Burial of the Count of Orgaz* (ills. 162, 163).

In the painting, El Greco visually narrates a miracle that occurred in the fourteenth century, when the remains of the count of Orgaz were taken to be buried in the church of Santo Tomé. The nobles of the city who followed the procession on foot saw, as Francisco de Pisa relates in his *Description of the Imperial City of Toledo* (1612):

> . . . the visible and real descent from the heavens of Saint Stephen before his martyrdom and of Saint Augustine, whom everyone recognized by his appearance and dress. Arriving to where his body was, they carried him to his tomb; in the presence of everyone there they set him down, saying, "This is the reward for whoever serves God and His saints," and then they disappeared, leaving the church filled with celestial fragrance and aroma.

According to Francisco de Pisa, El Greco's painting was already in its time taken to be:

> . . . one of the most excellent [paintings] that exist in Spain. . . . Many visitors come to see it with particular admiration, while residents of the city never tire of doing so, always finding new things to contemplate in it, for many of the most distinguished men of our time are vividly portrayed there.

In spite of such recognition, El Greco did not have a lot of work, so he sought to widen his clientele in other cities, among them Seville, Cáceres, and Madrid, where he was hired to paint the high altarpiece of the College or Seminary of the Incarnation (also known by the name of its founder, María de Aragón), which he completed between 1596 and 1600. Thereafter, El Greco worked on paintings destined exclusively for Toledo and its environs: the high altarpiece and the two side altars of the Chapel of Saint Joseph (1597–99); the altarpiece for the Franciscan college of Saint Bernardino (1603); the commission for the Hospital de la Caridad in Illescas (1603–05), the execution of which was the "best and most perfect in Spain," El Greco claimed during the long legal conflict between him and the patrons of the hospital); the canvases done for the Ovalle chapel in Saint Vincent Martyr (1607–13); and the paintings for the Tavera Hospital (1608–14). He died suddenly while working on the latter. Besides these monumental works, El Greco satisfied the high demand for devotional canvases for parishes, monasteries, and private clients, for whom he, along with his studio, repeated subjects such as the Penitent Mary Magdalene, the Tears of Saint Peter, and the saints (especially Francis, Jerome, and Dominic), the Holy Family, and scenes of the Passion of Christ. Such paintings, though turned out routinely, are of consistently high quality.

The city of Toledo itself—then full of minor nobility, rogues, and beggars, dominated by the religious orders, and without any imperial role—did not seem to inspire El Greco. Unlike the painters who had worked in the Veneto and were drawn visually and sentimentally to picture Venice in some of their paintings and use it as the subject of others, El Greco's paintings of Toledo (ill. 164) are not *vedute*—views of the city—but rather landscapes of the torments of the soul.

PRECEDING PAGES:
162. Domenikos Theotokopoulos, called El Greco
1586–88
The Burial of the Count of Orgaz.
Church of Santo Tomé, Toledo.

163. Domenikos Theotokopoulos, called El Greco
1586–88
Detail of *The Burial of the Count of Orgaz.*
Church of Santo Tomé, Toledo.

LEFT:
164. Domenikos Theotokopoulos, called El Greco
c. 1600
View of Toledo.
Metropolitan Museum of Art, New York.

LAOCOÖN

In spite of his time in Venice, El Greco was not drawn to paint either rural or urban landscapes, even as backdrops to other subjects. Having forged his art in the general and universal realm of the individual, he saw the human being as a landscape of essences and sentiments, of presences and absences, of passions and serenity, of visions of transcendence and everyday realities; man, in sum, both grand and hopeless. He portrays groups ("the most distinguished men of our time are vividly portrayed there," Alonso de Villega wrote about the figures assembled for the burial of the Count of Orgaz), and he portrays the individual in solitude faced with himself and those who observe him. He does so in the portrait of the impassive gentleman with a hand on his chest (c. 1580), his sweet face and absent gaze framed by a detailed ruff. He does so in portrayals of stubborn, heartless men, as suggested by the set of the lips and uneasy gaze of Cardinal Fernando Niño de Guevara behind the pince-nez, wearing the pompous crimson of the vestments of a general inquisitor who later became archbishop of Seville (ill. 165). He does so as well as in the portrait based on the death mask of Cardinal Tavera (c. 1610), and in the poetic grandeur of the Trinitarian friar Hortensio Félix de Paravicino (c. 1605).

El Greco plunges beneath the surface to portray the individual in depth, even in his *Laocoön,* the only mythological subject he ever painted. The inventory of El Greco's possessions drawn up after his death lists three versions of the *Laocoön,* although only the one described as "large" still exists (National Gallery of Art, Washington, D.C., ills. 166, 167). In the second part of *The Aeneid,* Virgil describes the Trojan Laocoön, the priest of Apollo who was punished for attacking with his spear the enormous wooden horse with which the Greeks had planned to conquer Troy. Apollo summoned two great serpents from the sea to kill Laocoön and his two sons. El Greco does not strictly follow Virgil's narrative, but draws some of the intense drama of the painting from the poet's words. He paints with rapture a dynamic chorus of distorted nudes in unstable poses who express the suffering of *Laocoön* with an immediacy seldom seen in El Greco's oeuvre.

The composition perhaps also reflects the tight interlacing of figures found in the antique sculpture discovered in 1506 that has occasionally been thought to be the work of Michelangelo himself (ill. 168). The supplication of the son who lifts his head to the sky while trying to fend off the fatal bite to his side; Laocoön's terrified expression; his fallen body about to lose its struggle against the serpent; and the still body of his other son are all circumscribed by an invisible circle. The curves and countercurves of the figural composition contrast with the verticality of the mysterious presences on the right and the soft contour of the horizon. The harmonious gray tones, unlike the dark stone and warm touches of color seen in *View of Toledo* (ill. 164), set off the sinuous silhouettes of the figures and model their musculature with its intermittent shadows, recalling the marmoreal surface of the Hellenistic sculpture. The man and woman on the right side of the composition do not appear in the myth. El Greco creates them as witnesses to the injustice of divine retribution. On the distant horizon, beneath a cloud-charged sky, Toledo, a modern Troy, lies undaunted, while in the center of the narrative space, between Laocoön and the city gate, the Puerta Nueva de Bisagra, we see the troublesome horse.

In 1611, when El Greco was putting the last touches on the *Laocoön*, Francisco Pacheco, Velázquez's father-in-law, who was a painter, theorist, and art censor of the Inquisition, visited El Greco's studio. Pacheco's attitude toward El Greco's art, expressed in a number of passages in *The Art of Painting,* is one of surprise and ambiguity. Pacheco was critical of El Greco, but his comments reveal a lack of understanding. Above all he accused El Greco of not having mastered drawing and criticized his technique of painting with what looked to Pacheco like mere blobs. Pacheco was a staunch believer in the primacy of drawing and understood sketches, as did many of his contemporaries, to be merely studies for what would be the refined surface of the finished painting. The "sketchy" style of El Greco's

RIGHT:
165. Domenikos Theotokopoulos, called El Greco
c. 1600
Cardinal Fernando Niño de Guevara.
Metropolitan Museum of Art, New York.

FOLLOWING PAGES:
166. Domenikos Theotokopoulos, called El Greco
c. 1610
Laocoön.
National Gallery of Art, Washington, D.C.

167. Domenikos Theotokopoulos, called El Greco
c. 1610
Detail of *Laocoön.*
National Gallery of Art, Washington, D.C.

168. Hagesandrus, Polydorus, and Athenodorus of Rhodes
Second half of the first century B.C.
Detail of *Laocoön and His Two Sons,*
marble.
Pio-Clementino Museum, Vatican.

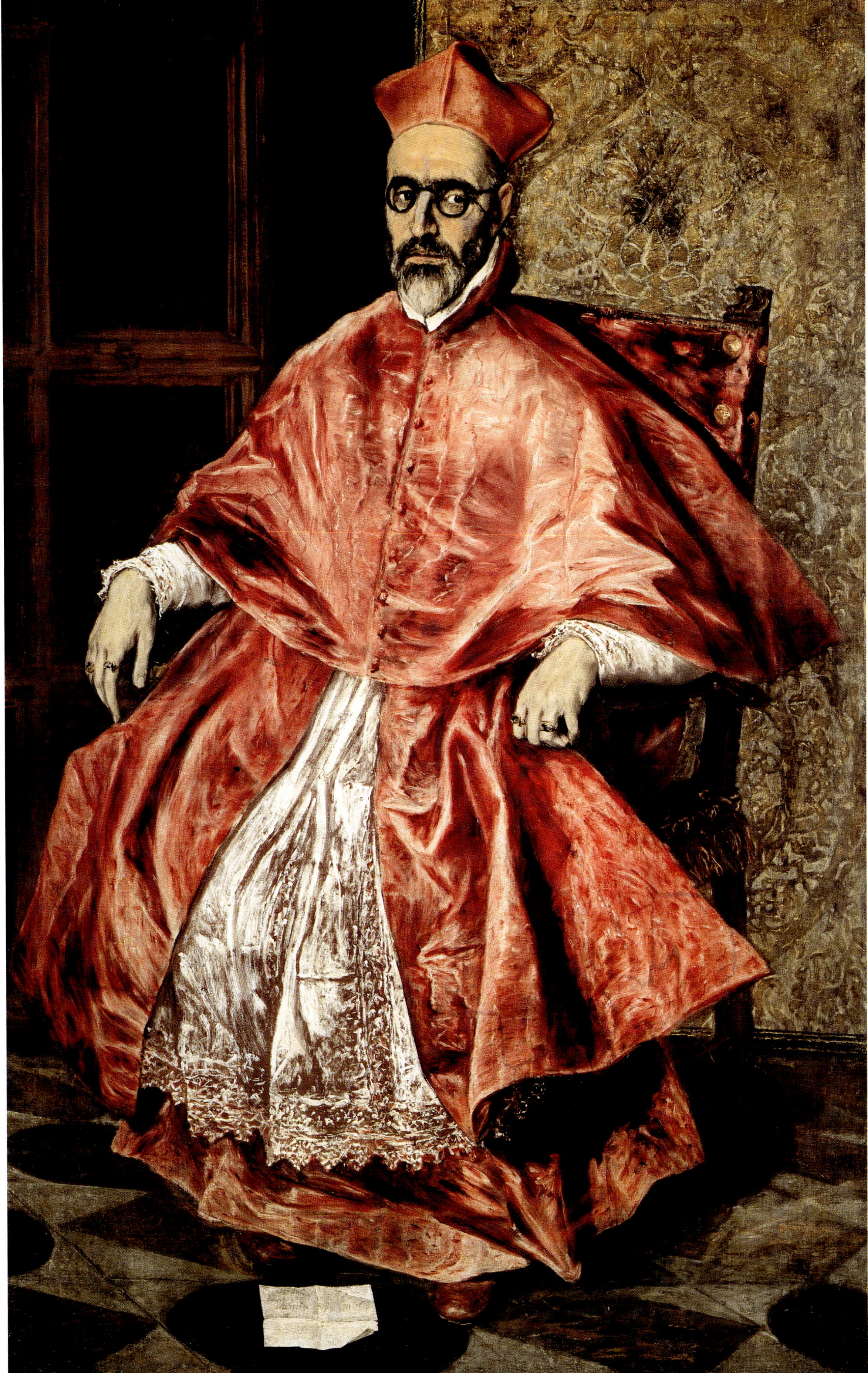

finished paintings left Pacheco unimpressed: "Who would believe that Domenico Greco works on his paintings over and over again, and retouches them again and again to leave a variety of disunited colors and add those cruel sketches to affect brio? This is what I call working to look bad."

According to Pacheco, the Trojan priest and his sons are sketches that do not result from a control of color, but from the desire to have the design suppress geometrical, or in this case anatomical, truth, the canon that the Renaissance had relied on to reproduce beauty.

For El Greco, truth was something else. The *Laocoön* is a visionary painting in which the figures, like those in his painting called the *The Vision of Saint John,* or *The Opening of the Fifth Seal* (The Metropolitan Museum of Art, New York), are stains of color almost without drawing, without contours. The forms are agitated and elongated until they are far from canonical, and gesture and light are used as expressive elements. This cannot be understood without the blending of east and west, of classical and mannerist styles, without the desire to convert painting into pure thought, distancing it from the "truth" as perceived by the human eye.

After El Greco's death, his followers found themselves before a radiant orb that paradoxically could only illuminate tenebrous shadows. We know very little about the Toledan studio of El Greco. The artistic personality of the Italian Francisco Preboste, who may have joined the Roman workshop of the Cretan painter and stayed with him at least until 1607, is quite unknown. Similarly, the hand of El Greco's son, Jorge Manuel Theotokopoulos, who probably started out as a simple studio assistant, could not be identified until he began to work alone on the canvases of the Madrid altarpiece of Titulcia, or Bayona de Tajuña (1607–21). There his work reveals him to be a docile follower of his father's late style. The sole example of an immediate follower of El Greco is Luis Tristán, who might have been influenced by his master between 1603 and 1607, when he left for Italy. Tristán's later production shifted toward the Caravaggesque naturalism he had the opportunity to learn in Italy.

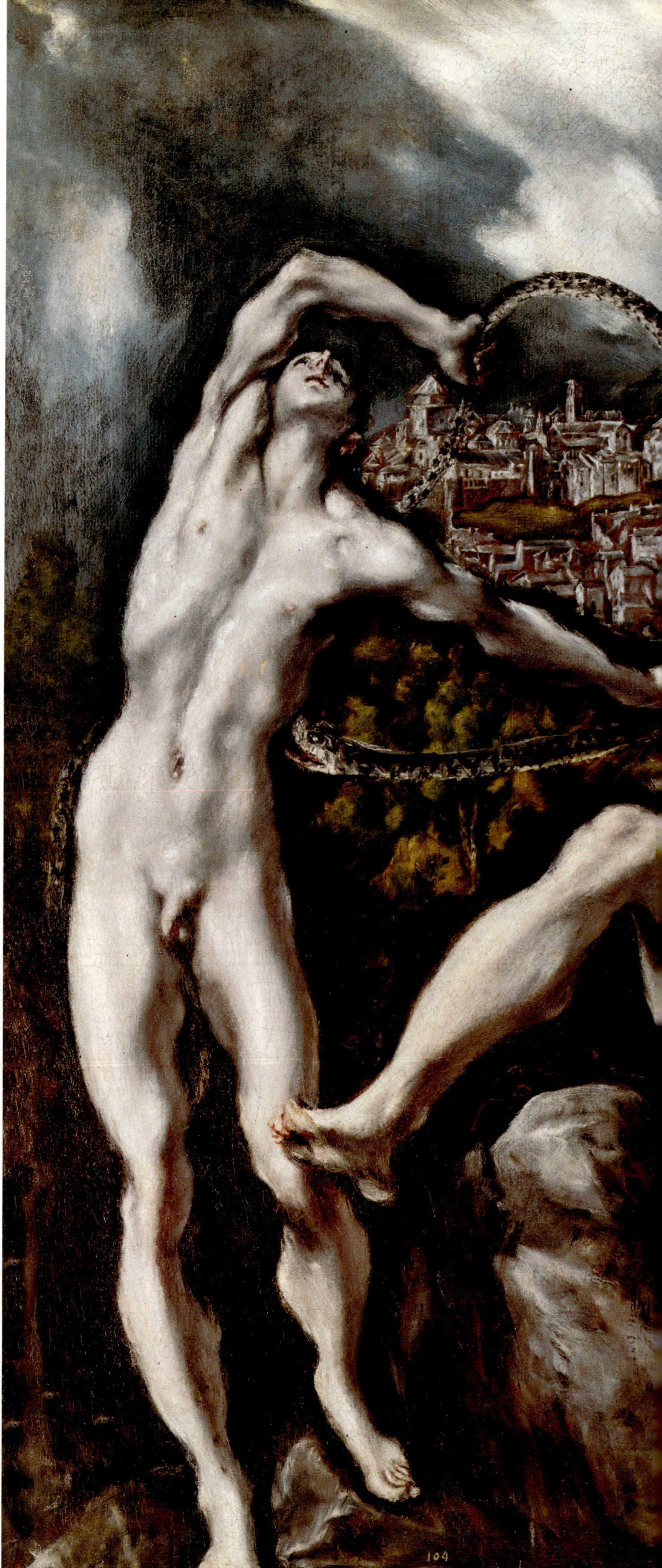

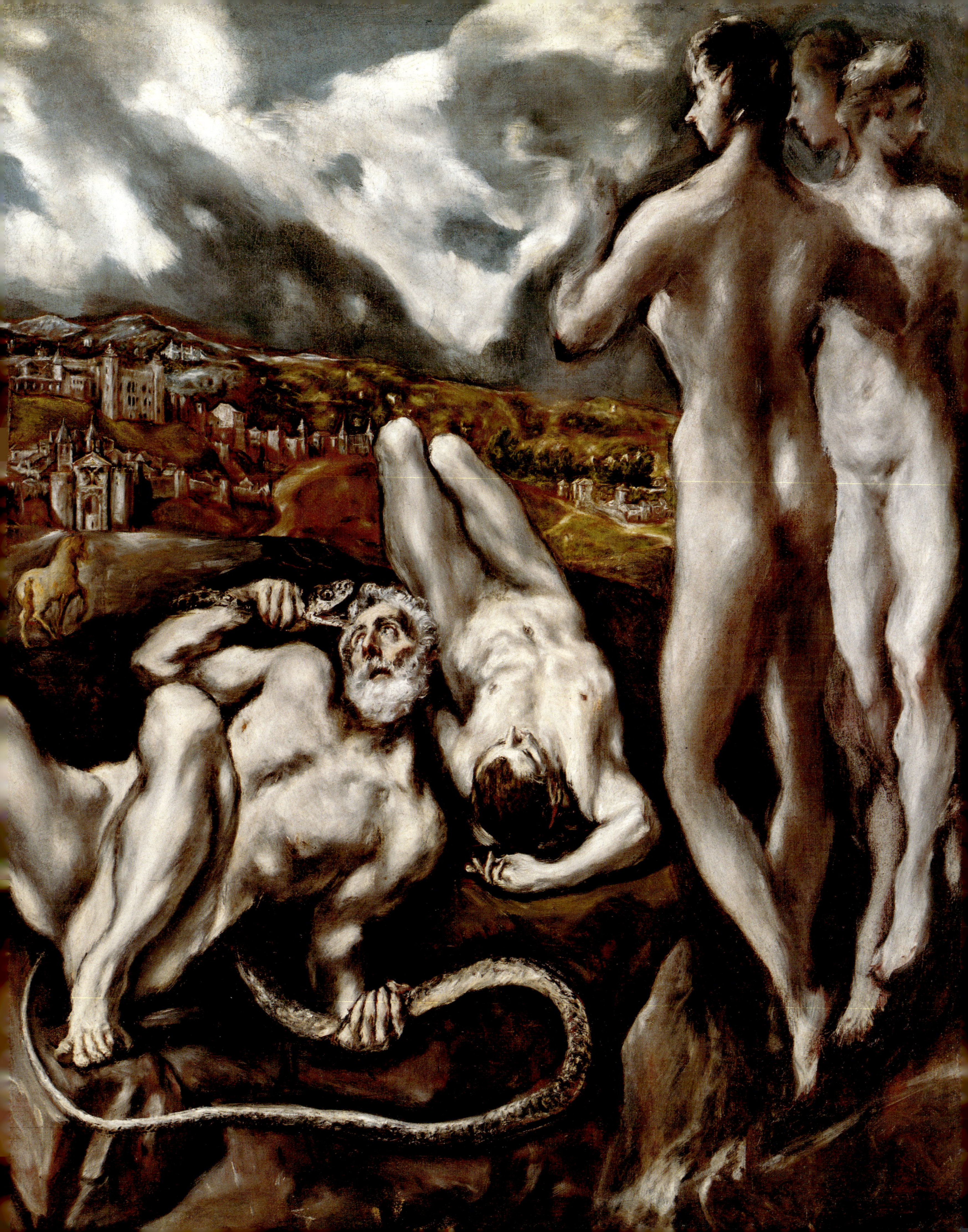

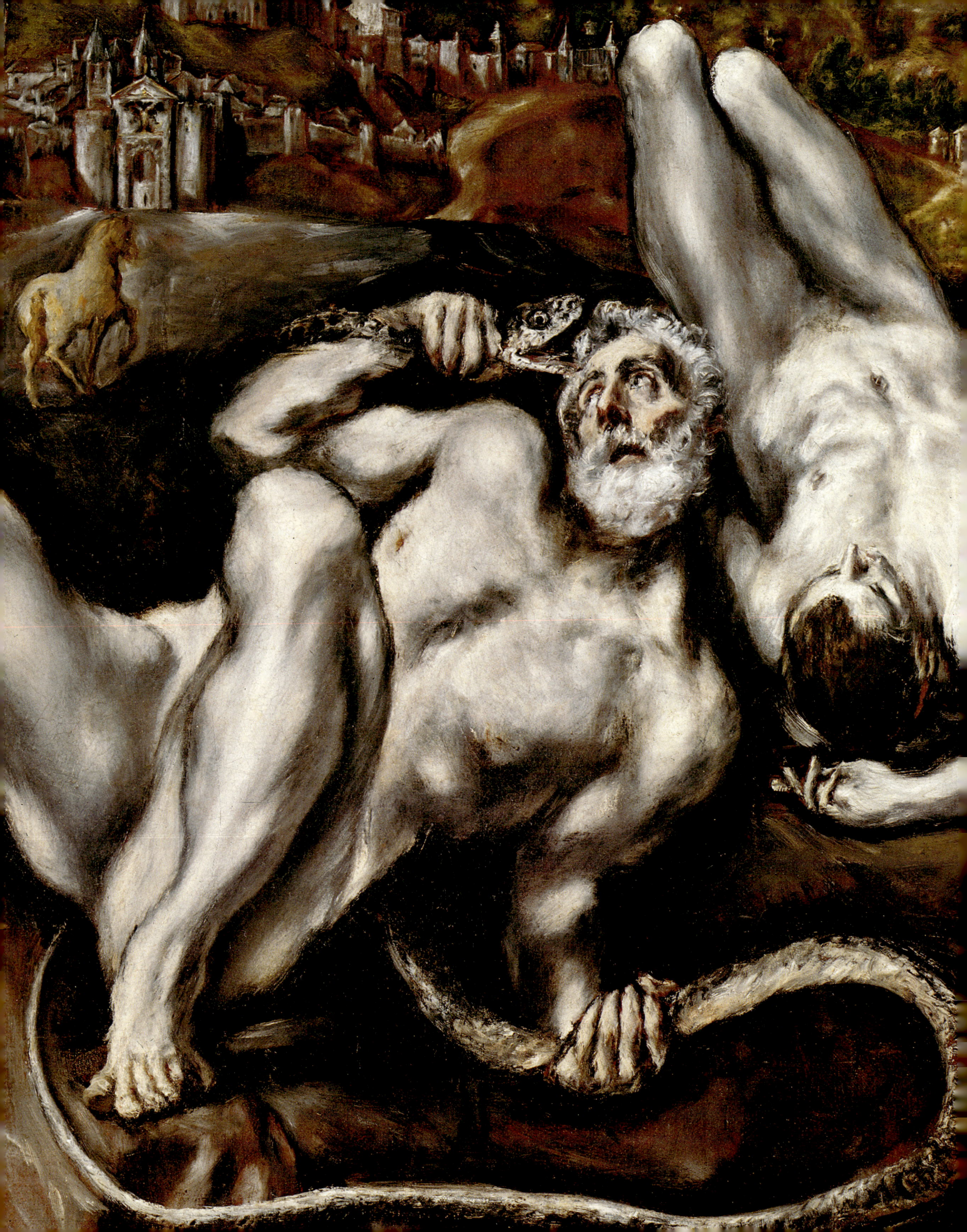

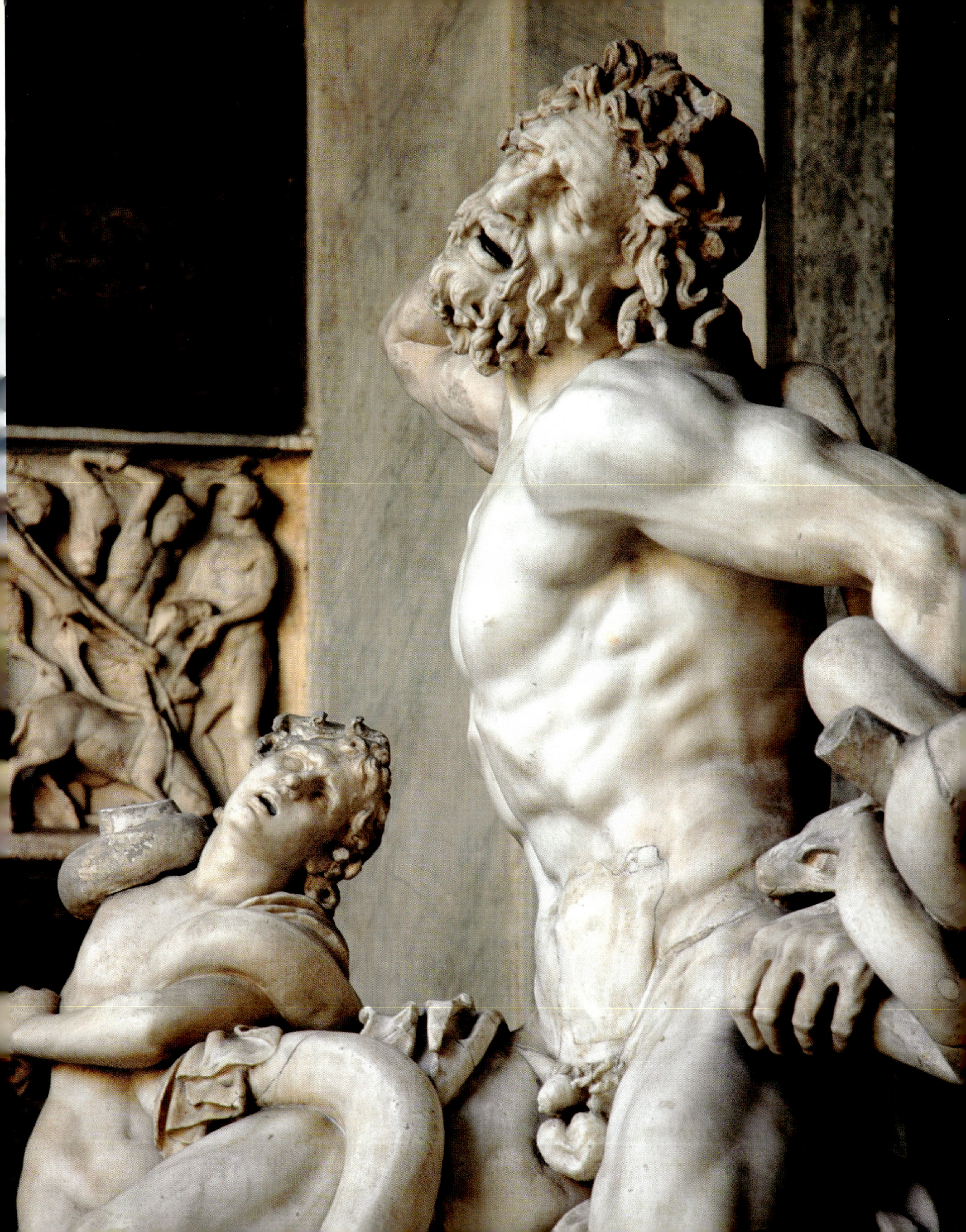

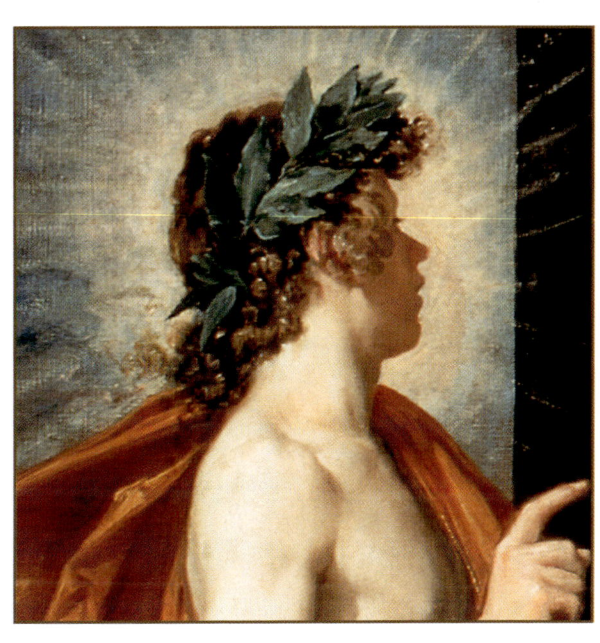

VELÁZQUEZ, PAINTER AND CHAMBERLAIN

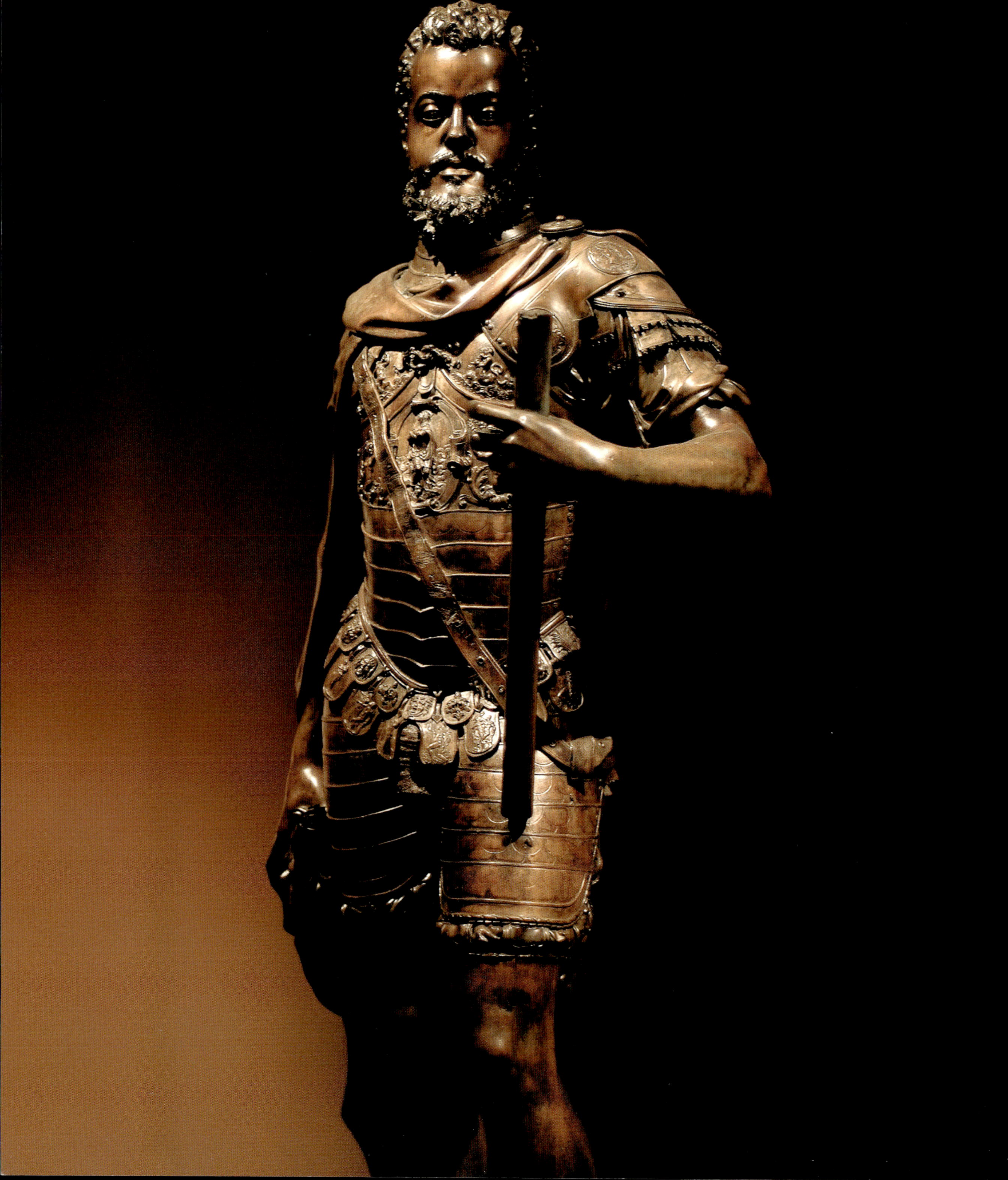

5

VELÁZQUEZ, PAINTER AND CHAMBERLAIN

His ability to create beautiful portraits
done with art in great likeness grew
so greatly that they were marvelled at,
both by painters and by men of good taste.

—JUSEPE MARTÍNEZ, *Practical Discourses on the Very Noble Art of Painting*, 1682

A few hours before dawn on September 13, 1598, the stones of the Escorial, whipped by strong, searing winds coming off the mountains, were shaken by the death of Philip II, first-born son of Charles V and Isabella of Portugal and the most powerful monarch of his time. Long before Valdés Leal painted the *Hieroglyphs of the Four Last Things* (see ills. 72–74), the king himself had endured them; his pain-stricken body was consumed by cancer, riddled with open sores, a drainage hole in his stomach. He died in a foul-smelling room filled with relics, among them six unicorn horns, which the monarch, in his last will and testament, had requested to accompany the "successors to these realms"; candles; and the crucifix that Charles V had held to his breast when he died.

The entire Hispanic world mourned. Seville prepared the funeral rites of the man known as the Julius Caesar of the Alameda de Hercules: "Great Prince, and Highly Noble Restorer of this Colony of Romulus" read the inscription on the base of the statue bearing his likeness. In imitation of the "temple of San Lorenzo el Real, in the town of El Escorial," the city put up the most ostentatious, expensive, and solemn funerary monument ever, a marvelous structure made of wood and canvas. Its maker, Jerónimo Collado wrote:

> not a single stone was taken from the church . . . for the funerary monument . . . it was not supported by anything, nor was a single nail driven into any part of it; yet this structure was as sturdy and strong as though it had been made of stone.

This ephemeral monument was primarily the work of master architects, including its principal designer, Juan de Oviedo, and Juan Martínez, Diego López, and Martín Infante; the participating sculptors were Juan Martínez Montañes and Gaspar Núñez Delgado; the painters, Alonso Vázquez, Francisco Pacheco, Vasco Pereira, and Juan Salcedo. The catafalque, whose overall invention can be attributed to Pacheco, a prebendary of the cathedral, was on view in the Cathedral of

PRECEDING PAGE:
169. Diego Velázquez
1630
Detail of *The Forge of Vulcan*.
Museo Nacional del Prado, Madrid.

LEFT:
170. Leone Leoni and Pompeo Leoni
1551–53
Philip II, bronze.
Museo Nacional del Prado, Madrid.

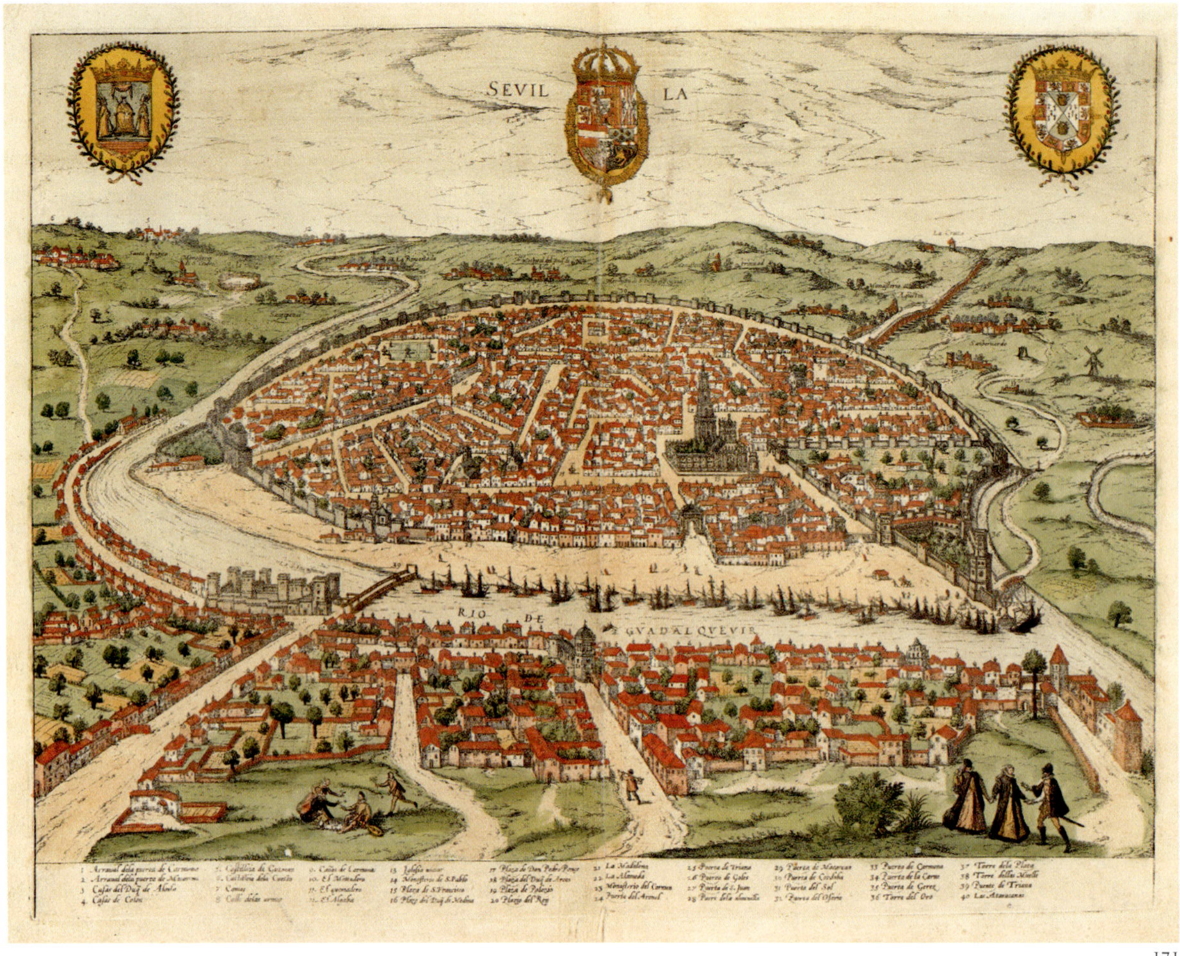

171

Seville for the exceptionally long period of thirty-five days, and it attracted the awe and admiration of visitors from near and far. Among them was Miguel de Cervantes Saavedra, a tax collector from the National Treasury, as well as a soldier and a writer of prose and poetry, who was commissioned to compose a poem in royal couplets dedicated to the death of Philip II. He also wrote a satirical sonnet about the ephemeral monument, which had cost 15,000 ducats:

> I swear to God that this grandeur frightens me
> and would give a doubloon to describe it;
> for who is not surprised and astonished
> by this notable machine, this richness?
>
> By Jesus Christ alive, each piece
> is worth more than a million, and it is sure
> that it will not last a century. Oh, great Seville!
> Triumphant Rome in soul and nobility.
>
> I will bet that the soul of the deceased
> so as to enjoy this site, has now left
> the glory where he lives eternally.
>
> A braggart heard this, and said: "It is true
> what you say, sir soldier,
> And whoever says the contrary lies."
>
> And later, unchastened,
> he firmly placed his hat, sought out his sword,
> took a sidelong glance, went away, and there was
> nothing.

DIEGO

It did not last a century—in fact, not even a year. A few months after the statue was dismantled, on June 6, 1599, the eldest child of Juan Rodríguez de Silva and Jerónima Velázquez was baptized in the parish church of San Pedro in Seville (ill. 171) and given the name of his paternal grandfather. Diego Velázquez grew up on a little street named Gorgoja in a city that had enjoyed its moment of greatness, thanks in good part to the gold and silver from the Americas that had paid for its adornment throughout the sixteenth century. However, an economic crisis was just around the corner, and it was to affect

171. 1599
View of Seville in the *Civitatis Orbis Terrarum* by Georg Braun and Frans Hogenberg,
colored engraving.
Biblioteca Universitaria, Seville.

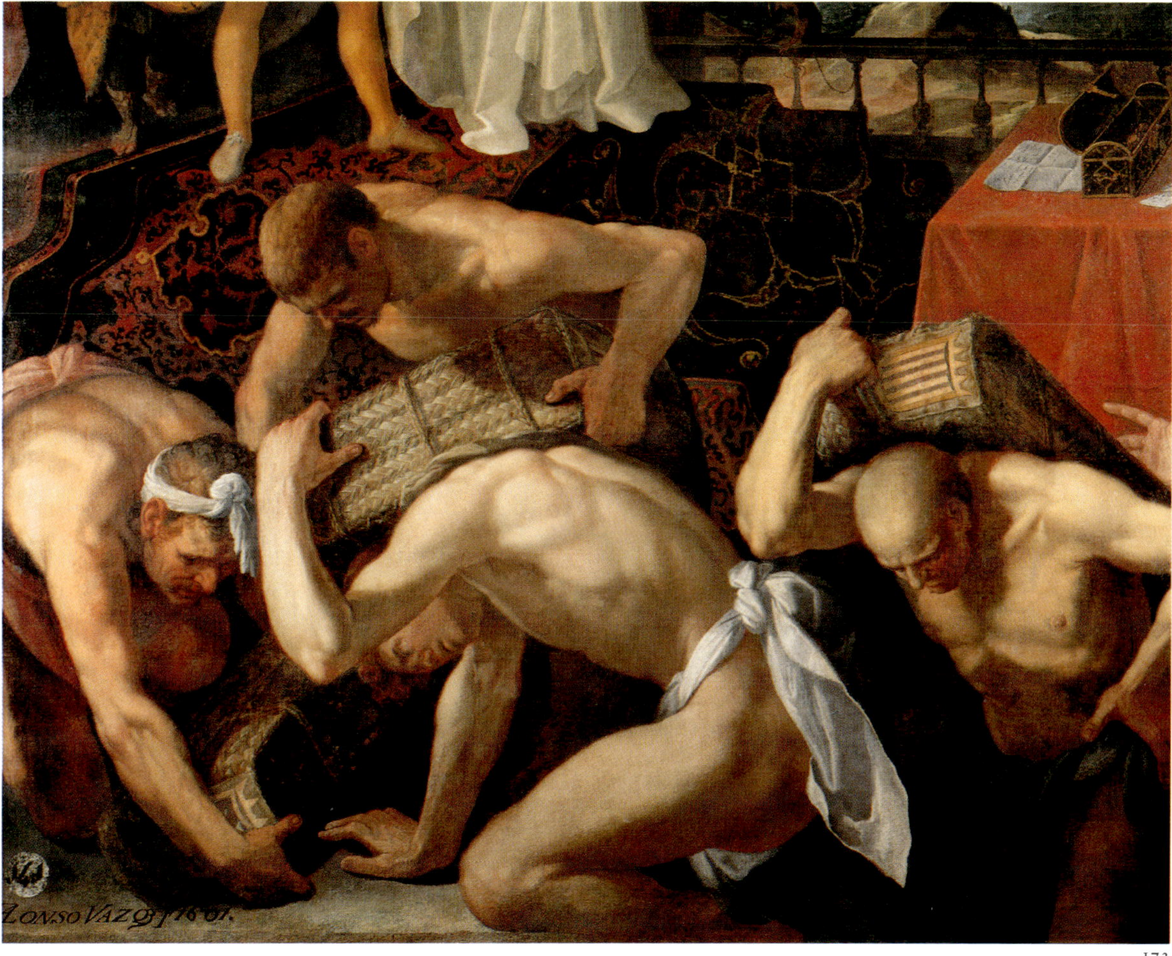

172

not only Seville. At the beginning of the seventeenth century not a single new bank would open anywhere in Spain, and Seville was a city in decline. Its port was less busy, and business transacted at the once-thriving fairs and markets had slacked off. The lack of activity meant that many people had to leave town, and many homes were abandoned and brought to ruin. Seville teemed with rogues, vagabonds, and shifty gamblers.

Nothing is known about the boyhood of Diego or his six younger siblings—only one of them, Juana, a girl—until he was twelve years old. In fact, nothing much would be known about practically any Sevillian boy of the time. His father's family had roots in nearby Oporto, Portugal. After studying with the Jesuits and most likely having been subjected to the discipline of the painter Francisco de Herrera the Elder, Velázquez's talent for drawing enabled him to enter the workshop of the aforementioned Francisco Pacheco as an apprentice. Pacheco was a faithful follower of Tridentine orthodoxy in religious art, and in 1616 was appointed a censor of works of art by the Inquisition in Seville.

Diego Velázquez had access to the paintings and knowledge of both Herrera and Pacheco, as well as to the paintings of Alonso Vázquez (who was in turn indebted to both Venetian and Flemish art, ill. 172), Mateo Pérez de Alesio from Rome, the Portuguese artist Vasco Pereira, and the naturalistic works of Juan de Roelas. Thanks to all of this exposure, Diego learned to appreciate the reality of things and of people. Yet neither these influences, nor the paintings of Jusepe Ribera and Caravaggio that he had surely seen when they arrived in Seville from Italy, nor works by El Greco, Luis Tristán, and possibly Rómulo Cincinnato, can explain how he came to transform what he saw around him into painting. In Seville, young Diego shaped his intellect, his eye, and his hand so that he could fully understand reality and be able to paint it. We do not know what guided him along the path of apparent ease that would always govern his painting.

We know little about how Diego lived and worked during his apprenticeship. In *The Art of*

172. Alonso Vázquez
1601
Detail of *San Pedro Nolasco Bidding Farewell to Jaime I.*
Museo de Bellas Artes, Seville.

OVERLEAF:
173. Diego Velázquez
c. 1616–17
Old Woman Cooking Eggs.
National Gallery of Scotland, Edinburgh.

Painting Francisco Pacheco describes his charge as a working "lad," more interested in the human than the divine, who "had coerced an apprentice from a village to model various movements and poses, sometimes crying and sometimes laughing, though never shirking the difficulty of what he had to do." It is quite likely that we see this young assistant growing older in various works that are attributed to the young Diego, from *Three Musicians* (ill. 174) to *The Water Seller of Seville* (Apsley House, The Wellington Museum, London).

Velázquez married Pacheco's daughter, Juana, in 1618, and we may presume that the master no longer referred to him as a "lad"; however, these early paintings were done when Diego was still more an apprentice than a full-fledged artist. The everyday subject matter and his insistence on the character and individuality of the objects, utensils, and figures suggest that such works are pictorial exercises more than anything else, Velázquez put his technique to work pulling out objects and figures from dense semi-darkness with an austere, rather dry brushstroke. Light anxiously seeks out linen tablecloths, glasses, jars, earthenware pitchers, cups, jugs, plates, knives, melons, pomegranates, onions, turnips, fried eggs, fish, tunics, shirts, and above all faces (ill. 173).

DIEGO VELÁZQUEZ, YOUNG ARTIST IN MADRID

On March 14, 1617, Velázquez obtained his license to practice the art of painting anywhere in Spain. Now that he was a master painter, he could have apprentices like Diego Melgar, who entered Velázquez's studio in 1620. Francisco Pacheco's young son-in-law most likely made a living through portraiture and religious paintings featuring the Virgin of the Immaculate Conception, saints, and narrative subjects such as the *Adoration of the Magi* (Museo del Prado), probably painted in 1619 for the Jesuit novitiate of San Luis in Seville. Without any loss of density or depth, Velázquez's painting had become somewhat more fluid and his figures took on a monumental presence.

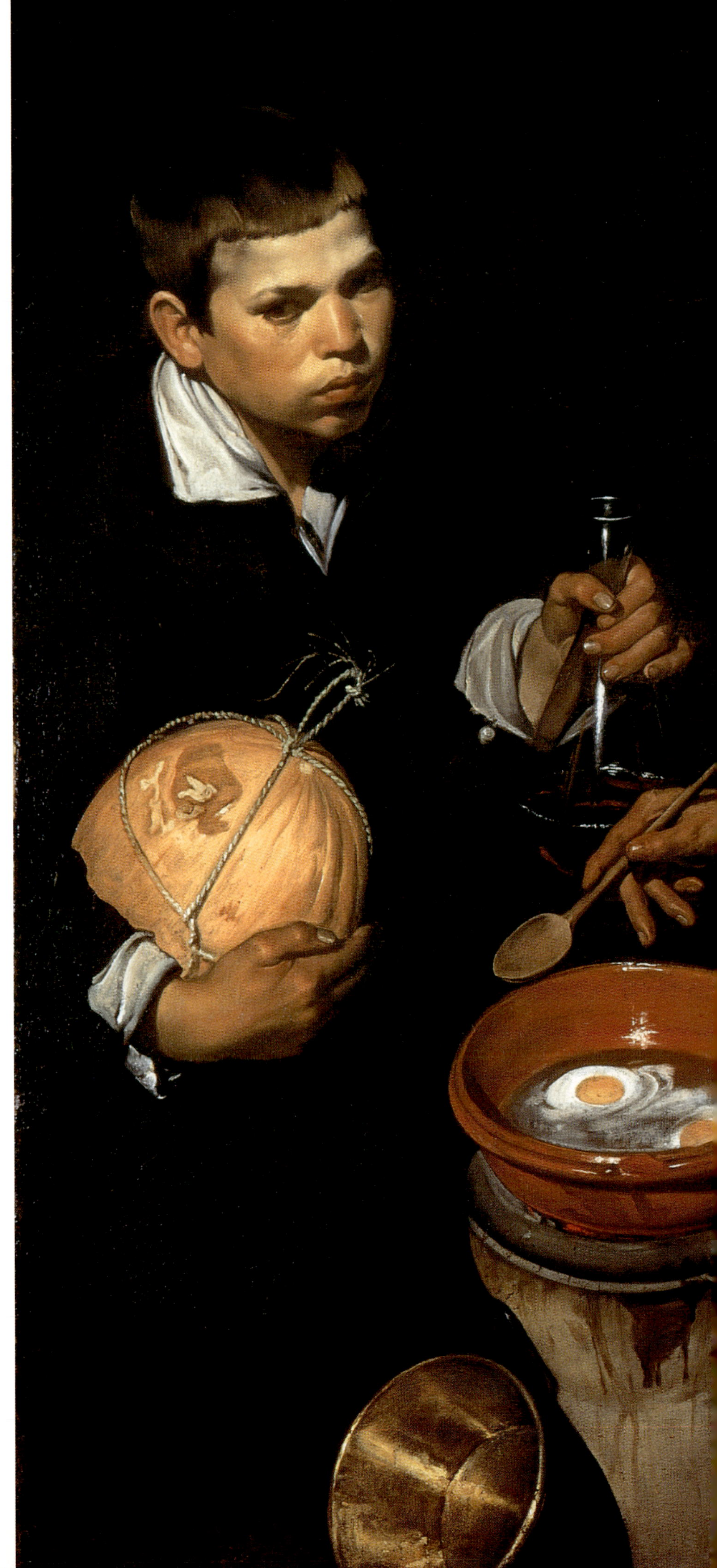

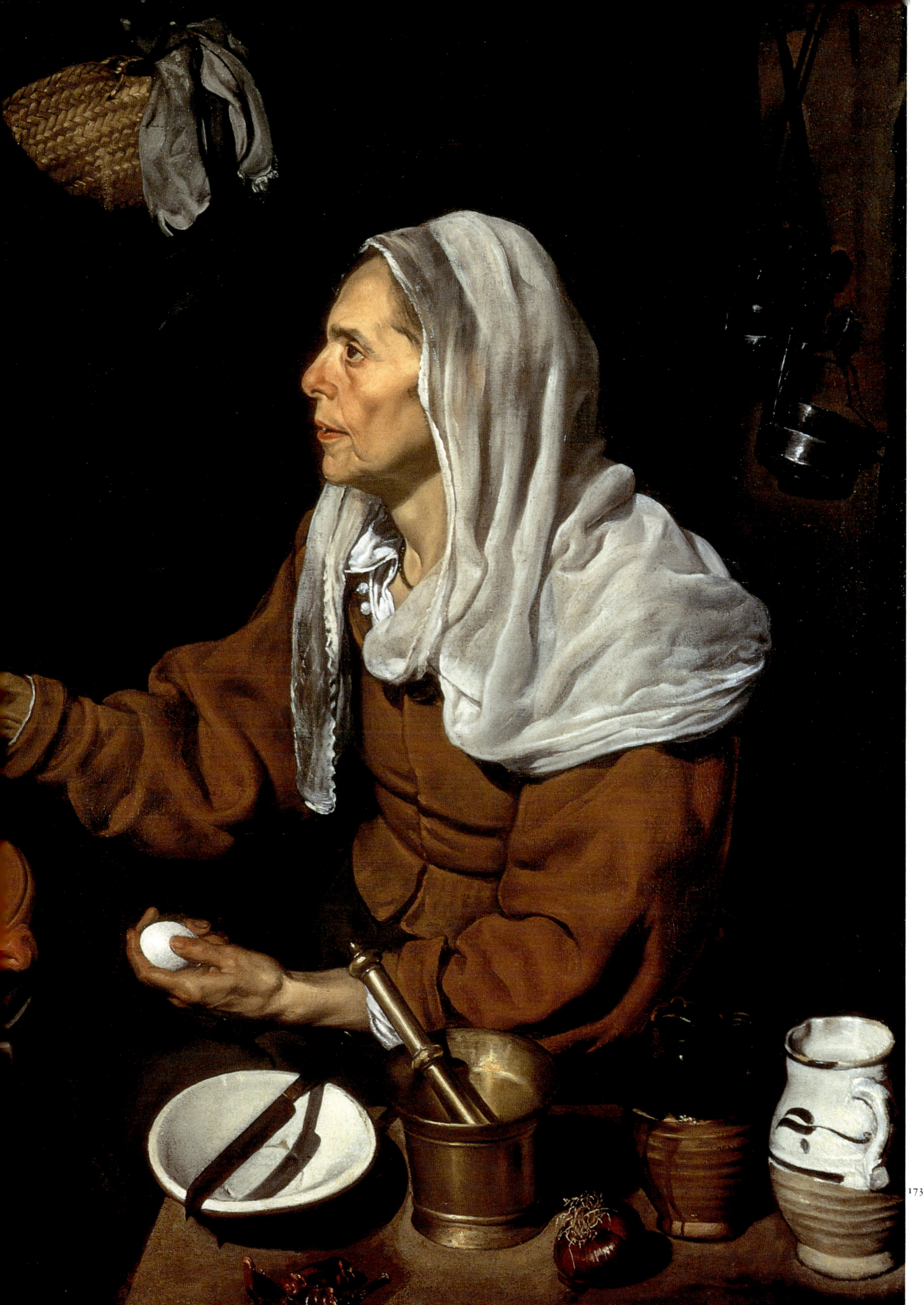

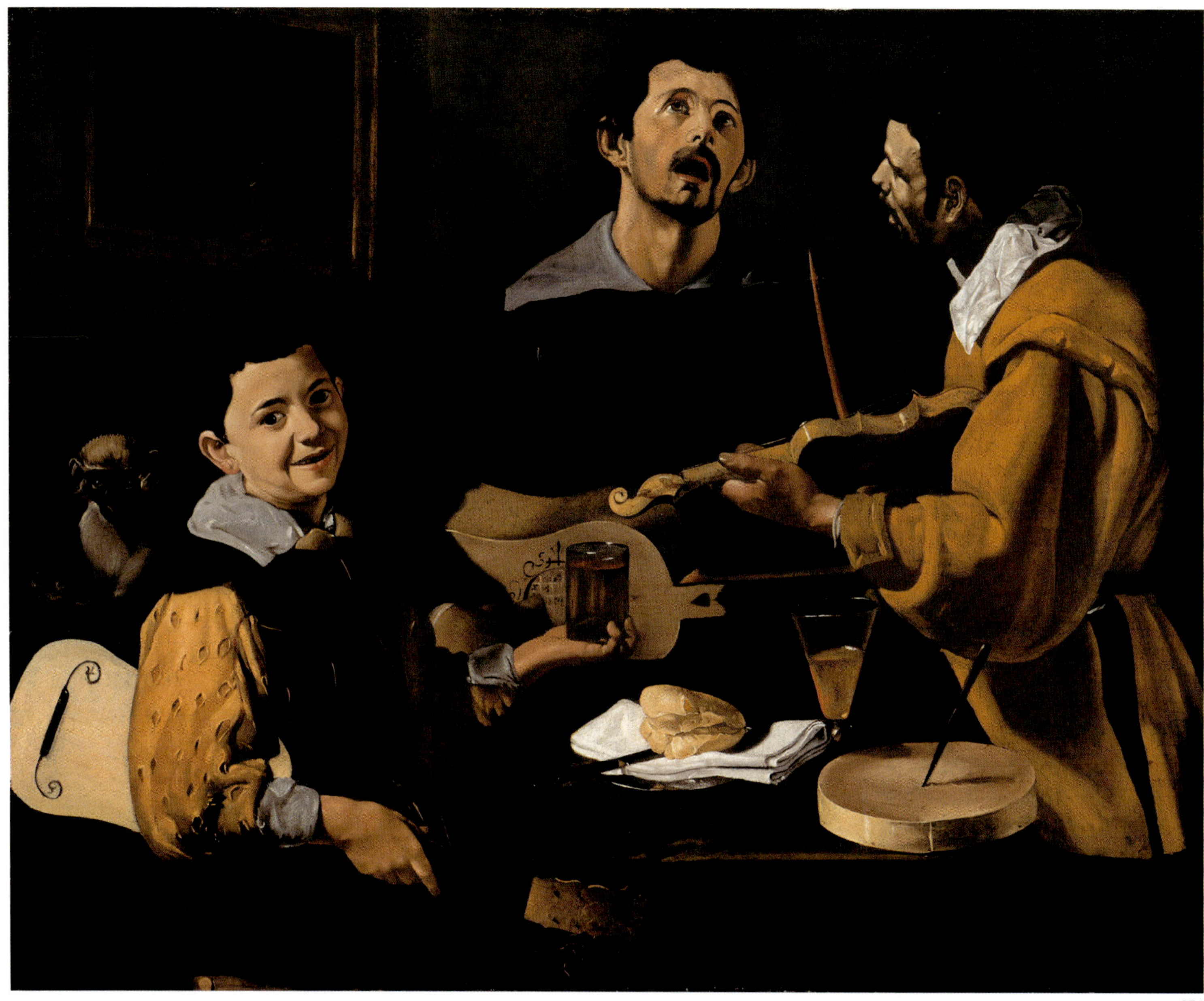

174

His compositions left behind the minimal, closed spaces of his earlier works, opening themselves up to a limitless visual depth in which the dark is penetrated by flashes of intense light.

Francisco Pacheco undoubtedly recognized that the student was beginning to excel the master, but he took it well, noting that "Leonardo da Vinci lost nothing by having Raphael as his disciple, nor did Giorgione with Titian, nor Plato with Aristotle," and encouraged Velázquez to try his luck at court. He might not have been able to do so if, after the death of Philip III in March 1621, his son and successor, Philip IV (ills. 176, 178), had not handed the reins of government to the ambitious but highly cultivated Gaspar de Guzmán y Pimentel, count of Olivares and later duke of Sanlúcar la Mayor. The count-duke, who had been born in Rome, had a home in Seville that he often visited between 1607 and 1615. There he befriended intellectuals and artists, including the priest Francisco de Rioja, the distinguished poet who sang in verse to the burning rose, quoted in Chapter 2, and was a frequent visitor to Pacheco's studio.

When the count-duke restaffed the court for the new king's rule, he cleared out some old retainers and brought a number of faithful Sevillian friends to Madrid, including Francisco de Rioja. In

174. Diego Velázquez
c. 1615–17
Three Musicians.
Gemäldegalerie, Berlin.

so doing, Olivares established Seville's power at court, which in turn afforded Velázquez entrée. He traveled to Madrid in 1622 as a portrait painter with hopes of portraying the young sovereign. Velázquez was not able to achieve that goal immediately, but he did paint one of the most powerful portraits of his entire career, that of the poet Luis de Góngora y Argote (ill. 177). Velázquez was then just twenty-three years old: Góngora was sixty or sixty-one. The poet, who served the court as royal chaplain, had not had an easy time of it in Madrid. He arrived there in 1617 from his native Córdoba, full of ambition. At the court, however, he found himself harassed by envy, drawn into controversies with Lope de Vega and Quevedo, and plagued by misunderstandings and economic hardship. In Velázquez's portrait (there are several versions, but the original is probably the one in the Museum of Fine Arts, Boston) Góngora's stern face is bisected by the light falling on it, his mouth is curved in a bitter rictus, and his eyes, set beneath arching eyebrows, gaze sharply and critically at the viewer. Velázquez at first planned to paint the poet wearing a laurel wreath, but rather than give the sitter refuge behind that emblem of glory, he left him sheltered only by his black clothing, a black relieved solely by the intense white shirt that lends his face a certain aura. This poet in shadows and light lived for only a few years after Velázquez portrayed him with death already sketched on his face. Góngora died on April 27, 1627, after returning—broke and ill—to Córdoba, the city he had passionately sung about in his youth:

> Exalted walls, battlements crowned
> with honor, courage, majesty!
> Great river! Great king of Andalusia,
> Of noble if not golden sands!
>
> O fertile plains, O high sierras
> Which heaven favors and day gilds!
> O my hometown forever glorious
> With pen no less than with the sword!
>
> If mid those ruins and spoils enriched
> by Genil, lapped by Dauro, your memory
> cease to be my sustenance,
> never may my distant eyes behold
> your walls, battlements, rivers, plain,
> O my hometown, O flower of Spain!

Velazquéz's portrait of Góngora did not bring the young painter immediate recognition, but he gave the court another try, this time accompanied to Madrid by Pacheco himself, who relates in *The Art of Painting* that Velázquez was:

> . . . summoned by Don Juan [Juan de Fonseca] himself, by order of the count-duke; he stayed in his home, where he was looked after and indulged, and did his portrait. A son of the count of Peñaranda, a servant of the cardinal-infante [the king's brother], took the painting that night to the palace, and in an hour everyone at court saw it, including the crown princes and princesses and the king, and it was greatly admired. Velázquez was ordered to do a portrait of the Infante. It seemed more appropriate to do one of His Majesty first, but that was delayed because of the monarch's obligations. In effect, Velázquez's first portrait of the king was finally done on August 30, 1623, to the pleasure of His Majesty, the princes and princesses, and the count-duke, who stated that the king had not had his portrait done until that time. . . . He also did a sketch of the Prince of Wales, who gave him a hundred *escudos* for it. His Excellency the count-duke spoke to him for the first time, encouraging him to honor his homeland, and making him promise that he would do portraits only of His Majesty and others that would be commissioned.

Philip IV must have been pleased by the portraits done of him, since on October 6, 1623, Velázquez joined the king's staff "so as to dedicate himself to all that was required of his profession." Just three years later it would be Diego Velázquez himself, "painter of Your Highness," who would request from the king the post of royal painter for his "father" Francisco Pacheco. Velázquez was connected to the court from 1623 to 1660, the year of his death.

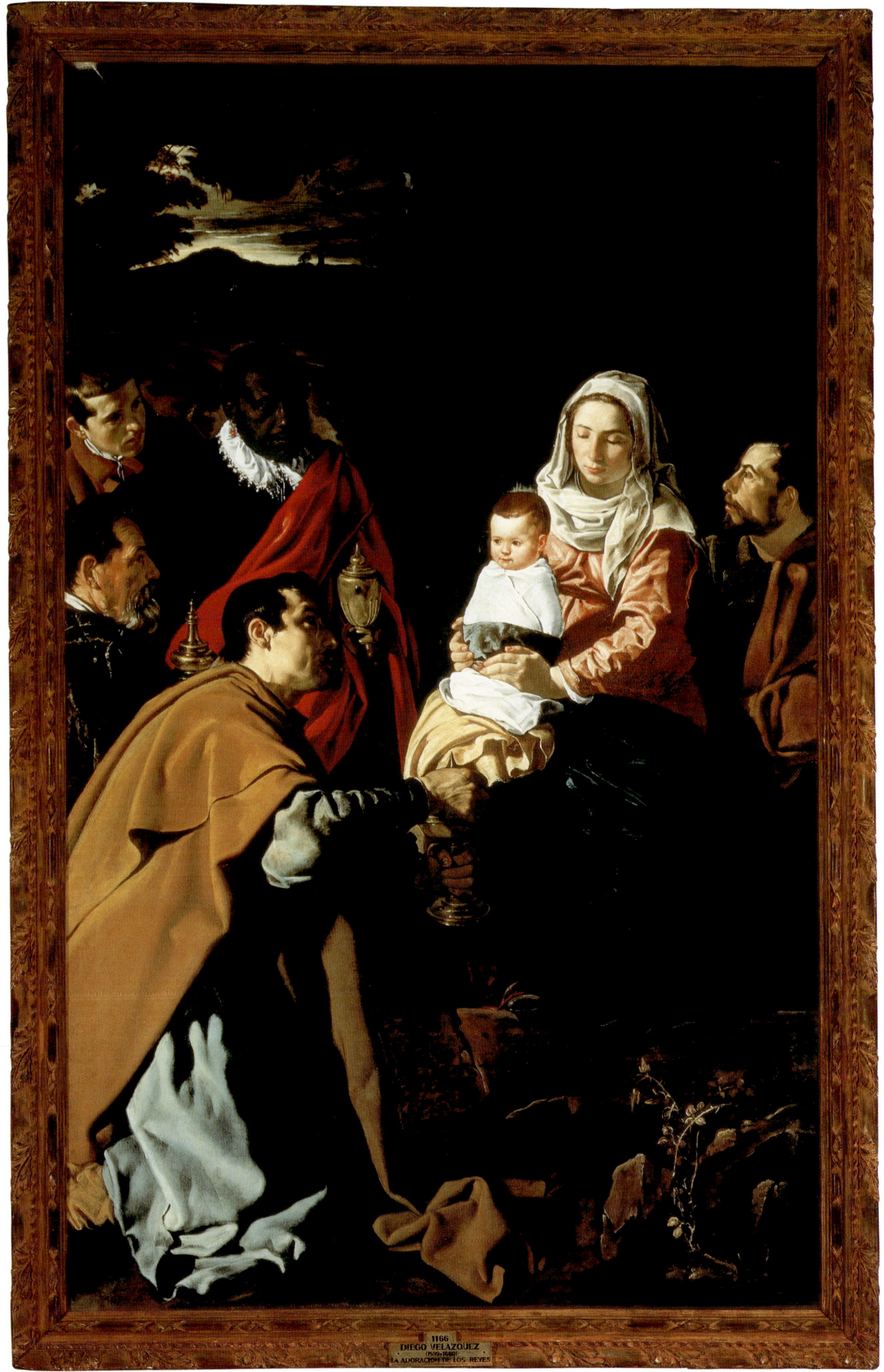
1166
DIEGO VELAZQUEZ
LA ADORACION DE LOS REYES

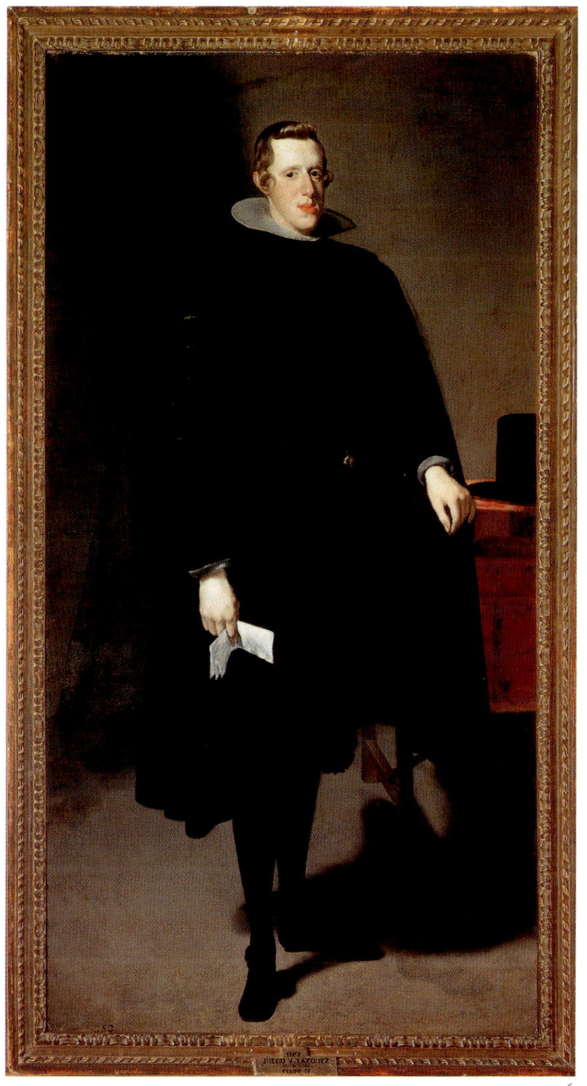

176

PAINTER AND COURTIER

The next several decades of Velázquez's life at court were marked by his assignment to a number of administrative posts: Gentleman Usher (1627), Gentleman of the Wardrobe (1634), Gentleman of the Bedchamber (1638), Chamber Assistant and Works Superintendent (1643), Chamber Assistant with Trade (1646), Viewer and Counter of Works (1647), and Senior Lodger (1652). The royal collection of art afforded Velázquez his discovery of sixteenth-century Italian painting. He was impressed by Titian's ability to express the intensity and sensuality of the visible and of what lies beneath the surface through color and light, shifting between the interior of a human being and the world around him.

LEFT:
175. Diego Velázquez
1619
The Adoration of the Magi,
probably from the novitiate of San Luis de los jesuitas, Seville.
Museo Nacional del Prado, Madrid.

ABOVE:
176. Diego Velázquez
1623–28
Philip IV.
Museo Nacional del Prado, Madrid.

In his early years at court, Velázquez was busy painting portraits of the king and the count-duke (the royal "favorite"), both always portrayed standing full-length in slightly affected, repetitive poses that nevertheless do not prevent the act of painting from slowly taking control of the canvases. However, it was the subject painted rather than the manner of painting that impressed his contemporaries (even though it was reality that his contemporaries took particular note of). García de Salzedo Coronel, a nobleman from Santiago de Compostela, wrote:

> If you paint Heaven,
> a grateful Heaven turns,
> and if the Sun,
> the handsome sun shines,
> and if you picture the wind,
> the wind breathes.

Only a few of Velázquez's first portraits of Philip IV, the "Planet King," are extant, and none of those that were most praised in their day, such as the equestrian portrait that, in emulation of the artists of antiquity, was on public view in Madrid's Calle Mayor facing the church of San Felipe. This portrait awakened the "admiration of the entire court and the envy of the art world," according to Pacheco. Poets praised the painting, as Jerónimo González de Villanueva's elegant verses attest :

> To your image they incline, sovereign
> oh great lord of the Christian people!
> When astride a strong horse armored in steel
> happily they look on you, those who adore your
> name,
> the fierce Persian of the indomitable front,
> the threatening arm of the Ottoman.
> Now the new light of a breaking dawn,
> now, Spanish Caesar, like an African
> gilds the fifth sphere of your rays.

Even though many paintings from this period have been lost, those that remain show us how Velázquez's painting distances itself more and more from a reliance on chiaroscuro and color, favoring increased subtlety. He constructs space on the blank

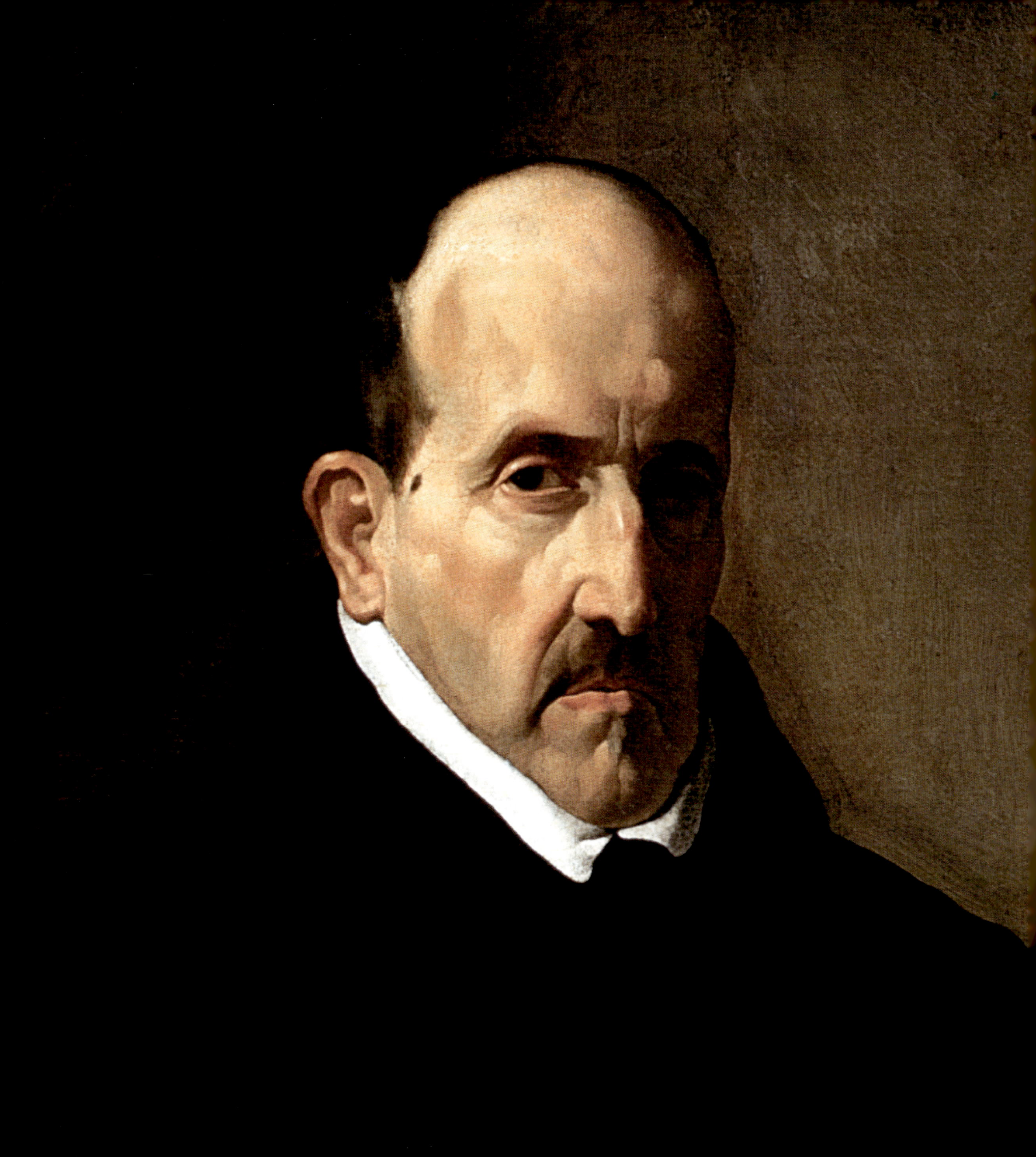

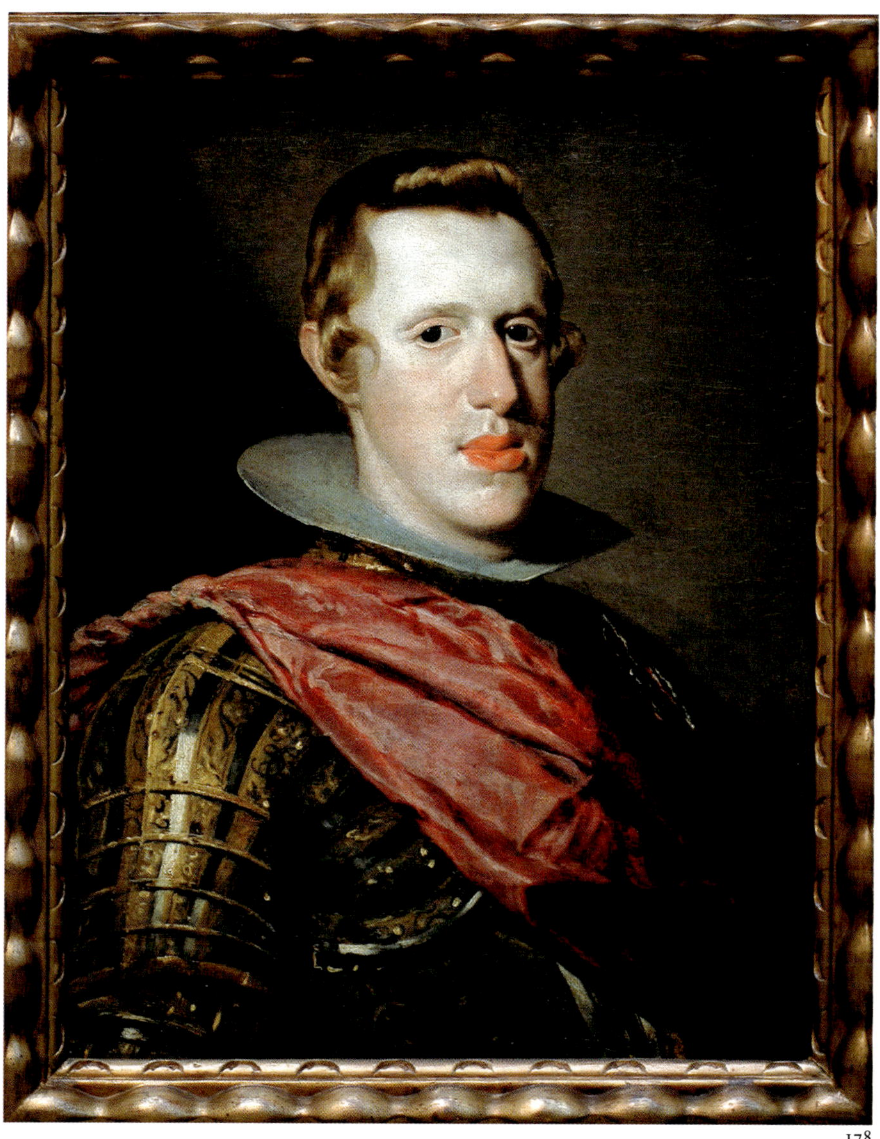

178

LEFT:
177. Diego Velázquez
1622
Luis de Góngora y Argote.
Museum of Fine Arts, Boston.

ABOVE:
178. Diego Velázquez
c. 1628
Philip IV.
Museo Nacional del Prado, Madrid.

surface of the canvas simply through the use of shadows that stretch away from the figures across the floor. This kind of painting distinguishes itself from the formulaic definition of portraits as "counterfeits of important persons, whose appearance and likeness thus remains for the memory of centuries to come," as defined in the 1611 Castilian dictionary by Sebastián de Covarrubias. The portrait painter almost never leaves his own role, not even in works such as the *The Triumph of Bacchus*, called *The Drunkards* (ill. 179), in which Velázquez clothes a mythological subject in the everyday, naturalistic warmth that typified his Seville years, though not without reference as well to Titian and Peter Paul Rubens. The fact that Velázquez was thought of as a "portrayer" (or painter who seemed limited to painting just what he sees) was considered a discredit by jealous court artists such as the Florentine Vicente Carducho. Velázquez's naturalism caused Carducho to dismiss him as a mere imitator of nature capable only of "painting heads."

This accusation was of course completely unfair. Velázquez—whose art had first been shaped in Seville, a city dedicated to copying nature, and later at the court in Madrid, which offered fine collections to study—was capable of so much more. Peter Paul Rubens surely perceived Velázquez's potential when he came to Madrid in 1628, sent from Antwerp as a diplomat to negotiate an end to the war between Spain and Holland and Holland's ally England. This was the war in which the Genoese Ambrogio Spinola, major general of the Spanish troops in Flanders, took control of Breda in 1626, a subject later painted by Velázquez (see ill. 22). Rubens, the painter of an elaborate, stunning, triumphant, and earthly Baroque style, took no time at all in advising Velázquez to travel to Italy, where he would be able to learn from the Venetians, Emilians, and Romans. By thus drinking from the founts of classicism, and studying historical and mythological paintings, Velázquez would be able to let go of the shackles of naturalism once and for all.

ITALY

In the archives of the Royal Palace in Madrid is a document dated June 28, 1629, in which Philip IV authorizes his painter to travel to Italy without any loss of benefits or salary. The Italian ambassadors in Madrid made an effort to inform their authorities at home about the trip. A diplomat from Parma wrote to Italy that, under the pretext of improving his craft, Velázquez "viene per spiare" (is coming to spy). The ambassador from Venice, Alvise Mocenigo, was more prudent. He wrote to the Council of Ten to clarify the situation, given the suspicions that had arisen: "This painter is young, and for this reason, in my view, his voyage cannot be suspect; it is only, I am convinced, to acquire greater knowledge of his profession that he has received permission

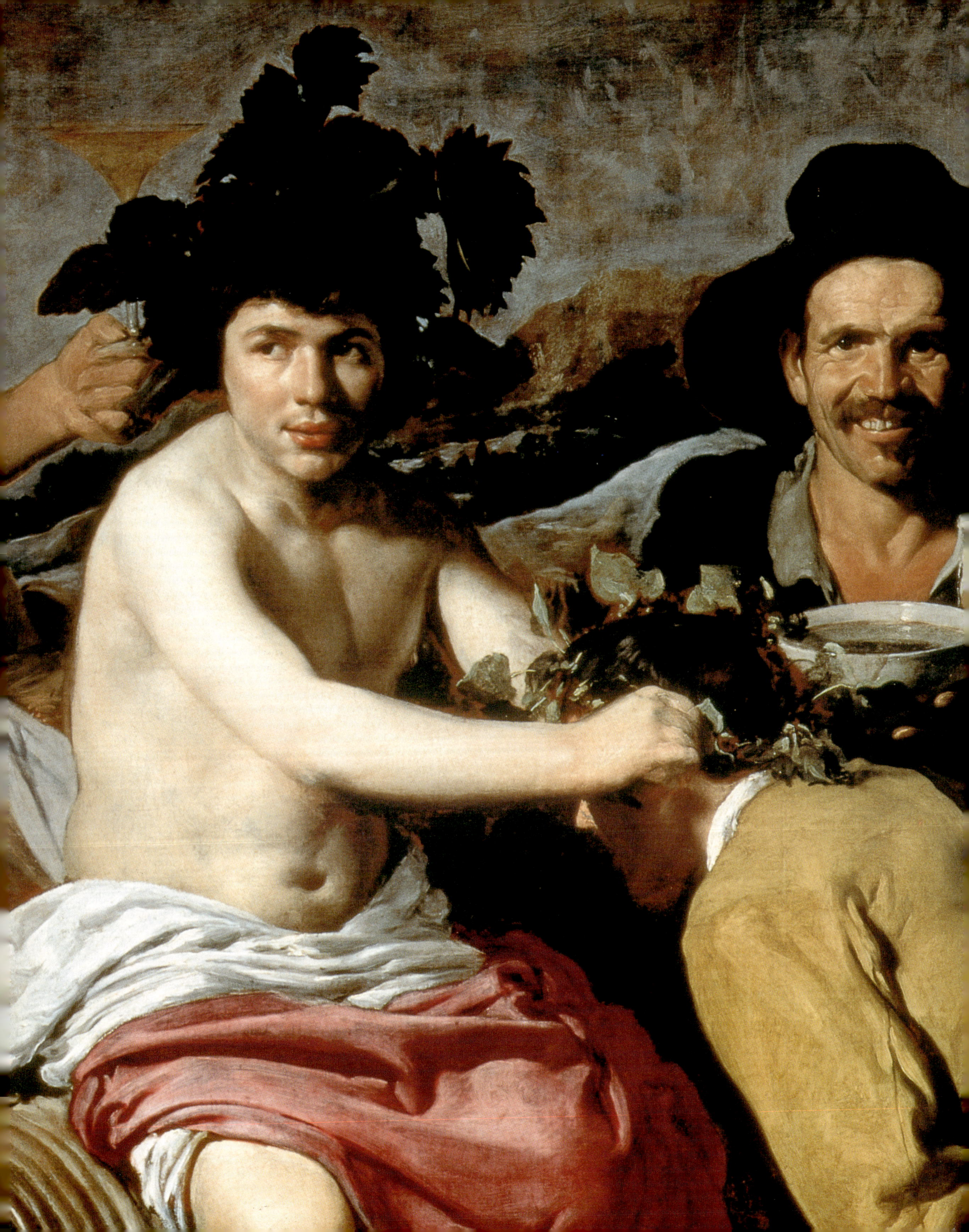

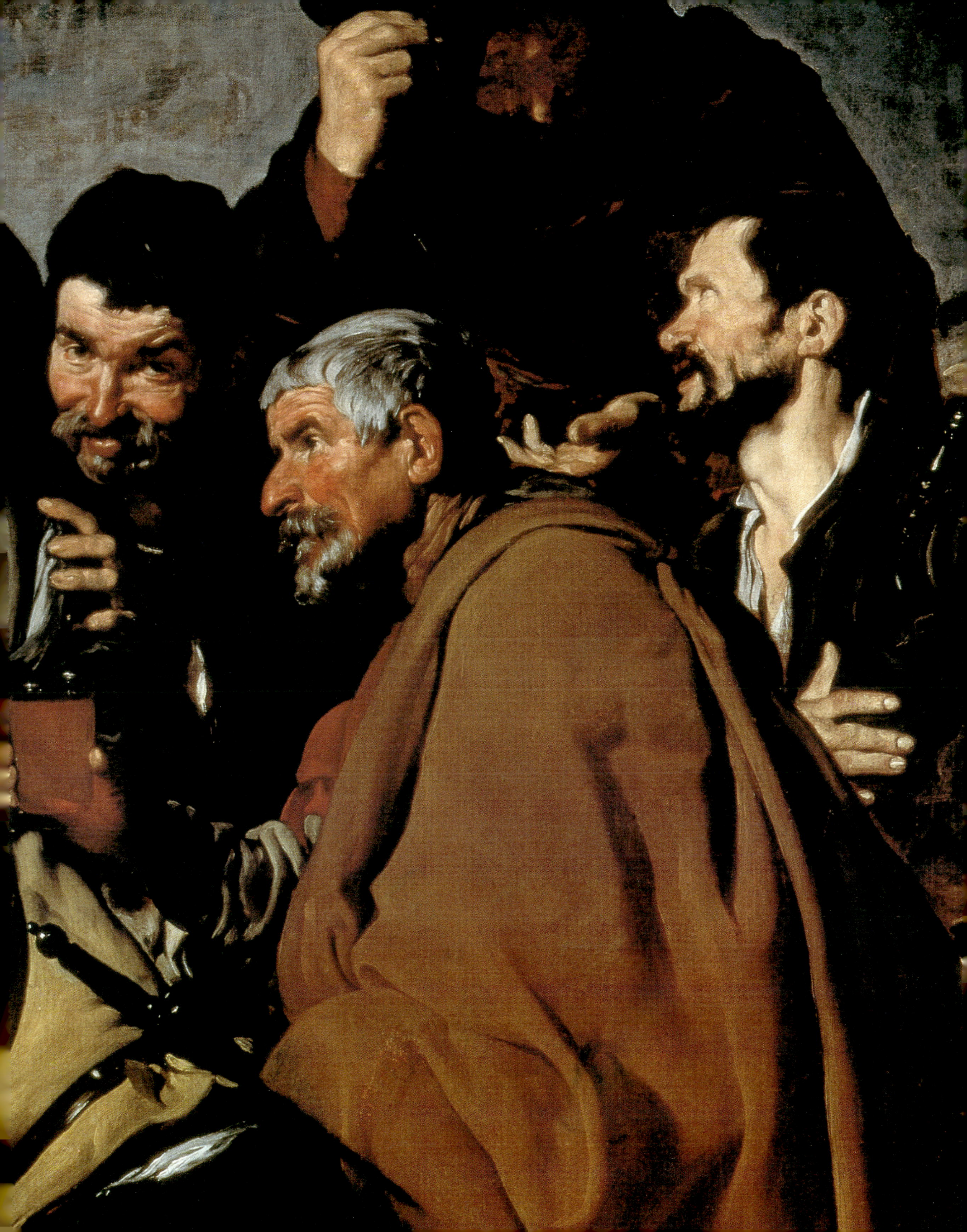

from the king to see the principal cities of Italy and their noteworthy works of art."

Preparations for the voyage were quickly arranged. On August 10, 1629, the feast day of Saint Lawrence and a comfortable time of year to sail, Velázquez set off from the port of Barcelona for Italy. A few weeks earlier he had left Madrid in the company of Ambrogio Spinola, who had been commissioned to take charge of the Spanish troops at Mantua. Velázquez did not board ship empty-handed; he left Spain with a servant, four hundred silver ducats, two hundred gold ducats, and many letters of introduction addressed to ambassadors, cardinals, and dukes so that he would be well received everywhere. We know nothing of his sea voyage and little about his trip to Italy, apart from diplomatic and court documents gathered by Pacheco, which he published in *The Art of Painting.* There are a few other documents relating to the trip in Palomino's eighteenth-century biography of Velázquez, but we do not know their source.

According to Pacheco, the first city Velázquez planned to visit was Venice, but his ship landed in Genoa, and there he was able to see the progress that had been made on the mural decoration of the Spinola Palace, where Lazzaro Tavarone was finishing off a series depicting the Flemish campaigns of Ambrogio Spinola, among which was a *Surrender of Breda.* Today these frescoes are barely visible, but Lazzaro Tavarone's compositions can be studied in the nearly identical versions painted by Gian Andrea Ansaldo in the Villa Spinola at San Pietro in Genoa-Sampierdarena.

Velázquez left Genoa for Venice, skipping over some important centers like Milan (he could not have seen Leonardo da Vinci's *Last Supper* there, as it had deteriorated considerably by then). In Venice he was lodged in the residence of the Spanish ambassador Cristóbal de Benavente, "who honored him greatly and sat him at his table; and because of the wars that were taking place, he sent his servants with him when he went out to see the city so as to protect him." Pacheco does not comment on what Velázquez might have seen and admired in Venice; Palomino, for his part, has him visiting the Doges' Palace, St. Mark's Basilica, and the Academy of Saint Luke, especially admiring Tintoretto and Titian, looking at many other artists whose works could be enjoyed, from Bellini to the Bassani, and taking in Sebastiano del Piombo and Sansovino along the way.

From Venice Velázquez went to Rome, with a brief visit to Ferrara, a city under papal control and governed by Cardinal Giulio Sacchetti, a lover of the arts and patron of such artists as Andrea Sacchi and Pietro da Cortona. The cardinal had served as papal nuncio in Spain from 1624 to 1626. Pacheco wrote:

> He received him very well and insisted that while Velázquez was in the city he should stay in Sacchetti's palace and eat with him. Velázquez modestly excused himself, saying that he did not eat at regular hours, though that if it would please his illustrious host he would obey and would change his customs. Given this, a Spanish gentleman, one of many who attended to the cardinal, was ordered to take good care of Velázquez, to arrange quarters for the artist and his servant, to serve him the same dishes found on the gentleman's own table, and to show him the most worthy sites of the city. Velázquez was there for two days. . . .

Thus Velázquez was put up in the ancient castle that had belonged to the Este family, former rulers of Ferrara. When the city came under papal control, the castle became home to papal governors, beginning with Cardinal Legati in 1598. Without leaving the castle Velázquez could study some remarkable works of art, including the paintings in what was called the Game Room and those in the small Salon of the Bacchanalia. We do not know what else he saw in the company of the Spanish gentleman. It is not unlikely that he was taken to the Schifanoia palace, another former residence of the Este family that then belonged to the Scandiana family. There Velázquez would have been amazed by the murals of Ercole de Roberti, painted from 1469 to1472 in what was called the Hall of the Months. These shared a celebration of the profane and the worldly

PRECEDING PAGES:
179. Diego Velázquez
1628–29
Detail of *The Triumph of Bacchus*, or *The Drunkards.*
Museo Nacional del Prado, Madrid.

in a style that might have seemed bizarre to the artist from Seville, for the bodies of the figures such as Vulcan and the three Cyclops representing the month of September, twist about on the surface as though driven by an unimaginable force (ill. 180).

Velázquez set off on his journey once again, making a brief stop in Cento—perhaps to meet Guercino—but traveling through Bologna without stopping. After visiting Loreto, he finally arrived in Rome, where he enjoyed the protection of Cardinal Francesco Barberini, nephew of Pope Urban VIII. At first he was lodged in the Vatican palaces, where he attentively studied Michelangelo's frescoes in the Sistine Chapel and works by Raphael. Later he requested, and was granted, permission (thanks to the intervention of Manuel de Fonseca y Zúñiga, the count of Monterrey, who was the Spanish ambassador to Rome) to stay instead in the Villa Medici, "so as to spend the summer there, it being located in the highest and breeziest part of Rome, and there being in it excellent ancient statues for study." He resided in the Villa Medici for two months, until an illness caused him to "go down to be near the home of the count."

Pacheco mentions the "studies" that Velázquez painted in Rome, but without being more specific. Pacheco does cite "one of his famous portraits," which has not been identified. Palomino, however, writing much later, refers to "the celebrated painting of the brothers of Joseph" and the one picturing the "fable of Vulcan when Apollo informed him of his disgrace due to the adultery of Venus with Mars, where we see Vulcan . . . so bewildered that it seems like he cannot breathe." *The Forge of Vulcan* (ills. 181, 182) was in fact one of the "studies" painted by Velázquez in Rome, most likely done for the sheer pleasure of freely practicing his art. Velázquez was evidently the first Spanish artist to paint the subject: Apollo's announcement to Vulcan of the infidelity of his wife. It has often been noted that Velázquez's composition may reflect the influence of an etching by Antonio Tempesta for an edition of Ovid's *Metamorphoses* (Antwerp, 1606). The novelty of Tempesta's composition is in depicting the announcement of the infidelity separately from the image of Mars and Venus in bed, which Velázquez could have seen in the Schifanoia palace.

Velázquez here painted a sort of profane Annunciation that allowed him to explore the physical reactions of human beings when surprised. His study of classical statuary is reflected in his painting of the bodies. Vulcan and Apollo are woven into a tense dialogue that is even more skillfully resolved than in Caravaggio's dramatic *Calling of Saint Matthew*, painted more than a quarter century earlier for the Contarelli Chapel in San Luigi dei Francesi in Rome. However, Velázquez's depiction of human anatomy based on his study of the statues, reliefs, and paintings in the Vatican and elsewhere in Rome does not overshadow his interest in the detailed, silent description of the objects in the forge—the hammers and anvils, the shiny armor, the surprisingly white porcelain ewer on the mantel of the chimney, and even the glowing red-hot iron being worked by a stunned Vulcan. However, iron, porcelain, and armor—ordinary,everyday things—cannot compete visually with Apollo and his halo of light, a figure seemingly created out of light itself. Apollo's form, cloak, and laurel wreath show that Velázquez had already assimilated the full grandeur of painting that took antiquity as its model.

During Velázquez's first sojourn in Italy, his inquisitive gaze (which had not taken in Florence or the Neapolitan naturalism so similar to what he had learned in Seville) absorbed all the painting and sculpture of the *maniera moderna* from Michelangelo to Titian, from Tintoretto to Bernini, from Correggio to Guido Reni, and the full glory of the art of antiquity. Velázquez would never have been the artist whom poets called the Apelles of the century without this visit to Italy.

While there, Velázquez practiced new ways of working and opened up paths that had not been taken by painters before. His concept of art was no longer limited to an agile, *sprezzante* hand that turns the canvas into a painting, a universe that encompasses both nature and history itself. *Joseph's Bloody Tunic, The Forge of Vulcan,* and the views—more than

FOLLOWING PAGES:
180. Ercole de Roberti
1469–70
Vulcan and the Three Cyclops, fresco.
Top register of the month of September, the Hall of the Months, Palazzo Schifanoia, Ferrara.

181. Diego Velázquez
1630
Detail of *The Forge of Vulcan*.
Museo Nacional del Prado, Madrid.

182. Diego Velázquez
1630
The Forge of Vulcan.
Museo Nacional del Prado, Madrid.

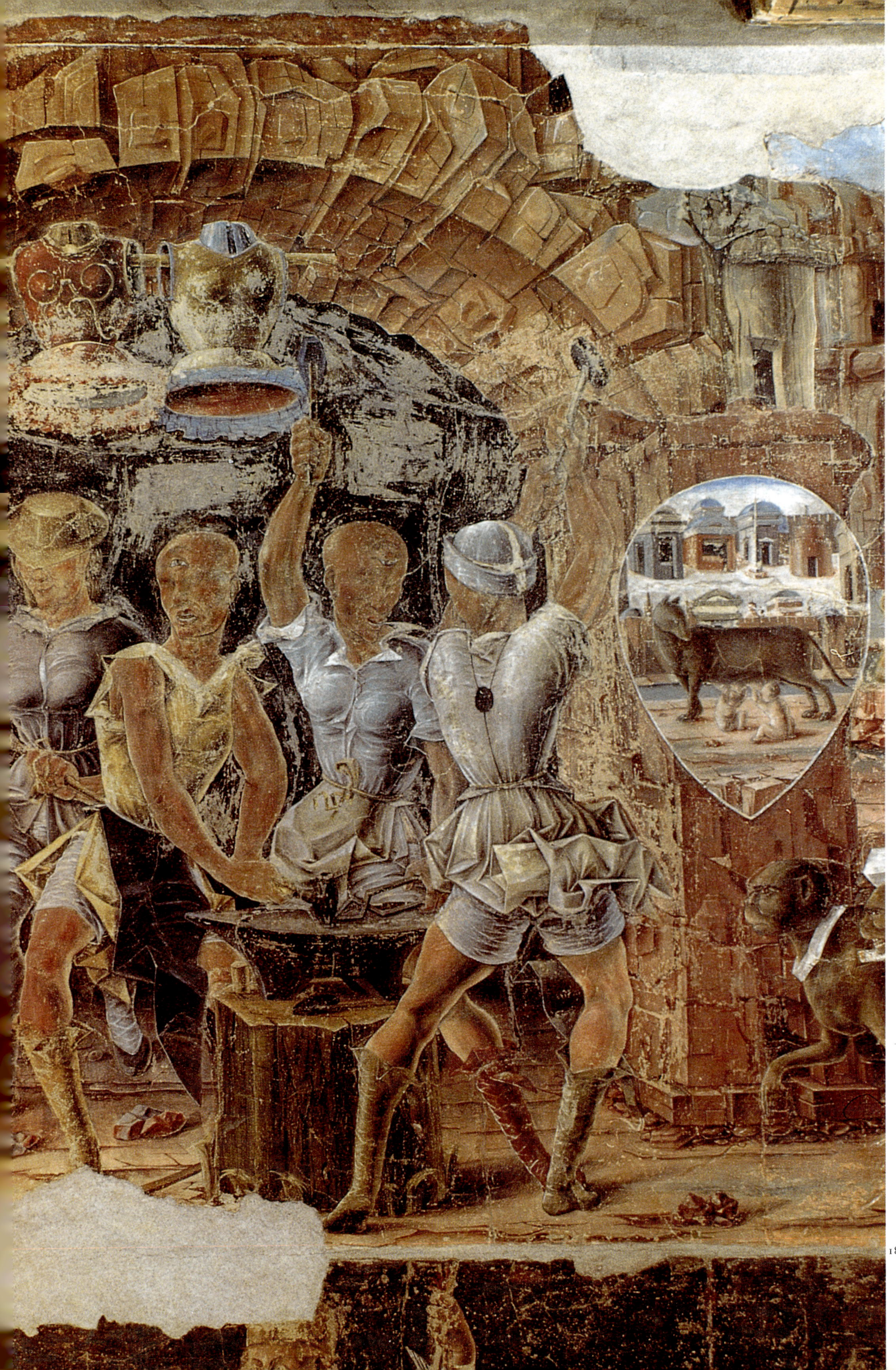

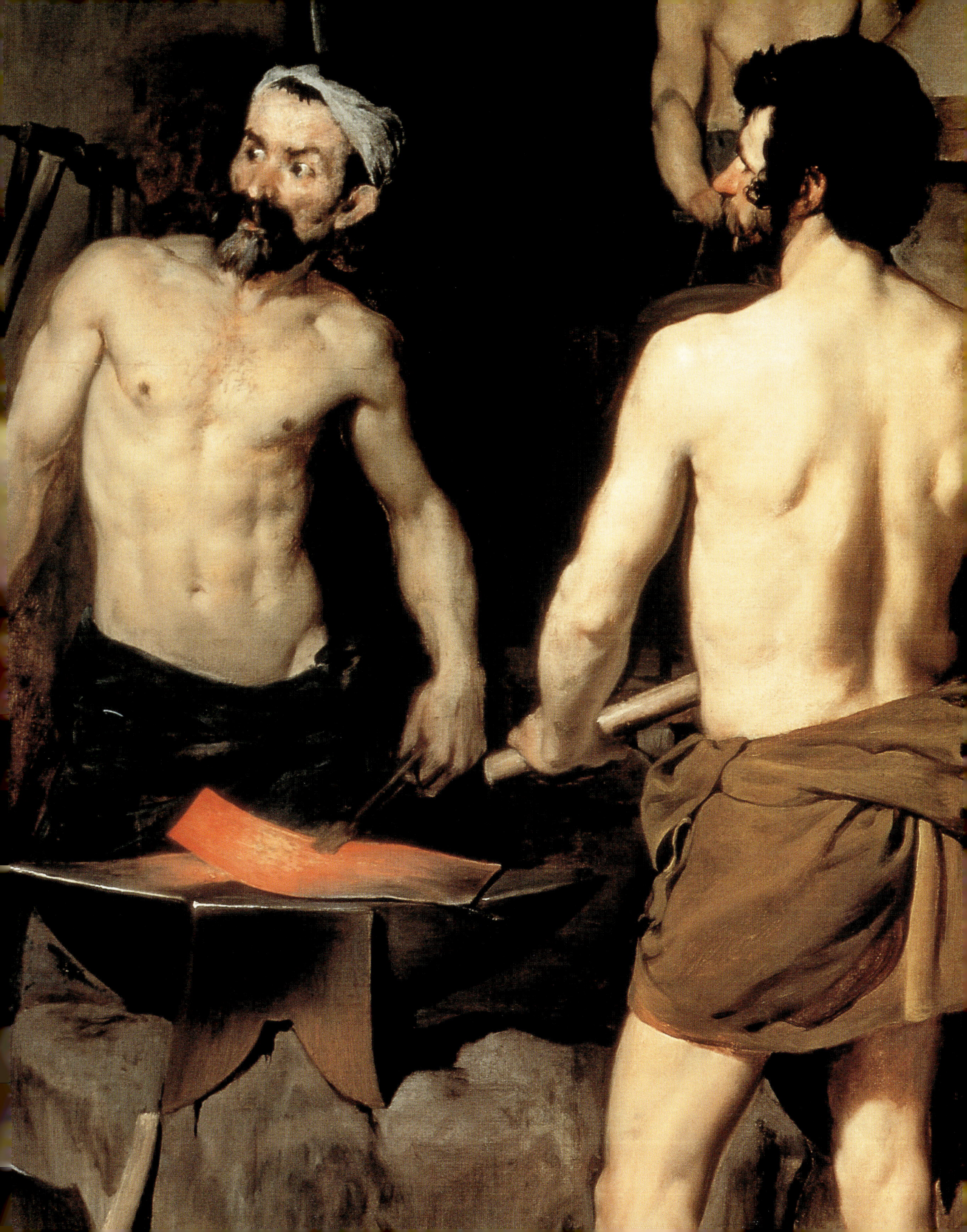

mere landscapes, they are evocations of Rome through the spirit of the ruins—of the Villa Medici, including *The Grotto-Loggia Façade* (ill. 183) and *The Cleopatra-Ariadne Pavilion,* the latter three in the Prado Museum, are unquestionable high points of this new way of working. Thick impasto and the touches of light bring out the thin layers of color that do not hide the preparation of the canvas. Velázquez was no longer painting reality. Instead, he was creating painting that, paradoxically, by being so obvious in its austerity, simplicity, composition, drawing (with many *pentimenti,* or overpainting strokes, made after careful consideration), quick and precise touches of color, and stains, no longer appears to the eyes of the viewer as artifice.

THE GLORY OF THE COURT

Francisco Pacheco reported in *The Art of Painting* that Velázquez "returned to Madrid after an absence of a year and a half, arriving in early 1631. He was warmly received by the count-duke [of Olivares], who sent him to kiss the hand of His Majesty, whom he thanked profusely for not allowing any other artist to paint his portrait, and agreed to paint a portrait of the Prince, which he soon did, and His Majesty was greatly relieved by his return."

With the freedom he had enjoyed in Rome now behind him, Velázquez returned to working as a member of the Madrid court. This might well have turned him into a conventional, repetitive artist, but it did not. He began instead to explore religious subjects that he had rarely painted before. The high point of this exploration is the *Christ Crucified* that was commissioned in 1632 by the notary of Aragon Jerónimo González de Villanueva for Madrid's San Plácido monastery (ill. 184). The body of Christ, his feet and hands pierced by nails, looks like a synthesis of Apollo and the blacksmiths in *The Forge of Vulcan.* Velázquez shapes the painted surface much in the same way as Spanish Baroque sculptors, such as Juan Martínez Montañés, infused their wooden forms with passion. Velázquez does this to move the faithful now faced with the tragic death of

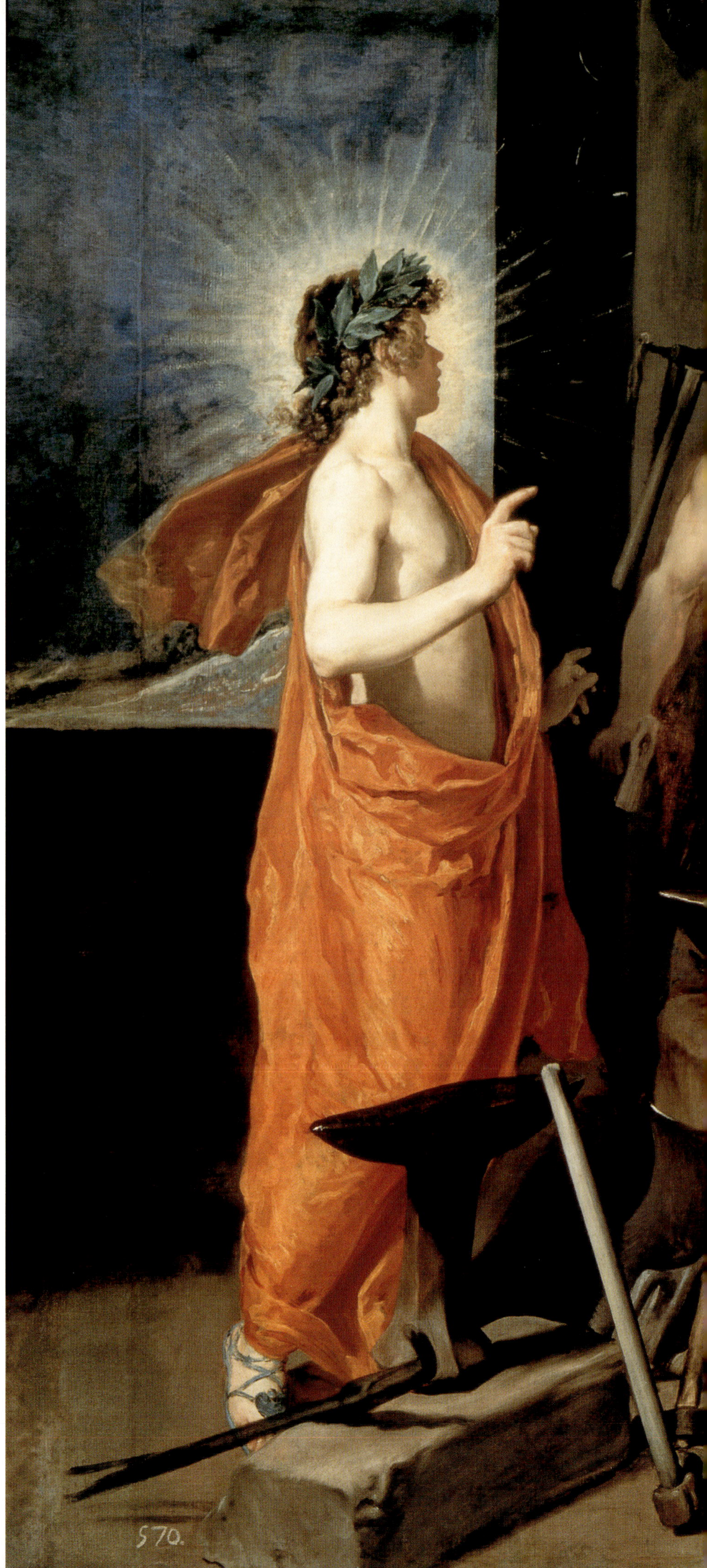

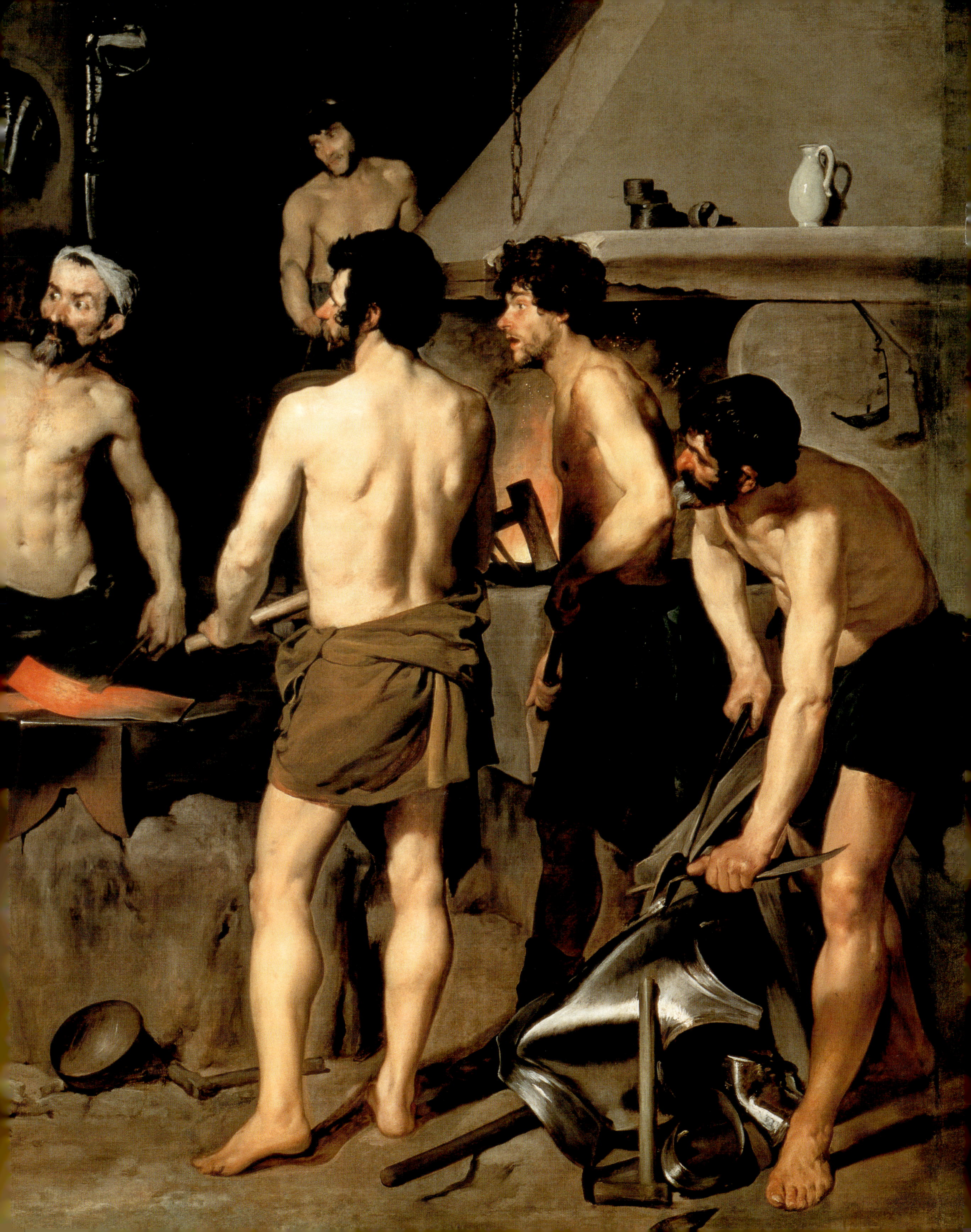

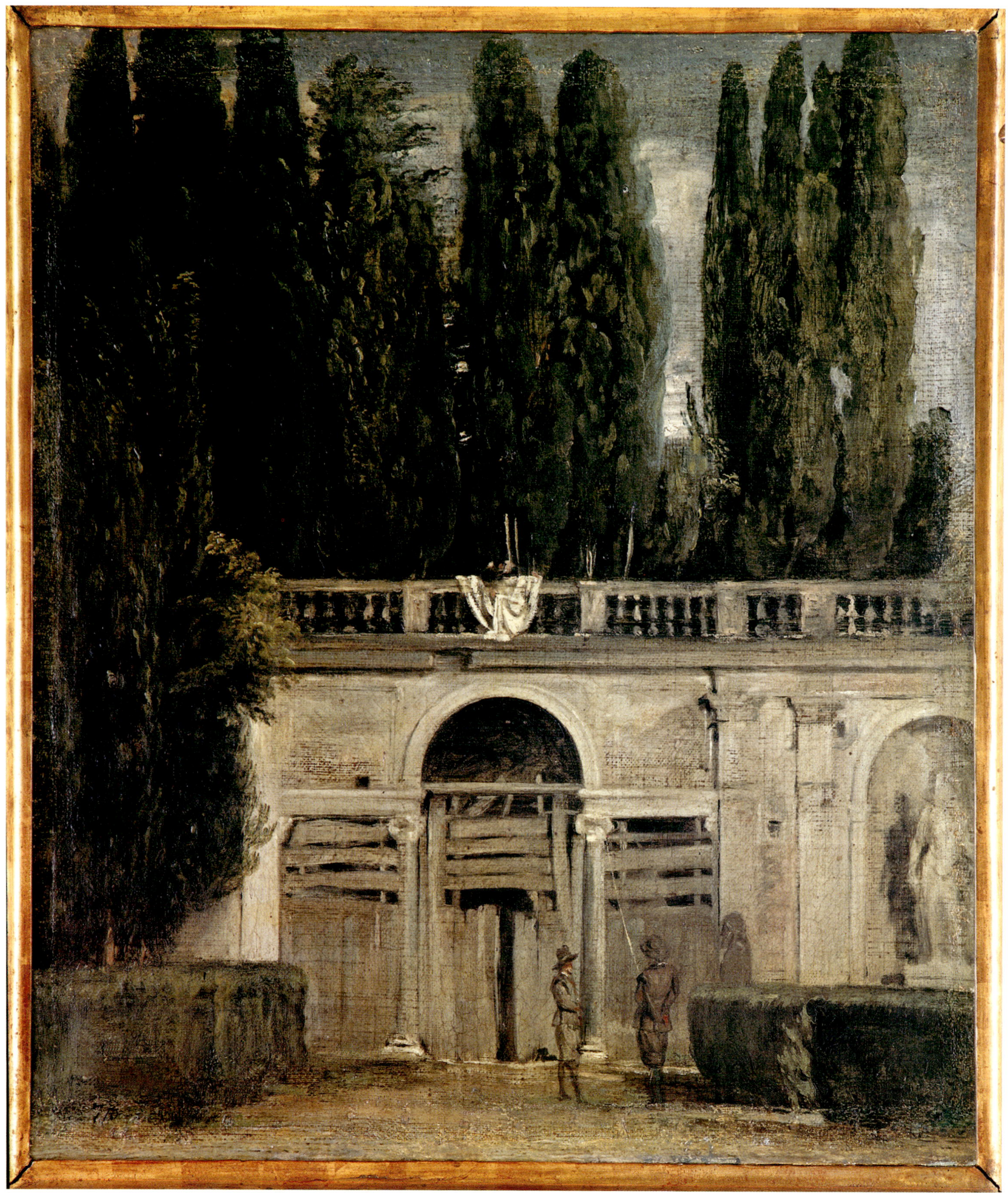

Christ. Experiencing such emotions was but one of the ways to the pastures of eternal life, to the immense sea of divinity, a guide to the soul and the divine portal that Christ represented for the believers of the period.

In Baroque imagery, the Passion of Christ is a shout that escapes from the throat after the Last Supper and the Prayer in the Garden of Gethsemane, when a pure body, born out of love and tortured by human ignorance, begins to die. Velázquez's vision of Christ on the cross stifles the Baroque shout of the Passion; the sun has set, the skies have darkened, and people have fled in fear. Silence and solitude are the only companions of this dead man nailed to a cross, dense blood oozing from the palms of his hands and flowing from the nails piercing his feet, running down the wood of the cross. It is not just a promise of paradise that moves the believer before this image of Christ; it is a selfless love for he who died for love, his glorious body lacerated by wounds. It is the exalted love reflected in one of the most beautiful sonnets in all of Spanish literature, attributed variously to Saint John of the Cross, Saint Teresa, Father Torres (a Capuchin monk), and the Franciscan priest Antonio Panes:

> I am not moved, my God, to love you
> by the heaven you have promised me;
> nor am I moved by feared hell
> to stop from offending you.
>
> You move me, Lord; I am moved to see you
> nailed to a cross and tortured;
> moved to see your wounded body;
> moved by your humiliation and your death.
>
> I am moved, in sum, by your love, and so much so
> that even if heaven did not exist I would love you,
> and even without hell I would fear you.
>
> You do not have to give me anything because I
> love you,
> just as for all I await I would not be expecting,
> in the same way as I love you and would love you.

Velázquez continued to paint religious subjects after his return from Italy, though not all of them

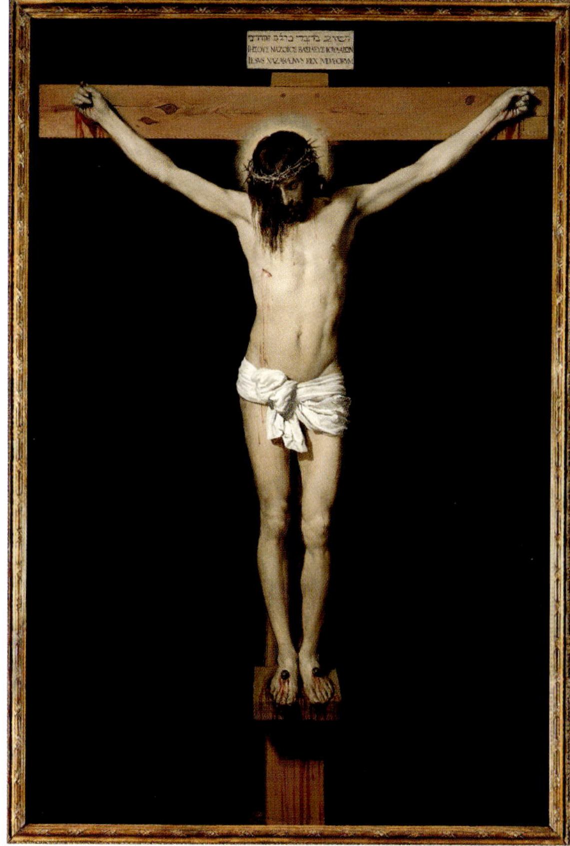

184

with the conviction of the *Christ Crucified.* He was mostly busy with painting portraits, not only of the king but of Prince Baltasar Carlos, born in 1629 to Isabella of Bourbon (ill. 189), and of other members of the court. With the exception of the Rubens-influenced equestrian portraits of the royal family painted for the Hall of Realms in the Buen Retiro palace, Velázquez distanced himself from the prevalent High Baroque style, as he did with the *Christ Crucified.* The same was true of his portraits of the king, as though he were not as interested in penetrating the character of his subject as he was in the portraits of the count-duke and, later on, in the portraits of Juan de Pareja (Metropolitan Museum of Art, New York), a painter who was Velázquéz's slave, as well as in his portrait of Pope Innocent X.

Nevertheless, over the years Velázquez's portraits delicately record changes in King Philip's face. Whether the king is pictured indoors or outside, whether dressed in stiff black silk with a wide ruff, in the raiment of a military commander or a hunter, the portraits reveal how the king's self-confidence

LEFT:
183. Diego Velázquez
1630
The Garden at the Villa Medici (The Grotto-Loggia Façade).
Museo Nacional del Prado, Madrid.

ABOVE:
184. Diego Velázquez
c. 1632
Christ Crucified.
Museo Nacional del Prado, Madrid.

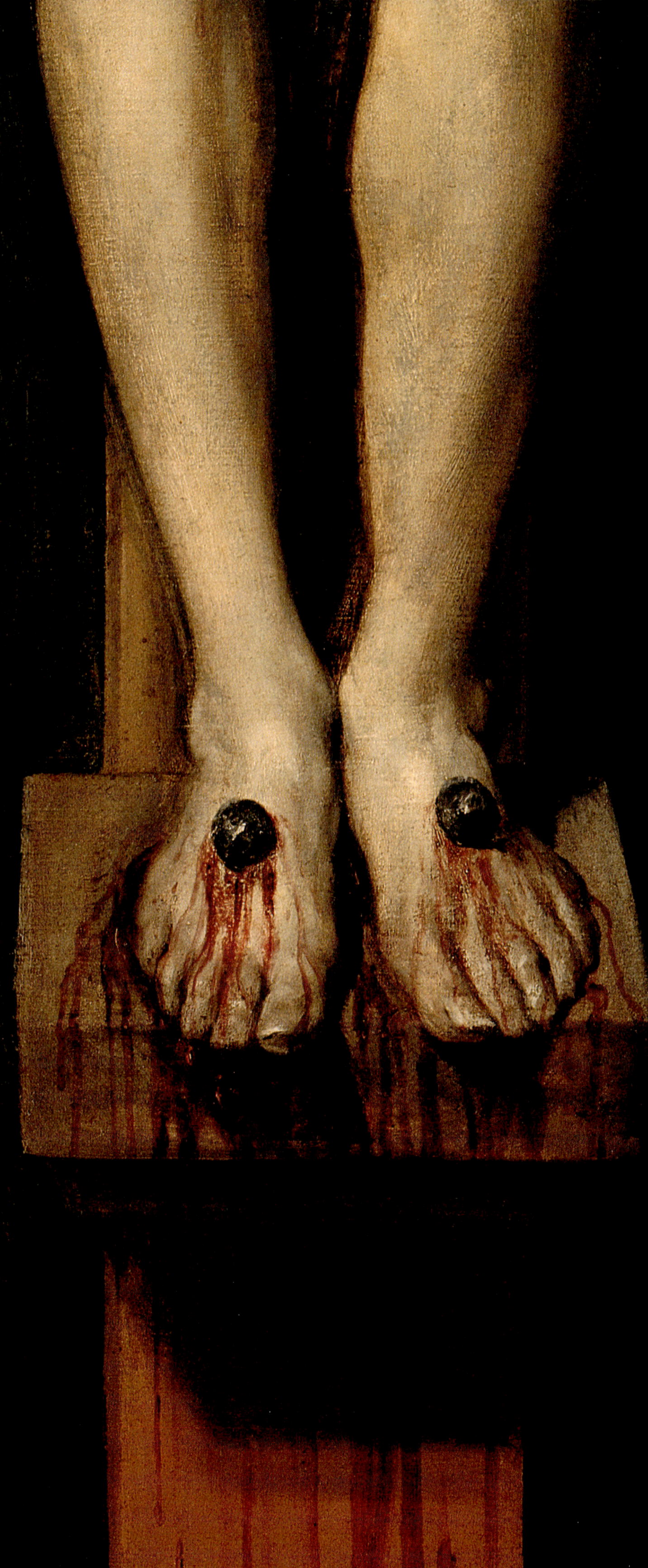

was gradually replaced by weariness and disappointment. Philip IV's spirit was continually tormented by doubts, for which he found solace over a period of twenty years in his correspondence with a nun, Sister María de Jesús de Ágreda. The court that Velázquez paints, not just the king, is melancholy despite its festivities, seamy despite its joys, a court of buffoons with an heir to the throne its only hope.

THE PALACE OF THE BUEN RETIRO

This hope for an heir inspired the paintings created for the Buen Retiro palace and for the Torre de la Parada, a hunting lodge in the forest surrounding El Pardo palace. These paintings, now in the Museo del Prado, were intended for sites dedicated to the relaxation and entertainment of the Spanish Habsburgs at a time when the dynasty was on a speedy course of decline.

In 1667 Jean Muret, the extraordinary ambassador of Louis XIV to the Spanish court, wrote a letter to Michel de Marillac, Lord of Ollainville, describing his visit to the Buen Retiro palace on January 10 of that year:

> Since you have asked me to describe the first country houses I have seen, I must tell you about the royal one in the Retiro, where nothing suitable for pleasure and magnificence has been omitted. . . . The interior of this fortress [is] a treasury of all the most precious things produced in the Indies, such as carpets made from the bark of trees, costumes of Montezuma and of the Incas of Peru, strangely shaped cabinets, stone [obsidian] mirrors, bed curtains made up of feathers, and innumerable other furnishings. . . . From here to the great palace you move through arbors formed of extremely long trained vines. . . . One has to admire the bronze horse that undoubtedly has no equal in Europe. . . . In the castle we were amazed by the great number of paintings hung from the entrance onward. . . . In one place we saw all of the modern battles that have taken place, while in another there were the most unusual antiquities. In still another place there were various history paintings depicting both sacred and profane subjects, while elsewhere one came upon an infinity of caprices, the boldest of nudes, and to round it off, a selection showing the genius and taste of each painter.

185. Diego Velázquez
c. 1632
Detail of *Christ Crucified.*
Museo Nacional del Prado, Madrid.

Foreign travelers to Madrid in the seventeenth century rarely mentioned the Palace of the Buen Retiro except in regard to the festivities that took place there. Hence, our interest in the description of the French ambassador, who was stunned by the gardens and the cabinets of curiosities holding treasures of the Indies; by the equestrian statue of Philip IV, which was cast in Florence by Pietro Tacca; and by the paintings, among them the depictions of "the modern battles" hung in the palace's throne room, called the Hall of Realms.

The room had initially been conceived as a type of royal loge from whose balconies could be viewed festivals, celebrations, and performances taking place in the gardens and courtyards below. Later, this room became the throne room of a palace built more on the initiative of the count-duke of Olivares than of the king himself. The salon, which is in the center of the north wing, has an elongated rectangular floor plan with balconies along the two long walls and doors in the end walls. The building and decoration of the Buen Retiro palace was done with great speed: the decoration of the throne room was begun in 1634 and finished on April 28, 1635 (ills. 186,187).

The ceiling was decorated in the Roman style with grotesques covering the entire surface. Rimming the ceiling on all four sides were twenty-four coats of arms of the realms and provinces of the Spanish monarchy, symbols of the vast territory ruled by Philip IV. These coats of arms gave the "Great Hall," known also as *salón de las comedias* or Throne Room, the more familiar apellation—Hall of Realms. Philip IV intended the decoration of the walls to serve as a mirror of the virtues and proper education of a prince for his eldest son, Baltasar Carlos, Prince of Asturias. Toward that end, Philip IV wanted the decoration to represent the two pillars of the Spanish monarchy: dynastic continuity and its role as defender of the Catholic faith against heretics and reformers. The idea was to exalt the

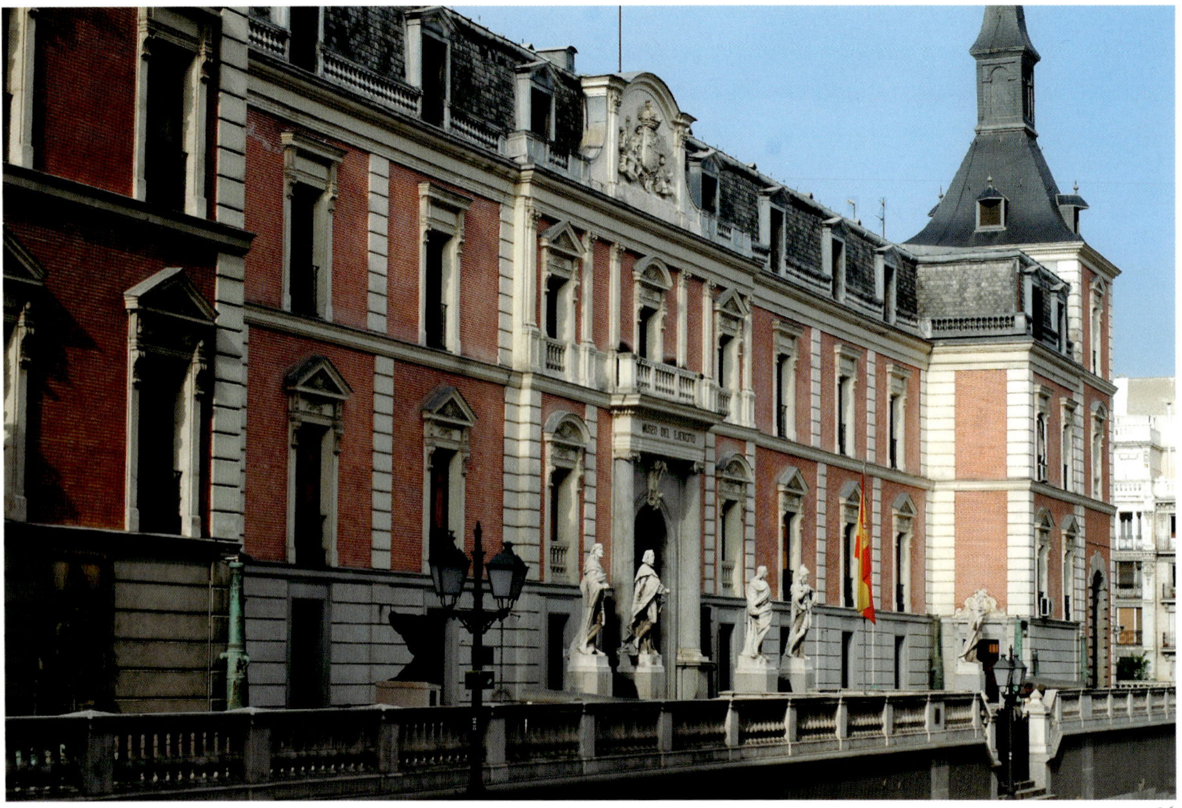

186

186. Detail of the north wing of the main plaza of the Buen Retiro palace (now Museo del Ejército), Madrid, built by Giovanni Battista Crescenzi and Alonso Carbonel, 1633–40.

187. Reconstruction, according to J. Álvarez Lopera (2005), of the arrangement of the paintings in the Hall of Realms of the Buen Retiro palace, Madrid, which differs from other reconstructions.

TOP: THE NORTH WALL, FROM WEST TO EAST:
Missing. *The Death of Hercules*, by Francisco de Zurbarán.
The Siege of Rheinfelden, by Vicente Carducho.
Hercules Slaying Geryon, by Francisco de Zurbarán.
The Relief of Brisach, by Jusepe Leonardo.
Hercules in the Straits of Gibraltar, by Francisco de Zurbarán.
The Relief of Constanza, by Vicente Carducho.
Hercules Slaying the Nemean Lion, by Francisco de Zurbarán.
The Recapture of San Juan de Puerto Rico, by Eugenio Cajés.
Hercules Struggling with the Hydra of Lerna, by Francisco de Zurbarán.
The Recapture of San Cristobal, by Félix Castelo.

CENTER: THE SOUTH WALL, FROM EAST TO WEST:
The Recapture of Bahía de Todos los Santos, by Juan Bautista Maino.
Hercules Struggling with the Cretan Bull, by Francisco de Zurbarán.
The Relief of Genoa, by Antonio de Pereda.
Hercules and Antaeus, by Francisco de Zurbarán.
The Victory of Fleurus, by Vicente Carducho.

power, glory, and fame of the Spanish Habsburg dynasty for the benefit of the young prince, but the count-duke may have had a hand in the decoration, hoping it would spur King Philip IV himself to play a more decisive role. Philip IV, a deeply learned and cultured ruler, was perhaps better suited to playing the violin than to wielding a sword. In 1633, when the work on the Buen Retiro began, he had just completed his translation of Books VIII and IX of the monumental *History of Italy* by Guicciardini. The king wrote in the epilogue:

> . . . I conclude that what I most desire is to leave to the Prince, my son, and all others that God Our Lord may choose to give me, a living example and some practical advice concerning how they, in order to be worthy of governing, must work from the moment they have use of reason, busying themselves in the art of government, which is truly very difficult and involves a great deal of knowledge and thus great learning. And how necessary it is for them to read history, for they will find in it great assistance and relief in directing and controlling the matters that arise during their reigns; and how important it is to love knowledge and learning, striving to overcome that disinclination of youth to study, and to judge the benefit that can be had from those studies, after all the time spent on them, when they are older, as studying will assist them in handling the many things they will be confronted with.

The equestrian portraits of the family were hung on the eastern and western walls of the Hall of Realms: Philip III and Margarita of Austria (on the western side) and Philip IV and Isabella of Bourbon (on the eastern), with the equestrian portrait of Prince Baltasar Carlos placed above a doorway between them, thus presiding over the ensemble (ills. 187, 189). In that portrait Velázquez expressed the energy, guilelessness, and gallantry of the young prince to whom the future of the weakened dynasty would be entrusted. Velázquez had never achieved anything like this before. The extremely loose painting style creates a majestic tonal symphony that deceives both the eye and the mind.

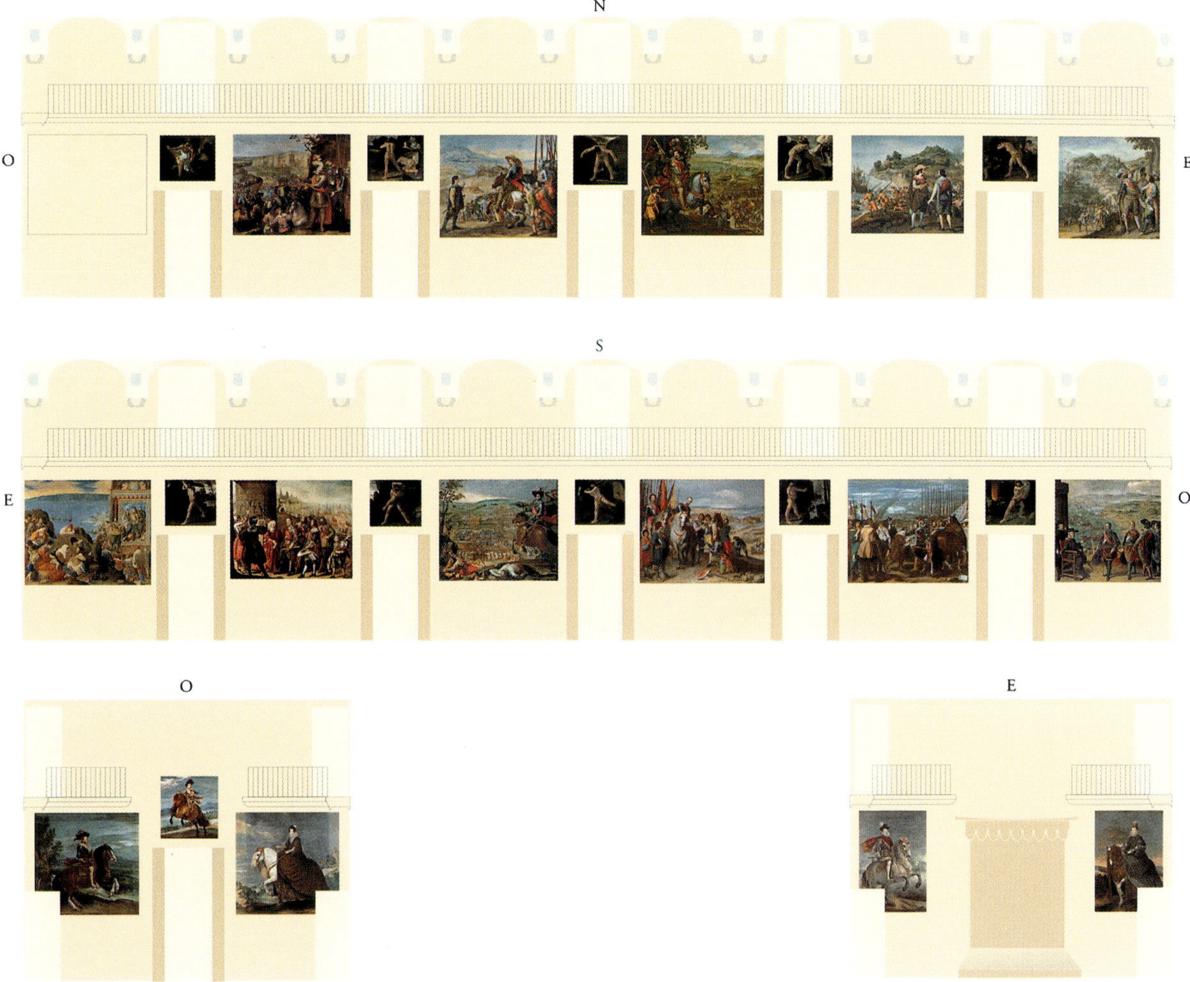

187

Hercules Struggling with the Erymanthian Boar, by Francisco de Zurbarán.
The Surrender of Juliers, by Jusepe Leonardo.
Hercules Diverts the River Alpheus, by Francisco de Zurbarán.
The Surrender of Breda, or *The Lances*, by Diego Velázquez.
Hercules and Cerberus, by Francisco de Zurbarán.
The Defense of Cadiz, by Francisco de Zurbarán.

BOTTOM LEFT: THE WEST WALL:
Equestrian Portrait of Philip IV, by Diego Velázquez.
Equestrian Portrait of Prince Baltasar Carlos, by Diego Velázquez.
Equestrian Portrait of Queen Isabella of Bourbon, completed by Diego Velázquez and his studio.

BOTTOM RIGHT: THE EAST WALL:
Equestrian Portrait of Philip III, completed by Diego Velázquez and his studio.
Margarita of Austria, completed by Diego Velázquez and his studio.

All of these paintings are now held in the Museo Nacional del Prado, Madrid.

OVERLEAF:
188. Diego Velázquez
1634
Equestrian Portrait of the Count-Duke of Olivares.
Museo Nacional del Prado, Madrid.

189. Diego Velázquez
1634–35
Equestrian Portrait of Prince Baltasar Carlos, Hall of Realms, the Buen Retiro palace, Madrid.
Museo Nacional del Prado, Madrid.

On the long walls of the room were hung twelve paintings representing the principal military victories of Philip IV's armies. These were painted by the best Spanish artists of the time, with unequal results. The Aragonese artist Jusepe Leonardo painted the siege of the Lower Rhenish city of Jülich, or Juliers, by the troops of Ambrogio Spinola (1622). The Florentine Vicente Carducho was given the task of depicting the victory of Gonzalo de Córdoba over the Protestant German armies at Fleurus (1622). Diego Velázquez painted *The Surrender of Breda* (1625, see ills. 110, 111), the unquestioned masterpiece of the series. Other Habsburg triumphs included the expulsion of the Dutch from Brazil by the expedition under Fadrique de Toledo (1625), painted by the Dominican friar Juan Bautista Maino; the expulsion of the Dutch from San Juan, Puerto Rico, by the governor Juan de Haro (1625) was handled by the Tuscan painter Eugenio Cajés; the aid to the fleet that the second marquis of Santa Cruz offered to Genoa when the city allied with Spain was under siege by armies of Savoy and France (1625) was painted by Antonio de Pereda; the resistance of Cadiz, organized by Fernando Girón against the attack of Lord Wimbledon (1625), was painted by Francisco de Zurbarán; the expulsion by Fadrique de Toledo of the French and English colonizers of the Caribbean island of San Cristóbal (1629) was depicted by Félix Castello; Cajés was also commissioned to paint the expulsion by the marquis of Cadereita (1633) of the colonizers from the island of Saint Martin in the Caribbean (the painting has not survived); and, finally, the victories of the duke of Feria in 1633 in German lands (Constanza, Rheinfelden, and Breisach) were painted by Carducho (the first two) and by Leonardo (the third).

The military campaigns glorified in the Hall of Realms were largely ineffective; military leaders like Ambrogio Spinola had died, and others fell out of favor with the count-duke. Between these scenes of victory were hung Zurbarán's depictions of the Labors of Hercules, whose battles against evil symbolized the battle of the Spanish kings against the Protestants.

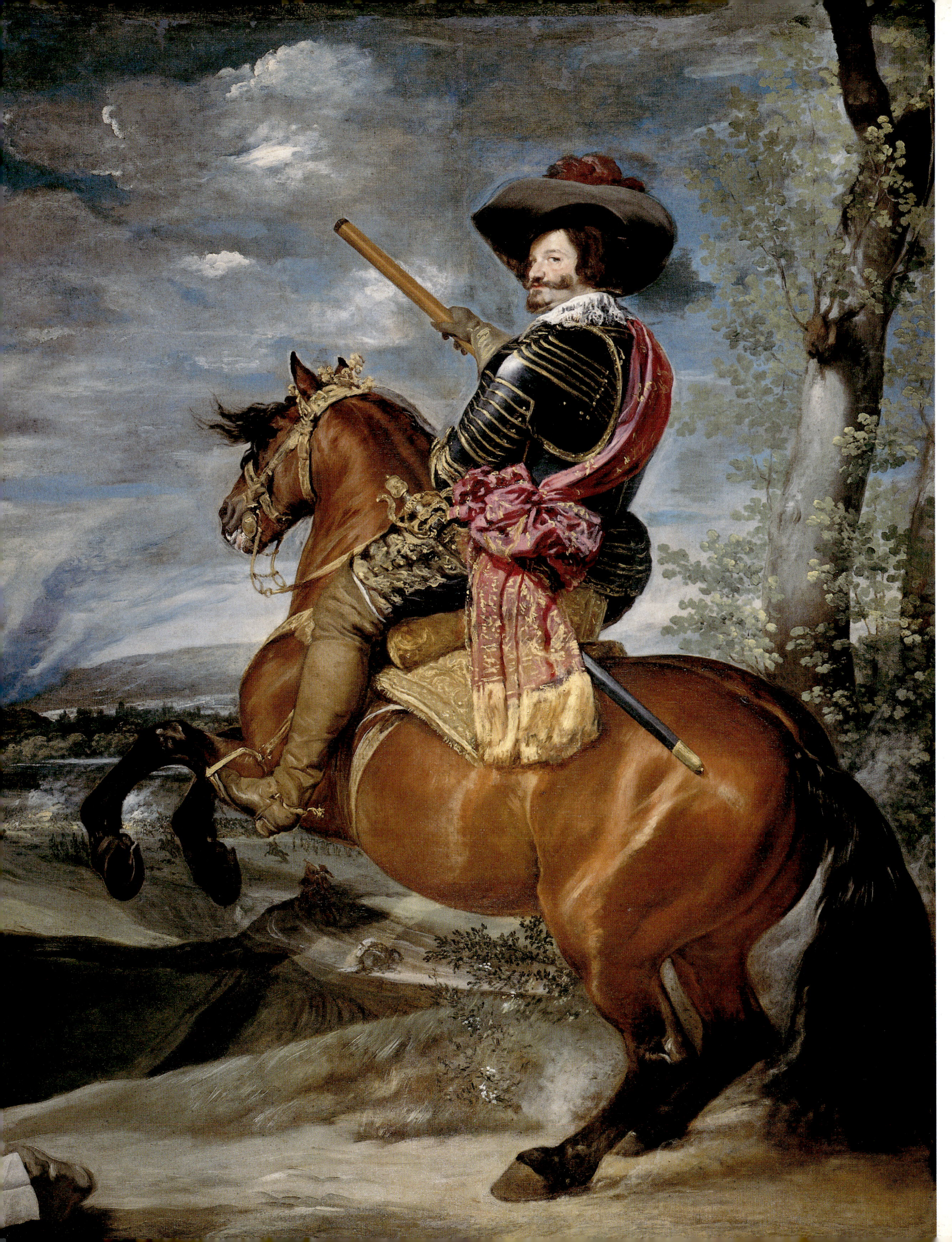

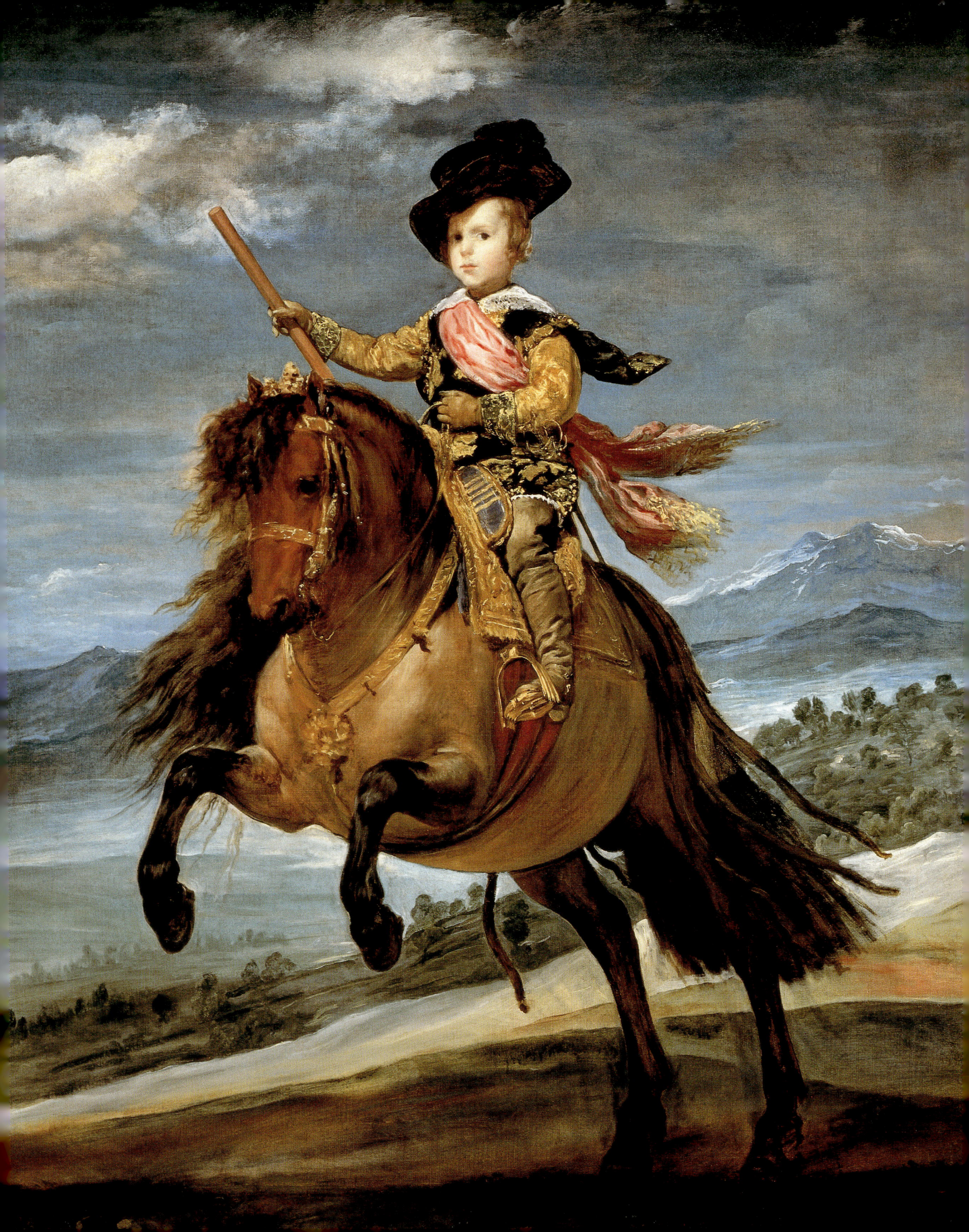

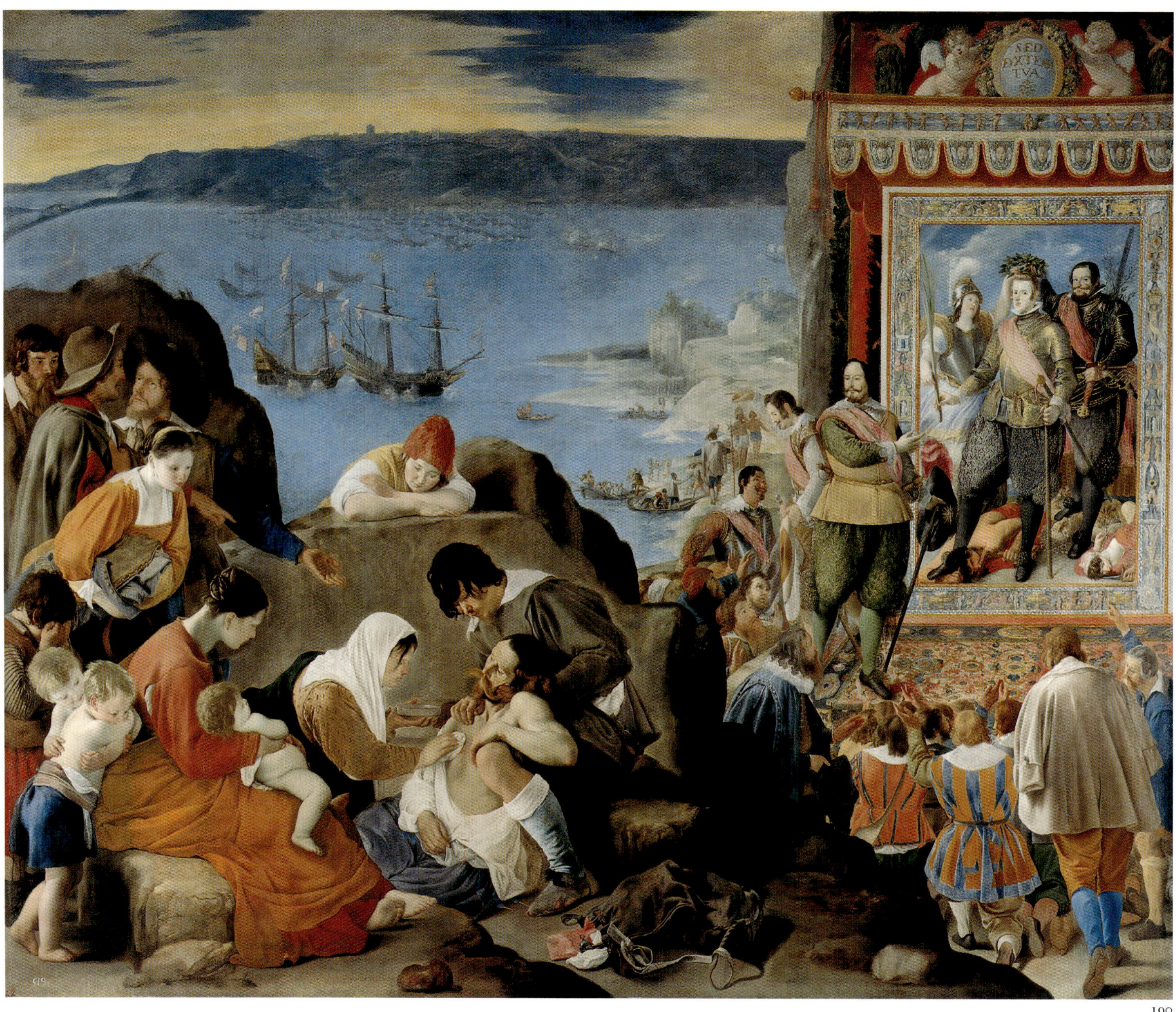

190

The Equestrian Portrait of Philip IV (1635–36) was the only portrait besides the one of Baltasar Carlos for the Hall of Realms that was painted entirely by Velázquez. This portrait of the king is quite grave and formal, but a simpler, more natural treatment can be seen in the portraits of the king, his brother, and Baltasar Carlos that Velázquez painted for the remodeled Torre de la Parada. (Rubens was commissioned to create the main decoration of that hunting lodge with some fifty canvases based on Ovid's *Metamorphoses*.) Velázquez also applied a simple, direct approach to the portraits he did of the common but unique people who lived at court—dwarfs and jesters (Francisco Lezcano, known as the Niño de Vallecas [see ill. 136]; Diego de Acedo, called el Primo [see ill. 132]; Juan Calabazas; Sebastián de Morra [see ill. 137]; and Pablillos de Valladolid). Velázquez's paintings of the philosophers Menippus and Aesop for the Torre de la Parada at first glance make them appear to be street people, and in his painting of Mars, the god is shown disheveled and exhausted. In these portraits the protocols of court—so obligatory in the portraits of dignitaries—can be disregarded by the artist in favor of the simple dignity of the common man.

190. Juan Bautista Maino
1634–35
The Recapture of Bahía de Todos los Santos, Hall of Realms, the Buen Retiro palace, Madrid.
Museo Nacional del Prado, Madrid.

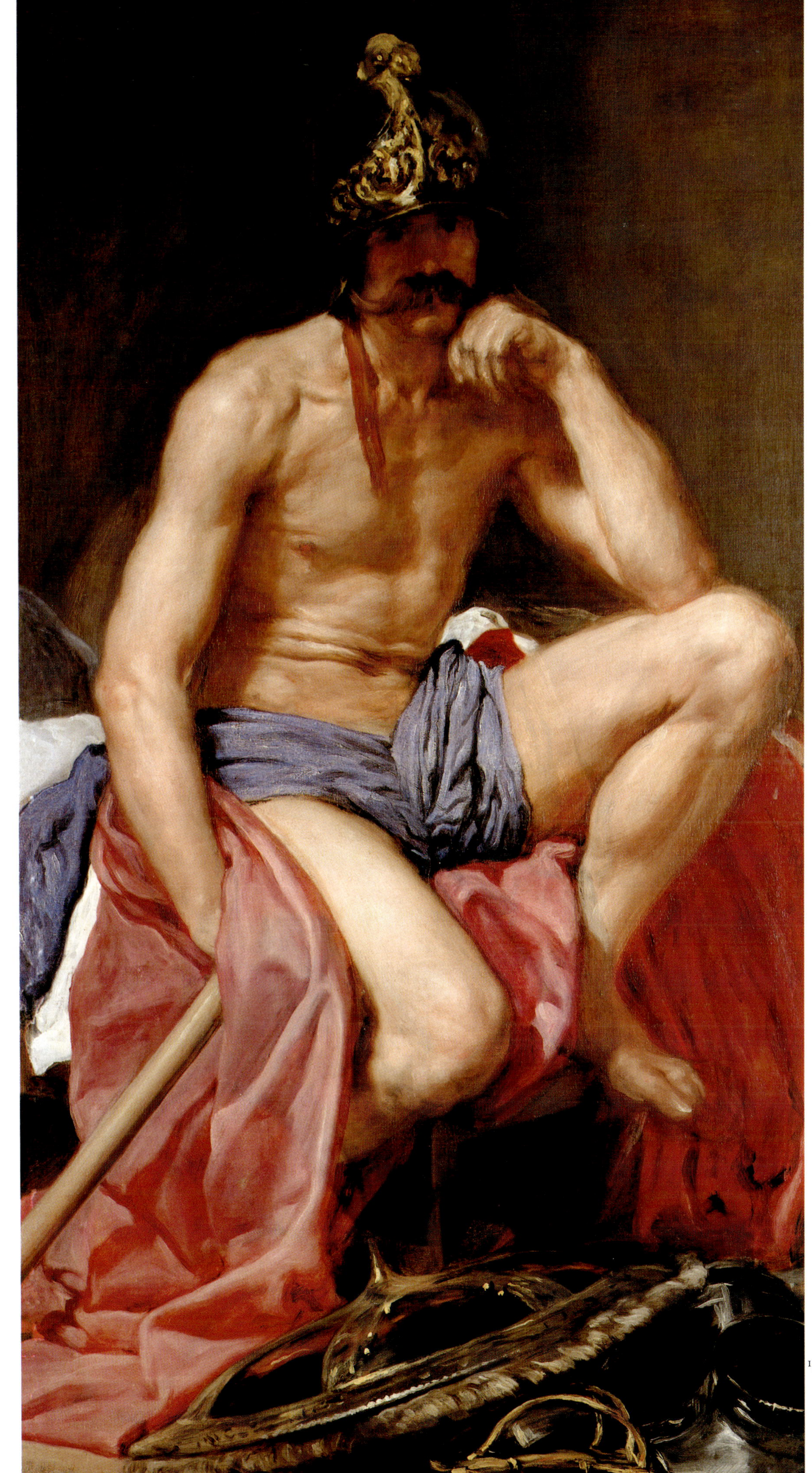

191. Diego Velázquez
c. 1639–41
Mars.
Museo Nacional del Prado,
Madrid.

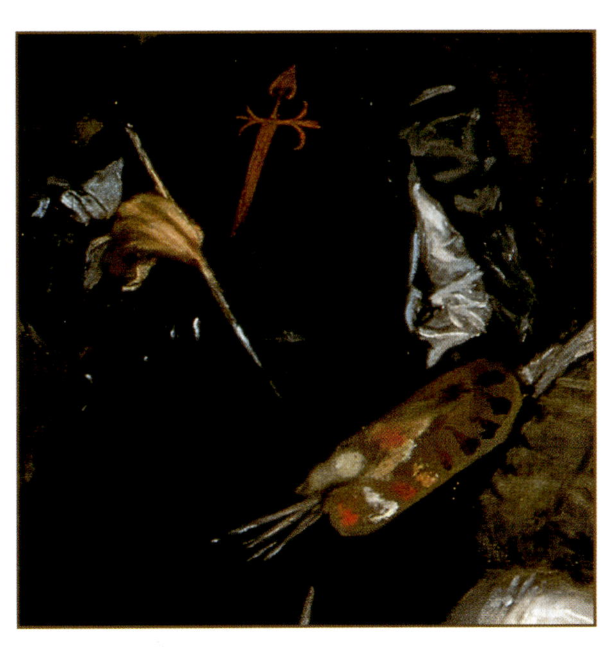

BUT WHERE IS THE PAINTING?

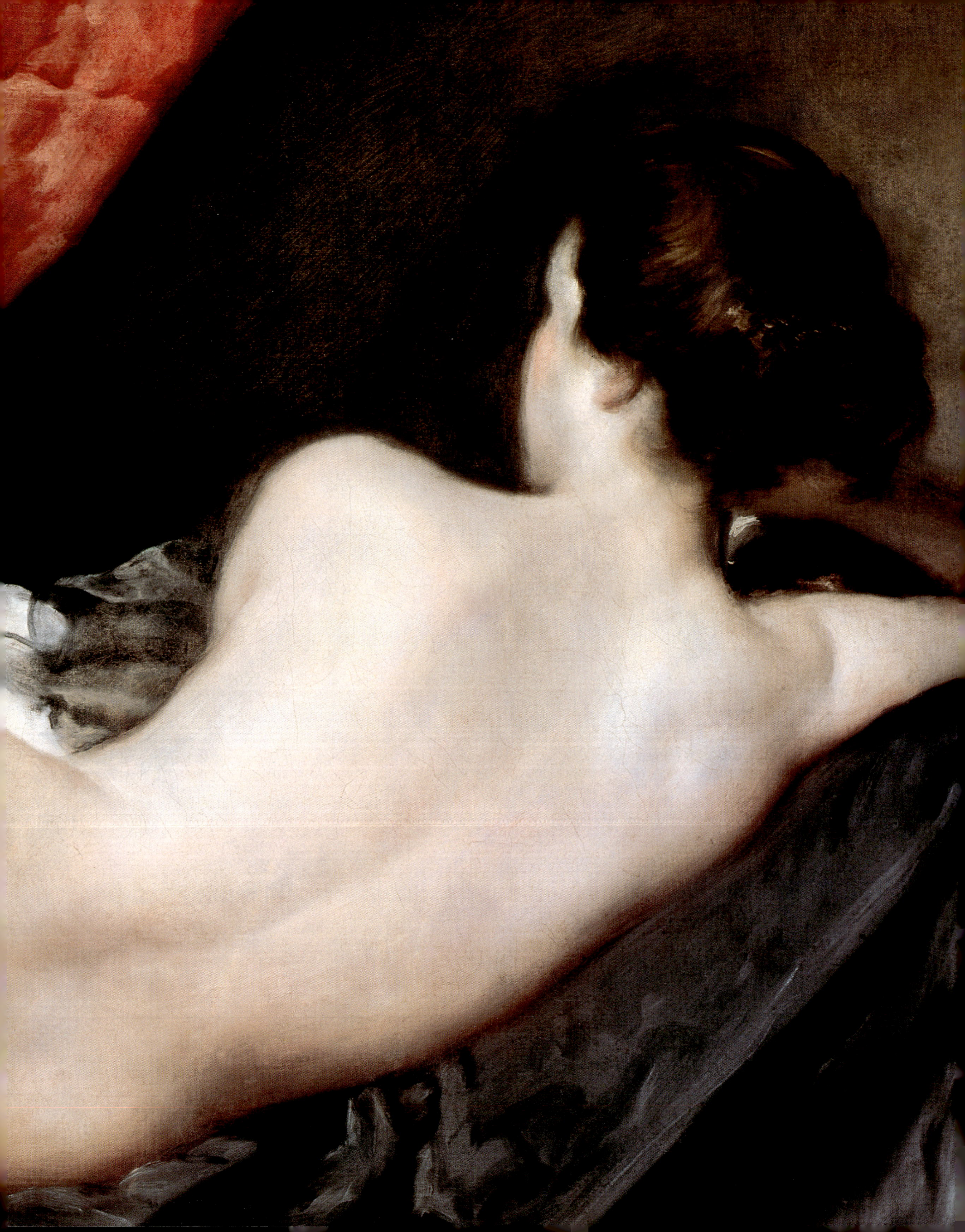

6

But Where Is the Painting?

> Velázquez undoubtedly came closest to capturing truth itself in his painting *The Spinners*, created during his later years and executed in such a way that it seems that the hand played no part in it, as if it was painted through will alone.
>
> —ANTON RAPHAEL MENGS, *Letter to Antonio Ponz*, 1776

The 1640s was a period of upheaval at the court of Philip IV because of both foreign affairs (the Peace of the Pyrenees, the treaties of Westphalia) and events at home. The count-duke of Olivares fell from favor early in 1643; Isabella of Bourbon died late the following year; and two years later Prince Baltasar Carlos, in whom everyone including Velázquez had placed their hopes for the future of the Monarchy, died.

PRECEDING PAGE:
192. Diego Velázquez
c. 1656–57
Detail of the self-portrait in *Las Meninas (The Family of Philip IV)*.
Museo Nacional del Prado, Madrid.

LEFT:
193. Diego Velázquez
c. 1650
Detail of *Venus at Her Mirror*.
National Gallery, London.

TO ITALY AGAIN

In 1649 the widowed king was married to his niece the Archduchess Mariana of Austria. The duke of Maqueda y Nájera led the delegation to Trent to accompany the future queen back to Spain. The expedition sailed from the port of Málaga bound for Genoa on Thursday, January 21, 1649. Diego de Velázquez sailed with it on a mission to purchase paintings and sculptures in Italy and to hire painters for the decoration of the old royal palace, the Alcázar. The search for works of art took Velázquez and his servant Juan de Pareja to Milan, Venice (where he acquired works by Titian and Veronese), Parma, Bologna, Florence, and Modena, where he visited the nearby Este palace at Sassuolo. While in Modena, he persuaded the fresco painters Agostino Mitelli and Angelo Michele Colonna to travel back to Madrid with him (having failed to engage the services of Pietro da Cortona). He also traveled to Rome, where he spent a long time, and to Naples.

By 1649 Velázquez was no longer the young artist he had been on his first journey to Italy, but a renowned painter, the royal portraitist who enjoyed the full support of Philip IV's diplomatic connections. Velázquez was not sent to Italy as a painter, however, but as an art connoisseur in the king's employ. Nevertheless, in Rome, after not picking up a brush for a number of months, Velázquez painted a portrait of Juan de Pareja, an exercise that resulted in one of his most superb portraits (Metropolitan Museum of Art, New York) and brought him a number of Roman commissions. Velázquez's work was so admired by his fellow painters that he was admitted to their Academy of Saint Luke and to the Congregazione dei Virtuosi at the Pantheon. He painted a portrait of Pope Innocent X (ill. 195) with extremely fluid reds, whites. and golds, thinning out the pigment so that the paint could engage in a dialogue with the grain of the canvas. Velázquez captured a severe, suspicious, restless, and challenging personality who posed without hiding his soul. When the pope saw himself reflected in the mirror of Velázquez's portrait, his comment was *"troppo vero"* (too true).

On his second trip to Italy Velázquez spent a lot of time looking but found nothing he wanted to learn. Instead he challenged the great Venetian painters whom he so admired by painting a naked woman—the only extant Velázquez nude, though not the only one he painted. The meaning of Velázquez's *Venus at Her Mirror* (ills 139, 193, 196) is of little importance, whether it represents an allegory of vanity—love conquered by beauty; a portrait of Velázquez's lover; a portrait of Damiana, the mistress of the marquis of Heliche; or a portrait of the ancient Roman painter Flaminia Triva. When he painted this Venus, Velázquez did not try to equate—through allegory—things, personalities, or concepts that are in fact opposites. He did not consult books or learned men to discover the truth about Venus, that goddess who, in a sonnet by Lope de Vega, faced Pallas Athena, the goddess of war, and reminded her: "When you dare, you will see how much more soundly you are defeated by the weapons of the one who first defeated you naked."

He did not probe into the truth of Venus; rather, in his creation of a naked woman seen from behind, Velázquez penetrated the baroque dream of truth itself, making an impossible painting out of an intimate reality, which by being impossible was more real than any other. This is one of the most beautiful female nudes painted in the seventeenth century. It is situated at the unattainable point of convergence between idealism and naturalism; a woman before a mirror that, paradoxically, reflects only the dreamy expression of an ardent peasant woman trapped, perhaps unwillingly, in the truth carried by a Cupid, the sweet victim of the silk ribbons that tie his hands and force him to his knees as the slave of the dialogue between idea and nature.

Nothing separates the eyes of the voyeur from the woman's body, nor does any drape need to be drawn aside to reveal it. We are together with this woman in a room closed off by a crimson curtain that prevents any gaze from beyond the canvas from contemplating her nakedness. This woman has little to do with those painted by Titian, or with the bronze hermaphrodite that Velázquez saw in Rome, or with the nudes in the Sistine Chapel, or even with the theme of the goddess in her boudoir (the "toi-

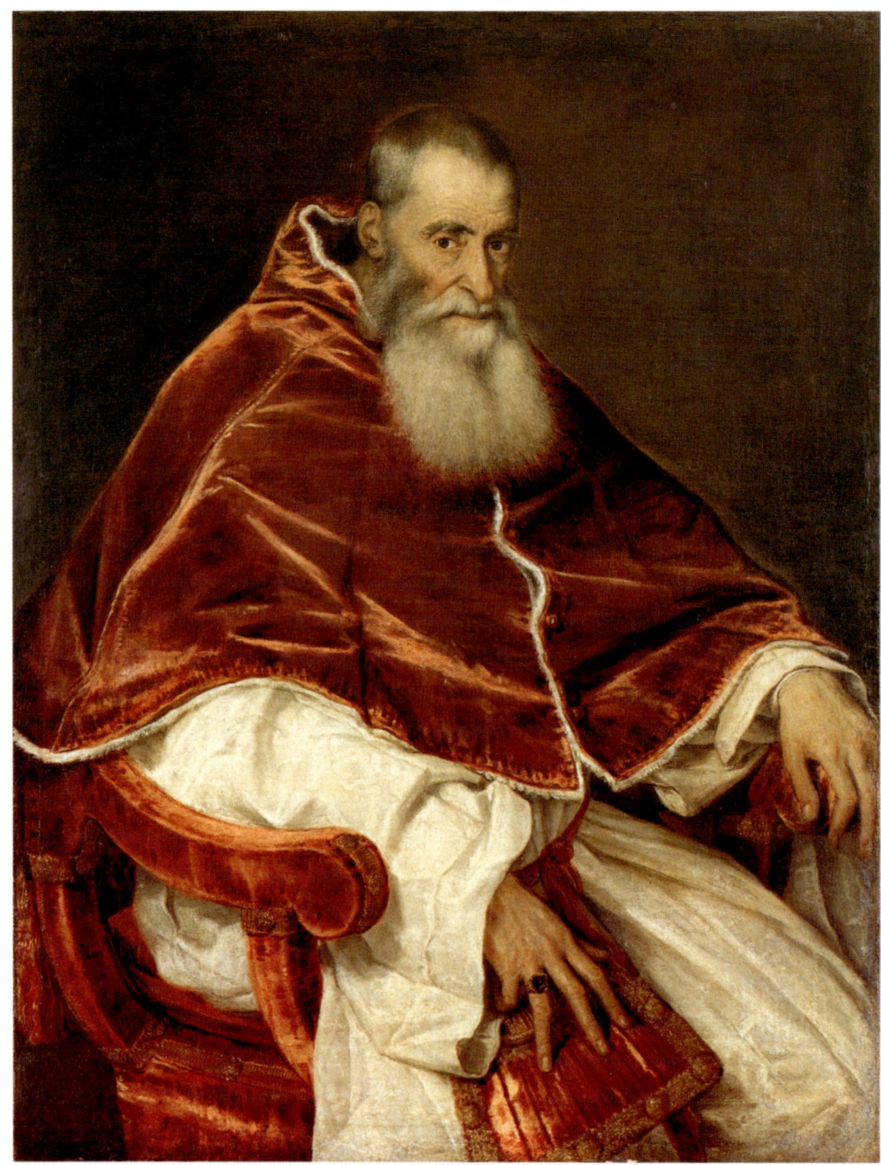
194

ABOVE:
194. Titian
1543
Portrait of Pope Paul III.
Museo di Capodimonte, Naples.

RIGHT:
195. Diego Velázquez
1650
Detail of *Portrait of Pope Innocent X.*
Galleria Doria Pamphili, Rome.

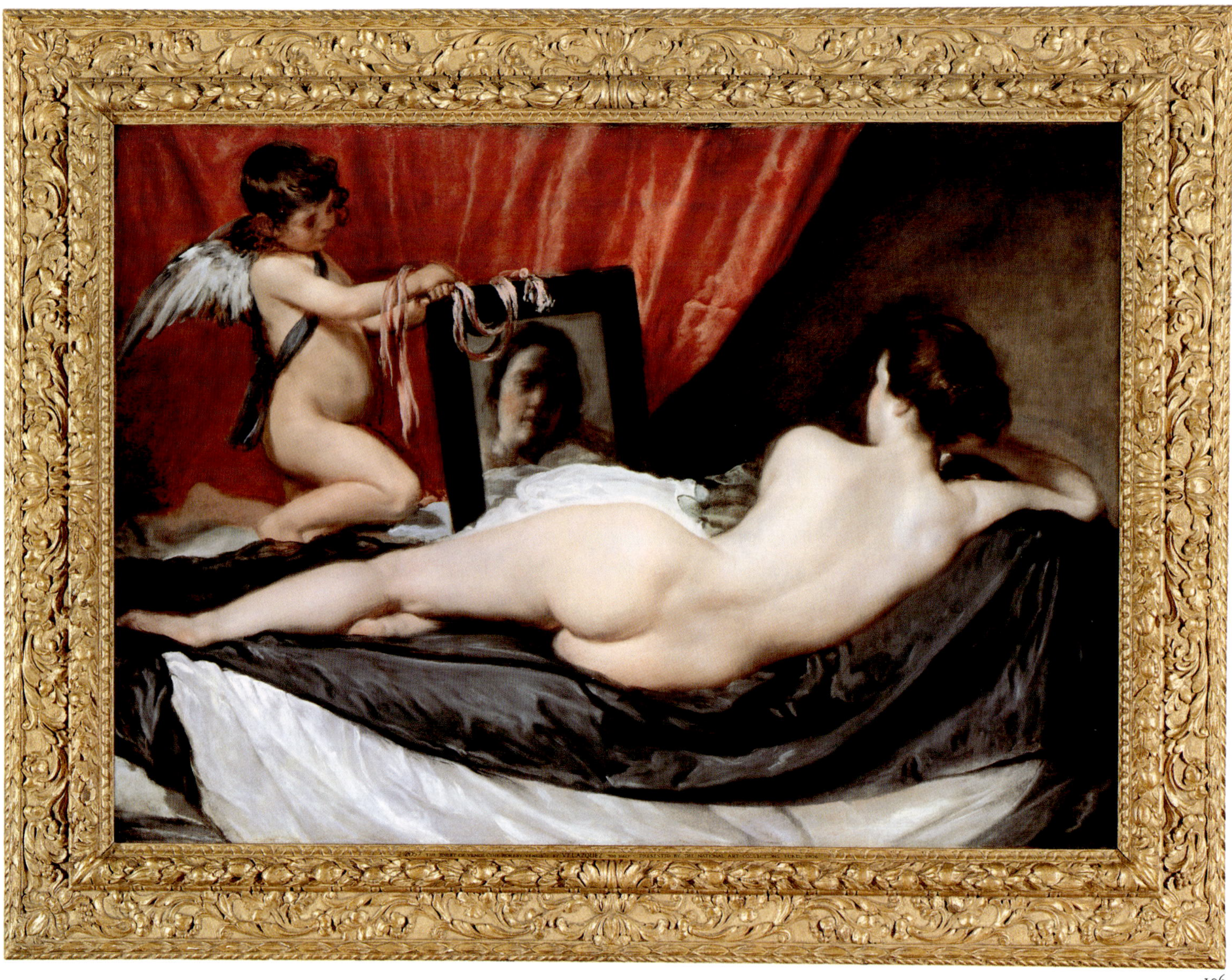

196

lette of Venus"), which had become a common subject in art after Giovanni Bellini introduced it. We do not know whether Velázquez painted this Venus for himself or for Don Gaspar Méndez de Haro y Guzmán, the marquis of Heliche, whose inventory of worldly goods dated June 1, 1651, includes "a painting on canvas by Velázquez of a naked recumbent woman with her back to us, leaning on her right arm and contemplating herself in a mirror held by a child." In the Spain of the Counter-Reformation, a land agonizing under the weight of mystical love, Velázquez painted a poem in which everything is sensual, especially the silky white and gray drapes that caress the woman's flesh. She brazenly delights in her own body, knowing that before it is taken by the one who will part the crimson drapery, it is our object of desire.

One might caress the pearly flesh of the beautiful young woman, or, as the art historian Enrique Lafuente Ferrari once wrote, trace with one's fingers the "linear undulation that links the narrow waist with the opulent guitar curve of her thighs"; one might slip one's hands among the folds of the gray silk, white linen, and red velvet; one might contemplate oneself with her in the mirror (although she is really the one observing us); and one might, like Cupid, become enraptured by the beauty of her body and her face, her tied-back hair, her black eyes,

196. Diego Velázquez
c. 1650
Venus at Her Mirror.
National Gallery, London.

her mouth, a glimpse of the soul in which beauty reigns, and her ruddy cheeks like those of the exotic Semiramis, portrayed by Calderón in *The Daughter of the Air.* The presence of Cupid (the love god Eros) identifies this woman as Venus, but what Velázquez really painted was a woman who came to the mirror to be enraptured and enrapture us, daring to do so without moral compunctions, something that Lope de Vega did not manage to achieve when in one of his sonnets he sang the praises of a woman and her reflection in the mirror:

> If to the mirror you come to be enraptured,
> you must break it not to be offended,
> or because in many pieces you might see yourself
> and it, in many others, may portray you.
>
> If your eyes seek no shame,
> you cannot be safe from yourself;
> for on seeing yourself so beautiful
> envy may overcome you.
>
> The mold from which you sprang
> broke when nature formed you,
> the repeated action of your mirror.
>
> To smash the mirror was flattery and artifice,
> for being your reflection, not even painted
> could it equal your beauty.

Velázquez was very comfortable in Rome, so much so that he keep putting off his return to Spain. The duke of Infantado, Spanish ambassador in Rome, received several letters from Philip IV during 1650 and early the next year, requesting him to press Velázquez to return to Madrid, which he eventually did in mid-1651.

CHIEF CHAMBERLAIN AND PAINTER

Though Velázquez had tarried so long, the king apparently did not hold it against him and paid him his full salary as Gentleman of the Bedchamber. Furthermore, on March 8, 1652, Philip appointed him Chief Chamberlain of the Palace. This was the high point of Velázquez's career as a courtier, but, although the position brought him close to the king, it left him with little time to devote to his art. He painted the occasional portrait of Queen Mariana of Austria, of the Infanta María Teresa, then heiress to the Spanish throne (and later Queen of France, as wife of Louis XIV), and of Philip IV, who after 1652 refused to have his portrait painted in order to avoid seeing himself mirrored by time *("troppo vero,"* he must have thought, like Pope Innocent X). In his later years, Velázquez also painted Prince Felipe Próspero, who was born in 1657.

Velázquez found his ideal sitter, however, in the Infanta Margarita Maria, born on July 12, 1651, who eventually became Empress of the Holy Roman Empire. He painted her in 1654, 1656, 1659 (in three portraits now in the Kunsthistorisches Museum, Vienna), and 1660 (this canvas, now in the Museo del Prado, was completed by Velázquez's son-in-law, Juan Bautista del Mazo). Velázquez also used the Infanta to convey the very essence of painting in a large canvas known as *Las Meninas* (The Maids of Honor, ills. 197–200, 204, 205).

Antonio Palomino de Castro y Velasco, who was born in 1655, just one year before Velázquez painted the canvas, was the first to provide a detailed description of the work, specifically in his *Museo Pictórico y Escala Óptica* (1715–24):

> Among the marvelous paintings by Don Diego Velázquez was the large picture with the portrait of the Empress Margarita María of Austria when she was very young (then still Infanta of Spain). There are no words to describe her great charm, liveliness and beauty, but her portrait itself is the best panegyric. At her feet kneels Doña María Agustina, one of the Queen's *meninas* and daughter of Don Diego Sarmiento, serving her water from a clay jug. At her other side is Doña Isabel de Velasco, daughter of Don Bernardino López de Ayala y Velasco, Count of Fuensalida and His Majesty's gentleman of the bedchamber, also a *menina* and later lady of honor, in an attitude and with a movement precisely as if she were speaking. In the foreground is a dog lying down and next to it is the midget Nicolasito Pertusato, who treads on it so as to show, together with the ferociousness of its appearance,

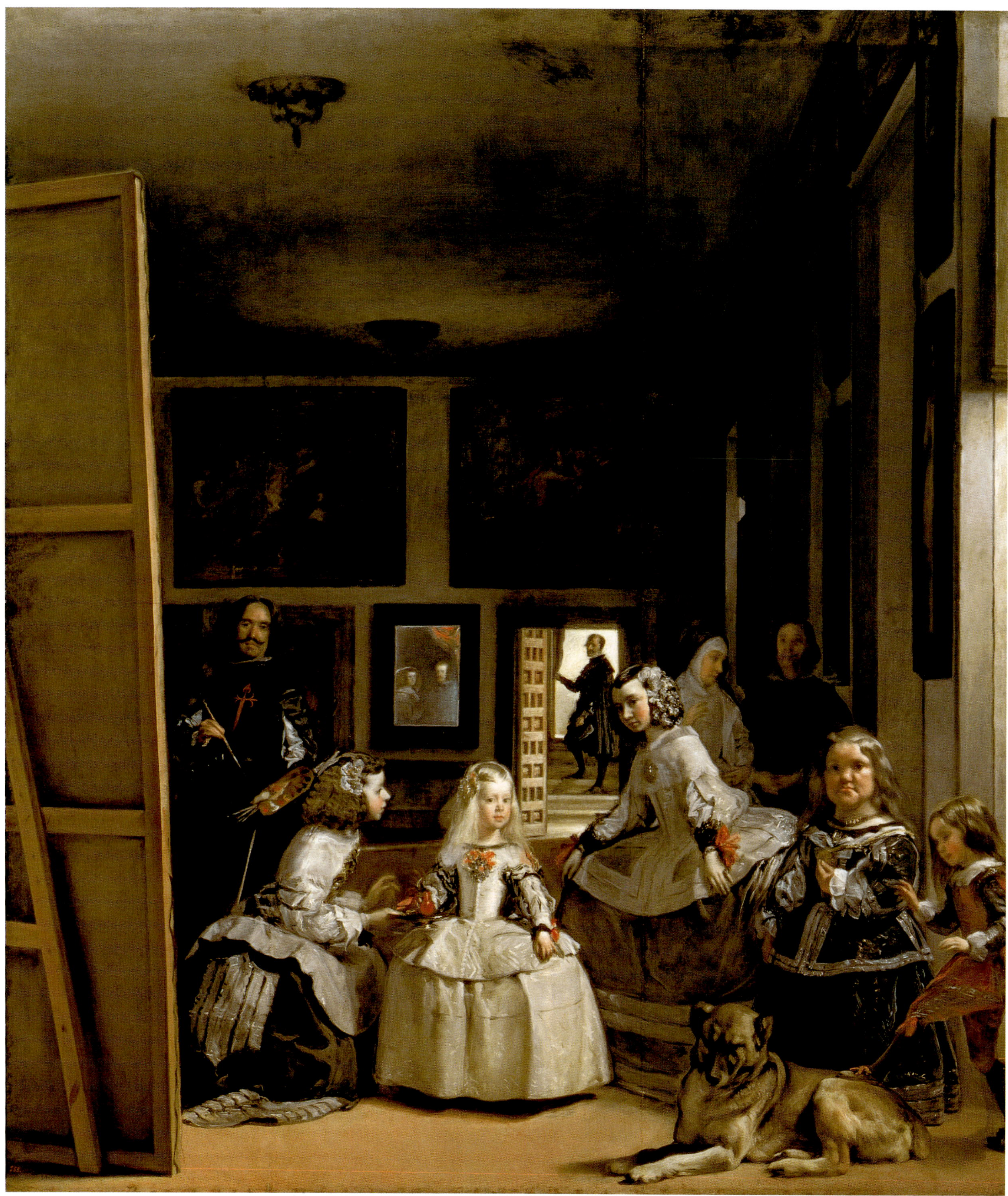

its tameness and gentleness when tried; for when it was being painted it remained motionless in whatever attitude it was placed. This figure is dark and prominent and gives great harmony to the composition. Behind it is Mari Bárbola, a dwarf of formidable aspect; farther back and in half-shadow is Doña Marcela de Ulloa, lady of honor . . . who gives a marvelous effect to the figural composition. On the other side is the painter himself, Don Diego Velázquez. . . . The canvas on which he is painting is large and nothing of what is painted on it can be seen, as it is viewed from the back. . . . Velázquez brilliantly revealed what he was painting through the ingenious device of a mirror at the back of the gallery facing the picture, where the reflection of our Catholic King and Queen, Philip and Mariana, is represented. On the walls of the room depicted here—the Prince's apartments—various dimly lit pictures can be seen. They can be recognized as representing scenes from Ovid's *Metamorphoses* by Rubens. This room has several windows that diminish in size, creating a perspective; the light enters through only the first and last from the left. The floor is plain and laid out with such good perspective that it looks as if one could walk on it; the same applies to the ceiling. To the left of the mirror is an open door leading to a staircase, and there stands José Nieto, the Queen's chamberlain; the resemblance is great despite the distance and the diminution in size and light where Velázquez assumes him to be. Air flows among the figures, the composition is superb, the idea totally new; in brief, there is no praise that can match the taste and skill of this work, for it is reality and not painting.

In the face of this "reality and not painting" the French critic Théophile Gautier exclaimed, "But where is the painting?" There is no painting; there is no representation in *Las Meninas,* only truth, a truth that Zeuxis applied to his beautiful Penelope: *In visurum aliquem, facilius, quam imitaturum* (it would be easier to envy it than to imitate it). It is the same truth that, years before, the courtier Luis Vélez de Guevara praised in a sonnet dedicated to one of Velázquez's portraits of the king:

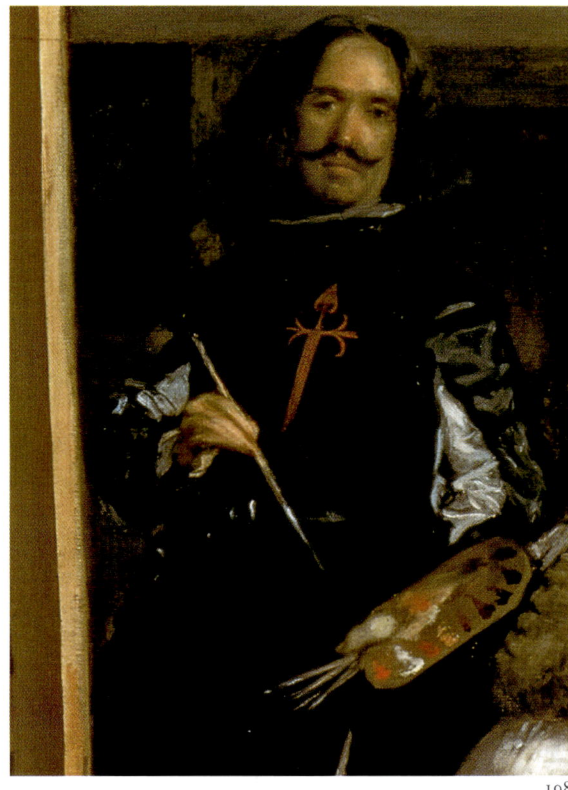

198

Oh brush, you render boldness and strength
with a fullness so well simulated
that you make ferocity fearful
and gentleness appear pleasurable.

Say, do you paint a portrait or bring it to life?
For this royal image is so surpassingly executed
that I would judge the canvas to be as alive
as insensible things are dead.

This portrait so splendidly reveals
the royal authority it is heir to
that it even commands the eye.

And since you have made it a likeness of power,
you have imitated what is most difficult,
for to be obeyed is easier.

Velázquez painted *Las Meninas* in the old Alcázar of Madrid. Palomino tells us that the picture was much admired by the king, who visited the studio often to watch its progress, as did Queen Mariana of Austria and the Infantas and ladies-in-waiting, that is, all the individuals who appear in the painting. They did not visit the studio to pose, but rather for pleasure and entertainment. Once

LEFT:
197. Diego Velázquez
c. 1656–57
Las Meninas (The Family of Philip IV).
Museo Nacional del Prado, Madrid.

ABOVE:
198. Diego Velázquez
c. 1656–57
Self-portrait, detail of *Las Meninas (The Family of Philip IV).*
Museo Nacional del Prado, Madrid.

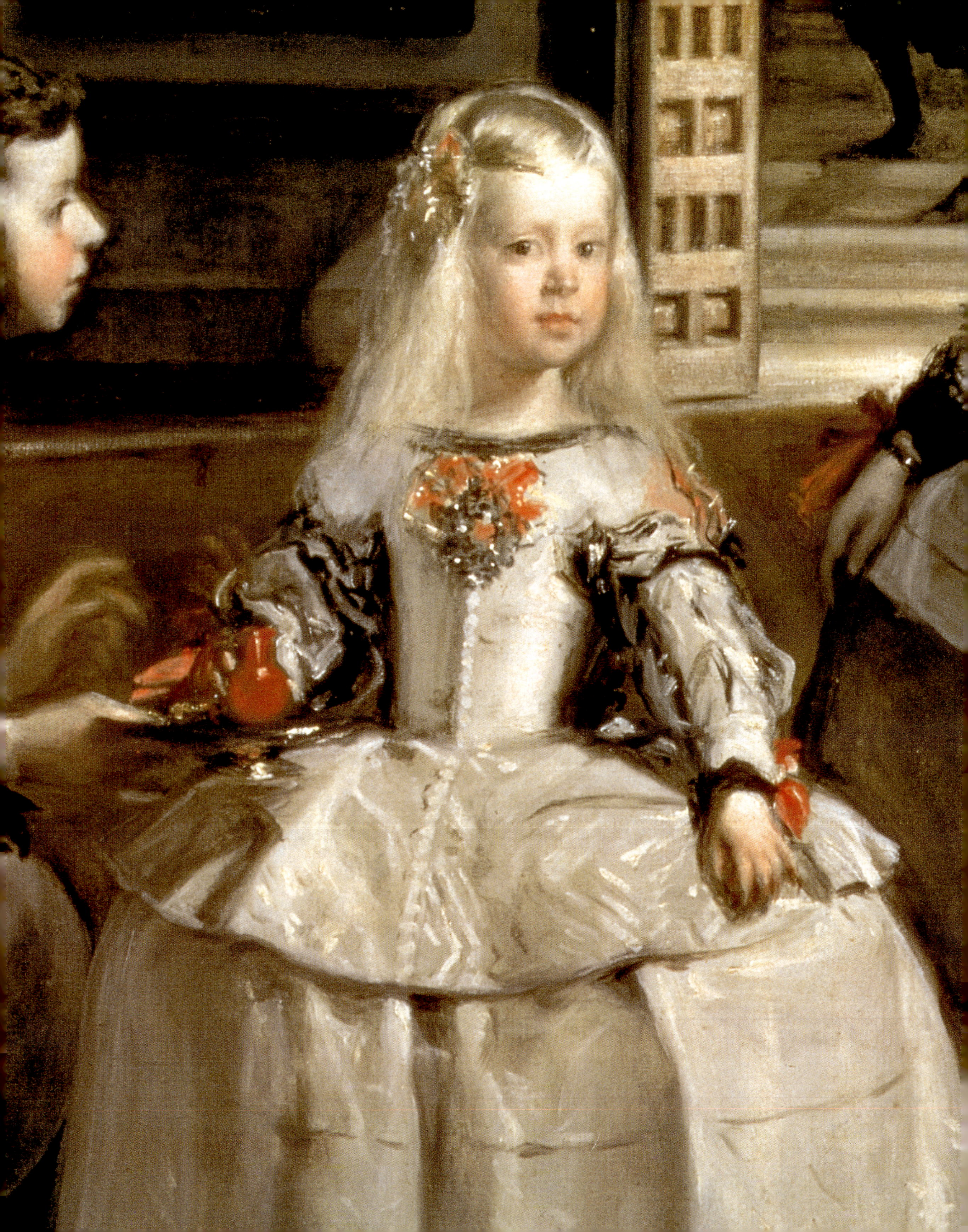

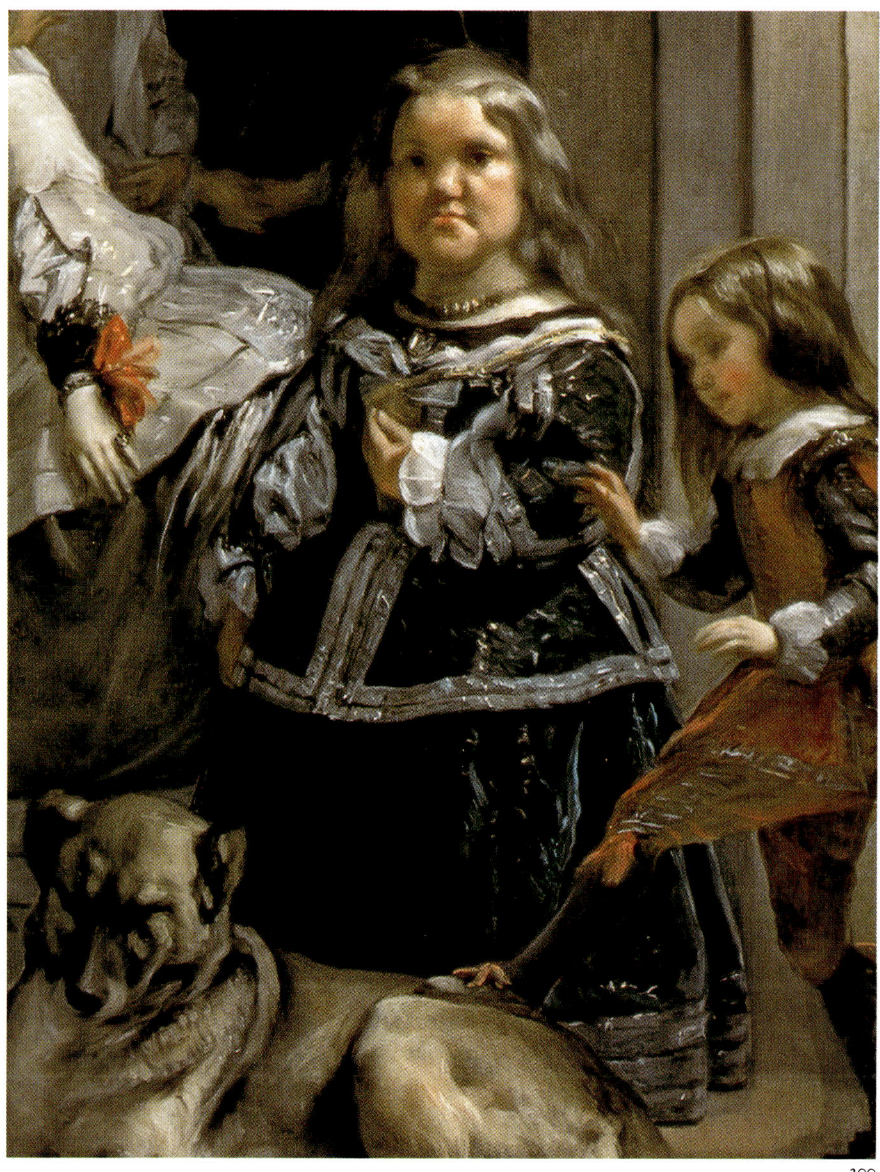

200

LEFT:
199. Diego Velázquez
c. 1656–57
The Infanta Margarita Maria of Austria, detail of *Las Meninas (The Family of Philip IV)*.
Museo Nacional del Prado, Madrid.

ABOVE:
200. Diego Velázquez
c. 1656–57
Mari Bárbola and Nicolasito Pertusato, detail of *Las Meninas (The Family of Philip IV)*.
Museo Nacional del Prado, Madrid.

finished, the canvas was hung in "His Majesty's lower room," that is, in a room on the lower floor of the Alcázar, which was closed to the public and where the monarch sought respite from the heat of summer. *Las Meninas* was hung there, along with paintings by Tintoretto, Rubens, Van Dyck, Titian, and Ribera, all of them purely for the king's enjoyment. For Velázquez himself, the painting was a new invention, a *capricho*, something out of the ordinary in painting, a royal "family portrait" without the conventional protocol. Indeed, "a painting of the family" was how it was described in 1666. The title *Las Meninas* appeared for the first time in a catalogue of the paintings in the Museo del Prado published in 1843.

The concept of newness is relative, of course, since the distinction between truth and fiction was a constant issue in the thought and creation of the time. Velázquez might have studied the play between the real and the fictional in a fifteenth-century panel painting by the Netherlandish artist Jan van Eyck depicting Giovanni Arnolfini and his wife (ill. 201), which was at that time in the Alcázar. In a royal inventory drawn up in 1700 Jan van Eyck's painting was described as:

> A painting on wood with doors that close and a frame of gilded wood; some verses from Ovid are on the frame of the painting, which is of a pregnant German woman dressed in green and giving her hand to a young man. It appears that they are marrying at night and the lines describe how they deceive each other. The doors are of wood painted to resemble jasper: valued at sixteen doubloons.

The doors and the frame with the lines describing the deceit have disappeared, possibly in the fire that ravaged the Alcázar in 1734. However, whether or not the man and woman were deceiving each other, whether or not they were proclaiming that what we see is false and what we read—which, paradoxically, has disappeared—is true, Velázquez undoubtedly understood that the artist who painted that panel had tried to represent the infinity of an open space by reflecting the concrete, finite quality of a room in a concave mirror.

Las Meninas has sometimes been regarded as a riddle and has been subjected to many different interpretations. Palomino reported that the Italian painter Luca Giordano described *Las Meninas* as the "theology of painting." Various scholars have considered it the consummation of seventeenth-century studies of perspective; the symbol of the social pretensions of the baroque artist; the exaltation of painting; the paragon of the arts; the speculum (mirror) of princes that the painter dedicated to Philip IV; Velázquez's way of requesting the king's permission to paint his portrait; and a host of other things. But perhaps all that Velázquez did in *Las Meninas* was to earn his salary and play with painting, converting the act of painting into entertainment and caprice—a game of true and false, of verity and deceit, of what is real and what is illusion.

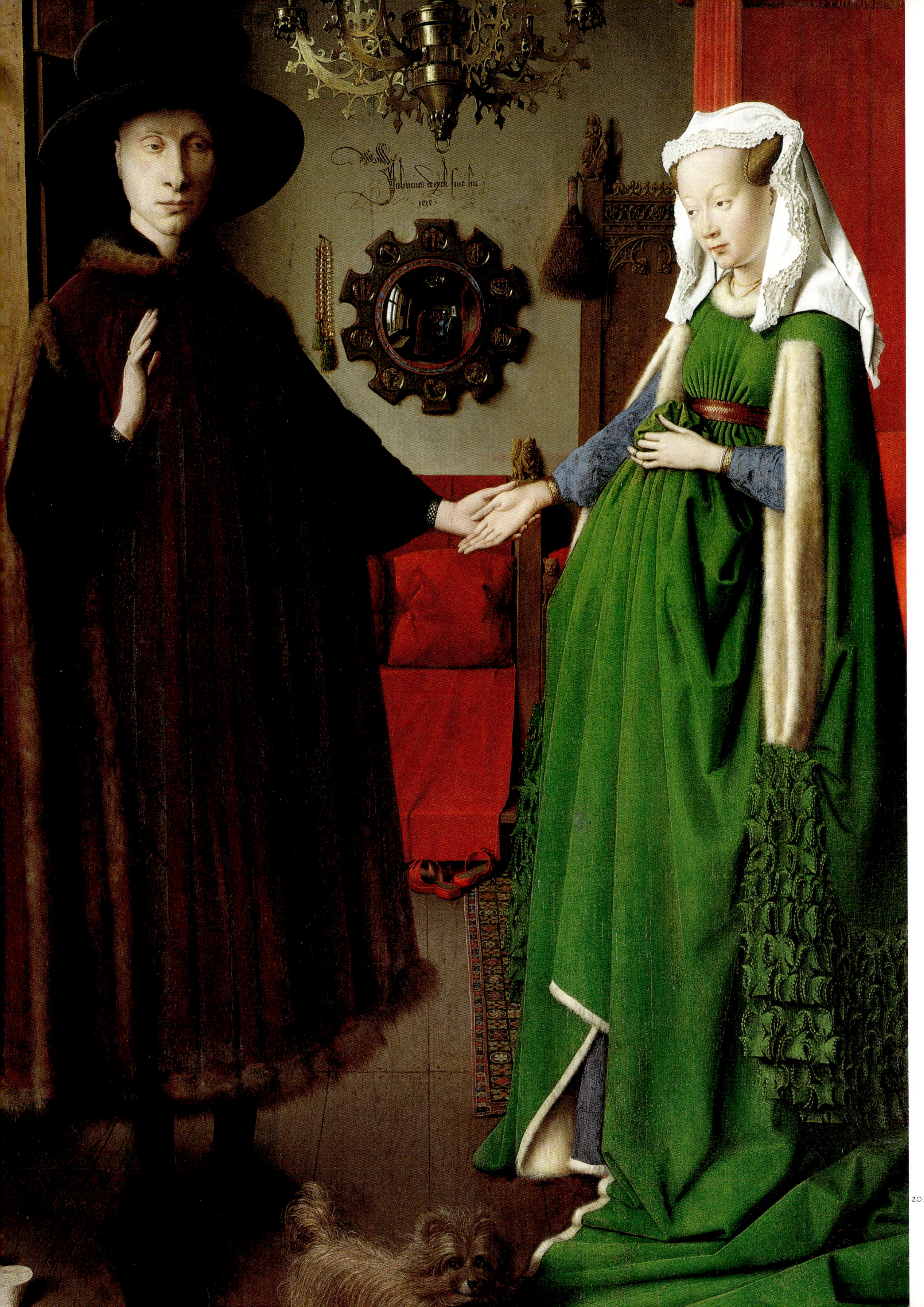

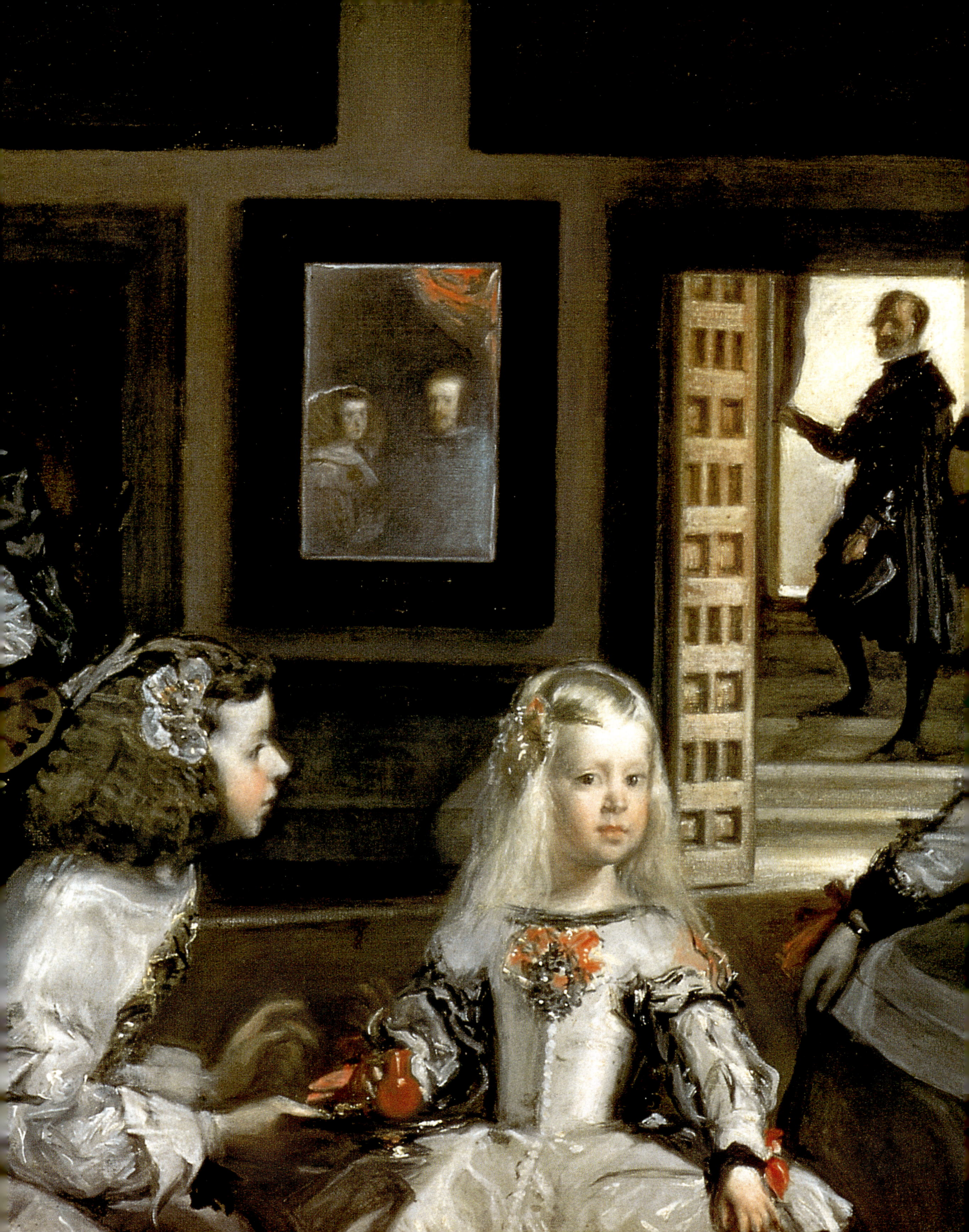

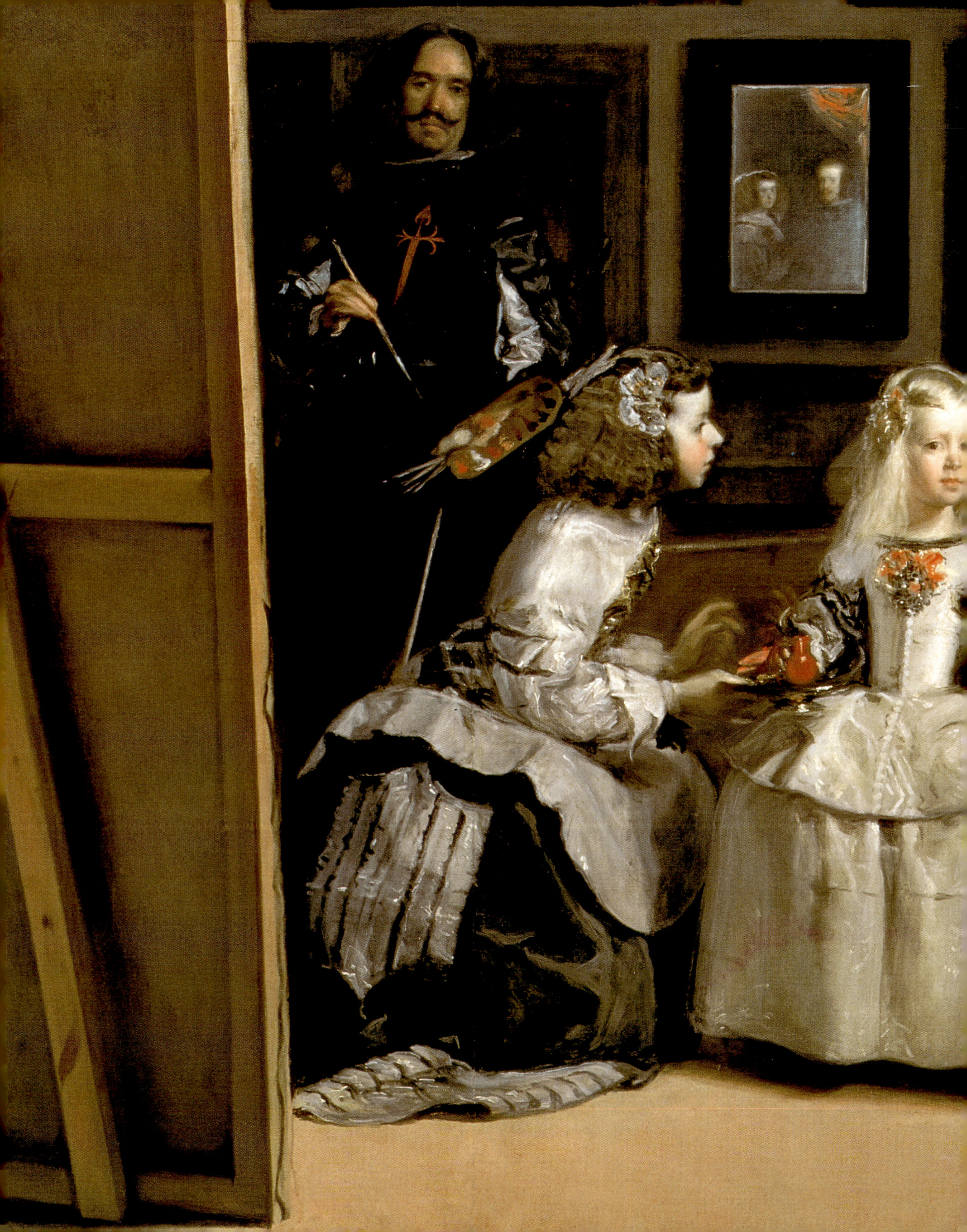

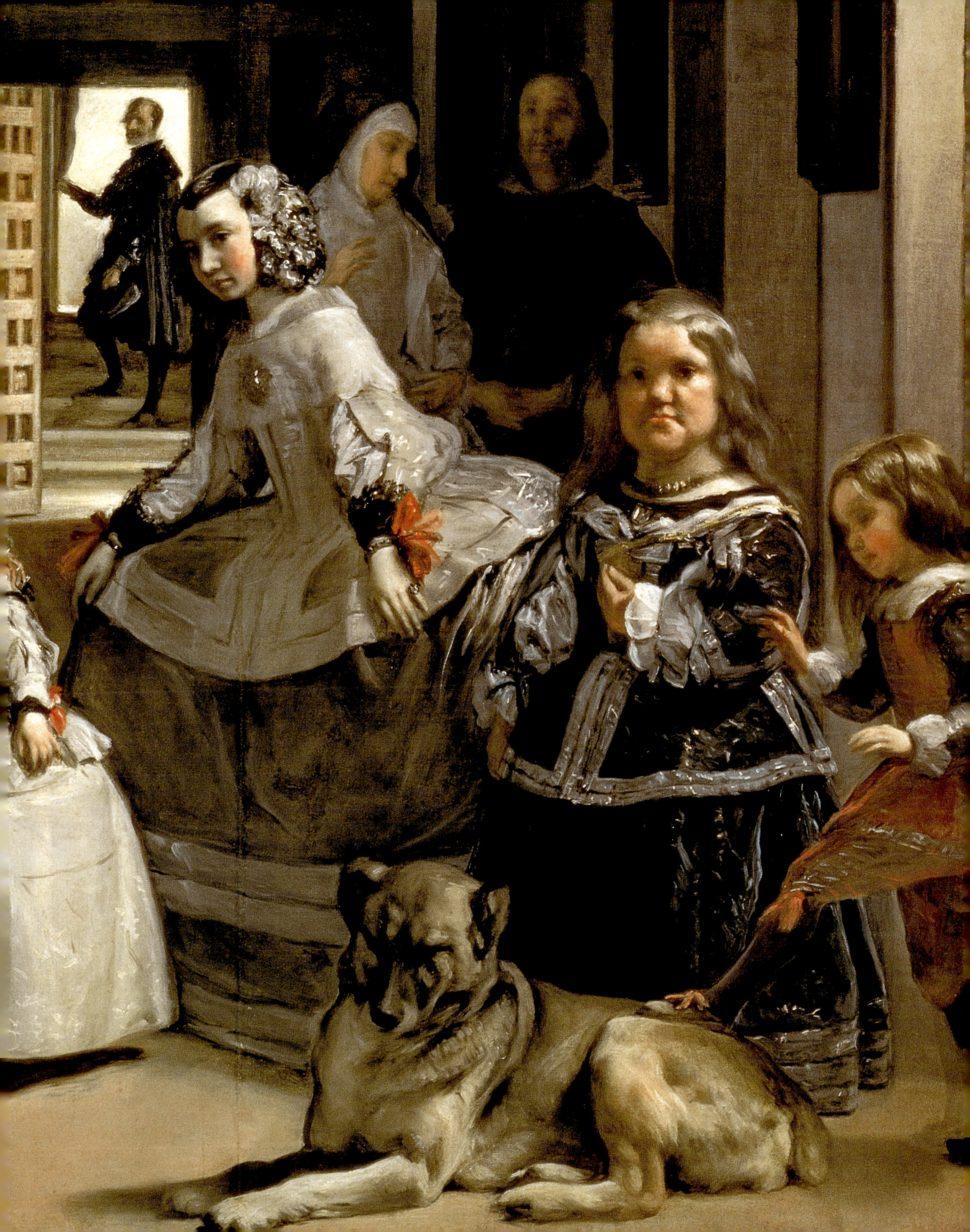

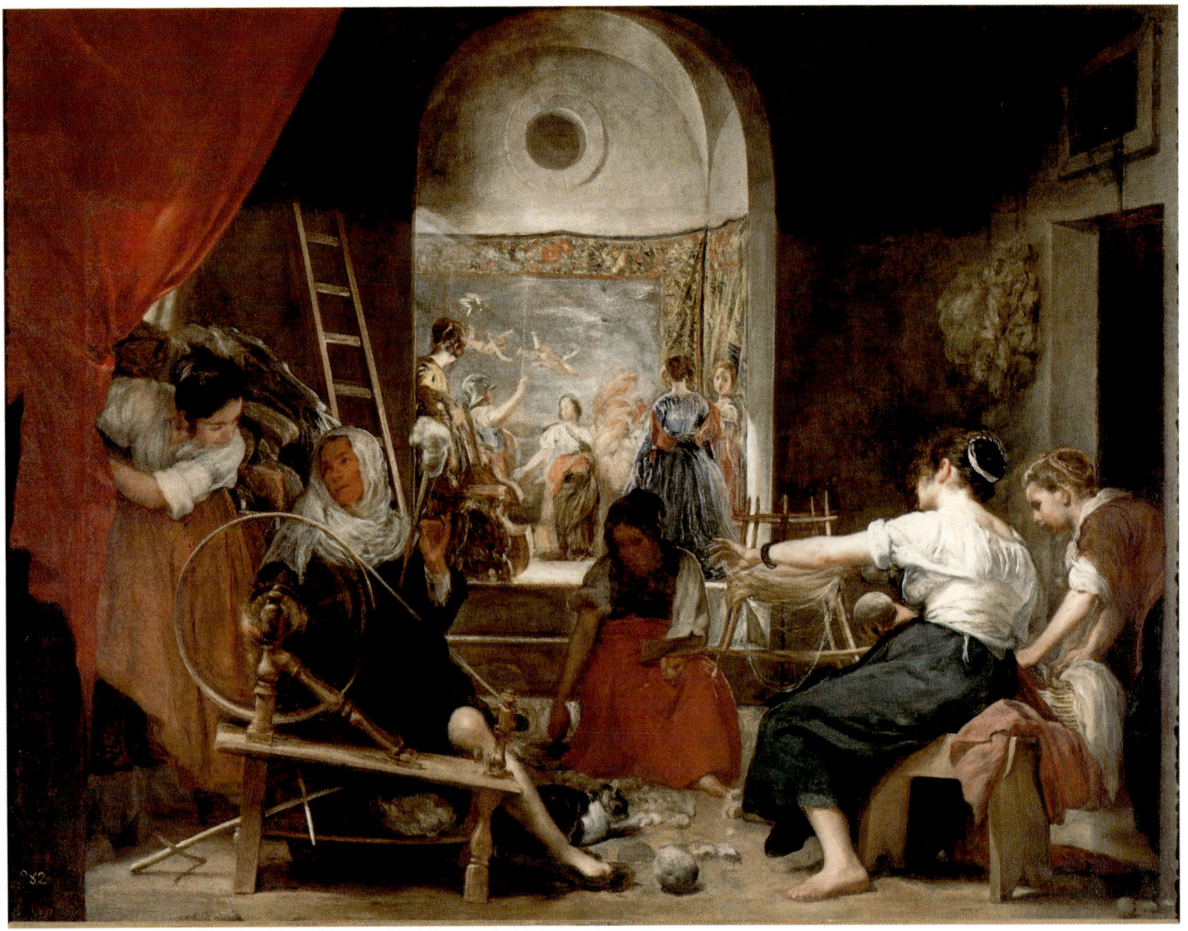

204

Perhaps at first it did not even occur to him to paint himself painting, as his face is painted on top of another, entirely different face. In the end, *Las Meninas* cannot be anything other than *Las Meninas* that the painter whom Velázquez depicts in *Las Meninas* is painting. Nobody before Velázquez had ever painted painting with reality as a pretext.

THE DAUGHTERS OF MINYAS

Velázquez does this not only in *Las Meninas* but also in *The Spinners* (ills. 46, 204, 206, 208–210, 212), a canvas that until 1945 was described in Museo del Prado catalogues as "a spinning and winding workshop at the tapestry manufacture of Santa Isabel, in Madrid. Five women working. In the upper room, three ladies contemplate a tapestry of a mythological theme, in which can be seen Minerva and Juno." After 1945, the catalogues add: "Later it was realized that the subject was the contest between Pallas Athena and Arachne. In Book VI of the *Metamorphoses,* Ovid relates the story of Athena and the mortal weaver Arachne, who had challenged the goddess to a competition in which she hoped to prove that her tapestry would be superior to that of Athena. The competition ended in a draw, with Arachne's tapestry deemed equal to the one woven by the goddess. Athena, enraged, turned Arachne into a spider.

However, Athena already had reason to be annoyed with Arachne, for that mortal weaver had created a series of tapestries depicting the mortal loves of Zeus, as exemplified by the tapestry on the rear wall of Velázquez's painting, a fictive tapestry woven after Titian's *Rape of Europa* (1559–62, Isabella Stewart Gardner Museum, Boston) in the Spanish royal collection, a highly esteemed painting copied by Peter Paul Rubens (ill. 207).

Velázquez situates Ovid's story in a light-flooded room at the rear of the composition that may be understood as Arachne's studio. She is portrayed as an elegant artist whose atelier is visited by finely clothed women, as well as by the helmeted, angrily gesturing figure of Athena. In the foreground is a scene perhaps inspired by a visit to the royal tapestry factory in Madrid. Five weavers set about spinning and carding the wool, executing their mundane, repetitive tasks

PRECEDING PAGES:
201. Jan van Eyck
1434
The Arnolfini Portrait,
oil on panel.
National Gallery, London.

202. Diego Velázquez
c.1656–57
Detail of *Las Meninas (The Family of Philip IV).*
Museo Nacional del Prado, Madrid.

203. Diego Velázquez
c.1656–57
Detail of *Las Meninas (The Family of Philip IV).*
Museo Nacional del Prado, Madrid.

ABOVE:
204. Diego Velázquez
c.1655
The Spinners, or *The Fable of Arachne.*
Museo Nacional del Prado, Madrid.

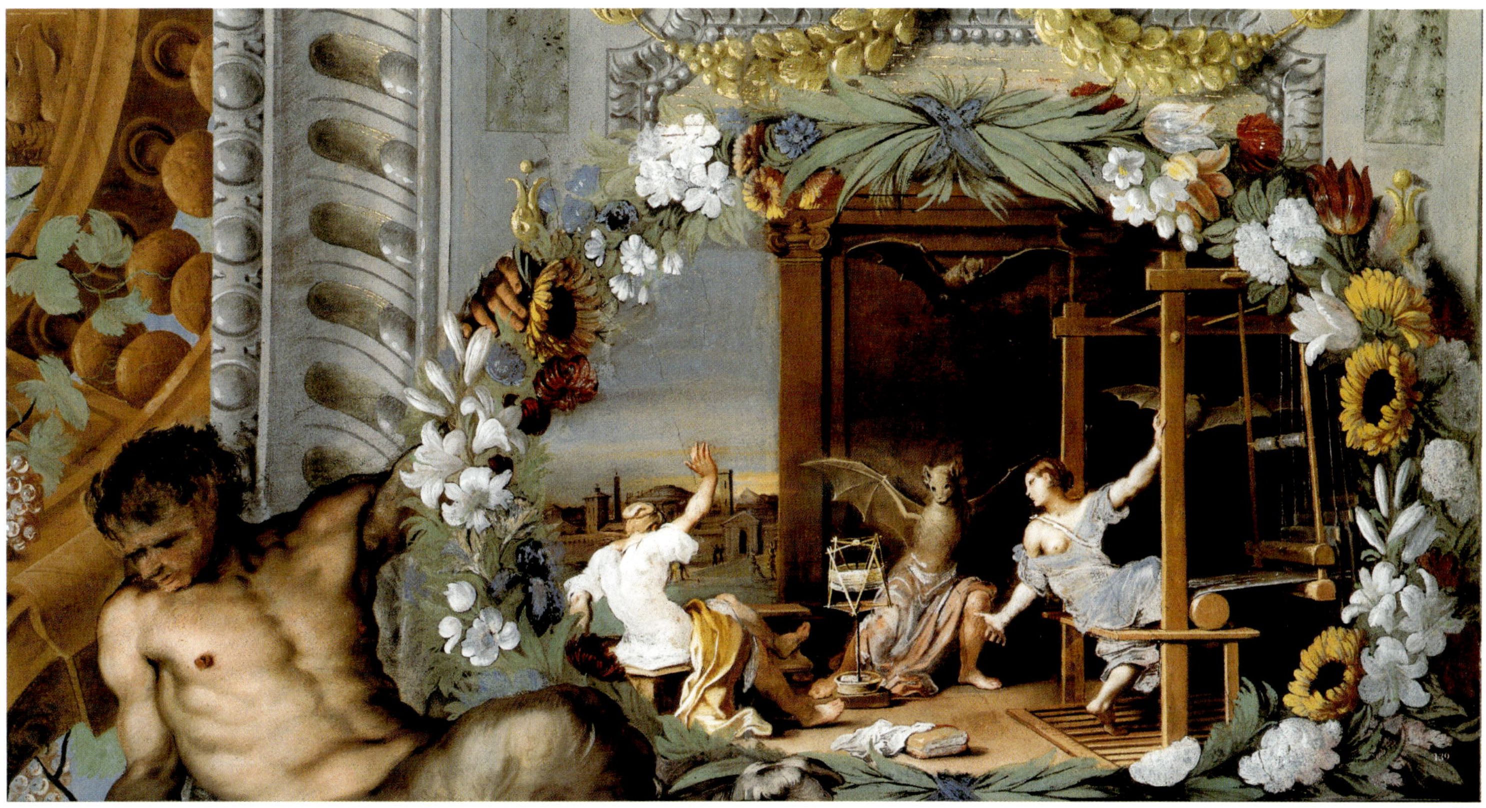

205

through Velázquez's exquisitely bravura brushwork. The sense of movement conjured by the spinning wheel is one of the most remarked details in all of the painter's oeuvre.

The interpretation of *The Spinners* as depicting the story of Athena and Arachne has not been questioned in recent decades, although it has been refined and more fully developed. Everything in the painting suggests that the subject is at least related to the fable of Arachne, although Velázquez rendered it very differently from other painters of the time. The versions by Rubens and Luca Giordano, for example, emphasize the themes of challenge and vengeance. In Velázquez's *The Spinners*, the composition perhaps inspired by an engraving by Philip Galle after Hendrick Goltzius's painting of the Roman Lucretia, there is neither challenge nor vengeance. Some believe that the canvas is a manifestation of the triumph of the fine arts, those seen in the background, over the applied arts, as depicted in the foreground. The painting has also been interpreted as representing the triumph of "modern" artists (Arachne) over those of antiquity (Athena). Yet others see a hidden moralizing meaning whose purpose was to warn Philip IV of the vices he must avoid, particularly adulation, pride, and carnal sin, in order to be a good ruler.

In fact, *The Spinners* was most probably not intended for the monarch, since it appears in the inventory of paintings belonging to Philip IV's chamberlain and equerry, Pedro de Arce, that was drawn up in 1664 by the painter Pedro de Villafranca. A few years after it was painted, and four years after the death of Velázquez, the painting is mentioned with an allusion to the fable of Arachne that was later forgotten. In the 1711 inventory of the estate of Don Luis de Cerda, ninth duke of Medinaceli, it is described only as a genre painting. In the 1794 inventory of the New Palace in Madrid it appeared for the first time as *The Spinners*. The dimensions of the canvas belonging to Don Pedro de Arce differ slightly from those of the painting on view at the Museo del Prado since 1819, but that does not mean that they are not the same work. It is probable that sections were added to the original painting to make it fit into a different frame after the Alcázar was destroyed by fire in 1734.

205. Agostino Mitelli, Gian Giacomo Monti, Baldassare Bianchi, Pier Francesco Cittadini, Carlo Cittadini, Jean Boulanger, and Olivier Dauphin
Begun in 1650
The Daughters of Minyas, fresco.
Bacchus Gallery, Ducal Palace, Sassuolo.

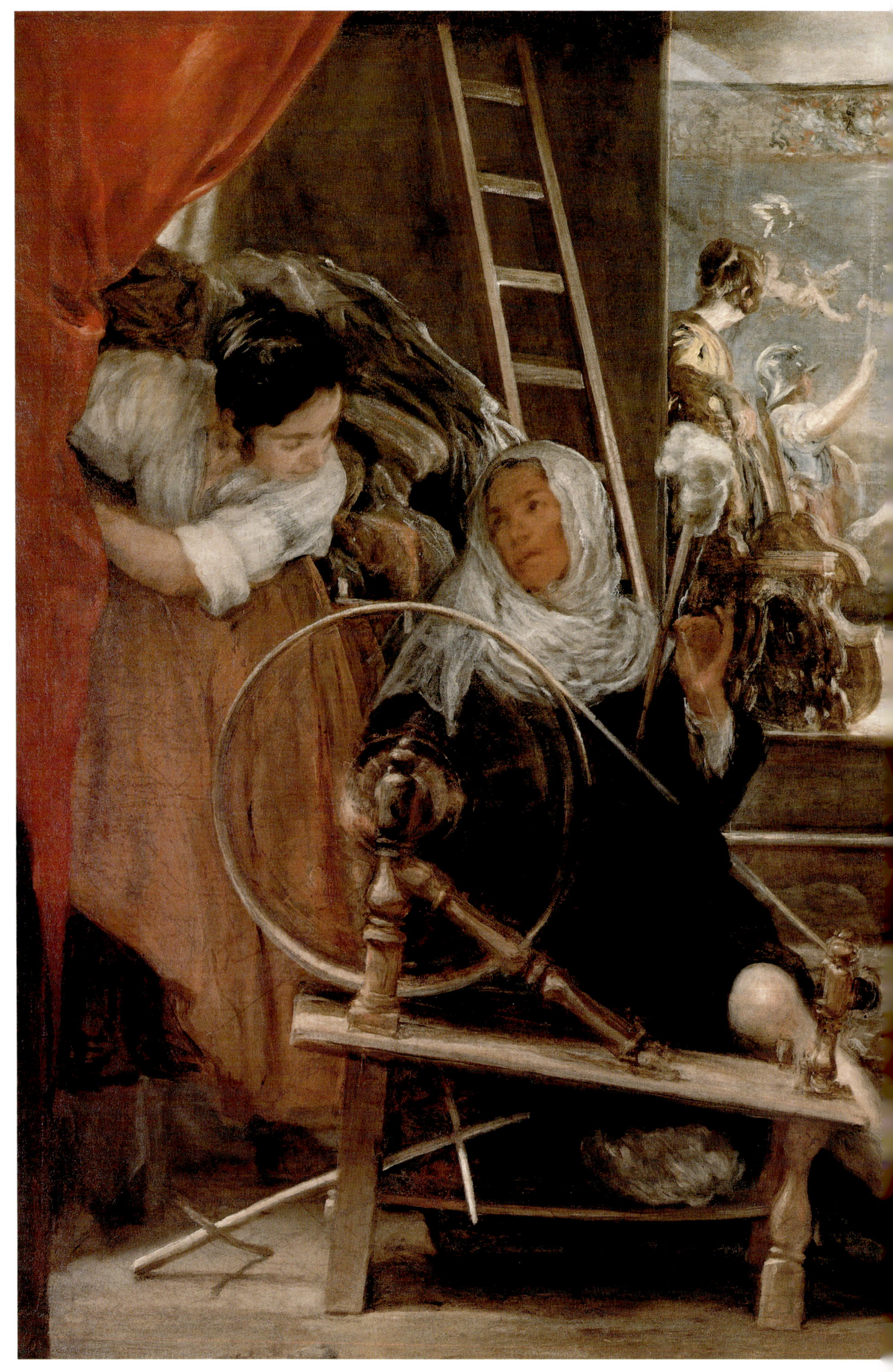

206. Diego Velázquez
c. 1655
The Spinners, without the top and left-hand-side strips that were presumably added after fire destroyed the Alcázar at Madrid in 1734.
Museo Nacional del Prado, Madrid.

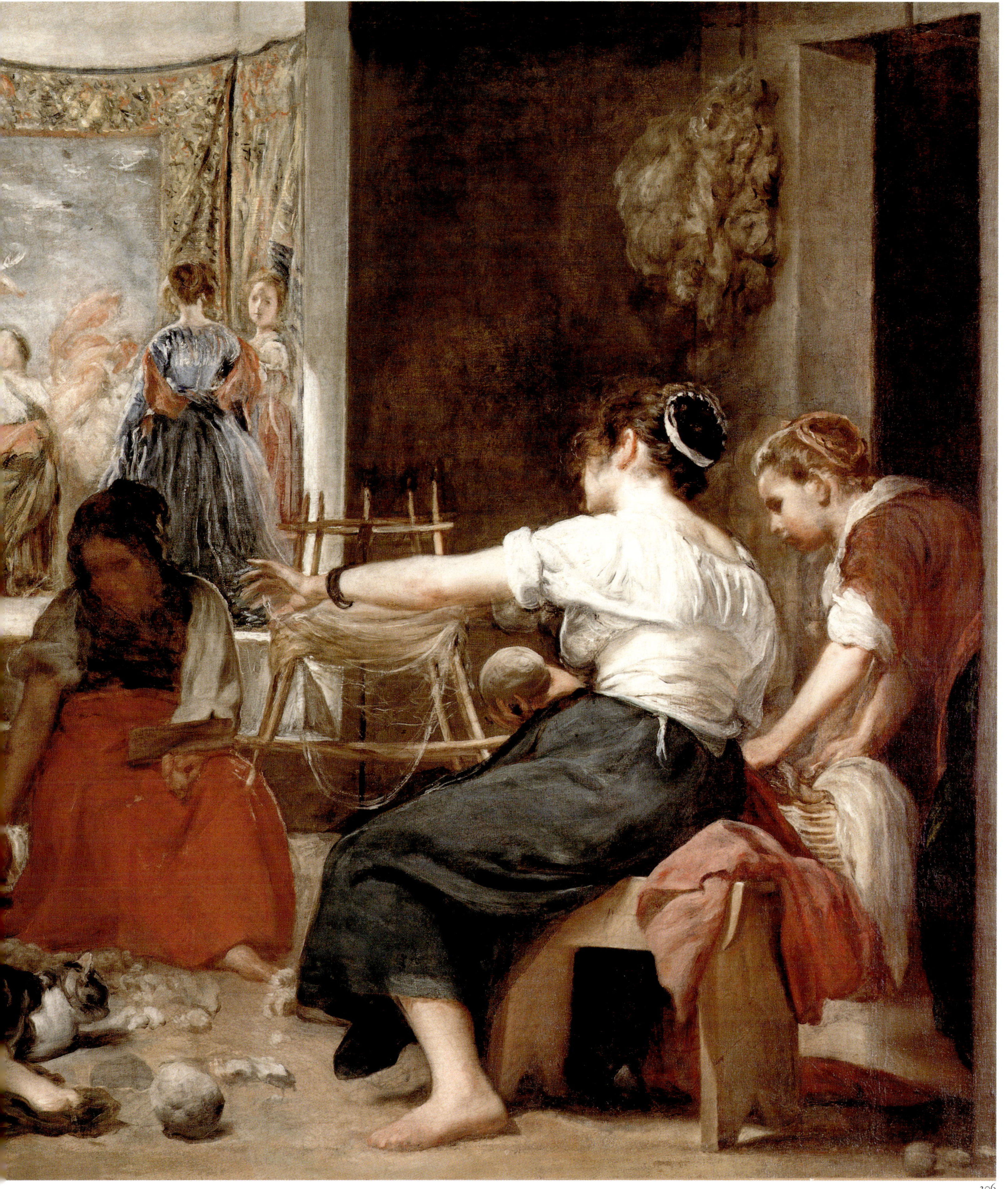

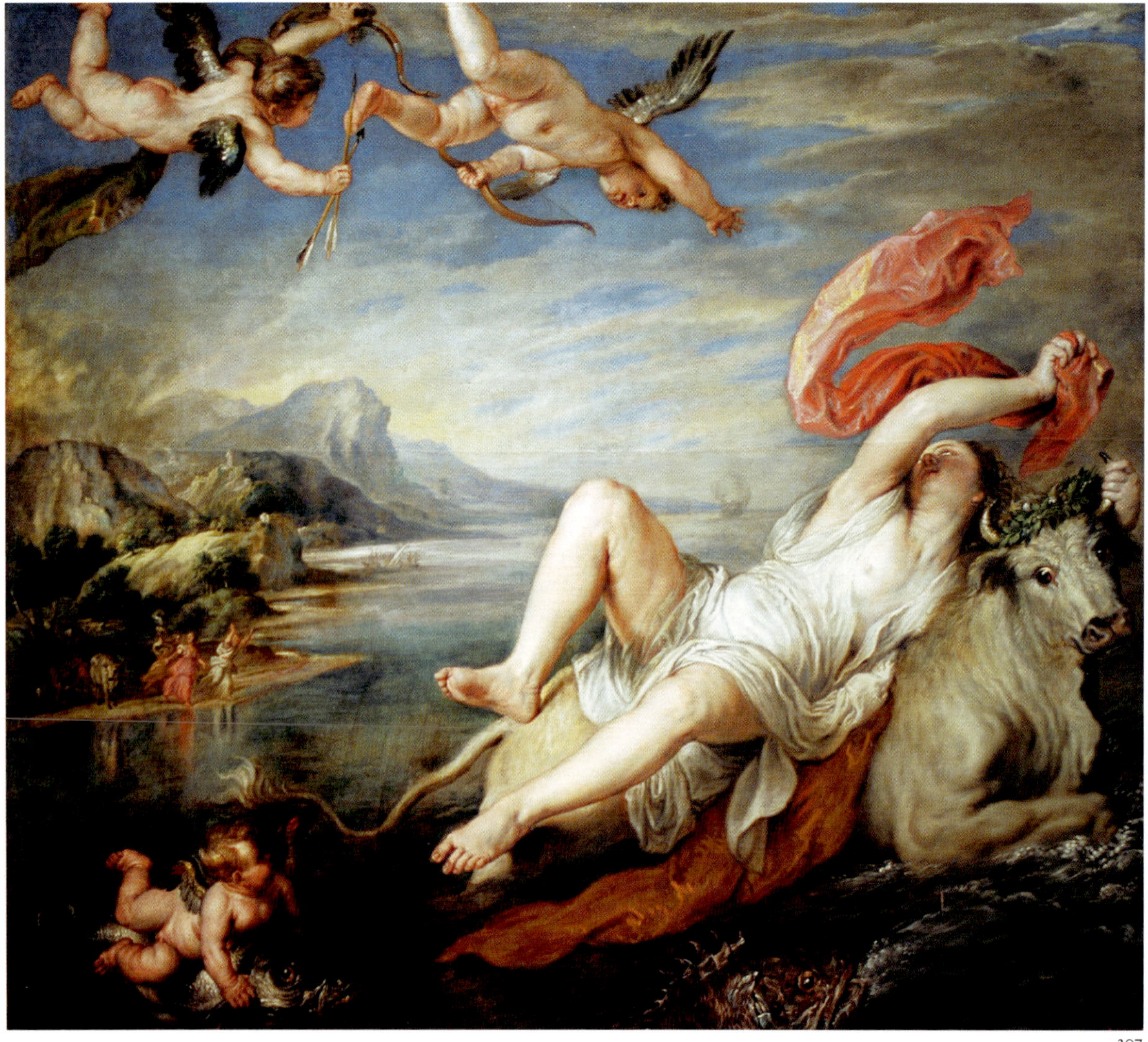

207

It is possible that the weavers pictured in the foreground of the painting, rather than simply being part of a genre scene, as it has been interpreted, may reflect another reading of Ovid found in Book IV of the *Metamorphoses,* the story about Leucippe, Arsippe, and Alcathoë, the daughters of Minyas, the mythical king of Orchomenos, who were punished for not taking part in the feasts of Bacchus. According to Euripides, Bacchus was one of the most important gods on Olympus, the one who relieved the sorrows of poor mortals not only with wine but also with theater and masquerades.

According to Ovid, while the nymphs and maenads—the ladies and servants of Orchomenos—celebrated Bacchus with dances, songs, and music, the daughters of Minyas spoiled the feasts by attending instead to their work for Athena—spinning. They guided the wool with their fingers and worked at their looms, urging the serving women to help them, as they seem to urge the spinners in Velázquez's painting. One of the sisters, Ovid continues, nimbly drawing threads, says:

> While others idly rove, and Gods revere, their fancy'd Gods! They know not who, or where; let us, whom Pallas [Athena] taught her better arts, still working, cheer with mirthful chat our hearts, and to deceive the time, let me prevail with each by turns to tell some antique tale (Book IV, 36-43).

The sisters were punished for rejecting the cult of Bacchus by being changed into bats: this transformation seems to take possession of the spinner in the center of Velázquez's composition.

Whatever the case, there can be no doubt that Velázquez created two different universes through his use of light. The light that penetrates the fictitious space of the workshop through a window on our left makes the bodies and objects in the background lose

207. Peter Paul Rubens
1628
The Rape of Europa.
Museo Nacional del Prado, Madrid.

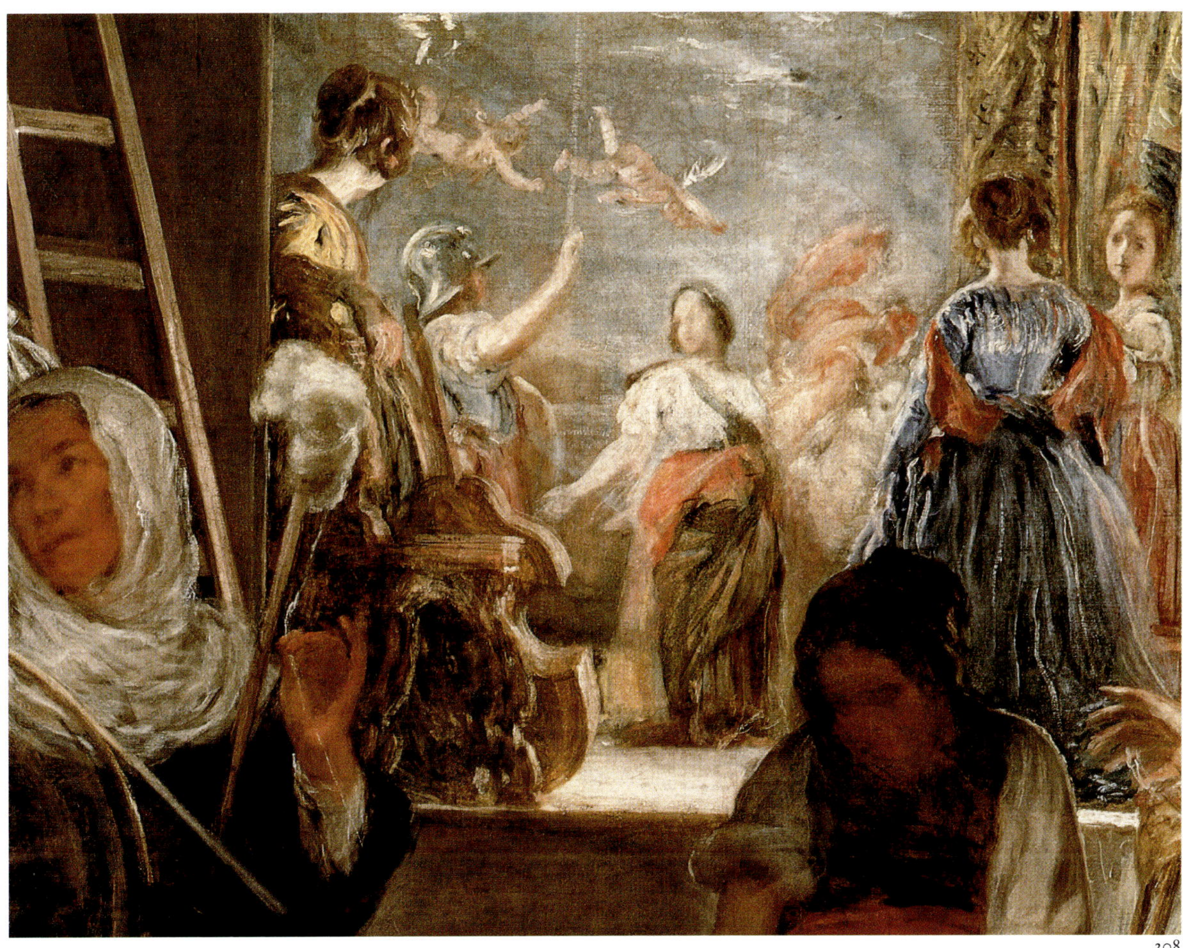

208

substance until they themselves become transformed into light. In the foreground, matter has weight, as weighty as the reds, greens, blacks, or whites, although some of the latter, like the white touches that caress the body and clothing of the young spinner, also seek transformation into light.

In fact, though, Velázquez created not two but three spaces, since the servant drawing aside the heavy red curtain (ill. 209) reveals that we, the observers, are included in the representation. We inhabit a space that the artist does not describe but merely frames with simple architecture or with the bench on which rests the illuminated beauty in whose pose some see a reflection of one of the *ignudi* that Michelangelo painted almost a century and a half earlier on the ceiling of the Sistine Chapel (ill. 211).

These spaces are different universes in which the concept of truth is as elusive as that of light, although Velázquez, despite the potent, sober architecture that separates them (which has become much less forceful because of the eighteenth-century additions to the canvas), employs other elements, such as the ladder, to bring them closer together. Among the elements that connect the two main spaces, the most powerful is the glance of the lady in the background who turns her gaze toward the space that is not hers, for it belongs to us. She is a lady who might easily have been praised by Góngora in one of his sonnets, had she lived in his time:

> Sacred temple of sheer modesty,
> whose handsome base and graceful wall
> were masoned by some hand divine
> from hard alabaster and white nacre;
>
> narrow gate of prized coral,
> bright lights of reassuring look
> that, changed to monstrances, have seized
> upon the pure green of the fine emerald;

208. Diego Velázquez
c. 1655
Detail of *The Spinners*, or *The Fable of Arachne*.
Museo Nacional del Prado, Madrid.

OVERLEAF:
209 and 210. Diego Velázquez
c. 1655
Details of *The Spinners*, or *The Fable of Arachne*.
Museo Nacional del Prado, Madrid.

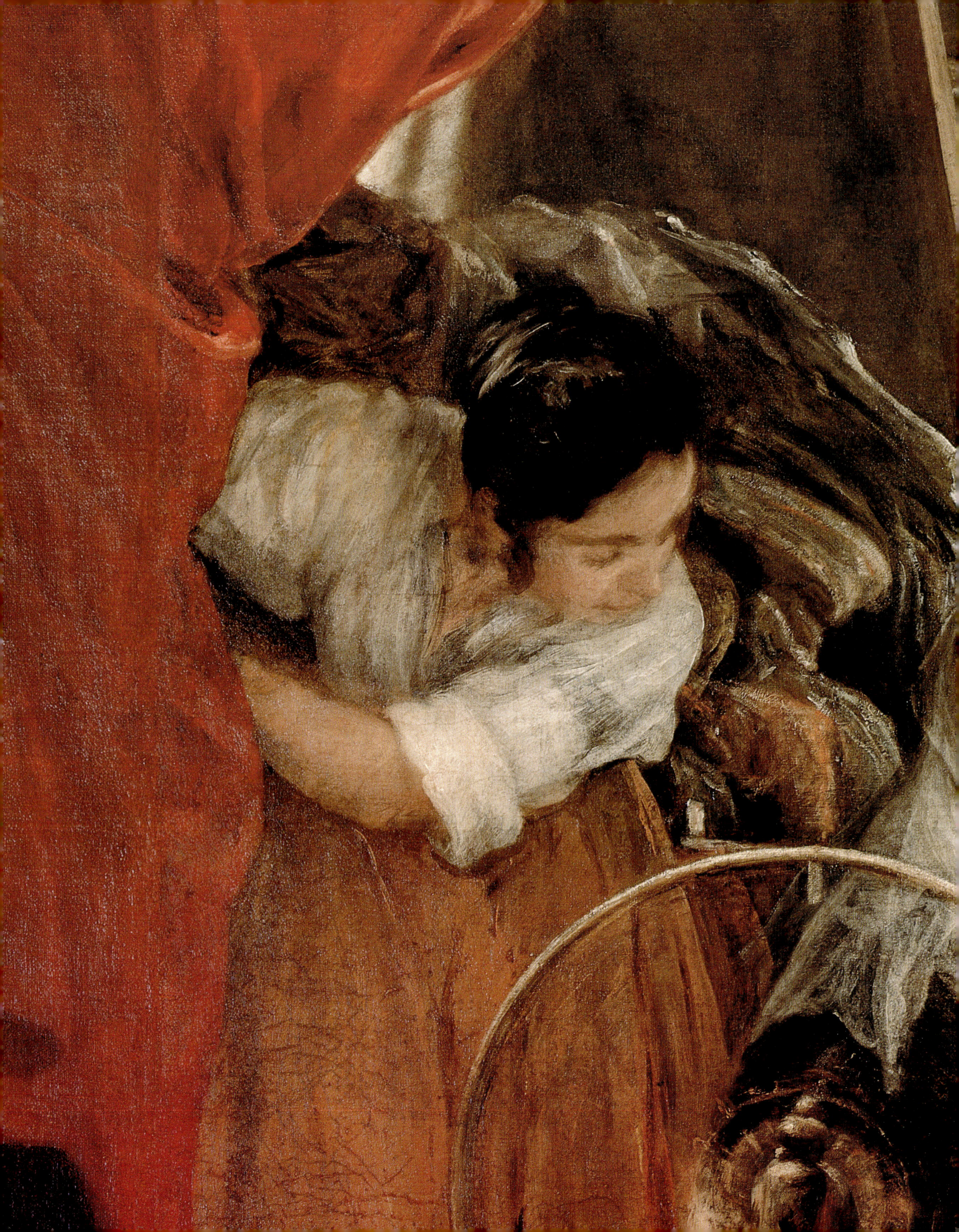

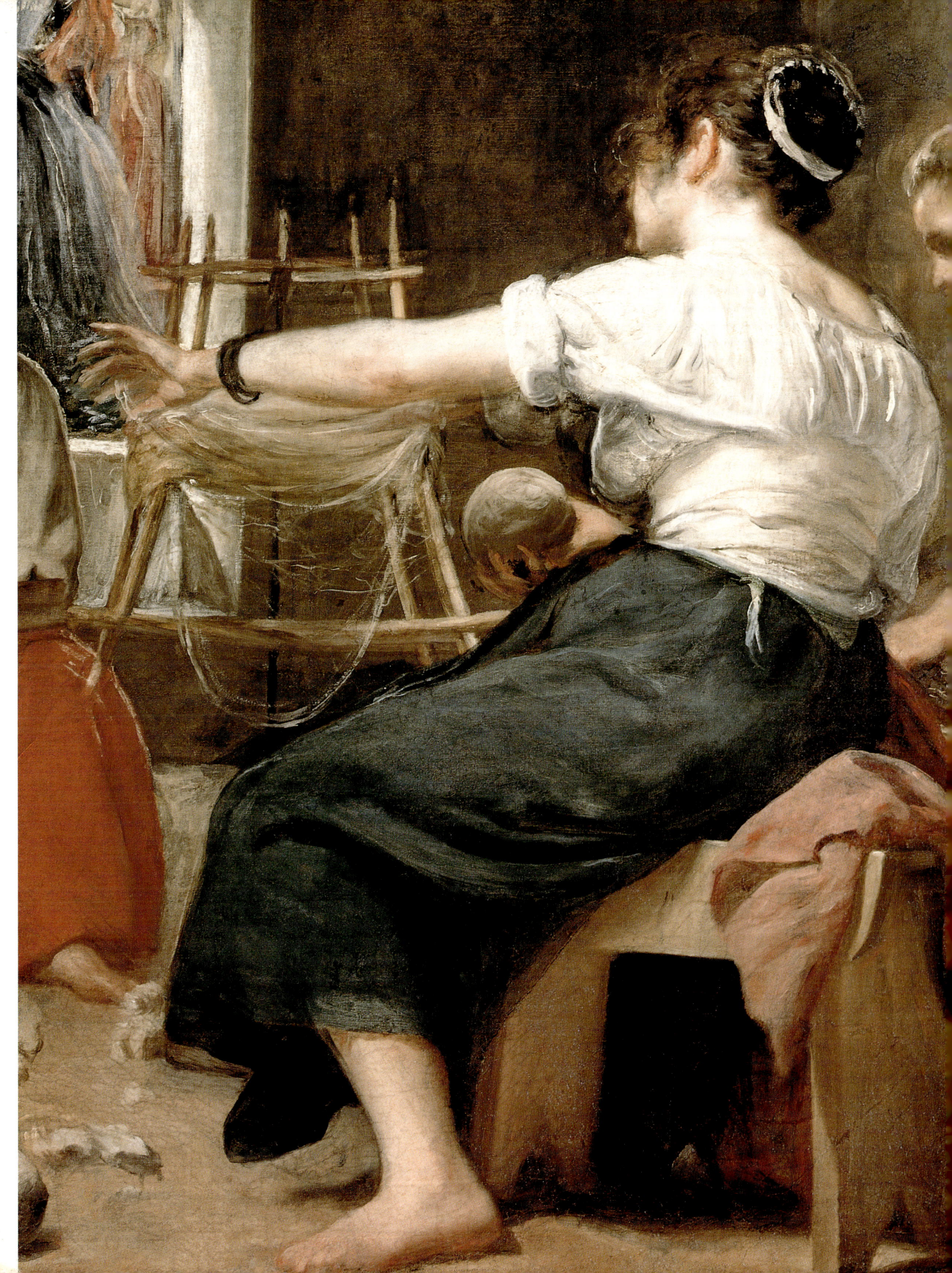

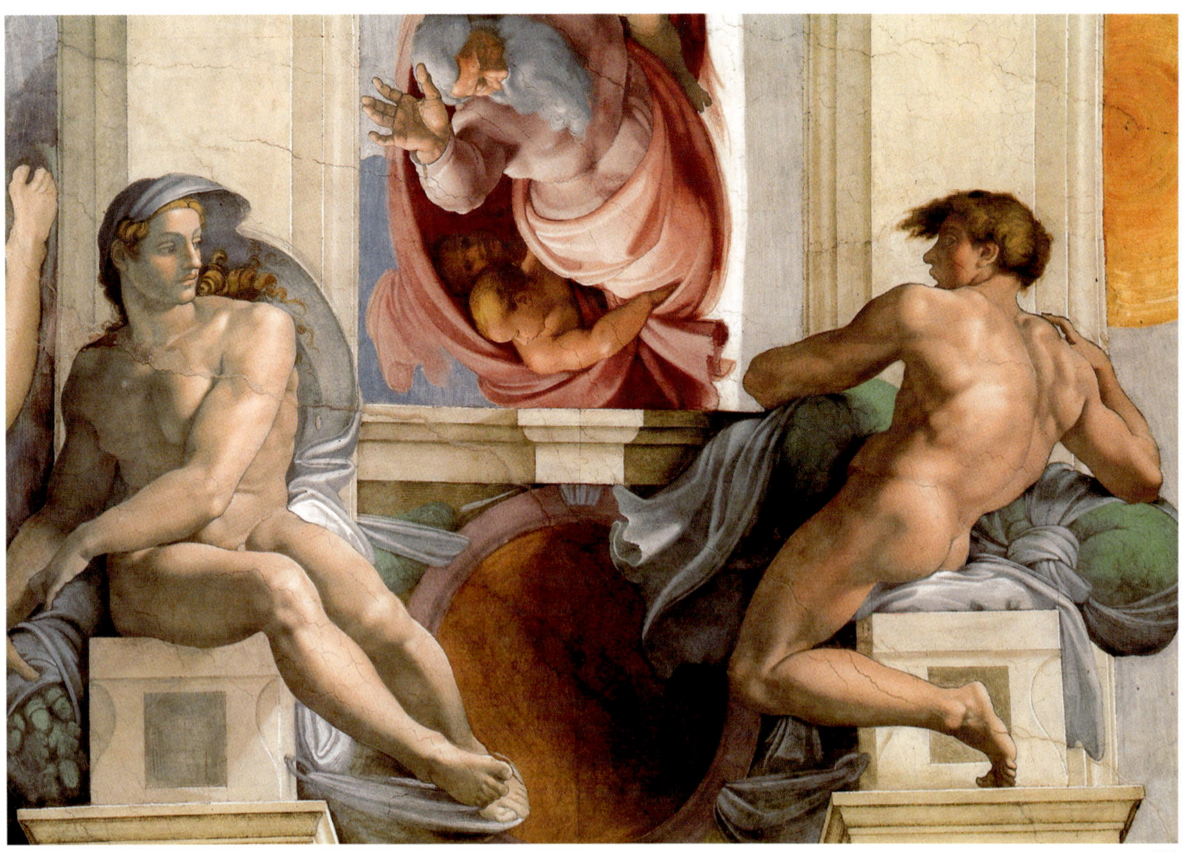

211

> proud ceiling whose beams of gold
> adorn with light and crown with beauty
> the lucent sun in all that wheels;
>
> lovely idol humbly I adore:
> hear him kindly who heaves sighs for you,
> sings your hymns, your virtues lauds.

Both *The Spinners* and *Las Meninas* are masterpieces of painting more interested in the metamorphosis of space than in the metamorphoses of the Minyades or Arachne; painting that studies movement, the passage of time and, above all, the effects of light; painting that shapes bodies and dissolves bodies, brings them closer or moves them apart; painting that confounds our perception of what is real and what is dream or illusion.

BORN A PAUPER, DIED A NOBLEMAN

On November 28, 1659, Velázquez was ennobled by royal letters patent:

> As a result of the investigations conducted further to my proposal of making Don Diego de Silva Velázquez a member of the Order of Santiago . . . it was established that he was not a noble by paternal and maternal lineage. His Holiness, however, decreed that despite this inconvenience he be allowed to take the habit [of the order]. But since it would be most unfortunate should it come to light that he is a commoner, by these royal letters patent and by virtue of my absolute power as monarch over temporal matters I hereby declare Don Diego de Silva *hidalgo* [gentleman] for the above-mentioned cause and grant him the right to enjoy the privileges, exemptions and freedoms due to all gentlemen.

Diego Velázquez a gentleman? Those of true noble blood continued to regard him as a commoner. He did not belong to their class, he was not of noble ancestry, he was not a *hidalgo de cuatro costados* (on four sides, that is, with four grandparents of noble birth). Neither could he be described as a *hidalgo de bragueta*, a title granted to commoners who produced eleven male offspring. When Velázquez was near death (which took place only months later, on August 6, 1660) after thirty-six years of service at court, Philip IV granted him the privilege of nobility, the lack of which had proscribed the Pope from

211. Michelangelo Buonarroti
1508–12
Detail of *Separation of the Earth from the Waters,* fresco.
Ceiling of the Sistine Chapel, Vatican.

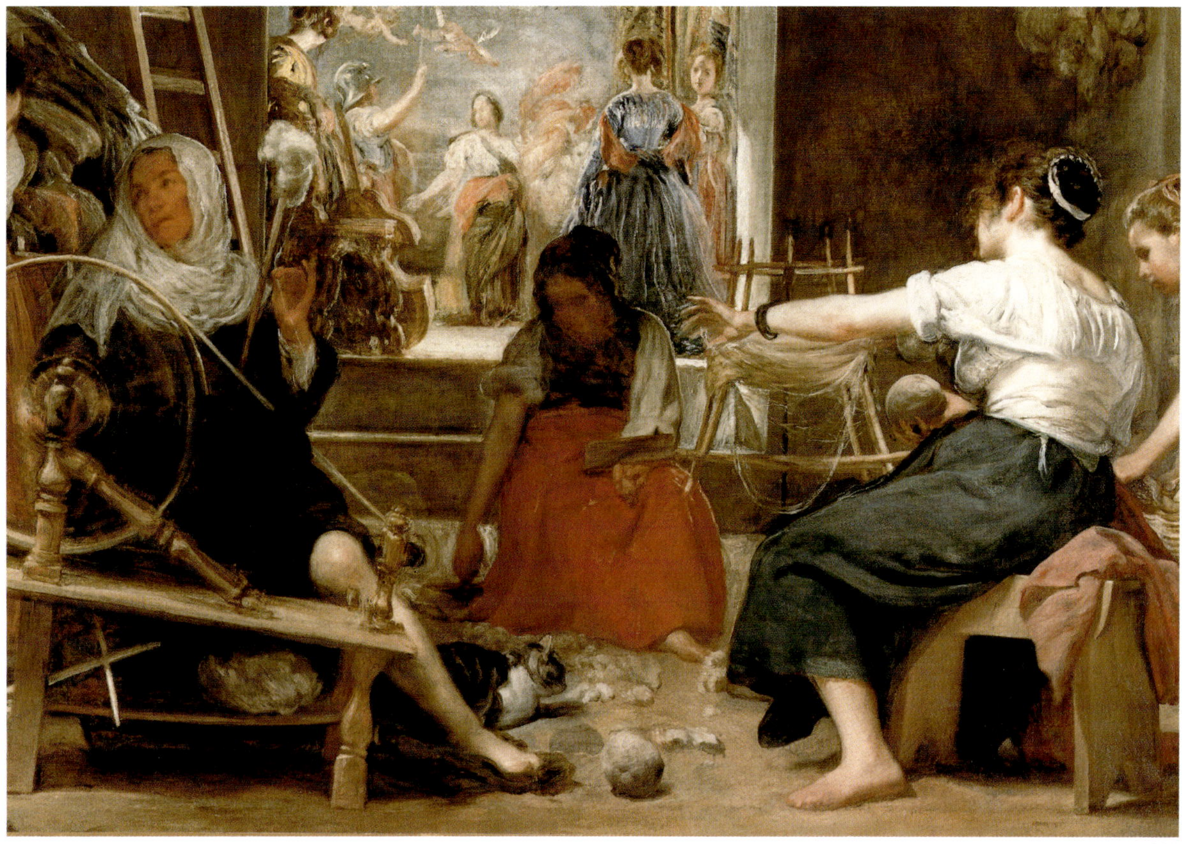

212

212. Diego Velázquez
c. 1655
Detail of *The Spinners,* or *The Fable of Arachne.*
Museo Nacional del Prado, Madrid.

permitting him to join the Order of Santiago. Velázquez had long cherished an ambition to join that order. Francisco Pacheco had taught him that painting was a noble art, and he had practiced that art without claiming nobility for himself until 1658, when the king offered him entry into the Alcántara, Calatrava, or Santiago Order. Despite the king's offer, Velázquez still had to prove his nobility, his purity of blood, and his *limpieza de oficio* (purity of metier). The first he was unable to prove, for neither his paternal grandmother nor his maternal grandparents were members of the *hidalguía.* He *was* able to prove the second (which meant the absence of Jewish blood), and *limpieza de oficio*, which essentially meant complying with the order's rule that nobody may don the habit who "themselves, their parents, or their grandparents had engaged, on their own or on behalf of others, in certain lowly or mechanical trades herein declared, . . . namely silversmith, painter, embroiderer, stonemason, innkeeper, tavern keeper, and scribe other than secretary to the King." Velázquez was able to "prove" *limpieza de oficio* with the somewhat false witness of fellow artists such as Alonso Cano, Francisco de Zurbarán and Juan Carreño de Miranda, among others.

Velázquez pushed his pretensions to nobility too far, though no further than Titian and Rubens, who had also been accepted into an order. But he had gone too far in a Spain where the commoner, even though he may have amassed a reasonable fortune, was meant to die as he had been born, and to associate only with his own kind if he was not to come to a bad end. Francisco Santos wrote in his *Life in Madrid* (1603) about the honorable but unfortunate cobbler Juanillo, who wanted to become a gentleman:

> Seeing that he had amassed a reasonable fortune and his daughter was not bad looking . . . and considering that if he married her to a craftsman his fortune would soon greatly decrease, he married her to a swindler, who had spread the word that he was of noble birth. He gave him not only his daughter but also most of his fortune, and by and by all of it. So good a spendthrift was the son-in-law that in a few days all the money was gone . . . after which he left his wife. The father, unable to take care of her, put her into service while he went back to his former trade. Now his fellow shoemakers mock him, calling him "Don,"

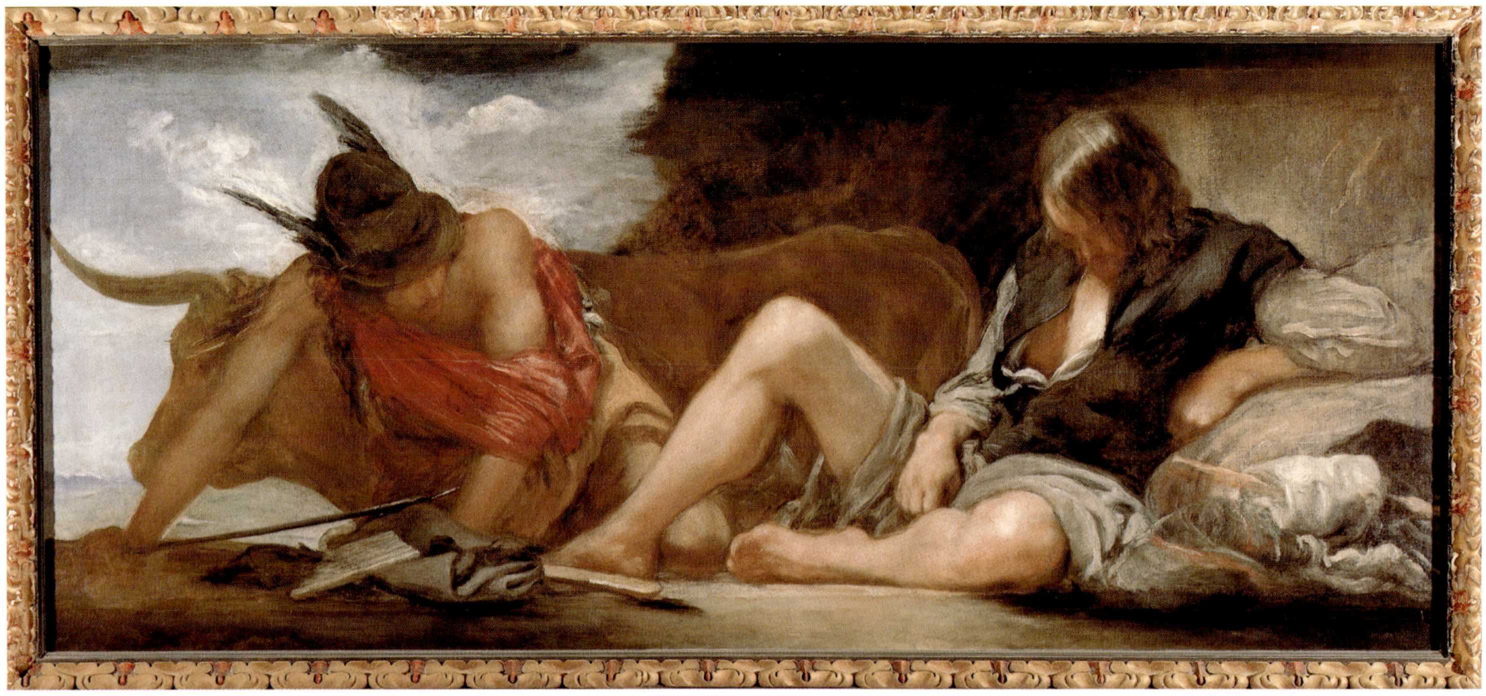

213

and although he has fallen so low, this still sounds good to his ears. . . . If he was not born for it, the poor man who desires to become a gentleman ends up begging for alms, the cause being the wish to live ostentatiously above one's means, to engage in lavish revelry, and enjoy the choicest delicacies. Rather than attempting to build castles in the air, it is better for the poor man to accept his station in life and not aspire to more.

During the last years of his life, although Diego Velázquez painted little, he produced highly notable works, including a number of portraits and his *Mercury and Argos* for the Hall of Mirrors at the Alcázar in Madrid (ills. 213, 214). His duties as royal chamberlain forced him to travel more than he desired. On one of these journeys, in which Philip IV traveled to the Isle of Pheasants to offer his daughter Maria Teresa's hand to Louis XIV of France, the painter suffered from extreme fatigue. On his return to the palace he fell ill and died, as told in a manuscript entitled *History and Nobility of the Kingdom of Leon and the Principality of Asturias* by Lázaro Díaz del Valle:

On August 6 at three in the afternoon Diego de Silva y Velázquez died in Madrid. [He was] court painter to our Lord King, his Gentleman of the Bedchamber and Chief Chamberlain whom His Majesty loved well by virtue of his superior talents in the art of painting and for other services rendered to him, for all of which His Majesty honored him with the habit of the military Order of the Knights of Santiago, whose emblem this great artist wore on his breast, and he was granted the award he deserved for his virtues and the services he rendered His Majesty for many years. He was an illustrious painter, above all of portraits. He now lies beneath the vaults of the parish church of San Juan Bautista in the city of Madrid. In him I lost a good friend for we had much in common.

Velázquez was supreme in the art of painting, to the extent that the artists who worked with him were completely eclipsed by his talent. Even his son-in-law, the able painter Juan Bautista del Mazo, was unable to emerge from beneath the shadow of the master.

ABOVE AND RIGHT:
213 and 214. Diego Velázquez
c. 1659
Mercury and Argos and detail, Hall of Mirrors, the Alcázar, Madrid.
Museo Nacional del Prado, Madrid.

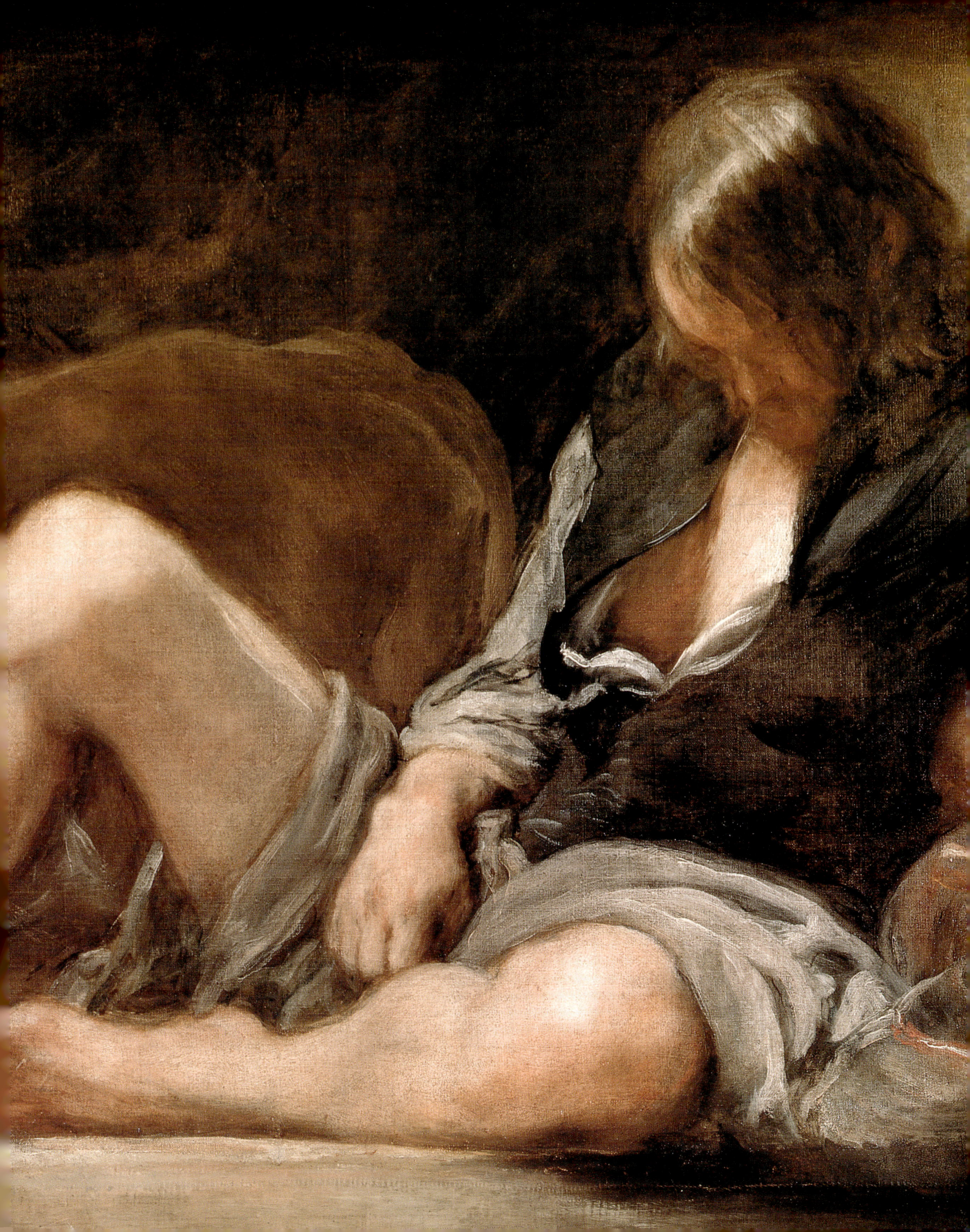

Selected Bibliography

Given the wealth of publications about the Spanish Golden Age, the following bibliography is limited to books and essays that have been fundamental to our understanding of the subjects dealt with in the book. With a few exceptions, they have all been published after 1980. Many of the literary works cited in the book have been published numerous times; when that is the case, no particular editions are given. A number of exhibition catalogues have been published by the State Society for the Commemoration of the reigns of Philip II and Charles V; only those closely related to the themes in this volume have been included in the bibliography.

To better evaluate the cultural context of the author and moment of publication, we normally cite the first edition in the original language or those that the reader can easily find in a Spanish version or, in their stead, another modern version. To make the bibliographical search easier and more fluid, in the case of volumes by multiple authors, whether catalogues or symposium proceedings, the creators or curators of the exhibitions and the coordinators, editors, and publishers are not listed, barring a few exceptions. Nor do we include, except in special cases, chapter titles or individual articles of the mentioned publications.

ABAD NEBOT, F. "Materiales para la historia del concepto de 'Siglo de Oro' en la literatura española," in *Analecta malacitana,* III, 2, 1980, pp. 309–30.

ABELLÁN, J. L. *Historia crítica del pensamiento español,* Book III: *Del Barroco a la Ilustración (siglos XVII y XVIII).* Madrid, 1981.

ALBARDONEDO FREIRE, A. J. *El urbanismo de Sevilla durante el reinado de Felipe II.* Seville, 2002.

Alonso Cano: Espiritualidad y Modernidad Artística (exhibition catalogue). Granada, 2001.

Alonso Sánchez Coello y el retrato en la corte de Felipe II (exhibition catalogue). Madrid, 1990.

ÁLVAREZ LOPERA, J. *De Ceán a Cossío. La fortuna crítica del Greco en el siglo XIX.* Madrid, 1987.

ANGULO, D. *Murillo.* Madrid, 1971.

———. *Velázquez. Cómo compuso sus principales cuadros.* Seville, 1947.

Antiquity in the Renaissance (exhibition catalogue). Northampton, Mass., 1978.

Arquitectura del Renacimiento en Andalucía. Andrés de Vandelvira y su época (exhibition catalogue). Jaén, 1992.

El Arte en Cataluña y los reinos hispanos en tiempos de Carlos I (exhibition catalogue). Madrid, 2001.

Arte y diplomacia de la monarquía hispánica en el siglo XVII (exhibition catalogue). Madrid, 2003.

AUBRUN, Ch. V. *La comedia española 1600/1680.* Madrid 1981.

AZANZA, J. J. (ed.). *Emblemata aurea. La emblemática en el arte y la literatura del Siglo de Oro.* Madrid, 2000.

Barroco (exhibition catalogue). Madrid, 2004.

Bartra, R. *Cultura y melancolía. Las enfermedades del alma en la España del Siglo de Oro.* Barcelona, 2001.

Bassegoda y Hugas, B. *El Escorial como museo: la decoración pictórica mueble en el monasterio de El Escorial desde Diego Velázquez hasta Frédéric Quilliet (1809).* Barcelona, Girona, and Lleida, 2002.

Benigno, F. *L'ombra del re: ministri e lotta politica nella Spagna del Seicento.* Venice, 1992.

Benito, F., and Berchez, J. *Presència del Renaixement a València.* Valencia, 1982.

Bennasar, B. *Un siècle d'or espagnol (vers 1525–vers 1648).* Paris, 1982.

Bennasar, B., and Vincent, B. *España: los Siglos de Oro.* Barcelona, 2000.

Bergström, I. *Maestros españoles de bodegones y floreros del siglo XVI.* Madrid, 1970.

Bernis, C. "La moda en los retratos de Velázquez," in *El retrato en el Museo del Prado,* Madrid, 1994, pp. 271–301.

Beruete, A. de. *Velázquez.* Paris, 1898.

Bieber, M. *Laocoön: The Influence of the Group since Its Rediscovery.* Detroit, 1967.

Blázquez Mateos, E. "El peinador de la Reina en La Alhambra. Los paisajes testimoniales de Conquista," in *Cuadernos de arte de la Universidad de Granada,* XXV, 1994, pp. 11–23.

———. *Viajes al Paraíso. La representación de la naturaleza en el Renacimiento.* Salamanca, 2004.

Bouwsma, W. J. *The Waning of the Renaissance, 1550–1640.* New Haven and London, 2000.

Brooke, X., and Cherry, P. *Murillo: Scenes of Childhood* (exhibition catalogue). London, 2001.

Brown, J. *Images and Ideas in Seventeenth-Century Spanish Painting.* Princeton, 1978.

———. *Velázquez: Painter and Courtier.* New Haven and London, 1986.

———. *The Golden Age of Painting in Spain.* New Haven, 1990.

———. *La Sala de Batallas de El Escorial: la obra de arte como artefacto cultural.* Salamanca, 1998.

Bryson, N. *Looking at the Overlooked: Four Essays on Still Life Painting,* Cambridge, Mass.,1990.

Bury, J. *Juan de Herrera y El Escorial.* Madrid, 1994.

Bustamante García, A. *La octava maravilla del mundo: estudio histórico sobre El Escorial de Felipe II.* Madrid, 1994.

Caballero Porras, G. *Poéticas de la metamorfosis. Tradición clásica, Siglo de Oro y modernidad.* Málaga, 2003.

Cali, M. *Da Michelangelo all'Escorial. Momenti del dibattito religioso nell'arte del Cinquecento.* Turin, 1980.

Calvo Serraller, F. *Teoría de la pintura del Siglo de Oro.* Madrid, 1981.

———. *El Greco: el Entierro del conde de Orgaz.* Madrid, 1994.

Cámara Muñoz, A. *Arquitectura y sociedad en el Siglo de Oro: idea, traza y edificio.* Madrid, 1989.

Carlos V: las armas y las letras (exhibition catalogue). Madrid, 2000.

Carlos V y la Alhambra (exhibition catalogue). Granada, 2000.

Carlos V y las artes: promoción artística y familia imperial (exhibition catalogue). Valladolid, 2000.

Carolus (exhibition catalogue). Toledo, 2001.

Carolvs V Imperator (exhibition catalogue). Barcelona, 1999.

Carrillo Castillo, J. *Tecnología e imperio: ingenios y leyendas del Siglo de Oro.* Madrid, 2002.

Castilla Pérez, R. *Las mujeres en la sociedad española del Siglo de Oro: ficción teatral y realidad histórica.* Granada, 1998.

Castillejo, D. *El corral de comedias: escenarios, sociedad, actores.* Madrid, 1984.

Caturla. M. L. *Francisco de Zurbarán.* Paris, 1994.

Centenario de Alonso Cano en Granada (exhibition catalogue). Granada, 1970.

Centenario de Alonso Cano en Granada: estudios (exhibition catalogue). Granada, 1969.

Chamorro, M. I., *Gastronomía del Siglo de Oro español.*

Checa Cremades, F. *Pintura y escultura del Renacimiento en España: 1450/1600.* Madrid, 1983.

———. *Felipe II mecenas de las artes.* Madrid 1992.

———. *Carlos V: la imagen del poder en el Renacimiento.* Madrid, 1999.

Cherry, P. *Arte y Naturaleza: el bodegón español en el Siglo de Oro.* Aranjuez, 2000.

Constantoudaki, M. "Domenikos Théotocopoulos de Candie à Venice. Documents inédites (1566–1568)," in *Thesaurimata,* 12, 1975, pp. 292–308.

Corpvs Velazqueño. Documentos y textos. Madrid, 2000.

Cossio, M. B. *El Greco.* Madrid, 1908.

Cristóbal de Villalpando: catálogo razonado. Mexico City, 1997.

Dacos, N. *Le Logge di Raffaello: maestro e bottega di fronte all'antico.* Roma, 1976.

———. *Roma quanta fuit. Tre pittori fiamminghi nella Domus Aurea.* Rome, 1995.

DaCosta Kaufmann, T. *The Mastery of Nature: Aspects of Art. Science, and Humanism in the Renaissance.* Princeton, 1993.

Dandelet, T. J. *Spanish Rome, 1500–1700.* New Haven, 2001.

Da Tiziano a El Greco: Per la storia del Manierismo a Venezia (1540–1590) (exhibition catalogue). Milan, 1981.

Davidson, N. S. *The Counter-Reformation.* London, 1987.

Delenda, O. *Sur la terre comme au ciel, Zurbarán.* Paris, 1999.

Dickens, A. G. *The Age of Humanism and Reformation.* New York, 1977.

Díez del Corral, R. *Arquitectura y mecenazgo: la imagen de Toledo en el Renacimiento.* Madrid, 1987.

Díez de Revenga, F. J. *La tradición áurea: sobre la recepción del Siglo de Oro en poetas contemporáneos.* Madrid, 2003.

El Divino Pintor: La creación de María de Guadalupe en el taller celestial (exhibition catalogue). Mexico City, 2002.

Documentos para la historia del Monasterio de San Lorenzo el Real de El Escorial (exhibition catalogue). Madrid, 1962.

Domínguez Ortiz, A. *La Sevilla del siglo XVII.* Seville, 1984.

Dubini, R. *Geografie dello sguardo: visione e paesaggio in età moderna.* Turin, 1994.

Duvenger, C. *Pierres métisses: l'art sacré des indiens du Mexique au XVIe siècle.* Paris, 2003.

Ebert-Schifferer, S. *Geschichte des Stillebens.* Munich, 1998.

Egido, A. *De la mano de Artemia: literatura, emblemática, mnemotecnia y arte en el Siglo de Oro.* Barcelona, 2004.

Elliot, J. H. *Imperial Spain: 1469–1716.* London, 1963.

Elliot, J. H., and Brown, J. *A Palace for a King: The Buen Retiro and the Court of Philip IV.* New Haven and London, 1980.

En torno al teatro del Siglo de Oro (exhibition catalogue). Almería, 1996.

La época de Murillo: antecedentes y consecuentes de su pintura (exhibition catalogue). Seville, 1982.

El Escorial en la Biblioteca Nacional en el IV Centenario del Monasterio de El Escorial (exhibition catalogue). Madrid, 1985.

El Escorial, IV Centenario del Monasterio de El Escorial (exhibition catalogue). El Escorial, 1986.

ETTLINGER, L. D. "Exemplum doloris, Reflections on the Laocoon Group," in *De artibus opuscula XL. Essays in Honor of Erwin Panofsky*. New York, 1961, pp. 121–26.

FAVARETTO, I. "La Tradizione del Laocoonte nell'arte veneta," in *Atti dell'Istituto Veneto di Scienze, Lettere ed Arti,* CXLI Classe di scienze morali, lettere ed arti, 1982–83, pp. 75–92.

Felipe II: un monarca y su época. La Monarquía Hispánica (exhibition catalogue). Madrid, 1998.

Felipe II: un monarca y su época. Las tierras y los hombres del rey (exhibition catalogue). Madrid, 1999.

Felipe II: un monarca y su época. Un Príncipe del Renacimiento (exhibition catalogue). Madrid, 1999.

Felipe II y las artes (exhibition catalogue). Madrid, 2000.

FERNÁNDEZ ÁLVAREZ, M. *La sociedad española en el Siglo de Oro.* Madrid, 1989.

———. *Felipe II y su tiempo.* Madrid, 1998.

———. *Carlos V, el César y el Hombre.* Madrid, 1999.

FERNÁNDEZ GÓMEZ, M. *Codex Escurialensis 28-II-12: Libro de dibujos o antigüedades.* Madrid, 2000.

FEROS, A., and GELABERT, J. (eds). *España en tiempos del Quijote.* Madrid, 2004.

FERRARINO, L. *Tiziano e la Corte di Spagna nei documenti dell'Archivio generale di Simancas.* Madrid 1975.

La fiesta en la Europa de Carlos V (exhibition catalogue). Madrid, 2000.

Figuras e imágenes del Barroco: estudios sobre el Barroco español y sobre la obra de Alonso Cano V (exhibition catalogue). Madrid, 1999.

Figures of Thought: El Greco as Interpreter of History: Tradition and Ideas (exhibition catalogue). Washington, D.C., 1984.

Francisco de Zurbarán, 1598–1664 (exhibition catalogue). Seville, 1998.

Los frescos italianos de El Escorial (exhibition catalogue). Madrid, 1993.

GABAUDAN, P. *Iconografía renacentista de la Universidad de Salamanca.* Salamanca, 2005.

GÁLLEGO, J. *Visión y símbolos de la pintura española del Siglo de Oro.* Madrid, 1972.

———. *El pintor de artesano a artista.* Granada, 1976.

———. *El cuadro dentro del cuadro.* Madrid, 1984.

———. *Velázquez en Sevilla.* Seville, 1994.

GÁLLEGO, J., and GUDIOL, J. *Zurbarán 1598–1664.* Barcelona, 1976.

GARCÍA ÁLVAREZ, C. *El simbolismo del grutesco renacentista.* León, 2001.

GARCÍA DE LA CONCHA, V. "Barroco: categoría, sistema e historia literaria," in *Estado actual de los estudios sobre el Siglo de Oro* (Actas del II Congreso Internacional de Hispanistas del Siglo de Oro, I). Salamanca, 1993, pp. 70–73.

GARCÍA FELGUERA, M. S. *Viajeros, eruditos y artistas. Los europeos ante la pintura española del Siglo de Oro.* Madrid, 1991.

GARCÍA MARTÍN, M. *Estado actual de los estudios sobre el Siglo de Oro.* Salamanca, 1993.

GARCÍA TAPIA, N. *Ingeniería y arquitectura en el Renacimiento español.* Valladolid, 1990.

GARRIDO, C. *Velázquez. Técnica y evolución.* Madrid, 1992.

GARRIGA, J. *L'Època del Renaixement s. XVI.* Barcelona, 1986.

GAVAZZA, E. *La grande decorazione a Genova.* Genoa, 1974.

GENTILI, A. *Da Tiziano a Tiziano: mito e allegoria nella cultura veneziana del Cinquecento.* Milan, 1980.

GIL, J. *Hidalgos y samurais. España y Japón en los siglos XVI y XVII.* Madrid, 1991.

GIL FERNÁNDEZ, L. *Panorama social del humanismo español (1500–1800).* Madrid, 1997.

GLACKEN, C. J. *Traces on the Rhodian Shore: Nature and Culture in Western Thought from Ancient Times to the End of the Eighteenth Century.* Berkeley, Calif., 1967.

GÓMEZ MORENO, M. *Las águilas del Renacimiento español.*1941 (1983).

Governare il mondo, l'impero spagnolo dal XV al XIX secolo (exhibition catalogue). Palermo, 1991.

El Greco de Toledo (exhibition catalogue). Madrid, 1982.

El Greco: identidad y transformación (exhibition catalogue). Madrid, 1999.

El Greco in Italy and Italian Art (exhibition catalogue). Athens, 1995.

El Greco of Crete (exhibition catalogue). Heraklion, 1990.

El Greco: su revalorización por el Modernismo catalán (exhibition catalogue). Barcelona, 1996.

GREEN, V.H.H. *Renaissance and Reformation.* London, 1952.

GREUB, T. *Las Meninas im Spiegel der Deutungen. Eine Einführung in die Methoden der Kunstgeschichte.* Berlin, 2001.

GRUZINSKI, S. *La colonisation de l'imaginaire: sociétés indigènes et occidentalisation dans la Mexique espagnol XVe–XVIIe siècle,* Paris, 1988.

———. *L'Aigle et la Sybille: fresques indiennes du Mexique.* Paris, 1994.

GUDIOL, J. *Doménikos Theotokopoulos El Greco.* Barcelona, 1973.

———. *Velázquez.* Barcelona, 1973.

GUINARD, P. *Zurbarán et le peintres espagnols de la vie monastique.* Paris, 1960 (edition updated by C. Ressort, Paris, 1988).

HALE, J. R., *War and Society in Renaissance Europe, 1450–1620.* New York, 1985.

HARRIS, E. *Velázquez.* Oxford, 1982.

HELLWIG, K. *Die spanische Kunstliteratur im 17.Jahrhundert.* Frankfurt, 1996.

———. "Interpretaciones iconográficas de las Hilanderas hasta Aby Warburg y Angulo Íniguez," in *Boletín del Museo del Prado,* XXII, 40, 2004, pp. 38–53.

HORN, H. J. *Jan Cornelisz Vermeyen, Painter of Charles V and His Conquest of Tunis: Paintings, Etchings, Drawings, Cartoons and Tapestries.* Doornspijk, 1989.

HUBER-REBENICH, G. "L'iconografia della mitologia tra Quattro e Cinquecento: edizioni illustrate delle *Metamorfosi* di Ovidio," in *Studi umanistici piceni,* 12, 1992, pp. 123–133.

La Imagen triunfal del Emperador: La jornada de la coronación imperial de Carlos V en Bolonia y el friso del Ayuntamiento de Tarazona. Madrid, 2000.

La Imitación de la naturaleza: los bodegones de Sánchez Cotán. Madrid, 1992.

Inmaculada (exhibition catalogue). Madrid, 2005.

JIMÉNEZ DÍAZ, P. *El coleccionismo manierista de los Austrias entre Felipe II y Rodolfo II.* Madrid, 2001.

JORDAN, W. B. *La imitación de la naturaleza. Los bodegones de Sánchez Cotán.* Madrid, 1992.

Juan de Valdés Leal (exhibition catalogue). Seville, 1991.

JUSTI, C. *Diego Velázquez und sein Jahrhundert.* Bonn, 1903.

KAGANE, L. *Spain in the Hermitage, Leningrad: Western European Painting of the 13th to the 18th Centuries.* Leningrad, 1989.

KAMEN, H. *Spain, 1468–1714: A Society of Conflict.* London, 1983.

———. *Cambio cultural en la Sociedad del Siglo de Oro. Cataluña y Castilla, siglos XVI–XVII.* Madrid, 1998.

———. *Imperio: la forja de España como potencia mundial.* Madrid, 2003.

KELEMEN, P. *El Greco Revisited: Candia, Venice and Toledo.* New York, 1961.

KUBLER, G. *Building the Escorial.* Princeton, 1982.

LAFUENTE FERRARI, E. *Velázquez: Complete Edition.* London, 1943.

LAFUENTE FERRARI, E., and PITA ANDRADE, J. M. *Il Greco di Toledo e il suo espressionismo estremo.* Milan, 1969.

LARA GARRIDO, J. *Del Siglo de Oro: métodos y relecciones.* Madrid, 1997.

Los Leoni (1509–1608): escultores del Renacimiento italiano al servicio de la corte de España (exhibition catalogue). Madrid, 1994.

LLEÓ CAÑAL, V. *Nueva Roma: Mitología y Humanismo en el Renacimiento sevillano.* Seville, 1979.

Loca ficta. Los espacios de la maravilla en la Edad Media y Siglo de Oro (exhibition catalogue). Madrid, 2003.

LÓPEZ, F. *Juan Pablo Forner et la crise de la conscience espagnole au XVIIIe siècle.* Bordeaux, 1976.

———. "Comment l'Espagne eclairé invent le Siècle d'Or," in *Hommage des hispanistes français à Noël Salomon,* Barcelona, 1979, pp. 517–25.

LÓPEZ REY, J. *Velázquez: A Catalogue Raisonné of His Oeuvre.* London, 1963.

LÓPEZ TORRIJOS, R. *La mitología en la pintura española del Siglo de Oro.* Madrid, 1985.

LYNCH, J. *Carlos V y su tiempo.* Barcelona and Madrid, 2000.

MAGNANI, L. *Luca Cambiaso da Genova all'Escorial.* Genoa, 1995.

MANN, R. G. *El Greco and his Patrons.* Cambridge, 1986.

MARAVALL, J. A. *La cultura del Barroco.* Barcelona, 1975.

MARÍAS, F. *El largo siglo XVI.* Madrid, 1989.

———. *El Greco, biografía de un pintor extravagante.* Madrid, 1997.

——— *Velázquez, pintor y criado del rey.* Madrid, 1999.

MARÍAS, F. (ed.). *Otras Meninas.* Madrid, 1995.

MARÍAS, F., and BUSTAMANTE, A. *Las ideas artísticas de El Greco. Comentarios a un texto inédito.* Madrid, 1981.

MARÍN LÓPEZ, N. "Decadencia y Siglo de Oro," in *Estudios literarios sobre el Siglo de Oro* (posthumous version by Agustín de la Granja). Granada, 1988, pp. 11–29.

———. "Meditación del Siglo de Oro," in *Estudios literarios sobre el Siglo de Oro* (posthumous version by Agustín de la Granja). Granada, 1988, pp. 511–27.

MARTÍNEZ, J. *Discursos practicables del nobilísimo arte de la pintura.* Madrid, 1866.

MARTÍN GONZÁLEZ, J. J. *Escultura barroca castellana.* Madrid, 1959.

———. *El escultor Gregorio Fernández.* Madrid, 1980.

MAYANS Y SISCAR, G. *Arte de pintar.* 1776.

MCKIM-SMITH, G., and NEWMANN, R. *Ciencia e Historia del Arte: Velázquez en el Prado.* Madrid, 1993.

MENA, M., and VALDIVIESO, E. *Murillo* (exhibition catalogue). Madrid, 1982.

MILICUA, J. "Velázquez y el paisaje," in *Los Paisajes del Prado.* Madrid, 1995, pp. 207—22.

El Monasterio de El Escorial y la pintura (symposium proceedings). San Lorenzo de El Escorial, 1999.

MORALES, A. J. *La obra renacentista del Ayuntamiento de Sevilla.* Seville, 1981.

MORÁN TURINA, M., and PORTÚS PÉREZ, J. *El arte de mirar. La pintura y su público en la España de Velázquez.* Madrid, 1997.

MORENO, A. *Zurbarán.* Madrid, 1998.

MORENO MENDOZA, A. *Mentalidad y pintura en la Sevilla del Siglo de Oro.* Madrid, 1997.

MULCAHY, R. *The Decoration of the Royal Basilica of El Escorial.* Cambridge, 1994.

El mundo de Carlos V: de la España medieval al Siglo de Oro (exhibition catalogue). Madrid, 2000.

NAVARRETE PRIETO, B. *La pintura andaluza del siglo XVII y sus fuentes grabadas.* Madrid, 1998.

NIETO, V., MORALES, A., and CHECA, F. *Arquitectura del Renacimiento en España.* Madrid, 1989.

O'GORMAN, E. *La invención de América.* Mexico City, 1984.

OLLÉ, M. *La empresa de China: de la Armada invencible al galeón de Manila.* Barcelona, 2002.

OROZCO DÍAZ, E. *Introducción al Barroco.* Granada, 1987.

———. *Manierismo y Barroco.* Madrid, 1988.

ORSO, S. N. *Philip IV and the Decoration of the Alcázar of Madrid.* Princeton, 1986.

———. *Velázquez. Los Borrachos and Painting at the Court of Philip IV.* Cambridge, 1993.

OSTEN SACKEN, C. VON DER. *El Escorial. Estudio iconológico.* Bilbao 1984.

PACHECO, F. *Arte de la pintura, su Antigüedad y Grandeza.* Seville, 1649.

El Palacio de Carlos V: un siglo para la recuperación de un monumento (exhibition catalogue). Granada, 1995.

El Palacio del Buen Retiro y el nuevo Museo del Prado (exhibition catalogue). Madrid, 2000.

El Palacio del Rey Planeta: Felipe IV y el Buen Retiro (exhibition catalogue). Madrid, 2005.

PALOMINO DE CASTRO, A. *El Museo Pictórico y Escala Óptica.* Madrid, 1724.

PELORSON, J. M. "Cómo se representaba a sí misma la 'sociedad' española del Siglo de Oro," in M. Tuñón de Lara (ed.), *Historia de España,* V: *La frustración de un imperio (1476–1714).* Barcelona, 1984, pp. 295–301.

PÉREZ SAMPER, M. A., *La alimentación en la España del Siglo de Oro.* 1998.

PÉREZ SÁNCHEZ, A. E. *Pintura Barroca en España (1600–1750).* Madrid, 1992.

———. *De pintura y pintores. La configuración de los modelos visuales en la pintura española.* Madrid, 1993.

PFANDL, L. *Introducción al Siglo de Oro: Cultura y costumbres del pueblo Español de los siglos XVI y XVII.* Madrid, 1929 (1994).

PHILIPP, F. "El Greco's *Entombment of the Count of Orgaz* and Spanish Medieval Tomb Art," in *Journal of the Warburg and Courtauld Institutes,* vol. XLIV, 1981, pp. 76–89.

PHILIPPVS II REX (exhibition catalogue). Barcelona, 1998.

PITA ANDRADE, J. M. "Dominico Greco y sus obras a lo largo de los siglos XVII y XVIII." Entry speech to the Academia de San Fernando, Madrid, 1984.

PORTÚS PÉREZ, J. *Pintura y pensamiento en la España de Lope de Vega.* Madrid, 1999.

———. *Entre dos centenarios. Bibliografía crítica y antológica de Velázquez: 1962–1999.* Seville, 2000.

———. *Pinturas mitológicas de Velázquez.* Madrid, 2002.

PRAY BOBER, P., and OLITSKY RUBINSTEIN, R. *Renaissance Artists and Antique Sculpture: A Handbook of Sources.* London and Oxford, 1986.

Rafael en España (exhibition catalogue). Madrid, 1985.

El Real Alcázar de Madrid (exhibition catalogue). Madrid, 1994.

REDONDO CANTERA, M. J. *El sepulcro en España en el siglo XVI: tipología e iconografía.* Madrid, 1987.

REDONDO CANTERA, M. J. (coord.). *El modelo italiano en las artes plásticas de la Península ibérica durante el Renacimiento.* Valladolid, 2004.

REGALADO, A. *Calderón: los orígenes de la modernidad en la España del Siglo de Oro.* Barcelona, 1995.

El retrato en el Museo del Prado (exhibition catalogue). Madrid, 1994.

REY HAZAS, A. (ed.). *Artes de bien morir. Ars moriendi de la Edad Media y del Siglo de Oro.* Madrid, 2003.

REYES-VALERIO, C. *Arte Indocristiano.* Mexico City, 2000.

Reyes y Mecenas: los Reyes católicos - Maximiliano I y los inicios de la casa de Austria en España (exhibition catalogue). Madrid, 1992.

Los Ribalta y la pintura valenciana de su tiempo (exhibition catalogue). Valencia, 1987.

Ribera 1591–1652 (exhibition catalogue). Madrid, 1992.

RIBOT, L. *Felipe II. Un monarca y su época. Las tierras y los hombres del rey* (exhibition catalogue). Valladolid, 1998.

RÍO PARRA, E. DEL. *Una era de monstruos: representación de lo deforme en el Siglo de Oro español.* Madrid, 2003.

RIVERA BLANCO, J. J. *Juan Bautista de Toledo y Felipe II: la implantación del clasicismo en España.* Valladolid, 1984.

RODRÍGUEZ MARÍN, F. *Francisco Pacheco, maestro de Velázquez.* Madrid, 1923.

ROJO VEGA, A. *El Siglo de Oro: inventario de una época.* Salamanca, 1996.

ROMOJARO, R. *Las funciones del mito clásico en el Siglo de Oro: Garcilaso, Góngora, Lope de Vega, Quevedo.* Barcelona, 1998.

ROSENTHAL, E. *The Palace of Charles V in Granada.* Princeton, 1985.

ROZAS, J. M. "Siglo de Oro: historia de un concepto, la acuñación de un término," in *Estudios sobre el Siglo de Oro. Homenaje al profesor Francisco Ynduráin.* Madrid, 1984, pp. 413–28.

SÁENZ DE MIERA, J. *De obra insigne y heroica a octava maravilla del mundo: la fama de El Escorial en el siglo XVI.* Madrid, 2001.

SALAS, X. DE, and MARÍAS, F. *El Greco y el arte de su tiempo. Las notas de El Greco a Vasari.* Madrid, 1992.

SALORT PONS, S., *Velázquez en Italia.* Madrid, 2002.

Sevilla en el Siglo XVII (exhibition catalogue). Seville, 1983.

El Siglo de Oro de la pintura española (exhibition catalogue). Madrid, 1991.

El Siglo del Quijote (exhibition catalogue). Madrid, 1996.

SIGÜENZA, J. DE. *Fundación del Monasterio de El Escorial.* Madrid, 1605.

SOLER DEL CAMPO, A. *Real Armería Palacio Real.* Madrid, 2000.

SORIA, M. *The Paintings of Zurbarán.* London, 1953.

Spanish Still Life from Velázquez to Goya (exhibition catalogue) London, 1995.

Sterling, C. *La nature morte de l'antiquité au* XX*e siècle.* Paris, 1985.

Stoichita, V. I. *Das mystische Auge. Vision und Malerei im Spanien des goldenen Zeitalters.* Munich, 1997 *(El ojo místico: pintura y visión religiosa en el Siglo de Oro español.* Madrid, 1996).

Stradling, R. A., *Philip IV and the Government of Spain, 1621–1665.* Cambridge, 1988.

Sullivan, E. J. *Baroque Painting in Madrid: The Contribution of Claudio Coello, with a Catalogue Raisonné of His Works.* Columbia, Mo., 1986.

Sureda, J. "Pere Fernández," in *Catalunya genio a genio.* Barcelona, 1995, pp. 81–96.

Sureda, J. (ed.). *La España Imperial: Renacimiento y Humanismo. Historia del Arte Español,* VI. Barcelona, 1995.

———. *El Siglo de Oro: el sentimiento de lo barroco. Historia del Arte Español,* VII, Barcelona, 1996.

———. *El Manierismo y la expansión del Renacimiento. SVMMA PICTORICA,* V, Barcelona, 1999.

———. *El Siglo de Oro de la Pintura Española. SVMMA PICTORICA,* VII, Barcelona, 2000.

Symposium Internacional Velázquez. Seville, 2004.

Tapices y armaduras del Renacimiento. Joyas de las colecciones reales (exhibition catalogue). Barcelona, 1992.

El Toledo de El Greco (exhibition catalogue). Toledo, 1982.

Tolnay, C. "Velázquez' *Las Hilanderas* and *Las Meninas.* An Interpretation," *Gazette des Beaux-Arts,* 35, 1949, pp. 21–38.

Trevisani, F. (ed.). *Il Palazzo di Sassuolo, delizia dei Duchi d' Este.* Parma, 2004.

Triadó, J. R. *El bodegón en la pintura española del siglo* XVII. Barcelona, 1982.

———. *Carlos V y su época: arte y cultura.* Barcelona, 1999.

Úbeda de los Cobos, A. *Pensamiento artístico español del siglo* XVIII*: de Antonio Palomino a Francisco de Goya.* Madrid, 2001.

Valbuena Prat, A. *El teatro español en el Siglo de Oro.* Barcelona, 1969.

Valdivieso, E. *Juan de Valdés Leal.* Seville, 1988.

———. *Francisco Pacheco.* Seville, 1990.

———. *La pintura sevillana de los Siglos de Oro.* Seville, 1991.

———. *Vanidades y desengaños en la pintura española del Siglo de Oro.* Madrid, 2002.

Valdivieso, E., and Serrera, J. M. *Pintura sevillana del primer tercio del siglo* XVII. Madrid, 1985.

Varey, J. E. *Cosmovisión y escenografía: el teatro español en el Siglo de Oro.* Madrid, 1987.

Varia Velazqueña. Madrid, 1960.

Velázquez (exhibition catalogue). Madrid, 1990.

Velázquez (exhibition catalogue). Madrid, 1999.

Velázquez (exhibition catalogue). Rome, 2001.

Velázquez in Seville (exhibition catalogue). Edinburgh, 1996.

Velázquez y el arte de su tiempo (exhibition catalogue). Madrid, 1991.

Velázquez y lo velazqueño (exhibition catalogue). Madrid, 1960.

Velázquez y Sevilla (exhibition catalogue). Seville, 1999.

Vetter, E. "El Greco's Laokoon reconsidered," in *Pantheon,* XXVII, 1969, pp. 295–98.

Vidaurre, A.C.V. *Figuras de la alteridad: el mito del "convidado de piedra."* Guadalajara, 1997.

La visión del mundo clásico en el arte español (exhibition catalogue). Madrid, 1993.

Vossler, K. *Algunos caracteres de la cultura española.* Madrid, 1941.

Vosters, S. A. *Rubens y España.* Madrid, 1990.

Wardropper, B. W. "Temas y problemas del Barroco español," in F. Rico (ed.), *Historia y crítica de la literatura española,* III: *Siglos de Oro: Barroco.* Barcelona, 1983, pp. 5–48.

Wethey, H. *El Greco and His School.* Princeton, 1962.

Wilkinson-Zerner, C. *Juan de Herrera, Architect to Philip II of Spain.* New Haven and London, 1993.

Wind, B. *Velázquez's Bodegones.* Fairfax, 1987.

Winner, M. "Zum Nachleben des Laokoon in der Renaissance," in *Jahrbuch der Berliner Museen,* XVI, 1974, pp. 83–121.

Yarza, J. *Los Reyes Católicos: paisaje artístico de una monarquía.* Madrid, 1993.

Ynduráin, D. *Humanismo y Renacimiento en España.* Madrid, 1994.

Young, E. "New Perspectives on Spanish Still Life Painting of the Golden Age," in *Burlington Magazine,* CXVIII, 1976, pp. 203–14.

Zurbarán (exhibition catalogue). Paris, 1988.

Index

Photo Credits

Numbers indicate pages

Aisa: 179, 192–93

Album/Erich Lessing: 103, 104, 105

Archivo Fotográfico Fournier Artes Gráficas, S.A.: 13, 53, 72, 74, 177, 180, 182, 187, 222–23, 224, 248, 260, 262, 263, 264, 266, 267, 268, 269, 270. 271, 272, 273

Archivo Lunwerg: 28–29, 60, 204, 205, 206, 275

Biblioteca Nacional, Madrid: 25 left

A. Bracchetti/P. Zigrossi: 208

Matiás Briansó: 96, 97, 117, 126, 130–31, 132

Bridgeman Art Library/Alinari: 209

Corbis/Burstein Collection: 238

Joaquín Cortés: 230

Jordi Cuxart: 10

Foto Scala, Florence: 17, 78, 79, 207

Foto Scala, Florence/Bildarchiv Preussischer Kulturbesitz, Berlin: 234

Laurentian Library, Florence: 21, 26, 27

Marc Llimargas I Casas: 9, 14–15, 18, 22, 33, 54, 61, 70, 86, 88, 90–91, 94–95, 99, 113, 114, 115, 118–19, 120–21, 123, 127, 133, 134, 135, 136, 137, 139, 141, 142–43, 144, 159, 161, 164, 165, 166, 176, 197, 200, 202–03, 210, 231

Mauro Magliani: 34, 36, 37

Ramon Masats: 19, 122, 145

Domi Mora: 40, 83, 84, 106–07, 140, 146, 169, 171, 172, 173, 181, 189

Museo Nacional del Prado, Madrid: 16, 31, 38, 39, 64, 65, 67, 69, 71, 80, 81, 147, 149, 150, 154, 155, 158, 162, 163, 174, 175, 183, 184, 185, 190, 194, 198, 227, 236, 237, 240–41, 245, 246–47, 249, 250, 254, 255, 256, 257, 259, 274, 276–77, 279, 280, 281, 283, 284, 285

National Gallery, London: 167

National Gallery of Scotland, Edinburgh: 232–33

Norton Simon Foundation, Pasadena: 62

Francisco Ontañón: 92, 124–25, 212, 213, 214–15, 216, 217

Oronoz: 51, 75, 101, 102, 168, 191, 195, 218, 221

Patrimonio Nacional, Madrid: 24, 42, 47

Prisma: 129

Real Academia de Bellas Artes de San Fernando, Madrid: 108, 109, 110

RMN, Paris: 76–77

Joan Sureda: 41, 43, 44, 45, 48–49, 50, 56, 58, 151, 152, 153, 156, 157, 188, 196, 225, 228, 239, 244, 252, 278

Vatican Library: 25 right